The Social Impact of the Novel

A Reference Guide

Claudia Durst Johnson and Vernon Johnson

GREENWOOD PRESS
Westport, Connecticut • London

Library of Congress Cataloging-in-Publication Data

Johnson, Claudia D.
    The social impact of the novel : a reference guide / Claudia Durst Johnson and Vernon Johnson.
      p. cm.
    Includes bibliographical references and indexes.
    ISBN 0–313–31818–2 (alk. paper)
    1. Fiction—Social aspects. 2. Fiction—20th century—History and criticism. I. Johnson,
Vernon E. (Vernon Elso), 1921– II. Title.
PN3344.J64 2002
    809.3'9355—dc21   2001055624

British Library Cataloguing in Publication Data is available.

Library of Congress Catalog Card Number: 2001055624
ISBN: 0–313–31818–2

First published in 2002

Greenwood Press, 88 Post Road West, Westport, CT 06881
An imprint of Greenwood Publishing Group, Inc.
www.greenwood.com

Printed in the United States of America

The paper used in this book complies with the
Permanent Paper Standard issued by the National
Information Standards Organization (Z39.48–1984).

10 9 8 7 6 5 4 3 2 1

116987

Contents

CONTENTS

Introduction

The modern novel, a comparatively new literary form, has, from its beginnings, shown itself to be exceptionally well suited to the exploration of social ideas and social protest, lending itself, more than any other genre, to transformation in society and changes in the hearts and minds of readers.

One of the most dramatic stories of the power of the novel to initiate graphic change began in the United States in the spring of 1939 with the publication of John Steinbeck's *The Grapes of Wrath*. Steinbeck's novel appeared at the end of a decade encompassing the Great Depression. The hardships suffered by so many in the 1930s were acutely felt by the hundreds of thousands of dispossessed families from the Midwest who had been lured to the California agricultural fields with the promise of work. Seeking Paradise, most thought they had landed in hell. In California's San Joaquin Valley alone, welfare organizations estimated that 70,000 transient farmworkers were starving to death in 1937. In this land of plenty, many of them lived in woods and caves like wild animals. Their fates were in the hands of a powerful group, the Associated Farmers, organized by wealthy owners of large farms. These men, who controlled money, politics, and law enforcement in California, resisted reforms and used local police to put down, by violent means, any attempts on the part of farm-

workers to organize for decent wages and living and working conditions. While many reformers had called the state and federal governments' attention to the plight of these workers, the power wielded by the Associated Farmers had managed to stalemate any relief. When the National Recovery Administration Act was passed in 1933 to alleviate the hardships of workers, its provisions did not extend to farmworkers.

John Steinbeck's novel, which followed a family through their tribulations in the Dust Bowl of Oklahoma and their disastrous experiences moving from wretched camp to camp in California, looking for work, was said to have been like dropping a match in a powder keg. News of the novel spread like wildfire throughout the United States. Sales kept it near the top of the bestseller list for a year; newspapers large and small publicized the situation described in the novel; national magazines like *Fortune, Collier's*, and *Life* ran articles on the situation; and one of the most highly acclaimed motion pictures of all time was promptly made from the novel. The minds of Americans were enlightened and their hearts touched by the human tragedy of these workers who were being treated like subhuman animals by their employers and the government.

The novel precipitated immediate action. After the novel's publication, the once-struggling committee, set up earlier by Congressman Robert LaFollette to investigate farmworkers, was immediately empowered to open hearings in San Francisco and Los Angeles on the Associated Farmers' abrogation of the civil rights of migratory workers and the organization's use of violence in putting down strikes.

In response to reams of persuasive testimony sympathetic to the workers, the Associated Farmers bombarded lawmakers and the public with claims that Steinbeck's amazing story was grossly exaggerated, stalemating effective measures in the U.S. legislature. The turning point came one year after the novel's publication when First Lady Eleanor Roosevelt, inspired by the novel, decided to visit farm laborers' camps in California to assess the situation for herself. Her public comment was that she had never doubted the truth of Steinbeck's novel. In May, after her return to Washington, Congress promptly empowered a committee on Interstate Migration to hold hearings on the West Coast.

Even without the passage of effective legislation, public opinion and the findings of the LaFollette and Toland committees forced the Associated Farmers and the state of California to change their police state tactics. Furthermore, the Associated Farmers abandoned all further attempts to extend its empire into other western states. The novel also gave new confidence to union organizers in the fields.

This example of the power of one novel to effect change, though striking, is scarcely an anomaly. Some critics argue that *every* successful novel has in some degree changed the thinking of its audience. Literary critic Lionel Trilling noted that "*every* novelist is dealing with a transitional society. A movement from one set of values to another set" (from his 1954 lecture notes in an article titled "Reality, Unreality, and the Novel," in *The New Republic*, February 5, 2001, p. 25). Some novels, more than others, however, have, like *The Grapes of Wrath*, inspired distinct and measurable changes in their readership.

THE NOVEL AS SOCIAL PROTEST

This volume examines 200 of the many novels that have had an impact on the way people regard themselves and their society. Most of these works occupy prominent positions in the intellectual and social history of the world.

In the eighteenth century the appearance of the modern novel, with its appeal for social reform, is inextricably tied to social shifts and the toleration of social and ideological change. To understand the enormity of these changes in both life and literature in the crucial periods of the eighteenth and nineteenth centuries when the novel began to flourish, it is important to grasp the general social situation as it had existed for centuries. The state of affairs in England and France can serve as illustration of the general climate across the Western world. In England, a handful of families owned half the land and controlled the country's economics and politics. No longer responsible to the king above, not yet troubled by great masses below, they lived in a world of pride and splendor celebrated by song and story. In this rigid class system, the poor were regarded as morally inferior, unimprovable, and rightly destined by God to live in abject poverty. In France, taxes and all other expenses to support a careless and irresponsible ruling class also fell to the peasants.

At the same time, beginning at about mid-eighteenth century, the Industrial Revolution brought fabulous wealth to new mill owners and entrepreneurs, while creating bleak factory towns of what were called "dark Satanic mills," resulting in working conditions for the poor so filled with horror and dark, relentless inhumanity as to defy description. Outrage over these long-standing conditions led to the eruption in Europe of an indescribable conflagration.

The eruptions in Western world society began in 1776, not in Europe but in the New World, with the American Revolution. The Americans not only secured their independence from England, but they set up a government on the principle that all men are created equal. While this did not result in universal suffrage, it was a clear rejection of monarchy and an officially sanctioned class hierarchy. It also extended the vote to most white males in an astounding broadening of suffrage.

The American Revolution was followed in 1789 by the French Revolution, which overthrew the monarchy and gradually led throughout England to a century of rebellions and social reforms based on the revolution's rallying cry of "Liberty, Equality, Fraternity."

Rising to prominence in the eighteenth century, in this time of earthshaking change, was the modern novel, a genre that itself would become an appropriate agent for social change and ideological challenge. Unlike poetry—the genre that had dominated literature up to this time and that so often focused on the sublime—the novel is usually situated in this world: in human society and psychology and in the problems of the common man, not just nobility. Unlike the older genre of drama, which is so often tempered by dramatic conventions, economic imperatives, and the obligation to entertain, the novel can be more expansive and more selective in its exploration of ideas and criticism of culture and can simmer slowly for years, waiting to catch fire.

The modern novel from the first, as with Samuel Richardson's *Clarissa* (1747–48), began to introduce sympathetic lower- and middle-class characters with which a broader audience could identify—characters of a type that were most interested in reform. The novel also typically diverged from poetry in its accessibility. While the language of the other arts was often arcane, frequently filled with French and Latin references to be appreciated by the intelligentsia, the humblest citizens, with little education, could appreciate the novel.

The novelists' opportunities to effect change through their work were encouraged by developments in their position. One of the most significant changes in society that led to the rise of the novel was the great increase in literacy, especially among the middle and lower classes. This, of course, swelled the audience for the novel and greatly affected both the independence of the novelist and the subjects that novelists were willing to write about. There were, as well, technical advances in printing and the concomitant increase in printed matter and the availability of books in lending libraries and, serially, in magazines. These created an enormous readership and demand for novels. Released from the old economic necessity of relying on upper-class patronage, writers became more willing to challenge entrenched ideas and social practices.

VARIETIES OF INFLUENCE

The kinds of influence these novels exerted on readers and society as a whole vary, ranging from the specific to the general. Novels that protest specific conditions in a given time provoke immediate responses and often bring tangible changes in policies and laws. Into this category falls Herman Melville's 1850 *White Jacket*, which was instrumental in having Congress outlaw flogging on U.S. military vessels, and Harriet Beecher Stowe's 1852 *Uncle Tom's Cabin*, credited with mobilizing the Union to fight a war to end slavery. Emile Zola's *Germinal*, published in France in 1885, inspired reform of working conditions in the mines. Helen Hunt Jackson's *Ramona*, published in the United States in the same year, was responsible for the passage of the Dawes Severalty Act that awarded land to Native American families. Another such novel was Upton Sinclair's *The Jungle* (1906), which was directly responsible for the Pure Food and Drug Act, enforcing decent standards and effective inspection of the meatpacking industry. Discovery that Ray Bradbury's 1953 novel on censorship, *Fahrenheit 451*, had itself been censored by his publisher led to the formation of the Intellectual Freedom Committee of the American Library Association to monitor book censorship. Sawako Arijoshi's *The Twilight Years*

(1972) resulted in expanded nursing home care in Japan. And, finally, environmental activism was born in the United States with Edward Abbey's 1975 novel *The Monkey Wrench Gang*.

A somewhat broader category of influence is found in novels that target not a specific grievance, like slavery or environmentalism, but a pervasive socioeconomic system such as capitalism or fascism. Such novels include George Gissing's *The Unclassed* and Charles Dickens's *Bleak House*.

Novels that attack or promote a particular ideology flowered especially in late-nineteenth- and early-twentieth-century Europe with the rise of Marxism. Labeled "socialist realism," they were written with the express purpose of promoting socialism or communism by exposing the abuses of the old landed nobility. A prime example is Mikhail Sholokhov's *Quiet Flows the Don*, written about the years after the fall of czarist Russia. Other Russian novels that attacked abusive systems were Nikolai Gogol's *Dead Souls* in 1842 and Maxim Gorky's *Mother* in 1906.

Later, at the opposite end of the political spectrum, collectivism (group control of farms and businesses) and socialism's threat to individuality was denounced in George Orwell's 1945 *Animal Farm*, in Russian-born Ayn Rand's 1957 *Atlas Shrugged*, and in Aleksandr Solzhenitsyn's *One Day in the Life of Ivan Denisovich* in 1962.

Other such novels that cover the entire political spectrum include H.G. Wells's attack on capitalistic materialism in his 1908 satire *Tono-Bungay* and Theodore Dreiser's *An American Tragedy*, published in 1925. Christa Wolf promoted the Marxism of East Germany in her 1963 novel *Divided Heaven*, whereas Bei Dao attacked Chinese communism and its cultural revolution in *Waves* in 1979.

Another category of influence is less situation specific and less broad in philosophic scope than social realism. These novels illuminate particular groups of people who often have not had a voice, bringing attention to their existence and our shared humanity. One example is Herman Melville's *Typee*, published in the United States in 1846, which brought to the attention of his Victorian audience the humanity of primitive peoples who had been regarded as little more than brutes. Charlotte Brontë's *Jane Eyre*, published in England the next year, drew attention to the plight of poor middle-class women. In 1861, Rebecca Harding Davis became one of the first novelists to represent factory workers in her novel *Life in the Iron Mills*. Mulk Raj Anand's *Untouchable* revealed a despised group of pariahs at the bottom of the social rung in India. Books from Israel Zangwill's *Children of the Ghetto* (1892) to Chaim Potok's *The Chosen* (1967) opened the public's eyes to the life and problems of Jewish communities.

One of the most important changes that novelists have made has been in their mainstream audiences' perception of people of different races. Modern readers have seen and been changed by portrayals of Native Americans in North America by the novels of Helen Hunt Jackson (*Ramona*), N. Scott Momaday (*House Made of Dawn*), and Leslie Silko (*Ceremony*). In 1941, Ciro Alegría's *Broad and Alien Is the World* led to a reevaluation of Peru's Native Americans. *Coonardoo*, Katherine Susannah Prichard's 1929 portrait of native peoples in Australia, changed the world's view of their circumstances. Novels written in the United States, as early as William Wells Brown's *Clotel* in 1853, and followed by the novels of James Weldon Johnson, Zora Neale Hurston, Richard Wright, James Baldwin, Ralph Ellison, and Ernest Gaines, have influenced the way readers view the African American experience. In the 1980s, the attention of audiences was drawn to the Hispanic experience in the United States in *The House on Mango Street* by Sandra Cisneros and to the Chinese American experience in Amy Tan's *The Joy Luck Club*.

Many novels have guided cultures by challenging stereotypes or creating mythic figures and heroes to inspire imitation, some even giving rise to cultist followings. The myth of the romantic fencer with windmills in Miguel de Cervantes's *Don Quixote* continues to define and inspire Western culture, as does the metaphoric Pilgrim in John Bunyan's *The Pilgrim's Progress*, the story of the Christian's spiritual journey. The myth of the romantic clansman in Sir Walter Scott's *Waverley* novels inspired the romantic values of the Old South in the nineteenth century as surely as it did in England. Mark Twain provided an equally powerful but distinctly American countermyth in the figure of the unpolished, natural man, Huckleberry Finn, in his *Adventures of Huckleberry Finn*. In France, one finds Rodolphe, the caped crusader of Eugène Sue's *The Mysteries of Paris*. And in Australia, there is Rolf Boldrewood's Captain Starlight, the outlaw hero of his 1888 *Robbery under Arms*. Lu Xun's Ah-Q in his novel *The True Story of Ah-Q* was an equally enduring and formative myth of the accommodating Chinese peasant, the influence of which even survived China's Cultural Revolution. In the United States one also finds the immensely influential national myths—of the mad rager against God in Melville's Ahab in *Moby-Dick*, the western gunman in Owen Wister's *The Virginian*, the Southern belle in Margaret Mitchell's *Gone With the Wind*, and the liberal Southerner in Harper Lee's *To Kill a Mockingbird*.

For 300 years, groups of readers have turned to fictional characters and societies for their models of behavior in a fervor that has reached the extreme of cultist imitation. Goethe's *The Sorrows of Young Werther*, which Napoleon admitted to having read seven times, inspired fanatical devotion, peculiar dress, and even suicide in imitation of the novel's main character. The cult of Bram Stoker's *Dracula* has never been as frenzied as it is at the turn of the twenty-first century when small groups of young people imitate the Gothic dress, decoration, and even the grisly habits of Stoker's vampire. In the 1960s, with increased interest in Asian religion and drugs, cults arose around Herman Hesse's *Steppenwolf* and Jack Kerouac's *On the Road*. In the mid-twentieth century, antiheroes who challenged authority and the whole adult world—J. D. Salinger's *Catcher in the Rye* is the prime example—also reached cult status.

Finally, one finds novels that provoke a reevaluation of entrenched values, including Cervantes's attack on medieval romanticism in 1605 in *Don Quixote*, Chateaubriand's attack on the Age of Reason in 1802 in *René*, George Sand's criticism of the lack of equality in marriage in 1843 in *Consuelo*, and the challenge of Victorian values in works by George Gissing in 1884—*The Unclassed*—and Samuel Butler in 1903—*The Way of All Flesh*.

SELECTION CRITERIA AND RANGE OF ISSUES

All successful novels impact the thinking of their readers to some degree, and no single volume, including this one, can encompass all the world's novels or claim to have identified *the* 200 most influential novels. What can be assumed with confidence is that this volume explores 200 *of* those novels that have had a profound impact on the way individuals think and society acts, either at the time of their appearance or when they were revived at a later time. Our choices were based on a number of practical as well as scholarly factors, with a bias toward those works that had an impact on Western culture and those that were reasonably available in English.

The landmark novels included here cover a wide range of issues, reflecting the history of different cultures since the development of the novel in the eighteenth century. A comprehensive list of issues included in this volume can be found in the "Issues Index" at the end of the volume. Just a few examples of key issues, illustrated by a single title, include the following:

- educational reform in Jean-Jacques Rousseau's *Émile* (1762)
- the legal and penal system in Charles Dickens's *Bleak House* (1853)
- victimized workers in Charles Dickens's *Hard Times* (1854)

- alcoholism in Timothy Shay Arthur's *Ten Nights in a Bar-room and What I Saw There* (1854)
- the treatment of animals in Anna Sewall's *Black Beauty* (1877)
- industrial monopolies in Frank Norris's *The Octopus. The Story of California* (1901)
- war in Henri Barbusse's *Under Fire: The Story of a Squad* (1916)
- homosexuality in André Gide's *The Counterfeiters* (1925)
- the medical profession in A.J. Cronin's *The Citadel* (1937)
- racial discrimination and apartheid in South Africa in Alan Paton's *Cry, the Beloved Country* (1948)
- racial discrimination in the United States in Ralph Ellison's *Invisible Man* (1952)
- nuclear weapons in Nevil Shute's *On the Beach* (1956)
- mental institutions in Ken Kesey's *One Flew Over the Cuckoo's Nest* (1962)
- the treatment of Muslim women in Mariaba Ba's *So Long a Letter* (1980)
- feminism in Margaret Atwood's *The Handmaid's Tale* (1985)

EVENTS THAT INSPIRED INFLUENTIAL NOVELS

In studying the broad spectrum of novels of social impact, it becomes apparent that various historical events have been particular incentives to the creation of such literary works. These include the rise of industrialism and slums in England in the 1840s, which sparked many of the social novels of Charles Dickens, George Gissing, and Charles Kingsley. In France, many novels were incited by the French Revolution and conditions of the Second Empire during the reign of Napoleon III. European colonialism produced both nineteenth-century English novels and twentieth-century African novels, including those of Joseph Conrad, E.M. Forster, and Chinua Achebe. The Boxer Rebellion in China and revolutions against the Manchu Dynasty constituted the setting of Tseng P'u's *Flower in an Ocean of Sin* in 1905–1907. Prerevolutionary Russia produced in-

fluential novels by Leo Tolstoy and Fyodor Dostoevsky. Other notable inspiring novels included World War I, the Great Depression in the 1930s, the rise of fascism, the Spanish Civil War, World War II and the Holocaust, Soviet aggression, the Cuban Revolution, and the civil rights struggle in the United States.

Novelists lead their readers to reinterpret historical events. One such event is the Shanghai Massacre of 1927 in which the forces of Chiang Kai-shek murdered hundreds of communists and supposed communists during a labor uprising. In 1933, André Malraux, in *Man's Fate*, uses the event to comment on survival in an existential world. Another such novel is Albert Camus's *The Plague* (1947). With his oblique references to the spread of fascism prior to World War II, couched in a story of a spreading village plague, Camus drew attention to a tragedy, the fall of France, that could have been averted. Similar statements about the same historical moment before World War II have been drawn by Heinrich Boll in his 1959 *Billiards at Half-Past Nine* and, from the point of view of a German dissident, by Günter Grass in *The Tin Drum* (1959). In the same time period, Elie Wiesel's *Night* (1958), about the Holocaust of World War II, reminded the world to be vigilant of creeping fascism and not to underestimate the lengths to which racial hatred can carry destruction.

With opposition to the Vietnam War beginning in the mid-1960s, antiwar novels like Kurt Vonnegut's *Slaughterhouse-Five* (1969) appeared on the scene, and antiwar novels about earlier conflicts—like Stephen Crane's *The Red Badge of Courage* (1895) and Joseph Heller's *Catch-22* (1961)—reemerged in popularity to serve the antiwar cause.

BANNED WORKS AND PERSECUTED AUTHORS

Although most of the novels with lasting impact caused little apprehension in the societies into which they were introduced, a significant group of novels did raise an alarm, resulting in book banning, book burning, and the persecution of their creators. Such situations serve to illustrate the power of the novel to upset powerful entities within a society. Authors in this group used the genre as a means of questioning the established order. Some works, like Voltaire's *Candide* and Johann Wolgang von Goethe's *The Sorrows of Young Werther* were banned chiefly for religious reasons in the eighteenth century. In the nineteenth century, Gustave Flaubert's masterpiece *Madame Bovary* was taken to court on grounds of obscenity.

Many novels throughout the ages have been banned for political reasons. In Nazi Germany and other fascist countries in the 1930s, novels, including Jaroslav Hasek's *The Good Soldier Sveijk* and Ignazio Silone's *Bread and Wine*, were not only banned but burned. In Russia influential books were banned by both czars and communists. A few examples are Maxim Gorky's *Mother* in the 1920S and 1930s, Mikhail Bulgakov's *The Master and Margarita* in the 1960s, and the Czech Milan Kundera's *The Unbearable Lightness of Being* in 1984.

While democracies have been less subject to censorship, even James Joyce's modernist masterpiece *Ulysses* was seized by U.S. customs officials and destroyed in the 1930s; and despite the First Amendment to the Constitution of the United States, individual communities have banned and burned books because they challenged traditional ideas. The list includes such classics as Nathaniel Hawthorne's *The Scarlet Letter*, Mark Twain's *Adventures of Huckleberry Finn*, J.D. Salinger's *The Catcher in the Rye*, and Harper Lee's *To Kill a Mockingbird*.

Novelists throughout the world have been met with ostracism, harassment, exile, and imprisonment. Ironically, Thomas Mann (*The Magic Mountain*) and Lion Feuchtwanger (*Success*), both exiled from Nazi Germany because of the antifascist positions they took in their novels, were then hounded after World War II by communist hunters in the United States because they publicly opposed fascism. Other exiles barred at some time from their own countries include Voltaire (*Candide*), Honoré de Balzac (*Père Goriot*),

Ignazio Silone (*Bread and Wine*), Ciro Alegria (*Broad and Alien Is the World*), Nuruddin Farah (*Close Sesame*), Isabel Allende (*The House of the Spirits*), Jorge Amado (*Gabriela, Clove and Cinnamon*), and Bei Dao (*Waves*), to cite a few.

One of the most notorious cases, ongoing into the twenty-first century, of a writer persecuted because of his novel is Salman Rushdie. Rushdie has been under a death threat from members of the Muslim world since 1988. Over seventy people have been killed in various demonstrations over his novel *The Satanic Verses*.

Many novelists represented in this volume have been imprisoned for opposing political tyranny in their countries. These include Pramoedya Ananta Toer, author of *This Earth of Mankind*, who was, until the twenty-first century, under city arrest in Indonesia; Wole Soyinka of Nigeria, who was jailed shortly after the publication of *The Interpreters*; Kenyan Ngugi wa Thiong'o, author of *Petals of Blood*; and Brazilian Jorge Amado, author of *Gabriela, Clove and Cinnamon*.

We attempted to represent an inclusive range of writers, both women and minority writers as well as a wide variety of issues. Even though we concentrated on novels that had an impact on Western thought, we tried to represent as many cultures as possible, including some important works from every continent—Africa, Asia, Australia, Europe, and North and South America. The reader will discover, however, that some major countries are unrepresented or underrepresented in this volume. These omissions are attributable to a combination of circumstances. One is the paucity of novels of social purpose; another is lack of accessibility in English translation for the general reader. Among European texts, for instance, Scandinavian, Swiss, and Dutch novels of social criticism are not represented in this volume. The novel itself was late in developing in these countries, taking a backseat to drama, poetry, the essay, and short story. When the genre did come into its own, well into the twentieth century, it took the form of the historical romance, the pastoral idyll, local color fiction, the family saga, or the psychological study, rather than adopting subject matter to effect change. Eventually, especially after World War II, a few novels of social import did emerge in Norway, Finland, Sweden, Denmark, Switzerland, and the Netherlands, but they have rarely been available in English except for the occasional, out-of-print university press translations.

Similarly, Asian countries of Korea, Cambodia, and Vietnam are missing entirely from these selections, and novels from Japan, China, and Indonesia are few in number. The first three of these Asian countries have long-standing strengths in many artistic areas but not the novel. In Korea and Cambodia, until the most recent times, literature—usually the short story, essay, or poetry—was read only by males of the privileged class. Attempts to develop novels of social purpose in South Korea have been suppressed, and nothing is known outside Cambodia and North Korea of any novels or novelists of any kind. In Vietnam, a few novelists emulated the historical style of Western novelists, and in North Vietnam, after 1954, as Ho Chi Minh solidified his power a few anonymous novelists wrote of the happiness of living within a communist state, but neither country produced novels of social criticism until after the Vietnam War. Some novels, analyzing the devastation of that war, have emerged, but they have not been translated into English. Translations of the rich literature of China and Japan are also difficult to secure.

In some cases, major countries are underrepresented in this volume because other kinds of novels—the historical romance, the family saga, the spiritual quest, the psychological novel, the children's idyll—have been slow to give way to the novel of social purpose. This has been true in India, where the English novel completely dominated that country's literature for so long, and in Canada, where few novels of social import have had an impact outside the region.

This work should not be viewed as a traditional literary history of a genre. We did not choose novels on the basis of their literary merit or their impact on the development of the novel or their influence on the style of other novelists. Our intent was to focus on works that impacted society as a whole or individual members of a general readership. Thus, the reader will find some obscure novels in the list alongside more familiar fiction.

Literary critics have typically disparaged many novels represented in this volume, often because the message tended to outweigh the artistry of the work or because they were written for the ordinary reader rather than a more sophisticated audience. Such has been the fate of works by Eugène Sue (*The Mysteries of Paris*), Robert Tressell (*The Ragged Trousered Philanthropists*), Horatio Alger (*Ragged Dick*), and Timothy Shay Arthur (*Ten Nights in a Bar-room*), despite their phenomenal popularity and influence on a wide readership. Other novels that have had a decided impact on society have been despised by the literary establishment because they are not in keeping with the artistic traditions of the country. Erich Maria Remarque was damned by German critics precisely because his anti-military novel *All Quiet on the Western Front* was too popular. It appealed to the masses; thus, they argued, it could not possibly possess artistic merit. Sometimes, of course, critical disdain derives from or is coupled with political disapproval of a work. Thus, *Untouchable*, the novel of Mahatma Gandhi's disciple Mulk Raj Anand, was condemned by the Indian literati, and Anand himself was expelled from India's association of writers. Likewise, *The Cabin* by Spanish political activist Vincente Blasco Ibáñez, whose works had been consistently in demand by Spanish readers, was banned as subversive by the Spanish government and ignored by Spanish literary critics.

We have also included novels that had little influence at the time of publication and vanished shortly after they were written but that reemerged long afterward to exert great influence. Franz Kafka's *The Trial*, first published in 1925, did not become a classic until it was republished in the 1950s, perhaps because of the broader appeal of existentialism at a later date. Herman Hesse's *Steppenwolf*, first published in 1927, did not emerge to sensational popularity until the 1960s when interest in Eastern philosophy and psychedelic drugs was rampant. Much of this resurgence has resulted from the growth of women's studies and African American studies in the 1960s and 1970s. Kate Chopin's *The Awakening* virtually disappeared after its publication in 1899, only to be received as an enduring classic after its republication in 1961. The same fate was in store for Miles Franklin's *My Brilliant Career*, published in Australia in 1901 and reintroduced in 1970. James Weldon Johnson's *The Autobiography of an Ex-Colored Man* disappeared from view shortly after its publication in 1912, as did Zora Neale Hurston's *Their Eyes Were Watching God*, published in 1937. Both, along with other works by African American writers, reappeared in the 1960s and 1970s when they achieved prominence and inspired the reevaluation of race in America.

ORGANIZATION OF THE BOOK

This volume is composed of two hundred entries organized geographically to help facilitate using the work. Entries are sequentially numbered throughout the work and grouped alphabetically by continent—Africa, Asia, Australia, Europe, North America, and South America; within continents, countries are organized alphabetically. Under country, the works are arranged chronologically by date of publication. Under countries where there are a large number of entries—England, France, and the United States—the entries are further divided into time periods. Preceding each group of a country's novels is a timeline of events pertinent to the works that immediately follow which places the literature in historical perspective.

Each entry includes its title in English, followed (in the case of non-English works) by the title under which it first appeared. The title is followed by the name of the author. The author's native country—and, if different, country relevant to publication—and original publication date appear in parentheses. With few exceptions, the country cited is the author's native land, that is, the country in which he or she grew to maturity, which provided the language and perspective of the work, and the place with which histories generally identify the author. Several complicated exceptions involving expatriate writers require explanation: These are Joseph Conrad, Samuel Beckett, and Elie Wiesel. Although Conrad was born and reared in Poland, he is listed under England because all of his great works were written in English and have become a recognized part of the English literary tradition. The same can be said of Samuel Beckett, a native Irishman whose novel *Molloy* is here listed under France. Beckett lived in France for most of his life, wrote in French, and is identified with the modern French literary tradition and absurdist philosophy of France.

Elie Wiesel is another complex case in point. Although he is generally listed as a "French/American" author in standard references, a number of countries could lay claim to him: Romania, where he was born; Poland, which is the setting for his novel *Night*; and the United States, where he has lived for forty-five years. We have chosen to list Wiesel's *Night* under France because the novel was written and published in France, where Wiesel was educated and was working at the time, and most important, because it was first published in the French language and thus read by a French audience.

Entries generally follow a pattern, beginning with an identification of the pertinent historical context, moving to an assessment of the public's reaction to the novel and its influence, and ending with bibliographical citations pertinent to the work itself and to its historical background.

An appendix titled "Additional Protest Novels" is included for further exploration and is arranged by country. Though far from exhaustive, the list allows the reader to pursue further interests in a particular national literature or an issue.

Four indexes, each keyed to entry numbers, appear at the end of the volume to facilitate the reader's use of this material:

- An author index listing author and title
- A title index listing title and author
- A geographical index by country listing author and title
- An issues index listing title

The indexes and the national timelines that appear before each group of entries thus allow the reader to access the material according to his or her interests: literary, historical, and ideological. By consulting the author or title index, the student is led to an entry describing the social impact of a particular figure or work, which supplements a reading of the novel by providing context and influence. By consulting the timelines, readers can compare the historical contexts across cultures. For example, they can become aware of the national political climate and literary re-sponse in England in the late nineteenth century and compare it with what was occurring in France in the same years. And by consulting the issues index, the student can pursue a particular social or political interest. An interest in education reform, for example, would quickly lead students to a number of entries.

The volume is intended as a reference tool for librarians, for teachers of humanities and social sciences, for students at the high school and college levels, and for general readers. In the entries, written with this audience in mind, literary and contextual material is presented in a straightforward, concise manner. Attempts have been made to define all specialized terms and proper names when they appear.

AFRICA

Egypt

༺ঌ

Naguib Mahfouz, *The Cairo Trilogy*, 1956–57
Nawāl El Saadawi, *God Dies by the Nile*, 1974

༺ঌ

TIMELINE

A.D. 647   Arabs conquer Egypt, bringing with them the religion of Islam.

1869   The Suez Canal opens.

1870   Egypt goes bankrupt, leaving itself open to control by its European creditors, France and England.

1882   Beginning of British occupation and rule in Egypt.

1904   Egypt's debt to Europe repaid, but the English presence in Egypt officially recognized and sanctioned by Europe.

1914   In an effort to continue its control over the Suez Canal, Britain declares Egypt to be a British protectorate.

1919   A nationalist rebellion for independence from England erupts in violence.

1922   England concedes to an independent Egyptian monarchy but remains as a presence in Egypt.

1941–45   Political agitation subsides during World War II.

Starvation in Egypt is widespread.

1948   Despite protests, the playboy, Farouk, becomes king of Egypt.

1952   In an Egyptian Revolution, the army deposes Farouk.

1953   Egypt is declared a republic.

1954   Gamal Abdel Nasser, who had been the virtual leader of Egypt since the revolution, becomes its official leader.

1956–57   Nasser joins with the rest of the Arab and African world, opposing European and American influence.

Naguib Mahfouz publishes *The Cairo Trilogy*.

1968   The Aswan Dam is completed.

1970   Anwar Sadat succeeds Nasser.

1976   Feminist physician Nawāl El Saadawi publishes *God Dies by the Nile*.

1981   El Saadawi, along with hundreds who have opposed Sadat, is arrested.

Sadat is assassinated and succeeded by Hosni Mubarak.

1984 El Saadawi publishes *Memoirs from the Women's Prison.*

1988 Naguib Mahfouz wins the Nobel Prize for Literature.

1992 Muslim fundamentalists mount attacks on the government, Christians, and unveiled women.

El Saadawi leaves Egypt in exile.

1994 Islamic extremists kidnap and wound Mahfouz.

1. *The Cairo Trilogy* (*al-Thulathiyya*), by Naguib Mahfouz (Egypt, 1956–57). This trilogy of Egyptian life, one of the few Arab novels to be translated into languages outside the Arab world, is by a 1988 Nobel novelist, universally acknowledged as the father of modern Arab fiction. Its importance and influence derive from its setting in the early decades of the twentieth century leading up to the 1952 Egyptian Revolution, considered to be the critical turning point and defining moment in the Middle East.

The stories of three generations of family life in Cairo from 1917 to 1944 occur against a vivid political background in which the 1950s resonate. In the background is the oppressive British colonial occupation of Egypt since 1882, the inflation and starvation brought on the peasants during World War I, the false promises of independence, the 1919 rebellion waged for Egyptian independence, and continuous communist and Muslim attempts to free Egypt of British control.

No other problem so permeates *Palace Walk*, the first novel about a Cairo family, as the Muslim view and treatment of women and the tyranny of husbands: the ability of husbands to take more than one wife, to take mistresses, to beat and mutilate their wives, to throw them out at will where they become pariahs, to forbid them from ever leaving the house, and to control their children's marriages. The modern world begins to impinge with the death of the oldest son in the family in the rebellion of 1919.

In *Palace of Desire*, the second novel,

modern ideas including Darwinism, are introduced into the family by Kamal the second son, whose college education leads him to challenge tradition. In *Sugar Street*, the third novel, the third generation of women have left the house to become educated alongside men.

Within this fiction, Mahfouz represents and discusses competing ideologies present in most of the Arab world. These include colonialism, communism, socialism, Muslim extremists, Muslim traditionalists, and rationalism.

Mahfouz articulated for his Arab readers the competing internal political philosophies that surfaced before the revolution and continued afterward. They saw reflected there their mounting frustration with lingering colonialism, Western culture, and Western military might confirmed, but many were unhappy with Mahfouz's definition of Arab life somewhat removed from the struggle with Israel. More important, they saw in this rich texture of Cairo's society a people divided along generational and gender lines over ancient Muslim tradition and insurgent modernism, the latter somehow represented by eventual building of the Aswan Dam. No other Arab novel to this time had voiced these tensions. There is grim but concrete proof of the perceived power of Mahfouz's work, particularly the trilogy, on the Arab world: In 1994, he survived an attack by a group of Islamic extremists who attempted to kidnap him and stabbed him in the neck.

Not only was the trilogy important in Egypt; through it the Western world heard the Arab voice for the first time. As Egypt joined the international political scene, with the rise of Nasser, the world found expression of a land they previously knew only from the Arabian Nights. Readers exchanged the mystery of the Sultan's harem for Mahfouz's realistic treatment of the twentieth-century homes and markets of middle-class families sorting through political realities.

Additional Readings: Roger Allen, *The Arabic Novel: An Historical and Critical Introduction* (Syracuse, NY: Syracuse University Press, 1995);

Andre Raymond, *Cairo* (Cambridge: Harvard University Press, 2000); Sasson Somekh, *The Changing Rhythm: A Study of Najib Mahfuz's Novels* (Leiden: Brill, 1973).

2. *God Dies by the Nile* (*Mawt al-rajul al-waḥīd ʿalā 'l-ard*), by Nawāl El Saadawi (Egypt, 1974).

God Dies by the Nile was written during the political administration in Egypt of Anwar al-Sadat, a man who made massive positive changes for the better in Egyptian life after decades of totalitarian tyranny by his predecessors King Farouk and Gamal Abdel Nasser. However, many outsiders were unaware of the extent to which the Sadat administration silently continued to tolerate inhumane practices based on class and gender discrimination. *God Dies by the Nile*, set in modern Egypt, fictionally explored a scenario that El Saadawi was well aware of from her interviews with women prisoners: the rape of peasant girls by powerful men who were often, in turn, murdered by their victims or their victims' relatives, and the government's execution of these rape victims, without any attempt to end the vicious cycle of abuse.

The powerful character in the novel is the mayor who has absolute power over the lives of the citizens of his small village. He may tax them, arrest them, spy upon them, and with the help of his three henchmen, entrap young girls to satisfy his voracious sexual appetite. He is a man who claims to be highly religious but is, in fact, the worst kind of immoral animal. The story begins when he orders one of the village peasants, Kafrawi, to send his daughter, Nefissa, to work in his house. Kafrawi, unaware of the mayor's true intentions, complies. There she is raped, then cast out because she carries the mayor's child, although the village is convinced she has become pregnant by another peasant. When the mayor then sends for Nefissa's younger sister, Zeinab, she refuses to go. In retaliation the mayor frames their father for murder, causing Zakeya, the aunt who has reared them, to go insane. The priests tell the family that the only cure for the aunt's insanity is Zeinab's willingness to serve in the house of the mayor. This she does and is also forced into sexual relations with the mayor. The villagers blame the year's crop failure on the immoral pollution of the older sister and her illegitimate child, whom they kill. The younger sister, Zeinab, marries and leaves the mayor's house, whereupon the mayor frames her husband for a crime and kidnaps her. She is presumed to have been murdered. In retribution, Zakeya, the girls' aunt, murders the mayor in broad daylight and is arrested for murder. Referring to the mayor's death, Zakeya declares that God has died on the banks of the Nile. Though she will be executed, her murderous defiance gives other peasants in the town courage, and the prospect of rebellion against entrenched injustice rises among the populace.

The novel was a revelation to the rest of the world of the continuing exploitation of women and peasants in Egypt, often justified by Muslim law, even during the more enlightened administration of Anwar Sadat. Few of El Saadawi's readers were aware of the extent to which Arab women continued to be regarded as property. Few were aware of the extent to which lower-class women, in particular, were raped, outcast, and mutilated. Although El Saadawi was honored throughout the world for her courage, she was finally arrested in 1981 by Sadat and imprisoned for thirteen months simply because of her writing. When she emerged from prison, she was constantly followed and has since been consistently on the "death list" of Islamic extremists. The association for women she had organized was closed by administrative order, and the magazine she had founded was confiscated. In 1992, she left Egypt in exile. Back in Egypt in 2001, El Saadawi is being brought to trial in two courts for transgressions against Islam and for apostasy. The verdicts in both cases had not been rendered at the time this volume went to press, but should she be found guilty, the government of Egypt will dissolve her marriage of thirty-seven years. El Saadawi and her husband have, however, declared that whatever the verdicts they will remain together in Egypt.

Additional Readings: Janet L. Abu-Lughod, *Cairo* (Princeton, New Jersey: Princeton University Press, 1971); Fedwa Malti-Douglas, *Men, Women and God(s): Nawal El Saadawi and Arab Feminist Poetics* (Berkeley: University of California Press, 1995); Joseph Zeidan, *Arab Women Novelists* (Albany: State University of New York Press, 1995).

Kenya

๛

Ngugi wa Thiong'o, *Petals of Blood*, 1977

๛

TIMELINE

1886–90 British begin their takeover of Kenya, adding sections to the west in 1902, the south in 1908, and the north in 1918.

1902 European families begin moving into Kenya in great numbers, taking over native land and, through heavy taxation of natives, forcing them into labor on European farms.

1914 Danish writer Isak Dinesen moved with her husband to Kenya, where she remained until 1931.

1918 British secure control of all of Kenya.

1920 Kenya is made a colony of Britain, to be administered by a British governor. Black Africans are forbidden to vote or hold office.

1924 The Kikuju Central Association, the first of several effective native movements for liberation and reform, begins advocating the return of Kenyan land to natives.

1937 Isak Dinesen's *Out of Africa* is published.

1940s As hostilities among different natives and between natives and the British continue, Jomo Kenyatta rises to power, and for the first time, native Africans in Kenya are allowed to vote. A few can also hold office.

1952 The Mau Mau rebellion begins in resistance to British rule in Kenya.

1956 The British successfully suppress the Mau Mau rebellion, killing 10,000 Africans in the process.

1963 Kenya becomes independent. Jomo Kenyatta is the first president.

1964 Kenya becomes a republic.

1964–78 Kenya is ruled by Kenyatta. Although this is a period of great economic growth, Kenyatta uses tyrannical tactics like the suspending of civil liberties and wholesale imprisonments to suppress all who oppose his pro-Western stance.

1972 Writer and scholar Ngugi wa Thiong'o becomes chair of the Department of Literature at the University of Nairobi, Kenya.

1977   Ngugi wa Thiong'o publishes *Petals of Blood*, sharply criticizing Kenyatta.

1978   Ngugi wa Thiong'o is arrested and loses his position at the University of Nairobi.

        Kenyatta dies and is replaced by Daniel arap Moi, who begins his administration as a populist.

1981   Ngugi wa Thiong'o publishes *Detained: A Writer's Prison Diary*.

1982   Moi's government, having abandoned its populist stance, declares Kenya to be a one-party country.

        Kenya slides into ever-deepening economic disaster.

        Ngugi wa Thiong'o is exiled from Kenya.

1992   Ngugi wa Thiong'o becomes professor of comparative literature at New York University.

3. *Petals of Blood*, by Ngugi wa Thiong'o (Kenya, 1977). This fourth and most controversial novel by Ngugi wa Thiong'o, considered one of East Africa's first and best-known novelists, appeared and has its setting in the 1970s after Kenya had gained independence. Besides being a commentary on timely issues, the narrative looks back to events in Kenya's colonial past in which members of Ngugi's family were implicated. Between 1886 and 1890, Britain gained control of coastal Kenya, designating it a protectorate. However, it was not until just after World War I that the British were able to assume administrative control of interior Kenya, in large measure by pitting native tribes against one another and by encouraging European settlement of Kenya. Gradually, heavy colonial taxes were placed on tribes, and laws were enacted requiring them to work on European farms. The administration, overseen by a British governor, did not allow native Africans to vote or participate in government until the mid-1940s. Even then only a small group of blacks were appointed by the British—not elected—to serve in the legislature. Discontent grew over unjust policies, loss of land, and the squalid conditions

under which Africans had lived since the turn of the century. The undisputed African leader during this period was Jomo Kenyatta. Finally in the 1950s, violent rebellion broke out when poorer tribes, under the leadership of the Mau Mau army, warred with the British as well as with the natives whom colonialism had enriched. In May 1963, Kenya was given independence, and Kenyatta became the country's first president.

Kenyatta's presidency was far from peaceful, however. Opposition parties were formed to protest Kenyatta's Western leanings and capitalist sympathies. To squelch this opposition, Kenyatta began using tyrannical tactics such as packing his own supporters into all positions of power and detaining suspected opponents without warrant and trial. When Kenyatta died in 1978, Daniel arap Moi, a controversial figure whom he had groomed as his successor, took over the government. Although Moi began his administration as a populist, he, too, altered his course in the 1980s to put down all opposition by any means.

Ngugi's *Petals of Blood* appeared in the last year of Kenyatta's presidency. The novel's four main characters are three men—a schoolteacher, a former freedom fighter, a union organizer—and a woman of questionable character. All three converge on a tiny village to which they have come to escape their pasts. The history of Kenya is related in the course of unveiling their pasts. But attention is also given to the deplorable state of Kenyan life in the 1970s under Kenyatta, with the author's suggestion that in important ways life is no better than it was before independence was declared. His particular focus is on the state of education, the administrative corruption, the prohibition of free expression, the disenfranchisement of peasants who had fought for independence, the subjugation of women, the encouragement of a capitalistic system thriving on starvation wages, and the appropriation of the land of freedom fighters by the wealthy men in government who had spent their time receiving training when the others were fighting.

Ngugi's novel was one of the first fictional

criticisms of a postcolonial African government to reach large numbers of readers in
Europe and America. His audience saw
clearly that the problem in many newly independent Third World countries was what
he described as a multinational colonialism.
Economic interests on the part of major
world powers collaborated with a few
wealthy and unscrupulous natives to exploit
and disenfranchise the majority of a country's
citizens. Colonialism still existed; it had just
taken a different form. Largely as a result of
Ngugi's attack in this novel on Kenyatta, he
was arrested in December 1977 and detained
in prison until the death of Kenyatta in December 1978. He had, in the meantime, lost
his position as professor and head of the Department of Literature at the University of
Nairobi. After his release from prison, he was
unable to secure a teaching position in Kenya
again. While on a lecture tour in London in
1982, word reached him that he would be
arrested if he returned to Kenya. He has been
living in exile ever since.

Additional Readings: Charles Cantalupo, ed.,
The World of Ngugi wa Thiong'o (Kirksville:
Northeast Missouri State University, 1993);
Simon Gikandi, *Ngugi wa Thiong'o* (Cambridge:
Cambridge University Press, 1998); Carol Sich-
erman, *Ngugi wa Thiong'o: The Making of a Rebel*
(London: Hans Zell, 1990); Mwangi Wa-
Githumo, *Land and Nationalism* (Washington,
DC: University Press of America, 1981).

Nigeria and Senegal

༛

Chinua Achebe, *Things Fall Apart*, 1958
Wole Soyinka, *The Interpreters*, 1965
Mariama Ba, *So Long a Letter*, 1980

༛

TIMELINE

1500s–1800s	Muslims spread across West Africa.
1700s	Portuguese control Nigeria and its extensive slave trade.
1800s	European missionaries arrive in Nigeria.
1860s	Al-Hajj Umar creates a Muslim empire in Senegal-Gambia region.
1884	After European powers divided Africa among themselves at the Berlin West Africa Conference, Britain lays claim to Nigeria. The resistance among native peoples is widespread and often ends in violence.
1900	Britain secures the last section of Nigeria and divides all of Nigeria into two British Protectorates.
1903	Britain puts down resistance from rebels and establishes indirect rule by British-appointed native leaders whose chief function is tax collection.
1914–18	Armed resistance and strikes, especially in mines and railroads, are regular occurrences.
1929	A battle against taxation is fought chiefly by Igbo women.
1930s–40s	There is persistent passive resistance to British rule and policies.
1945	A major strike disrupts commerce and contributes to the rise of nationalist political parties urging independence. The most prominent of these are the National Council of Nigeria and the Cameroons and the Action Group.
1947	Internal and external pressure prompts Britain to divide the country again and institute a new constitution.
1958	Chinua Acebe's *Things Fall Apart* is published.
1960	Nigeria achieves independence, but ethnic tensions rise, frequently escalating into violence. The new

prime minister, Abukakar Tafawa Balewa, meets all criticism with brutal repression.

1965   Wole Soyinka's novel *The Interpreters* is published.

1966   Balewa and other officials are killed by junior officers in the Nigerian army. General Johnson Aguiyi-Ironsi takes control, suspending the constitution and taking authority away from regional governments. He is assassinated before his first year is out and followed by another military ruler, Yakubu Gowon.

1967   Wole Soyinka is arrested and placed in solitary confinement for two years.

        Civil War breaks out between Biafra, a newly formed, largely Igbo state, and the rest of Nigeria.

1970   The war ends with Gowon still in charge as military ruler.

1975   Reformer Brigadier General Murtala Ramat Muhammed overthrows Gowon.

1976   Muhammed is assassinated in a failed coup attempt, but his government continues in power under reformer General Olusegun Obasanjo, who creates Nigeria's Second Republic under constitutional parliamentary law.

1978   Alhaji Shehu Shagari and the National Party of Nigeria win the election, a result that many question.

1980   Senegal writer Miriama Ba's *So Long a Letter* is published. Her target is predicament of women within a Muslim tradition. At this point, 90 percent of Senegal is Muslim.

1983   The army overthrows Shagari and General Muhammadu Buhari assumes leadership, bringing in some reforms but also much repression and censorship.

1985   Buhari is overthrown by another general, Ibrahim Babangida.

1986   Wole Soyinka of Nigeria becomes the first African writer and first black writer to win the Nobel Prize for Literature.

1989   The constitution is restored and elections guaranteed.

1993   The elections of 1992 are annulled by the military, and General Sani Abacha assumes control, subsequently forbidding all political activity.

1994   Wole Soyinka goes into exile.

1995   Eight political activists are hanged, and many others are imprisoned by Abacha.

1997   Nigeria charges Wole Soyinka with treason.

1998   Abacha dies of a heart attack.

        Charges against Soyinka are dropped.

4. *Things Fall Apart*, by Chinua Achebe (Nigeria, 1958). Chinua Achebe's novel appeared during years of intense struggle in Africa for independence from European colonialists. Though it is set in the closing years of the nineteenth century during the height of colonialism, it speaks to the 1950s. The first European incursions into Africa were made by Portuguese traders and navigators, who exported slaves to Europe and America to satisfy the need for more and more labor created by the Industrial Revolution. In 1830 alone, 135,000 Nigerians a year were exported. Between 1880 and 1887, Britain acquired Nigeria, building up military forces there to protect economic interests. European missionaries came in the eighteenth and nineteenth centuries, their purpose to save the natives from their own religion. As Achebe points out, missionaries brought some necessary and desirable changes in tribal practice, but at the expense of the total destruction of native culture. A vast bureaucracy of white governmental institutions followed: prisons, courts, police, and military garrisons. At the time of the novel's appearance, Nigeria was in a struggle for independence, a goal it reached two years later in 1960.

The hero of the novel is humbly born Okonkwo, who after much vicissitude rises to become a lord of a clan in Umofia. After he viciously beats his wife and then murders two men, his position is taken from him, and he is exiled to Mbanta. Here Okonkwo learns of the effects of the European presence in surrounding areas. While he is in exile, the British forces kill large numbers of the Abaeme tribe, and European missionaries in Umofia convince many people to abandon their native religion. Later, the missionaries come to Mbanta as well, and Okonkwo's son is converted. When Okonkwo has served out his term in exile and returns home, he finds the Europeans fully ensconced, some native conversion to Christianity, but much conflict between natives and Europeans. In the course of the friction between Okonkwo and the British, he kills an emissary and hangs himself. On the heels of this event, the District Commissioner makes plans to write a skewed history of the Igbo people.

Achebe's novel has to date sold over 8 million copies and been translated into fifty languages. It had a tremendous immediate impact and has continued to exert a huge influence, especially in Africa where the book is required reading in most high schools. As many African intellectuals have pointed out, Achebe's novel has become a major factor in shaping the young African's more accurate picture of his or her own past and is in marked contrast to the distortions still propagated in many African schools and pulpits.

Much of the enduring influence of Achebe's novel can be credited to his use of an African protagonist and African characters in a nineteenth-century tribal setting, in marked contrast to Joseph Conrad's *Heart of Darkness*, the other major work that criticizes nineteenth-century colonialism in Africa. Readers for the first time saw tribal Africans during the time of beginning English colonization as humans with intelligence, fami-

lies, emotional dimension, and their own religion and culture that were just as sacred to them as Christianity was to the missionaries. For many readers, the book is a celebration of difference.

The most important influence the book has had on readers—African and European— is to dispel the European's justification of colonialism. The book shows that Africa was not a savage "void" before the arrival of Europeans. It had a history, its own arts, and its own religion. Yet most have declared Achebe's view to be balanced. At the same time that he uncovers the fallaciousness of the European argument for colonization, he reveals that Africans, in many traditions and in their reaction to colonialism, also contributed to the condition in which Africa found itself in the 1950s.

Additional Readings: David Carroll, *Chinua Achebe* (New York: Twayne, 1970); Kalu Ogbaa, *Gods, Oracles, and Divination* (Trenton, NJ: Africa-World, 1992); Kalu Ogbaa, *Understanding Things Fall Apart* (Westport, CT: Greenwood, 1999); Dike K. Onwuka, *100 Years of British Rule in Nigeria 1851–1951* (Lago: Federal Information Service, 1958).

5. *The Interpreters,* by Wole Soyinka (Nigeria, 1965). Wole Soyinka, who in 1986 became the first black person and the first African to win the Nobel Prize for Literature, was already an established writer when he wrote his first novel, *The Interpreters.* The setting of the novel is the 1960s when Nigerians were living through the bloody power struggles that followed Nigerian independence from British rule on October 1, 1960. Democracy, however, did not arrive with independence. Regional and tribal tensions erupted. The country's first prime minister began a policy of arresting those he considered politically unfriendly, and violence erupted during most elections, which were viewed as dishonest. Several military coups, massacres, and assassinations occurred throughout the 1960s.

Soyinka's novel, set during these turbulent years in an academic Nigerian community, satirizes the country's leaders, the military, the press, and the country's intelligentsia. The story involves five characters, university graduates, who meet on a return to their alma mater. The narrative flashes back to their past lives, moving forward to the thorough disillusionment each feels with the results of Nigerian independence. Each of the men represents a different, critical profession. Sagoe is a journalist; Sekoni, an engineer; Ebgo, a foreign office worker and heir to a fiefdom. Kola is an artist, and Bandele, a university lecturer. Each *interprets* the country, hence the title. Though each is in a profession that has the potential to shape national affairs, and each claims to oppose corruption and collaborators, none are in positions of power, and their responses to the political situation are different.

The corrupt individuals whom Soyinka satirizes include a doctor who only performs abortions for those women who will grant him sexual favors and a professor who rants against "bad girls" while fathering illegitimate children.

The response of the disillusioned professionals to the corruption around them is to withdraw into their own obsessions, chiefly art and religion, which ignores responsibility for the society they live in. Only the engineer Sekoni remains politically engaged. He is soon broken by the government, banished, and disowned by his family and friends. His sincere efforts to help the common people are thwarted, and he goes mad, a fate that leads to the further isolation of his friends.

Noah, a poor boy who seems to represent the masses of Nigerians, is pursued by the five professionals because he can be useful to them individually. He is sought out as a model by the artist and as the subject of a feature article by the journalist. Ever obsessed with "interpreting," no one actually helps him. When he is eventually killed, only Bandele accepts guilt for his fate.

The Interpreters, largely banned in Africa, was shortly regarded as an African classic and was largely responsible for the choice of Soyinka as a 1986 winner of the Nobel Prize. The novel also had responsibility for the arrest of Soyinka in 1967. For the next two years, he remained in solitary confinement. The novel has also been criticized by African nationalists for being too accommodating to the West and insufficiently radical in outlook.

Still, readers all over the world have found that the novel opened their eyes to the tribal nature of Africa and to the corruption that these competing entities engendered. For Africans the novel focused on the need for Africans themselves to take an active role in fighting internal corruption rather than concentrating wholly on Western intervention.

The potential influence of the novel as well as of Soyinka's dramas can be seen in the threat that they posed to the various regimes that fought for power after the Nigerian civil war. By 1994, Soyinka had been forced into exile, and in 1997 he was charged with treason, a charge that was dropped in 1998 with a change in political leadership.

Additional Readings: David William Cohen, *The Combing of History* (Chicago: University of Chicago Press, 1994); Gerald Moore, *Wole Soyinka* (London: Evans Brothers, 1978); Derek Wright, *Wole Solinka Revisited* (New York: Twayne, 1993).

6. *So Long a Letter* (*Une si longue lettre*), by Mariama Ba (Senegal, 1980). Although Mariama Ba only wrote two novels, her *So Long a Letter* drew attention to practices and attitudes with regard to women, specifically polygamy and female circumcision, widespread in North Africa, that until that time were spoken about only in whispers and lost in the maze of other political problems in modern Africa.

Drawing from her own experiences with a marriage that disintegrated, Mariama Ba's novel, generally considered her major one, is a study of Muslim marriages in the form of a "so long a letter" written by the newly widowed Ramatoulaye to her friend Aissatou. A third woman, Jacqueline, is also a major character in the drama. These women are distinguished from many other Muslim wives and the older generation of wives because they have been educated. Their marriages began outside the usual Muslim traditions in that they, rather than their families, had chosen their husbands. However much they realized that Muslim male entitlement could not be overridden, all were shocked at the indignities and limitations of married life in the modern world. Each of the women is finally "despised, relegated, or exchanged" as their husbands' yen for sexual variety leads them to take other, younger wives. And the first wives' situations are made even worse in that their in-laws invariably support the husbands' behavior and in all three cases are resentful of the highly educated first wives. The whole matter of caste also complicates Muslim marriages, for even though Aissatou is highly educated, she is of a lower caste than her husband Mawdo. His mother, who has voiced her strong disapproval of the union from the start, immediately begins searching for a more suitable wife from a higher caste for her married son. Aissatou's in-laws go so far as to put pressure on their son to get rid of Aissatou altogether. Other Muslim customs make the women apprehensive: At the death of Ramatoulaye's husband, his brother moves to force both his brother's widows to marry him.

All three react differently to their husbands' taking of additional wives. Ramatoulaye forces her husband to leave the house but refuses to allow the marriage to be dissolved. Aissatou ends the marriage and leaves with her four sons. But Jacqueline suffers a nervous breakdown.

Mariama Ba's readers also became aware of the psychological tensions created in modern marriages when two diametrically opposed cultures—Western society and Middle-Eastern society—are in conflict. The woman, who receives a Western education, expects that she will be treated as an equal partner and an only wife and companion. Yet the Muslim tradition she inherits insists that she is no more than an object to be given to her husband. She is to be completely subservient to him. To the older Muslim families, love has little or nothing to do with marriage. Young marriageable women are used by their families to secure status, money, stability, and children.

Mariama Ba articulated for her Middle Eastern readers the problem of the subjugation of women that is endemic to Muslim religion—men having total freedom and women living as prisoners within their households. In this sense, her "letter" is not just to one character but to all Muslim women who experienced the same emotions, were silenced by Muslim law, and had no one to speak with about their heartbreak.

For the international community the book was a revelation about abuses that were difficult to correct because they were so long-standing and dictated by holy writ. Yet it was one of the main initiatives in gaining international support for Arab women interested in more humane reforms.

Additional Readings: Judith Njage, *Notes on Mariama Ba's "So Long a Letter"* (Nairobi: Heinemann Educational Books, 1984); Melanie Stephens, *Gender and Solidarity: A Village in Rural Senegal* (Cambridge: Harvard University Archives, 1987); Florence Stratton, *Contemporary African Literature and the Politics of Gender* (London: Routledge, 1994).

Somalia

❦

Nuruddin Farah, *Close Sesame*, 1983

❦

TIMELINE

1947   After World War II, Italy, which had controlled Somalia, was forced to renounce its African territories, and Somalia was placed under British control.

1950   Somalia is transferred to Italian control.

1960   Somalia is granted independence. The first president is Aden Abdullah Osman Daar. This marks the beginning of nine years of turmoil.

1967   Daar is defeated in an election by Abdi Rashid Ali Shirmarke.

1969   Shirmarke is assassinated. Major General Mohamed Siad Barre assumes control, instituting military rule.

1970   Barre declares Somalia a socialist state and nationalizes the economy.

1974–75 General drought and starvation plague Somalia.

1976   Somalian writer Nuruddin Farah learns while traveling abroad that he faces arrest and a thirty-year imprisonment if he returns to Somalia. This forces him into exile.

1982   Civil war ensues between Somalia's clans.

1983   Nuruddin Farah's novel *Close Sesame* is published, pronounced a dangerous book, and immediately banned in Somalia.

1991   Barre is deposed, but Somalia continues into the twenty-first century to be plagued by internal fighting between clans, despite UN peacekeeping efforts. Killing floods and famine have also taken their toll on the country.

7. *Close Sesame*, by Nuruddin Farah (Somalia, 1983). The primary political theme of the novels of Nuruddin Farah, one of the foremost novelists of North Africa, has been the oppression of the peoples in his native Somalia. *Close Sesame*, his most influential and well-known work, is the last novel of a trilogy set in Somalia.

In 1945, when Farah was born, Somalia was in a transition period during which administration of the country was being transferred from postwar British occupation to a provisional Italian administration. In 1960,

Somalia was granted independence. A turbulent ten-year political period followed, ending in 1969 with a military coup led by Major General Mohamed Siad Barre who then took over the leadership of Somalia. Although many people, like Farah, were encouraged at first by Barre's declared policies such as waging war on corruption, illiteracy, and poverty, they were soon rudely awakened by Barre's methods. In the name of Marxism and Islam, Barre created a police state to protect him and the narrow interests of the tribes to which he felt loyal. Those who criticized Barre were summarily executed; a police force trained by the KGB used Stalinist tactics to spy on citizens, indoctrinate youth, and torture political dissidents. Speech and literature were heavily censored. When it became more convenient for his purposes to switch allegiances, Barre traded his close connections with the Soviets for Western capitalism, with almost no perceived difference in his mode of operation. He was not deposed until 1991.

Close Sesame is a direct challenge to Barre's dictatorship, portraying it as just as objectionable as the earlier Italian and British colonial governments in Somalia. The novel's protagonist is an old gentleman named Deeriye, who has a well-earned reputation as a freedom fighter. He was sent to prison for fighting the Italian fascists in World War II and, as part of the liberation movement, actively helped in the establishment of Somalian independence. His difficulties begin, however, when his son joins a group planning to assassinate the general who runs the country. After the government arrests one of Deeriye's close friends and his son's best friend, Deeriye is placed under suspicion and begins to be harassed secretly, even though the government is afraid to confront such a symbol of liberation openly. The tyranny that parents exercise over their children and the tyranny that husbands and parents exercise over wives and daughters are directly compared to the tyranny of the country's dictator.

Deeriye trades his symbolism for activism when his son is killed by the government. In response, he decides to kill the dictator himself, but at the last moment he is himself killed by the dictator's body guards when he extracts prayer beads, which they mistake for a pistol, from his clothes. The reader is left to speculate about the ending. Has Deeriye been maddened by grief? Or has he deliberately made a politically useful martyr of himself?

For twenty years, because it was perceived as one of the most dangerous of books, Farah's *Close Sesame* was banned in Somalia. Despite this, it has had an important impact in the Somalian underground where it is transmitted through the ancient oral tradition. The novel has also had a measurable impact in areas outside of Africa. Farah's novel literally changed the way in which many people viewed the volatile situation in North Africa in that Farah refused to follow blindly any one political line. His readers saw that blame for oppression in Africa could be laid to multiple factors in the African and European traditions, yet both traditions had also contributed positively to Somalia. The target of much of his criticism, for example, is African tribalism, Islam, and Marxism, all of which have been used to destroy justice and freedom in Somalia.

In 1976, Farah, who was returning home to Somalia from a two-year stay in England, chanced to meet the Somalian Minister of Justice in the Rome airport. He was told that he would be arrested and face a thirty-year prison sentence when he set foot in Somalia. Understandably, he changed his plans and did not return. Since that time, he has lived in exile. *Close Sesame*, published eight years later, was regarded by the Barre government as the most dangerous of Farah's books because it laid bare the heart of the problem in Somalia. This novel confirmed his exile because it articulated to the rest of the world the complex set of forces that, he writes, cause most Somalians to live in exile within the boundaries of their own country.

Additional Readings: Jamil Abdulla Mubarak, *From Bad Policy to Chaos in Somalia* (Westport, CT: Praeger, 1996); Derek Wright, *The Novels of Nuruddin Farah* (Bayreuth, Germany: Bayreuth University Press, 1994).

South Africa

❧

Olive Schreiner, *The Story of an African Farm*, 1883
Alan Paton, *Cry, the Beloved Country*, 1948
Peter Abrahams, *The Path of Thunder*, 1948
Nadine Gordimer, *The Conservationist*, 1974

❧

TIMELINE

1652   The Dutch East India Company establishes a fort at the Cape of Good Hope, eventually bringing in Dutch farmers who appropriate tribal lands and use slaves from the Khoikhoi people.

1680   French Huguenots begin arriving to farm in the Cape Colony.

1700   By this time the Khoikhoi had lost most of their land to European settlers.

1770   Bantu-speaking Zulus begin settling in the northern and eastern portions of present South Africa.

1781   Xhosa settle in the north.

1814   The British buy Cape Town from the Dutch.

1820   The English begin migrating to South Africa in great numbers.

        The English abolish slavery, which angers the Dutch or Afrikaners.

1835–40 Dutch displeasure over English policies starts a migration of the Afrikaners to the north where they are continually engaged in territorial wars with the Xhosa.

1838   Afrikaners defeat the Zulus in a territorial war.

1858   Separate Afrikaner and English colonies are established in the region.

1883   Olive Schreiner's *The Story of an African Farm* is published.

1886   Gold is discovered in South Africa.

1902   Afrikaner colonies are forced to become British colonies.

1910   The British Parliament becomes the final authority in South Africa. Afrikaner Louis Botha becomes prime minister.

        Policies of segregation and discrimination toward black Africans, "coloreds," and Indians remain in place in what are now four areas of South

Africa. Black Africans are restricted to reserves.

1912   A group of black Africans organize as the African National Congress (ANC) to protest legal and work discrimination, segregation, and their lack of suffrage and representation.

Mohandas Gandhi works for Indian rights in South Africa.

1913   Congress passes the Natives Land Act, specifying that blacks can buy land only on reserves, which make up only 7 percent of the country's land.

1921   The gold mining industry replaces all white workers with blacks to save money on labor costs.

The Rand Revolt results in the exclusion of black workers from managerial positions.

1939   Writer Peter Abrahams leaves South Africa.

1940–44   Writer and minister Alan Paton is attacked by the government for writing on its unjust treatment of blacks.

1945–47   Paton goes on a world tour lecturing on the bad situation in South Africa.

1948   Paton's *Cry, the Beloved Country* is published. From this moment Paton is stalked, harassed, and spied upon.

Peter Abraham's *The Path of Thunder* is published.

South Africa's long-standing practices of segregation and racial discrimination are written into law, known as apartheid.

1950   The Group Areas Act passes, mandating separate living areas for whites, for blacks, for coloreds, and for Asians.

Under the leadership of Nelson Mandela, the ANC increases its peaceful demonstrations against government policies.

1952   Pass Laws are enacted to limit and control the entry of nonwhites in white areas.

The ANC and Indian Congress join to oppose apartheid laws.

1959   Blacks are allowed limited self-government within the boundaries of their own reserves, or Bantustans, and government no longer assumes responsibility for providing services to these areas.

1960   Paton loses his travel privileges. His passport will not be restored for five years.

During a peaceful demonstration by the ANC in Sharpeville, police kill sixty-nine people and wound many more.

Both the ANC and the more militant Pan-Africanist Congress are banned.

Stephen Biko organizes the Black Consciousness Movement.

1963   Nelson Mandela and other resistance leaders are sentenced to life in prison.

Passage of the Unlawful Organizations Act allows the government to detain anyone for ninety days without trial.

1967   The Terrorism Act allows indefinite detention without trial.

1974   *The Conservationist* by Nadine Gordimer is published.

South Africa is suspended from the United Nations General Assembly.

1976   Black students hold a demonstration in Soweto protesting the necessity of using Afrikaner in required classes. In a confrontation with police, 574 people are killed.

1977   Stephen Biko dies while detained by police.

1981   Blacks are finally given the right to unionize.

1983   In response to economic boycotts from every quarter of the world, President P.W. Botha introduces limited reforms, but the establishment of three separate congresses by race still excludes blacks and is controlled by the white congress.

1989   F.W. de Klerk becomes president of South Africa.

1990   Nelson Mandela is released from prison.

1991   Nadine Gordimer wins the Nobel Prize for Literature.

1993   In the transfer of power to the black majority and the end of apartheid, the government establishes a policy of one person, one vote.

1994   The first democratic election is held. Nelson Mandela is elected president, with F.W. de Klerk and Thabo Mbeki as deputy presidents.

8. *The Story of an African Farm*, by Olive Schreiner (South Africa, 1883). Olive Schreiner's *The Story of an African Farm*, one of the most highly acclaimed novels of its day, brought her instant celebrity in England, Europe, and Africa. What is unusual about the novel is that its clear social thesis has little to do with the extraordinary racial situation in South Africa. Instead, she addresses the universal issue of what came to be known as "the Woman Question," which was just as applicable to England or America as it was to South Africa. The novel appeared at a time before women had a right to vote, before they were able to receive the kind of general or professional educations available to men, when women were expected to marry, to remain confined to home and church, and to try not to exercise their brains, God having not made them for intellectual endeavors.

The Story of an African Farm has as its main characters Waldo, an idealistic young man; his soul mate, a beautiful and strong-willed young woman in her late teens named Lyndall; Em, a sweet and fairly passive young woman about the same age; and Gregory Rose, an effeminate young man who, like Waldo, is in love with Lyndall. Lyndall, the heroine of the story, violates every possible expectation of womanhood in the course of her short life. At the first she insists on an education but comes home convinced that the usual boarding school education pro-

vided for girls does, indeed, "finish" them. She violates other taboos by becoming an adherent of Natural Religion, by leaving home to explore the larger world, and by becoming pregnant and then refusing to marry her child's father. Gregory Rose finds her and dresses as a woman in order to live with and take care of her. But she and the baby both die shortly after the birth. Gregory returns to the home place to marry Em, and Waldo, Lyndall's soul mate, dies, seemingly of a broken heart.

Schreiner's celebrity in the usual literary and intellectual circles was instantaneous. For the rest of her life, she was treated as a famous person, all on the basis of this one novel. Moreover, she received hundreds of letters each year from young women who found that her messages in the novel hit a chord with them and believed that she alone understood the problems they were going through. At issue was Lyndall's courage in defying the expectations that her family and society had of women, especially with regard to religion, education, and marriage. Many of those who wrote to Schreiner were still struggling with their families to receive the kinds of education afforded to the men in their families. Many of them, both men and women, were grappling with religious doubts and trying to bring the new science of the day, especially Darwinism, into harmony with a new religion. Many of them, like Lyndall and Schreiner herself, were disillusioned with what they saw as worn-out, hypocritical sexual mores and the mindless and inflexible insistence on the form of marriage without the spirit of love.

The novel has been credited with being a forerunner of twentieth-century feminism with a landmark model of the New Woman.

Additional Readings: Joyce Berkman, *The Healing Imagination of Olive Schreiner* (Amherst: University of Massachusetts Press, 1989); Cherry Clayton, *Olive Schreiner* (New York: Twayne, 1997); Gerald Monsman, *Olive Schreiner's Fiction* (New Brunswick, NJ: Rutgers University Press, 1991); Robert Ross, *A Concise History of South Africa* (Cambridge: Cambridge University Press, 1999).

9. *Cry, the Beloved Country,* by Alan Paton (South Africa, 1948). Alan Paton's phenomenally successful novel evolved from his efforts to reform many aspects of South African life, beginning with the system of reform school education for young black men and gradually embracing attempts to tear down impediments blacks faced in receiving education, justice, social acceptance, suffrage, and economic opportunities. The novel appeared in the year that apartheid became law, making official the rigid separation of the races that had been tradition and practice since the Europeans settled South Africa in the seventeenth century. For decades, all nonwhites had been relegated to reserves, comprising about 7 percent of all land, established on the least desirable South African land. Government passes were required of them to move from one area to another. The Natives Land Act of 1913, which prevented them from buying land outside the reserves, merely funneled black labor into the mines and other physical and domestic labor inside the cities. In essence, they became migrants, having to live on reserves but having to work in the cities.

In the early 1940s, when Paton was maliciously attacked at home for writing on the economic and political injustice in the treatment of those black South Africans who were in the majority and actually native to the area, and for offering his plans to bring them into the mainstream of South African life, he decided that he had to seek a wider platform. This brought him to a worldwide tour in 1945–47 to gather support. It was while he was on tour that the idea for the novel came to him.

Cry, the Beloved Country is the story of a black Anglican priest, the Reverend Stephen Kumalo, who goes from his very poor reserve in rural South Africa to find his son and his sister who have been swallowed up in the city of Johannesburg where they had gone to look for work. After an intense and heartrending search, he finds that his sister Gertrude has become a prostitute in order to exist and that his son Absalom is in prison awaiting trial for the murder of the son of a well-to-do white farmer, James Jarvis. Kumalo must return to his village without either his sister or his son, who will be executed. But he brings back with him Gertrude's young son and Absalom's wife and unborn baby, wondering what can be done to keep these children from being destroyed by the system that took their parents. Despite the tragedy, the novel ends on a hopeful note as Kumalo and Jarvis, fathers of the murderer and the murdered son, are reconciled and together plan to bring the changes to the black community that will interrupt a pattern of hopelessness and crime.

That Paton's novel reached a wide circle of readers can be seen in its sales—more than 15 million by 1988 and 100,000 in 1991 alone. In 1951, it was the subject of a popular film in Great Britain, directed by Zoltan Korda, and in 1995 a film made in the United States by Darrell James Roodt. Despite, or because of, the continued popularity and influence of the book, it was perceived as a threat by the white South African establishment, especially Hendrik F. Verwoerd, the Nationalist Party official who engineered the policy of apartheid. In 1960, after a twelve-year campaign of harassment, Paton lost his traveling privileges. His passport was not restored for ten years. Paton, who never wavered in his convictions and could never be silenced, was constantly followed; his house was periodically searched, his phone tapped, his mail intercepted, and his car destroyed.

Paton's book was the first one to inform the general public about the lives of black people in a white African world and was for a decade the only book presenting such a perspective on South Africa. The book was the first written as a clear plea for economic, social, and political justice in South Africa. As people knowledgeable of conditions in South Africa noted, Paton was able to convey something of every conceivable racial wrong in the country, including the abominable conditions in the mines, the unspeakable poverty in the reserves, the poverty of the city that led to crime, the dissolution of the controlling and ordering traditions of tribal life, and the subsequent chaos that ensues.

Paton's book brought many of its readers to the conclusion he suggested: that the inevitable result of the treatment of blacks would be continent-wide violence.

Additional Reading: Peter F. Alexander, *Alan Paton: A Biography* (London: Oxford University Press, 1994); Joshua Brown, ed., *History of South Africa* (Philadelphia: Temple University Press, 1991); Edward Cullan, *"Cry the Beloved Country": A Novel of South Africa* (Boston: Twayne, 1991).

10. *The Path of Thunder*, by Peter Abrahams (South Africa, 1948). Peter Abrahams has been described by critic Andrew Peek, in an article on Abrahams in *African Writers*, as "the first black African author to produce a considerable body of work that synthesizes African and western narrative traditions in a distinctly modern idiom." Abrahams's novel *The Path of Thunder* is one of his most popular and influential works specifically designed to show English readers the social impediments and humiliations under which black and mixed-race South Africans labored. The novel was published in 1948, the year that traditions of segregation and discrimination officially became the law of the land in South Africa, under the title of "apartheid." Although the action of the novel takes place in the 1940s, it looks both to the future of South Africa and back on the history of the country. In 1650, when the existing tribes in South Africa included the Khoikhoi and the San, the Dutch East India Company established a fort and trading post at the Cape of Good Hope. The Dutch farmers, called Boers, who were imported by the Dutch to settle the area, began confiscating for their personal ownership more and more of the land occupied by the natives. To cultivate their land, the Boers used slaves imported from Asia and from the native Khoikhoi tribes. Many tribes were simply wiped out. The British entered the picture in 1814, and there were many frontier wars between British, Dutch, and natives. Life in South Africa changed drastically with the discovery of gold there in 1886, for the Euro-

peans made fortunes and the natives did the mining for them under dangerous working conditions and for pittances.

From the beginning, blacks, Indians, and peoples of mixed race were not allowed to vote, hold office, or mix with other races. Most were relegated to reserves where education was nonexistent. The only jobs available to them were the lowliest, demanding hard physical labor. In 1913, the Natives Land Act prevented black people from buying land outside their reserves, which comprised only 7 percent of the total land and was the least desirable in the country.

This rigid segregation of the races is the subject of *The Path of Thunder*, which has often been compared with the story of Romeo and Juliet and has perhaps accounted for its popularity. One of the star-crossed lovers is Lanny Swartz, a young man classified as "Colored," who has received an education in Cape Town and returns to his home reserve of Stilleveld to repay the community by setting up a school. There he falls in love with Sarie Villier, a young woman adopted by the Afrikaner family whose mansion overlooks Lanny's colored settlement and a black settlement. The two are killed by the Afrikaners who attempt to thwart their elopement to Portuguese East Africa. The ironic discovery made after their deaths is that Sarie was also colored, not white, and that Lanny was the product of a union between a black person and a member of the Afrikaner Villier family.

Readers attracted to the novel by its Gothic romance were introduced for the first time to a realistic rendering of the rigid racial system of segregation in South Africa, including the attempts to hide the sexual exploitation by Afrikaners of black and mixed-race women, the Afrikaner conviction that no black or mixed-race person should be educated because it gives them false aspirations, and the Afrikaners' clear economic exploitation of natives whom they regarded as animals.

Its influence is shown in its having been translated into twenty-six languages and its continuing high volume of sales.

Additional Readings: Robert Ensor, *The Novels of Peter Abrahams* (Essen, Germany: Verlag die, Blaue Erle, 1994); Allister Haddon Sparks, *The Mind of South Africa* (London: Heinemann, 1990); Michael Wade, *Peter Abrahams* (London: Evans Brothers, 1972).

11. *The Conservationist,* by Nadine Gordimer (South Africa, 1974). *The Conservationist* established Nadine Gordimer as a novelist of international importance, winning the prestigious British award the Booker Prize in 1974 and leading to her 1991 award of the Nobel Prize in Literature.

The Union of South Africa, where Gordimer lives and of which she writes in *The Conservationist*, was established in 1910 when the British Parliament assumed authority over the country, once tribal lands colonized by the British in the nineteenth century. Although they were in the majority, black Africans in the country could not vote or hold office and were restricted to poor, segregated areas. For decades prior to the action of Gordimer's novel, black workers were restricted to the lowest form of physical labor in the country's rich mines and lucrative factories. The African National Congress, the major organization of nonviolent resistance to minority white role and its policies of racial discrimination, was formed in 1912. Under strong leadership, black and white South Africans in this and other resistance organizations continued the fight for reform, suggesting that the establishment of majority rule was only a matter of time.

The main character of Gordimer's novel is Mehring, a white South African industrialist and international entrepreneur who makes his fortune on the backs of his black workers and spends his leisure hours in the pastoral setting of his South African farm, ironically calling himself a conservationist. His interior monologues reveal the attitudes of racial and cultural superiority, typical of apartheid-era South Africa, as well as blindness to the validity of African culture and its power to reassert itself in South Africa. There is tangible evidence that the political winds are changing throughout the country when Mehring's laborers take over his farm in his absence. The symbol of the reemergence of the black African in Africa is represented by the body of a black man that rises to the surface from its burial site during torrential rains and has to be buried again.

Feminism, a major issue of the novel, is shown in the similarities between the exploited and repressed white women of the novel and the abused, oppressed black workers, between colonial power and sexual power.

It has often been said of *The Conservationist* that like the dead body that rises to the surface the novel exposes much that lay hidden in South African life. Through Mehring's monologue we see not only the idea of the blind racial superiority of the South African but also the inability of white liberal reform to effect satisfactory changes. Gordimer's novel was one of the first to predict the enforced political reversal of South Africa's power, from white to the black majority.

The novel was also one of the first by a white African to incorporate black African culture into the form and message of the novel. Zulu myths, especially involving rainmaking and possession by spirits, serve the progress of the plot as well as a basis for the symbolic meaning of the novel.

One of those hidden truths that the novel surfaced was the blind belief of many well-meaning white South Africans that they could remain unpolitical, seeking only a peaceful, comfortable existence for themselves.

Unlike many white South African radicals, Gordimer has been determined to stay in her country, a decision that, as a result of *The Conservationist* and other works that followed it, have exacted a price. This book, for example, was banned in South Africa before majority rule changed the character of government. Nor was Gordimer's work, especially this one, given the attention and approval of the nation's white literary establishment, even though she was finally awarded the Nobel Prize by the international community. Although she was never arrested, in the 1960s she was under constant police surveillance.

Additional Readings: Stephen Clingman, *The Novels of Nadine Gordimer: History from the Inside* (Amherst: University of Massachusetts Press, 1992); Judie Newman, *Nadine Gordimer* (London: Routledge, 1988); Robert Ross, *A Concise History of South Africa* (Cambridge: Cambridge University Press, 1999).

Zimbabwe

∽

Doris Lessing, *Children of Violence*, 1952–69

∽

TIMELINE

1890   An area of Southern Africa, made an English protectorate under the direction of Cecil Rhodes, came to be named Southern Rhodesia. Rhodes exploited the natural resources of the area and brought in European farmers to take away the land of natives and force them to work for Rhodes in the mines and other endeavors. Though technically a protectorate, Southern Rhodesia was ruled independent of England by a white minority. Blacks were segregated, allowed no vote, and discriminated against with regard to jobs.

1930s–40s   These years of Doris Lessing's young girlhood in Southern Rhodesia provided the setting for *Children of Violence.*

1949   Lessing moves to England.

1952–69   Lessing publishes her five-novel sequence under the title of *Children of Violence.*

1956   Upon her visit to her homeland from England, Lessing finds that she has been designated a "prohibited immigrant" and is barred from returning to her country again.

1965   Pressed by England to widen suffrage, Southern Rhodesia declares itself independent of England.

1980   After years of conflict, Southern Rhodesia is forced to accept majority rule. Robert Mugabe becomes its leader, and its name is changed to Zimbabwe.

1982   Doris Lessing is allowed to return to her native land.

12. *Children of Violence*, by Doris Lessing (Zimbabwe, England, 1952–69). Lessing's series of five novels called *Children of Violence* is a semiautobiographical work set largely in Africa's Southern Rhodesia, where she grew up and spent her first thirty years, and London, England, where she moved in 1949. Although Lessing has felt that she cannot or should not speak for African blacks in her novels, the political upheaval and racial injustice in her country shaped her own life as a political activist and novelist.

The country in which the first three *Children of Violence* novels unfold was settled by the British in 1890, under the leadership of adventurer-capitalist Cecil Rhodes, who was interested in mining the country for its wealth of natural resources. The people he brought with him wanted to make their fortunes running plantations, which they did by displacing small tribal farmers who were needed as labor in Rhodes's enterprises. Although technically classified as a British protectorate, Southern Rhodesia was in fact a self-governing entity, ruled entirely by the white minority. Policies there were very similar to those in nearby South Africa: Blacks could not vote or hold office, were rarely educated, were completely segregated from whites, were allowed to perform only the most menial and servile jobs, and were subject to curfews and travel restrictions and to economic, social, and political discrimination. When England ordered the ruling whites to change their policies and admit majority rule, Southern Rhodesia declared itself in 1965 to be free and independent of England. Subsequently, two black political parties, one of them Marxist, waged a war for majority rule. Finally, in 1980, majority rule was secured and Robert Mugabe, a black Marxist, came to power. Afterward, many large landholdings, which had been confiscated from black farmers 100 years earlier, were returned to black ownership in the form of small farms. But many whites retained their land and remained in the country. When black majority rule was instigated, the name changed from Southern Rhodesia to Zimbabwe. Difficulties in neighboring countries—Mozambique which was Zimbabwe's link to the sea, and South Africa, whose apartheid continued until 1994—destabilized the new country.

Children of Violence initially takes place in Southern Rhodesia in the 1930s and 1940s, when Lessing still lived there and white majority rule was at its height. The first four books were written before the establishment of majority rule. The last novel, with futuristic elements, takes place in London and is the only one of the series written after majority rule became a reality.

The book follows Martha Quest, a woman very like Lessing herself, from the time she is a teenager in Africa where she fights with her bigoted mother over the country's racial and social injustice. Finally, she leaves at the age of seventeen for a large city, where she fails to find the work she has dreamed of having and makes a marriage of convenience that ends shortly. She becomes increasingly involved with communists and their efforts to address discrimination in Africa. After spending a number of years exploring other social and political theories, she leaves for England, where she continues an interest in spiritualism. In the final book, which shows an apocalyptic nuclear war that Martha has predicted, she dies of radiation poisoning.

The first two books of Lessing's series, which explored racism, including anti-Semitism, in Southern Rhodesia, were perceived as subversive and dangerous in that country. In 1956, when she returned to the country of her childhood for a visit, she was declared to be a "prohibited immigrant" and barred from coming back. Nor were her books allowed to be sold in Southern Rhodesia. Not until 1982, after the founding of Zimbabwe, was she allowed to return.

Although Lessing did not have as her main purpose the uncovering and correcting of racial wrongs in her country, as, say, did South Africa's Alan Paton and Nadine Gordimer, her story, set in Southern Rhodesia, necessarily involved considerable involvement with what was happening to blacks. And many readers saw, for the first time, a white African perspective that was sympathetic to blacks.

Lessing's main subject, however, was colonial displacement of both blacks and whites, like herself. As a person out of sync with her own people and thrown out of her home, her main character, Martha, typified for many readers the general rootlessness and loneliness of all contemporary life. They saw her search through many political and social philosophies and causes, as well as psychiatry and mysticism, as a reflection of their own search for meaning in a universe that seemed to be coming to an end.

Readers who were influenced by the realism and incipient feminism of the early novels of *Children of Violence* were disappointed in the futurism and mysticism of the last two in the series. Nevertheless, her new readers, more interested in science fiction and apocalyptic visions, raised her popularity to cult status in the 1970s. Many twentieth-century writers used science fiction for satire and escapism, but she was one of the first modern novelists seriously to link spiritualism, psychiatry, and telepathy to science fiction.

Additional Readings: Gayle Greene, *Doris Lessing* (Ann Arbor: University of Michigan Press, 1994; Margaret Roan Martin, *Doris Lessing* (New York: St. Martin's Press, 1994); P.E.N. Tindall, *A History of Central Africa* (London: Longmans, 1968).

ASIA

China

෧෨

Ts'ao Hsueh-ch'in, *Dream of the Red Chamber*, ca. 1769

Tseng P'u, *Flower in an Ocean of Sin*, 1905–1907

Lu Xun, *The True Story of Ah-Q*, 1921

Bei Dao, *Waves*, 1979

෧෨

TIMELINE

1368–1644 The Ming Dynasty rules China, reasserting Chinese culture after a long period of Mongol rule.

Mid-1400s The power of the Ming Dynasty begins to wane.

Repeated wars are waged with invading Mongolians and Japanese pirates.

1514 Portuguese explorers and traders enter China, beginning what will be centuries of Western exploitation of China.

Late 1500s Jesuit missionaries enter China, assuming some positions of importance, but meet with limited success in converting the Chinese.

1570 Trade opens up with the Philippines.

1619 The Dutch are allowed into Chinese Formosa as traders.

1630s–40s Widespread natural catastrophes produce national starvation and economic collapse and leave the Ming Dynasty open to attack from outside and inside China.

1644 Rebels from the provinces are driven from Beijing by Ming soldiers assisted by invading Manchus. But Manchus also drive the Ming regime from Beijing, forcing the bureaucrats to flee south. The new Manchu dynasty is known as the Qing Dynasty.

1645 In an action that humiliates the Chinese, the Manchus force all males to shave their heads in front and wear pigtails in the Manchurian manner.

The Manchus establish an elaborate system of administrative bureaucracy that will remain in place for centuries. Exams open to young men will allow them to enter positions of leadership in the civil service.

1670	The emperor issues the Imperial Edict of Chinese Confucian teaching, which applies Confucianism to aspects of public life.
1673	Civil war breaks out between the Manchus and old Ming sympathizers.
1679	The Qing Dynasty mobilizes scholars in an immense literary effort. Chosen by exam, these scholars write histories, dictionaries, and encyclopedias.
1681	The Manchus successfully put down rebellion.
1683	Formosa is invaded and incorporated into the Manchu (Qing) Dynasty.
1736	Emperor Qianlong redoubles the projects of scholarship.
1769	Ts'ao Hsueh-ch'in's *Dream of the Red Chamber* is published around this time, set in the late 1600s.
1780s	Trade flourishes between China and Western nations, particularly Britain, France, and the United States. The balance of trade is at first in China's favor, but Britain reverses this when it introduces Indian opium to China at gunpoint. Soon opium becomes the major import into China and profoundly alters Chinese society.
1799	Qianlong dies, and the Qing Dynasty begins to weaken.
1800s	Japan and Western nations push to enlarge trade with China.

Britain intensifies opium importation to China and insists that it be allowed to do trade in China's interior. |
| 1839 | China, seeking to stop the opium trade, confiscates and destroys opium on British ships in the harbor.

Armed hostilities break out between British and Chinese and between Chinese factions. |

1842	China loses the first of the Opium Wars with Britain.

The Treaty of Nanking forces China to agree to treaties with England detrimental to China. Similar treaties with France and the United States follow. |
| 1850 | The Taiping Rebellion breaks out and is defeated. It is led by Hung Xiu-quan, an applicant who had failed to secure a civil service position. Having studied under the Jesuits, he believed himself to be the younger brother of Jesus and amassed a following. |
| 1856–60 | China loses the Second Opium War with Britain, France, and the United States and is forced to enter into even more undesirable treaties.

Eventually the English force China to cede Hong Kong and Kowloon to them.

By the 1860s, the Chinese economy is completely controlled by foreign powers. |
1860–95	Manchus attempt to revitalize Confucianism and the government by reorganizing the civil service.
1884–85	The Sino-French War results in French takeover of Vietnam and British takeover of Burma.
1890	Western landgrabs in China continue as Russia secures the maritime provinces of northern Manchuria.
1895	After China's defeat in the Sino-Japanese War, Japan ends the system of tribute that Korea paid to the Chinese and takes Taiwan from Chinese jurisdiction.
1898	The Western powers among themselves carve up China into trading territories, and Russia constructs railroads on the Chinese mainland.

Reformers seek to modernize China and to introduce a constitutional monarchy. They are defeated by the dynasty, but sympathy for reform spreads across China. |

1900	In the famous Boxer Rebellion, a society antagonistic to Western incursions rises to counter foreign influence, including the opium trade, and is put down by an eight-nation alliance supporting English against China.
1902	Manchus yield somewhat to reformers and adopt an extremely limited constitutional monarchy.
1905–1907	Tseng P'u's *Flower in an Ocean of Sin* is published. It has a setting between 1870 and 1900.
1911	The Chinese Imperial government is overthrown in a successful rebellion led by Sun Yat-sen.
1912	China becomes a republic under the leadership of General Yüan Shih-kai, a notorious warlord.
1913–16	Sun Yat-sen and his Nationalist Party, or Kuomintang, attempt to overthrow the increasingly tyrannical Yuan and his warlords.
1915	Japan succeeds in securing jurisdiction over China.
1917	The West, especially the United States, which had previously promised China protection from the Japanese, refuses to come to China's aid.
1919	An anti-Japanese protest, known as the May 4th Movement, spreads throughout China. It is the result of a new awakening in China and inspired by intelligentsia and reformers. Its intent is to open a conversation with the Western world, partially through the exchange of students.
1921	In part as a reaction to decades of capitalistic imperialism, Chinese reformers look to the thought of Marx and Lenin. The Chinese Communist Party is formed in Shanghai.
	Lu Xun's *The True Story of Ah-Q*, with a setting in 1911, is published.
1923	Sun Yat-sen reorganizes the old Kuomintang to unify China against imperialists.
1925	Sun Yat-sen dies, and Chiang Kai-shek assumes leadership of the Kuonmintang. Chiang joins with Communists in an unsuccessful uprising against the government.
1927	A similar rebellion through a Communist and Nationalist alliance occurs. With success assured this time, Chiang turns against his Communist allies and slaughters them.
1928	Chiang Kai-shek's Nationalist Party gains control of five Chinese provinces.
1930s	Communists work underground to overthrow the Nationalists and remaining warlords.
1931	Japanese seize all of Manchuria.
1933	Japanese seize all of China's Inner Mongolia.
1934	Chiang fights Communists instead of warlords and the Japanese.
	Mao Zedong leads his "Long March" of Communists toward eventual takeover of China.
1936	Chiang is kidnapped and held imprisoned by one of his own generals.
1937	When he is released, Chiang has finally been forced into the decision to have his Nationalist Party join the Communists in a short-lived alliance in the fight against Japan.
1937–38	The battles against the Japanese are waged on the Chinese mainland, and China loses land. The central government retreats to Nanking.
1939	During the war, the Communists and the Red Army gain strength.
1945	The Japanese surrender, and World War II ends, but the Chiang's Nationalists and Mao's Communists continue to fight in China.
1947	Civil war breaks out throughout China.
1948	The Communists are victorious in the northern region in the civil war.

1949	After the Nationalists collapse, they move to Taiwan.
	Mao Zedong is the head of state of the People's Republic of China.
1949–51	The Communists execute between 1 and 2 million Chinese counterrevolutionaries.
1950	China invades and conquors Tibet, taking back territory that had traditionally been Chinese.
1950s	China severs all ties with the Western world.
1950–53	The Chinese Communists come to the aid of North Korea during the Korean War.
1953	The death of Stalin deeply impacts China, providing Mao with the opportunity to independently project himself and China as leaders of the Communist world.
1966–76	China gradually severs ties with the USSR.
	Mao Zedong and his closest associates declare and maintain a "Great Proletarian Cultural Revolution," to purge Chinese society of upper- and middle-class influence and Western culture. The Red Guards, an elite force of young students, take the lead in harassing and imprisoning members of the intelligentsia, former members of the aristocracy and business class.
1971	Lin Biao, chosen by Mao as his successor, is later charged with treason and dies under mysterious circumstances.
	China is admitted to the United Nations.
1976	Mao dies. Hua Guofeng becomes premier.
	"The Gang of Four," close and radical advisers to Mao, including his widow Jiang Qung, are arrested, eventually tried, and imprisoned.
1979	Bei Dao's *Waves* is published in China, causing an immediate uproar.
	Trade and other agreements are made with Japan and other countries in the West.
1989	A formidable student prodemocracy protest is mounted in Tiananmen Square. The Red Army kills thousands of peaceful protesters, many of whom have been inspired by *Waves*.
	Bei Dao is out of the country when he hears of the prodemocracy debacle and immediately makes the choice to go into exile, where he remains.

13. *Dream of the Red Chamber* (*Honglou meng*), by Ts'ao Hsueh-ch'in (China, ca. 1769).

Dream of the Red Chamber, also translated as *The Story of the Stone*, is universally acknowledged as China's greatest novel. Set during the late seventeenth century at the height of the Qing Dynasty, it is in many ways a reflection of the story of the dynasty—its oppressive authoritarianism, its gluttony for opulence, its appreciation of fine art, its class structure, and its decline.

The dynastic social structure included, at the top, an elite class comprising 10 to 15 percent of the total population. The three levels of the elite class included, first, the imperial class holding hereditary titles; second, the government officials called mandarins, who gained their positions after passing difficult examinations; and finally, a class of wealthy, educated men.

Theoretically, women were subordinated to men at every level. They were rarely educated and, at the elite level, did not have careers or hold official government positions. However, many mature women had such influence within their clans and families that they were regarded as the "powers behind the throne." Such women made all the crucial decisions within the family.

In wealthy families, the chief occupations were the cultivation of the arts and learning, the shaping of their homes and gardens, and the cultivation of policies and alliances that buttressed family power and finances.

By the mid-eighteenth century, the Qing

Dynasty was on the decline as a result of greed and corruption among government officials and a massive population explosion that also drained government resources.

Ts'ao Hsueh-ch'in's novel is the story of a wealthy and influential imperial family, the House of Chia, whose fall parallels that of the Qing Dynasty of which it was a part. The word "family" or "house" denoted an extended family of grandparents, all their grown children, and all their grandchildren, who lived together within one large mansion, each nuclear family having its own compound within the mansion, and the teenage children enjoying their own suites and servants. So grown and married brothers and sisters and their families lived in the mansion together, and an army of first cousins grew up together.

Much of the novel consists of a documentation of daily life in the family, with vivid, detailed descriptions of their living quarters and gardens, their passion for poetry reading and composition, their flirtations with their servants and each other, and the many intrigues and manipulations inspired by love, lust, and greed.

The major plot interest is the passionate love of the novel's young hero Pao-yu and his cousin Black Jade. They are, however, star-crossed lovers, for the tyrannical family matriarch, their grandmother, has firmly made up her mind that they will not marry. Several other love affairs comprise subplots. The novel ends unhappily with Black Jade's death of a broken heart and the ruin of the family brought on by the greedy matriarch's dishonorable decision to practice usury.

Dream of the Red Chamber has much of the same standing in Asian culture as Shakespeare's plays enjoy in the West. Readers regard it universally as the greatest of all Chinese novels. Yet when it first appeared, it was classified as an "outlaw" novel because of its realistic treatment of a social theme. It was not, as most highly regarded Chinese literature was at the time, solely a lyrical myth of spiritual quest. It was the first novel to present an important family unit, so central to Chinese society at the time. Readers em-

braced it as the first literary mirror of a life they actually knew. Whether they were members of the elite or servants, they could actually see their own society and someone very like themselves reflected in the novel. As a result, many readers felt that the novel influenced their lives by interpreting, discussing, and laying bare essential relationships that they had experienced but never intellectualized.

On an individual level, Chinese readers saw reflected in the work the cultural difficulty they experienced in communicating true feelings and belief as well as the difficulty of leading a life of the spirit in such a mundane world.

On a social level, the novel threw light for the first time on subjects that were usually suppressed in literature and discussion: the taking of concubines and the fates of their children, the licentiousness within the family unit, the tyranny of the matriarchies, and the exploitation of the children by their elders.

The novel was said to have continued to have a particularly strong influence on the children of the intelligentsia, but its general popularity over the years with all classes of readers has promoted it to the status of a national epic.

The grand scale and inclusiveness of the novel, as well as its ambiguities, have led to its being claimed by each of the major religious groups in China. Adherents of Buddhism, Taoism, and Confucianism have all seen their own philosophy as central to the spiritual quests within the novel.

Even in the twentieth century, there are what the Chinese call "Red Chamber fanatics" who have made a cult of the novel. A number of scholars and ordinary citizens even now devote their lives to the study of the novel, often trying to document in it particular references to their own religious persuasions.

The novel has lived through the ages in stage, film, and television adaptations. A more unusual testimony of its continuing influence is that ever since the publication of the novel mansions and gardens, identical to those described in such detail in *Dream of the*

Red Chamber have been continually reconstructed in public areas across the country.

Additional Readings: Robert E. Hegel, *The Novel in Seventeenth-Century China* (New York: Columbia University Press, 1985); Andrew H. Plaks, *Archetype and Allegory in the "Dream of the Red Chamber"* (Princeton, NJ: Princeton University Press, 1976).

14. *Flower in an Ocean of Sin (Nieh-hai hua)*, by Tseng P'u (China, 1905–1907). Tseng P'u, a scholar, writer, and political figure in the early decades of twentieth-century China, sets his novel, one of the most influential works of modern China, between 1870 and 1900, a time of turbulent cultural and political change. The weakening of the old world China, developed in the novel, was exacerbated by three major events: the defeat of China in the Sino-Japanese War of 1894–95, showing the collapse of official policies; the Hundred Day's Reform Movement of 1898, which showed the inability to make needed changes from within established culture; and the Boxer Uprising of 1900, which showed the helplessness of subcultures in China in the face of European influence. In the last decades of the century, the long-standing oppression and exploitation of the common people by the ruling class had reached intolerable levels. And in 1905, the date of the novel's publication, the downhill slide of Chinese influence and the impairment of government and the military by corruption and inertia seem to mark China for disaster.

Tseng P'u's novel traces the rise and fall of Chin Wen-ch'ing, an important Chinese scholar/diplomat who is emblematic of the fall of China itself. The plot follows Chin Wen-ch'ing's rise as a scholar into the ranks of the most revered society in China, the *chuang-yuan*, his appointment as a special envoy to Russia, Germany, Holland, and Austria where he travels, taking with him his young concubine, Fu Ts'ai-yun. He seems to lose none of his reputation for wisdom and competence in China, even though his experiences as a diplomat are a disaster: He is cheated out of large sums of money, bum-blingly cedes Chinese land and influence to the Russians and Germans by using a faulty map he has bought at great personal cost, and cowers in his quarters while his concubine sleeps with numerous men. He returns to China to occupy a high government position and bask in the hedonist, decadent social whirl of Peking, but a series of events undermines his happiness, and he dies a premature death, made particularly horrible by hallucinations and memories of his betrayals and ineptitude.

The immediate public response to Tseng P'u's novel was overwhelmingly positive on the part of the public and general readership. Fifty thousand copies sold; it was reprinted fifteen times; and it produced a steady stream of imitations, adaptations, and argumentative commentary. As much as the novel was praised by the general public, it was severely criticized by traditional scholars, critics, and the government for its revolutionary sympathies, its reproach of scholars and the government, and its picture of a hard-drinking, self-indulgent, pleasure-seeking society. Many critics who admired the novel still took the author to task for presenting an unflattering picture of China to Western readers.

This novel of the late Ch'ing Period is classified as a "castigatory novel." For most traditional scholars, this was a term of derision, noting that the political purpose had overtaken the artistic one. They disparaged the novel not only for its criticism of government but for its criticism of the traditional Chinese education, its mandatory examinations that directed the life of young men, and other social conventions. But more progressive readers, even among scholars, called it the best revolutionary novel of the period, specifically because it embodied the democratic values leading up to the Revolution of Sun Yat-sen. Tseng P'u's novel exposed for the first time abuses and weaknesses in government that had long created unhappiness in the general populace. The resultant ideological stance, which gained increasing support among the Chinese, was highly antiimperial and antifeudal. He was also very suspicious of Western capitalistic attempts to influence Chinese government.

Later revolutionaries would claim that the author was insufficiently radical and far too conciliatory as a reformer.

Additional Readings: Peter Li, *Tseng P'u* (Boston: Twayne, 1980); Colin Mackerras, *China in Transformation 1900–1949* (London: Longmans, 1998); Donald S. Willis, "The *Nieh-hai hua* and Its Place in the Late Ch'ing Social Novel of Protest" (Ph.D. diss. University of Washington, 1951).

15. *The True Story of Ah-Q (AQ zheng-zhuan)*, by Lu Xun (China, 1921). Lu Xun has been called, by the Chinese Communist establishment, the father of modern Chinese literature and the greatest standard bearer of the Chinese cultural revolution—this last a title that few Chinese in the twenty-first century would consider praiseworthy. His greatest novel, *The True Story of Ah-Q*, has a clear historical setting in China in 1911. Rural China at the time had changed little in 200 years. The peasants had steadily, since the mid-eighteenth century, lost economic ground and were largely at the mercy of a few landholders in every village. The Manchu government, using appointed provincial leaders, had been able to retain power for the few and resist implementing any land reforms or constitutional government, despite rebellions throughout the nineteenth century. Life for the rural peasant was made difficult by all-powerful bureaucrats, chosen through an ancient civil service examination system, who were uninterested in reforms of any kind. Nor was the country served by the Imperial government's alliances and concessions to the West.

The rebellion against Manchu rule mentioned in the novel began in 1911, originally against a railroad nationalization scheme and then spread to central China and other provinces under the leadership of Sun Yat-Sen. This was the first democratic effort to limit Manchu power. But the new leader, General Yüan Shih-kai betrayed the democratic cause by refusing to limit his own power. At his death in 1916, political power went to pro-

vincial warlords, who ruled China until the mid-1920s. By 1921, the year of the novel's publication, revolution was in the air. Many Chinese were looking to Russia and Marxism to solve their ancient problems, and the Chinese Communist Party was founded in Shanghai in 1921.

The topical references in Lu Xun's 1921 novel, set in 1911, are critical. These include Ah-Q's hatred of those young men from privileged families whose success in passing their civil service exams is understood to be a ticket to corruption and Ah-Q's hatred of the "Imitation Foreign Devil," who has been educated in Europe. Other references are to the dependence of Ah-Q and others on the local gentry and the arrival of the revolutionaries.

It is a fiction within a fiction, the story of a writer who records the life of a simple peasant named Ah-Q, who has no last name and no discernible ancestry. Ah-Q, who lives by doing odd jobs, is the village whipping boy. Again and again his tormentors grab his pigtail and bang his head against the nearest wall. He responds by uttering curses underneath his breath and only picking on people weaker than himself. Though he is cursed, beaten, and cheated, he always finds some way to believe he is not defeated or dishonored. After making an indecent proposal to a maid servant, he is no longer hired in the village. Desperation leads him to steal several turnips from the local convent before leaving the village for the city where he has some success as a petty thief. His reappearance in the village with a few silk goods and stories of executions to relate buy him a small measure of respect. But village interest in him soon turns to rumors of revolutionaries whose chief reform is wearing their pigtails coiled up on their heads. Ah-Q, eager for further attention, coils his own pigtail on top of his head, securing it with a chopstick. When he attempts to join the three or four local middle-class revolutionaries, they run him off. He is later arrested after a robbery and shot. The villagers decide that because he was shot and because he didn't have the spirit to sing operatic arias as he was being driven to his execution that he must be a bad man.

The True Story of Ah-Q has been open to several interpretations. On one level, readers viewed it as a hilarious satire of provincial life and revolution. But socialists insisted on a more profound meaning, seeing it as an excoriation of provincial Chinese characteristics of fearfulness, timidity, and acquiescence. In Ah-Q, many readers found a ludicrous but lovable antihero who, like the typical Chinese character of the time, is made a buffoon by his self-delusion. To him and the people of his world, the revolution makes no difference whatsoever.

But the social realism of the novel was reinterpreted by post–World War II Maoists as a myth of revolution: Ah-Q is the starving peasant under local warlord control who is also victimized by the middle-class revolutionaries who refuse to let him join the fight. The novel was clearly seen by many readers as a rallying cry for Chinese communism. The advertisement on the cover of a translation printed in Beijing states the following: "It was the author's sincere hope that the broad masses of peasants, victims of feudal oppression and imperialist aggression, might be aroused and rise in resistance against them."

Additional Readings: Milena Dolezelova-Velingerova, ed., *A Selective Guide to Chinese Literature, 1900–1949*, vol. 1, *The Novel* (New York: Brill, 1988); Colin Mackerras, *China in Transformation 1900–1949* (London: Longman, 1998); Winston Yang and Nathan K. Mao, eds., *Modern Chinese Fiction: A Guide to Its Study and Appreciation* (Boston: G.K. Hall, 1981).

16. *Waves* (*Bodong*), by Bei Dao (China, 1979). From 1966 until 1976, China, under communist rule since 1949, underwent what its leader Mao Zedong called a "Cultural Revolution." The purpose of the movement was to erase all traces of European influence and all traces of upper-class, middle-class, and intellectual Chinese culture of a traditional nature, unless it was deemed by the authorities to serve the new communist state in a practical and unmistakable way. Thus,

traditional books considered to be feudal in sentiment were burned and banned. All modern literature except for that of Lu Xun and, later, works expressly commissioned by the Mao government were banned. European classical music and "feudal" Asian music were banned. The Red Guard, for instance, confiscated pianos in the houses of the elite, often throwing them down stairs and out of windows. Along with this cultural censorship came the obliteration of the whole system of education in China. Very few Chinese people were allowed schooling. The government shipped most young people to farm collectives to do hard labor in their early teens. Those who were allowed education usually received only vocational training. The government prohibited the study of foreign languages, except for Russian, and all subjects relating to non-Chinese nations or to traditional Chinese culture. A critical step in cultural "cleansing" was the complete ruin of members of the intellectual and upper classes whom the government stripped of all possessions and brutally humiliated.

The Cultural Revolution came to an end with the death of Mao in 1976, after which time the rebuilding of the educational system and the culture of modern China slowly began. Still, inexorable damage done to a generation of young Chinese men and women was deep and irreversible.

The first and most celebrated novel to appear after Mao's death was *Waves*, by Bei Dao, a poet generally described as an "underground writer" in a journal with which he was associated but that was not government approved. For a brief period, as power was being sorted out after Mao's death in the 1970s, the government permitted such unauthorized publications to be distributed.

In a complex journey told from multiple points of view, the protagonist of *Waves* rebels against all official directives and all prescribed mores of the socialist state to seek his own spiritual meaning.

The circulation of *Waves* caused an astounding sensation in a China that had been required to revere and obey Mao Zedong for the previous thirty years. The novel was the first work of literature that had been allowed to appear since Mao assumed control of China openly to criticize Maoist socialist principles. Thus, it was the only such work that the vast majority of Chinese readers had ever seen.

Its readers saw for the first time a fierce condemnation of a Cultural Revolution whose effects had set the Chinese people adrift in a sea without faith or tradition. Chinese citizens, who felt intensely the literal and psychological rootlessness of postrevolutionary life, believed that they had found in Bei Dao a voice and a representative to express all the angst of their tortured and empty lives.

The novel undermined other sacred cows of the revolution. It placed collectivism and accommodation to the group in a decidedly bad light, as minor in importance to the individual's private quest. The pragmatism of communism was demeaned as petty in comparison with the needs of the spirit. Many heard their own suspicions corroborated and articulated in the suggestion that the revolution's narrow social realism had crippled the populace psychologically.

For the first time since the Cultural Revolution began, readers were exposed to a work of art that had ordinary, flawed but sympathetic people at its center rather than party functionaries. They saw issues raised that were treated as more important than Mao's version of a class struggle and that validated the importance of personal relationships.

The effect of *Waves* was to open up to its readers worlds with which they had no experience. Unfortunately, its effect was too great, and when Deng Xiaoping came to power, the book, which had been under continual attack by old party-liners, was suppressed.

It is widely acknowledged, both in and out of China, that *Waves* paved the way for the student movement that erupted in Tiananmen Square in 1989 and continues to plague Communist China. Fortunately, Bei Dao was in Berlin at the time that the demonstration and subsequent massacre occurred. He did not return to China but now lives in exile in the United States.

Additional Readings: Anita Chan, *Children of Mao* (Seattle: University of Washington Press, 1985); Key Ray Chong, *Americans and Chinese Reform and Revolution 1898–1922* (Lanham, MD: University Press of America, 1984); Edward Gunn, *Rewriting Chinese: Style and Innovation in Twentieth-Century Chinese Prose* (Stanford, CA: Stanford University Press, 1991).

India

∾

Mulk Raj Anand, *Untouchable*, 1935
Salman Rushdie, *The Satanic Verses*, 1988

∾

TIMELINE

1500 B.C.
Aryan-speaking nomads migrate to northern India, bringing with them a social system that includes at the bottom the Harijans or Untouchables made up of original Indians in addition to pariahs who had been cast out of the castes into which they had been born.

563–483 B.C.
Buddhism develops in northeastern India. It rejects the notion of caste.

200 B.C.–A.D. 100
Priests write the *Law of Manu*, giving the systems of castes the authority of divine inspiration and making it part of the Hindu religion.

1893
Mohandas Gandhi, reared in British India and educated in England, takes a position in South Africa. Here he develops a philosophy of civil disobedience and passive resistance to address the appalling discrimination against Indians there. He is jailed repeatedly over a twenty-year period.

1914
Having secured some concessions from the South African government, primarily forcing the government to recognize Indian marriages and abolish the poll tax, Gandhi returns to India, where he spearheads the fight for civil rights for Indians and independence from Britain.

1921
Mulk Anand, who has joined Gandhi's civil disobedience campaign, is arrested and jailed during a demonstration.

1930s
A strain of militant Islamic fundamentalism makes itself known and grows steadily throughout the twentieth century. The philosophy behind the growing terrorism

waged by militant groups is that those who kill non-Muslims, especially in the West, will be regarded as martyrs and rewarded in the afterlife.

1932 Gandhi begins a "fast unto death" to address the conditions of the Untouchables.

Mulk Anand, a close associate of Gandhi's, finally sees his novel *Untouchable* into print after repeated rejections.

Anand's novel is immediately banned in India by the British.

1934 Gandhi leaves political position but continues to devote his energies to end the untouchability.

1935 Gandhi drafts a constitution for India in which the station of the Untouchables is forbidden.

1936 Jawaharlal Nehru's *Toward Freedom* is published.

1945 Anand returns from Europe to make his home in his native India.

1947 India is granted independence.

Nehru elected as first prime minister of independent India.

Gandhi is assassinated.

1948 The constitution written by Gandhi is published. In it, he abolishes untouchability.

The major writers' group in India, the Bombay Group of the Progressive Writers' Association, expels Anand from its group and denounces him as a decadent because of his criticism of caste and colonialism.

1952 Anand is awarded the International Peace Prize of the World Peace Council.

1960s–70s Sporadic wars rage between Muslims and Hindus in India.

1961 V.S. Naipaul, a novelist born in Trinidad of Indian ancestry, publishes *A House for Mr. Biswas.*

1979 Militant Islamic Shiite fundamentalists, led by the Ayatollah Khomeni, assumes power in Iran.

The new government takes sixty-six Americans hostage.

1981 American hostages in Iran are finally released.

1984 A government battle with Sikh terrorists in India ends with over 1,000 dead.

Indira Gandhi, head of India, is assassinated by a Sikh. An aftermath of reprisals against Sikhs followed.

1987 The Intifada movement is born among Islamic Palestinians and mounts a campaign of terror.

Jihad terrorism increases.

1988 Salman Rushdie's *The Satanic Verses* is published.

Violent anti-Rushdie demonstrations are launched throughout the world, and his book is banned in India, Pakistan, South Africa, and most Arab countries, including Egypt and Saudi Arabia.

A Pan Am airlines flight is bombed by an Arab terrorist group.

1989 The Ayatollah Khomeni of Iran issues an Islamic edict against Rushdie, ordering Muslims to kill him and offering a reward for his death.

Rushdie, under tight security, goes into hiding in London until 1991.

1991   A Japanese translator of *The Satanic Verses* is stabbed to death.

1992   The bounty on Rushdie reaches $5 million.

1993   The new Iranian leader, Hashemi Rafsanjani, renews the death sentence of Rushdie.

In New York City, the World Trade Center is bombed by Islamic radicals.

1998   A new, more moderate leader in Iran backs off from the death threat against Rushdie.

2001   Militant Muslims in Iran reassert the execution order of Rushdie, avowing that no one can cancel Khomeni's decree.

17. *Untouchable*, by Mulk Raj Anand (India, 1935). The 3,000-year-old caste system in India, devised by Hindu priests according to their reading of holy scripture, consists of four hereditary divisions. In descending order of importance, they are (1) the priestly caste called Brahmans, (2) the warrior caste, (3) the caste of farmers and merchants, and (4) the caste of laborers born to servants of the other three castes. Persons born into a particular caste are to remain within a fixed place in society. Therefore, one must marry only someone in one's caste, choose an occupation suitable for one's caste, and restrict one's contact to members of one's caste. At the bottom, outside any caste are the "Untouchables"—the aboriginal Indians. This bottom-level group also includes pariahs, consisting of people who have been expelled from the higher castes for religious or social misbehavior. The Untouchables are, as a result, a despised and miserable lot who inhabit India's city slums, even now typically without access to medical attention or clean water.

Traditionally, the jobs relegated to the Untouchables were clearing the cities of human excrement, and they were required to announce themselves with cries of "Unclean!" so that no persons of caste would be contaminated by touching them.

The system of castes and Untouchables was perpetuated by Hindu reincarnation and karma, understood as the quality of one's actions. According to Hindu belief, one can be reborn into a higher caste only if one has remained within his or her God-given caste in his previous life and has been obedient to caste rules. Obviously, this is a discouragement to any kind of rebellion.

Mohandas Gandhi made the first real national effort on behalf of the Untouchables, in September 1932, beginning a fast unto death to improve the lives of the Untouchables. In the constitution he created in 1935, the class of Untouchables was to be abolished, and any attempt to maintain such a group and continue the long-standing social practices toward Untouchables or any group of people was forbidden. Nevertheless, such a lower order persists, and murderous attacks on Untouchables by members of higher castes are still reported in the press in the twenty-first century.

Mulk Raj Anand wrote a first draft of his first novel *Untouchable* in 1932 while he was living with Mohandas Gandhi. In the following year, the completed novel was rejected by nineteen publishers before finally being accepted and printed. The novel follows one typical, physically and psychologically excruciating day in the life of Bakha, a youthful Untouchable. Bakha's daily routine begins very early as he goes about the endless task of collecting and carrying away excrement from the city streets. In the course of his duties, as a consequence of accidentally touching a higher-class Hindu, he is attacked by a mob. Later in the morning he learns that his sister, after having been helped by a priest at the crowded watering hole, is the object of the priest's sexual advances. When she repels him, he screams, "Polluted! polluted!" as if *she* were the one who had violated *him*. In the afternoon, when Bakha helps an injured hockey player get to his home, the boy's mother castigates Bakha for polluting her son and her house. Following this, his own father scolds and expels him for questioning his lot in life. As his day comes to a close, he hears three possible ways of offering relief to Untouchables: A missionary declares that conversion to Christianity will free Untouchables from the restraints of caste; Mohandas Gandhi tells the audience that untouchability can be eliminated politically; a third speaker believes that the lowly and despised job of cleaning up excrement will be unnecessary with the implementation of modern plumbing and, thus, eliminate Untouchables as a class.

The first reaction to Anand's novel, making an Untouchable his hero, was consternation and outrage. It was, at the time, a revolutionary action, as scandalous as a nineteenth-century novelist making a prostitute a protagonist. Especially shocking was Anand's portrayal of an Untouchable as not silently passive but angry, even thinking of one of their upper-class tormentors, the priest: "I will kill him!" Equally daring to his Indian readers was his having his Untouchable protagonist dream of being a white *sahib*, or master. For all these reasons, the novel was banned by the British government in India.

He received as little sympathy from anti-colonialists as he did from the British because his work targeted injustices of the Hindu-inspired caste system, rather than showing that all India's social ills sprang from the British occupation of India.

Unlike most caste Indians, Anand had, from childhood until adulthood, associated as a friend with members of the Untouchables; so he had information and perspectives new to other Indians who kept clear of this lowly group as pariahs. *Untouchable* was the first major work of Indian literature that was a realistic treatment of that country's social problems. Usually, fiction written in the many Indian languages was concerned entirely with the upper and middle castes. For the first time, readers in and out of India saw an Untouchable treated as a human being,

with the sensitivity to be wounded by attitudes he faces daily and the intelligence to understand how the progressive ideas, presented at the end, might change his life.

Untouchable must be given much of the credit for India's finally removing official sanction from the perpetuation of this pariah class. Anand, chiefly on the strength of this, his first book, was widely lauded in left-wing circles abroad but was castigated as a "propagandist" in India. After a period of exile in England, he chose to return, to make his home in India, even though he would likely have been more welcomed and celebrated in any other place. Upon the occasion of his return, the Bombay Progressive Writers' Association denounced him as a "decadent" who had turned his back on traditional Indian religion.

Additional Readings: Margaret Berry, *Mulk Raj Anand: The Man and the Novelist* (Amsterdam: Oriental Press, 1971); Hermann Kulke, *A History of India* (London: Routledge, 1998).

18. *The Satanic Verses,* **by Salman Rushdie (India, England, 1988).** No book of the modern age has elicited the intensity of reaction provoked by Indian-born British author Salman Rushdie's *The Satanic Verses,* a novel that primarily explores the constructing of identity on the part of people of color, former British colonials, who have moved to England.

The novel, with its foundation in fantasy, follows a variety of characters, primarily from India and Pakistan, who seek to adjust to England where most receive their formal educations and, at the same time, continue to cling to their cultures. At every turn they are humiliated and thwarted in England. This struggle forms the basic theme of the novel.

The fantastic overlay, however, is what made the novel controversial. The two main characters, at the level of fantasy, are an Indian movie star and a voice-over artist. Both of them, while flying over England in an Air India plane, are thrown into the air when the plane is blown up by Sikh terrorists. Like immigrants below in England, they find themselves in another realm and are metamorphosed into different creatures. The movie star becomes an adviser to Mohammed, relaying revelations to him. The voice-over artist becomes a devil. The latter, like the immigrants to England, must change himself into a more acceptable character, deserving of grace. An Anglophile, he denounces his passion for everything English, abandons his plans to marry an English wife, goes back to India to be reconciled with his dying father, and takes an Indian lover.

The Satanic Verses burst on the scene with all the force of a literary bombshell. In Britain, where it was praised by the literary establishment, it received the Whitbread Prize. In Germany, the novel gained Rushdie the honor of being named author of the year. Similar honors were forthcoming throughout Europe.

But followers of Islam in countries throughout the world were enraged by the book for a number of reasons. One of the characters in the book is a prophet named Mahound, an insulting name for Mohammed. One character dreams of a brothel where the prostitutes give themselves the names of Mohammed's wives in order to arouse their visitors. The Indian movie star provides Mohammed with many of his revelations, including the Satanic Verses, allowing veneration of female gods. In short, believers found that Rushdie had ridiculed the Islamic faith, religious revelation, and the character of Mohammed.

Islamic objections to *The Satanic Verses* were expressed in violent massive demonstrations and acts of terror throughout the world. The recommendation of a huge noisy mob in Hyde Park in London was that Rushdie be killed. Five Iranians were killed in Islamabad in the midst of demonstrations; sixty Indians died in Kashmir; six Pakistanis died in the melee of another demonstration. Copies of the book were publicly burned. Largely to quell demonstrations, India, Pakistan, South Africa, Egypt, and Saudi Arabia banished the book from library and book shelves and banned it.

But the most bizarre event was yet to come. In February 1989, the Ayatollah Khomeni of Iran ordered an execution of Rushdie and all people who had any part in the novel's publication. His decree read in part: "I call on all zealous Muslims to execute them quickly. . . . God willing, whoever is killed on this path is a martyr." The bounty placed on Rushdie's head reached $5 million. Rushdie was forced into deep hiding for two years. After this time he gradually began to make some appearances and interview, always unscheduled and unannounced.

Rushdie was not the only one to suffer from the Ayatollah's order. In 1991 a Japanese man who had translated *The Satanic Verses* was stabbed to death. The Italian translator of the novel narrowly survived a stabbing, and the Norwegian publisher of the novel was ambushed and caught, but not killed, in the resulting shooting spree.

Yet for many readers the revelations of the novel were those Rushdie most stressed: the difficulty of having one's life and character torn between two cultures and the ignominy of living as a despised culture in an arrogant land. The danger of losing self in such a situation is suggested in his fantastic portrait of an institution in England peopled with many immigrants who have been changed into beasts. The idea is that it is easy to turn oneself into the image that the dominant culture projects.

Additional Readings: Karen Armstrong, *Islam* (New York: Modern Library, 2000); Timothy Brennan, *Salman Rushdie and the Third World: Myths of the Nation* (New York: St. Martin's Press, 1989); Daniel Pipes, *The Rushdie Affair: The Novel, the Ayatollah, and the West* (New York: Carol, 1990).

Indonesia

༄

Pramoedya Ananta Toer, *This Earth of Mankind*, 1980

༄

TIMELINE

1500	The Dutch enter Indonesia for the purpose of trading.
1744	The Dutch secure control of most of the Indonesian islands.
1811–16	The English assume control in much of Indonesia.
1816–42	The Dutch resume their interests and control of most of the cities in Indonesia.
1825–30	An armed rebellion intended to dislodge the Dutch in the area is unsuccessful.
1912	A growing Islamic movement continues to challenge Dutch leadership and wins some concessions.
1926–27	An unsuccessful communist-led revolt prompts the Dutch to introduce more repressive measures in the areas under their control.
1927	An antigovernment leader named Sukarno emerges on the political scene and establishes the Indonesian Nationalist Party, which worked for independence from the Dutch.
1929–31	Sukarno is arrested and exiled. The Indonesian Nationalist Party is outlawed.
1942	During World War II, Japan occupies Indonesia, a time of enforced labor and repression. The Japanese took this opportunity to militarize young Indonesians.
1945	After the Japanese surrender, Sukarno and other rebel leaders set up an Indonesian republic. An agreement is reached with the Dutch briefly.
1947	The Dutch break the agreement, attack Indonesia, and reassert control over key areas. They also blockade areas over which they have not been able to assume control.
	Pramoedya Ananta Toer is arrested by the Dutch Colonial Army for his involvement in the struggle for independence.
1948	The Dutch renew attacks on independent areas of Indonesia and arrest rebel leaders.

1949	Indonesia achieves independence from the Dutch.

The new government is plagued by an inability to bring under central control the many competing areas, cultures, interests, and political ideologies that divide the area.

From the first, the government is corrupt and repressive in dealing with Indonesian differences. |
1950	Sukarno, as president, establishes the Unitary State of Indonesia. There are continual rebellions on the part of Muslims in West Java and Aceh and the Dutch in Sulawesi and the Moluccas.
1955	Illustrative of the diversity of interests, in the elections there is no clear majority.
1956	Sukarno puts in place a policy of "Guided Democracy" that provides him with greater power.
1956–61	These years are marked by repeated, unsuccessful rebel attempts to topple Sukarno's government and continual guerrilla activity in many antigovernment areas of Indonesia.
1958	An organization called the Revolutionary Government of the Republic of Indonesia, with encouragement by the United States, launches an unsuccessful coup attempt.
1965	Another coup attempt is tried, this time involving the palace guard.
1966	General Suharto is able to defeat the coup attempt. Then he ousts Sukarno himself and takes over the leadership of the country.

Some 300,000 to 1 million people, primarily suspected communists, are killed in retaliation for the coup; 120,000 people are arrested.

Toer is one of the 800 prisoners imprisoned without trial. His property is destroyed and confiscated. |
| 1966–74 | Toer remains in prison where he writes *This Earth of Mankind*. |
| 1968 | General Suharto is officially inaugurated. |

1971	General elections are held but tightly controlled by Suharto's supporters.
1971–2001	Various parts of Indonesia, which have never securely come under control, continue to fight for their own independence from the central government.
1974–2002	After his release from prison, Toer is forbidden to leave Jakarta. He remains under city arrest to this day.
1980	*This Earth of Mankind* by Toer is published. Although it will be celebrated throughout the world, it is immediately banned in Indonesia and still forbidden over twenty years later.
1981	Toer's publisher is imprisoned in Indonesia.
1998	Antigovernment riots occur continually.

Suharto resigns in May, and his deputy, Bucharuddin Jusuf Habibie, becomes president, a term to run until 2003. |

19. *This Earth of Mankind* (*Bumi Manusia*), by Pramoedya Ananta Toer (Indonesia, Java, 1980). Toer's novel, one of a series titled *The Buru Quartet*, is set on the Indonesian island of Java at the end of the nineteenth century, during the centuries-old colonization of Indonesia by the Dutch. Half the country's population live in Java, the largest island of the group comprising Indonesia. Jakarta, the capital of Indonesia, is located there. In the sixteenth century, the Dutch moved into Indonesia for commercial reasons, and by 1755, they controlled huge portions of the islands. After a brief, six-year period of English control, Indonesia was returned to the Dutch in 1816, where they remained until the Japanese occupation in 1942. After the defeat of Japan and the return of the islands to the Dutch, there were armed struggles for independence within the islands. These movements for independence flourished throughout Toer's childhood and youth. In 1947 he was arrested by the Dutch Colonial Army for his political activities in the cause of independence. Indonesia finally achieved independence in 1949. But oppression and corruption continued in the aftermath of independent Indonesia, and many military coups were launched unsuccessfully. Finally, in 1965, a coup came close to overthrowing the government. It also was put down, however, and blame was placed on communist factions. In the brutal reprisals that followed in 1966, close to 1 million people were killed and some 120,000 arrested. Only 800 of these received trials. Included among those imprisoned without trial was Pramoedya Ananta Toer, who spent eight years in prison. There he composed *This Earth of Mankind*.

His story begins in late-nineteenth-century Java. Its main character is an eighteen-year-old native Javanese boy named Minke who is privileged to be attending an excellent Dutch school that is open to a handful of natives. Minke displeases the Dutch officials with his popular journalistic articles on the island's people and with his outstanding academic performance, which outstrips that of the school's European students. He gets into further trouble when he dates and then marries a young woman named Annalies, daughter of a native Javanese courtesan and a wealthy Dutchman. The plot is complicated by the poisoning of Annalies's father, the vitriolic racism of her two half brothers, and her rape by her half brother. Annalies's European half brother is successful in having her marriage to Minke annulled and having her sent to the Netherlands, despite a fight to the end by Minke and Annalies's mother.

The impression that most Europeans and Americans had of Dutch rule in Indonesia was that the Dutch had been benevolent rulers who had liberally modernized Java, making it a much better place to live for both its native and Dutch inhabitants. Toer's novel certainly dispelled that impression. However, the novel was also read as a statement about attitudes toward race and the oppression of women in the 1980s. The novel suggested that a caste system based on skin color kept most underclass natives and almost all women from being educated, skewed the law in favor of light-skinned men, and kept land and wealth in the hands of a few who tightly controlled speech and political activity.

Javanese readers saw Annalies's rape by her half brother as a figure for the abuse of power in modern Indonesia.

Despite the couple's suffering and final defeat when Annalies is sent to Europe, many readers viewed the novel as affirmative and hopeful. Minke, at least, did prevail in small ways: He was able to attend a good school and excel; he built a base of support through his writings; when the Dutch expelled him from school, he was able to get himself reinstated; and he was able to fight the good fight for his marriage. Likewise, Annalies and her mother were able to overcome many of their adversities.

As dissidents were informed and inspired by this—one of the most powerful of Asian novels—so the Indonesian government viewed and still views it as a perpetual threat. A ban was placed on Toer's book by the prosecutor general, declaring that it had the power to incite reactions that threatened public order. Furthermore, the book, it was alleged, secretly advanced "forbidden ideologies" that posed a threat to the good of the state. Not surprisingly, the book is still banned in Indonesia. After Toer's release from prison, he was placed under city arrest and to this time is forbidden to leave Jakarta. The government has also continued to refuse to return property that was taken from him at the time of his arrest. His papers were burned. Even the translator of his works has been forced to flee the city. For copublishing the works of Pramoedya Ananta Toer, Joesoef Isak was imprisoned for months in Indonesia in October 1981.

Additional Readings: Nancy K. Florida, *Writing the Past: History as Prophecy in Colonial Java* (Durham, NC: Duke University Press, 1995); John Ingleson, *In Search of Justice: Workers and Unions in Colonial Java* (New York: Oxford University Press, 1986); Max Lane's "Introduction" to Pramoedya Ananta Toer's *This Earth of Mankind* (Ringwood, Victoria: Penguin Books of Australia, 1982).

Japan

෧෧

Shusaku Endo, *Silence*, 1966

Sawako Ariyoshi, *The Twilight Years*, 1972

෧෧

TIMELINE

1549   Jesuit missionary Francis Xavier introduces Christianity to Japan, a country where the state religion is Shintoism with its nature and ancestor worship.

1549–1600   In a fifty-year period, some 300,000 Japanese are converted to Christianity.

Westerners from Portugal, Spain, and the Netherlands increase their trade with Japan, bringing with them their Roman Catholic religion.

1612   The occasional instances of religious persecution of Christians becomes official state policy, resulting in numerous massacres and imprisonment of Christians.

1642   Fearful that the Western world is using Christianity and trade as a stepping stone to colonizing Japan, the Japanese empire makes the first of many steps to isolate itself from the West, barring the entry of foreign ships and Japanese travel abroad.

Western books are also forbidden.

1860s   As Japan was reluctantly brought into trade with Western nations, attacks on foreign ships increased and a strong anti-Western force developed, increasing attacks on Christians.

1945   Following the defeat of the Japanese by the United States in World War II, the United States occupied Japan with the intention of fostering democracy and building the economy.

1956   Now as Japan's independence is restored, it is admitted to the United Nations, and its economy begins to grow.

1960s   Japan's economy and industry grow faster than those of any country in the world. This leads to overcrowding, pollution, and disruption of old social traditions.

1966   Shusaku Endo's *Silence*, set in the sixteenth and seventeenth centuries, is published.

1972   Sawako Ariyoshi's *The Twilight Years* is published.

1973   Japan begins to expand its social services for the elderly and their caregivers and to expand and improve nursing homes.

20. *Silence* (*Chimmoku*), by Shusaku Endo (Japan, 1966). The subject of this well-known novel by Shusaku Endo is Japan's historical resistance to Christianity and the acceptance, suitability, and promise of grafting Western culture onto Eastern countries.

The chief religions of Japan include over 200 sects of Shinto and 207 sects of Buddhism. Shintoism has for centuries been treated unofficially, at times officially, as a state religion. About 1 percent of the population is Protestant, Roman Catholic, and Greek Orthodox. Yet the influence of Christianity has been remarkably strong in Japan. Shusaku Endo, the author, was converted to Roman Catholicism when he was eleven years old and was educated by Roman Catholics. By his own admission, his chief literary influences were French Roman Catholic writers, and he remained a fairly independent but devout Roman Catholic until his death. *Silence* has been described as a novel written by a Japanese man with a Christian sensibility.

The novel, set in the sixteenth and seventeenth centuries in Japan, has as its topic the persecution of Christians in Japan. The plot concerns Sebastian Rodrigues, a Portuguese priest, who goes in search of his teacher, Ferreira. Rumor has it that Ferreira has, under torture in Japan, renounced his Christian faith. When Rodrigues reaches Japan, he goes into hiding and secretly searches for Ferreira. In the process he learns that Christianity has been banned in Japan, and Christians are routinely tortured and executed. Eventually Rodrigues is found out and arrested. He, like his old teacher, is urged to renounce his faith by stepping on a picture of Jesus. Until he agrees, he is told, faithful Christians will be tortured and killed. But despite the dreadful consequences, Rodrigues remains unmoved from his position. Then

Ferreira, now assimilated into Japanese society, is brought to convince him that outer actions are only empty, meaningless forms and that by doing what the torturers ask he can save lives and halt suffering. So Rodrigues, convinced, does as he is asked and steps on a picture of Jesus. However, contrary to his teacher's assurance, he finds that his inner faith vanishes with this outward action. So Rodrigues, too, joins Ferreira in growing old in Japan.

Few modern Asian novels have been so controversial as *Silence*. Its immediate effect was to bring many practicing Christians among the Japanese into the sunlight, astounding the general populace with their fervor and numbers.

The ambiguity of the novel has generated discussion that has been ongoing ever since its publication, chiefly about the appropriateness of aspects of Western culture, particularly Christianity, to Japan. Controversy has even raged over Endo's intention in the novel. And readers applied Endo's sixteenth-century story to contemporary Japan.

Much of the controversy centers on the novel's metaphor of the tree, understood to be a symbol of Christianity, and the soil, symbolic of Japan. In the novel, the tree withers. Readers have argued that it is, as Rodrigues believes, because it hasn't been nurtured—that is, Christianity doesn't flourish in Japan because the Japanese discourage it. Others believe the tree died because such a Western religion could not survive in an Eastern culture: that is, Christianity and Japanese culture just do not mix. Many believed that in *Silence* Endo was searching for a form of Christianity more compatible with Japanese culture.

The novel also placed on the table the conflict between Christians and non-Christians in the country and thus generated discussion over religious persecution.

Additional Reading: Mark B. Williams, *Endō Shūsaku: A Literature of Reconciliation* (London: Routledge, 1999).

21. *The Twilight Years* (*Kokotsu no hito*), by Sawako Ariyoshi (Japan, 1972). Japanese writers who published in the 1940s and 1950s, just after World War II, often chose the subject of the war itself and alienation. By the 1950s, however, what was known as the economic miracle in Japan was creating affluence throughout the country, and many novelists turned away from social subjects. Yet distressing social issues touching all citizens at all economic levels remained to be addressed. Specifically, these involved rampant inflation, which placed strenuous burdens on families, even when both parents worked hard at jobs outside the household; the attitudes toward and treatment of women in Japan; and the problems facing the elderly and their families. The problems on the last two issues arose from diametrically opposed attitudes toward these two populations in Japan. While women were denigrated and humiliated as a matter of course (even in language, male children are given greater titles of respect than are women), the elderly are so venerated that their families expect and are expected to care for them without advice and assistance. The two problems merge in that care of the elderly usually falls on younger women in the family. This is the subject of *The Twilight Years*.

The plot involves an extended family consisting of Akiko, a young mother who must work as a secretary to help augment the family income; Nobutoshi, her husband; Shigezo, her recently widowed father-in-law who has Alzheimer's disease; her son, a student at the university; and a couple of radical university students who are eventually hired to help care for Shigezo.

As Shigezo's disease progresses, his care officially falls to Nobutoshi, his eldest son. But the son's lack of attentiveness and capability means that practically the burden falls on Akiko, who had always had a strained relationship with the old man. These are duties she must assume in addition to her full-time job and all the household duties such as cooking, cleaning, and laundering, which Japanese men are by tradition forbidden from doing.

Soon, however, Shigezo's mental condi-

tion creates insurmountable problems for Akiko, even when, to give the old man more of her time, she quits full-time work to assume a part-time position, thereby placing the family's economic survival in jeopardy. Since, as a matter of honor in Japan, the families of the aged are expected to assume the full burden of care themselves, no agencies or services are available to help them. Finally, to help them with the old man, the politically conservative Akiko and her husband hire a young couple who are activists at their son's university.

In the course of Akiko and Nobutoshi's discussions with friends and their search for ways to take care of Shigezo, whom Akiko has come to love, the inadequacies of Japan's care for the elderly become apparent.

The importance of *The Twilight Years* is attested to by the way in which it generated discussion of widespread and ever-growing problems that had been neglected in Japan. Readers learned from Akiko's and Nobutoshi's research, for example, that Japan by the twenty-first century would be a nation of elderly, with over 30 million people over sixty years of age in a country of 126 million.

Moreover, the novel occupies a rare place in history as one of those works of literature that provoked fundamental changes in national policy. Ariyoshi's novel, for example, resulted in expanded nursing home care specifically designed for the elderly and human services intended to assist the caregivers of the elderly.

As other of Ariyoshi's novels would do, *The Twilight Years* also brought to the table for debate the burdens shouldered by working mothers in Japan. One critic asserted that there was no Japanese novel in English translation that depicted so faithfully the picture of the daily lives of Japanese families.

Additional Readings: Yoshiko Yokochi Samuel, "Ariyoshi Sawako," in *Japanese Women Writers: A Bio-Critical Sourcebook*, ed. Chieko I. Mulhern (Westport, CT: Greenwood Press, 1994), pp. 8–18; Mildred Tahara, "Ariyoshi Sawako: A Novelist," in *Heroic with Grace: Legendary Women of Japan*, ed. Chieko I. Mulhern (Armonk, NY: Sharpe, 1991), pp. 297–322.

AUSTRALIA

Australia

෨෨

Marcus Clarke, *For the Term of His Natural Life*, 1874

Rolf Boldrewood, *Robbery under Arms*, 1888

Miles Franklin, *My Brilliant Career*, 1901

Katherine Susannah Prichard, *Coonardoo*, 1929

Nevil Shute, *On the Beach*, 1956

෨෨

TIMELINE

1768	English explorer Captain James Cooke lands in Australia.
1770s	The British claim the continent.
1787	The British establish their first Australian penal colony in Sydney.
	Captain Arthur Phillip rules the first penal colony until 1782.
1788	European and British settlers begin arriving in Australia, the home of 300,000 Aborigines.
1792	Australia is overseen by the often corrupt and out-of-control New South Wales Corps soldiers.
Late 1700s	Bushrangers, escaped convicts turned highwaymen, begin to plague the free settlers.
1804	A rebellion by Irish convicts is put down by the New South Wales Corps.
1806–08	The governor of New South Wales is Captain William Bligh.
1810	The growing of Merino sheep—and the exportation of wool—is proposed as an Australian industry.
1814	The settlement of free farmers in Australia increases.
1815	The criminal escapades of the bushrangers become so threatening that the colony declares martial law.
1830	Australia passes the Bushranging Act, the intent of which is to curb the activities of highwaymen by imposing severe punishments.
1850–52	After exporting criminals to Australia for over sixty years, England abolishes its use of Australia as a penal colony. During this time, over 150,000 convicts had been exported to Australia.
1851	The discovery of gold in Australia increases the activities of bushrangers.

1870s–80s	Famous outlaw Ned Kelly is most active.
1874	Marcus Clarke sees into print *For the Term of His Natural Life*. It has an 1820–40 setting.
1880	Ned Kelly is caught and executed.
1888	Rolf Bolderwood's *Robbery under Arms* is printed.
1901	Australia becomes an independent commonwealth.
	Miles Franklin's *My Brilliant Career* is published and soon disappears from view.
1905	After excoriating reviews of her book, Franklin leaves Australia in exile for thirty years.
1920s	The number of Aborigines has declined from 300,000 in 1788 to 60,000.
1929	Katharine Susannah Prichard's *Coonardoo* is published.
1930	The Aborigines Department begins offering legislation to protect Aborigines by forbidding the use of slave labor and criminalizing the sexual exploitation of Aboriginal women.
1945	World War II ends in the Pacific after two atomic bombs are dropped on Japan.
1950	The British make a highly successful film series of *Robbery under Arms*.
1952	The United States explodes the first hydrogen bomb.
1956	Nevil Shute's *On the Beach* is published.
1959	*On the Beach* is adapted for film into an award-winning movie.
1960s	The creation of the Strategic Arms Limitation Talks results in treaties limiting the development, testing, and use of nuclear arms.
1968	The Nuclear Nonproliferation Treaty is passed.
1970s	Miles Franklin's novels are reprinted.
1979	A film version of Franklin's *My Brilliant Career* revives interest in her novels.

22. *For the Term of His Natural Life*, by Marcus Clarke (Australia, 1874). Marcus Clarke's novel is a faithful historical chronicle of events that occurred some forty to sixty years earlier in the British penal colony in Australia, where the English government begins its penal colony at Botany Bay. By the early 1850s, when the exportation of criminals to Australian penal colonies was abolished, over 150,000 convicts had been sent to Tasmania and New South Wales. The large majority of these were the very poor. Only half of the convict population could read or write. Most were repeat, petty offenders. Twenty percent were women, large numbers of whom were prostitutes. One third of the convicts were Irish.

As one governor described it, Australia and its islands were the perfect penal colonies. The treacherous water, the remoteness from home, and the interior desert made it almost impossible for a convict to escape. The penal colony became, in effect, a place without hope, without humane impulses, without God.

Physical conditions in the colony were extremely harsh at this time for both convicts and free settlers alike. The soil did not seem to support edible vegetation or products to export in exchange for imports; so food shortages were acute. Records indicate that all had to live largely on fish and kangaroo flesh.

The treatment of convicts swung from one extreme to the other, both extremes tending to brutalize the convicts. At one stage, they were given license to behave as they wished. The results were chronic drunkenness, alcoholism, prostitution, disease, and lawlessness. Free settlers were terrorized by the marauding convicts, and no one protected convicts from one another. Rape of both male and female convicts was a commonplace, occasionally mentioned in official reports. At the other end of the spectrum were governors sent in to correct convict lawlessness. Even the most minor theft, for example, was punished with 200 lashes of a cat-o-nine-tails.

The action of Clarke's novel begins in the 1820s when the treatment of convicts was at its most brutal. Shortly after a young aristocrat, Richard Devine, learns that he is illegitimate, he is sentenced to the penal colony in Australia for a murder he did not commit. To conceal his disgraceful birth, he changes his name to Rufus Dawes, and sails to Tasmania on a ship with most of the other important characters in the novel. John Rex, another felon, turns out to be Dawes's half brother. It is he who has killed their father, the crime for which Dawes was convicted. Major Vickers is headed to Tasmania to be the new prison governor. His young daughter Sylvia will be rescued by Dawes and grow up to fall in love with him and die with him in a shipwreck. The Vickers family maid Sarah Purfoy is a former prostitute who entraps the villainous Rex and tries to cash in on the Devine fortune. Maurice Frere is a soldier and Sarah's lover.

The melodrama includes descriptions of the sadistic treatment of convicts, the brutal landscape, and the isolation on a continent that is perfect as a penal colony, according to Major Vickers.

Clarke's was the first widely read fictional account of the convict ships and their perilous existence on the penal colony. In what is often described as an angry book, he accomplished what he intended to do, which was to force Englishmen and Australians to come to terms with a horrendous history that the English had perpetrated and the Australians had either facilitated or suffered through and were attempting to sweep under the carpet.

The book was also specifically intended as a warning to any country that was maintaining or planning to use deportation as punishment, particularly the English in India and the French at New Caledonia.

The reaction of many Englishmen to the novel was to deride the book as a polemic exaggeration. Australians, for their part, took him to task for failing to point out the beauties of the continent and happy convict stories, illustrating how difficult it was for Australians to face their past.

Additional Readings: Barry Argyle, *An Introduction to the Australian Novel, 1830–1930* (Oxford: Clarendon Press, 1972); Laurie Hergenhan, *Unnatural Lives: Studies in Australian Fiction about the Convicts, from James Tucker to Patrick White* (St. Lucia: University of Queensland Press, 1983); Ernest Scott, ed., *Australia* (Cambridge: Cambridge University Press).

23. *Robbery under Arms,* by Rolf Boldrewood (Australia, 1888). *Robbery under Arms: A Story of Life and Adventure in the Bush and in the Gold-fields of Australia* (3 vols), one of the most famous and popular works of Australian literature, was written under the pseudonym of Rolf Boldrewood by Thomas Alexander Browne, a college-educated man who as an Australian adventurer, squatter, pioneer, miner, rancher, and lawman had firsthand experience with the Australian outback and the bushrangers about whom he wrote.

Australia was used by the British as a penal colony from 1803 to about 1850. In the nineteenth century, many convicts who escaped the penal colony hid out in wooded, unsettled areas called the bush and became highwaymen or robbers, preying on and terrorizing settlers. From the name of the place they hid in, the bush, they earned the name "bushrangers." A variety of legislation passed to punish bushranging did little to halt their activities. The discovery of gold in Australia in 1851 gave bushrangers even greater opportunities and impetus to rob gold shipments and banks.

The most famous of the bushrangers was outlaw Ned Kelly who went on a two-year rampage and even constructed a homemade suit of armor. In the minds of many Australians he was a Robin Hood–type hero, pitted against the despised British colonial government and law enforcers. When he was finally caught, 30,000 people signed a petition for his reprieve, to no avail. He was executed in 1880, just two years before the first installment of Boldrewood's novel appeared.

Robbery under Arms is a fast-paced tale of

bushrangers who roam the outback and occasionally invade the cities in the southwestern quarter of the continent. They raid cattle and rob banks full of the newly discovered Australian gold, taking whatever they can with a sense of the panache, self-confidence, and romance typical of frontier days wherever incipient civilization has met a wild and woolly frontier. Their leader is a dashing upper-class Englishman named Starlight, who is part Robin Hood and part Edmund Dantes from *The Count of Monte Cristo*. His cunning, disguises, and ability to hobnob with the authorities at horse races and masked balls protect him from capture. The story is told by Dick Marston, one of the bushranger gang who has been caught and is awaiting execution. Significantly, Marston was born in Australia; thus, he is a local product, not a convict imported from abroad. One finds the past, however, in the figure of his father Ben, who was a transported convict. Also present are Dick's mother and his sister Aileen, both of whom are decent Catholics (Boldrewood's only mention of Anglo-Irish relations in Australia). Starlight falls in love with Aileen, but this comes only to a dramatic ending when Starlight at last is killed, dying with her name on his lips. In his death scene, Captain Starlight (without ever confessing his real identity) reveals in a single sentence that the titled policeman who has brought him down was long ago his friend.

Robbery under Arms ran for over a year in the *Sydney Mail* before being published as a book in 1888. It became an international success, earning for Boldrewood enduring fame as the chronicler of a particular time in Australian history. The serial was immensely popular, and readers eagerly awaited the next chapter, just as they did for Charles Dickens's works in London and for Eugène Sue's in Paris. Once when the paper did not arrive, because of a flood, a group of readers had an entire chapter telegraphed to them. At another place, there was almost a riot when the paper failed to arrive. A stranger accosted the author once on a train to tell him how exciting the story was. He had, he said, called up the postmaster of a township to find out "how Starlight got on."

Rolf Boldrewood suddenly became famous throughout the English-speaking world—in America, Canada, India, England, and of course, Australia. He made a small fortune, something like 10,000 pounds (roughly equivalent to 9,000 U.S. dollars), from the many editions of his book. The Oxford University Press published it with great success in its World Classics series. Thomas Wood, in the introduction to this edition, considered the author's treatment of animals so skillful that he thought the real hero of the tale was Starlight's horse Rainbow. It continued to be published in inexpensive editions to the end of the twentieth century.

The story was also dramatized on stage in 1890, was made into a film with the advent of movies, and became a BBC serial as late as 1950.

The tremendous success of the book is attributable to Boldrewood's thorough knowledge of his subject, his use of realistic details, and his ability to tell a good story, filled with picaresque adventures and action. Part of its success is also attributable to timing: It came close on the heels of Ned Kelly's execution, Kelly's dying last words still echoing: "Tell 'em I died game."

More than any other book, *Robbery under Arms* has given the world an indelible picture of nineteenth-century life in Australia, not only in the outback but in the cities and goldfields. In what might be called an Australian epic, *Robbery under Arms*, with its embrace of so many types of characters and so many aspects of society unique to the country, gave expression to an Australian myth. Generations of Australians looked upon this as their earliest idea of what it meant to be Australian. For many others abroad it also gave their most vivid and lasting image of early Australia, as it was shifting from colonialism to national independence.

Additional Readings: Barry Argyle, *An Introduction to the Australian Novel* (Oxford: Clarendon Press, 1972); Laurie Clancy, *A Reader's Guide to Australian Fiction* (Melbourne: Oxford University Press, 1992); F.G. Clarke, *Australia*

(South Melbourne: Oxford University Press, 1989).

24. *My Brilliant Career*, **by Miles Franklin (Australia, 1901).** *My Brilliant Career*, often called the first "true" Australian novel, was written by Miles Franklin when she was in her late teens and published when she was twenty-one. The story came to life in a period of great nationalistic feeling in Australia, a time of emerging cultural and political independence and pride. On January 1, 1901, the same year in which the novel was published, spirited political efforts came to fruition when Australia finally became an independent commonwealth. This hope and national pride, felt by one born and bred in the Australian bush, was clearly in evidence in the novel.

But another, less positive Australian reality was also in the background of the novel. This was the position of Australian women in a society founded primarily by male convicts and settlers, where the most precious bonds were still considered to be between "mates" and the most cherished values were macho ones of physical adventure and toughness on a wild frontier. There was little place for girls or women in the cultural history of such a place. Women, far outnumbered by men, were regarded by Australian society and portrayed by its writers as existing solely as dependent sources of pleasure and work for men. The country's one great female writer at the time—Ethel Florence Lindesay Richardson, who wrote as Henry Handel Richardson—published under a male nom de plume, just as Sarah Miles Franklin would.

The central character in this Australian story is Sybylla Melvyn, a plain but brilliant and tomboyish young girl, who lives in a remote, isolated bush hut with her family: her alcoholic father, who has squandered what money he has made; her cold mother, occupied constantly with keeping the family alive; and her prettier and more valued younger sisters. Sybylla expresses her divided feelings about her environment. At the same time that she glories in the peculiar beauty of her home and declares her pride in her country, she rebels against its narrowness. She betrays a humorous interest, even affection at times, for the people around her but despairs of their ignorance and limitations, as she illustrates in her conversation with one of their neighbors, Mrs. M'Swat:

> "Did you ever hear of Gladstone?" I inquired.
> "No; where is that place?"
> "Did you ever hear of Jesus Christ?"
> "Sure, yes; he's got something to do with God, ain't he?"

Most of all, she despairs of her own circumscribed, seemingly hopeless life, filled with all the longings, frustrations, and dreams of adolescence. She is, she writes, like a duck in a desert, "ever wildly longing for water."

An opportunity presents itself when she goes on an extended visit to relatives. There she meets a wealthy landowner who recognizes her sterling qualities, falls in love with her, and asks her to marry him. She returns his love, and they become secretly engaged. But upon reflection, she breaks their engagement, knowing that he will always control her and never treat her as an equal partner. She also tells him that she is something that an Australian man will never forgive in a woman—she is a writer.

Even under a pseudonym, Franklin could not get her book published in Australia, but a leading literary figure of the day was engaged by her manuscript and took it with him to England, from where it was published. It was an immediate, enthusiastic success and bestseller in both Australia and England and afforded the twenty-one-year-old limited entry into Sydney's literary society. Most of the reviews were extremely positive.

In a time of great national feeling, a substantial readership welcomed it as the first real Australian novel, written by one who was not an "interloper" or an "immigrant," one who used the Australian tongue, the Australian landscape, authentic Australian characters, and an Australian point of view.

But the negative response to the novel was

also great, far too overwhelming for the young author. Her friends and family were furious and appalled at what they regarded as a libelous autobiography, rather than the fiction she insisted it was. People with whom she associated were certain that they recognized themselves in her book, and she was inundated with letters of outrage from people all over Australia. The most painful was a letter from her grandmother, whom she described as writing her: "She had hoped that her eyelids would be closed in death before such a disgrace had been brought upon her" ("Introduction" to the novel, Angus and Robertson Australian Classic Edition, 1980, p. 11).

Coupled with this negative reaction was a review by one of the most awe-inspiring newcomers to Australia, the famous psychiatrist Havelock Ellis. He criticized the novel as crude, its egotism and bitterness so great as to be pathological.

Moreover, the second novel, which Franklin had completed within the year of the first one's publication, was rejected by publishers as "too extreme." This book, a corrective of the young Sybylla's adolescent excesses, did not find a publisher for forty-five years.

As a result, Franklin withdrew her book from any further editions and left Australia in exile for thirty years.

My Brilliant Career was a book decidedly ahead of its time. Its real influence came many years later with a reprinting in the 1970s and with the highly successful film made of it in 1979. Like Louisa May Alcott's *Little Women*, it has been said that young men and women from every walk of life, in every country, recognized themselves in Sybylla, found their own youthful angst and rebellion expressed in Franklin's portrait, and as a consequence, felt less lonely.

Additional Readings: Laurie Clancy, *A Reader's Guide to Australian Fiction* (Melbourne: Oxford University Press, 1992); F.G. Clarke, *Australia* (South Melbourne: Oxford University Press, 1989); Leonie Kramer, ed., *The Oxford History of Australian Literature* (Melbourne: Oxford University Press, 1981).

25. *Coonardoo*, by Katharine Susannah Prichard (Australia, 1929). *Coonardoo*, the first serious full-length novelistic study of an Aboriginal woman, was written in the late 1920s, a time between the wars when old values and old concepts were beginning to change throughout the Western world. At the time of European settlement of Australia in the late eighteenth century, some 300,000 Aboriginal peoples lived there. By the 1920s, when *Coonardoo* was published, the introduction of diseases, brutal mistreatment, and social disruptions had reduced the population to 60,000. Aborigines were regarded as little more than lower animals by the invading Europeans. In isolated settlements, both male and female Aborigines were worked as slaves, and in an Australian society where white men far outnumbered white women, Aboriginal women were sexually misused as a matter of course.

The setting of *Coonardoo* is a cattle run called Wytaliba in the northwestern part of the continent, a place where the mail comes in once every three months, by horse-drawn vehicle. It is a frontier, several weeks' distance from Geraldtown, where the people have a world of their own—a place where whites and native blacks associate freely but carry with them the traditions and the prejudices of the times.

The story in the main concerns a long-enduring friendship and love affair between a white man and a native woman who has grown up as his slave, his playmate, and companion. The owner of the run is Mrs. Bessie Watt, an ex-schoolteacher who tossed her stationary respectable life to the winds to run off with an illiterate drover and, after his death, wound up owning Wytaliba. She becomes a mother figure to the native tribe, treating them decently while refraining from proselytizing.

Her son Hugh grows up with a native girl, Coonardoo, as his daily playmate and, later, his lover. When Hugh goes away to town to be educated, Coonardoo mourns. After Bessie, now ill with cancer, goes to town to see a doctor and to bring Hugh back home, he returns with a girl, Jessica, whom he intends to marry. Coonardoo, meanwhile, has become the second wife of Warienda, a man of her tribe, and has borne two children. Jessica, totally revolted by crude frontier life, returns to the city. Bessie, now dying, obtains from the blacks, and especially from Coonardoo, a pledge that they will look after her son while telling them, in turn, that she will return as a white cockatoo to guard against his neglect. Hugh, devastated by his mother's death, disappears into the bush where Coonardoo finds and saves him. He contracts typhoid, is cared for by Coonardoo, and is finally taken off by the worthless villain, Sam Geary. When Hugh returns with a wife, Mollie, a hard-working maid from Geraldtown, they are greeted by Coonardoo, carrying her and Hugh's child Winni in her arms. Mollie sticks it out for some time, but at last, learning the truth about the child and having wearied of frontier life, she screams that she was better off scrubbing pots and returns with her three daughters for the life she had left. At a time years later, when Hugh is away, Sam Geary, in a drunken fit, rapes Coonardoo. When Hugh learns of this, he rejects Coonardoo angrily and thrusts her into the fire.

Coonardoo "goes bush," has her wounds dressed, and begins to deteriorate. Hugh loses Wytaliba, which goes to Sam Geary. Deciding to prospect for gold, Hugh offers Winni a chance to go with him, but she declines, instead accepting five pounds and taking off into the bush to find her mother. After being wasted away by men and disease, Coonardoo at last comes back to die in the place where she began, finding everything in ruin and deserted by all except the white cockatoos.

Prichard's novel, which demonstrated a more profound understanding and sympathy for the Aborigine than had ever been presented before, was highly successful and garnered a considerable following in Australia. It is credited with actually changing the public perception of the Aborigine by dispelling the old stereotypes. The novel not only presents a serious study of a native woman, but it treats her with great sympathy and understanding, as a fully developed human being with complex passions and ideas. Critics had commented on the influence the book had in showing sympathetically the nobility of the Aborigine in his or her natural state and in painting an understanding picture of native religion and culture.

In presenting for the first time in Australian literature the love between a white man and an Aboriginal woman, she exposed a complication that was a decided reality in white enclaves in the bush, using the situation to show the inevitable clash of cultures.

In bringing attention to the plight of Coonardoo, the novel played a decisive role in bringing about legislation by the Aborigines Department designed to prevent the kind of actions perpetrated by Geary and to protect Aboriginal women from being preyed upon and used by white men, making it illegal, for example, for white frontiersmen to take Aboriginal or half-caste women to hotels for sex. The book also garnered public support for abolishing de facto slavery in frontier camps and insisting that Aboriginal "stockmen" be paid.

Additional Readings: F.G. Clarke, *Australia* (South Melbourne: Oxford University Press, 1989); Ken Goodwin, *A History of Australian Literature* (New York: St. Martin's Press, 1986); H.M. Green, *A History of Australian Literature* (Sydney: Angus and Robertson, 1961).

26. *On The Beach*, by Nevil Shute (Australia, 1956). *On the Beach*, one of Nevil Shute's last novels, was written less than three years before his death in 1960 at age sixty-one on the theme of the end of human society. It was a moral tale, written in the atmosphere of tension between the USSR and the West following World War II.

World War II began for England in 1939 when Nazi Germany invaded Poland as the last, fatal step in a design to dominate all of Europe and, eventually, the world. America entered the war in December 1941, when the Japanese attacked Pearl Harbor by surprise. The war in Europe had ended in May

1945 with the surrender of Germany. It ended in the Pacific in August 1945, following America's dropping of two atomic bombs on the mainland of Japan. In the postwar euphoria that followed, America dramatically dismantled its armies and navies, while retaining nuclear weapons and even developing a more destructive hydrogen bomb to replace the primitive atomic ones. The USSR also developed nuclear weapons, as well as formidable air, ground, and naval forces, with the avowed intention of crushing all forms of capitalism and "burying" the West. The subsequent tension was called the Cold War.

The bitter hatred prevailing on all sides, throughout the world in the following years, provoked numerous armed conflicts. In 1949, the communist Mao Tse-tung successfully rose to power in China. In Korea, the communist North invaded the South, and the United Nations, with the USSR temporarily abstaining, officially intervened, with forces led overwhelmingly by the United States. Throughout the world, violence and bloodshed continued, led always by the devotion either to the USSR or to the West, called the "Free World" in the popular press.

In this atmosphere, Nevil Shute produced his novel *On the Beach*. His strength of character gave the novel a strong moral tone and his experience as an engineer gave the story credibility. Shute was trained at Balliol College, Oxford, had worked at the de Haviland Aircraft Company, served as deputy chief engineer at an airship company, and joined the Royal Navy in World War II, where he served as head of engineering in the Department of Miscellaneous Weapons Development. At the same time over the years he was writing novels. The idea for *On the Beach* came in the early 1950s, after he moved to Australia, where an early and unsound theory once held that in case of nuclear devastation Australia would be spared because the trade winds would divert the spread of radiation. Shute, upon discovering that this was false, had the basis of his novel.

The plot is simple. It shows its characters waiting in Melbourne, Australia, for the inevitable cloud of doom to reach the south-ernmost city of the southernmost continent, following a totally devastating war that has already happened when the novel begins. The war had been the result of a misunderstanding: Egyptians, following a demonstration flight by Americans and British over Cairo, bomb Washington in Russian-made planes. Americans retaliate against Russia. Retaliatory bombing continues, with nobody knowing exactly how it all began. As deadly clouds of radiation sweep over the globe, the human race is slowly being destroyed. Australians, one of the last remaining people alive, wait for their turn.

The characters include Dwight Lionel Towers, an American submarine captain, a man with a strong sense of duty and order who still feels himself married to his now-dead wife in Connecticut; Moira Davidson, an independent, freewheeling Australian woman generally unhampered by traditional morality; John Osborne, a physicist who loves racing; and Peter and Mary Holmes, a typical young married couple. From summer to the following spring, each makes his own quietus as they all await a slow death.

On the Beach was a sensational bestseller and in 1959 was scripted as a successful movie, produced by Stanley Kramer, one of the outstanding filmmakers of his day. Critics of the Cold War were especially impressed by Shute's novel. Philip Wylie, American commentator on society and politics, even went so far as to suggest that *On the Beach* be required reading at American military academies (Julian Smith, *Nevil Shute* [New York: Twayne, 1976], p. 134).

The novel's considerable impact came from its being the first major fiction, in the middle of the ideological breast-beating of the Cold War, to sound an alarm: For the first time in the history of the world, it had become truly possible for mankind to totally destroy all human life on earth. A whole generation, old and young, were led by this novel to the very real and horrifying possibility that the military powers could extinguish the human race. Furthermore, it was more than a sermon or a tale of threatening doom told at the fading of the first millennium. It was a carefully calculated scenario based on scientific facts and carrying all the weight of scientific expertise wedded to what his every reader knew of human folly and Cold War politics. Shute's novel dramatized that given man's brutality, complacency, and limited vision, given the suspicious frenzy on all sides and the unchecked growth of weapons at the time, the scenario of the novel *would* become a reality—unless the pattern of life changed.

Moreover, this novelist, as more than one observer has noted, did more than any other writer to bring his generation to the realization that this is indeed One World and that we all, after the invention of the bomb, share a common fate. As a consequence, the novel helped create an atmosphere that would eventually be favorable to the meaningful reduction of nuclear arms.

Additional Readings: Cathy Giffuni, *Nevil Shute: A Bibliography* (Adelaide: Auslib Press, 1988); Ernest Scott, ed., *Australia* (Cambridge: Cambridge University Press, 1988).

EUROPE

Czechoslovakia

❧

Jaroslav Hašek, *The Good Soldier Švejk and His Fortunes in the World War*, 1921–23

Franz Kafka, *The Trial*, 1925

Milan Kundera, *The Unbearable Lightness of Being*, 1984

❧

TIMELINE

1899	What will be Czechoslovakia is now part of the Austro-Hungarian Empire.
	Hague Conference is unsuccessful in attempt to get European countries to limit arms.
1907	A second attempt at disarmament fails in light of growing aggressive nationalism and rivalries.
	Two alliances face each other: One is Germany, Austria-Hungary, and Italy; the other is Britain, France, and Russia.
1908	Austria-Hungary annexes Bosnia and Herzegovina, leading Serbia to threaten war.
1912–13	The Balkan Wars encourage arms buildups throughout Europe.
1914	World War I begins when Austro-Hungarian Archduke Franz Ferdinand is assassinated by a Serb.

In retaliation and to put an end to Greater Serbia's movement to annex part of the Austro-Hungarian Empire, which includes a high population of Serbs, Austria-Hungary declares war on Serbia.

Germany enters the war by declaring war on Russia and then France. England declares war on Germany, and Italy declares war on Austria-Hungary.

Russia invades Austria and Hungary, and Austria-Hungary makes two unsuccessful attempts to invade Serbia.

1915	Germany and Austria-Hungary defeat Serbia.
1916	Austria-Hungary conquers Romania.
1917	The United States enters the war.
1918	At the battle of Vittorio Veneto, the Austrian army is destroyed by the Allies.

The Austro-Hungarian Empire is destroyed, and the Czechs and Slovaks in the former empire join to create a separate state called Czechoslovakia. Hungary and Austria become separate countries.

Germany is defeated and forced to form a republic.

1921–23   Jaroslav Hasek's *The Good Soldier Svejk and His Fortunes in the World War* is published.

1925   The Czech Army bans Hasek's novel.

Franz Kafka's *The Trial* is published posthumously.

1928   Poland bans Hasek's novel.

1933   Hitler comes to power in Germany and burns Hasek's book.

1935   Bulgaria bans Hasek's book.

1948   After World War II the Czech Communist Party, to which Milan Kundera belongs, gains control of the government.

1950   Kundera is expelled from the Party and the university because of his criticism of Stalin. He is eventually reinstated.

The Czech government comes increasingly under the control of the USSR.

1960   West Germany makes a film of *The Good Soldier Švejk*, which wins a Golden Glove Award for Best Foreign Language Film.

1968   Alexander Dubcek, in a move independent of the USSR, takes control of Czechoslovakia.

Before the year is out, Russian tanks roll into the country to reassert the authority of the USSR and arrest Dubcek.

1969   Milan Kundera's works are banned by the Russia-controlled Czechs. He is fired from his job and loses his travel privileges.

1975   Kundera flees to France.

1978   Kundera loses his Czech citizenship after having defected to France.

1984   Kundera's *The Unbearable Lightness of Being*, set in the 1960s, is published.

1988   *The Unbearable Lightness of Being* is adapted to film.

1989   Communism is overthrown in Czechoslovakia.

27. *The Good Soldier Švejk and His Fortunes in the World War* (*Osudy dobreho vojaka Svejka za svetove valky*), by Jaroslav Hasek (Czechoslovakia, 1921–23). *The Good Soldier Svejk* is the story of a reluctant private in the Austro-Hungarian army, fighting on the side of Germany during World War I. This was a war that had its beginning in comic opera, progressed with tragedies of slaughter, stupefying in their enormity, and ended in a theater of the absurd, with every possible value, every comforting certainty, and most of the old governments crumbling into dust. For those who survived it, the war had made a sad, sick joke of life in the modern world. The enormous loss of life in World War I—over 6 million Germans killed and some 250,000 Austrian casualties in a single battle—began over the assassination in June 1914 of Austro-Hungarian Archduke Franz Ferdinand.

It is into this war that Svejk is conscripted even though the army has previously classified him as an "imbecile." At the time the war breaks out, he is making his living by selling dogs, for whom he constructs false papers. When he receives the news from a charwoman that "Ferdinand" (the Archduke Franz Ferdinand) has been assassinated, he replies that he knows only two Ferdinands: one who by mistake drank a bottle of hair oil and one who collects dog manure. And neither, he notes, "is any loss." This opening episode sets up the satirical tone and comical character of the novel.

Svejk is arrested, imprisoned, examined in a lunatic asylum, freed, and finally drafted into the army. Hampered by rheumatism, he is branded a malingerer; but being a bit cleverer than he seems, he survives. He becomes a lowly "batman" for a chaplain and then for a lieutenant—taking care of their pack horses. Sent into action on the Galician front, Svejk is taken prisoner and condemned to death; but again he survives, ultimately being sent back to his unit.

Appearing only three years after the end of the war, Hasek's novel immediately became a great favorite with ordinary readers, if not with military and the political authorities. Hasek had articulated for readers, especially the common soldiers, what they had sensed and discussed privately—that patriotic bombast, military tradition, heroic pretensions, and military bureaucracy were ludicrous at bottom.

Hasek gave readers an antihero with whom they could identify. He is the poor dumb clod, familiar to every soldier, who stumbles at every task and somehow, miraculously, manages to survive—in large part because of his own stupidity—and yet who, upon examination, proves to not be stupid at all. Readers found Svejk to be a simple, soldier-Everyman. In an idiotic war fought by an idiotic military, it is he, the cunning private, who is ironically branded an imbecile, because with a simple man's innate cleverness and naïveté, he manages to survive and even to flourish, while the official army and the entire Austro-Hungarian Empire is, in fact, crumbling all around him. Every private in any army at any time who has ever extricated himself from serious trouble by pretending to wide-eyed stupidity, too imbecilic actually to walk through a door, can understand Svejk's troubles and his techniques for survival. It is a fact of human existence that an officer will automatically "know" that a given private is totally dumb; and so clever privates (and other underlings), the world over, operate in a world of their own, one never penetrated by practitioners of arrogance and pretension. It is, in fact, something like the Emperor's New Clothes in reverse.

The great popularity of the novel no doubt stems from the fact that the book not only excoriates army bureaucracies but also reveals a great deal about ordinary life and ordinary people. Svejka not only represents the cunning and rebellious private but any underling on estate or in business who manages to subvert the system while maintaining a facade of ignorance.

It is a fine popular portrait with a missing center. It is never clear just what Svejk really is. At the heart of it, however, is the fact that it was a satire written to entertain and to puncture the clichés and the pretensions of everything that Svejk—or Hasek—encountered.

The negative response to the novel says much about its power to influence its audience. The new republic of Czechoslovakia found it objectionable, as an assault on their new independence; and a leading critic pronounced Svejk a "scoundrel." Another feared that Svejk's resistance to the military system would undermine the national will to fight. The Czechoslovak army banned the book in 1925. A Polish translation was confiscated in 1928. Bulgaria suppressed a translation of it in 1935. The Germans officially burned it in the Nazi bonfires of 1933. In the rest of Europe and in the English-speaking world, however, it achieved fame as well as praise. Ironically, it was through a German translation that the novel originally achieved international fame. And not until after World War II did Czech critics embrace it as serious literature. It has been translated into at least twelve languages and has been frequently adapted for stage and film.

Additional Readings: Jaroslav Krejci, *Czechoslovakia at the Crossroad and European History* (London: I.B. Tauris, 1990); Cecil Parrott, *The Bad Bohemian: The Life of Jaroslav Hasek, Creator of "The Good Soldier Svejk"* (London: Bodley Head, 1978).

28. *The Trial* (*Der Prozess*), by Franz Kafka (Czechoslovakia, 1925). Franz Kafka was one of the most influential European writers of the twentieth century. He was a German born in Prague in 1883, at a time when the city was part of the Austro-Hungarian Empire, a nation outwardly elegant and tranquil but internally fragmented. Its cities were overcrowded and simmering with political turmoil, problems that were to see the collapse of the empire following World War I, when Prague became part of a newly created nation, Czechoslovakia. Kafka lived briefly in Berlin, during 1923 and 1924, at a time when inflation was staggering, the ultimately doomed and unstable Weimar Republic itself was struggling, and the Nazis, led by Adolf Hitler, were beginning to be heard.

The plot of the novel has all the unknowable personal terror of a time after World War I when the world itself was in chaos, and mindless police states were looming throughout Europe. *The Trial*'s protagonist, Joseph K., having committed no offense so far as he is concerned, one morning finds himself arrested and made a ward of the court and his property confiscated by the state. His attempts to discover the reason for all this and to apply normal rules of logic and common sense to his situation come to nothing. He finds himself in a circular maze of legal traditions, procedures, and evasions and always ends up where he began: nowhere. The Court is all powerful, all intrusive, vague, and unreachable.

In the long, central part of the novel, Joseph K. learns the inscrutable ways of the Court. He encounters Huld, a lawyer pushed upon him by his Uncle Karl, and meets others—including Tradesman Block, a fellow victim of the Court who has all but lost his mind after years of useless litigation. A priest comes to explain a parable to Joseph K. before two men from the Court take him to be executed. The story ends in the same puzzlement and darkness with which it began. There is only the sensed directive, for those who have been subjected to such indecipherable torture in the name of justice or order, that: "This is the way it always works!" We are at the mercy of bureaucratic and dictatorial idiocy: perversion, darkness, and death, always in the name of some abstract law or tradition, and always pernicious.

Kafka died in 1924 and his great novel, *Der Prozess* translated as *The Trial*, was published posthumously in the next year. Although he had left instructions that his manuscripts were all to be destroyed, his friend Max Brod decided to publish them anyway. Kafka became a major figure after his

death, leaping into greatness and unsurpassed fame in the years after World War II. His succinctly brilliant but ambiguous novel of repression, ambiguity, fear, entrapment, and darkly lurking unknown danger seemed perfectly to embody the horror of the Third Reich, of Stalinism, and of the American landscape of the McCarthy years and the new conspiracies of the 1960s. His fame extended not only to literary figures; he was also treated seriously by theologians and philosophers, by such figures as Martin Buber.

Kafka's novel mirrored a specific historical moment but also the human condition in general—human weaknesses, emotional traumas, and the persistent sense of terror. This he examined and recorded in *The Trial*, which came to embody, for several generations, the terrible facelessness of a hostile and often brutal bureaucracy that seemed at times to encompass all the processes of so-called civilized man, with its subsequent loneliness and despair.

The ultimate proof of the influence of *The Trial* is that it added his name to the English language: "Kafkaesque" became a readily recognizable term, meaning hopelessly lost or confused in some indecipherable bureaucratic maze that offers no escape and no hope of victory. In the late twentieth century, a manuscript of *The Trial* was auctioned for $1.98 million.

Additional Readings: J.F.N. Bradley, *Czechoslovakia: A Short History* (Edinburgh: Edinburgh University Press, 1971); Arnold Heidsieck, *The Intellectual Contexts of Kafka's Fiction* (Columbia, SC: Camden House, 1994); Henry Sussman, *The Trial: Kafka's Unholy Trinity* (New York: Twayne, 1993).

29. *The Unbearable Lightness of Being* (*Nesnesitelna lehkost byti*), by Milan Kundera (Czechoslovakia, 1984). Kundera's novel is set in Czechoslovakia in the 1960s against the political turmoil of Soviet intervention and occupation through which Kundera had lived and suffered. In 1948 the Czech Communist Party, of which Kundera was a member, gained control of the government, but in 1950 he was thrown out of the

Party and the university he was attending, presumably for criticizing Stalinism. When Khrushchev came to power in the USSR and denounced Stalinism in the 1950s, Kundera was reinstated in the Party. But in 1967 he fell into disfavor when he published a Kafkaesque satire, calling life under communism a "joke." The work translated into English, appropriately, as *The Joke*. In this year he was a leading spokesman at an artists' symposium on encouraging Czech intellectuals to grow beyond their rigid national and political borders, an action for which he came under official sanction. In January 1968, the brief "Prague Spring" began under the leadership of Alexander Dubcek, a communist but independent of the Soviets. The openness of the regime was such that Kundera is even honored in Czechoslovakia for *The Joke*. But nine months later, the brief independence ended with the armed invasion of the country by the Soviets and the arrest of Dubcek. In 1969, the new government refused to allow publication of Kundera's new novel in the country, and in 1970, he was fired from his teaching job and lost all travel privileges. None of his books were allowed to be sold inside the country. His novels and plays were, however, published in the United States and France. When the French government pressured Czechoslovakia to allow him to lecture in France, he and his wife were granted an exception to leave the country. Once outside Czechoslovakia, they defected to France, lost their Czech citizenship in 1978, and became citizens of France in 1981.

The Unbearable Lightness of Being, published in 1984, some five years before the overthrow of communism in Czechoslovakia, is his best-known novel and was made into an award-winning film in 1988 by Philip Kaufman. The novel is a psychological study of a marriage against the backdrop of political upheaval and suppression. Tomas, a philandering Czech physician, is married to Teresa, a photojournalist. His political detachment is in contrast to her earlier courage in smuggling out pictures of Czech people reacting to the Russian tanks rolling into their country in 1968. The couple noted the not-so-subtle ways in which the Soviets have erased Czech history and culture. The streets, for example, have lost their old Czech names and now pay homage to Soviet heroes. The free radio broadcasts of Czech dissidents are doctored by the Soviets. The ruins of World War II and later revolt are purposefully left by the Soviets as reminders of humiliation. Closer to home, Teresa begins to worry that the government is spying on her. Tomas suddenly wakes up to the need to speak against his country's enslavement and writes a lengthy letter to the editor of a journal—a treatise that is finally more philosophical than political. His friends beg him to publicly retract his letter, but he refuses. In retaliation, he loses his post as a physician, can find no further work in his profession, and ends up becoming a window washer.

Although Kundera was already well known and praised in literary circles before 1984, *The Unbearable Lightness of Being* established his reputation as an international figure of wide influence. His message did not immediately reach a Czech audience, however, for it was banned until the overthrow of communism there in 1989.

A situation that had been masked in secrecy, that is, daily life behind Soviet bloc countries, was now a matter for examination from a writer who had been there. This was not a story, of which readers would see many, of leading dissidents who landed in prison; Kundera's characters were only marginally political and never leaders. Moreover, it was a portrait of considerable political ambiguity that challenged the simplistic black-and-white view held by both sides with regard to Eastern Europe and the Western world. Here was a country, with a strong sense of its own national traditions, that had embraced communism after World War II, was absorbed by the Soviets, and was able to have a brief (but still communist) moment of independence under Dubcek. The reader sees the Soviet invasion and Dubcek's defeat as the defining moment in the lives of his characters as well as in modern Czechoslovakia as a whole. In a real sense, it was the Soviets who defeated communism in Czechoslovakia.

The resistance to easy classification is seen in Kundera's disinclination to be classified with Russian dissidents and this novel's effect of angering many Russian dissidents with a portrayal that seems more anti-Russian than anticommunist.

The novel and the film made from the novel introduced his readers to the tragic situation in his native country where the ideal of national communism had given way to Soviet domination. Both had cut Czechoslovakia off from the rest of Europe. The novel showed his readers the weaknesses of both Eastern European countries and Western culture. Its effect was to bring Czechoslovakia into the modern Western European arena. With the publication of this novel with its universal themes, Czech culture came alive again after decades of morbidity and became a civilization to be dealt with on the international scene.

Additional Readings: Aron Aji, ed. *Milan Kundera* (New York: Garland Publishers, 1992); Maria Nemcova Banerjee, *Terminal Paradox: The Novels of Milan Kundera* (New York: Grove Weidenfeld, 1990); Alfred French, *Czech Writers and Politics: 1945–1969* (Boulder, CO: East European Monographs, 1982).

England

1600–1799

ᕙᕗ

John Bunyan, *The Pilgrim's Progress*, 1678, 1679, 1684
William Godwin, *Caleb Williams*, 1794

ᕙᕗ

1600–1799: TIMELINE

1591	The first Puritan Church is organized in England.
1603–25	James I rules England.
1605	Fanatical Roman Catholics are thwarted in their plan to blow up Parliament. This, the Gunpowder Plot, intensifies animosity against the Roman Church.
1620	Francis Bacon publishes *Novum organum*, which revolutionizes scientific thought by stressing accuracy and experimentation.
1628	The Petition of Right, largely drafted by jurist Sir Edward Coke, is passed by Parliament. This document places restrictions on the power of James I.
1629	Charles I becomes king of England.
1629–40	Charles governs for eleven years without calling Parliament. There is increasing tension throughout England regarding king, Parliament, Scotland, Independents, Dissenters, Puritans, and the Irish.
1633	Anti-Puritan William Laud becomes archbishop of Canterbury and supports legislation to limit freedom of religion.
1637	Puritans and other religious dissenters begin to suffer persecution at the hands of the government.
1640	Beset by private debts and private wars, Charles is forced to summon Parliament. When Parliament follows its own way, Charles dismisses them after three weeks in what comes to be known as the "Short Parliament."
1642–48	Civil war rages in England between revolutionary forces in Parliament led by Puritan Oliver Cromwell and those of the king, ending with Cromwell's triumph.

1649	The government executes Charles I, beginning the Commonwealth and the Protectorate.
1651	Thomas Hobbs publishes *Leviathan* in Paris. He enrages religious readers by making a distinction between faith and reason and attacking the papacy.
1653	Oliver Cromwell becomes Lord Protector under England's only written constitution.
1658	Cromwell dies.
1658–60	A period of governmental chaos occurs after Cromwell's death.
1660	Puritan rule ends, and Charles II, a Frenchman and a Roman Catholic, is restored to the throne in what comes to be known as the Restoration.
1660–69	Samuel Pepys keeps a diary that becomes a classic description of the age.
1660–72	John Bunyan is imprisoned for violating the Clarendon Code. While in prison he writes *Grace Abounding to the Chief of Sinners*, a private spiritual memoir.
1661–65	The Clarendon Code is passed. It is a series of laws designed to curb the power of all those outside the Church of England. It forces conformity to the Anglican prayer book and forbids the activity of dissenters.
1662	The Royal Society is granted a charter to promote the natural sciences.
1666	London burns and is rebuilt with designs by Christopher Wren.
1667	John Milton's *Paradise Lost* is published.
1672	Charles II in a Declaration of Indulgence allows limited religious freedom for Roman Catholics and dissenters.
1673	The Cavalier Parliament passes the Test Act, excluding from civil and military office all who have not taken the sacrament of the Church of England.
1675	Bunyan writes *The Pilgrim's Progress* during his six-month imprisonment.
	A system of political parties begins with what comes to be known as the Whig Party, established by a group of country gentleman. The opposing Tory Party is made up of the royal court.
1678, 1679, 1684	John Bunyan's *The Pilgrim's Progress* is published and is a bestselling title for over 200 years.
1685–88	James II rules England.
1687	Isaac Newton's *Principia Mathematica* is first published.
1688	John Bunyan dies. By this time 100,000 copies of his book have been sold.
	In what is known as the Glorious Revolution, James II is deposed.
	William and Mary come to the English throne.
1689	The Toleration Act gives freedom of worship to Protestant dissenters.
1690	John Locke publishes his *Essay Concerning Human Understanding* and *Two Treatises of Government*. By attacking the theory of the divine right of kings and insisting that sovereignty belongs with the people rather than the state, he provided the philosophical foundation for democratic government.
1700s	In the eighteenth century, following the Augustan Age, dominated by the philosophy of John Locke and Isaac Newton and the idea of balance and propriety in society, revolutions in agriculture, transportation, and industry produce the most momentous event of the modern age: the Industrial Revolution. The century was totally dominated by the aristocracy, who believed that every person should

stay in his proper place, forever. Thus it was a time of highly stratified society with power in the hands of a few and great masses of working poor at the bottom of society. Landed gentry lost much of its influence and land through heavy taxation. The growth of a wealthy merchant class gained more power, and a middle class of those in trades and professions became increasingly literate.

1701   Parliament passes the Act of Settlement, insuring that a Protestant monarch would follow Queen Anne on the throne.

1701–14   The War of the Spanish Succession pits England against France and Spain to prevent France's control of the Spanish throne.

1702–14   Queen Anne, the last of the Stuarts, rules England.

1707   The Act of Union joins Scotland with England under a single Parliament, forming Great Britain.

1713–14   The Peace of Utrecht, ending the War of Spanish Succession, gave Britain control of the Mediterranean, Gibralter, Nova Scotia, Newfoundland, and the Hudson Bay and a monopoly on the slave trade to Spanish colonies.

1714–27   The first Hanoverian king, George I, a German who speaks no English, rules England. The Hanoverian monarchs favor the Whig Party and suspect the Tories of being Jacobites sympathetic with descendants of James II.

1715   England successfully puts down a rebellion of Jacobites who supported the accession to the throne of a Catholic descendant of James II.

1719   Daniel DeFoe's *Robinson Crusoe* is published.

1721–42   One of the most influential Whig leaders, Robert Walpole, becomes

the leader of the House of Commons.

1727–60   George II rules England, chiefly relying, as his immediate predecessors did, on his ministers to make most of the decisions.

1733   John Kay revolutionizes the textile industry with the invention of the "flying shuttle."

1734   Alexander Pope's "Essay on Man" is published, stating the tenor of the age: "Whatever is, is right."

1739   John Wesley forms the Methodist Society.

1740–48   In the War of the Austrian Succession, Britain fights successfully to keep Maria Theresa on the throne and impede the influence of France and Spain.

1745–46   Charles Edward Stuart, a grandson of James II, leads a Jacobite rebellion but is defeated at Culloden Moor by the duke of Cumberland, a son of George II.

1747–48   Samuel Richardson's *Clarissa* is published.

1748   Scottish philosopher David Hume publishes his *Philosophical Essay on Human Understanding*, which introduces his age to his skepticism and empiricism.

1756–63   In the Seven Year's War Britain wins its fight with Spain, France, Russia, Austria, Sweden, and Saxony for colonial power.

1757   Battles in India under British military leader Robert Clive secure British control of India.

1760   George III becomes king of England and takes a more active role in running the country than his predecessors had done.

1763   As the French and Indian War ends, Britain secures control of Canada.

1764   Industry is impacted with James Hargreaves's invention of the "spinning jenny."

1765	The Stamp Act becomes one of the most controversial of the many duties placed on goods sold in the New World, leading to the American Revolutionary rallying cry of "No taxation without representation."
1768	James Cook begins his first voyage to the South Pacific.
1769	Industry is revolutionized by Richard Arkwright's invention of the "water frame" and James Watt's invention of the modern steam engine.
1770	James Cook claims New Zealand and part of Australia, New South Wales, for England.
1775	Edward Jenner begins work on a vaccination for smallpox.
1775–83	England loses in the war for American independence.
1776	Adam Smith's *The Wealth of Nations* becomes an important proponent of noninterference in commerce, free competition, and free trade.
1780	The London anti-Catholic Gordon riots continue for a week, leaving 700 dead.
1782	Francis Burney's *Cecelia* is published.
1783	William Pitt, the Younger, begins his first term leading the government.
1784	The India Act, written by Pitt, takes control of India from the East India Company and places it under English government.
1788	Pitt takes over the running of the government when George III is incapacitated with a physical and mental disorder.
1789	The Combination Acts forbid workers from organizing into unions.
	On a voyage to Tahiti, the crew of the HMS *Bounty* mutiny against

	Captain William Bligh and set him afloat at sea on a small boat.
1790s	Revolutionary activity is high in England. Edmund Burke's *Reflection on the Revolution in France* is published in denounciation of the French Revolution.
1791–92	Thomas Paine's incendiary *The Rights of Man* is published, refuting Edmund Burke's view of the French Revolution.
1792	Paine is indicted and found guilty of treason in absentia.
1792–93	The revolution in France inspires and frightens the English rulers, who suspend civil rights in England in 1792 in an attempt to squelch any revolutionary activity.
1793	William Godwin's *Enquiry Concerning Political Justice* is published.
	Eli Whitney invents the cotton gin.
	France declares war on Britain.
1794	William Godwin's *Caleb Williams* is published.
1795	Parliament allows anyone who criticizes the government to be imprisoned without trial.
1797	Mutinies at Spithead, the Nore, and Plymouth are a result of the abuses of working men and an indication of the rebellious spirit of the age.
1798	Antigovernment riots rage throughout Ireland and are put down by British troops.

30. *The Pilgrim's Progress,* by John Bunyan (England, 1678, 1679; pt. II, 1684). *The Pilgrim's Progress* is an allegorical account of a Christian Everyman's journey through all the trials of life, including Restoration England, to ultimate salvation in the Celestial City. Bunyan, an untrained tinker, was a Nonconformist preacher at a time when the Restoration government insisted on strict conformity. The book, while directed to the humble and lowly, enjoyed an extraordinary success immediately and went on to become one of the most popular and influential books in the English language.

In the background is Charles II's return to the throne of England in 1660 as a Catholic monarch, with French tastes and a licentious court, to reign in a Protestant country fearful of Catholics and determined to see that neither defeated Puritans nor Catholics rose to power again. While Charles largely floated with the tide in an effort to hold on to his throne, he issued Declarations of Indulgence that were alternately honored and rescinded by Parliament.

A Cavalier Parliament, dominated by old royalists and led by Edward Hyde, who became earl of Clarendon, sat for eighteen years. Among other actions, they passed a series of four laws called the Clarendon Code, designed to check the power of the former Dissenter rebels and anyone else outside the Church of England. These laws excluded all but Anglicans from corporations that governed cities; required that all clergy agree to every provision in the Prayer Book; imposed harsh penalties for anyone attending meetings or "conventicles" where any services other than Anglican were used; and prohibited any Dissenting minister from teaching school or even coming within five miles of a town unless he swore not to engage in any Dissenting activity, that is, not to "endeavor any alteration of Church or State."

Thus while the court and court life were dissolute and extravagant, much of the country was still Puritan or in other ways Dissenting, and the Code in effect stifled all Dissenting schools as well as churches.

One of those who refused to obey these laws strictly was the staunchly devout Nonconformist John Bunyan. He had served in the Parliamentary army, had been converted to Puritan piety under the influence of his wife, and after much inner turmoil, had devoured Nonconformist literature and become a preacher in 1657. In addition to mastering Puritan theology, he taught himself to write brilliantly. When he continued to preach and refused to say that he would cease doing so,

he was sent to prison on numerous occasions for years at a time. While there, he wrote a host of sermons and *The Pilgrim's Progress.*

Bunyan wrote prose that was direct, simple, and clear and sufficiently filled with figures of speech, allegories, and imaginative incidents to give *The Pilgrim's Progress* great power. The story is told as a dream or a vision. It is a metaphoric journey that his character, called Christian, who has been convinced that he must seek the Celestial City, takes alone, leaving his wife and family behind, a sign that one must seek salvation alone. He sets off on the hazardous path, encountering along the way all the perils that one meets in trying to live a Christian life.

The book, while designed for working-class people who shared his beliefs, nevertheless appealed to others as well. By the time Bunyan died in 1688, 100,000 copies had been sold. It went through fifty-nine editions in the first 100 years. Subsequent sales were in the millions. For more than 200 years it was a constant bestseller.

Critically, while it was scorned by such literari as Alexander Pope, Joseph Addison, John Gay, William Congreve, and other writers of the early eighteenth century, it was reevaluated and elevated toward the end of the century, when sensibility or emotion began to replace the earlier stress upon pure reason. Romantic writers such as Samuel Taylor Coleridge, Robert Southey, John Keats, Charles Lamb, and Sir Walter Scott praised it highly, for both its spiritual and its aesthetic qualities, and helped establish it as a classic.

The work spread to America with the Nonconformists who left England for the New World. When frontiersmen and settlers went west, they carried it with them. Phrases and concepts from the book became part of daily life. By the late nineteenth century, *The Pilgrim's Progress* was in almost every home, and its reputation and figures were known to virtually everyone. It was often said that American settlers needed only three books: the Bible, an almanac, and *The Pilgrim's Progress.* With those they conquered the West.

English Victorians as well as Americans

embraced both the ideas and the style. Charlotte Brontë, George Eliot, William Thackeray, Charles Dickens, Nathaniel Hawthorne, and Louisa May Alcott all made use of it. These authors transformed Bunyan's allegorical analysis of Christian's journey and his gradual growth and change as he nears his goal into the Bildungsroman novel, a type in which a young protagonist undergoes a series of spiritual, moral, and social crises that result in his growth into maturity. William Makepeace Thackeray titled his greatest work *Vanity Fair*, choosing his theme from an episode in Bunyan's book. When Theodore Roosevelt searched for a word with which to criticize journalists who, he thought, stressed too much the evil of current society, he called them Muckrakers, an image derived from Bunyan's book.

Additional Readings: Christopher Hill, *Puritanism and Revolution* (London: Secker and Warburg, 1958); Christopher Hill, *A Tinker and a Poor Man: John Bunyan and His Church, 1628–1688* (New York: Knopf, 1989); N.H. Keeble, ed., *John Bunyan: Conventicle and Parnassus: Tercentenary Essays* (Oxford: Clarendon Press, 1988).

31. *Caleb Williams*, by William Godwin (England, 1794). In the early 1790s, a young English minister, serving in small, rural parishes, suddenly came under the influence of the French philosophes, a group who did not necessarily have any need of God and who had, in theory at least, prepared the way for a revolution in France. The young cleric bolted the ministry, joined a club of "revolutionists," and produced a work in 1793 that was to make him the most influential philosopher of his day. Whatever followed him, concerning concrete or abstract considerations of English society or the equity of English governments, bore at least some mark of his influence. This was William Godwin; the work was *Enquiry Concerning Political Justice and Its Influence on General Virtue and Happiness*. His novel *Caleb Williams* was written the following year to illustrate the principles of his theory.

The context in which Godwin's philosophical novel appeared was one of gross social injustice and erupting revolution. For the great mass of people, it was a time of brutality, class prejudice, and injustice. Public morality and corruption characterized the age. Bribery was commonplace. A system of class oppression made petty crime inevitable and punishment doubly vicious for the poor. The crime that raged in every city made the streets perilous for every citizen. The police were corrupt, and courtrooms themselves were constant reminders of the chasm between rich and poor. The great unwashed masses carried with them such an odor that men with sensitive noses, including the court's justices, screened the smell of dirt and disease by breathing through cloths soaked in vinegar. It is not surprising that punishments were meted out in these courtrooms with blatant inconsistency. Aristocratic criminals could escape prison or execution by obtaining positions out of the country aboard ships. The poor, including debtors, were transported to penal colonies and publicly executed, often after being tortured. Such executions, which were attended as if they were circuses or fairs, in turn brutalized the public.

Class injustice resulted in rebellion everywhere. In 1789 Fletcher Christian led a mutiny on the HMS *Bounty* in the Pacific Ocean. Across the Channel in 1792–93, France had carried out its own revolution against long-standing privilege, and in a Reign of Terror, extremist leaders were executing aristocrats and "enemies of the state." At the same time, England, itself, was seething with near revolution. In 1797, just as ships were about to sail on Easter morning—in the midst of a war, just three years after the appearance of Godwin's novel—virtually the entire British fleet at Spithead, Nore, and Plymouth mutinied because of rotten conditions and years of abuse.

At every turn, revolutionary thought was met with repressive government measures. Under William Pitt, the government undertook a campaign to wipe out every hint of rebellion. Pitt passed post facto laws to inhibit dissent, hoping, for example, to jail the revolutionary thinker Thomas Paine. Pitt also sent government agents into every nook and cranny, trying to capture the poet/agitator John Thelwall.

Into this situation Godwin dropped his bombshell, the publication of *Caleb Williams*. It is a novel of suspense, secret crime, and terror. Caleb, the son of peasants, is employed as personal secretary to Count Ferdinando Falkland, who behaves mysteriously. Caleb sets out to watch his employer secretly, until one day Falkland reveals to him a terrible secret crime. But Falkland, realizing the power this knowledge has given Caleb, begins to hate and fear his secretary. Caleb flees, is falsely accused of theft, and soon finds himself the object of a nationwide pursuit, during which he adopts various disguises to avoid detection. The novel has two endings: The manuscript version has Caleb declared guilty and executed; in the printed version Falkland is found guilty and is executed, while the freed Caleb is haunted by a sense of responsibility for Falkland's death.

The book was an immense success, both as a novel and as an objectification of radical philosophical principles, principles that were picked up and carried to new heights of rebellion and protest by the following generations of Romantics, as in the example of Godwin's son-in-law poet Percy Bysshe Shelley. It continued to exert an influence on subsequent social and political thought, as well as on the literature of social protest, well into the nineteenth century. Throughout the twentieth century, it was still studied for its integral connection with radical thought and movements in the years following its publication.

Caleb Williams consciously served to promote Godwin's campaign for political justice through his philosophical vision of the individual's relationship to society. The novel was praised and studied as a de facto refutation of Edmund Burke's defense of traditionalist conservative views in *Reflections on the French Revolution*.

Godwin achieved his great influence in this novel by focusing on the English legal system: crime, English law, police detection, the courts, punishment, and the penal system. This system he shows to be the result and epitome of class injustice, which distorted every aspect of British life.

Additional Readings: Pamela Clemit, *The Godwinian Novel: The Rational Fictions of Godwin, Brockden Brown, Mary Shelley* (Oxford: Clarendon Press, 1993); E.J. Hobsbawm, *The Age of Revolution, 1789–1848* (New York: New American Library, 1962); Gary Kelly, *The English Jacobin Novel 1780–1805* (New York: Clarendon Press, 1976).

1800–1899

Jane Austen, *Pride and Prejudice*, 1813

Sir Walter Scott, *Waverley*, 1814–19

Mary Shelley, *Frankenstein*, 1818

Charlotte Brontë, *Jane Eyre*, 1847

Emily Brontë, *Wuthering Heights*, 1847

William Makepeace Thackeray, *Vanity Fair*, 1848

Mrs. (Elizabeth) Gaskell, *Mary Barton*, 1848

Charles Kingsley, *Alton Locke*, 1850

Charles Dickens, *David Copperfield*, 1850

Charles Dickens, *Bleak House*, 1853

Charles Dickens, *Hard Times*, 1854

George Eliot, *Silas Marner*, 1861

George Gissing, *The Unclassed*, 1884

George Meredith, *Diana of the Crossways*, 1885

Robert Louis Stevenson, *The Strange Case of Dr. Jekyll and Mr. Hyde*, 1886

Thomas Hardy, *Tess of the d'Urbervilles*, 1891

Israel Zangwill, *Children of the Ghetto*, 1892

Thomas Hardy, *Jude the Obscure*, 1895

∽

1800–1899: TIMELINE

1800   The long-standing British presence in India changed as the English became less tolerant of Indian custom and religion.

1802   The first Factor Act is passed, limiting working hours to no more than twelve hours a day for children and making modest improvements in sanitation.

1813   Jane Austen's *Pride and Prejudice* is published. It is set in the eighteenth century.

1814   The British defeat Napoleon and place him in exile in Elba, from which he escapes.

1814–19   Sir Walter Scott's *Waverley* novels are published.

1815   Napoleon is defeated by the English at Waterloo.

The Congress of Vienna redraws the map of Europe and recommends the end of the slave trade.

Industrialization has so flourished in England that the country is exporting 100 times more cotton products than it sold fifty years earlier.

In one of many Corn Laws, high tariffs are placed on grain to keep domestic prices high, creating a hardship on the poor who must buy grain for bread.

1816   Habeas corpus, a protection against arbitrary imprisonment, is extended beyond criminal acts alone.

1817   A repeal of income tax tends to benefit merchants and manufacturers and places an additional burden on the working poor.

1818   Mary Shelley's *Frankenstein* is published.

1819   The Peterloo Massacre occurs in Manchester. The government has cut back on services to the poor and working classes in order to pay high debts incurred in the Napoleonic wars. Some 50,000 to 60,000 workers demonstrate to appeal for reforms. They are attacked by government forces, and 11 workers are killed. As a response to this and the fears aroused by the French Revolution, Parliament passes Six Acts to restrict civil liberties. It limits freedom of the press and labor organization. Severe penalties are levied on violators.

1827   Jeremy Bentham's *Rationale for Judicial Evidence* is published.

1828   The Test Acts are repealed. These acts had discriminated against non-Anglicans by barring all Dissenters and Catholics from civil service, professions, and admission to universities.

Additions to the Corn Laws reinforce high import tariffs on grain to keep domestic prices elevated.

1829   Catholics become eligible to hold office. More than 190,000 small landowners are disenfranchised.

1830s   These years see the creation of two new political parties: the Liberal Party, dominated by the middle class, and the Conservative Party, dominated by the aristocracy.

1831   A Royal Commission is set up to investigate factories.

1832   The Reform Bill of 1832 grants suffrage to a rising middle class, including mill owners who are opposed to reforms of working-class living and working conditions. Passed under the guidance of P.M. Charles Grey, the measure decreased the amount of land a citizen needed to own in order to vote and redistributed House of Commons seats. Still, however, only 20 percent of the adult male population could vote.

1833   Parliament enacts the Factory Act, forbidding the employment of children under nine in silk mills and limiting the working hours of children in other industries.

Robert Owen forms the Grand National Consolidated Trades Union, the first comprehensive organization designed to consolidate the efforts of unions.

Slavery is abolished in British colonies.

1834   The New Poor Laws, one of the most bitterly opposed pieces of legislation of the century, eliminates assistance to the poor and establishes "poor houses," notoriously squalid institutions.

"Puseyites," named for Edward Pusey, leader of the Oxford Movement, grow in influence after publishing *Tracts for the Times*. Many people condemn these Anglican Oxford men for their Roman Catholic leanings with their beliefs in apostolic succession and confession.

1835   The British decree that English shall be the language of government in India.

1837   Poor harvests throughout the British Isles create even greater hardships for the poor.

The "People's Charter," presented by the Chartists, who were trade unionists, calls for an end to discrimination in legal and political arenas. Their six points include a demand for the vote for all males over twenty-one; election by secret ballot; and annual parliamentary elections. Their appeal is refused.

Thomas Carlyle's *French Revolution, a History* is published in which he enlarges on the problems of the poor.

1837–39   Charles Dickens publishes *Oliver Twist* serially.

1837–1867   These years are defined by laissez-faire economics and the "Victorian Compromise."

1837–1901   Queen Victoria's reign dominates most of the century.

1838–39   The Anti-Corn Law League is organized, led by reformers Richard Cobden and John Bright.

1839   A Chartist Petition, recommending voting reforms of the People's Charter, is presented and again refused after hundreds are injured and arrested.

An Anti-Corn League is organized.

1839–43   Britain engages in the first Opium War with China, which tries to halt the importation of opium into China.

1840s   Because of the widespread poverty throughout the British Isles, many writers call the decade the "Hungry Forties."

1841   Britain occupies Hong Kong.

1841–73   David Livingstone maps uncharted areas of Africa, and his efforts there as a medical missionary endear him to his African patients and encourage others to go on errands of mercy in Africa. Unintentionally, however, he also helps open Africa to European exploitation.

1842   A demonstration on the part of Chartists is two miles long.

Child labor protection laws extend for the first time to children working in the mines.

1844   English tailors publish a report regarding clothing made and contaminated in the slums.

1845   Bejamin Disraeli's *Sybil, or The Two Nations* is published, showing that England is composed of two worlds—one of the rich and one of the poor.

1845–47   John Henry Cardinal Newman, once an Oxfordian and Anglican convert to Roman Catholicism, publishes his *Essay on the Development of Christian Doctrine*.

1846   In response to widespread starvation, Prime Minister Robert Peel repeals English Corn Laws, excepting small tariffs on wheat.

The "Ten Hours Bill" is passed, limiting workers to a maximum number of work hours a day.

1847   Charlotte Brontë's *Jane Eyre* is published.

Emily Brontë's *Wuthering Heights* is published.

1848   William Makepeace Thackeray's *Vanity Fair* is published. The setting is England before and after the Battle of Waterloo.

Revolutions wage throughout Europe.

Mrs. (Elizabeth) Gaskell's *Mary Barton* is published.

Karl Marx and Friedrich Engel's *The Communist Manifesto* is published in London. It issues the call: "Workers of all countries, Unite!"

Another Chartist petition asks for broadening of suffrage. It is again turned aside, but all except the call for annual parliamentary elections will eventually become law.

1849   Britain adds the Punjab to its crown of colonial jewels.

1850   Charles Kingsley's pamphlet on the distressing conditions under which clothes are tailored is published as "Cheap Clothes and Nasty."

Charles Kingsley's *Alton Locke* is published.

Charles Dickens's *David Copperfield* is published.

1851   By mid-century there are more industrial than agricultural workers in England. The industrialism, an explosion in population, laissez-faire economics, and the unquestioned profit motive create unparalleled slums and disease-ridden living conditions in industrial towns. Workers are housed in decrepit shacks and unheated basements. It is not unusual to find as many as 215 people who must use one toilet.

1852   British imperialism seems secured with its final successful fight for control of Burma.

1853   Charles Dickens's *Bleak House* is published.

1854   Charles Dickens's *Hard Times* is published.

1854–56   Britain fights in the Crimean War.

1857   England's Ecclesiastical Courts are abolished. This automatically ends the requirement of seeking Church permission to receive a divorce.

In the Sepoy Rebellion, Indian revolutionaries war unsuccessfully against the British.

1859   Charles Darwin's *On the Origin of Species* is published.

John Stuart Mill's *On Liberty* provides a theoretical basis for his support of civil liberties.

1860   Benjamin Jowett's *Essays and Reviews* is published. This controversial Anglican minister translates and interprets the work of the Apostles, contributing further to a reevaluation of older religious concepts.

1861	George Eliot's *Silas Marner* is published.
1863	T.H. Huxley's *Zoological Evidences of Man's Place in Nature* is published, a work that more than any other clarifies and gives credence to Darwin.
	J.S. Mill publishes *Utilitarianism*, arguing for the public ownership of natural resources.
1867	The Fenians, a secret Irish society, work to overthrow British rule of Ireland. The charismatic Irish leader in Parliament is Charles Stuart Parnell.
	Benjamin Disraeli is largely responsible for the passage of the Reform Bill of 1867, extending the suffrage to many working-class men.
1867–95	The multivolume work by Karl Marx, *Das Kapital*, is published.
1868–94	William Gladstone, leader of the Liberal Party, is the prime mover in reforms. For fourteen of these years, he is prime minister of England.
1869	Physicist John Tyndall, along with Darwin and Huxley, promotes the New Science by disproving the theory of spontaneous generation.
	The Corn Laws are totally abolished.
1869–89	Henry Morton Stanley explores Africa, claiming areas of that continent for England and working for King Leopold of Belgium to exploit resources there.
1870	The Education Act of 1870 made elementary education compulsory for all.
1871	The government is finally forced to recognize the rights of workers to organize and strike.
	Stanley is successful in his goal of finding medical missionary David Livingstone.
1873	The enactment of the Judicature Act is a reform of the legal system.

Walter Horatio Pater's *Studies in the History of the Renaissance* is published, giving impetus to the aesthetic movement recommending that art be created for art's sake only, not for any social purpose.

1876	Victoria proclaims herself empress of India.
1880s	Several aspects of a Women's Property Act are passed, giving women the right to own property, to dispose of their own property in their wills, to sign contracts, to execute deeds, and to sue and be sued, none of which were available to them before.
1881–94	The British Empire is so extensive that the government can claim that the sun never sets on the British Isles. For most of its claims to Africa, England can thank Cecil Rhodes, the entrepreneur—or plunderer, depending on one's point of view—who dreamed of building a railroad that would go from South to North Africa on English possessions.
1882	England gains control of the Suez Canal.
1884	George Gissing's *The Unclassed* is published.
	The Third Reform Bill extends the vote to agricultural working men.
	A group of nonviolent, non-Marxist socialists, called the Fabians, are organized. The most illustrious members of this highly important group are playwright George Bernard Shaw, novelist H.G. Wells, and statesman Ramsey MacDonald.
	George Meredith's *Diana of the Crossways* is published.
1885	A group of English-educated Indians and their sympathizers form the Indian National Congress to secure an increased voice for Indians in their own affairs.
	The British annex Botswana.

The Congo is set up under the personal rule of Leopold of Belgium.

1886   Robert Lewis Stevenson's *The Strange Case of Dr. Jekyll and Mr. Hyde* is published.

1887   Queen Victoria and her subjects in England and around the world celebrate her Jubilee.

1888   In one of the most notorious crimes of all time, a murderer known as Jack-the-Ripper murders at least seven prostitutes, terrorizing London for three months. Among the suspects is Sir William Gull, personal physician to Queen Victoria.

Through Cecil Rhodes's successful securing of mining rights in Zimbabwe, the British secure control of that area of Africa.

1889   A bitter dock workers' strike results in a secured minimum wage and new political clout for labor unions.

The British take control of Zambia in Africa.

1890   General William Booth, who organized the Salvation Army and had worked for many years ministering to the poorest and most destitute inhabitants of London's slums, paints a portrait of what he has learned and come to recommend in *In Darkest England and the Way Out.*

Joseph Conrad works on the Congo River in Africa.

1891   Thomas Hardy's *Tess of the d'Urbervilles* is published.

1892   Israel Zangwill's *Children of the Ghetto* is published.

1893   Sigmund Freud's seminal work *Studies in Hysteria* is published.

1895   Thomas Hardy's *Jude the Obscure* is published.

1896   Freud designates his manner of exploring psychological disturbances as "psychoanalysis."

1899–1902   The Boer War, fought with Dutch settlers in South Africa, ends in Britain's favor.

32. *Pride and Prejudice*, by Jane Austen (England, 1813). Jane Austen's most famous novel is a study of the social milieu of which she was a part. The class system she writes about was divided into an aristocracy, a gentry, a merchant class, the respectable working poor, and the disreputable poor. Ordinarily, one associated with and married within one's own class, but mobility had become possible, and social mixing did sometimes occur, especially with changes in economic status.

Women were placed in especially precarious situations by the social system. If they had brothers, daughters rarely inherited from their fathers' estates. Any property that did come their way automatically became their husband's upon marriage. An unmarried woman with no means of support had very few occupational options open to her. So marriage became as much a matter of business and survival as of love and affection.

Set in eighteenth-century England, the story is of Elizabeth Bennet, the second oldest of five daughters of an English gentleman who supports his family from the income of an inherited estate. Such is their social standing and income that his daughters mingle in polite society, going to parties and receiving visitors in stations well above their own. However, it is well known that after Mr. Bennet dies because he has no sons, his estate will go to a male relative, a Mr. Collins. In this event, any of Mr. Bennet's unmarried daughters and his widow will be left with no visible means of support.

The action of the novel is fueled by the need, keenly felt by the daughters' flighty mother, to get the girls taken care of in marriage. The chief focus is on the courtship of the second daughter Elizabeth and her wealthy and aristocratic suitor Mr. Darcy. Although they are initially attracted to one another, their pride and prejudice and the actions of friends and family result in misunderstandings that delay their final reconciliation and marriage.

One subplot involves the eldest daughter's courtship, and another involves Lydia, Elizabeth's scatterbrained younger sister who brings dishonor to the whole family and jeopardizes the chances of marriage for her other sisters by running away with a scoundrel and fortune hunter named Wickham.

The novel sold only moderately well after its first publication but has always been highly regarded and has withstood the test of time as few other works have done. It has always been one of the chief subjects of literary study, it has been translated widely, and it has gone through many editions. It has also been the subject of a number of film and stage adaptations. In the 1990s, a tremendous surge of interest in Austen resulted in the issuing of a number of new, handsome editions and several award-winning dramatic adaptations by both English and American filmmakers.

The novel's great influence has come from its fictionalizing the predicament of the woman of marriageable age in the eighteenth century, a predicament that changed very little in degree in 150 years. In the late nineteenth century, it provided a powerful incentive for the passage of new inheritance laws in the United States that allowed wives to own and control the property they had inherited from their fathers. Although not overtly political, the novel impressed upon its readers critical issues of gender, class, and economics that figured in village life of the time, often ridiculing the ruling class and arguing for greater class and gender equity.

Although the whole point of the novel is to secure husbands, and therefore economic stability, for the Bennet girls, many readers could scarcely help noting that most of the marriages in the novel are far from ideal or even satisfactory: Mr. and Mrs. Bennet have little understanding or respect for one another; Elizabeth's friend Charlotte seems to marry the silly curate Collins out of desperation at being twenty-seven years old with no other prospects. And Charlotte is Collins's second or third choice. Elizabeth's sister

Lydia and Wickham's shotgun marriage is not the foundation of a long, mutually loving relationship, and the hypercritical reader has reason to wonder, financial considerations excepted, if Elizabeth wouldn't be better off maintaining the lowly and precarious status of a spinster, as Jane Austen did.

Additional Readings: Julia Prewitt Brown, *Jane Austen's Novels: Social Change and Literary Form* (Cambridge, MA: Harvard University Press, 1979); Marilyn Butler, *Jane Austen and the War of Ideas* (Oxford: Clarendon Press, 1975); Debra Teachman, *Understanding Pride and Prejudice* (Westport, CT: Greenwood Press, 1997).

33. *Waverley*, by Sir Walter Scott (England, 1814–19). Sir Walter Scott's influence on the development of Western thought is difficult to pinpoint, for it was so broad as to defy compaction. It is impossible to turn a page or to stir a thought without, somehow, touching his influence.

His first novel, in 1814, was titled *Waverley*, initiating a series called the "Waverley" novels because they were "by the author of *Waverley*," who was anonymous. The Waverley novels, which included *Rob Roy* and *Ivanhoe*, met with unparalleled success, lifting the subject of English history to new heights of respect, mythologizing the rise of modern England, and in the process, elucidating distinctive values and establishing a particular vision of the world, with its knights in armor and its Highland clansmen in emblematic conflicts.

Several historical periods are pertinent to the publication of the Waverley novels: medieval England and Scotland, the Jacobin rebellion of 1745, and the wars between England and France, contemporary with the first *Waverley*'s publication.

The earliest period Scott deals with is medieval England, the setting of one of the most famous Waverley novels, *Ivanhoe*. It was a time of knightly splendor, Robin Hood, and King Richard I.

Second is the time of his first historical novel during the last rebellion in the Highlands of pro-Catholic, pro-Highland, anti-British forces that gathered with fading, antique grandeur around the Clans, to fight once more for "Bonnie Prince Charlie," the last Jacobin pretender to the throne. The armies met at Culloden, the Highlanders sweeping down from the hills, the pro-English forces of the Duke of Cumberland marching up from London in 1745. After some uncertainty, the Duke of Cumberland prevailed. They slaughtered the Scots, scoured the field to kill the wounded and the dying, secured their prizes, and then, under orders, marched up into the Highlands, going into every cranny, glen, and hut to wipe out once and for all the last vestiges of Highland rebellion. It was one of the most brutal and most melancholy slaughters in English history. When it was over, George Frideric Handel wrote a composition, *Hail the Conquering Hero Comes*, about the Duke of Cumberland's triumphant march back to London.

The time of the publication of the first Waverley novel is also important to its influence. In the spring of 1814, after more than twenty years of conflict that had turned Europe into a slaughterhouse, England and most of Europe thought the days of the Napoleonic Wars were over. Following a disastrous retreat from Moscow in 1812, Napoleon continued to wage war. In April 1814, the French marshals finally quit, and Napoleon was sent to the isle of Elba. In that summer, England was momentarily free from conflict at last. In that same year, Walter Scott released his first Waverley novel.

Pulling from the example of Maria Edgeworth's *Castle Rackrent* and of his own knowledge of chapbooks, medieval romances, and Enlightenment views of history, which provided him with the bases of modern social and economic structure, plus his intimate awareness of Scottish history and culture, Scott set out not only to entertain and to sell books but also to teach his public something of what Britain and the British Empire should be after the Napoleonic Wars.

The story of Edward Waverley, replete with color and violence, is told from the omniscient third-person point of view, setting it off from the first-person, confessional type of narration, which had become the domain of more radical reformers. Waverley, an Englishman, becomes involved with the rebellion of 1745, entranced by the romantic pageantry of the lost cause, the fine aristocratic figures with their loyal plebeian followers, and the dashing Bonnie Prince, pretender to the English throne. He is especially enchanted by the noble, entirely fictional MacIvor and his sister Flora. Enlightened at last by the reality of a brutal war that included cruelty on both sides, Waverley gains a proper perspective, marries an attractive but unpretentious girl, settles down, and presumably lives wisely in the United Kingdom.

The most popular of the Waverley novels, *Ivanhoe*, represented a change in Scott's subjects and themes. With that, he left the recent past and went into the far Middle Ages, the time of the Crusades. It was this more than anything else that created a lasting mark in the public mind. While his theme in *Waverley* and the novels immediately following was the creation of a unified Britain, it was his romantic, eternally dashing picture of the Middle Ages with its knights and ladies in distress that captured the public remembrance.

The influence of the Waverley novels was so enormous as to be incalculable. The picture of knights in armor fighting jousts or defending the honor of a chaste heroine captured not only all of Britain but the United States and other countries as well. Sections of Chicago were even named after his novels.

But his influence in America is most associated with the South, where planters attempted to establish a new manorial society, borrowing from the images of Scott. They gave themselves and their homes knightly names and played analogous games on horseback.

At the core was the influence of a fictional society's values: upper-class heroic action, the meaningful flourish, the necessity of defending to the death even small points of honor, knightly competition, and seemingly mindless loyalty largely based on class or clan.

Mark Twain, disparaging this incalculable influence, portrayed a clannish slaughter in the *Adventures of Huckleberry Finn*, named a sinking ship of murderous thieves *The Walter Scott*, and declared on more than one occasion that Walter Scott had caused the Civil War.

Additional Readings: Katie Trumpener, *Bardic Nationalism: The Romantic Novel and the British Empire* (Princeton, NJ: Princeton University Press, 1997); Alexander Welsh, *The Hero of the Waverley Novels* (Princeton, NJ: Princeton University Press, 1992).

34. *Frankenstein*, by Mary Shelley (England, 1818). *Frankenstein*, published anonymously by Mary Shelley in 1818, dedicated to her father, the radical philosopher William Godwin, introduced by her husband Percy Shelley, and dealing as it did with fantastic and controversial subjects, was an instantaneous if qualified success.

In an unexpected way, Mary Shelley's novel is a reflection of the age. Immediately after the fall of the Bastille, the French Revolution with its grand ideals of liberty, equality, and fraternity for all people electrified Europe. William Wordsworth, one of the great English poets who was there, wrote in *The Prelude*: "Good was it in that time to be alive, But to be young was very heaven." The future of humankind looked bright with promise. But the wholesale execution of aristocrats, known as the Reign of Terror, the chaos of shifting governments, and ultimately the rise of Napoleon Bonaparte, along with endless wars, gradually led to profound disillusionment and despair. Mary Shelley, born in 1797, the daughter of William Godwin and Mary Wollstonecraft, absorbed the radical reformist philosophies of her parents and of those early hopes; but she saw also the fading of the dreams: In the world of 1818, with the end of wars, England faced enormous debts, growing problems of industrialism, labor, and the poor, wandering and often wounded and indigent veterans of the wars, and increased troubles abroad. The monster of her novel represents many aspects of the world in which it made its appearance.

All the world now knows the story of the monster and the monster's maker, but when it was first issued, it was something new and startling and morally and aesthetically questionable. It became an embodiment of man's eternal search for the secret of life, a Faustian quest fused with a utilitarian projection of pure science.

The story of the brilliant scientist who, like God (who is not mentioned in the story at all), learns to *create* a living human being (in this case, not from the dust of the earth but from fresh corpses) is told in a series of letters, layer upon layer of stories within stories, which together create a sense of immediacy and mounting suspense. At the same time, however, the complexity, along with the varied points of view, creates a sense of the imperceptible, like dense fog or mist.

The book had its champions and also its critics, who brought both its morals and its art into question. In the nineteenth century, it retained a large readership. In the twentieth century, especially after the phenomenally successful movie of the 1930s, its popularity soared. In the 1970s and afterward, with the rise of women's studies and of science fiction as an acceptable genre, it grew in stature in the academy.

There is scarcely an issue in the age that is not reflected in *Frankenstein*, a work described as a cross between a Godwinian tract and a terror novel. Implicitly, it treats such matters as egalitarianism, education, morality and the modern world, women's rights, the romantic stress on individualism, uncontrolled ambition, and utilitarianism.

Many radical readers saw in the novel a social statement. Percy Shelley, in a review published only after his death, noted that the clear moral of the story was: "Treat a person ill, and he will become wicked." Other readers found in it the first fictive analysis of the post-Revolutionary decline in France. Like the Revolution, in the beginning, the monster is an Innocent, inexperienced in the ways of the world; but it reacts quickly to slights or to mistreatment; and it becomes violently destructive—like the French Revolution itself.

But above all, the novel continues to articulate the problem of the New Science and the viability of scientific achievement in the modern world. In Mary Shelley's story, the scientist-creator Dr. Frankenstein, the seeker after infinite power, is completely removed from the moral views of the community. He lives in a world apart. His is the perfect dream of science, which has not only challenged all of morality, emulating God, but results not in wonder but in horror. The enormous influence of the story has in fact been implicit in its theme even from the first, and it remains especially significant in the current age. In the modern world, the scientist has typically been above or apart from morality. He does not deal in such subjective and emotional matters. He has to function in complete objectivity, in the realm of test tubes and quantifiable results. Otherwise, he is not a "scientist."

However, in the New Mexico desert in 1945, at White Sands, as Dr. Robert Oppenheimer and others watched the explosion of a bomb that could destroy the world, the scientist discovered morality. He was no longer above and apart from basic human activity. He was, and always had been, involved in the total human process.

The continuing significance of the novel in the modern consciousness has initiated a major industry of manufacturers and moviemakers attempting merely to satisfy public interest in the monster and his creator. It has, above all, become a modern myth, and the phrase "the creation of a Frankenstein's monster" has become a universal expression for the unexpected results of human actions, like the development of the atomic bomb.

Additional Readings: Harold Bloom, ed., *Mary Shelley's "Frankenstein"* (New York: Chelsea House, 1987); Ian Hedworth Gilmour, *Riot, Uprisings, and Revolution* (London: Hutchinson, 1992); Emily W. Sunstein, *Mary Shelley: Romance and Reality* (Boston: Little, Brown, 1989).

35. *Jane Eyre*, by Charlotte Brontë (England, 1847). Some of the contextual issues of England in 1847 that are pertinent to *Jane Eyre*, the novel that Charlotte Brontë saw into print that year under the pseudonym of Currer Bell, include the attitudes toward women at the time, the economic and vo-

cational limitations of educated, middle-class women, religious hypocrisy, and the position taken by England as a civilizing force over the dark-skinned people in their colonies. Charlotte Brontë, herself, had known the limitations of the typical educated woman. No matter what talents an unmarried educated woman had, the only profession open to her was teaching, usually as a governess to upper-class families who regarded her with the same disdain they had for their uneducated kitchen servants. The lower- and middle-class woman was expected to be humble, modest, quiet, and restrained. Most important, they were expected, in a culture so clearly patriarchal, to remain subservient to men of any class. The woman who aggressively challenged the code was often regarded as insane, a pariah, or a prostitute.

Brontë lived as the child of a curate in an age that was technically devout but sometimes hypocritical. The Industrial Revolution was often able to flourish with the help of the Protestant Church, which was inextricably tied to economics, many of its believers attesting to the spiritual worthlessness of the poor and the moral righteousness of the rich, who obviously, it was argued, would not be rich if God did not love them.

To many Englishmen in the nineteenth century, colonial peoples, being innocent of English civilization, were dark, dangerous barbarians. They represented the human species without the shaping restraints of English society.

These issues are addressed in *Jane Eyre*, the story of an orphan who is reared and educated in religious schools and goes on to the position of governess in the household of the mysterious Mr. Rochester. Jane and her employer fall in love but are thwarted by the revelation, made on their wedding day, that Rochester is already married to a madwoman he confines in his attic. Jane leaves, refusing to become his mistress, and returns several years later to marry Rochester, having inherited a comfortable income and having found that Rochester's wife had set fire to the house, which destroyed it, blinded him, and killed her.

Brontë's novel was an immediate commercial success, running to three editions before the end of the year and leading the *London Times* to say that the public was afflicted with *Jane Eyre* fever. Part of the interest arose from the mystery surrounding the author. While it appeared obvious to many that the author was a woman, at the same time, others believed the author had to be a man because its subject matter was unbefitting a woman writer.

When the identity of the author became known, however, negative reviews began to proliferate on the grounds that the vigor, power, and "coarseness" of the book were unspeakable from the pen of a woman. More fundamental to objections, however, was the "rebelliousness" central to the book at a time when the political establishment of England was looking with distaste and fear on revolutions in England and abroad. For this reason *Jane Eyre* was described as a dangerous book, which perpetuated evil, held up rebelliousness as a positive virtue, recommended the overthrow of authority, and sanctioned discontent.

While many people objected that the novel was sacrilegious, other readers warmly identified with the "plain" Jane Eyre, a sympathetic heroine who refused to submit quietly to the abuse of her religious teachers and insisted on speaking her own unorthodox religious opinions as a child. Readers also admired St. John, a contrast to the typical religious hypocrite and bigot in the novel and the man who asks Jane to share his life helping the less fortunate.

It was not just the novel's religious views that made it unorthodox. Readers saw a young, sympathetic heroine, very unlike the Victorian ideal. As governess, she refuses to play the subservient feminine charmer to Rochester's upper-class teasing. The mere fact that Jane, in complete ignorance, falls in love with a married man and that Rochester proposes that she become his mistress affected readers both negatively and positively. On the one hand, the mere inclusion of such a proposal on the part of a sympathetic character was considered scandalous. On the other hand, when Jane refuses, she is again defying the ruling patriarchy of Victorian England.

Brontë's readership remained constant and enthusiastic throughout the nineteenth and twentieth centuries, despite critics who disparaged it as thinly veiled autobiography or inferior to her sister Emily's *Wuthering Heights*. In the women's studies movement beginning in the 1960s, the influence of *Jane Eyre* spread from her ever-constant general readership to the academy, where the novel came to be recognized as a defense of the plight of poor women and an encouragement of female self-worth. Moreover, the text came to be read in a new light in the twentieth century. There was the impossible war waged between passion and duty within the female character, and the imprisonment of passion and difference, represented by Rochester's wife Bertha, "the madwoman in the attic."

Also, as the colonial glory of England came to an end, readers were prepared to see the way in which Bertha, the dark-complexioned Jamaican wife, was emblematic of the colonizer's fear of others unlike himself and also the ways in which Bertha represented that which Victorian women repressed.

Brontë's gripping tale has inspired numerous films and dramas based directly and indirectly on the novel, and the rich interpretive possibilities in *Jane Eyre* have inspired other fictions, the most successful of which is Jean Rhys's 1966 *Wide Sargasso Sea*, told from the point of view of Bertha. The novel also inspired a musical version that opened on Broadway in December 2000.

Additional Readings: Marjorie Chibnall, *Manners, Morals, and Class in England 1774–1858* (New York: St. Martin's Press, 1994); Inga Stina Ewbank, *Their Proper Sphere: A Study of the Brontë Sisters as Early Victorian Female Novelists* (Cambridge, MA: Harvard University Press, 1966); Sandra Gilbert and Susan Gubar, *The Madwoman in the Attic: The Woman Writer and the Nineteenth-Century Literary Imagination* (New Haven, CT: Yale University Press, 1979); Sally Shuttleworth, *Charlotte Brontë and Victorian Psychology* (Cambridge: Cambridge University Press, 1996).

36. *Wuthering Heights,* **by Emily Brontë (England, 1847).** The story of the strange owner of Wuthering Heights, a house on the Yorkshire moors, is told through letters, by a recent visitor named Lockwood and by a longtime servant named Nellie Dean. Thirty years before Lockwood's first visit to Wuthering Heights, Nellie Dean informs him that the owner of Wuthering Heights had been a Mr. Earnshaw who brought home with him from a trip to Liverpool a strange, dark child named Heathcliff. The boy is despised by Earnshaw's son Hindley but becomes the soul mate of Earnshaw's daughter Cathy.

After Mr. Earnshaw's death, Hindley, as new master of Wuthering Heights, treats Heathcliff abominably, but Cathy continues to wander the moors with him. When Hindley promotes the idea of marriage between Cathy and a wealthy neighbor, Edgar Linton, Heathcliff runs away, leaving Cathy to grieve herself sick. Nevertheless, when Heathcliff fails to return, Cathy marries Linton. Six months after their marriage, Heathcliff returns, now a grown man of great wealth.

His response to Cathy's marriage is to contribute to her brother Hindley's ruin. He elopes with Linton's sister Isabella, whom he does not love and treats as a slave. Cathy dies in giving birth to Linton's daughter, Catherine, and Isabella gives birth to Heathcliff's son, whom she names Linton. Meanwhile, Heathcliff secures Wuthering Heights as his own and makes a servant of Hindley's son Hareton.

Heathcliff's continuing plan to control both families and secure the hated, neighboring Linton's estate of Cathy's widower leads him to encourage the courtship between his own weakling son and Cathy and Linton's daughter, Catherine. Not long after the couple marry, the young groom dies; Catherine inherits her father's estate, which automatically ends up in the hands of Heathcliff, who keeps Cathy's daughter, the widowed Catherine, and Hindley's son, Hareton, as virtual prisoners at Wuthering Heights. When Heathcliff dies, his ghost can be seen joining the ghost of Cathy in wanderings on the moor for all eternity. The two surviving young people have fallen in love.

Brontë, under the name of Ellis Bell, in 1847, published *Wuthering Heights* in two volumes with a second-rate publishing house. Unlike *Jane Eyre*, written by her sister, Charlotte, Emily Brontë's novel was poorly received. The public at the time found it to be both unsettling and shocking. It was not until the end of the nineteenth century that her work began to rise in reputation, actually achieving greater critical stature than *Jane Eyre*. A film adaptation made at the height of the novel's popularity, starring Lawrence Olivier, increased the novel's appeal and critical acclaim, a position it held until mid-twentieth century when Charlotte's novel assumed ascendancy.

Wuthering Heights was a landmark novel in its counter to Victorian morality and hypocrisy. To its Church-centered Victorian readers, the world of the novel seemed empty, not only of any kind of organized religion or church (like the one Emily's father served as pastor) but of any kind of traditional deity. Furthermore, she presented one of the first novels in which the romantic hero is not just wronged against but is, in essence, a cruel, vengeful, God-defiant outlaw. By contrast, his enemies, the respectable, civilized people in the novel, are despicable. In this sense, the novel struck its first readers as irreligious and amoral.

Against civilization, the novel holds up as admirable the powerful forces of nature—not the quiet, beatific nature of the English Romantics like Wordsworth, but the fierce, dark, turbulent nature of Heathcliff.

After World War I and again during the 1930s, when the novel had renewed popularity, disillusionment with the ruling classes and governments was high and, in the 1930s, the public made cult heroes of many outlaws, whom they judged to be less heinous thieves that the big corporations who robbed the poor. So it is not surprising that readers in such times would find no difficulty in admiring Heathcliff, Emily Brontë's dark outlaw.

Additional Readings: C.W. Davis, "A Reading of *Wuthering Heights*," *Essays in Criticism* 19

2

(1969): 254–273; G.E. Mingay, *Rural Life in Victorian England* (London: Heinemann, 1977); J.F. Petit, ed., *Emily Brontë* (Harmondsworth: Penguin, 1973).

37. *Vanity Fair*, by William Makepeace Thackeray (England, 1848).

Thackeray wrote *Vanity Fair*, his first published novel, in the 1840s, called the Hungry Forties, a time of personal and national despair that enabled him to see the society of his age, the English upper class, with a clear and jaundiced eye.

Born in India to a family of wealth, educated in London and Cambridge, inured in his youth to travel abroad and to a sophisticated perception of life and friends, he lost his fortune in 1833 one year after the Reform Bill of 1832 had given the rising middle class new power in Parliament and initiated a century of struggle for supremacy between them and a dominant but politically endangered aristocracy. In the year of *Vanity Fair*'s publication, the great famine in Ireland sent waves of chaos through the British Isles, as well as through all of Europe. All these things enter inevitably, if subtly, into Thackeray's work, for they determine the vision of a man who, largely, had come to see life as a spectator and chronicler of disaster.

While written near mid-century, the novel takes place during the Napoleonic era and in the aftermath of Napoleon's defeat. One of the crucial and climactic scenes takes place during the battle of Waterloo, when a feckless and trivial class of domestic conspirators are partying, dancing, and arranging secret liaisons, while a few miles away, in the mud and the brutal slaughter of a battlefield, their countrymen are determining the fate of the empire and of all of Europe. That scene, in fact, gives a unique perspective to the entire novel.

While the title and the concept—"Vanity" fair, a place where all the people are vain and insensitive, in a useless round of activity that leads ultimately to nothing—stem directly from John Bunyan, the story itself focuses on the intertwining lives of two fast friends who, in the beginning, are graduating from a finishing school of the day: Amelia Sedley, a decent, kind young girl of the upper class who is also unusually naive, and Becky Sharpe, an intelligent, sexually magnetic, and ruthless girl from the lower classes who is deterred by no moral scruples at all and who has an eye for human vulnerability. Becky determines to manipulate, to marry, and to do whatever she must in order to survive and thrive in this corrupt world. Thackeray gives an indelible portrait, not just of a limited upper-class group of snobs but of the whole of British society.

At the very end of this sad chronicle of human waste, Becky has one grand moment of self-sacrifice. Her friend Amelia has refused to marry a decent and wholly faithful man who truly loves her because she is still faithful to the memory of a dead husband whom she idealizes but who was really a deceiver and a scoundrel. Becky at last intervenes, telling Amelia the truth even though it will ruin Becky's own chances for fortune. Amelia marries, happily, while Becky vanishes, somewhere in the dark recesses of the socially poisonous post-Napoleonic world of gamblers and wastrels.

Vanity Fair was not an instant success but quickly caught the eye of the British public. The readership for the novel in its first year of publication is estimated to have been around 10,000. Despite much critical acclaim at the time of the novel's appearance, many critics and readers reacted negatively to Thackeray's portrayal. While many readers responded to Thackeray's satire of human beings as self-seeking and silly, others were angered and disappointed that he showed that human beings are not basically good, that people are "scamps, scoundrels, or humbugs." One reviewer echoed the feelings of many in his distaste for a novel in which everyone is egotistical, faithless, or depraved.

Yet readers through the years have discovered it to be an unforgettable picture of a society and a people in a time of tumultuous change when wars and social chaos, and the inevitable corruption, cynicism, and waste of war, had left a society floating without anchors and without moral purpose.

The great cultural impact of the novel derives from its portrait of a society. It was a picture of life that attained the status of historical reality. More real in many ways than actual reality, it served as a shortcut to history.

The novel was also a formidable influence in showing how people become entrapped by the social roles into which they are born, even for those people who struggle to change their status. Readers were also encouraged by the novel to question the social orders that made up society, to discard their sacrosanct view of privileged social behavior.

One of the greatest measures of its impact comes through its clear influence on another novel: The characters Scarlett O'Hara and Melanie Wilkes in Margaret Mitchell's *Gone With the Wind* are echoes of Becky and Amelia. *Vanity Fair* was one of the two bestselling novels of the nineteenth century; *Gone With the Wind* was one of the fantastic bestsellers of the twentieth. And each, typical of its day and of a time, has come to epitomize epochs in history.

Additional Readings: Ina Ferris, *William Makepeace Thackeray* (Boston: Twayne, 1983); Glenn R. Hueckel, *The Napoleonic Wars* (New York: Garland, 1985).

38. *Mary Barton*, by Mrs. (Elizabeth) Gaskell (England, 1848). Mrs. [Elizabeth] Gaskell directed her novel *Mary Barton* to members of the middle and upper classes who seemed either unconscionably ignorant or cruel in their social attitudes. Her intent was to explain what caused working-class people to unionize, or to become Chartists, and to create some understanding of the lives of the poor, who lived universally on the verge of total desperation.

The novel takes place in the wake of the combined effects of the Factory Laws and the Poor Laws of 1834. The context is the inhumane conditions in which mill hands (a nonhuman term invented in this desolate period) worked and most immediately, the betrayal of the working man following the Reform Bill of 1832, when the London Workingman's Association, led by radicals

Francis Place and William Lovett, stimulated a protest that ultimately produced the "People's Charter." This called for six major reforms: universal suffrage, secret voting, equal electoral districts, elimination of property qualifications for election to Parliament, payment of members, and annual elections. The leader of the northern workers was Feargus O'Connor, a charismatic man with brilliant demagogic abilities who soon led the entire movement. In 1839, the Chartists presented a grand petition, which was ignored. In 1842, they demonstrated in a procession two miles long, presenting a second petition, with over 3 million signatures, and once again threw fear and hatred into the rulers of England. Thomas Babbington Macaulay, an English lord and prominent historian, declared "universal suffrage" to be "fatal to all purposes for which government exists." Civilization itself, he said, would collapse. Lord John Russell (the sponsor of the Reform Bill of 1832) said that merely to discuss such matters would be fatal to the country. Even some radicals in Parliament condemned the Chartists' proposals.

O'Connor then shifted Chartist actions from politics to formation of a land cooperative. The year was 1848. O'Connor organized a third petition. With the continental revolutions of that year remaining a threat to English rulers, the government organized 250,000 special constables who gathered in full force to hear Feargus O'Connor deliver a speech, after which the crowd dispersed. Following that, while the Chartists movement died, the hope did not. It was kept alive by loud and brilliant voices, including that manifest in protest novels like *Mary Barton*.

Gaskell, the wife of a Unitarian minister, worked for many years with the industrial poor and the destitute of Manchester. She wrote with an understanding and balance, giving an individualized and sympathetic treatment to her characters at a time when men, women, and children, in cold streets and unheated basements all over Europe and in England and Ireland, were starving or dying from malnutrition, disease, and all the other plagues that haunt the poor.

Although Mary Barton, John Barton's daughter, dominates the last chapters of the novel, John Barton is actually the main character around whom the chronicle of poverty, pain, and chronic unemployment evolve, in the face of middle- and upper-class callousness. Mrs. Gaskell begins her story with high tea among the poor, a pleasant, endearing ceremony, involving decent and kindly people, in a background setting of chill basements and shacks and slums, which she gradually reveals. She introduces John Barton and his family. Not until much later does she reveal that Barton is an organizer, a Chartist, a man theoretically devoted to violence as a last resort to achieve goals that he feels cannot be reached in any other way. The story proceeds with an increasing sense of desperation. A strike occurs. A grand and hopeful petition is presented. The failure is complete; and Barton's agony increases, until he murders Henry Carson, an owner. It is revealed, too, at last, that Barton, a deeply religious man, had come to feel unequivocally that his religion was a fraud, that God did not care, and that his church was only a device for keeping the poor eternally deprived and quiescent in their slavery.

Gaskell actually did not really approve of the Chartist movement; she felt that it only exacerbated class differences. Nevertheless, she presented a powerful—and highly influential—picture of the poor. She also produced scenes of remorse. Her influence lies in her decision to make a tragic hero of a member of the lower class and in producing sympathy, by stressing his provocation and subsequent remorse, for a social radical who commits a murder. John Barton deeply regrets his terrible act and dies in the arms of the old father of his victim.

Mary Barton was reviewed more as a document than as a novel, and many important readers were prompted by the novel to work for justice. In 1849 *The Westminster Review* considered it proof that "the ignorance, destitution and vice which pervade and corrupt our society must be got rid of." The reviewer in *Fraser's* noted that if the comfortable and rich wanted to learn why the poor hate the rich or why they turn Chartist, or wished to learn something about the science of starving, "Let them read Mary Barton." With only a few exceptions (some claiming it was unfair to mill owners), outstanding people of the day hailed it. Gaskell was even consulted by leading politicians about working-class problems. The powerful effect of the novel is seen in the practical reforms it was largely instrumental in bringing about. Except for holding annual elections, all the Chartists' proposals were ultimately enacted.

Additional Readings: John E. Archer, *Social Unrest and Popular Protest in England* (Cambridge: Cambridge University Press, 2000); Angus Easson, *Elizabeth Gaskell* (London: Routledge and Kegan Paul, 1979); Jenny Uglow, *Elizabeth Gaskell: A Habit of Stories* (London: Faber, 1993).

39. *Alton Locke*, by Charles Kingsley (England, 1850). *Alton Locke*, the fictional autobiography of a Chartist tailor turned Christian Socialist, presents clergyman Kingsley's passionate desire to rectify the conditions under which the poor worked in the bleak 1830s and 1840s and, in effect, to reform society. The novel appeared at a time when there was an intense awareness on the part of social thinkers that Britain was actually two nations, one of squalor and one of splendor. Behind the novel is also the fear of social unrest among the upper and middle classes, aroused by the trade unionists, or Chartists, and by revolutions throughout Europe. It was also a time when the rising middle-class mill owners and capitalists achieved power in Parliament and conditions of working-class Englishmen suffered a decline.

Kingsley portrays the system as productive of horrible working conditions, lack of sanitation, health, and education, and thriving gin palaces, all of which elicit no concern whatsoever on the part of mainstream English society. In 1850 he had researched and written about the grievances of tailors in a pamphlet titled "Cheap Clothes and Nasty." In Chapters II and X of *Alton Locke* he used the material he had gathered for that pamphlet. Kingsley also built into the plot of the novel the danger of contagion, when Alton's cousin dies of typhus fever he had contracted from a new coat manufactured in a Bermondsey house that earlier had been spread over three bodies dead of the disease. The idea of contagion from the slums was corroborated in a report instituted by the tailors themselves in 1844.

Kingsley shows the desperate reality of both rural and city slums. Alton discovers the abominable conditions of the agricultural poor when he is sent from London to a meeting of half-starved agricultural workers to see how far they will go to promote Chartism in 1845. What he finds is wretchedness and stultifying poverty, in a place where the owners use every device possible to gain the last bit of profit from the waste of human lives. Among the horrors of "sweated labor" or sweatshops and terrible hovels, Alton sees fat overstuffed animals and starving people. It is one of his most powerful scenes, an indictment not just of petty greed but of an entire society.

One of the crucial scenes occurs at a place called Jacob's Island, a festering area of slums in Bermondsey. It is surrounded not by running water but by a stagnant, filthy ditch, into which Thames water is introduced about twice a week. This carrier of disease and death is the source of water for drinking, washing, and cooking. Alton notes the terrible smell in this area; it is so intense that it makes Alton nauseated. It is literally a place where it was safer to drink gin than water.

In volume II, chapter 14, titled "The Lowest Depths," a former "sweater" or sweatshop operator named Jimmy Downes has been reduced to doing piecework at starvation wages. Downes is so beset with gin and despair that he contemplates suicide. He takes Alton to his own wretched quarters in Jacob's Island, where his wife and children are dying of typhus. In a crucial moment, Downes goes to the balcony to draw up a bucket of water, to have Alton drink it and thus experience for himself its terrible pollution; but he drunkenly falls into the ditch himself and drowns. Later Alton returns to the Downes living quarters to find women

covering the bodies of Downes's wife and children. Alton notes again the "heedless hypocrisy of the law."

The novel was a powerful and influential statement that established the very poor as a fit topic for philosophical, social, and scientific concern in the novel. It established the poor as human beings, with blood and sinews and passions—and basic human rights—no different from the rest: Knowledge, Kingsley believed, is the first step for reform.

The novel gave encouragement to practical reforms put forward by Kingsley: the boycotting of goods produced by industrial exploiters, the development of workers' cooperatives, and the transporting of clean drinking water to Jacob's Island.

Kingsley's graphic, unsentimental picture of the poor affected his readers' thinking as few other writers did, revealing that not only industry but government policy and the law itself were equally guilty for producing this indescribable inhuman horror.

Several years before the appearance of Charles Dickens's *Bleak House*, Kingsley impressed upon his readers a sobering truth: that the poor did not exist in isolation from other citizens but that contagion spread from the slums to the houses of the middle and upper classes.

Finally, Kingsley was one of the first writers to raise the issue of the folly of trying to do away with urban blight by tearing down the houses of the poor in order to build houses and warehouses for the wealthy.

Additional Readings: Kate Flint, ed., *The Victorian Novelist: Social Problems and Social Change* (London: Croom Helm, 1987); Barbara Kerr, *The Dispossessed: An Aspect of Victorian Social History* (London: Bader Publishers, 1974); Sheila Smith, *The Other Nation: The Poor in the English Novels of the 1840s and 1850s* (Oxford: Clarendon Press, 1980).

40. *David Copperfield*, by Charles Dickens (England, 1850). *David Copperfield*, written in 1850 at a time of turmoil in England, as in all of Europe, by a writer whose every work was, in effect, social commentary, takes the form of a "growing-up" novel, known as a Bildungsroman. It is a story that echoes the life of the author in a period of intense bitterness, covering the lowest depths of his poverty to the heights of his success. Here Dickens achieved the remarkable feat of being highly acclaimed by all classes while at the same time revealing the harsh realities of a desperate time.

In England, the "Hungry Forties" revealed the true horrors of the Industrial Revolution as it affected the lives of all lower classes. The New Poor Laws of 1834 eliminated the dole; Corn Laws protected the landed aristocracy while throwing the poor or unemployed upon the hands of fate; and the Reform Bill of 1832 gave all the powers of law to newly enfranchised mill owners bitterly opposed to reform. A series of bad seasons beginning in the late 1830s produced shortages of bread and massive starvation. Government actions crushed strikers and the Chartists who were working to organize labor. In 1846, a famine in Ireland impacted on the entire British world. By 1848, all of Europe was exploding with revolutions.

In the same year, Karl Marx issued the *Communist Manifesto*, with its ringing call for workers of the world to unite because they had "nothing to lose but their chains," while they had "a world to win."

In 1850, Victoria, dedicated to reigning over a society not disturbed by dramatic change, had been queen for thirteen years. In an arrangement known to historians as the "Victorian Compromise," the aristocracy and the middle class combined sufficiently to keep all power to themselves, to the exclusion of the working class. It was a time when lower classes were regarded by many thoughtful people as subhuman grinds not capable of true civilization. Government from 1837 to 1867 was based primarily on the philosophies of utilitarianism and laissez-faire economics. It was a world where war with its concomitant slaughter was seen as good because it eliminated those whom society considered dispensable—the great numbers of starving poor who were becoming restless. At the same time, it protected the idle wealthy.

In this atmosphere, many voices spoke out in protest. Charles Kingsley, a clergyman and a novelist, thundered against sweatshop labor and oppression of the agricultural poor and declared: "I assert that the business for which God sends a Christian priest into a Christian nation is to preach and practice liberty, equality and brotherhood" (quoted in Walter Phelps Hall, A *History of England* [Boston: Ginn and Co., 1946], p. 778). Cardinal Manning, a converted, conservative Roman Catholic, in a lecture titled "Rights and Dignities of Labor," echoed Marxian theory by declaring that all wealth comes from labor.

One of the loudest and most effective voices of the century was that of Charles Dickens.

The novel, narrated by an older and wiser David, begins with the hero's birth into a comfortable, solid family. He remembers his childhood, his lapse into terrible conditions of work as a factory laborer, his rise in the world through ingenuity and persistent ambition, and ultimately, the death of his first wife (the doll-like Dora) and his personal and philosophical recovery through marriage to the more suitable Agnes. At last, he explains his philosophical decision to follow his calling as a novelist. In addition, the novel contains great numbers of brilliantly drawn and memorable characters—Uriah Heep, the Micawber, Mrs. Gamp, Steerforth, and others.

Like Dickens himself, who worked in a blacking plant as a child, David works in a factory and becomes a freelance shorthand writer (Dickens invented his own style) and a parliamentary reporter, developing skills that ultimately lead to his career as novelist. An early biographer, John Foster, in his *Life of Dickens* in 1872 claimed that Dickens originally had planned the book as an autobiography.

At a time when lines of battle between social classes were sharply drawn and often erupted in violence, Dickens produced a work that, while vividly portraying the eternal disadvantages of life for the poor, succeeded in reaching all classes. *David Copperfield* was exceptionally well received in its day, and it went on to be recognized as one of the greatest novels of the century. Its influence was pervasive.

Dickens works in this novel in the cause of humanity. And the novel's influence on society and social reforms, on the tone and sentiment of Victorian England, has been incalculable. His enormous popularity carried the banner for reform for the remainder of the century.

In this, as in more specifically targeted novels, he wanted to arouse the conscience of his readers, not their fears.

Additional Readings: Barbara Hardy, *The Moral Art of Dickens* (New York: Oxford University Press, 1970); John Rule, *The Labouring Classes in Early Industrial England 1750–1850* (London: Longman, 1986).

41. *Bleak House*, by Charles Dickens (England, 1853). Dickens's comprehensive, multifaceted novel *Bleak House*, begins with a cold, dreary day of rain and fog covering that part of London that includes the Chancery, a dismal congery of alleyways, dim streets, slums, and other haunts of lawyers, criminals, and businessmen. The opening scene manages to capture, in a nutshell, the tone and the demeanor of the entire novel. Dickens, who always wrote about social injustice in one form or another, in this case focuses on the law: an interminable maze of legal traps and contradictions that make the mid-century legal system a spider's web of terror even for the wary and slow suffocation for the poor.

His target, however, is broader than that. He covers the life of London: religion, education, the class system, poverty, the innate troubles of grown-up foundlings, and the blindness of social "reformers" who focus on troubles far away while ignoring the terrible ones at home.

Alternating between the personal narration of Ellen Summerson, a young lady who does not know her parentage and who is trying to discover herself and define her life, and the omniscient point of view that covers a panorama of eccentric and bizarre people, the story of London life unfolds.

The setting is 1850. It begins in London, where the High Court of Chancery is hearing the case of Jarndyce and Jarndyce, a case that has lingered on for years and created unfathomable subsuits and tangled webs of obfuscation and greed. Opening scenes introduce Esther Summerson, Ada Clare, and Richard Carstone, all wards of John Jarndyce (whose home is called Bleak House), and Lady Deadlock, the wife of aristocratic Sir Leicester.

With the endless legal case always in the background, the story concerns the fate of Esther Summerson and the efforts of Lady Deadlock to hide from her husband and others the dreadful secret of her life: the existence years ago of a lover and the birth of an illegitimate child who presumably died at birth. Lady Deadlock, fortuitously seeing a note written by her former lover, asks Mr. Tulkinghorn, her attorney, to help find him, only to learn that he is now dead and that Esther is actually her daughter; when Tulkinghorn threatens to tell all, Lady Deadlock tells the truth to Esther, still keeping it a secret from her husband. Somebody murders Tulkinghorn and Lady Deadlock disappears; Sir Leicester hires a detective, Inspector Bucket, to find her, offering forgiveness. Bucket eventually discovers that Lady Deadlock was not the murderer. Ada marries Richard, who dies disappointed in his expected inheritance; Lady Deadlock is found dead on her lover's grave; and Esther, planning to marry Jarndyce out of duty, is released from her promise and marries Allan Woodcourt, the doctor who cared for her during a serious illness. The case of the mysterious estate is never solved, most or all of the money vanishing into legal fees.

Even though *Bleak House* was not as critically acclaimed as Dickens's other novels in his lifetime, it was one of the most read novels of the nineteenth century, Dickens attesting to its having more readers than any of his other books.

On a large scale, the novel has, through the years, given readers a graphic view of the dark side of Victorian life. Especially vivid are accounts of the abused and the neglected poor who swill out their lives in lonely darkness and stinking slums. Readers at the time were also made uncomfortably aware that they could not remain removed and protected from the poor, that the contagion that was allowed to fester in slums would make its way into every other aspect of nineteenth-century life. In this novel, and in all his others, Dickens pushed the theme that all people alike share a common fate. The misfortunes of one class will impinge on all the rest.

On a particular level, the novel was a powerful incentive to correct many abuses. Although Dickens was rarely the first writer to draw attention to a problem, he had an uncanny sense of when his fictionalizing of a problem would carry the greatest impact for positive change. As a result of this novel, a number of conditions that he addressed prompted changes in legislation and policy. These included a reformation or elimination of the Court of Chancery; improvement in education for all to eliminate widespread illiteracy; reform of the House of Corrections, which sent children to prison for stealing food; the cleaning up of slums; the alleviation of suffering among homeless children; a reevaluation of the cure and treatment of juvenile vagrancy; sanitary reform; the cleaning up of the pestiferous city graveyards; changes in the way in which executions were conducted; and improvements in London's police force. Each of these issues that arise in the novel were addressed by the authorities shortly after the popular novelist's book appeared.

The novel also led many readers to reexamine two cultural types that Dickens satirized in the novel. One is the do-gooder who is religiously devoted to public service, especially to African charities, but seriously neglects her daughter, her husband, and her own home. His other target was the Puseyite, members of a branch of the Church of England who pretentiously adopted the attitudes of the Roman Catholic Church.

Additional Readings: Richard Daniel Altick, *Victorian People and Ideas* (New York: Norton, 1973); Norman Page, *"Bleak House": A Novel of Connections* (Boston: Twayne, 1990); Graham Story, *Charles Dickens, "Bleak House"* (Cambridge: Cambridge University Press, 1987).

42. *Hard Times,* by Charles Dickens (England, 1854). *Hard Times* is a novel of industrial England in the "Hungry Forties," a time when a savage system had so combined as to produce for the poor unparalleled suffering and despair.

Earlier in the century, laborers had worked under conditions worse than slavery, under laws that protected newly rich factory owners who, in the beginning, had had hosts of orphans, children as young as five and six, shipped to factory towns to work in "dark Satanic mills" until they dropped or died. Children sometimes worked so hard and became so weary that they fell into the machinery. As time passed, they used entire families of the poor who worked under the same abysmal circumstances. It was a system that produced great masses whose only life was work in the mills, poverty, and death. Factory laws were ultimately passed, partially limiting the hours and minimum ages for working children, laws passed, ironically, by the Tories, over the objections of mill owners. But in a laissez-faire economy, there were no protections at all for adults.

Since the beginning of the industrial system there had been a constant and bitter war between the rising middle class dominated by the mill owners and the traditional landed aristocracy. The Reform Bill of 1832 at last broke the power of the aristocracy by extending the vote to the middle class, transferring power in Parliament to the mill owners. Collectively, they fought every change in a system that made them fabulously rich.

The laws and actions of the government triply hampered workers. The New Poor Laws of 1834 restricted government issue of free bread for the poor and instead established "poor houses," places designed to be so abominable that anything would be preferable. Concerted actions against the Chartists, who made union organization possible, severely hampered labor. In time government actions and the personal weaknesses of leader Daniel O'Connell eliminated the Chartists, but unionization remained. The Corn Laws provided a fluctuating tariff to protect aristocratic landowners in bad times, while letting the poor suffer the laws of the market: In bad years, there would be no cheap grain, no free bread, in effect no dole, and high unemployment. Then in 1837 poor harvests resulted in years of starvation and bitterness, running parallel to the potato famine in Ireland.

Hard Times is a story of growing labor troubles in a desolate factory town named Coketown, modeled on Preston in northern England. The chief characters are Thomas Gradgrind, who runs a school that teaches only *facts*, just facts; his children Tom Jr. and Louisa; Sissy Jupe, taken in by Gradgrind after being deserted by her father, a circus clown; Bounderby, the mill owner; and Stephen Blackpool, a power loom weaver at the mill. The cast is large and the story covers many years. As time passes, serious labor trouble arises. Louisa is virtually forced to marry Bounderby, a move that she eventually renounces. Tom Jr. gets into serious trouble and hides among the circus people, and Blackpool dies, after having been unjustly charged with robbery.

Although the end is moderately happy, in that Louisa discovers a social conscience and Sissy Jupe enjoys a happy marriage, the novel is actually a savage satire on the entire industrial system and on a host of related problems: popular utilitarian philosophy, current educational theory, industrial relations in general, and unjust divorce laws. In addition, it savages the idea of the "self-made man." In this complex of ideas, Sissy Jupe symbolizes an ideal domestic woman.

In one scene, Louisa, who has grown up in a privileged atmosphere, actually sees the poor as human beings rather than objects for the first time and is horrified. In another, the weaver Blackpool, who has refused to join the union because he sees the organizer, Slackbridge, as just as corrupt as the owners, in turn faces Bounderby, whom he castigates in blistering terms for making the life of the workers eternally hopeless.

Dickens had already sympathetically reported in *Household Words* on the strike at Preston and on the lives of the workers. But in the novel, he failed to include both the strike and unionization. Instead, he inserted Gradgrind's school with its stress on facts alone and on the purely utilitarian, a philosophy that Gradgrind himself comes to see as pernicious. Dickens thus takes out direct confrontation and puts the stress instead on the way of life, aiming his efforts at the human heart.

Social critics have argued over the effectiveness of the novel from the time of its first appearance. Social novelist George Gissing criticized the novel for making a villain of the union leader and, in effect, undermining the efforts of working people in England. Socialist George Bernard Shaw, on the other hand, believed that no novel had so trenchantly exposed the villainy of the mill owners and their supporters and so sympathetically revealed the living and working conditions of common laborers. History has tended to agree with Shaw, for the novel's influence has been wide and enduring. More than any other industrial novel of the time, this one has lived and has never ceased to reach and to move its audiences.

The novel also had an impact outside of England. The Russian Nikolai Chernyshevsky, author of the most radical and most influential Russian novel of the period (*What Is to Be Done?*), listed Dickens's *Hard Times* as a major influence on his work.

Additional Readings: Anne Digby and Peter Searby, *Children, Schools, and Society in Nineteenth-Century England* (New York: Macmillan, 1981); J. Hillis Miller, *Charles Dickens: The World of His Novels* (Cambridge, MA: Harvard University Press, 1958).

43. *Silas Marner*, by George Eliot (England, 1861). When George Eliot, the pen name of Marian Evans, wrote *Silas Marner*, the rural landscape in which the novel is set was rapidly giving way to an industrialized society, driven by capital, based on materialism, and characterized by competition and even fiercer class division than those that had prevailed earlier. There was not only loss of family and community but also loss of the old ties to nature. With the separation from the older way of life came a burdensome moral complexity.

Not all old rural values were laudable, as George Eliot herself had shown in two other novels, *Adam Bede* and *The Mill on the Floss*, and money had always given men status in any community, but those values that had sustained the best in human nature—the sympathy and support of community and family—were disappearing as the poor were increasingly being dispersed and displaced in being drawn of necessity to jobs in impersonal industrialized centers, where material success was deemed the greatest good.

Within this context, the events of George Eliot's novel take place. Its driving forces are gold, family, and community. Its tragedies derive from greed and alienation.

The main, title character is Silas Marner, who, in the story's beginning, is a religious man, living as a weaver in the industrial town of Lantern-Yard in northern England, and is engaged to be married. Catastrophe befalls him when his friend, William Dane, who wants Silas's girlfriend for himself, wrongly implicates Silas in the theft of someone else's money. Finding himself falsely accused of a crime, Silas, now friendless, is forced to leave his home, job, and fiancée. He resettles in Raveloe, a town in the south of England, far from the place of his misfortune. Here he isolates himself and through hard work at his trade as a weaver amasses a fortune in gold, the sole obsession of his existence. He is nearly destroyed again when his gold is stolen by a feckless young aristocrat. Good fortune follows bad, however, when a beautiful child miraculously appears in his house. With the help of a friend, Dolly Winthrop, Silas rears and adores the child, whom he calls Effie. Through Effie, Silas is reconnected to the world. Effie is actually the daughter of the brother of the man who had stolen Silas's gold. When Silas's gold is found and the identity of the real thief is discovered, Effie's father appears to claim her. But she refuses to leave Silas, whom she has come to regard as her father. Effie matures and marries the son of Dolly Winthrop. The couple live happily ever after with Silas in his house.

While several of Eliot's novels that preceded and followed *Silas Marner* were rejected by the public, this simple story, with its happy ending, had an enthusiastic readership. Eliot seemed to have captured the idyllic life of the child growing up in nature that her readers longed to rekindle. The author also memorialized the vanishing village community that, in the form of the patrons of the Rainbow tavern, offer clarification and encouragement. The novel's popularity also derived from its simplicity, in contrast to the moral complexity of *The Mill on the Floss*.

In contrast to Effie and Dolly and Silas, the villains of the story are motivated, as the new industrial barons were, by greed for gold, which turns them into thieves, betrayers, liars, and profligates. The heroes and heroines are nature's simple people, whose love and caring are rewarded in the novel's end.

The uplifting affirmation of the story, which attracted so many readers, derives from its theme of renewal and possibility, chiefly seen in the title character whose hardened heart is transformed, as he is united to another human being through love, joined with the community, and given meaning and purpose as a surrogate father.

Additional Readings: Harold Bloom, ed., *George Eliot* (New York: Chelsea House, 1986); George R. Creeger, *George Eliot: A Collection of Critical Essays* (Englewood Cliffs, NJ: Prentice-Hall, 1970); G.E. Mingay, *Rural Life in Victorian England* (London: Heinemann, 1977).

44. *The Unclassed*, **by George Gissing (England, 1884).** The unclassed of Gissing's title refers to London's bohemians, the intellectual and artistic poor who lived entirely outside traditional society and mores. One of the first portraits of the poor artist, the larger context of the novel is Victorian society, which Gissing viewed as adhering to a narrow, superficial morality, defined largely in terms of sexual behavior, while, at the same time, exploiting the poor in total disregard of economic and political responsibility. Within the artistic mainstream of these last decades of the Victorian era, the prevailing view was "art for art's sake," that is, the artist's freedom to abdicate social responsibility in the creation of art. *The Unclassed* criticizes both the skewed morality of the Victorians and the foolishness of the artist.

The protagonist of the novel is Osmond Waymark, once a radical novelist, who decides for a time to make a living by acquiescing to Victorian values and throwing to the winds his old quest for social justice. As a consequence, he becomes a rent collector in the city's slums.

Other important characters include a dreamy, spiritual-minded woman named Maud, who turns her back on the base world and becomes a nun; her opposite, the prostitute, Ida; and Osmond's artist friend, Casti. In the course of the story, Ida is falsely imprisoned for theft; Osmond's uncle, a slum lord, contracts a disease from the slums; and a pauper steals the rents that Osmond has collected from slum dwellers and for which he is responsible. As Gissing put it, "The slums have avenged themselves."

Gissing found it extremely difficult to even secure a publisher for his work, and having finally seen the novel into print, he was dismayed by the hostility with which it was greeted. His innovative portrait of a sympathetic prostitute was the single aspect of the novel that received the greatest criticism. It was charged that *The Unclassed* misled and corrupted youth. As a consequence of his portrait of Ida and his attacks on conventional religion and the church, many libraries throughout England and the United States banned the novel.

The Unclassed was the first and one of the most iconoclastic criticisms of Victorian idealism and morality, calling into question the sacredness of marriage, moral judgmentalism and hypocrisy, the value of materialism, and the elevation of science. In the wake of *The Unclassed*, a plethora of thinkers, from the Decadents to the Lost Generation, attacked Victorianism.

Gissing's novel also brought to the attention of his readers the futility of many reformist ideas in bringing positive change to the urban poor. Alone, neither philanthropy, representational government, nor mass edu-

cation were cure-alls for the inequities of British society.

Gissing was also one of the first writers to challenge the idea that art and the artist could responsibly and morally remove himself or herself from social questions.

Additional Readings: Hamid Bensaou, *From the Poetry of Complaint to the Novel of Protest* (Alger: Office des Public Universitaires, 1984); Barbara Kerr, *The Dispossessed: An Aspect of Victorian Social History* (London: J. Bader, 1974); John Stokes, *In the Nineties* (London: Harvester Wheatsheaf, 1989).

45. *Diana of the Crossways*, **by George Meredith (England, 1884).** The last decades in the nineteenth century, when George Meredith's novel appeared, were marked by the struggle of women for civil rights in both England and the United States. Society's view of women, perpetuated by both church and state, had deprived them of those rights on which any adult human being should have been able to lay claim. But the prevailing view of women as children needing to be under the control of father or husband had resulted in their having no legal identity. That is, they could not vote; they were prohibited from being a party in a lawsuit; and they could not serve on juries, write legally binding wills, hold property (even if it were specifically given to them by their fathers), sue for divorce, or successfully compete with their husbands for custody rights. Not until the 1880s were women successful in England in passing a Property Act that allowed them to hold their own property independent of their husbands. Only in 1917 were reformers successful in gaining limited suffrage for women in Great Britain. Not until 1928 did the laws for suffrage become the same for both men and women. Laws governing divorce and property when Meredith was writing had a profound effect on the novel he produced, and the novel had an immense influence on the struggle for women's rights that continued after the 1880s.

The Diana of the novel's title is a beautiful, intelligent young Irish woman who feels herself continually threatened by the aggressive males who are attracted to her. To escape further unwanted attention, she enters into an unwise marriage with a much older man, Mr. Warwick. The suspicious Warwick makes life even more miserable for her when he wrongly accuses her of infidelity and sues for divorce. But the trial vindicates Diana, proving her innocence and denying the couple a divorce. As a result, Diana moves away from her husband's house and decides to live alone, an act that, in itself, generates even more unjustified, scandalous rumors about her. Diana's plans to remain above romance and become an author go awry when she falls in love with Percy Dacier. But she cancels plans to run away with him at the last moment and refuses his propositions, despite the possibility that yielding would alleviate her pressing financial worries. He leaves her alone only when he finds that, in her distress, she revealed a critical political secret he has told her. Finally, the death of her husband sets her free, and she eventually marries a man whom she is convinced really loves her.

Diana of the Crossways was a great commercial success, in tremendous demand in both England and the United States where the struggle for women's rights was at its peak. The issues the novel raised were the very ones being debated in the public forum of both countries: marriage, divorce, sex, and the woman's place in society. With this unconventional story, Meredith's popularity finally freed him from dependence on what he regarded as the sanctimonious English publishing establishment and the serial magazines to which the fiction writer often felt enslaved.

The novel had tremendous influence on the "Woman Question" by presenting a sympathetic "New Woman" who is morally pure, a so-called Goddess of Chastity, who illustrated the vulnerable and inconsequential position of the intelligent woman in society. Diana shows, from a sympathetic point of view, various aspects of the true nature of such a woman: her need for her own self-sufficiency, her submerged sexuality, the dangers to which her lack of education exposes her, her need to be defined by her innate qualities rather than subservience to her husband or her social position.

In revealing Diana as basically pure, Meredith showed his readers, who were beginning to question society's values, that the so-called morality of the day was actually dirty-minded and coarse.

Meredith became a public figure with an immense following after the publication of *Diana of the Crossways.* He was seen as a great champion of women and a radical critic of his society who could advance his views effectively and calmly. In the years after the novel's publication, when he began to be confined to his estate from ill health, suffragettes were said to visit him for advice and encouragement, and journalists and men in public life sought his advice and opinions on a variety of matters.

Additional Readings: Gillian Beer, *Meredith: A Change of Masks: A Study of the Novels* (London: Athlone Press, 1970); Helen Blackburn, *Women's Suffrage* (London: Williams and Norgate, 1902); Mohammad Shaheen, *George Meredith: A Reappraisal of the Novels* (London: Macmillan, 1981).

46. *The Strange Case of Dr. Jekyll and Mr. Hyde,* **by Robert Louis Stevenson (England, 1886).** Stevenson's *The Strange Case of Dr. Jekyll and Mr. Hyde,* written in the late Victorian era at a time of great change in all phases of modern life, was a popular success from the time of its first publication. Furthermore, it has come with the passage of time to represent London's Victorian world with its suggestive mingling of Gothic horror, fogs, crime, strict control of morality and manners, and seething, dark suppressed sexuality waiting to leap out from the shadows. It also reflects an emerging science, a Darwinian ethos added to man's basic perceptions, and has also become a proverbial term for psychoanalytic probing of the divided soul, a synonym for all the dark evil that lurks in the human psyche, even in the best of men. Written at a time when the sensational Jack the Ripper murders were in the public mind, Jekyll and Hyde combines these elements in a novel that presents a significant perspective on good and evil and puts them both not as separate entities but in the same form: the good, respectable, and honored Dr. Jekyll and the evil, darkly brooding, deceitful, and murderous Mr. Hyde.

The story is one of the most widely recognized in the world. Dr. Jekyll, a scientist searching for the truth about human nature, secretly invents a chemical that separates good from evil. When Dr. Jekyll takes this drink, all goodness and kindness are filtered out, and he becomes the purely evil Mr. Hyde. A second drink, on the other hand, takes him back to his original form, Dr. Jekyll. The novel begins with the mysterious murder of Sir Danvers Carew and proceeds as a "case," with a lawyer-friend named Utterson serving as amateur detective. In his detective story, fraught with mystery, the author achieves multiple points of view by including such things as news stories, while the evil Hyde and the concomitant pursuit of vice and crime come to dominate the story. Thus the story proceeds in a dramatic alteration between the two until at last his magic potions being totally depleted, Hyde is trapped, no longer able to revert back to his respectable form, and both he and Jekyll perish.

Stevenson takes certain elements of Gothic horror—wedded in the previous century when the Gothic novel began to flourish—to external elements of fantasy, cruelty, and superstition, with the "other," as the enemy. Like others in the late Victorian age, Stevenson turns them inward, making them part of the architecture of the novel. He internalizes the "other" and, pulling from the rising interest in science and in Darwinian evolution, focuses on the human mind.

In *Dr. Jekyll and Mr. Hyde*, all these warring or changing elements come together in what has become a classic of Victorian horror. At the same time, in an age of psychoanalysis, it is distinctly modern. As subsequent critics have pointed out, it is pre-Freudian, yet it almost perfectly illustrates Freud's early work on the ego and the id.

Otto Rank specifically analyzes the story in a major work based on Freud's theories of projection and narcissism (*The Double: A Psychoanalytical Study* [Chapel Hill, NC: University of North Carolina Press, 1971]), concluding that the projections are one and that they are reflections of self-love. Stevenson, a great writer of adventure stories and of strange and exciting places, created the ultimate adventure story, which was inward, and the ultimately "exotic" place, the human mind.

Stevenson achieved what is perhaps the supreme accolade: He created a work that for more than a hundred years has never ceased to attract readers ranging from the very young, who look for adventure and suspense, to the most sophisticated, who look for light in the darkness of the human mind. It has become the ultimate, most immediately recognizable symbol for the divided soul, or the split self, on all levels, the term "Jekyll and Hyde" having become firmly entrenched in the English language.

One measure of the novel's influence is the extent to which is has been successfully and repeatedly adapted for stage and screen, including one in 1908 and one in 1912.

Additional Readings: J.R. Hammond, *A Robert Louis Stevenson Companion* (New York: Macmillan, 1984); Frank Mort, *Dangerous Sexualities* (London: Routledge and Kegan Paul, 1987); William Veeder and Gordon Hirsch, eds., *Dr. Jekyll and Mr. Hyde after One Hundred Years* (Chicago: University of Chicago Press, 1988).

47. *Tess of the d'Urbervilles*, by Thomas Hardy (England, 1891). Thomas Hardy's novel, set in rural England, was written in a time of great general optimism that social reforms, like the third reform bill of 1884, could significantly improve the lives of the English underclasses whom Hardy had seen starve to death in his native Dorset and live like animals in London's urban slums. Reformers energetically and hopefully approached the social problems with a variety of practical improvements, from extending the franchise to cleaning up the drains.

Against this background of optimism, Hardy wrote a bleak, pessimistic novel portraying the suffering of the rural poor, particularly its women, as represented by his title character, as no novelist had ever done. His plot centers on young Tess, whose weak and drunken parents send her as a commodity and a sacrifice to gain economic help from a rake, Alec, to whom they believe they are related. Tess is seduced by him and subsequently is abandoned and has a child who dies. Later, when her pious husband Angel learns of her past, he also abandons her. Alec returns to the scene, this time agreeing to support her starving family if she will become his mistress. In a moment of rage, Tess murders this man who has ruined her life. She is found guilty and executed by hanging. Angel, who has a change of heart, returns too late to help her.

Hardy's novel, which has since been regarded as a literary masterpiece, was rejected by his first publisher, forcing him to tone down several episodes that were considered indecent: the seduction scene, a night baptism of Tess's illegitimate infant, and a scene in which Angel carries milkmaids across a stream in his arms. In a preface to one of the editions, Hardy summarized the violent objections to the novel: the charge that sexual relations was not a fitting topic for a novel; that the novel encouraged immorality; and that the subtitle, "A Pure Woman," in referring to one who had borne an illegitimate child was outrageous.

However, *Tess* came to be one of the most influential late-nineteenth-century novels in many ways. First, it astounded its Victorian readers with its unmasked portrayal of sex, forever opening up the way in which mainstream readers talked about sex. The novel also provided his readers with a new way of seeing a wronged heroine. English novels from the time of Samuel Richardson, in the eighteenth century, had told the story of the fallen woman as a shameful, victimized creature, which Hardy called the doll of English fiction, which he was determined to demolish. Tess was one of the first counterportraits to the usual passive victim. Those, like Angel, who piously judge and condemn her are the despicable characters in the novel. And feminists, even in the late twentieth century,

have found that his portrait is an accurate and modern one.

Readers also came to challenge several sacred cows of Victorian society as a result of the novel. His view of the church and the clergy as hypocritical and mean-spirited outraged many members of an extremely religious, churchgoing public. But Hardy opened the way for many of his readers to question sacrosanct institutions like the church, which had enjoyed uncontested privilege and stood in the way of progressive social and scientific thought.

By implication, the novel was also a counterargument to progressive optimism, for it revealed that while reforms were, of course, necessary, they would not fundamentally change the human condition, which was dreary at best.

Finally, Hardy was the first major novelist to present his readers with a universe ruled by neither wisdom nor benevolence and thus helped prepare the way for existential thought in the twentieth century.

Additional Readings: François Bedarida, *A Social History of England* (New York: Routledge, 1991). Penny Boumelha, *Thomas Hardy and Women: Sexual Ideology and Narrative Form* (Madison: University of Wisconsin Press, 1985); R.P. Draper, ed. *Hardy, the Tragic Novels: A Casebook* (London: Macmillan, 1991).

48. *Children of the Ghetto*, by Israel Zangwill (England, 1892). *Children of the Ghetto* stands as the major work of a writer who revealed and explained the life of immigrant Jews in London toward the end of the nineteenth century. While Benjamin Disraeli, prime minister, novelist, and political representative of the British aristocracy, was a striking exception, Jews, at this time, were still largely segregated, were still barred from upper-class clubs and positions of significance in public life, and still existed, largely, in a separate world. It was Zangwill's fate to throw brilliant and humanizing light on this newly emerging and rapidly changing facet of English life.

Zangwill's *The Children of the Ghetto: A Study of a Peculiar People* was a highly regarded work that established him as the supreme spokesman for English Jews and earned him an enduring reputation as a chronicler of the life of the very poor.

In a complicated plot that shows various attempts to reconcile tenets of Judaism with the practical demands of modern life, the fate of two families living in the East End carries the main threads of action: the very poor Ansells and the more affluent Jacobses. Esther Ansell, who is intellectually curious and articulate, questions Jewish law without breaking it and even reads the New Testament surreptitiously. Ultimately, after ten years, Esther writes a novel on Jewish life titled *Mordecai Josephs*, which sparks a heated discussion on its treatment of Jewish ideals and characters. She falls in love with Raphael Leon, an Oxford man who edits a prominent Jewish paper and, while continuing to focus on the demands of Judaism in modern life, once even goes back to the ghetto to live. Raphael even calls Esther "an allegory of Judaism," which while carrying a glorious past and offering a rich future is "yet wasting with an inward canker." Ultimately, the two become engaged to marry, although at the end, Esther is on a boat bound for America, accompanied by a disillusioned rabbi who advocates a universal religion based on Judaism.

Hannah Jacobs, another character who is also troubled by the demands of Jewish law, wishes to marry a man who has rejected orthodox observance and is, in addition, a descendant of the priestly class, a position that bars him from marrying a divorced woman. Hannah had earlier engaged in what she thought was a mock marriage ceremony, which, unfortunately, turned out to be legally binding and required a religious divorce. Therefore, their union is forbidden. At one point, they plan to elope, but in the end, Hannah changes her mind and follows the demands of her Jewish heritage.

The novel, which sold well in both England and America, gave both audiences an inward and authentic view of the life of immigrant Jews in London at a time when the East End was a great, dark abyss, familiar to most readers only in fanciful tales of crime.

The East End had become a cliché place of opium dens, tales of Fu Manchu, and Jack the Ripper, and a bit later, it was described realistically in Jack London's journalistic *People of the Abyss*. By 1891, the Jewish community had grown considerably since the days of Jack the Ripper, but still the details of life there remained unknown, even to many Jews. Zangwill provided a taste of reality on wholly human terms.

Although the novel was a great success with readers, it received mixed critical reviews. In England, critics in *The Speaker, The London Times, The Spectator*, and the *Manchester Guardian* praised the novel both for its general excellence and for its portrayal of Jewish life. In America, on the other hand, it aroused considerable controversy, as in the pages of *The American Hebrew*, where some readers deplored the printing of realistic, unflattering details of Jewish life.

As a result of this novel, Zangwill was regarded as a major figure and was listened to as an international voice in the development of Jewish affairs until his death in 1926. In particular, in his novel, he gained an audience for his advocacy of the oppressed of the world, with a special emphasis on the matter of identity and of Jewish identity. Above all, in throwing light on a largely unknown or misunderstood and significant element in British life, with a strong sense of common humanity, he helped eliminate barriers based on ignorance that had stood for so long and that, in another part of Europe, were to explode in bitter chaos some forty years later with the rise of Adolf Hitler.

Additional Readings: Joseph Leftwich, *Israel Zangwill* (London: James Clark, 1957); John Stokes, *In the Nineties* (Chicago: University of Chicago Press, 1989); Joseph H. Udelson, *Dreamer of the Ghetto: The Life and Works of Israel Zangwill* (Tuscaloosa: University of Alabama Press, 1990).

49. *Jude the Obscure*, by Thomas Hardy (England, 1895). *Jude the Obscure*, Hardy's last and most controversial novel, dramatizes the social, intellectual, and spiritual malaise of the late nineteenth century. It is a work that generated more heat and more extended sound and fury than any other fictional work of the age. The reason for this was teleological: It hit sensitive spots in an age that was in the midst of traumatic change, at a time when culture itself was caught between two contradictory extremes of conduct and behavior. The Victorian world of tight control and restricted language and subjects was crumbling, and a new age was about to be born. In effect, Pandora's hand was on the box, and all the imps were about to escape irretrievably into the air. It was Hardy's fate to conjure up a sense of tragic ghosts.

Darwinian science had destroyed the peace and order of establishment Christianity. Queen Victoria, that bastion of order, was old, on the point of death. T.H. Huxley, Benjamin Jowett, John Tyndall, John Stuart Mill, and others had seriously shaken the old order. In this period of transition, Hardy created a novel that attacked marriage, sexual standards, educational hypocrisy and elitism, the repression of women, and in general, social malevolence.

His protagonist Jude, for example, while longing with all his heart to enter Christminster and ultimately to become a bishop, at the same time sees the great cathedral as "ten centuries of bigotry and gloom." He has an affair with his cousin Sue and then marries the sensual Arabella, who first meets him by throwing a pig's penis at him as she washes animal parts. He has one child with Arabella and two with Sue, at the same time that he longs for an idealized, "Shelleyan" relationship that is not physical and is as pure and thin as air, a dichotomy that is destined for sure catastrophe and that reflects, it is thought, the basic nature of Victorian values. The novel alternates between a condemnation of society and the Christian tradition, which he sees as warring with nature, and blaming the weaknesses of the characters themselves. It also alternates between farce and tragedy and concludes—passim—that all of humanity is cursed and is the plaything of "purblind doomsters." Hope, Hardy implies, can only destroy; that is the fate of Man.

The novel is divided into six parts. Each one begins with soaring hope and ends with despair. Part One ends in attempted suicide. Part Two ends in utter defeat for Jude. Part Three in desolation for Sue, after marriage to Phillotson. Part Four ends in a sexless union. Part Five ends in poverty and beggary, and Part Six ends in total doom. At the last, Jude's child with Arabella, called Father Time, kills the other two children and commits suicide. Of the chief players, Sue leaves Jude; Jude wastes away and dies at age thirty; and Arabella, finding his body, fails to report it until the next morning so she can have a night of fun at the festival with Jude's friends.

Obviously Hardy's philosophy was rooted in pessimism. He believed that "if a road to the better there be," it can be reached only by taking a hard look at the worst.

The critical response to this novel was almost universal outrage. The story was considered so scandalous that much of it was cut for *Harper's New Weekly* in America. Various reviewers in England called it a "grimy story," "steeped in sex," "wallowing in the mire," "degenerate," "a shameful nightmare to be forgotten as soon as possible," "foul in detail," and "disgusting." An Anglican bishop burned the book and urged others to do so as well. Circulating libraries generally removed it from their shelves. As a result of this reception, Hardy quit writing novels altogether and for the next thirty-three years wrote only poetry.

Jude was eventually adopted into the literary canon and became one of the most frequently studied novels of the modern period. It is credited with helping to break the barriers of censorship and to open up the Victorian and modern world for discussion of heretofore banned topics and ideas. It has stimulated, for readers ever since, provocative examinations of practices regarding sex and marriage, in particular, and has been used by Marxists as a critique of Victorian and capitalist society and by modern feminists as a relevant and powerful document concerning women's rights and the oppression of women in Victorian society.

Additional Readings: Gary Adelman, *Jude the Obscure* (New York: Twayne, 1992); Harold Bloom, *Thomas Hardy's* Jude the Obscure (New York: Chelsea House Publishers, 1987); Gertrude Hemmelsfarb, *The De-Moralization of Society* (New York: Knopf, 1995).

1900–1999

෴

Joseph Conrad, *Heart of Darkness*, 1902

Samuel Butler, *The Way of All Flesh*, 1903

H.G. Wells, *Tono-Bungay*, 1908

D.H. Lawrence, *Sons and Lovers*, 1913

Ford Madox Ford, *The Good Soldier*, 1915

E.M. Forster, *A Passage to India*, 1924

Virginia Woolf, *Mrs. Dalloway*, 1925

Aldous Huxley, *Brave New World*, 1932

Siegfried Sassoon, *The Complete Memoirs of George Sherston*, 1937

A.J. Cronin, *The Citadel*, 1937

George Orwell, *Animal Farm*, 1945

Graham Greene, *The Heart of the Matter*, 1948

William Golding, *Lord of the Flies*, 1954

Anthony Burgess, *A Clockwork Orange*, 1962

෴

1900–1999: TIMELINE

1899–1905	George Nathaniel Curzon, British viceroy to India at the peak of the British Empire, suppresses all agitation for broadened Indian participation in government and for independence from Britain.
1900	Fabian socialists are instrumental in founding the Labour Representation Committee, which will evolve into England's powerful Labour Party.
	The chief domestic issues for the first half of the century are the activities of trade unions, Irish Home Rule, and women's suffrage.
1901	The Taff Vale decision, which allows employers to sue unions for damages, seriously impedes the labor movement.
1901–10	Queen Victoria dies and her son Edward ascends the throne, reigning for nine years.

During this period wages decline, and the poor, many destitute, comprise one half of England's population.

1902	Joseph Conrad's *Heart of Darkness* is published.
1903	Emmeline Pankhurst founds the Women's Social and Political Union to fight for women's suffrage. For five years prior to World War I the women's movement for suffrage disrupts the country with hunger strikes, obstruction of traffic, and property damage. Women who go on hunger strikes in prison are tied down so that fluids can be poured through their noses.
	Samuel Butler's *The Way of All Flesh* is published.
1905	George Bernard Shaw's attack on private property, the play titled *Major Barbara*, is produced.

1906 — The Labour Party is formed to secure a voice for labor in Parliament by influencing elections. Ramsey MacDonald, a former Fabian, emerges as the new political party's leader.

Parliament passes a program of free meals for schoolchildren and an old-age pension bill.

The Workman's Compensation Act makes employers liable for injured workmen and those who contract occupational disease.

The Trades Disputes Act reverses the Taff Vale decision. The new act allows unions the right to peaceful demonstration.

A parliamentary report reveals that one eighth of the population possess half the wealth of the country. One third of the workmen earn less than twenty-five shillings a week. Six hundred thousand paupers live in England.

1908 — H.G. Wells's *Tono-Bungay* is published.

Parliament passes its first bill designed to provide care for the elderly.

Grassroots boycotts of foreign-made goods gives a boost to native Indian industry.

Outrages over the atrocities committed by Belgians working for King Leopold in the Congo force Leopold to relinquish his private control to the Belgian state.

1909 — Reformer David Lloyd George introduces "the people's budget," which raises taxes on the wealthy to pay for poor and workmen's relief. It passes the House of Lords only when King George V threatens to expand that body with liberal appointments if it is not passed.

The Labor Exchanges Act, an attack on unemployment, passes.

The Trades Boards Act attacks the problem of sweatshops.

The Housing and Town Planning Act attempts to demolish a number of slum houses and to hold landlords responsible for the condition of their houses.

The National Insurance Act, providing sickness and unemployment insurance, passes and is put into place in 1911.

1910 — Discussions are under way regarding the Parliament Bill, which would severely limit the power of the House of Lords. It will pass into law in 1911.

1911 — Britain transfers the capital of India from Calcutta to New Delhi.

1913 — The Trade Union Act affirms the right of unions to use their funds for political purposes.

1914 — D.H. Lawrence's *Sons and Lovers* is published. Bernard Shaw's *Pygmalion* is produced. It is a critical portrait of class distinctions in English society.

A general strike of key industries threatens the economy but provides additional clout for labor.

1915 — Britain declares war on Germany, and its involvement in World War I begins.

At Gallipoli in the Balkans the Allies meet the Turks in an invasion of Turkey. Two hundred and five thousand English soldiers die in a disastrous encounter.

Ford Madox Ford's *The Good Soldier* is published.

Mohandas Gandhi, already having secured a reputation as a civil rights activist in South Africa, returns to India and immediately becomes politically involved there.

1916 — In the Battle of the Somme the Germans lose 500,000 men, and the Allies lose 600,000; 420,000 of these are British soldiers. All this is over a few yards of earth.

The Russian Revolution results in the deposing of the czar and infects the rest of the world with both fear of revolution on the part of the ruling classes and commitment to social change on the part of reformers.

1918   T.E. Lawrence (Lawrence of Arabia) successfully leads Arab forces against the Turks, culminating in a triumphant entry into Damascus.

In defeat Germany signs an armistice with the Allies.

By the end of the war, England has suffered 2.5 million casualties and millions wounded or disabled.

In recognition of women's work during the war, they are now provided limited suffrage by Parliament. But war casualties had left the country with 2 million more women than men; so in fear of petticoat rule, the new bill only gives the vote to women over the age of thirty.

1919   The Treaty of Versailles, which settles postwar boundaries, establishes the League of Nations, reduces the German military, and forces Germany to pay reparations.

T.E. Lawrence is unsuccessful in arguing for Arab independence from Britain.

In the Government of India Act, the English allow limited Indian control of India by opening civil service and officer corps to Indians and by giving them greater representation in the legislative council. At the same time, the British impose on India the Rowlatt Acts, which permanently places the populous under wartime emergency measures intended to quell revolutionary activity.

Gandhi organizes civil disobedience to protest the Rowlatt Acts. At Amritsar, a Hindu celebration as well as the occasion of political demonstration, the British open fire on the crowd, killing 400 people.

Two thousand strikes by labor unions occur in a single year.

1921   The Bolsheviks win control of Russia.

In Britain 18 percent of the adult workers are unemployed.

Ten percent of the English people hold 90 percent of the wealth.

1922–24   Gandhi is in prison.

1924   E.M. Forster's *Passage to India* is published.

The Labour Party forms its first government, which will last less than a year.

V.I. Lenin, leader of the Bolsheviks, dies.

Interest in socialism and in changing society itself grows in Britain.

1925   Virginia Woolf's *Mrs. Dalloway* is published.

1926   A miners' strike escalates into a crippling general strike.

T.E. Lawrence's *Seven Pillars of Wisdom* is published.

1928   Edmund Blunden's *Undertones of War* and R.C. Sheriff's *Journey's End*, both antiwar books, are published.

Josef Stalin, after emerging as the leader of the Bolsheviks, institutes his five-year plan in the new USSR. His actions of replacing farms with industry and forming farm collectives result in the death from hunger of 7 million peasants.

Women over twenty-one are given the vote.

1929   Two other important antiwar memoirs are published: Robert Graves's *Goodbye to All That* and Richard Aldington's *Death of a Hero*.

The worldwide economic depression hits England.

1930   In protest of the English salt tax, Gandhi leads masses of people to break the law by making their own salt from the sea.

Stalin begins his purges of suspected critics of the state.

1931   The British colonies of Canada, Australia, New Zealand, and South Africa become independent countries within the Commonwealth.

1932   Aldous Huxley's *Brave New World* is published.

1933   In the heart of the economic depression, 3 million people are unemployed.

1935   The British Parliament approves the Government Act of India of 1935, increasing Indian representation in government but still refusing to grant independence.

1937   Siegfried Sassoon's *The Complete Memoirs of George Sherston* is published.

A.J. Cronin's *The Citadel* is published.

1939   After the German army invades Poland, Britain and France declare war on Germany.

Britain declares war on Germany in India's behalf without consultation with the India legislature.

Stalin signs a Non-Aggression Pact with Hitler.

1940   Hitler, now in control of most of Europe, concentrates on bringing England, virtually standing alone at this time, to its knees. Hoping to starve England out, Hitler blockades the country, attempting to keep the country from importing needed supplies.

In August, Germany begins trying to wipe out the British air force. Not only does Germany bomb military installations, but it conducts bombing raids on cities in the interior of England to draw the British air force into the open.

By the end of 1940, Hitler has abandoned his original plans to invade England.

German forces are beaten back when they attack British-held Egypt.

1940–41   The Germans make seventy-one bombing raids on London and fifty-six on other English cities.

1941   The British have significant victories over Italian forces in Africa but are driven back by the Germans.

The Japanese take British Hong Kong.

1942   Gandhi organizes the "Quit India" movement, asking for England's immediate withdrawal from India.

The Japanese take British Singapore.

1942–44   Gandhi is in prison.

1943   The Germans and Italians suffer defeats in North Africa from Anglo-American forces.

English and American forces invade Italy.

English and American forces begin to bomb Germany.

1944   Allies cross the Channel for an invasion in a massive invasion of Normandy in German-occupied France.

The Allies liberate Paris.

The last major German offensive is launched in the Battle of the Bulge.

1945   George Orwell's *Animal Farm* is published.

The Allies cross the Rhine and rapidly move toward Berlin.

The Allies bomb Dresden, Germany, killing 135,000 civilians and destroying 80 percent of the city.

Allied soldiers liberate Nazi death camps.

It will be discovered that the Nazis have murdered millions of civilians, including 6 million Jews.

Germany is forced to sign an unconditional surrender in May.

The bombing of Hiroshima kills 70,000 nonmilitary men, women, and children and destroys 68 percent of the city.

War ends in the Pacific.

In World War II, 4.5 million Englishmen serve in the military overseas; 3 million Englishmen serve in the military at home. In the bombings of London, some 60,000 civilians are killed and 50,000 injured; the destruction or serious damage of approximately 4 million homes leaves hundreds of thousands homeless. For five years, every English household is under blackout. Thousands of children from London are disrupted and separated from their families to live in less dangerous rural areas.

England begins to recuperate from the heavy losses inflicted by the war, including those suffered by the civilian population. In addition, England is left deeply in debt and must continue rationing long after the war is over.

1945–51	The Labour Party under Clement Atlee governs England. Broad programs of reform begin, including the nationalization of the Bank of England, of the iron and steel industries, of the railroad, and of the coal mines.
1946	Extensive social security programs are passed, pertinent to maternity, unemployment, disability, and old age.
1947	India secures independence from England.
1948	Graham Greene's *The Heart of the Matter* is published.

The book is immediately placed on the Roman Catholic's Index of forbidden books.

The National Health Service is finally put in place.

Britain withdraws from India. Following independence, wars between Indians and Pakistanis result in the deaths of between 250,000 and 500,000 people.

1952	Queen Elizabeth II comes to the throne.
1952–56	The British army kills 10,000 Mau Maus in Africa.
1954	William Golding's *Lord of the Flies* is published.
1956	England loses control of the Suez Canal.
1957	Sputnik sparks technological research.
1961	The British empire in Africa is becoming unraveled, with the loss of South Africa, Ghana, Nigeria, Uganda, and Kenya.
1962	Anthony Burgess's *A Clockwork Orange* is published.
1964–70	The Labour Party is in control in England.
1965–80s	As relations between the Republic of Ireland and England improve, the more radical Irish Republican Army (IRA) increases acts of terrorism, especially in Protestant-dominated Northern Ireland.
1966–67	Massive dock strikes cripple England.
1973	The IRA begins a policy of bombing public sites in England.
1979–90	Conservatives elect Margaret Thatcher as prime minister. What is known as the Thatcher Revolution proceeds. This includes the privatization of industry, the removal of many government subsidies, and the relaxation of government regulations.
1983	William Golding wins the Nobel Prize for Literature.

50. *Heart of Darkness*, by Joseph Conrad (England, 1902). *Heart of Darkness* is one of the most powerful, complex, and pessimistic novels of the modern age. It takes the form ostensibly of a postcolonial adventure novel, in which a representative of an industrially advanced country explores a more primitive land that is exotic and perilous. Conrad's setting is the Belgian Congo, operated as a private enterprise by King Leopold II of Belgium in the late nineteenth century. He presents a searing indictment of the brutal exploitation of African natives in a ruthless search for private gain, especially for ivory. At the same time, he castigates the entire colonial process, using it as a metaphor for a passionate, brooding journey into a personal darkness.

Following explorations of the Congo between 1874 and 1877 by Anglo-American journalist Henry Morton Stanley, the Belgian king Leopold II employed Stanley to return to the Congo to set up trading stations. The Congo Free State, under Leopold's personal sovereignty, was recognized by European powers in 1885. Set up to bring "civilization" to the center of darkest Africa, the organization instead brought plunder, torture, and death. Leopold personally laid claim to all the rubber trees and the ivory. Stations were established for collection of ivory. Taxes were levied on native peoples, to be paid only in rubber, while at the same time the Belgian colonial army forcibly stamped out the slave trade in the eastern Congo. Three mutinies by members of the Force Publique and minor uprisings throughout the region were suppressed with force. The result was a reign of unsurpassed brutality and horror, worse than legal slavery; it was massive extermination, conducted with callous disregard for everything except private gain. Deaths were numbered in the millions.

Between June and December 1890, Conrad worked for a Belgian firm possessing concession rights to all ivory and rubber along a thousand miles of the Congo River. There he came to know about Sir Roger Casement, an Irish aristocrat, later a revolutionary, who held consular posts in various parts of Africa, including the Congo from 1892 to 1903. Following this, he presented to the British government the results of a two-year study

accurately reporting what was happening in the Congo. In 1902, Conrad published *Heart of Darkness*, his own version of the horror. One of the characters in the novel is based on Sir Roger Casement.

The tale begins as four men sit in the yacht *Nellie* in the estuary of the Thames. When the subject turns to empire, one of the four, Marlow, tells the story of his journey up the Congo River to bring back an unusually successful trader named Kurtz. The tale is intense, subjective, filled with constant variations on light and dark, knowledge and ignorance, civilization and savagery, and with continuous plays on fogs and mists, on things that defy logic and even basic concepts of humanity itself; and always, from first to last, there is the brooding nature of Marlow himself, as he explores unknown, often horror-filled depths of his own soul. And always there is the constant, haunting image of dead or dying natives, existing like ghosts or shadows in an impenetrable darkness of the spirit.

Three points in the story have proved crucial for critical evaluation. First, at the bottom of the noble, idealistic letter that Kurtz has written about bringing light to the darkness, he has scrawled, at a later time: "Exterminate all the brutes." Then Kurtz's last words are, "The horror, the horror." Finally, when Marlow faces Kurtz's fiancée, he tells the lie she wants to hear, then walks out, noting that the entire world was a great heart of darkness.

Heart of Darkness received modest praise when it first appeared, but gradually it rose in status to become one of the solid masterpieces of modern literature. The novel, one of the first sustained studies of colonialism, exposed a view quite counter to the prevailing Western outlook. For the first time, Englishmen, proud of their empire, began to suspect the baseness that lay at the heart of colonization and to reevaluate the positions of Western nations in Africa and elsewhere. Conrad presents the hypocrisy of the colonizer who masks his need to dominate with a declaration of pious mission. His readers saw the colonizer as one who is corrupted by his greedy actions and then shifts blame for his corruption to the very people, the Africans, he is exploiting.

In the late twentieth century, Conrad was sometimes charged with racism because of his description of natives and native life, a charge that has been found by many to be wholly irrelevant, in that his entire focus is on the brutalizing effect of colonization on whites. His descriptions are not from the point of view of the author or an omniscient narrator but are the impressions of ironic narrators who are nineteenth-century whites. The reader sees what Marlow sees.

Heart of Darkness is perhaps the one novel that has come to pervade all of modern culture. It is the ultimate statement on colonial exploitation, the omnipresent metaphor for life without meaning, without cause, and without restraint—"civilization" without the policeman on the corner or God in His heaven. It is the ready image of the modern soul in extremis. Philosopher Bertrand Russell praised Conrad highly for his expression of truth about the modern human condition; Conrad portrays, he noted, "civilized and morally tolerable human life as a dangerous walk on a thin crust of barely cooled lava which at any moment might break and let the unwary sink into the fiery depths" (Gary Adelman, *Heart of Darkness* [Boston: Twayne, 1987], p. 7).

Additional Readings: Adam Hochschild, *King Leopold's Ghost* (Boston: Houghton Mifflin, 1998); J.H. Stape, ed., *The Cambridge Companion to Joseph Conrad* Cambridge: Cambridge University Press, 1996); Ian P. Watt, *Conrad in the Nineteenth Century* (Berkeley: University of California Press, 1979).

51. *The Way of All Flesh*, by Samuel Butler (England, 1903). Samuel Butler's most famous and influential novel was virtually completed in 1885 but was not published until 1912, the year after he died. In the background of the novel are theories of evolution and psychological theories bearing on the family, for Butler's story is one of the evolution of a family, as each generation is damaged by the previous one.

It is the story of Ernest Pontifex whose an-

cestors have declined from the vigorous carpenter, who was his great-grandfather, to his money-grubbing, social-climbing grandfather, and then to Ernest's bitter, self-righteous father, a man who was too weak to resist parental plans to push him into the ministry, a profession for which he is unfitted.

In dogged plans to shape Ernest into the socially proper, classically educated, pure Victorian gentleman his parents want him to be, they are unspeakably brutal to him even from infancy. The prudish, ambitious minister father and his wife humiliate, terrorize, and brutalize Ernest continually in every possible way.

Despite a deep-seated inner voice that tells Ernest that he is basically good and intelligent, his outer, intellectual self is convinced of the opinion of his parents that he is evil and stupid and deserves the beatings he routinely receives.

The young boy's only salvation is his aunt Alethea who oversees his education for a time. Despite scholastic success and an inheritance from his grandfather, Ernest yields to his parents' insistence, against his better instincts, that he become a minister. Both his financial independence and his clerical career come to an end, however, when he trusts his money to a high-placed cleric who promises to invest it for him and when he moves to the slums to study and help the poor. The cleric steals his money, and a decent woman in his boardinghouse whom he has mistaken for a prostitute has him arrested for attacking her.

He has a brief relationship and two children with his father's former maid, an alcoholic, whom he leaves when he finds that she is still married to someone else. He sends the children to be raised by others to escape what he fears is the Pontifex curse, makes his living as a tailor for a time, and is then hired by his wealthy godfather as a steward and secretary. Ernest finally has a life for himself, but it is not the one expected of a Victorian gentleman, in that he is without social position or a family. At the end, with the help of his aunt's inheritance, he becomes a writer.

The Way of all Flesh, sometimes called the greatest novel of the early twentieth century, had a large and enthusiastic audience. It sold extremely well, went through sixty-eight editions, and was translated into many languages before 1953 when the original manuscript was restored in a Riverside edition.

Coming at a time when readers were becoming more sceptical, the novel had great influence in corroborating the public's growing lack of commitment to traditional values. In his story, which late-twentieth-century studies have reinforced, Butler suggested that a child who is abused by his parents is much more likely to become an abuser himself.

The story of Ernest was a painful but affirming one for Butler's readers, many of whom felt that they had been damaged in some way by the old culture. What they saw was a story that undermined key elements in the Victorian code: the primacy of the family, the gentleman father, the pure mother, social ambition, and the church. The family in his novel is so brutal that the son decides he will dispense with a family of his own, farming his children out to a man who has no social standing at all. The father is a monster who is all piety, and the mother goes to any means to withhold affection and suppress her son's natural urges.

The church that his father represents is seen as even more suspect when a cleric runs off with Ernest's money. He finally comes to believe that atheism is a more humane position than Christianity.

Additional Readings: Lee E. Holt, *Samuel Butler* (Boston: Twayne, 1989); Thomas L. Jeffers, *Samuel Butler Revalued* (University Park: Pennsylvania State University Press, 1981).

52. *Tono-Bungay*, by H.G. Wells (England, 1908).

Tono-Bungay, a story of the rise to wealth and prominence of a lower-class man by means of his marketing of a worthless substance, is actually an indictment of all of British society in the Edwardian era, a time when, in retrospect, it is clear that the great days of Britain were over, and the empire was doomed to vanish as a relic of the past in a rapidly changing world.

In 1908, Britain was "the empire on which the sun never sets." Its upper classes could educate their sons at the best universities in the world, send them out to the farthest corners of the earth, and know that there they could rule, automatically. At the same time, while these few were holding fast to their privileges, the underprivileged, in England and throughout the world, were increasingly agitating for power and freedom.

Tono-Bungay chronicles the rise of George Ponderevo to a position of great wealth through the fantastic sale of a worthless product, "Tono-Bungay," invented by his uncle Edward. George grows up on the great estate of Bladesover, where his mother is a domestic; but eventually, being exiled from there, he sets out to improve himself, first by studying chemistry while living with Edward, then, after Edward goes broke, following him to London to sell Tono-Bungay. George falls in love, gets married, and experiments with airplanes; but as his fortunes rise, his marriage fails. Indeed, all human values fail for George. At one point, to recoup depleted fortunes, he goes to Africa for a radioactive cure-all called Quap. He even commits murder to sell Quap; however, Quap eats through the ship's hull and sinks it. George helps Edward, now in serious trouble, escape to France, where Edward dies.

In the end, George builds a destroyer and sails down the Thames for the open sea. He also decides that England is a despicable place.

Tono-Bungay particularly attacks failure to change outmoded traditions, and class distinctions, as well as various aspects of an emerging society in which clever marketing produces fantastic success for worthless products and ideas.

Wells in effect criticizes all of British society. From the first, George says that his purpose is "to say things I have come to feel intensely of the laws, traditions, usages and ideas we call society." It is a place that promotes greed and profit and destroys human values. George also, he says, is searching for that mysterious thing that transcends human expression, call it Truth or Science or something else. His aim in building the destroyer (identified as "X") is somehow to achieve that mysterious thing, the unknown entity that will provide man with answers.

At the time of this novel, Wells considered England to be still clinging to a diseased system, unwilling to change at a time when reality had outpaced the social framework. For several years, Wells, like George, was a Fabian socialist but broke with them because of philosophical differences. He remained a socialist, however, and a sharp critic.

Wells already had an immense popularity among a general readership whom he was able to influence with his social views of England in the first decades of the twentieth century. In *Tono-Bungay*, it has been observed, the reader found the focus to be more on England as a country than on any single character. In the narrow sense, the novel was an exposé of the patent medicine business, then booming in England. It was also an exposé of the world of capitalist ventures, then fraught with fraud and totally unregulated.

On the larger canvas, however, Wells was able to reach his vast readership with his view that English society was undergoing a crisis, a period during which the country was challenged to emerge from a rural past where a feudal mentality of class discrimination prevailed in both city and country alike. The novel held a mirror up to English society where a class of peasants were obeisantly and without question dependent on the ruling class. Wells's novel, through the social awakening of his main character, awakened his readers to the fact that this old order had passed and, as he wrote, "our fine foliage of pretenses lie glowing in the mire."

Tono-Bungay was a novel that also successfully challenged its readers to judge the kind of society that seemed doomed to take the place of the old feudal system. The materialistic, tasteless capitalism of Edward Ponderevo, which threatened to supplant the old order, was seen by Wells's readers as the ugly and insubstantial scheme he had portrayed.

His novel shows that working-class people will suffer under both old and modern worlds. The commercial one is identified with disease. "Each day one feels that the pressure of commerce grew, grew insensibly monstrous."

Additional Readings: John Batchelor, *H.G. Wells* (Cambridge: Cambridge University Press, 1985); François Bedarida, *A Social History of England* (London: Routledge, 1991); John Huntington, ed., *Critical Essays on H.G. Wells* (Boston: G.K. Hall, 1991).

53. *Sons and Lovers*, by D.H. Lawrence (England, 1913). The setting for D.H. Lawrence's story of a young artist's growth into manhood is a coal-mining village in the English midlands. While largely studied as a psychological novel in the modernist vein, the social setting of the novel is also of importance. Lawrence, himself, often saw *Sons and Lovers* in terms of its social setting and message, describing it as his "collier novel," referring to its setting in a mining town.

While the novel opens with the courtship and marriage of a young man's mother and father, the real focus is on Paul Morel, a clerk with a good education and aspirations to be a painter or designer. His father, who works in the mines, as do most of the other adult males in the community, has degenerated since his youth into a drunkard and wife abuser, whose children have turned against him. His overbearing mother, Gertrude, is from a higher social class than the father. Her preoccupation in life is to keep Paul from a life as a miner, to follow his artist's instincts, and to encourage him to rise in the world.

The three other characters central to the plot are his first love, Miriam Leivers, whom he finally persuades to sleep with him, despite her reluctance; Clara Dawes, an older married woman and suffragette with whom he has an affair; and Clara's husband, Baxter, a metal worker with whom Paul first has a violent encounter and then comes to admire.

When Paul's mother Gertrude, with whom he has a strong love-hate relationship, becomes ill with cancer, Paul commits euthanasia by giving her a fatal dose of morphine.

Sons and Lovers is the most famous and highly regarded of D.H. Lawrence's novels. However, the 1913 manuscript was highly censored by his publisher who was uneasy with the sexually explicit nature of the original. Not until 1992 did a copy of Lawrence's original manuscript see print. Despite the publisher's cutting, at the time of the novel's first appearance, Lawrence's explicit treatment of sex in the novel caused it to receive mixed reviews. It was also criticized from the first for its sympathetic presentation of a hero who misuses the women in his life.

The continuing influence of the novel is twofold. It is one of the most realistic pictures of working-class life in England before World War I. In choosing, as he did, the mining community of the midlands, Lawrence has provided one of the most vivid pictures of the disruption of rural society by the continuing growth of industry, which had overtaken village life. His novel also depicts the humiliation of class conflict based on capitalism in the story of a talented young man who is never able to break into the middle class.

Another aspect of the novel's influence has received far more discussion. That is its early, frank, and prophetic treatment of the sexual profile of a small community. Lawrence's readers found an early archetypical study of an oedipal triangle involving the dominant mother, a brutal father, and a young man whose own sex life is deeply affected by his emotional connection to his parents. Although scarcely explicit in its treatment, the novel was also one of the first oblique treatments of homoeroticism and one of the first modern novels to deal negatively with sexual repression in Western culture and to recommend sexual liberation, especially for women.

Additional Readings: James E. Cronin and Johnathan Schneer, *Social Conflict and the Political Order in Modern Britain* (New Brunswick, NJ: Rutgers University Press, 1982); Judith Faar, ed., *Twentieth-Century Interpretations of "Sons and Lovers": A Collection of Critical Essays* (Englewood Cliffs, NJ: Prentice-Hall, 1970); Julian Moynahan, ed., *"Sons and Lovers": Texts, Background, and Criticism* (New York: Penguin, 1977).

54. *The Good Soldier*, by Ford Madox Ford (England, 1915). *The Good Soldier*, now regarded as Ford Madox Ford's masterpiece, written when the author was forty-two years old, presents a psychological portrait of representative characters caught in a tangled pattern of deceit, pretense, and intrigue in the values of a dying era, written as a war that was thought would end all wars was just beginning. As such, it is the last significant Victorian/Edwardian work whose characters exist in the twilight of its dying.

The good soldier of the title is not a military man at all; he is an upper-class civilian who lives his daily life under a continuous façade of duty, honor, and congeniality, while his private life is one of betrayal, self-gratification, and weakness, very like the Victorian era itself. His whole life is devoted to maintaining an upright appearance, which his corrupt and treasonous actions belie. The original title of Ford's novel was "The Saddest Story," rejected by the publisher as not inclined to promote sales. In response, Ford, in line with the rising military atmosphere, suggested the ironic title "The Good Soldier," subtitled "A Tale of Passion."

The story concerns the close friendship of two mature couples, one American and one English. John Dowell and his wife Florence, the Americans, have for nine years been close and trusted companions of Edward Ashburnham and his wife Leonora. On the surface their lives have been honorable, and time has only brought them closer together. But all is not entirely well, because the marriage of Dowell and his wife has never been consummated, presumably because Florence has a weak heart. Her husband John, who loves her, understandingly lives with this reality. But on a fateful day, John Dowell learns that his wife had had an affair before they were married. Simultaneously, Florence's horror over the possibility that her affair will become known in her social clique leads her to kill herself. To further complicate the rosy picture of the past, Dowell learns that Florence had actually been having an affair with his best friend Edward Ashburnham throughout their marriage, throughout the couple's seeming idyllic friendship. There has never been anything physically wrong with her heart. Moreover, Ashburnham's wife, Leonora, had not only known of this affair all along; she had also known of many others and had even helped to procure young women for her husband.

Complications continue after Florence's death when another young woman named Nancy, a ward of Leonora's who looks upon Edward as a father, enters the picture. John falls in love with her. Although Leonora even attempts to procure her for Edward, he resists. Nancy, who is secretly in love with Edward, and shocked and confused by the predicament, is sent to India to join her father.

Disaster is heaped upon disaster as Edward, "the good soldier," upon receiving a misleading telegram from Nancy, kills himself, and Nancy, learning of his death, loses her mind. In the end, John Dowell is left to nurse Nancy, now a feeble-minded psychotic, whom he had once wanted to marry. Only Leonora, Edward's wife, emerges from the situation. She marries and starts a family, leaving Dowell, the unreliable and decent, if naive, narrator, to ponder the meaning of the tragedy alone. A Latin quotation from Psalm 119 is given as an epigraph to the novel: *beati immaculati*, meaning "blessed are the undefiled."

At the time of the novel's appearance and for most of the twentieth century, Ford received little critical acclaim. But even from the first, readers appreciated this one novel. Over the years, its reputation has risen, as, toward the last decades of the century, Ford's influence has received more attention. The novel garnered many more readers after a highly successful television dramatization by the same title in 1981.

The novel's influence derives from its position as a funeral oration for the Edwardian age in England that Edward Ashburnham and his American friend, John Dowell, embody. Readers correctly regarded Ashburnham as a representative of his age, which valued above all appearance, manners, social standing, tradition, and a shallow code among friends of one's own class. John Dowell, the foolish, cold narrator, like many of the Edwardian age, is blind to the perfidy all around him, as he continues to justify and admire Edward.

Ford was one of the first writers to expose the destructive emptiness of the so-called virtues of pre–World War I's ruling-class society, predating, as he did, the many English and American chronicles of disillusionment that followed the war.

In some sense, as critic Charles G. Hoffmann writes, readers at the time actually saw this as Ford's war novel, its characters representing not only prewar values but the nations involved in the war. The characters' entanglements, deceptions, suicides, and madness parallel the international alliances and intrigues leading to World War I. Moreover, the "good" people of the novel who comprise Europe's ruling class are the very ones who, through their actions, precipitated the war. The breakup of the four friends is, Hoffmann writes, the breakup of civilization as it was then constituted, finalized in the act of war, and personal destruction is parallel to national destruction, the values of this civilization causing its downfall.

Additional Readings: Charles G. Hoffmann, *Ford Madox Ford* (Boston: Twayne, 1990); Clive Irving, *True Brit* (London: Cape, 1974); John A. Meixner, *Ford Madox Ford's Novels: A Critical Study* (Minneapolis: University of Minnesota Press, 1962).

55. *A Passage to India,* **by E.M. Forster (England, 1924).** Forster's last novel, undoubtedly his best-known work, marks the end of British colonialism and the beginning of a postcolonial era of Indian independence. The work is deeply engaged, not only in the future hopes for a self-governing India but in the British domination of the Indian past.

In the background of Forster's story is the East India Company, a private British trading business, which had established firm control of most of India by the dawn of the nineteenth century. To mine the resources of the country, the company acted as a governmental body, assuming control of many provinces where they loosely shared power with the local aristocracy, raised armies and police, established its own legal system, and built forts. Even as early as the eighteenth century, some educated English viewed the British operation in India as a form of theft. In 1858, when the East India Company was abolished, the control it once exercised was transferred to the British crown. Virtually absolute power rested in a viceroy who served as a representative of the crown in India. The working arm of the crown in India was the Indian Civil Service, some 1,000 men, chiefly graduates of Oxford and Cambridge Universities, who received their commissions on a highly competitive basis. From the Civil Service came military leaders, police, teachers, doctors, and an immense administrative corps that controlled every aspect of Indian life, including the courts. The official language and culture of India became English. Among other things, Forster addresses the double standard that prevailed under the British, whereby the Civil Service had one code for dealing with Anglo-Indians and one code for dealing with Indians.

One of the most traumatic events in the colonization of India occurred in 1857 when a sizable portion of the population mounted a mutiny against British control. After the mutiny was put down, the British felt justified in enacting repressive measures in their dealings with most Indians, though some concessions were made to members of the Indian aristocracy. In 1885, the real tangible beginnings of the independence movement began with the Indian National Congress composed of Indian professionals who urged self-rule. Scant reforms followed, allowing the admission to the Civil Service of a few Indians.

By the time of Forster's novel, several conditions and events began to spell the end of the British ruling presence in India, notably the appearance of Gandhi and the policy of civil disobedience; the Rowlatt Acts, which dispensed with basic civil liberties; and the Amritsar Massacre, when 400 Indian demonstrators were killed and 1,000 were wounded.

Dramatized against this political background, *A Passage to India* is the story of the complex relationships between the English and Indian characters in the novel. It begins as two Englishwomen arrive in India on a visit. One is Adela Quested, a young woman engaged to a city magistrate in India. The other is her fiancé's mother, Mrs. Moore. Both women are eager to know Indians and the true India, which eventually leads them to the mysterious Malabar Caves, guided by an Indian named Dr. Aziz. In the intensely rarefied atmosphere of the caves, reached after a long, hot climb, Adela, in a hallucinatory panic, imagines that Dr. Aziz has assaulted her. Mrs. Moore hears a voice telling her, "Everything exists, nothing has value." Adela'a charges against Dr. Aziz occasion a trial in which he is acquitted. These events doom the hope of any trusting relationships between Indians and English. Even the once close friendship between Dr. Aziz and Fielding, the English principal of an Indian College, can no longer be sustained.

Forster's novel immediately received forty enthusiastic reviews from prestigious critics. By 1925, 17,000 copies had been sold in Britain and 53,000 in the United States. Now it is a staple of English literature, having found its way into the university curriculum.

Through the years it has also remained controversial. Indian writers have frequently praised the novel as the most faithful portrait of the last days of empire in India and for making India a respectable subject for study as well as fiction. On the other hand, some Hindus have expressed disappointment in Forster's choice of a Muslim instead of a Hindu for his central character. Likewise, many feminist readers saw in the novel an adequate expression of the parallel oppression of both Indians and women, while others have criticized the novel for its portrait of Adela as a hysterical accuser. Other readers of the novel have debated just how decidedly the novel supports the idea of independence, arguing that he underplayed the violence on both sides in India and suggested that personal interaction could somehow be a solution to problems of imperialism.

Forster's success in giving a human face to the colonized Indian for the first time and trying to convey something of the Indian mind has been attested to by many of his readers. Westerners also saw for the first time an attitude of sympathy for the Indian. The book changed forever the way the Western world viewed this large, complex society.

The book also raised the question of the possibility of friendship between members of the colonizing society and individuals who are being colonized and explored the extent to which such friendships can overcome political injustice and the extent to which social liberalism on the part of isolated members of the invading class is sustainable.

Additional Readings: Malcolm Bradbury, ed., *"A Passage to India": A Casebook* (London: Macmillan, 1970); Hermann Kulke, *A History of India* (London: Routledge, 1998); Judith Schere Herz, *A Passage to India: Nation and Narration* (New York: Twayne, 1993).

56. *Mrs. Dalloway*, by Virginia Woolf (England, 1925). *Mrs. Dalloway* is in the modernist tradition that emphasizes internal rather than external action. Nevertheless, in the background of the characters' musings is the full range of social issues pertinent to those years following World War I, the so-called Great War, which profoundly changed the demographics of England and demolished the values and traditions that belonged to the nineteenth century.

Before the war, England was an industrialized, capitalistic country, with sharp divisions based on economics between a wealthy class who owned the factories and the poor who worked in the factories. Even older and more rigid divisions separated the aristocracy from the lower classes. It was also a world in which honor, glory, and loyalty to God and country gave one meaning and united the populace. These values became the public motivation for entering into World War I, a war that many British intellectuals rejected vociferously to on the grounds that participation in a war was merely meant to line the pockets of industrialists. The need to defend the old values also provided those in power with a means of luring young soldiers to battle. Lower-class Britons also had their own motives for enthusiastic enlistment in the war: Many had the hope that in going to war they would find themselves united with all British people in a common cause that would transcend class discrimination. Instead, they found in the military and on the battlefield the most class-conscious world they had ever known. The staff officers, all from the upper classes, came to be despised by the commoners who provided the country with cannon fodder.

The soldiers who returned home were bitter about a war, prolonged by business interests, that had taken the lives of so many men and left others maimed, invalided, and too sick of body and mind to live normal lives. They were disillusioned about having sacrificed so much in a war that left England even more divided by class and wealth than ever. In 1921, there was 18 percent unemployment in England, and 10 percent of the people owned 90 percent of the wealth. The war seemed to have devastated the general population in order to benefit the rich. With the collapse of trust and hope came the collapse of other traditional, high-minded values that had lured soldiers to war.

The disillusionment with the traditional, class-conscious English society affected not just the oppressed working-class men but many women throughout England whose own sense of oppression had been sharpened by the war and had come to the surface as a result of their own newly won legal advances: the right to vote and enter more trades and professions.

The novel, which takes place in the backwash of World War I in London, England, is scant of plot and external action. The main character, Mrs. Clarissa Dalloway, a society wife of a conservative politician and the mother of a young daughter, proceeds throughout the one day encompassed by the novel to prepare for a party she is giving in the evening. She leaves the house in the morning on a mission to buy flowers to decorate her house. On her outing, she encounters several people in the park who seem in various ways to be alienated, to echo some aspect of her own state of mind, and to bring back her past. The sound of the clock, Big Ben, chiming the hour, connects these diverse individuals in the park, even as it connects all people in London within the sound of the bells.

In midmorning, Clarissa is visited by a former suitor, who later appears at her party with another of her old friends. In midafternoon, she and her conservative husband have a conversation. The centerpiece of her day is the party, and the point of emotional impact comes as she is told about the suicide of Septimus Warren Smith, a shell-shocked young veteran. The lower-class Smith seems to be the opposite of the upper-class Clarissa, but she feels great empathy for him, as if he is an echo of her own disturbed inner self. Like him, she feels destroyed by the social expectations she has allowed to take over her life. Like him, she longs to repudiate the traditions that have oppressed them.

Mrs. Dalloway was published in both England and the United States and received many favorable reviews. But from the 1930s to the 1950s, the novel was neglected. Not until the mid-century growth of women's studies did it begin receiving critical attention again.

Woolf's novel was influential in presenting the many aspects of post–World War I society—mental illness, social mores, class oppression, the alienation and emptiness—from a woman's perspective. She articulated the postwar malaise that had devastated England. Readers were struck by the way in which she captured the devastation of the war, the social and psychological changes that it had wrought, the spiritual bleakness of the modern world, as felt by Clarissa.

In following Clarissa on her walk along the ordinary byways of the city, Woolf also was able to make the city itself one of the main characters of her novel.

Moreover, the novel was the first to subtly impress on readers the impact of the war on the class structure in England by showing those, like the Dalloways, who had flourished after the war, in contrast to Septimus who is destroyed by it.

Additional Readings: Joan Bennett, *Virginia Woolf: Her Art as a Novelist* (Cambridge: Cambridge University Press, 1945); Alice van Buren Kelley, *The Novels of Virginia Woolf: Fact and Vision* (Chicago: University of Chicago Press, 1973); Nell Nehring, *Flowers in the Dustbin* (Ann Arbor: University of Michigan Press, 1993).

57. *Brave New World*, by Aldous Huxley (England, 1932). Huxley, in an impressive array of novels, attempted to define the atmosphere and the moral and ideological chaos of the postwar world of the 1920s. In *Brave New World*, he shifted to satire and produced one of the most phenomenally successful and influential science-fiction novels of the age.

Following the world war, all of Western society was adrift in a world that had rejected traditional values that had led to such a disaster but had as yet achieved no system on which to base a new world. In the vacuum, however, had emerged incipient fascism, communism, hedonism, and above all, technological and scientific advances that made mind control and the redefinition of a human being a looming reality.

At the same time, rebellions of the young and rich in the so-called Jazz Age in Europe and America, as well as revolutionary societies, had created an atmosphere of amorality. In Russia, for example, communists began their rule by outlawing bourgeois concepts of marriage. And in Europe wide-open cities, like Weimar Berlin, flaunted traditional morality. At the same time, the sophisticated European world was awash in social change, and for many, life was lived as if there were no tomorrow.

Huxley, indirectly at least, addresses all of these elements in his satire. In *Brave New World*, happiness is universal, and pain does not exist. Any problems that arise can be taken care of with conditioning, and if that fails, the drug soma produces happy oblivion. The world's new people engage in sex without emotion or love, only for pleasure. Women no longer give birth. Instead, new human beings are created in laboratories, where through genetic engineering, the intelligence of the child is predetermined. At the top are Alphas, those of superior abilities; at the bottom are the dim-witted Epsilons. Freudian dangers embedded in family life are avoided by abolishing families and emotional attachments.

The narrative shows Bernard Marx (an Alpha who was accidentally exposed to some Beta material and is thus "different") going on vacation to the Savage Reservation in New Mexico. He carries with him Lenina Crowne, an amplified beauty devoted to pleasure and soma. There they meet Linda, his boss's former girlfriend, who got accidentally stranded on the reservation twenty-five years earlier and who, without birth control or abortion centers, became pregnant and gave birth to a child. John, her son, grew up in the old-fashioned way, is devoted to Shakespeare, is susceptible to love and passion, and holds fairly traditional values. When John and his mother return to civilization, he, though initially enchanted, quickly becomes disillusioned. People here are without feeling, engage in promiscuous sex, and never think for themselves. They have no children or lovers. They know nothing of poetry and art and spend most of their time in a haze. Not long after John has left to become a hermit in disgust, he hangs himself. Linda dies in a soma haze, and Bernard is sent to Iceland, an exile for misfits.

The novel sold 13,000 copies in 1932, 10,000 the next year, and was translated into nineteen languages. Initial reviews were decidedly mixed regarding the implications of the satire. Readers and critics could not agree on the interpretations of this innovative and controversial novel.

Time has proved that Huxley prepared the world for many scientific and sociological developments that were the stuff of fantasy in 1932. Huxley extrapolated scientific and so-cial trends visible at the time in a dystopian vision of the future. At the turn of the present century, his visualization of genetic engineering, the total manipulation of people who have become more like machines than individual human beings, and the sense of drug-induced happiness, exemplified by calm acceptance of a caste system along with moral emptiness and sexual promiscuity, has merged into common reality. The novel was created as an antidote to more euphoric scientific utopian fantasies by H.G. Wells and others, emerging as far more pessimistic.

By the turn of the twenty-first century, cattle had been cloned and grain genetically altered (and disapproved for import by the European Union). The U.S. Supreme Court has approved genetically altered bacteria. The human genome has been analyzed, with genetic processes facing the possibility of patent. The test tube and incubator production of human beings had become a cliché image of modern fate, demonized.

While critics initially argued about the novel's merits, it was popular with readers from the first, has never been out of print, and has never waned in popularity. The extent of its influence is seen in the fact that the title itself and other references gleaned from the novel have entered Western mythology and the English language.

Additional Readings: Lawrence Brander, *Aldous Huxley* (London: Hart-Davis, 1970); Gertrude Hemmelharb, *The De-Moralization of Society* (New York: Knopf, 1995); Harold H. Watts, *Aldous Huxley* (New York: Twayne, 1969).

58. *The Complete Memoirs of George Sherston*, by Siegfried Sassoon (England, 1937). Sassoon's memories of World War I, cast first as poetry and then as autobiographical fiction, were among the most popular as well as the most startling and influential accounts of a conflict that began with heroic posturing and blind, political maneuvering and ended with universal revulsion, along with an unchallenged sense of waste and betrayal that changed the face of Europe. Originally published as separate novels—*Memoirs of a Fox-Hunting Man* (1928), *Memoirs of* *an Infantry Officer* (1930), and *Sherston's Progress* (1936)—all were collected as three parts of a single story in 1937.

There was a special tone to World War I, which began with a flourish and promised adventure. It was the ultimate challenge and the sign of manhood. Men rushed off eagerly to battle, as they had in the pages of romance, to prove their bravery. Those who shirked their duty were damned with the white feathers of ignominious cowardice. It did not take long for enlightenment to strike. Modern weapons had far outstripped old attitudes and old techniques of war. Men walked across open spaces into machine gun fire. They huddled in muddy, disease-infested trenches, and the bodies piled up, in unparalleled slaughter. In the first six months of war, the French lost 800,000 men. In the Battle of the Somme (in which Sassoon participated), the Germans lost half a million men; the Allies lost 600,000. The British alone lost some 420,000—all for a few yards of earth.

Sassoon's popular trilogy contains strong biographical elements. Like his protagonist, Sherston, Sassoon lived a life of upper-class wealth and privilege. Bored with university education at Cambridge, he spent his time reading, writing poetry, foxhunting, and playing golf. Like many other young men his age, he was more than half in love with the romance of war and rushed off to do battle in World War I, with a keen sense of personal and national honor.

Like many young men, his hero Sherston included, Sassoon ultimately had to come face to face with the reality of modern war as he made repeated trips to the front for extended service. His war experience left him physically and psychologically wounded and also brought him high honors for heroism. In battle, under fire, Sassoon rescued wounded comrades from no-man's-land. For his fearless feats, he earned the nickname Mad Jack, captured a German trench single-handedly, was recommended for the Victoria Cross, and was awarded the Military Cross.

At home, in a hospital, recuperating from wounds, he became an objector and a pacifist. He threw his Military Cross into the Mersey River and announced that he would not return to the front. Ultimately he did, however, having determined at last that it was not right that he should remain safe in England while his fellow soldiers and friends were undergoing such pain. So he returned to battle. The entire experience for Sassoon was a horror that haunted him for a lifetime.

It was this that he wrote about in his poetry, bringing him the reputation of the leading war poet of England. The three books of the trilogy give a realistic view of the kind of life that Sassoon had led, from the pleasant, rare, and privileged days as a foxhunter on a grand estate in fading Edwardian England, on through the brutalizing experience of the war, and finally the efforts of his protagonists, George Sherston, to pull his life together. The third volume of the trilogy, *Sherston's Progress*, is a deliberate echo of John Bunyan's *The Pilgrim's Progress*, as the hero makes his way from the City of Destruction to the City of Zion. The story ends with Sherston in the hospital, speaking to Dr. Rivers, making the desolate and lonely observation: "It is only from the innermost silence of the heart that we know the world for what it is, and ourselves for what the world had made us."

Memoirs of a Fox-Hunting Man had enormous success in both England and America. It won both the Hawthornden Prize and the James Tait Black Memorial Prize; the following volumes and the publication of the trilogy were also successful. From the first, this established Sassoon as one of the finest prose writers of the era.

The first of the trilogy is a chronicle of the late Victorian era, a fading, twilight world in which, for a time at least, the daily routines of life, for that rare and privileged few, presented all that this world allows. Sassoon's book gives a rare and realistic glimpse into the world before moving to the universal catastrophe that followed.

Just as Sassoon's war poetry shocked England into realization of the truth of war and paved the way for such poets as Wilfred Owen and Robert Graves, so his prose fictional memoir paved the way for a host of antiwar novels, memoirs, and dramas that were to follow. In its wake came works by R.C. Sheriff (*Journey's End*, 1928), Robert Graves (*Good-bye to All That*, 1929). Richard Aldington (*Death of a Hero*, 1929), and Ernest Hemingway (*A Farewell to Arms*, 1929). Former soldiers felt that Sassoon had opened the floodgates, had freed them to at last write what would have been unthinkable before. Perhaps more than any one author, Sassoon shaped the modern world's view of war. The work stands, both stylistically and contextually, as one of the major and most influential works of the age.

Additional Readings: Paul Fussell, *The Great War and Modern Memory* (New York: Oxford University Press, 1975); Brock Millman, *Managing Domestic Dissent in First World War Britain* (London: Frank Cass, 2000); Sanford Sternlicht, *Siegfried Sassoon* (New York: Twayne, 1993).

59. *The Citadel*, by A.J. Cronin (England, 1937). *The Citadel*, the most popular novel of a physician turned novelist, tells a story quite obviously drawn from experiences in his own life. Written during the heart of the Great Depression, when most of the Western world was still suffering from deprivation and neglect and war clouds were slowly gathering over Europe, the novel provided a bracing touch of honesty and crusading idealism for a world eagerly searching for both.

After his own medical training (which included degrees from Glasgow University Medical School, a Ph.D. in 1923, admission to the Royal College of Physicians in 1924, and an M.D. with honors in 1925), Cronin practiced in several Welsh mining towns and served as a medical inspector for the Ministry of Mines before ultimately working in 1925 as a general practitioner in London's fashionable West End. In 1930, while in Inveraray to recuperate from gastric ulcers, he began writing novels. His fifth novel, *The Citadel*, was not only enormously successful; it also led to significant examinations of medical practices of his day.

The hero of the story, Andrew Manson, arrives in Blaenelly, Wales, to assist Dr. Ed-

ward Page, only to discover that Page is unable to work because he is partially paralyzed. Yet Page and his wife perpetuate the illusion that he is "temporarily" ill in order to continue collecting fees. In the mining community, though Manson also faces ignorance, prejudice, and poor facilities, he does his job, even at times performing heroically. He dynamites a sewer to prevent a typhoid epidemic; contradicts a superior to save a minor from the asylum. In the course of his stay, he meets an honest, competent, and bitter friend, Dr. Philip Denny, and meets and marries a young schoolteacher, Christine Barlow.

On his next job for a large mining company, Manson's encounter with jealousy, incompetence, venality, and corruption cause him to resign here as well. He moves from here to the Coal and Metalliferous Mines Fatigue Board in London. Finding this mostly a façade for neglect and pretense, he resigns once more, this time, however, with his ideals wearing thin and his desire to make money growing. In London, after setting up a small practice and struggling to pay debts, he begins to reach the very wealthy and to become friends with wealthy and careless physicians. He begins to become one of them (his wife tells him at one point that she liked him better in his boots, in the old days) until one day when he sees a careless colleague with a bloated reputation blunderingly cause the death of a patient on the operating table. His old sense of integrity returns, and he abruptly breaks with the cream of English physicians.

As a direct result of his break, he is accused of unethical conduct by a nurse and a jealous physician and faces a trial board. In a dramatic defense he gives a blistering indictment of a medical system based on greed and fierce competition rather than cooperative effort. At last he sets up an ideal clinic in a small town with like-minded colleagues.

The reading public in both England and America eagerly devoured the story of the idealistic struggle of a young doctor and Cronin's authentic view of the medical profession from the inside. The novel continued to sell sensationally week after week. In America, it was third on the bestseller list for 1937 and second for 1938. The official views of the book were a bit chillier.

The *Journal of the American Medical Association* condemned the book as unfair to the medical profession. The British Medical Profession, meeting at the time of its publication, erupted in furious controversy, most of it overwhelmingly critical of the author. Serious and official investigations were launched to censor Cronin and remove him from the profession. James Agate in the London *Daily Express* deplored Cronin's attack on Harley Street. Cronin considered that he had attacked the abuses, not the street. But when the London edition of the novel came out, Cronin stated that the entire street should be obliterated for the good of the profession and of mankind.

Few novels have ever had such an immediate impact that produced such practical results. The London *Leader* called for an immediate investigation. Letters to editors were indignant. The Glasgow *Forward* called for a reorganization of the profession along "scientific" lines. And the British Ministry of Health began an inquiry into fee-splitting and started a fund to have 2,000 physicians take postgraduate courses.

In the United States, Dr. Mabel Ulrich, in the *Saturday Review of Literature*, noted that Cronin had "cut through the romanticism that still surrounds the medical profession" and had exposed the "potentialities of charlatanism and dishonesty" in a system in which men "depend for economic security on the real or fancied suffering of others." Dr. Hugh Cabot of the Mayo Clinic wrote, "It is a great book which may easily have a profound influence on the future of society" and concluded that "there is no important situation which he draws, the counterpart of which cannot be found in this country and probably more frequently."

The novel exerted a tremendous effect on the English public. Its most profound impact was felt in the attitudes it changed, leading not only to immediate reform but ultimately to the establishment of the National Health Service.

It continued to be widely read and discussed for decades. In 1938, it was made into a successful film starring Robert Donat, one of the most popular British actors of the day; and in 1983 it appeared as a ten-part miniseries for British TV, one of the most highly acclaimed of the era.

Additional Readings: Nigel Barley, *Native Land* (New York: Viking, 1989); Dale Selwak, *A.J. Cronin* (Boston: Twayne, 1985).

60. *Animal Farm*, **by George Orwell (England, 1945).** George Orwell's *Animal Farm* is an allegorical fable recounting the history of the Union of Soviet Socialist Republics from the Russian Revolution to the Tehran Conference of 1943. The first phase of the revolution, which brought down the Russian czar in February 1917, was a reaction against long-standing grievances of the working class. In the struggles for control of Russia that ensued, every side was guilty of atrocities. The Bolsheviks won control of Russia in 1921 after a civil war between White and Red Russians, the last led by Leon Trotsky. But Trotsky was replaced by Vladimir Lenin, a professional revolutionary who, with Marxism as his ideology and Bolshevism as his political party, had come from exile into Russia to help complete the overthrow of the ruling class by the proletariat. Other world powers afforded the revolutionary government formal recognition throughout the 1920s and early 1930s. Lenin's sickness and his death in 1924 provoked a bitter struggle for Russian leadership between Trotsky and Stalin, resulting in Stalin's victory and Trotsky's exile. From the first, Stalin used every means possible to retain power as dictator and to shape the USSR as he liked. In 1928, he instituted the USSR's Five-Year Plan, based on Marxist economic principles, whereby he planned to bring all farms into collectives and to replace much of the agrarian culture with industrialism. The coercive speed with which this was accomplished brought on famine, urban poverty, and dissent. In the process, some 7 million peasants died from hunger and disease. Throughout the 1930s, Stalin dealt brutally with anyone who disagreed with him, initiating an era of terror-filled purges through executions, imprisonment, and exile. Some 1 million people were shot, and 2 million died in prison camps.

One of the striking historical moments in *Animal Farm* concerns Stalin's decision in 1939 to sign a Non-Aggression Pact with Germany, a country that had begun to threaten the rest of Europe. Throughout the rest of the year, the Soviet Union greatly expanded its empire by invading or supporting sympathetic governments in parts of Poland, Latvia, Lithuania, and Estonia. Stalin's ill-considered pact with Germany finally came to an end with the German invasion of Russia in June 1941. It has been estimated that Soviet losses in World War II reached 28 million people.

The postwar arrangements made by the Allies allowed Stalin to further the Soviet empire by assuming control of Eastern Europe.

With the use of an animal fable, Orwell comments on the history of Lenin, Trotsky, Stalin, Hitler, and the Soviet Union. The setting of the narrative, Manor Farm, owned by a farmer who abuses his animals, is equivalent to the prerevolutionary days of feudal Russia where aristocratic landlords continued to treat their serfs like slaves, long after slavery had been abolished. In an incident equivalent to the revolution of 1917 and the subsequent changes in landownership, the animals revolt and run Farmer Jones off his farm. They then proceed to set up a new system guided by an idealistic ideology, the basis of which is that all animals are created equal. Soon, idealism falls to rivalry and greed, as the pig Napoleon (Stalin) wrests control for himself alone and becomes as much of a dictator as Farmer Jones was. Napoleon and his cohorts, who call themselves "comrade," kill anyone who opposes them and break all the idealistic commandments behind the revolution until they come to resemble the oppressive landlords from whom they had wrenched power.

Animal Farm, in general, is an indictment of the bestiality of all human beings and of the corruption of human beings by power. In particular, however, it is an indictment—

the first and still the most powerful indictment—of communist leaders and the revolution in Russia.

The marked swings in official reaction to the novel are a lesson in world politics. After Orwell finished his manuscript in early 1944, the official reaction was so decidedly negative that over twenty British and American publishers refused to consider it for publication. The reason for this reception was clearly the reluctance of Britain and America to attack one of their Allies at a time when they were engaged in war against Germany. Moreover, the economic travail created throughout the world in the 1930s by unbridled capitalism had generated great sympathy for the communist experiment in the Soviet Union. Publishers who read Orwell's manuscript believed that he had greatly exaggerated his case against the Soviet Union in *Animal Farm*.

But the novel was clearly prophetic of the Cold War that developed after World War II, between Western powers and the Soviet Union. It became an immediate bestseller after its publication in 1945. Within two years, it sold one-half million copies, had been translated into sixty languages, and had been a Book-of-the-Month Club choice in the United States.

In the Cold War, the official reception of the book turned even more positive, as *Animal Farm* was chosen to serve as propaganda. The U.S. Information Agency sponsored translation of the book in thirty languages; the Voice of America broadcast it to Eastern Europe; and the Central Intelligence Agency sponsored it in South America and Eastern Europe.

Ironically, *Animal Farm*, one of the most frequently banned books in the United States, is continually objected to by private citizens and right-wing groups, like the John Birch Society, on the grounds that it advocates communism, rather than the opposite.

By 1990, it had sold 20 million copies in seventy languages; was on the required list of readings in most U.S. high schools; in the top-twenty bestsellers of all time, and was repeatedly dramatized. Dramas include a 1955

British film directed by Joy Batchelor and John Halas, and a 1999 U.S. made-for-television movie starring Kelsey Grammar, Patrick Stewart, and Peter Ustinov.

Its power to influence was apparent in the Soviet Union where it was seen as a threat for forty years after its publication. In 1987, at an international book fair in Russia, it was removed from all booksellers' exhibits, and in 1989 a dramatization of it was cut from the program of an International Theater Festival, at Soviet request.

Additional Readings: Robert Hewison, *British Culture in the Cold War* (New York: Oxford University Press, 1981); John Rodden, ed., *Understanding* Animal Farm (Westport, CT: Greenwood Press, 1999); Raymond Williams, *Marxism and Literature* (Oxford: Oxford University Press, 1977).

61. *The Heart of the Matter*, by Graham Greene (England, 1948). A novel set in the West African colony of Sierra Leone, this novel, regarded as one of Graham Greene's most powerful and provocative, places the protagonist in a setting remote from Western, Roman Catholic strongholds in order to explore the meaning of Christianity. The novel is an attempt to go beyond official dogma to investigate the way in which faith is joined to pity and the love of God and evolves as a result of our own experiences.

The protagonist of the novel is Major Scobie, a highly religious Roman Catholic policeman in British West Africa who, as a failure at most things he has attempted, never has been able to advance in his career or to achieve any level of distinction. Still Scobie clings to his religion from which arises his overwhelming pity for his fellow human beings and his all-consuming love of God. Two turns of events bring his life from mere failure to outright catastrophe. First, lacking the money to provide adequately for his wife Louise, he borrows money from an unscrupulous and dangerous local merchant named Yusef. When Yusef secures control over the policeman, he carries out his plan to blackmail Scobie into helping him smuggle diamonds for him. The second event is his

betrayal of his wife in an affair with a woman named Helen whom he has come to love devotedly and passionately. His wife Louise eventually discovers the affair and urges him to seek forgiveness in the confessional and Holy Communion of the Church. Scobie comes to see, however, that his part in the diamond smuggling and blackmail is corrupt and leads to his own further corruption and the corruption of others. At his lowest moral point, he allows Yusef's henchman to murder his houseboy Ali to keep Ali, he says, from bringing further grief to the two women in his life, Louise and Helen. Finally, the only way he can spare those he loves is to take his own life. He rationalizes his suicide by deciding that if he lives, he will continue to crucify the God that he so fervently loves and he will harm further the people close to him whom he both loves and pities. Despite the hard and fast dogma of the Roman Catholic Church that holds that suicides are damned to hell because they have fallen into despair, an unforgivable sin, at the novel's end, the local priest who comforts the family holds out hope that Scobie is saved, that he has not damned himself by his suicide in that he has done it from his love for God.

The novel created a storm of controversy, especially among Roman Catholic readers. The immediate official reaction of the Church was to place *The Heart of the Matter* on the Index of forbidden books. The reason was the Church's perception that Greene had condoned the protagonist's transgressions and had implied that God condoned them, too.

Writing from a Catholic point of view in *Commonweal*, British author Evelyn Waugh expressed the disgust of many Catholics who read the book: "To me the ideal of willing my own damnation for the love of God is either a very loose poetical expression or a mad blasphemy, for the God who accepted that sacrifice could be neither just nor lovable."

Other artists and intellectuals criticized the novel for the opposite reason, that Greene seemed to be preaching a particular brand of religion rather than creating a work of art, despite his protest that *The Heart of the Matter*, unlike his *The Power and the Glory* (1940), was no thesis novel.

Even though the novel was damned by many, it made a positive impression on many of its readers as a thinking man's approach to religion, free of dogma. For them, Greene corroborated much of what they had suspected all along, that God concerned himself with important, heartfelt issues—"the heart of the matter"—not most transgressions. Many of Greene's readers felt liberated by what they considered to be his rational vision of God, his acknowledgment of the complicated nature of morality and salvation, and his sympathetic view of human nature, so at odds with established Christianity.

Additional Readings: A.A. DeVitis, *Graham Greene* (Boston: Twayne, 1986); Robert H. Miller, *Understanding Graham Greene* (Columbia: University of South Carolina Press, 1990).

62. *Lord of the Flies,* by William Golding (England, 1954).

Golding's novel, which contradicted the myth of human innocence, appeared in 1954 at a time when the horrors of World War II were fresh in the minds of people throughout the world. Golding's position was that one could scarcely argue that human beings were basically good in light of the devastation of civilians—women, children, the sick, and the old—during the war. In the bombing blitz on London, 30,000 civilians had died; 50,000 had been injured; and hundreds of thousands had been rendered homeless. German women and children had suffered similar losses when on February 13, 1945, Allied firebombing of Dresden had killed 135,000 civilians and destroyed 80 percent of the city. And in the bombing of Hiroshima, as many as 70,000 nonmilitary citizens, most of them women and children, were killed or missing, and 68 percent of the city was destroyed.

The full extent of humankind's capacity for evil was uncovered only after the war when it was discovered that almost 6 million Jewish civilians alone had perished in ghettos and concentration camps, even more having suffered unspeakably. Millions more people considered to be ethnically or politically tainted also died.

Other conflicts gave the lie to the myth of innocence as well. In 1947, 150,000 people died in hostilities between India and Pakistan, and between 1952 and 1956, British soldiers put down a rebellion by killing 10,000 members of the Mau Mau tribe in Africa.

To illustrate what he saw as the truth of human nature, Golding places his characters in a natural setting, untouched by civilization. Young boys being transported by plane in World War II crash in a remote, uninhabited area. In the initial days of cooperation, three boys emerge as leaders: Ralph, the charismatic young fellow with social skills, takes the lead; Piggy, a chubby boy with glasses, derided by the others, becomes, nevertheless, the intellect behind Ralph; and Jack, the young, physically adroit boy who is knowledgeable about nature, becomes the hunter of pigs to feed the boys.

After the first stage of cooperation, human nature goes awry, as Jack begins to return to savagery, senselessly slaughtering animals while whooping and dressing in war paint. He begins to challenge Ralph's leadership. His followers' accidental killing of another boy releases their animalism, and they hunt down Piggy, crush his glasses, and eventually kill him. At the same time, they terrorize the rest of Ralph's followers into joining Jack.

Their next prey is Ralph himself whom they decide to kill and decapitate. In the process of capturing him, however, they are discovered by a naval officer who at first thinks they are engaged in childish play, like cowboys and Indians. But his presence immediately reduces them to children, and they begin to weep.

Golding's manuscript, which was rejected by twenty-one publishers before it was finally accepted, received a fairly cool reception from the literary critics. It was the public who immediately recognized the worth of the novel. Within a year, it had over 1 million copies in sales. It quickly came to be regarded as a classic, and Golding became a celebrity. Its influence has spread through its presence on school reading lists and the two film adaptations (1963, United Kingdom; 1990, United States) of the novel. In 1983, chiefly on the strength of this novel, Golding received the Nobel Prize for Literature, and in 1988, he was knighted by Queen Elizabeth.

The novel's chief influence came from the debate and discussion it stimulated over the romantic, pastoral ideal, borne of Émile Rousseau and Ralph Waldo Emerson, that children and nature are basically innocent and that it is society that corrupts human nature, a view coupled with the idea of the Noble Savage, that the uncivilized human being closest to nature and removed from society is the noblest. Readers saw from Golding's novel the possibility that human nature is depraved, that isolation from civilization leads to superstition, savagery, and evil, and that violence and class distinctions are inevitable.

The novel came to be the means for understanding what had happened in World War II and, furthermore, generated discussion of the nature of leadership and power.

Politically, the novel spoke against anarchism as a political theory, against humanistic optimism as an approach, and against the welfare state as a panacea.

Additional Readings: Robert Hewison, *British Culture in the Cold War* (New York: Oxford University Press, 1981); Kirsten Olsen, *Understanding Lord of the Flies* (Westport, CT: Greenwood Press, 2000); Patrick Reilly, *Lord of the Flies* (New York: Twayne, 1992).

63. *A Clockwork Orange*, by Anthony Burgess (England, 1962). Anthony Burgess's shocking futuristic novel is firmly grounded in the international affairs of the late 1950s and early 1960s, especially the single-minded focus in the United States and the USSR on technological and scientific advances, along with evidences throughout the world of a social collapse. Burgess noted that during a time of space exploration, with the increased international competition that came with the launching of Sputnik, so-called modernized countries had begun to ignore the everyday needs of people on earth.

This had, in his view, contributed to a social collapse that he saw graphically represented in the inability of law and order to deal effectively and humanely with the consequences of misplaced government priorities—the outlaw gangs of youth on the rise in the USSR and Britain. In Leningrad, gangs called *stilyagi* roamed the city on senseless and destructively violent forays. In London, similar gangs arose, called teddy boys.

In Burgess's novel, Alex, a member of such a gang in a country that seems a mixture of Russia and the United States, is a portrait of unmitigated evil. Alex, who is inclined toward sadism and classical music, tells the story of his several transformations by technological conditioning. At the beginning, he and members of his gang delight in terrorizing the populace with torture, rape, and murder. But his career as a criminal is interrupted when a friend knocks him over the head at a crime scene and calls the police.

To protect society, the government puts him through their new antiviolence program by giving him a drug that makes him sick at the same time he is forced to view violent films and listen to classical music. The program is a success in that Alex is conditioned to avoid both violence and classical music and is subsequently freed.

Now Alex becomes a victim himself. He is beaten up repeatedly by other gang members and taken in by a man he recognizes as one of the victims of his own violence when he was a gang member. His benefactor, F. Alexander, who doesn't immediately recognize Alex as one of the boys who had raped and murdered his wife, plans to use Alex in his campaign against the government and its antiviolence conditioning. Alex's new friend has written a book called "The Clockwork Orange," which argues that people, like oranges, are organic and should not be mechanically programmed. Thus, he argues, Alex has been brutalized, has had his humanity taken away when the government took his choice away. To prove the antigovernment argument, F. Alexander and his followers try to drive Alex to suicide.

But Alex survives his leap out a window and is deprogrammed by the government, which is eager to avoid further unflattering public relations. Alex is sent home as the same kind of person he was when he was first arrested: He is violent, and he loves classical music.

In the American edition, this is how the story ends, but in the English edition, Alex has an enlightenment and is redeemed, deciding that he will get an ordinary, harmless job and raise a family.

What has been described as Burgess's dystopian nightmare was an immediate success, its popularity and impact doubling with the Stanley Kubrick film made in 1971, which did not include the redemptive ending and, it has been charged, was soon suppressed because of its excessive violence.

On one level, the novel impressed on its readers the dangers of a cold technological society that leads to urban decay, easy drug access, and mindless materialism, which in turn produces monsters like Alex. It was also seen as an antigovernment novel in the tradition of George Orwell, but it was actually just as critical of rebellions against government.

On another level, Alex and his gang, despite their evil, were seen as compelling characters in a deadening society. Something of a minor cult developed around Alex's character with his private language, "nadsat," and his stylized dress.

Burgess's book also prophetically preceded large-scale interest in, and many sociological studies of, the nature of the urban gang.

Additional Readings: James E. Cronin and Jonathan Schneer, *Social Conflict and the Political Order in Modern Britain* (New Brunswick, NJ: Rutgers University Press, 1982); A.A. Vitis, *Anthony Burgess* (New York: Twayne, 1972).

France

1700–1799

⁇

Abbé Prévost, *Manon Lescaut*, 1731

Voltaire, *Candide; or, Optimism*, 1759

Jean-Jacques Rousseau, *Julie, or the New Heloise*, 1761

Jean-Jacques Rousseau, *Émile*, 1762

Pierre Choderlos de Laclos, *Dangerous Liaisons*, 1782

Bernardin de Saint Pierre, *Paul and Virginia*, 1788

Marquis de Sade, *Justine; or The Misfortunes of Virtue*, 1791

⁇

1700–1799: TIMELINE

1637   René Descartes's *Discourse on Method* is published.

1643   Louis XIV comes to power in France as the epitome of the divine right to absolute power.

1648   Civil war in France is waged by bourgeois and workers in protest of Louis's unscrupulous collection of taxes.

1667–68   Louis must go to war against a European Triple Alliance, waged over Louis's European imperialism.

1672–78   Louis attacks the Dutch Republic.

1685   Louis revokes the religious toleration set forth in the Edict of Nantes. Protestant worship is henceforth outlawed, prompting 300,000 valued workers to leave France.

1689–97   France's economy is placed under further strain by the War of the League of Augsburg.

1702–13   The War of Spanish Succession over the dispensation of the Spanish kingdom ends with Louis's grandson on the throne of Spain but without the union of Spain and France that he had hoped for.

1708   Bishop Jacques Bossuet publishes his *Politics Drawn from the Very Words of Scripture*, in which he argues for the absolute divine power of the king.

1715	Louis XIV dies and is succeeded by Louis XV.
1731	Abbé Prévost's *Manon Lescaut* is published.
1740–48	The War of Austrian Succession further drains France's economy.
1748	Montesquieu publishes *The Spirit of Laws.*
1751	Denis Diderot publishes his *Encyclopedea.*
1755	All of Europe is traumatized by the All Saints' Day earthquake in Lisbon, killing 30,000, including holy men and women of the church.
1756–63	France is involved in the Seven Years' War in both Europe and North America. It ends with France's loss of its colonies in India and America.
1759	Voltaire's *Candide* is published.
1760	The Council of Geneva orders *Candide* burned, and the Catholic Church denounces it as heresy.
	Louis XV ends the right of *parlement* to veto his decrees.
1761	Jean-Jacques Rousseau publishes *Julie.*
1762	Jean-Jacques Rousseau publishes *The Social Contract* and *Émile.*
1774	Louis XIV comes to the French throne.
1778	France comes to the aid of the Americans in their war of independence from Britain, once more incurring great debts. Intolerable taxes are placed on the lower classes, and the new and powerful middle class becomes increasingly dissatisfied.
1782	Pierre Choderlos de Laclos's *Dangerous Liaisons* is published.
1788	Louis strips *parlement* of its power.
	Bernardin de Saint-Pierre's *Paul and Virginia* is published.
	Along with mounting problems in France, there are years of bad crops and shortages of bread.
1789	The Estates-General, though long since officially stripped of its power, meets in a state of national crisis. The National Assembly of France is created.
	French peasants storm the Bastille: The French Revolution is under way.
	The "Declaration of the Rights of Man and Citizen" is issued.
1790	Edmund Burke writes *Reflections on the Revolution in France.*
1791	The Marquis de Sade's *Justine* is published.
1791–92	Tom Paine writes *The Rights of Man* in answer to Burke.
1792	The French monarchy is overthrown, and the First French Republic is formed.
1793	The king is executed in January, and the Reign of Terror under the Jacobins begins.
	By March 1793, France is at war with all of Europe.
1795	The government called the Directory rules France until 1799.
1799	A military coup led by Napoleon unseats the Directory and establishes a Consulate under Napoleon's leadership.

64. *Manon Lescaut*, by Abbé Prévost (France, 1731). *Manon Lescaut*, set in the eighteenth century during the Regency in the France of Philippe d'Orleans, is a story of obsession in a dissolute, libertine society. The action takes place in both France and the French colony of New Orleans in the New World.

The French Regency, which was in control after Louis XIV died and before the young king, a child, could assume the throne, was one of the most corrupt in French history. Over the years, the royal court, in collaboration with the nobility, had constructed a system consisting of a small group of privileged and parasitic aristocracy at the top of the social scale who set examples of utter immorality and exploitation. At the bottom were masses of starving, tax-burdened peasants. The resulting class animosity was intense and bitter.

In such a licentious atmosphere at the top, with such poverty at the bottom, prostitution flourished. Among aristocrats, prostitution was often condoned as a means of gaining more palatial homes, more elegant clothes, more prestigious contacts. Among the poor, it was often a necessity, as an option to slow death. It has been estimated that Paris had from 40,000 to 60,000 prostitutes during the Regency. In rare cases, when a prostitute was arrested, her hair was cut off. If she offended someone of importance or in other ways made herself unpopular, she would be sent to the French colony in Louisiana.

Manon (volume VII of a series called *Memoirs and Adventures of a Man of Quality*), published in Paris in 1731, was originally titled *The Adventures of the Chevalier Des Grieux et de Manon Lescaut, by Monsieur D.* In the story, a nameless marquis witnesses a group of girls being sent to Louisiana and is struck by the unusual beauty of one (Manon). He also notices that a man, the Chevalier Des Grieux, is in obvious despair over her departure. The marquis gives Des Grieux some money, thus enabling him to follow his lover, Manon, to Louisiana. Two years later, the marquis encounters Des Grieux again and listens to his story, which forms the basis of the novel.

In brief, Des Grieux met Manon when he was seventeen, she fifteen. She had been forced into a nunnery but escaped. They ran off together to Paris, considering themselves married but without benefit of the church. Des Grieux's brother found him and took him back home. Some time later when Des Grieux went back to Paris to join his lover, he discovered that Manon had already become the mistress of a wealthy banker, Monsieur B. Des Grieux was then found by his father who persuaded him to take holy orders. But Manon found him just as he was taking his vows, and they once more ran away together. Again and again, as time passed, Manon temporarily slept with other men or became someone else's mistress for a

time. Each time Des Grieux was devastated, and each time he believed her when she declared: "I *had* to do it. . . . I did it for you!"

At the last, he had followed her to Louisiana, where after further misadventures, he and Manon escaped from New Orleans into the "desert" of Louisiana. There, at last, she died. The story portrays the disintegration of a once-respectable man because of an obsession with a woman who sets pleasure and comfort above all else and who makes her way through the world horizontally, all the while retaining the inescapable hold she has on him.

The novel was a sensation in Paris. Prévost was singular in being able to gain sympathy for the morally dissolute characters in *Manon*, especially among his many court readers. No one had ever been so frank or had so sympathetically portrayed a courtesan. Unlike subsequent literary portrayals of prostitutes, Manon was not regarded as a victim. Though Prévost intended Des Grieux as his main focus, readers shared Des Grieux's obsession with Manon. The much longer original title of the novel eventually became shortened to just *Manon*. While some readers were obsessively admiring of Manon, others deplored Prévost's inherent sympathy for an amoral character.

The story marked another change in that though the story is about relationships between men and women, there is little in it that could be called love, in the traditional sense. Manon primarily uses sex as a commodity, a medium of exchange, while Des Grieux's passion might more accurately be labeled sick obsession, rather than love. For an audience used to tales of romantic, courtly love, *Manon* represented a distinct departure.

Its impact can be seen in its literary influence and in its adaptations and imitations, notably Alexander Dumas's *Camille* in 1848 and Prosper Merimée's *Carmen* in 1846. It still lives in the opera called simply *Manon*. In more modern times, the movie *The Blue Angel*, produced in Berlin in the early 1930s, with a script by Carl Zuckmeyer, starring Marlene Dietrich and directed by Joseph von

Sternberg, is clearly in the tradition of *Manon*.

Additional Readings: James P. Gilroy, *The Romantic Manon and Des Grieux: Images of Prévost's Heroine and Hero in French Literature* (Sherbrooke, Quebec: Noaman, 1980); Richard B. Smernoff, *L'Abbé Prévost* (Boston: Twayne, 1985).

65. *Candide; or, Optimism (Candide; ou, L'Optimisme)*, by Voltaire (France, 1759).

The most influential and famous work by Voltaire, the pen name of François-Marie Arouet, the figure who shaped his age, was the rollicking satire *Candide*.

Voltaire found much in his age to satirize. The eighteenth century was a time of scientific, geographic, and intellectual expansion. So important were its rational philosophical achievements that it is labeled the Age of Reason. Man, it was posited, could solve all of his problems with reason alone. In France, it was the age of the philosophes, who provided the intellectual bases for future social revolts, and of the encyclopedists, who would collect all man's significant knowledge into one series of volumes.

It was also an age of skepticism, poverty, and wars and of a relentless industrial process called the Industrial Revolution that ground down the poor and spilled their blood wherever their European monarchs directed their guns. It was an age of burdensome taxes, unjustly levied, which, along with the seething resentment of embittered masses and their leaders, armed with the new philosophical artillery, made the revolution inevitable.

It was a time of natural disasters as well as human ones. On November 1, 1755, on All Saints' Day, at nine in the morning, Mother Earth sent a quake that (in six and a half minutes) killed 15,000 people, fatally wounded 15,000 more, and destroyed thirty churches, on the very morning of a holy festival when great numbers of people were attending Mass. Devastated churchmen wondered with private anguish why God had thus unleashed His wrath upon them and

had killed or wounded so many of the faithful, including many nuns and priests.

Despite the wars and poverty, the economic and political instability, and the natural disasters, there was also endless optimism. Alexander Pope, the English poet, in a moment of heady optimism, typical of the age wrote in the "Essay on Man": "Whatever is, is right" (line 94). And the seventeenth century thinker Gottfried Wilhelm von Leibniz philosophized, "This is the best of all possible worlds" *Theodicy* [La Salle, IL: Open Court Publishing Co., 1985]).

Voltaire's reaction to the disasters of the age was in total opposition to Leibniz's. A few months after the All Saints' Day earthquake, Voltaire wrote an angry poem, in part a reaction to a general sense of optimism that he himself had shared earlier: "On the Lisbon Disaster, or An Examination of the Axiom 'All Is Well.' " But his most famous response to the earthquake is his blistering satire *Candide*, ridiculing virtually every philosophical idea in the eighteenth century but chiefly its indomitable optimism in the face of multiple disasters.

It is the story of the naive hero Candide, who learns at the knee of his optimistic mentor, Dr. Pangloss, and pines for the eternally evasive heroine Cunegonde (a word with a libidinous connotation). It is told in the manner of the old courtly love tales and is fraught with every imaginable disaster. Candide lives through an earthquake; he is impressed into fighting in a battle where most of the soldiers are maimed or die; he returns to find that half of Dr. Pangloss's face is missing, the result of a case of syphilis; and he learns that his beloved Cunegonde has been raped and taken as a slave. In the course of their journeys, he and Dr. Pangloss are shipwrecked, and Dr. Pangloss is arrested and hanged, though he survives. Still, after all this death and devastation, Pangloss assures him that all is well and that they must cultivate their garden.

The immediate reaction to the satire was swift and unfriendly. Almost before the book was out, the Great Council of Geneva ordered it to be burned. The book enraged

Voltaire's readers, especially political and religious leaders, with its ridicule of everything they held dear: the Church, the caste system, the criminal code, slavery, war, and above all, optimism. In 1806 Pope Pius VII placed *Candide* on the Roman Index of books prohibited by the Roman Catholic Church, and as recently as 1928, copies of the novel were seized by U.S. customs officials in Boston.

Yet for many readers at the time it was an exposé of all they had come to deplore in a society that cheerfully sent out cannon fodder for the wars of the monarchs and smugly declared that class and economic injustice were just meant to be.

The ending was variously interpreted by the age: Some readers believed that Dr. Pangloss's final decision to just "tend his own garden" was the voice of Voltaire, recommending resignation in the face of universal human and natural disaster. You just make your own life and the lives of others worse to struggle against the inevitable. Others found that Voltaire was satirizing such an abdication of responsibility for everything beyond one's own isolated "garden."

However one interprets the ending of *Candide*, Voltaire's satire, which stands as one of the grand achievements of the eighteenth century, it helped defame the erroneous pretensions of the age in the face of disaster.

Despite its continued notoriety among religious leaders, *Candide* has remained one of the most widely read works in modern literature and a consistently studied work in courses on the history of ideas and world literature.

Additional Readings: Hadyn Mason, *Voltaire* (New York: St. Martin's Press, 1975); Renee Waldinger, ed., *Approaches to Teaching Voltaire's "Candide"* (New York: Modern Language Association of America, 1987).

66. *Julie, or the New Heloise* (*La Nouvelle Heloise*), by Jean-Jacques Rousseau (France, 1761).

The focus of *Julie*, one of the most popular works in European literature, is not on plot but rather on ideas, primarily the concept of virtue and how it relates to tenderness, sentiment, and passion. Marriage itself at this time among the aristocracy and the wealthy bourgeoisie was a matter of contractual and financial convenience, as it had been for centuries, and adultery was an accepted way of life, so long as the women, at least, were discreet. In the eighteenth century at the time of the Regency, the duchesse of Chaulnes explained to her son, when he vehemently objected to being forced to marry the daughter of a rich merchant to get money into the family, that "to marry advantageously beneath oneself is merely taking dung to manure one's acres" (Louis Ducros, *French Society in the Eighteenth Century* [London: G. Bell, 1926], p. 61). This vignette tells something of the way the aristocratic mind worked in the days of the Old Regime. True love and sentiment were of little importance; marriage was entirely about money and social station. It suggests why Rousseau's novel was so distinctive and so popular and why the *ideas* in the work made it a precursor of what was to come in the next half century.

The story is simple. Seventeen-year-old Julie is the daughter of Baron d'Etrange. Saint-Pierre is her tutor. They fall passionately in love and ultimately consummate their love, after which both are guilt-ridden. Julie at last confesses her sin to her parents. Her father, brutally aware that marriage cannot be considered with a "lower-class" person, beats her severely, causing a miscarriage. Her mother dies of heartbreak. Julie, forgiving her father, at his bidding marries Wolmar, an older, extremely honorable man whom she does not love. At last she confesses to him, too, but he assures her that this was no sin and even invites Saint-Pierre to be the tutor of their children, knowing that, being wholly virtuous people, the two former lovers will not betray his trust. Amazingly, they do remain virtuous. In the end, when Julie dies, she sends a letter to Saint-Pierre declaring that he is the only man she ever truly loved.

Readers in a society where adultery on the part of wives and husbands and casual sex were commonplace found Rousseau's novel about virtuous characters, to be, quite literally, revolutionary. Rousseau had painted a picture of true love as natural love. What twists the course of true love is the violent prejudice of society itself and the pervasive evil in those who ruled society by smothering the human heart.

The immediate reception to *Julie* was sensational. It was one of the most rapidly selling books in history and the bestseller of the entire eighteenth century. The public clamored for it hysterically, paying higher prices than usual for the chance to read and own it. When they couldn't purchase it, they even rented it at exorbitant prices. By the end of the century, it had gone through seventy-two editions and was still selling phenomenally well. Rousseau was even mobbed by the ladies of Paris. Furthermore, *Julie*, rivaling only Goethe's *Young Werther* and Benardin de Saint-Pierre's *Paul and Virginia* in popularity, stimulated a major industry in the production of artifacts and mementos.

The concrete and comprehensive influences of Rousseau on the Western world are so immense as to be beyond calculation: On the global level, he stimulated the romanticism that flourished in the nineteenth century. On a national level, he contributed to the French Revolution. On an individual level, he changed the course of child rearing.

Julie clearly is not just a love story. In the novel, Rousseau discusses the famous ideas that were to rock his world: on religion, justice, social prejudice, music, atheism, education, and nature, to name a few. Fundamental to all his philosophy is the conviction that nature is good, and society and urban life are wretched and corrupting. The prejudice that tears lovers apart is a monstrosity. The enforced celibacy of Catholic priests is unnatural and wrong. Faith provides strength and salvation. In the novel, it is a diligent adherence to the Protestant church that saves Julie. At the same time, Wolmar, who demonstrates saintly understanding and honor, is an atheist. So the author demonstrates the efficacy of toleration and recommends intellectual independence. Although Rousseau had already expressed some of these basic ideas in previous works, this is the novel that propelled him into fame and that distributed those ideas to all of Europe.

His romanticism can be seen in the value he places on nature over civilization, on sentiment over reason, on individualism over society, and on the present rather than the past.

His antiauthoritarian approach, which recommends dispensing with old forms and traditions, helped bring about the French Revolution. Shortly after the revolution, it was a commonly accepted notion that Rousseau's ideas, especially as they were promulgated in this popular novel, were major forces in inciting revolution.

On a more individual level, readers of the novel adopted his radical theories of child rearing and education, all based on his conviction that children are uncorrupted beings and that whatever is considered natural is always what is best. For example, he writes that children should not be treated as little adults; don't "reason" with them until after puberty. In the daily newspaper columns on child rearing and in colleges of education, theories based on Rousseau's beliefs are still argued today, especially with regard to discipline and toleration of a child's individual inclinations.

Additional Readings: James F. Jones, Jr., "*La Nouvelle Heloise*": *Rousseau and Utopia* (Geneva: Droz, 1978); Peggy Kamuf, *Fiction and Feminine Desire: Disclosures of Heloise* (Lincoln: University of Nebraska Press, 1982).

67. *Émile*, by Jean-Jacques Rousseau (France, 1762). When eighteenth-century philosopher Immanuel Kant first picked up Rousseau's *Émile*, he reportedly became so entranced that he forgot to take his daily walk. It is a tribute to Rousseau, not only that he changed the thinking of his own time but that he has mesmerized individual readers of every nationality for centuries with his 450-page treatise on education. This treatise, masquerading as a novel, begins as an effort to advise a woman, Mme. D'Epinay, on the best way to educate her son; but then gradually the scene transmogrifies as Rousseau introduces, for the purpose of making it concrete and objectively real, the figure of a boy and a tutor. Rousseau thought of it as a sequel to *Julia, or the New Heloise*: How should Julia's children be educated? Thus the importance of the book lies in its ideas.

Rousseau begins, first, with a revolt against civilization. Nature is good; children are close to nature and are deformed by civilization with its stupefying tradition of facts and rote memory. That training is best that gets farthest away from then-current practices. The first line in the book iterates and summarizes his often-repeated thesis: "Everything is good as it comes from the hands of the Creator; everything degenerates in the hands of man." This is actually a more trenchant, though less dramatic, observation than the more famous one of *The Social Contract* (1762): "Man was born free, but everywhere he is in chains."

Rousseau takes his fictive Émile through several "natural" stages of development: (1) the period of infancy, from birth to age five; (2) childhood, from five to twelve; (3) the age of reason, from twelve to fifteen; and (4) the social or mature stage, from fifteen to twenty.

In infancy, one is to follow nature by allowing freedom from restraint. Mothers are to breast-feed their babies, not turn them over to wet nurses. The stress is on nature and independence, along with free self-expression. In the second stage, the operative idea is experience; one learns from natural activities, from *doing*, not reasoning. The inner person should be allowed to emerge. In the third stage, conventional education begins in the manner of *Robinson Crusoe*: Here one learns practical things about the world of nature. The important subjects are geography, astronomy, physical science, and practical arts. The main concern should be learning not mere facts but rather methods of thought. Nothing is to be acquired from authority. In the last stage, such problems as sex, social life, beauty, morality, religion, and the higher virtues are studied. The emerging student would, specifically, *not* be a musician, actor, or writer. He might, however, be a "gentleman carpenter," a notion that greatly amused pre–French Revolution aristocrats.

Speaking about the education for girls,

Rousseau, while noting that females are by nature subordinated to males, recommends, nevertheless, that young women be prepared for life's realities.

> Is a woman able to pass by sudden alterations from one mode of life to another without risk or danger? Can she be a nurse today, an Amazon tomorrow? . . . How long has it been since men concerned themselves with the education of girls? Who debars their mothers from bringing them up in whatever manner they please? . . . The more their sex tries to resemble ours, the less influence they will have over us; and then it is that we shall be really their masters.

It should be noted, too, that Émile rises early; he loves the morning chill; and he washes often. Winter and summer, he bathes in ice-cold water.

Émile resulted in some interesting practical changes: It encouraged a trend for bathing in cold water, as a matter of good health and a stimulation to the spirit, and it caused mothers of the time suddenly to begin breast-feeding their babies: Among other things, he noted, this established a bond between mother and child; otherwise, the bond would be established between wet nurse and child.

In a period of fifteen months, Rousseau published three books that shook the world and that have continued to shape human behavior. As historians have noted, after 1761, Rousseau *owned* the eighteenth century.

Virtually every experimental movement in education since that time has, in one way or another, owed a debt to Rousseau's novel. Modern educational theory begins with *Émile*. Before *Émile*, conventional education in Europe consisted in studies of Greek and Latin literature, some smattering of Renaissance science memorized, along with lists of facts, and holdovers of medieval Scholasticism, largely unchanged since the days of Abelard. Discipline at the time was severe. Rousseau virtually eliminated it. Conventional religion said that man was "bad," born with a corrupt heart. Rousseau maintained that man was born good, and it was "civilization" that corrupted him. Conventional wisdom, in addition, tried to protect children from risky adventures. Rousseau recommended that they take risks and that they learn by doing, not just by listening.

In every possible way, Rousseau challenged the wisdom and the practices of the times. Thinkers and earthshakers of subsequent years could disagree with Rousseau, and they could rail at his inadequacies or his absurdities, but they could never ignore him.

Additional Readings: Carol Blum, *Rousseau and the Republic of Virtue: The Language of Politics in the French Revolution* (Ithaca, NY: Cornell University Press, 1986); English Showalter, *The Evolution of the French Novel (1641–1782)* (Princeton, NJ: Princeton University Press, 1972).

68. *Dangerous Liaisons* (*Les Liaisons dangereuses*), by Pierre Choderlos de Laclos (France, 1782).

France, at the time of Laclos's novel, was facing an increasingly intense series of crises. The coffers were bare, the state was nearing financial bankruptcy, and public and private morality, especially among the upper classes who alone ruled the country, had been disintegrating for most of the century. The Seven Years' War had depleted the treasury, dangerously increasing taxes chiefly paid by the poor and making the nation vulnerable to attack. At the same time, a further drain on the budget was created when the government of Louis XVI, as part of its long-standing conflict with England, had given serious aid to rebelling American colonies.

For centuries now the Church as an organization had been under attack; and for two generations, the best minds of the day had attacked all supernatural beliefs, thus undermining the fundamental principles on which traditional morality was based. The number of monasteries was dwindling, as was the number of monks within them. As the nation was nearing financial chaos, the Church, as an organization, was rolling in wealth. At the same time the parish priests, like their parishioners, lived in extreme poverty but gave most of their money in tithes to the bishops, whom they watched live in

luxury. Even many priests and bishops, scattered throughout the country, had ceased truly to believe in God and were retaining pretense of their beliefs to control the public, for "utility," or to preserve their own positions. The king, Louis XVI, reportedly refused to let a priest teach his son because he was afraid that the son would thus lose his belief in God. Six years after Laclos's novel, a peasant wrote to a government official: "The poor suffer from cold and hunger while the canons feast and think of nothing but fattening themselves like pigs that are to be killed for Easter" (quoted by Will Durant in *Rousseau and Revolution* [New York: Simon and Schuster, 1967], p. 902). The serious minds of the day debated whether the great mass of people could ever be held to standards of morality after their belief in God had been undermined or destroyed.

Rousseau's *Nouvelle Heloise* had been written twenty-one years earlier. His novel was still popular, still being read widely and favorably, when *Dangerous Liaisons* came out. It was General Laclos's only novel and only comment on the disintegrating society of his day.

This novel shows scandalous intrigues among a corrupt ruling class only a few years from total collapse. The titillated aristocrats here, for example, exchange notes on successful techniques of seduction and plan how to have a fifteen-year-old girl deflowered as she leaves a convent. The leading figure argues that most men are kept from fulfilling their evil desires only because they are intimidated by moral traditions and that one should, therefore, pursue whatever gives him pleasure.

While the epistolary form shows exchanges of letters among twelve uniquely portrayed writers, the chief machinator is Mme. de Merteuil, a dissolute woman who shows genuine respect for hardly anyone and who expresses patent contempt for other women. Addressing one letter to a man, she declares that she intends to "avenge" her own sex and to "dominate yours." Thus she proceeds to manipulate both the men and the women whom she encounters. The story shows a universal process of deception and of slow disintegration. It also shows an atmosphere in which people pursue only their own passions and their own desires to control and manipulate, and to use other people in this pursuit, without consideration of morality or the welfare of others as human beings.

The novel was written to shock the audience with its story of the mean-spirited machinations, undertaken by jaded adults to sexually assault a virginal young girl. And shock it did. The audience was appalled to see the characters declare that the pleasure of sexual conquest would be much less if the girl, being too willing, turned it into more of a seduction than an assault.

Unfortunately, while many readers were shocked, they reacted in ways the author did not intend nor anticipate. Many missed his irony altogether and either denounced him as a shameless admirer of the ruthless society he portrayed or lauded him for providing them with lighthearted, pleasurably wicked amusement.

Although it is a parody of Rousseau's *Julie*, it is also, like the body of Rousseau's work, part of the canon that inspired romanticism—but in a wholly ironic, negative sense, for it shows just how cruel and depraved sexual relations without love and sentiment can be.

The importance of Laclos's novel is that it held up a mirror to his time. It succeeded in forever characterizing late-eighteenth-century France as utterly degenerate and without the least moral scruples or guilt.

While causing a sensation in the eighteenth century, it was subsequently neglected for most of the nineteenth. It was, however, revived to form the basis of a highly successful American movie in 1988.

Additional Readings: Lloyd Free, ed., *Laclos: Critical Approaches to "Les Liaisons dangereuses"* (Madrid: José Porrua Turanzas, 1978); Ronald Rosbottom, *Choderlos de Laclos* (Boston: Twayne, 1978).

69. *Paul and Virginia*, by Bernardin de Saint-Pierre (France, 1788).

Paul and Virginia was written in 1788, during the last gasp of the Old Regime in France. A century of wars had bankrupted France. In particular, the Seven Years' War had depleted the treasury and lost an empire in India and in America. Furthermore, France had, largely to spite their ancient enemies the British, provided extensive aid to the rebelling American colonies. The time seemed ripe for revolution. The feckless and corrupt ruling class was represented by a wildly extravagant queen, Marie Antoinette. In contrast, the great masses of common people were starving. For the peasants there were failing crops and an oppressive, medieval tax system. A peasant paid taxes to the state, the lord, and the Church. He was taxed if he crossed a bridge or owned a fireplace, while French nobility were virtually immune. A peasant could not kill a game bird or animal—that was reserved for aristocratic hunters, who did not pay for trampling the peasant's crops or destroying his fences. There were bread shortages, and lack of bread meant starvation. Tension and violence were in the air. Troops were assembled. Pamphlets deriding the queen were passed out in the streets. And on July 14, 1789, one year after the publication of Saint-Pierre's novel, the commoners of Paris occupied the Bastille. The revolution had begun.

The vision of life in *Paul and Virginia* is as far removed from the chaos and corruption of 1788 Paris as it could possibly be. Saint-Pierre, a follower of Rousseau and a believer in the natural man and the virtue of the simple, natural life, sets his story on a subtropical island in the Indian Ocean. Two pregnant French women living on the island give birth to a boy and a girl, Paul and Virginia. They grow up together, weathering various childhood adventures at each other's side. Eventually, they realize their love for each other. The idyll does not last forever, for their lives are complicated with Virginia's return to France, where she has unexpectedly inherited a fortune. After a time, she turns her back on the offer of an advantageous marriage, as well as great wealth, to return to Paul. As her ship approaches the shore, however, it runs into shallows and is hit by a storm, and she drowns, trying to reach the shore. Paul dies a year later of a broken heart.

In its praise of natural virtues, *Paul and Virginia* is one of the indisputable precursors of nineteenth-century romanticism. Despite, or because of, its attack on prevailing attitudes of the court, *Paul and Virginia* was one of the most popular works in France for over a century. In an age of cynicism, it assured its readers of the efficacy of virtue as a counterweight to depraved court life in the city. In an age of artifice and sophistication, the novel provided the antidote of romanticism with its admiration of sensibility and nature.

In France, Virginia is exploited; on the idyllic island, she is loved and valued as a human being; so it is not surprising that women, especially, believed that Saint-Pierre articulated for them something about their lives that they had felt but not expressed: that sophisticated civilization degraded them. In France, men tyrannized over women by giving them in marriage without love to indifferent or old or incompetent husbands.

Many readers also found in *Paul and Virginia* expression for the weariness and distaste that they had long felt, but not dared express, with modern society, especially the prevailing sophisticated view that actions close to and in harmony with nature were despicable and that work with one's hands, especially farming, was demeaning.

Paul and Virginia was one of the few works whose immense popularity was not altered by the revolution. Like Rousseau's works, this novel continued to enjoy great popularity with the ladies of Paris. It is a measure of the novel's continued influence that Gustave Flaubert has Emma Roualt reading *Paul and Virginia* in *Madame Bovary*.

Another proof of its popularity is found in its stimulation of a market in popular arts connected to it. French readers for a century collected mementos and artifacts, ranging from dinner plates to engraved prints and tapestries decorated with scenes and characters from *Paul and Virginia*.

Additional Readings: Angelica Goodden, *The Complete Lover: Eros, Nature, and Artifice in the Eighteenth-Century Novel* (Oxford: Clarendon Press, 1989); E.J. Hobsbawn, *The Age of Revolution, 1789–1848* (New York: New American Library, 1962); Vivienne Mylne, *The Eighteenth-Century French Novel: Techniques of Illusion* (Manchester: Manchester University Press, 1965).

70. *Justine; or The Misfortunes of Virtue (Justine ou Les Malheurs de la vertu)*, **by Marquis de Sade (France, 1791).** Donatien Alphonse François, Marquis de Sade, a titled member of the nobility, a onetime army officer, and an acknowledged adventurer and predator, spent thirty years in prison, died in an insane asylum, and wrote books that because of their sexual perversity have had a life of their own and have added Sade's name—"sadism"—as an adjective to the English language.

Justine stands as the last of an era, the production of a man guilty of murder, flagellation, and torture, who would turn his crimes into a way of life and a philosophy. Written at the same general period as Bernadin de Saint-Pierre's *Paul and Virginia*, the work stands as a striking contrast to that work in its view of human society and the human heart. In a paean to virtue, Saint-Pierre writes of idyllic love on a subtropical island far removed from the innate corruption of great cities and stifling governments. Sade, thematically, at least, portrays a world unrelieved by virtue or anything remotely resembling it. It is a world of cosmic and human emptiness and brutality. In Justine's world, there is no kindness, no brotherhood, no trust, no holding out a hand to a neighbor or a fellow being in distress.

Two sisters, twelve-year-old Justine (representing Virtue) and fifteen-year-old Juliette (representing Vice), are cast out of a convent and forced to part. After many years, they are reunited, just when Justine is to be executed for crimes she did not commit and Juliette is now the wife of Count de Lorsange as well as the mistress of another wealthy man. Justine then tells the story of her unfortunate life consisting of a long series of brutal assaults. Each time, Justine attempts to stop the assaults of her torturers, which include many learned men, by persuading them of the superior merits of virtue—but to no avail. Thus the author injects philosophical discussions into the story.

The initial reaction to *Justine* was disgust, but many readers claimed to have found Sade's philosophy in the novel very liberating, in that it freed them from the guilt usually associated with the pursuit of pleasure. The novel repudiated the idea that God will somehow protect the virtuous and the good in this life and reward them in the next. *Justine* conveyed to them, in effect, that there is no God; that we construct our own guilty consciences; and that virtuous people only invite evil and cruel people to take advantage of them. In short, to be virtuous is to be a victim and spend one's life being imposed upon and tortured. His readers came away with the impression that the very concept of crime was only a temporary social convention. In the 1960s, Sade was revived by those with a skewed reading of situational ethics.

Justine renewed philosophical discussion of the implication of eighteenth-century speculation. Philosophers had considered whether society could exist if there were no concept of God. Would morality, the cement that holds society together, totally collapse for the common people, given such a view? Denis Diderot, among others, had spent much of his life trying to devise a workable system of *natural* morality and had failed. Others, at the same time, arrived at what was called Deism, the idea of a clockmaker God that, in effect, retained the idea of God and Christian morality while discarding supernatural elements. Sade's novel pushed the processes of eighteenth-century reasoning to the extreme, as a kind of reductio ad absurdum: If there is no God, and to Sade there is not, then any kind of human behavior is possible. What results, inevitably, he suggests, is the pleasure of torture. Like Dracula, to which Sade gave rise later, Sade's creations represent the darkness of the human soul and the bankruptcy of all human values. In a world without God, the characters in *Justine* can justify their personal pleasure, which is torture. *Justine* opened up a great abyss in the human mind and soul, projecting a dismal future born of disbelief.

Such a view also, it was thought, removed any protection of the underclasses, including women, who could now be exploited by the upper classes without fear of guilt in this life or punishment in the next.

Although initial reaction to the novel was disgust, Sade did find sympathetic readers in the eighteenth century. In the nineteenth, *Justine* was universally banned, though it had an influence on Gustave Flaubert, Charles Baudelaire, and Algernon Chanes Swinburne. In the twentieth, he inspired Jean Genet and Henry Miller. He has been called the spirit of both leftist rebellion and fascist terror.

Additional Readings: Timo Airaksinen, *The Philosophy of the Marquis de Sade* (New York: Routledge, 1995); Georges Bataille, *Literature and Evil* (London: Calder and Boyars, 1973); Geoffrey Gorer, *The Life and Ideas of the Marquis de Sade* (London: Panther Books, 1953).

1800–1899

෨

Madame Anne Louise Germaine Necker de Staël, *Delphine*, 1802

François-René, Vicomte de Chateaubriand, *René*, 1802

Honoré de Balzac, *Père Goriot*, 1835

Eugène Sue, *The Mysteries of Paris*, 1843, 1844

George Sand, *Consuelo*, 1843

Gustave Flaubert, *Madame Bovary*, 1857

Victor-Marie Hugo, *Les Misérables*, 1862

Gustave Flaubert, *A Sentimental Education*, 1869
Jules Verne, *Twenty Thousand Leagues under the Sea*, 1869–1870
Émile Zola, *Germinal*, 1885

1800–1899: TIMELINE

1800   Robert Fulton invents a primitive submarine, the *Nautilus.*

1801   Napoleon Bonaparte negotiates with the pope to make the Catholic Church France's state church.

The Napoleonic Code enforces civil liberties and freedom of conscience but institutionalizes lack of equality for women.

1802   François-René, Vicomte de Chateaubriand publishes *René.*

Madame Anne Louise Germaine Necker de Staël's *Delphine* is published.

1803   Madame de Staël is banished from Paris by Napoleon.

1804   Napoleon crowns himself emperor.

1805–07   Napoleon launches his campaign to master Europe.

1806–08   Education is centralized in France.

1807   Madame de Staël is banished again after the publication of her novel *Corinne.*

1809   An early theory of evolution is published in Jean Baptiste Lamarck's *Zoological Philosophy.*

1814   Napoleon, defeated in battle, abdicates, surrenders to the allies, and is exiled to Elba.

A monarchy is established in France under the leadership of Louis XVIII.

1815   King Louis XVIII flees, and Napoleon returns as leader, reestablishing the empire.

Napoleon is defeated by the British at Waterloo and is sent into exile on St. Helena.

Louis XVIII returns to the throne of France—the Second Restoration.

1815–22   Jean Baptiste Lamarck's *The Natural History of Animals without Backbones* is published.

1817   George Cuvier's *Le regne animal*, a system of scientific classification, is published.

1821   Napoleon dies.

1824   Louis XVIII dies, and Charles X assumes the throne of France.

1830   Charles X institutes repressive measures, and the Chamber of Deputies votes no confidence in the king. He dismisses the Chamber.

In July, in what is known as the "July Revolution," workers, artisans, students, and writers barricade the streets for three days and defy the army and the police, forcing Charles to abdicate.

Louis Philippe ascends the throne, bringing modest reforms and economic growth.

1833   The postrevolutionary government passes laws to bring literature and education to the masses, but the lower classes are increasingly alienated. Seething resentment of the nouveau riche and aristocracy mounts.

1835   Honoré de Balzac's *Père Goriot* is published.

1840   Napoleon Bonaparte's remains are brought to Paris and entombed in a shrine.

1843   Eugène Sue's *The Mysteries of Paris* is published.

George Sand's *Consuelo* is published.

1848	There is 65 percent unemployment in the construction trades and 51 percent in the textile industry.
	After two days of rioting in late February, Louis Philippe abdicates.
	In June, riots occur again in Pairs. Some 13,000 people are killed and 12,000 are arrested and sent to labor camps in Algeria.
	The Second Republic is instituted under the presidency of Louis Napoleon Bonaparte, Napoleon's nephew.
1851	Victor Hugo goes into exile from France to protest the government of Napoleon III.
1852	Louis Napoleon declares France to be an empire and gives himself the title of Napoleon III.
1857	Gustave Flaubert's *Madame Bovary* is published and is followed by an obscenity trial.
1859	Charles Darwin's *On the Origin of Species* is published.
1862	Victor Hugo's *Les Misérables* is published.
1864	The Roman Catholic Church places *Les Misérables* on its Index of forbidden books.
1867	The French senate attempts to have all the novels of George Sand removed from all public libraries.
1869	Gustave Flaubert's *A Sentimental Education* is published.
1869–70	Jules Verne's *Twenty Thousand Leagues under the Sea* is published.
1870	The Second Empire falls and a Third Republic is established.
	Victor Hugo returns to France from exile.
1870–71	France is at war with Germany. Napoleon loses a battle and surrenders to the Germans.

1871	Civil war rages in France between the military and radical Republicans; the Republic prevails.
1872	The French Association for the Advancement of Science is established.
1880s	Ferry Laws establish separation between church and state schools and make education free and compulsory.
1885	Emile Zola's *Germinal* is published.
1886	Massive labor strikes occur in French mines, largely inspired by Zola's *Germinal*.
1890	Alfred Dreyfus, a Jewish officer, is unjustly convicted of espionage and sentenced to prison. He is later pardoned, through the efforts of Zola.

71. *Delphine*, by Madame Anne Louise Germaine Necker de Staël (France, 1802).

Madame de Staël's *Delphine*, universally recognized as one of the great novels of nineteenth-century France, is richly imbued with the gender political questions that are as timely at the turn of the twenty-first century as they were at the turn of the nineteenth.

At the time of the appearance of this, her first important novel, the political climate of Paris was decidedly turbulent, and Madame de Staël was at the center of the storm. She had at first admired Napoleon Bonaparte, leader of postrevolutionary France, but several issues had arisen that caused her to change her mind and to speak so frankly to her influential friends that she became his chief domestic enemy, his "nemesis," as Will and Ariel Durant wrote in their *Age of Napoleon* (Simon and Schuster, 1975). She openly opposed his policy of brutally crushing all political opposition, his widespread censorship of all literature he considered harmful to his reign, his scorn of and refusal to accept the advice of intellectuals, his scarcely concealed view of women as breeders and/or playthings, and his infringement of powers rightfully belonging to the legislature.

If Napoleon was irritated by Madame de Staël before her famous novel, he was enraged afterward. *Delphine* is the story of a virtuous young woman about whom untrue and malicious rumors are spread about numerous love affairs. She loves and is loved by an aristocratic young man named Leonce who because of the rumors avoids her and marries another. He is tricked into marrying Matilde de Vernon, a woman he doesn't love, by her mother, a diabolical schemer. As a consequence of his rejection, Delphine enters a convent where she takes a sacred vow of chastity for life. Too late, Leonce finds that Delphine has been innocent of the accusations all along and that his wife is physically and spiritually loveless. He knows, however, that the Catholic Church will never abide his putting aside his wife for another and that his career will be ruined. Luckily for Leonce, Matilde dies, leaving him free to pry Delphine from the convent. She elopes with him and becomes his lover briefly. But he deserts her, is captured and condemned to death, and is shot before she can rush to save his life. As he is shot, she falls dead as well.

What interested de Staël's readers in this patently absurd narrative was not the twists and turns of a one-sided love story but the social and political commentary that she was able to weave into it. To her audience, for instance, the malicious mother of Matilde is a hilarious parody of Talleyrand, her former supporter and minister of foreign affairs under Napoleon. Leonce is Narbonne, a former lover whose politics began to disappoint her. Other of Napoleon's advisory council were parodied as well.

She also took this opportunity to discuss a variety of issues on which she and the emperor disagreed. These included the legitimacy of divorce, the intolerance of the Roman Catholic Church, the rights of women, the double sexual standard, and class prejudice as opposed to individual conscience.

Napoleon was furious at her book, especially with her attack on Catholicism and her personal parodies. Nor was he pleased that the Parisian intelligentsia began praising the book. In the fall, following the book's December publication, he gave an order banishing her from Paris. She was not able to return to her home until his defeat at Waterloo twelve years later.

Despite Napoleon's well-orchestrated attack on the novel, it was immensely popular in the France over which he reigned. For those interested in ideas, the novel opened up a discussion of the old order that was passing away, society's repression of women, and the double standards that thwarted a fulfilling relationship between men and women.

The growth of women's studies and feminism revived interest in the ideas of de Staël's *Delphine*, not only as a mirror of politics in postrevolutionary France but as a statement of the problems of gender politics in the twentieth century, particularly the pressures of society that go against woman's conscience, the continuing exclusion of women from an equal place in the political sphere, and the reluctance of both Catholic and Protestant churches to accord women equality with men.

Additional Readings: Gretchen Rous Besser, *Germaine de Staël Revisited* (New York: Twayne, 1994); Madelyn Gutwirth, *Madame de Staël, Novelist: The Emergence of the Artist as Woman* (Urbana: University of Illinois Press, 1978).

72. *René* in *The Genius of Christianity* (*Le Genie du Christianisme*), 5 vols., by **François-René Vicomte de Chateaubriand (France, 1802).** Chateaubriand's novel *René*, and the larger work in which it appeared, *The Genius of Christianity*, are credited with helping to rehabilitate the Christian Church in postrevolutionary France and with stimulating French Romanticism. As such, these works were reactions to the excessive rationalism and social disintegration that occurred during and after the French Revolution.

When the French Revolution swept away the government of aristocrats, the Church, which had been integrally allied with the oppressors, went down with them. Leaders of the Church had been among the chief villains, for while they had joined the aristocrats in rule of the country, enjoying all the luxuries of privilege and caste, they had at the same time maintained an iron grip on the organization that, by itself alone, offered spiritual ease, hope for eternity, and justice in this world and the next. For a period following the revolution, the Church, as a viable organization, vanished, as did the morals and the manners and the accumulated customs associated with its past—all displaced by new ideals of liberty, equality, and fraternity, which electrified all of Europe. In addition, the eighteenth-century philosophes, in establishing an Age of Reason, had largely undermined the philosophical bases of Christianity. The Deists, while attempting to retain the moral and social values of Christianity, discarded organized religion and religious supernaturalism. In the face of all this a sense of malaise set in as the age of Napoleon replaced the Republic. Christianity was dead, and philosophy had proven to be empty. Even the Republic was dying and was beset on all sides by hostile armies.

Chateaubriand, as an aristocrat, supported the royalists and fought against Napoleon; and he especially opposed the revolutionary excesses and the confiscation of property. Returning to France in 1800, he published a lengthy treatise telling of the demise of the Church and expressing the belief that it could never recover from the assaults of the Age of Reason. Then, feeling the heat of violent objections from sympathetic believers, and in an effort to compensate for the seeming betrayal of the cause that he honored, he set out to examine the characteristics of Christianity and its critical place in Western civilization. It was not so much a rational defense as an exploration containing history and illustrations of diverse points. *The Genius of Christianity*, a five-volume work, included the novel *René*. While the name of the larger volume would seem to suggest a reaffirmation of Christianity, and while it is credited with revitalizing Christianity after the bleak period of excessive rationalism and disbelief, the novel *René* is a stronger endorsement of natural religion and romanticism than it is of Christianity. Many readers

suspected that Chateaubriand had grafted a Christian moral onto a narrative written earlier.

The plot is decidedly romantic. René is a young Frenchman who passionately loves his sister. He tries to free himself of his incestuous obsession by emersing himself in the Paris social whirl and, when that fails, appealing to nature and then to the Church, seeking relief. His sister, Amelia, who returns his passion, learns of his desperation and his plans to kill himself and joins him in Paris for three months of idyllic, but seemingly chaste, love. Nevertheless, her guilt then drives her to a convent. He, on the other hand, tries to escape his passion and what he perceives as a corrupt civilization by fleeing to America, there living the life of a natural man among the Indians. Before he dies, a missionary advises him to return to face reality and spend his life doing good to others.

Throughout the novel Chateaubriand presented brilliant pieces on the value of nature (a healer, a constant inspiration, and second only to God in service to ailing mankind), along with the worthiness of the rural, natural world as opposed to the citified and thus corrupted life. He stressed the necessity of man's becoming simple and direct once more in his search for meaning.

There can be no doubt of the enormous effect of *The Genius of Christianity*. Because of this work (along with Napoleon's decision to consent to the operation of the Catholic Church in France), Paris and the rest of Europe could once again, at least nominally, adhere to the Church.

René lives equally as a precursor of Romanticism. It has often been said that Chateaubriand followed Rousseau, and Europe followed Chateaubriand. *René*'s readers were influenced by three aspects of the romanticism of the novel: its unabashed sentiment, its idealization of nature and the natural man, and its expression of the romantic *maladie du siècle*, or what has been described as soul weariness.

After the spiritual emptiness that came in the wake of the Revolution, and after so many stifling years of unrelieved reason, Europe seemed ready for *feeling* once more. *René* expressed this need and unabashedly elicited from its readers the very emotion and sentiment that had been missing in their lives.

The novel also excoriated established society while elevating nature as the universal healer. It is credited with idealizing the American wilderness for its readers as emblematic of the goodness and beauty of nature, a kind of Eden before the fall. Consistent with this philosophy was Chateaubriand's elevation and idealization of the Noble Savage.

The novel's readers also swooned over this highly popular novel, as Johann Wolfgang von Goethe's readers had swooned over *The Sorrows of Young Werther* because it validated and encouraged a soul weariness or self-torment so essential to romanticism. As René says, he finds great satisfaction in his suffering, which is the most lasting thing in his life.

Additional Readings: E.J. Hobsbawm, *The Age of Revolution 1788–1848* (New York: New American Library, 1962); George D. Painter, *Chateaubriand: A Biography* (London: Chatto and Windus, 1977); Charles A. Porter, *Chateaubriand: Composition, Imagination, and Poetry* (Saratoga, CA: ANMA Libri, 1978).

73. *Père Goriot*, by Honoré de Balzac (France, 1835).

Père Goriot is the most famous and influential of the novels of Honoré de Balzac. A story of greed and passion set in the chaos of postrevolutionary France, it was one of the first of a series of novels, called *The Human Comedy*, by a man destined to dominate the fiction in his age as no other ever had and to exert his influence in the much larger society.

Following the defeat of Napoleon and the restoration of the Bourbon monarchy, France became one of the most disrupted and unstable nations in Europe. The country had been bled dry by wars; society was chaotically divided between the old and the new; there were thousands of veterans of old battles and their descendants and families, now dispossessed; and the new world of the cities was emerging. In addition, although the Old Regime had been swept away by the revolution, the aristocrats, in the new society, still held immense power.

Honoré de Balzac wrote scientifically about this world, and like a scientist, he viewed it completely: provincial, urban, high, and low. Balzac borrowed the word "milieu" from zoology to more effectively show exactly what he was attempting. *Père Goriot*, appropriately enough, was even dedicated to a scientist. The result, *The Human Comedy*, was a series of ninety loosely connected stories and novels in which Balzac attempted to probe the social, political, and economic aspects of French society.

The setting of *Père Goriot* is a run-down section of Paris where a varied group of people live in a seedy pension. Some residents, like the students, are on their way up. Some, like Goriot, are on their way down. Old Goriot is a retired merchant. Once a man of great wealth, he has sacrificed everything for his careless, self-absorbed daughters who are now married and so avoid him.

Rastignac, a student, learns quickly that it takes more than talent to rise in Parisian society and so seeks help from his aunt, a ruling figure in aristocratic Parisian society. Her advice is that he should cultivate one of Goriot's daughters who, though wealthy, is married to a Jew and would give her soul to enter into Mme. Beauseant's elevated circles. The archcriminal Vautrin gives other advice: Rastignac should marry a certain girl living in the pension because she will be rich after the death of her brother in a duel, which Vautrin will arrange.

At the conclusion of the novel, all leave the pension in one way or another. Vautrin is arrested. Goriot dies, devastated by his daughters' ingratitude, with only Rastignac and one other present at his death; Rastignac even has to pay for the funeral. The daughters send only their fine emblazoned carriages. Rastignac vows that he will succeed in the Parisian world, no matter what he has to do or what he has to sacrifice.

Père Goriot is a landmark novel because in it Balzac created a new sociology that had never appeared before, in which individuals only existed as integral parts of the society they inhabited. In such a world, every physical detail of the environment assumed enormous importance in the creation and development of the human being. The novel literally changed the way in which in every conceivable way conclusions based on social science were drawn about human beings.

For example, he used techniques and devices now regarded as sociological standards in the analysis of cities and groups of people. He intended especially to show the interrelationship of environment and character.

He is now classified as an early environmental determinist, one who showed his audience the way in which the external world shapes a life. In doing this, in *Père Goriot*, for example, he places an unusual emphasis on descriptions of the house, the neighborhood, the furniture, the clothes, and the tastes of the people in the pension where his main characters live. It has been remarked that Balzac is the only writer to have his men spend more time worrying about how their clothes look than about how their mistress will receive them. For Balzac, the clothes literally make the man. The sleepy neighborhood, and the pension, is more than a setting; it tells something significant about the people who live there, and they in turn reflect something of their milieu, in a symbiotic relationship.

The novel also expressed for its audience for the first time an economic determinism or historical materialism, the overwhelming importance in the modern world of money and class in shaping human behavior. Friedrich Engels and Karl Marx claimed that Balzac taught them more than all the economists, historians, and social theorists they had encountered (Sandy Petrey, "The French Novel: 1800–1850" in Paul Schellinger, ed. *Encyclopedia of the Novel* [Chicago: Fitzroy Dearborn, 1998], p. 446).

The novel has always inspired strong positive and negative responses. Libraries report that Balzac is still the most often published and read of French authors. On the other hand, *Père Goriot* was placed on the Catholic Index of Prohibited Books in 1841, where it has remained since the last Index was issued in 1948. And in the twentieth century, his name was still used (in *The Music Man*, for example) as a symbol of all that is forbidden and dangerously infectious.

Additional Readings: David Bellos, *Honoré de Balzac: "Old Goriot"* (Cambridge: Cambridge University Press, 1987); Harry Levin, *The Gates of Horn* (London: Oxford University Press, 1963).

74. *The Mysteries of Paris* (*Les Mystères de Paris*), by Eugène Sue (France, 1843). In the second third of the nineteenth century, a series of coincidences, connected to postrevolutionary ideals, produced one of the century's astonishing literary events. In 1833, laws intended to bring literacy and education to the masses were passed by the new post revolutionary government. Within a decade, the nature of the reading public in France had gone through a momentous change. In 1829, only 45 percent of the French population were literate. By 1847, after the reforms, 64 percent of the French public could read. So a vast new reading public, hungry for materials, was growing by leaps and bounds. Furthermore, the character of the new readers was totally unlike the usual intellectual aristocrat who had gone before: The new readers were not devoted to slow, agonizing lucubrations of aesthetes or arcane philosophy. They wanted fast action, plain language, relevant characters, and excitement.

The newspapers catered to the tastes of the new reading audience by carrying serialized novels, printing them chapter by chapter. And popular writers soon learned to cater to the needs of the new reading public, even developing a technique designed to capitalize on the demands of the new audience for exciting serials: They ended each section with high suspense. Newspapers printed each new chapter on a bottom section of the paper, originally called the feuilleton, or "leaf," which was designed to be pulled off. The result was a much larger audience both for the newspapers and for the novelists.

The popularity of the feuilletons was legend. It was said that literate apprentices would read to fellow laborers while they worked; similarly, that janitors would read to audiences gathered about or in buildings. Libraries rented copies of a paper for ten centimes per half hour to those readers who could not afford to subscribe for forty francs a year. Maids were said to burn meals while reading latest episodes. Patients were said to delay dying, in order to read the next chapter.

At the same time that the reading public was being democratized, Marie-Joseph Sue, the son of a wealthy, upper-middle-class surgeon, returned to Paris after a stint in the navy and turned to the writing of novels and serialized stories about the sea to pay his mounting debts. The privileged Sue, writing under the pen name Eugène, had also become changed by the new ideas of equality and fraternity and had taken up socialism. When a friend pointed out to Sue that a socialist who wrote for the amusement of the wealthy was an anomaly, he decided to write a novel about the less privileged residents of Paris, conducting research by revisiting Parisian scenes frequented by those who were down and out, criminals, petty thieves, the failures and rejects of society. His expressed purpose was to draw attention to the poor and afflicted of French society, advocate needed reforms, and advance socialist ideals.

The result was *The Mysteries of Paris*. The hero of *Mysteries* is Rodolphe, the prince of Gerolstein, a resourceful, mysterious man of great strength, infinite wealth, superior intelligence, and a desire privately to correct the world's wrongs. In his wanderings around the streets of Paris, disguised as a painter of fans, he encounters unjust situations that require his services.

The inventive technique Sue adopted was like nothing in the literary field before or since. While writing the serial version, he received floods of mail from readers, telling him what they liked or didn't like about the chapters and what they would like to see in the future. Sue actually shaped his future chapters based on suggestions made by his readers, in effect, asking them to join him in the creative process. As a result, the final product more accurately reflected the dark side of Paris life that he wanted to capture.

The immediate response to Sue's novel was nothing short of phenomenal. Sales of the paper in which he published his novel increased 100-fold. The average feuilleton writer received from 75 centimes to 1 franc per line, but Sue was given 100,000 francs for his next novel and received a contract for 100,000 francs per year for fourteen years. It has been estimated that *The Mysteries of Paris* was read or heard by as many as 800,000 Frenchmen during the run of the series. It became the bestselling book of the century.

Sue's novel was one of the great turning points in literary history. As a kind of caped crusader of the 1840s, his protagonist is said to have inspired similar figures—Cyrano de Bergerac, D'Artagnan, and the modern-day Zorro and Superman. Among those it influenced were Charles Dickens, Victor Hugo, and Alexander Dumas.

Its influence, however, goes beyond literary history. The fear of the mob during and just after the revolution had made a greater chasm than ever between the very poor and all the rest of French society. This widely read novel, written by a socialist, served to dispel much of that fear and created sympathy and understanding for its characters whose situations and injustices were disclosed to the public for the first time.

Furthermore, Rodolphe struck a chord in the breasts of those sympathetic with the poor, inspiring them to selfless acts of benevolence. Charity was no longer unfashionable.

Because of its unusual authenticity, later readers would treat the novel, as well as the 1,100 extant letters to Sue, generated by the novel, as serious sociological texts. Its influence reached the fathers of modern communism, Marx and Engels, who addressed *The Mysteries of Paris* seriously in their works. Because of the topicality of the novel, it lost its readership by the early twentieth century, but with the rise of interest in popular literature in the 1960s, interest in Sue and *The Mysteries of Paris* has revived.

Additional Readings: Peter David Citkowitz, *Beyond Chevalier* (Cambridge: Harvard University Thesis, 1983; Christophe Lamiot, *Litterature et hopital en France* (Chilly-Mazarin: Sens, 1999).

75. *Consuelo,* by George Sand (France, 1843).

George Sand, one of the most prolific, influential, and wildly acclaimed writers of the nineteenth century, was born Amantine-Aurore-Lucile Dupen. At a time when few women were educated, much less able to pursue an intellectual life, George Sand wrote eighty novels, twenty-four plays, three books of short fiction, and numerous political tracts. In her novel *Consuelo*, still called France's most important portrait of the female artist and considered to be her most far-reaching in influence, she opposed the continuing political tyrannies, social castes, and religious intolerance in Europe and the gender restrictions of the Napoleonic Code of her native France, while at the same time presenting an idealistic, utopian marriage and theories of socialist reform to counter oppressive practices of her own day.

The title character of her novel, a talented, high-minded young singer who is unable to accept the immorality of theatrical life, abandons her life as a performer to become a tutor in a household of enlightened, socially progressive aristocrats whose son Albert shares her love of music and her commitment to the betterment of society. Although she and Albert are drawn in love and similar beliefs, the family is not so liberal as to ignore her humble social class, and she leaves their household. But Albert's dire health brings Consuelo back to the estate where his family now agrees to their marriage, believing that despite Consuelo's unsuitable social standing their union may save Albert's life. Nevertheless, he dies, and Consuelo leaves again, promising never to use the family name or title. For a third time, she begins her career as a musician, this time in Berlin. But she is exploited again by the ruling class: Frederick the Great has her imprisoned when she spurns his advances. While she is in prison, a secret society, to which Albert and his family belonged and which had pledged to fight tyrants like her imprisoner, investigates her character to see if she is eligible to join their ranks. When she is found to be worthy, Albert, who has not died after all, rescues her, his mother now agreeing to welcome her into the family, and she becomes a member of the secret society of rebels. For the rest of her life, she and her husband and children roam Europe, seeking to reform society through instruction in politics and music.

Sand's novel, through Consuelo and Albert's ideological discussions, has been credited with enhancing political awareness in its arguments against tyranny not only in France but also in Prussia and Czarist Russia. The novel affirms a benevolent socialism in which members of all classes are educated and can take their stands in society on an equal footing. Indeed, her now devoted readers found in *Consuelo* daring perspectives on several other themes. First, the novel dramatized for them the cruelty that the rigid class system brings on individuals like Consuelo and Albert, oppression that has nothing to do with love or intelligence or talent or opinion. Second, the novel contained a strong role model for women and was an inspiration for both male and female readers. Consuelo was seen as a woman who maintains her integrity in a paternalistic world, epitomized by Frederick the Great, who is only willing to tolerate her if she is forthcoming with sexual favors and feminine wiles, neither of which she is willing to exploit. Third, her readers commended her for providing in the novel a positive, utopian model of marriage, a union at once harmonious and fulfilling for both partners because it is founded on equality between equal partners, both of whom retain their individuality in the union.

As with all her other novels, *Consuelo* sold exceptionally well throughout Europe in 1843. The novel received unqualified praise from such diverse artists as Leo Tolstoy and Elizabeth Barrett Browning, who declared that it showed Sand to be a woman of genius, who had no equal in history. Dostoevsky was especially taken with her utopian vision, and Dumas declared that, in 1860, she was more highly regarded than Charles Dickens in most of Europe. In the year of the novel's appearance, a friend visiting Russia wrote to her describing her fame there, a fame that seemed to blossom in the same way in most European cities: "Your books are in everybody's hands, your portraits are everywhere to be seen, you are ceaselessly talked about . . ." (Robert Godwin-Jones, *Romantic Visions*, p. ix).

The sheer sociopolitical power of Sand's novel is demonstrated by the threat the work was felt to pose to the status quo. Despite her popularity, there was scarcely a country where her work was not banned at some time, by the state or by the church. In 1867 the French Senate, for instance, tried to remove her novels from the country's public libraries. In the final decades of the nineteenth century, as Romanticism gave way to Victorianism, her notorious private life had eclipsed her literary production, and few people read *Consuelo*.

However, a revival of Sand's novels, including *Consuelo*, occurred in the 1960s with the rise of feminism and new interest in recovering the work of radical writers. The novel has been found again to be timely, even at the beginning of the twenty-first century, challenging, as it does, ideas of gender, class, political, and artistic authority and presenting a possibility of ideal human relationships, free of oppression.

Additional Readings: Robert Godwin-Jones, *Romantic Vision: The Novels of George Sand* (Birmingham, AL: Summa, 1995); Isabelle Hoog Naginski, *George Sand: Writing for Her Life* (New Brunswick, NJ: Rutgers University Press, 1991); David Powell, *George Sand* (Boston: Twayne, 1990).

76. *Madame Bovary*, by Gustave Flaubert (France, 1857). Gustave Flaubert's *Madame Bovary*, generally considered one of Europe's greatest novels, reveals the author's growing realism and his disillusionment with the romantic politics and culture of the middle class in France. Louis-Napoleon, who came to power in 1851, was eager to place his stamp on France and was not above securing his goal of setting a new moral tone for

France with tyrannical means. His government insisted upon order and the appearance of morality while permitting corruption at every level. In the process, he alienated many artists who dared to question tradition and authority. His vision for moral order included a particular view of works of art, which he insisted must be uplifting and contain moral lessons. It was into this intellectual climate that Flaubert's famous novel appeared.

Madame Bovary is the story of a young woman, ill-prepared for real life by her convent education and her voracious reading of the literature of romance. Consumed with a yearning for a larger life, she consents to marriage to a man more educated than herself, whom she gradually finds is devoted but lacking in spirit, sensitivity, and discernment. In pursuit of a larger life than the one she seems destined to live in the provinces with her husband, she entraps herself in illicit affairs and incurs financial difficulties, a situation from which she finally can escape only by suicide.

The initial reaction to Flaubert's famous novel was resounding disapproval. The imperial prosecutor brought the author to trial for writing an offensive book that was an outrage to religion and morality. Flaubert, it was charged, had made a poetry of adultery, a heroine of an adulteress. His picture of life was true and authentic, but nowhere did he at any time condemn his characters' adultery or Emma's sin of suicide. Flaubert was eventually dismissed with a rebuke for his failure to pass judgment on his realistically drawn characters. His publishers were also charged with immorality and acquitted, guaranteeing impressive sales of the novel. What the imperial prosecutor deplored was, in fact, Flaubert's innovative vision and contribution to letters, namely, realism.

The practical effect of the trial was to ensure phenomenal sales of Flaubert's book. *Madame Bovary* has never been out of print and has continued to maintain its importance as a landmark in literary history, the most popular and well known of all French novels. It has been translated into every major language of the world, with fourteen versions in English alone.

While *Madame Bovary*'s importance is usually discussed in terms of its influence on other writers, the novel can be said to have introduced to the general public a new way of regarding character and action, nonfictional as well as fictional. This point of view is best described as objectivity mixed with empathy. On the positive side, it is a nonjudgmental, non-self-righteous way of regarding one's fellow human beings. On the other hand, stressing Flaubert's scientific bent, critics have described the outlook he encourages as cold and clinical. That is, he never enters into the story as author. Instead, he supplemented his portrait with figures of speech, juxtaposition of elements and images: When Rodolph is romancing Emma at the agricultural fair, the author does not comment, but a nearby barker, praising agriculture, shouts out, "Manure!" And when Emma is facing a final reckoning, the image of a blind beggar haunting her carriage conveys an unforgettable sense of doom.

The novel provided a point of reference for a certain type of self-destructive and pernicious romanticism.

With its portrait of ordinary people, living mundane lives, *Madame Bovary* undercut a romanticized view of the world, which appeared in the novel as both destructive and silly, as when Emma Bovary, who is obsessed with romantic novels, seems gleefully to anticipate the possibility of her husband having a duel with her lover.

At the same time, Emma Bovary showed Flaubert's readers, as nothing had before, the real anguish of a small, empty life, shared with dull, insensitive companions, and the tragedy in her misguided search for a more vibrant existence. Taught by romances, she looks for meaning in all the wrong places and without success—in excitement, in the forbidden, in the dangerous, in the fanciful.

The idea of a human being fatally trapped by deceptive illusions was given a fully developed, dramatic form for the first time by Flaubert. As the century passed, the idea itself stimulated more and more attempts to explain it; and what eventually emerged, in the form of conscious and unconscious illusions, individually and socially, was historical materialism and the psychoanalysis of Sigmund Freud.

Additional Readings: Victor Brombert, *The Novels of Flaubert: A Study of Themes and Techniques* (Princeton, NJ: Princeton University Press, 1966); Alison Fairlie, *Flaubert: Madame Bovary* (London: Arnold and Woodbury, 1962).

77. *Les Misérables*, **by Victor-Marie Hugo (France, 1862).** Hugo's massive portrayal of the miserable ones of French life in the early part of the nineteenth century covered details of degradation and injustice as well as the triumph of the human spirit and exerted an enormous influence on life in France in particular and the Western world in general. Written in Hugo's maturity, while he was in a nineteen-year exile from Napoleon III's Second Empire, his novel was an instant success and has remained one of the most widely read novels of all time.

In *Les Misérables*, a story of redemption, Hugo portrays an escaped convict, Jean Valjean, who rises from utter debasement to a useful life, a high position in society, and a higher morality. An ordinary worker, he is arrested for stealing a loaf of bread and is sentenced to serve as a galley slave, an unusually severe but common punishment. He ultimately escapes, becomes a model citizen, even a saintly figure, after an encounter with a bishop who saves his life by telling police that he has "given" Valjean the candle sticks that Valjean has actually stolen. Over a period of many years and in several guises, but always keeping just ahead of the police, Jean Valjean redeems himself by maintaining his integrity. He adopts a child named Cosette, the daughter of Fantine, a dying prostitute. When Cosette, whom he loves as his own child, grows into a young lady, he saves the life of the one she loves while the Revolution of 1830 is in progress, by carrying the unconscious man through the sewers of Paris.

The unbending, book-bound Detective Javert, the merciless figure of law upheld by the establishment of trade and piety, trails

Valjean to the end—only to see, finally, the true moral superiority and saintliness of the man he has hounded for so many years. Realizing at the same time his own vicious nature, Javert plunges into the Seine.

The immediate enthusiasm for the novel bordered on the hysterical. The price went up 33 percent on the first day of publication. Three days after the first volumes appeared, it was entirely sold out in Paris, and reading rooms rented it by the hour. Published simultaneously in cities throughout Europe and in Rio de Janerio, it was an instant success, with readers on every level of society. But at the time and for at least 100 years, it was routinely attacked by literary critics as unwieldy and in poor taste.

When one critic, at the publication of the novel, expressed utter scorn of Hugo, a more sympathetic reader, himself a writer, retorted that Hugo had taught him everything he knew, whereas ten years working for a newspaper that scorned Hugo had taught him nothing. He noted also that all the world was reading Hugo's *Les Misérables* and that while others of his generation were doing nothing, Hugo had created a monument.

One of the most immediate effects of the novel was to mobilize opposition to the reign of Napoleon III in its implied, but clear, satire of the dictator's reign. In the novel's prerevolutionary police state, his readers saw the tyranny of Napoleon III. In its depiction of the suffering of the poor before the revolution, they saw the class hostility and poverty of the Second Empire.

Through the novel, Hugo was able to marshal sympathy for the lowest levels of society, which had been feared and despised by the country's leaders ever since the mob's participation in overthrowing the monarchy in the French Revolution. Hugo portrayed the poor, and his audience saw them not as subhuman degenerates to be feared but as sympathetic human beings who were morally superior to those who oppressed them.

More than this, as critic Catherine M. Grossman writes, "*Les Misérables* is among the most widely read novels of all time"

("Victor-Marie Hugo" in *Encylopedia of the Novel*, p. 565).

The novel's great power to influence the public to sympathize with the downtrodden and overturn tyranny is made known by its enemies. The supporters of the Second Empire, including the French Roman Catholic Church, for instance, were outraged at Hugo's satire and took whatever measures they could to suppress the book. In 1864 the Church placed it on its Index of forbidden books.

The book was even found to be dangerous at the turn of the twentieth century by defenders of a repressive Third Republic and as late as the 1930s and 1940s by proponents of fascism.

On the other hand, *Les Misérables* has been held up as a rallying cry by revolutionaries throughout the twentieth century. In communist countries it was made required reading for schoolchildren. In 1951, in Red China alone, 5 million copies had been published. It was one of the most popular books in colonial India.

The 1950s saw a resurgence in interest in *Les Misérables* by both literary critics and social activists who found that the novel articulated positions that continue to be controversial: opposition to capital punishment, opposition to the exploitation of child and female labor, support for prison reform and realistic measures for dealing with prostitution.

Between 1950 and 1984, over 5 million volumes of the novel were sold in France. And between 1982 and 1993, Penguin sold over 200,000 copies. It has also been made into numerous films, one of the most successful musicals of the twentieth-century theater, and a highly praised television drama in 2001.

When Hugo died, he was given a state funeral where he was eulogized as the leading writer and humanitarian of his age. He was said to have incorporated in his works all the various hopes of the century and to have given voice in *Les Misérables* to oppressed peoples in every age throughout the world.

Additional Readings: Victor Brombert, *Victor*

Hugo and the Visionary Novel (Cambridge, MA: Harvard University Press, 1984); Catharine M. Grossman, *"Les Misérables": Conversion, Revolution, Redemption* (New York: Twayne, 1996).

78. *A Sentimental Education (L'Éducation sentimentale),* by Gustave Flaubert (France, 1869).

Flaubert's novel is at once a novel of youthful discovery, a satirical picture of the world of artistic society of Paris at mid-century, an undermining of the tradition of "sentimental" education, and a picture of the ineffectualness of an individual when faced with the furious world of politics around him. Written near the end of the reign of Napoleon III, *A Sentimental Education* inspired a new realism and naturalism that influenced the development of modernism.

The setting is in mid-nineteenth-century France when, in 1848, a violent revolution in France overthrew the monarch Louis Philippe, producing a stormy Second Republic and raising the hopes of idealistic reformers. The disillusionment that followed led to a well-staged coup that enthroned Louis Bonaparte, Napoleon III, a despised mediocrity who ruled over a long period of material progress and moral degradation. Napoleon III's France was one of unbridled capitalism, based on money and big industry. Great new wealth was much in evidence, which created and was created by technical inventions, railways, waterways, an increased flow of goods, and a generous system of credit. As a result, his army could be used to suppress the lower classes but not the upper middle classes, which provided his capital and his support. Socially, the period resulted in even greater chasms between poor and privileged classes and a ten-year prohibition of all labor movements.

It was, for idealists and reformers, one of the most desolate periods in modern French history, a time when the best young minds went into commercial ventures. Although the revolution of 1848 had initially inspired intellectuals, they quickly became disillusioned with the demise of democracy, freedom of the press, and intellectual freedom.

Many artists retreated into their art and artistic societies largely isolated from the real world and from the public. France's reputation as a center for great art was replaced with its reputation for shallow and ostentatious entertainment.

The setting of Flaubert's novel is the world of Parisian artists in which a young idealist, Frederic Moreau, hopes for an education that will bring him fulfillment, success, and love. Unfortunately he arrives in Paris with an impossible idealism and is further educated by artistic pretenders. So fulfillment eludes him as his journey through artistic society brings him into contact only with a superficial and sham world. Love also eludes him as he has many romances but never love. His idealism is represented by a young woman to whom he is attracted as his journey begins and with whom he is obsessed but considers untouchable. His sentimentality has rendered him so out of touch with reality that when he sees the revolution of 1848 brewing and then erupting around him, he is oblivious. At the end of the novel, Frederic, in reflection, romanticizes, as one of the grand moments of his life, an adolescent, first, unsatisfactory visit to a whore house.

The art world that Flaubert wrote about understandably gave a cool reception to this novel, now considered one of the masterpieces of the nineteenth century. But society as a whole at the time and since has recognized its influence in undermining what he considered to be silly idealism, sentimentalism, and the pretentious isolation of the artist from reality.

The earlier literary Romantics had generally felt detached from ruling society and thus stressed individual feeling or sensitivity, the suffering soul fighting against the world. In a culture that had been shaped by romantic idealism, the scene of Moreau, waiting for romantic love while standing, completely oblivious to the scene of one of the most momentous events in French history, impressed upon his audience the sad and ludicrous attempt to escape the real world into romantic dreams. The result of escape is, as in Moreau's case, to see life waste away into ineptitude, aimlessness, and emptiness.

In Moreau's obsession with his untouchable ideal, audiences saw another perfect symbol for idealizations that can never be realized in the real world. For the real world at the time was the searing ineptitude of Louis Philippe's monarchy and the disillusionment following the revolution of 1848.

Like other of Flaubert's novels, this one devastatingly unmasked for its readers the dangers of a sentimental education or the frame of mind, so prevalent in the nineteenth century, especially in the form of novels, that led to grand, idealized, and totally unrealistic expectations.

Readers of the novel throughout the nineteenth and twentieth centuries have also been forced by the novel to a reevaluation of artistic society, feeding on its own sentimentality and aesthetic self-absorption. In Flaubert's portrait, the useless society of artists was merely a reflection of the larger culture.

What his readers see is that the results are aimlessness and emptiness for the culture as a whole, for the artists who should be providing some vision for the culture, and for the individual, like Moreau.

Additional Readings: Victor Brombert, *The Novels of Flaubert: A Study of Themes and Techniques* (Princeton, NJ: Princeton University Press, 1966); Richard Terdiman, *The Dialectics of Isolation: Self and Society in the French Novel from the Realists to Proust* (New Haven, CT: Yale University Press, 1976); Anthony Thorlby, *Gustave Flaubert and the Art of Realism* (New Haven, CT: Yale University Press, 1957).

79. *Twenty Thousand Leagues under the Sea* (*Vingt milles lieues sous les mers*), **by Jules Verne (France, 1869–70).** To understand the impact of the work of Jules Verne, it is necessary to realize that the clash of religion and science dominated the nineteenth century. Science had changed from meaning merely "knowledge acquired through study" to the more restricted modern concept of a systematic and precise study of the natural world. Moreover, Charles Darwin's *The Origin of Species*, which appeared in 1859, pro-

voked vehement and bitter conflict. At the same time, the Catholic Church, which controlled French education, regarded science with suspicion and neglected it in the schools.

Into this situation stepped Jules Verne, one who saw infinite hope for the future of mankind in the marvels of science and who, with the help of a publisher named Hetzel, produced an unparalleled series of successful works in a new genre, something called science fiction. His novels combined adventure and futuristic projections of scientific inventions with acceptable moral codes. The first of these was *Five Weeks in a Balloon*. Sales were so good that Hetzel gave Verne a ten-year contract to produce two similar novels each year. The books were gathered under a series called *Voyages extraordinaires*. From the first Hetzel insisted that entertainment have a moral. While Verne sometimes chafed at the limitations Hetzel placed upon him, he leaped into the project with eagerness and infectious optimism.

In *Twenty Thousand Leagues under the Sea*, a shipwreck brings a group of people in contact with a mysterious person, Captain Nemo ("No-one"), commander of a fantastically equipped vehicle of the future, a submarine. And as usual with Verne, the story proceeds (like *Robinson Crusoe*) as nineteenth-century citizens encounter a different and challenging culture, a world that is totally alien to them. Nemo, belonging to no country, has developed scientific marvels that give him immense power for good or bad; and thus his decisions involve the moral question of power (What is the ethical course to take?). To this end, Nemo is a challenger of society and champion of oppressed peoples. One reflection on politics comes when they encounter a swimmer who is, they learn, a Greek freedom fighter; so they give him a sack of gold and set him free to pursue his fight.

Verne was not a trained scientist, but he was an apt researcher and was advised by his brother, an engineer. Thus, using his powerful creative imagination, he was able to extrapolate from known scientific facts a vision of future marvels. For his fantastic machine in *Twenty Thousand Leagues under the Sea*, he drew on a far more rudimentary submarine called the *Nautilus*, developed by Robert Fulton in 1800.

The immediate success of the work was phenomenal. Verne became the rage of Paris and a household name. His book sold by the millions and was translated into many languages. There is considerable irony in the fact that Verne's novel sold better than Darwin's *The Origin of Species*. By the end of the century, fine editions embossed in red and gold were selling unusually well as Christmas gifts. Theatrical adaptations of the novel played to full houses night after night. "Jules Verne" became one of the most recognized names in the Western world, so widespread as to have entered the language as an adjective for scientific, fictionalized, and often fantastically accurate visions of the future.

The novel continued to have a general readership and remained popular among young people. Young readers for generations grew up reading *Twenty Thousand Leagues under the Sea*. At the same time, in the early twentieth century, his reputation among critics suffered primarily as a result of many bad translations and bowdlerized editions published over the years. One in Britain, for example, cut out all the science and emphasized the sensational elements. Verne also became stereotyped as a boys' writer of shallow adventure books and science fiction. Beginning in the 1960s, however, after years of neglect, he was revived by the academic marketplace as a serious writer. Between 1975 and 2001, numerous biographies and critical books on Verne were published, along with primary and secondary bibliographies and literally dozens of scholarly articles, university dissertations, and theses. Verne, who had suddenly leaped into prominence, became regarded as an author of vision, style, and linguistic sophistication. One hundred years after his initial publication, he was once again the rage of Paris. Prestigious publishing houses produced fine editions of his work, and two French towns engaged in heated battle for the privilege of maintaining his papers. Two

major movies were made of the novel, both popular, and one a classic.

Verne was a cofounder (with H.G. Wells) of modern science fiction This novel exercised its greatest influence by countering much of the ignorance and antagonism toward science in church-based French education at the time of its publication. The novel, along with other of Verne's works, generated and continues to generate an intense interest in science and the future it projects, especially among young people. Consequently, the novel stimulated scientific inquiry and education. Even today, many successful physicists, astronomers, and engineers throughout the twentieth century credit Verne with inspiring their first interest in science. The renewed appeal of his work in the middle of the twentieth century sparked a flood of science fiction and fantasy that had not abated as the twenty-first century approached.

Additional Readings: Paul K. Alkon, *Origins of Futuristic Fiction* (Athens: University of Georgia Press, 1987); William Sims Bainbridge, *Dimensions in Science Fiction* (Cambridge: Harvard University Press, 1986).

80. *Germinal*, **by Emile Zola (France, 1885).** For the setting of his *Rougon-Macquart* series of novels, Zola chose the period of the Second Empire in France, which ended in 1870. During this time the Industrial Revolution began in France, bringing with it technological progress, enormous profits, and urban factories run by depressed workers who lived lives of inexpressible squalor and desperation. They were categorized with criminals by the country's elite and were called the "dangerous classes." These were Zola's subjects, and he knew intimately the hopeless poverty about which he wrote. He had experienced it as a boy and had seen it as a reporter for the city's newspapers.

The science that made the Industrial Revolution possible also introduced methodologies for modern chemistry, physics, and biology. It was this that Zola chose as his literary model. He would adapt the scientific method literarily, seeing urban society as his laboratory and his characters as subjects, while assuming an objective approach to his material. He was especially drawn to genetics and the idea of an inherited disposition to alcoholism, known as the disease of the poor,

For his series *Les Rougon-Macquart*, Zola planned twenty novels to follow the fortunes of two families. One of the most influential of these novels, and one with which French workers identified Zola, was *Germinal*, the story of a French mining community. As he had earlier characterized urban factories and businesses as monsters devouring the workers, so in *Germinal* the mine is a voracious animal, consuming workers and then spewing out their spent bodies. Conditions have become so desperate that many of them are ready to strike, led by a man familiar with socialist political philosophy. Their misery is made all the more apparent by the contrast between the wealthy Gregoire family who own shares in the mines and the Maheu family who work in them. The striking miners suffer a humiliating failure as their strike is broken, and they are compelled to return to the mines in even worse circumstances than before.

Despite their defeat, however, the novel ends on an affirmative note, an effect reinforced by the title of the work. *Germinal* is the month of the French calendar in which many eighteenth-century revolutionary events had occurred. It denotes a springlike renewal, suggesting that the seeds of revolution are again germinating, this time in the mining town, and that the day will come when the miners, indeed all workers, will see reforms.

Germinal was a radically new form of literature in that it made humans and heroes of a class of individuals who had usually been treated in literature as objects of ridicule and farce. Moreover, political conservatives feared, with good reason, that the work was intended as a call to revolution. For decades, the novel was also derided by literary critics as being tasteless, vulgar, and having little beauty or artistic merit. However, the book was a phenomenal success among the general public at the time of its appearance and has continued to have a huge following among

working people. In 1886, miners were impressed with the accuracy of his portrayal and his implied sympathy with the downtrodden. As conservatives feared, the novel inspired working people throughout France to retain the hope that their struggles for decent treatment would not finally be in vain.

While literary critics up to the 1950s generally demeaned the novel, *Germinal* has retained its place as one of the bestselling, most frequently read works of nineteenth-century literature. *Germinal* was one of Zola's books studied regularly in working-class night schools at the turn of the twentieth century, and in 1979 Zola was listed most often by French college students as the writer who had most influenced their lives. Only with a reassessment of Zola, beginning in the 1950s, has his great influence begun to be acknowledged by scholars. It is a testament to the power of Zola's work that between 1952 and 1980 more than 2,600 new books and articles were published about him.

Zola's novels, *Germinal* in particular, exposed details about the victims at the bottom of the Industrial Revolution in an unflinching and thorough way, as no other work had done. No one could accuse Zola of ignorance of his material, for he was first among writers to do exhaustive, firsthand research of his subjects on the site. For *Germinal* he pretended to be a mining engineer to document his portrayal of life in the mining community accurately. As a result of *Germinal*, reforms were made in the mining industry.

Despite Zola's innovative stance as a spokesman for the laboring poor of nineteenth-century France and the changes he effected in their lives, his most profound intellectual contribution to modern culture and to the dispossessed of every age was his introduction to literature of the scientific method of meticulous observation and assumed objectivity, a method that earned him the title of "Father of Naturalism."

Zola's method as well as his characterizations also had a profound influence on Sigmund Freud, the father of modern psychology, who devoured his novels voraciously and incorporated Zola's system of observation into his own revolutionary theories. Zola also influenced the application of science to the fields of crowd psychology, history, and economics and is credited with transforming modern sociology. In literature, this first great strike novel, a precursor to Spain's Vincente Blasco Ibáñez and America's John Steinbeck, gave writers for the next fifty years the tools for improving the lives of the working classes.

Zola's dramatic funeral was a testament to his novel's tremendous impact on society: In the impressive procession at his public funeral in October 1902 marched a large delegation of miners, raising what had become a rallying cry for action: "Germinal! Germinal!"

Additional Readings: David Baguley, ed., *Critical Essays on Emile Zola* (Boston: G.K. Hall, 1986); Alan Schom, *Emile Zola: A Bourgeois Rebel* (London: MacDonald, 1987); Philip Walker, *"Germinal" and Zola's Philosophical and Religious Thought* (Philadelphia: John Benjamins, 1984).

1900–1999

Marcel Proust, *Remembrance of Things Past*, 1913–27

Henri Barbusse, *Under Fire: The Story of a Squad*, 1916

André Gide, *The Counterfeiters*, 1925

André Malraux, *Man's Fate*, 1933

Jean-Paul Sartre, *Nausea*, 1938

Albert Camus, *The Plague*, 1947

Samuel Beckett, *Molloy*, 1951

Simone de Beauvoir, *The Mandarins*, 1954

Elie Wiesel, *Night*, 1958

Pierre Boulle, *The Planet of the Apes*, 1963

1900–1999: TIMELINE

1900   France enters into alliances with Britain as defense against Germany's aggression.

France continues to strengthen its hold on colonies throughout Africa and the Near East.

These are the optimistic years of the belle epoque.

1913–27   Marcel Proust's *Remembrance of Things Past* is published.

1914   France enters World War I.

1915   Henri Barbusse, after being wounded repeatedly, is awarded the Croix de Guerre for bravery under fire.

1916   Henri Barbusse's antiwar novel *Under Fire* is published.

1917   Mutinies plague the French army.

1918   French troops, buttressed by the American army, defeat Germany, ending the war. The war has left 8,538,315 soldiers dead and 21,219,451 wounded.

1919   The Treaty of Versailles gives France Alsace-Lorraine and forces Germany to demilitarize the Rhineland.

1920   Separate Socialist and Communist political parties are established in France.

1925   André Gide's *The Counterfeiters* is published.

1930s	France builds a line of defenses called the Maginot Line to protect the country from Germany.	1943	Jean-Paul Sartre's seminal existential masterwork *Being and Nothingness* is published.

1930s — France builds a line of defenses called the Maginot Line to protect the country from Germany.

French colonial holdings have grown to an area twenty times the size of France itself with twice the population of France.

1931 — The economic depression that had devastated the rest of the world hits France.

1932 — The Radicals win the French government. Socialists win 131 seats and Communists win 10.

1933 — André Malraux's *Man's Fate* is published.

1935 — The Popular Front, a coalition of Communists, Socialists, and Radicals, forms to combat the increasing threat of fascism in Europe.

1936 — Adolf Hitler, now leader of Germany, remilitarizes the Rhineland.

The Popular Front achieves control of the government.

1938 — France accepts without military protest Germany's invasions of Austria and Czechoslovakia.

Jean-Paul Sartre's *Nausea* is published.

1939 — Germany's invasion of Poland finally brings France and Britain into World War II.

1940 — Germany attacks France in May, and within six weeks France falls. A puppet government, ultimately controlled by the Nazis, is set up in Vichy, France, under an aged French general, Marshall Petain.

1940–44 — In active collaboration with the Nazis, the Vichy government rounds up 75,000 French Jews and sends them to German-run death camps in Poland.

A French underground movement, nominally under the leadership of General Charles de Gaulle, resists the Nazis in France.

1941 — Germany decides on a policy of ethnic cleansing and extermination throughout Europe.

1943 — Jean-Paul Sartre's seminal existential masterwork *Being and Nothingness* is published.

1944 — On June 6, Allied troops begin invading the beaches at Normandy. In August Paris is liberated, and de Gaulle leads France. With the fall of the Nazi Vichy government, 10,000 French collaborators are executed and 40,000 are sent to prison.

The fall of Nazi Germany and the liberation of concentration camps give the world graphic evidence of the Holocaust.

1945 — The French provisional government institutes reforms, only at this time extending the vote to women.

1946 — The Fourth Republic is created with a parliamentary form of government.

1946–62 — France is forced to give up power abroad and colonies in Indochina and Algeria after bloody fights abroad for independence.

1947 — Albert Camus's *The Plague* is published.

1951 — Samuel Beckett's *Molloy* is published.

1953 — Simone de Beauvoir's important feminist text *The Second Sex* is published.

1954 — Simone de Beauvoir's *The Mandarins* is published.

Samuel Beckett's Absurdist masterpiece, his play *Waiting for Godot*, is translated into English.

1957 — Albert Camus's *The Rebel* attacks Stalinism.

Camus receives the Nobel Prize for Literature.

1958 — The Fourth Republic gives way to the Fifth Republic.

Elie Wiesel's *Night* is published.

1962 — The Evian Accords provide for referendum in Algeria, resulting in Algerian independence.

1963 — Pierre Boulle's *The Planet of the Apes* is published.

1964	Jean-Paul Sartre is awarded and refuses the Nobel Prize for Literature.
1968	A massive student protest and national strike result in educational reforms and wage increases.
1969	De Gaulle resigns after his proposal for the senate is rejected. He is followed by Georges Pompidou, a friend of big business.
	Samuel Beckett receives the Nobel Prize for Literature.
1974	Valery Giscard d'Estaing's government of right-of-center Independent Republicans assumes power.
1981	François Mitterrand and his Socialist Party assume leadership in France.
1985	Elie Wiesel receives the Nobel Prize for Literature.

81. *Remembrance of Things Past* or *In Search of Lost Time* (*À la recherche du temps perdu*), by Marcel Proust (France, 1913–27). Often judged to be the greatest French author of the twentieth century, Marcel Proust is best known for his multivolume work titled *Remembrance of Things Past*. The monumental epic in poetic prose is at once a groundbreaking psychological study and a portrait of a social class. Proust cannot be said to have changed the social thinking of his readers, for though his characters include members of every social class and profession, the main characters are the idle rich and their servants. But in the social sphere, his readers are impressed with the instability of upper- and middle-class standing, which tends to vary according to a variety of events, despite their continuing privileged status above others. Proust's real influence is of a different sort, having to do with the way we view our own lives.

Basically, *Remembrance of Things Past* is about the life of a man called Swann from his childhood to middle age. The primary business of his young manhood is his courtship and eventual marriage to a courtesan named Odette, all the while moving from one social circle to another. There are the circles that revolve around the Verdurins, bourgeois intellectual snobs, and those that circulate around the Faubourge Saint-Germain household from which Odette is excluded. One of the strongest emotions that Swann feels is jealousy. And always there is the experience and sensation opening him to memory.

Proust's readers were introduced to the complexity and preciousness of memory, to the operations of the unconscious mind, to the inspiration of the moment. The memory spoken of in the title carries several different meanings. There are the memories that are conveyed to us by others about life before we were born or before we can ourselves remember. The second type are "voluntary" memories we choose to conjure up repeatedly. The most striking of these are scenes from childhood. Swann chooses, for example, to remember again and again various times in his life when he is beginning to go to sleep, dreaming, and waking up, as times of disorientation, as if by so doing he will awake to his true artistic self. He remembers repeatedly his mother coming to kiss him as he goes to sleep. But the most valuable memory, and one to which Proust introduced his readers, is "involuntary," those hidden memories that suddenly and unexpectedly come to the fore for the first time through some sensation. The sip of tea, for instance, suddenly brings to Swann a buried memory of his aunt feeding him a small cake called a madeleine when he was a boy. Indeed, every precious detail in the town of his boyhood "sprang into being, town and gardens alike, from my cup of tea," he writes. Thus, Proust changed his readers' way of thinking by heightening, moderniziing with psychology, and valuing above all the romantic notion of introspection. Even love in his novel becomes most important as an opportunity for introspection.

In summing up Proust's influence, Arnold Hauser writes: "Proust is the first to see in contemplation, in remembrance and in art not only one possible form, but the only possible form in which we can possess life" (*The Social History of Art*, vol. 4, Vintage Books, 1958, p. 225).

Proust gave his readers an entirely new concept of time from the one they received from earlier novelists. Time was not a destroyer but a reviver. It is a means of gaining a hold on the spirit and even life itself. We are the result of all our times past, not just of the present moment. So the past gives us substance, and happiness comes from recapturing that.

As such, Proust challenged his readers to dispense with viewing the story of ourselves and others in a conventionally chronological or causal way. After Proust, people tended to view events as not having a clear, single cause but having complex multiple motivations and causes—causes that would seem to cancel each other out on first view.

Proust also undermined factual information, logic, and rigid pattern in a person's search for self, in favor of impression and sensation. Yet he shows through Swann that the unconscious and memory are useless until analyzed by intellect.

Additional Readings: Germane Bree, *The World of Marcel Proust* (Boston: Houghton Mifflin, 1966); Renee Girard, ed., *Proust: A Collection of Critical Essays* (Englewood Cliffs, NJ: Prentice-Hall, 1962).

82. *Under Fire: The Story of a Squad* (*Le Feu: Journal d'une escouade*), **by Henri Barbusse (France, 1916).** Henri Barbusse wrote *Under Fire* as an attempt to shed light on a dark event: a disastrous war in progress at the time of the novel's publication. For centuries, from Homer to Shakespeare, from the Napoleonic Wars to modern times, it was the custom of civilized man to wrap wars and its victims in banners of romance and glory. And afterward, governments and civilization in general could close their eyes and forget the slaughter. World War I was an exception. The slaughter was so great, the execution so bloody, and the motivation so monstrous, the entire action so useless, that it changed the face of Europe. A war that began when a Serb nationalist assassinated an Austrian archduke escalated in an atmosphere of intense nationalism into conflagration involving thirty-two nations. By the end, four years

after the war had begun and two years after the publication of Barbusse's novel, 57.6 percent of the mobilized forces were casualties—a total of 8,538,315 soldiers were dead, and 21,219,451 wounded. Over 73 percent of Barbusse's fellow soldiers in the French army were dead, wounded, or missing by the end of the war. Close to 10 million civilians died in the war.

To appreciate the impact and originality of Barbusse's work, it is important to know the way in which war was generally written about before 1914. Histories and analytical articles describing war (true even now, but much more so before World War I) typically took a sweeping, godlike view of history, resulting in a point of view that was cold, dry, and detached. The higher the chronicler was removed above the battle and the broader his vision, the more detached he became. Like old generals, such writers saw and thought in terms of sweeping movements, the soldiers being like figures on a chessboard. In such a perspective, individual reality gets lost—the view seen by those at the bottom who actually fight the battles, who live in the mud and the horror until it begins to soak into their souls. Even the word *war* in the typical reports is a sweeping, generalized term, eternally detached from reality and genuine feeling. Instead, it becomes synonymous with *glory, heroism*, and *honor* or, at worst, *romantic loss* and *sacrifice for duty*, like something out of a Walter Scott novel.

Barbusse, however, wrote a new kind of novel, unlike the old romantic war sagas that both reflected and helped bring about a disturbing, abysmal truth. Barbusse's veracity and credentials are unimpeachable: He had served in the military in 1893 and 1894; in 1914 he served, willingly, as a combat infantryman and was wounded several times, but each time he made his way back into action, and in 1915 he was honored with the Croix de Guerre. By 1915, however, his patriotism had turned to anger; his diary began to be a record of the butchery, injustice, and incompetence he saw around him. This diary he transformed into his novel. It was the first to bring to many French readers, and English and German as well, a glimpse of reality: a ghastly account of life in the trenches, where the fire of artillery is mixed with constant cold rain and mud, where soldiers, more like puppets or prehistoric barbarians than human beings, are moved from one place of slaughter to another by some unseen hand, and where the squalor of their conditions reduces them to animals who will kill each other over a scrap of food.

In addition to accounts of hellish slaughter, Barbusse brought to light the war profiteering and criminal negligence on the part of French officers, contrasting the sordid truth of battle with the patriotic romances appearing in the press. *Under Fire* also carries a sociopolitical message: the representative nature of the men who make up the squad, along with their representative thoughts regarding such concepts as liberty, equality, and fraternity, ideas that they are beginning to comprehend now in practical, life-and-death terms.

One thing that makes Barbusse's antiwar statement so unusual is that it appeared in the fall of 1916, in the middle of patriotic fervor concerning the war. Even more amazing, in 1917, still at the height of the war, this indictment of World War I was awarded France's top literary prize, the Prix Goncourt. By the end of the war, it had sold over 250,000 copies.

It was the first and still stands as the most influential antiwar novel of France in the Great War. Its influence on future war stories and on the thinking of people who read it was enormous. It is generally conceded that no other novel of World War I ever achieved the power of Barbusse's view of life in the trenches.

In the 1920s, following Barbusse's example, a flood of memoirs and novels expressing disillusionment and condemnation of everything the war represented began to appear. Among contemporaries greatly impressed by *Under Fire* was Siegfried Sassoon, the English poet, and Robert Graves, each of whom wrote strong antiwar memoirs or novels. Sassoon received a copy of Barbusse's novel when he was in an English hospital recuper-

ating from wounds received in action, a time when he, too, after being honored for unusual bravery, was sorting out his thoughts about the war and deciding on moral grounds that he would not go back to the front.

Additional Readings: Frank Field, *Three French Writers and the Great War: Studies in the Rise of Communism and Fascism* (Cambridge: Cambridge University Press, 1975), pp. 21–29; J.H. King, *The First World War in Fiction*, ed. H.M. Klein (London: Macmillan, 1976), pp. 43–52.

83. *The Counterfeiters* (*Les Faux-Monnayeurs*), by André Gide (France, 1925). André Gide's *The Counterfeiters*, regarded as the major French novel of the 1920s, has frequently been hailed as an emancipation proclamation, an inspiration to his readers to free themselves of all sorts of social constraints but to adhere to a self-constructed morality. It is important to realize that in the 1920s, despite the reputation that the decade turned conventional morality upside down, there was scarcely a gay person to be found who was not closeted. Homosexuality was not only secretive but almost universally prosecutable.

The Counterfeiters, which raises a variety of daring social issues and challenged the value of the family, was based in part on a number of court cases involving juvenile delinquency and counterfeiting. It is set in Paris and Switzerland. And the main characters include the chief point of view, Edouard; his antagonist, the novelist Passavant; his nephew, Olivier; a minor cast of juveniles including the haunted Boris; a young woman named Laura; and her friend Bernard. The major theme of the novel, a subject that many readers were seeing discussed openly for the first time, was homosexuality. Its intent was to explore the morality of various interpersonal behaviors, including those between homosexual lovers and between parents and children.

The immediate reaction to the novel was extremely hostile because of its antifamily stance and its sympathetic and open treatment of homosexuality. But many readers were introduced for the first time to the radical possibility that a homosexual relationship could be as ethical as any other so-called normal relationship. The tenderness and mutual love of the protagonist's homosexual relationship is portrayed as eminently more moral than the psychologically brutal manner in which parents, especially Bernard's father, treat their children and each other in the novel. The nuclear family in the novel is tyrannical, oppressive, materialistic, laying a foundation for moral corruption. Yet Gide took pains to make clear that not all homosexual relationships are benign. The novel portrays a destructive homosexual relationship as well.

The novel led its readers to associate counterfeiting with falsity, fascades, hypocrisy, and automatic devotion to traditional, unexamined values.

Open-minded readers have discovered the great irony in this novel, which opened Gide to the charge of being a corrupter of youth: Its expressed and profound intent, as Bernard and Laura make clear, is to locate right values and sound ethics, to determine, independent of social dictates, what constitutes moral actions. Furthermore, one is to work hard and honestly in taking responsibility for behaving in accordance with one's morality. Despite Boris's suicide, which ends the novel, its message is finally hopeful and comforting: One can be free of traditional values and still lead a moral, humane life.

Integrity, the novel suggests, is to be foremost in approaching a number of social problems primarily concerned with youth: delinquency, education, illegitimacy, and parental tyranny.

Perhaps the greatest influence that Gide had was in frankly considering very real and ancient problems in an open and honest way and encouraging his readers to rid themselves of inherited ideas in order to think independently about them.

On an individual level, Gide's correspondence reveals that many young homosexuals believed that Gide's novel had saved them from despair and self-loathing.

Additional Readings: Germaine Bree, *Gide*

(New Brunswick, NJ: Rutgers University Press, 1963); Albert J. Guerard, *André Gide* (Cambridge, MA: Harvard University Press, 1951); G.W. Ireland, *André Gide: A Study of His Creative Writings* (Oxford: Clarendon Press, 1970).

84. *Man's Fate* (*La Condition humaine*), by André Malraux (France, 1933). The setting for *Man's Fate* is Shanghai in northern China in March 1927. Since the foreign commercial and industrial developments at the turn of the century, Shanghai had been an international city inhabited not only by people from all over China but from the rest of Asia and Europe as well. In part because of this international perspective, the people of Shanghai grew impatient with oppression at an early stage and were exposed to political philosophies from all over the world. In 1911 they had overthrown the Imperial government of China and in 1913, 1915, and 1916 had waged rebellions against warlords of seemingly unlimited hereditary power. It is not surprising to learn that the Chinese Communist Party was born in Shanghai, in 1921, and that an unsuccessful communist revolutionary uprising occurred there in 1925, supported by Chiang Kai-shek's Nationalists or the Kuomintang. In 1927, however, another communist uprising took place in Shanghai. This time, Chiang Kai-shek, whose Nationalists had taken other key territory and held the upper hand, turned on the local communists, ordered their wholescale liquidation, and slaughtered them brutally. This is the setting for *Man's Fate* which appeared only six years after the Shanghai Massacre.

The political struggle that occurs in the novel is among the "White" Shanghai government, the "Blue" Chiang Kai-shek Nationalists, the local communists within the city, and the international communists headquartered in Hankow. A general strike is going on in the city of Shanghai when two men, one Kyo Gisors, a native of Shanghai, and one Katov, a Russian, manage to sidetrack a shipment of weapons and turn the strike into a revolution. Within a day and a half they take the city. These local communists had been able to count on the powerful Chiang Kai-shek and his Nationalist Party to support them in earlier conflicts, but this time Chiang moves in, turns against them, and orders them to surrender their weapons. Their appeals for help from the international communists in Hankow fall on deaf ears, so they return to Shanghai, determined to continue their fight, this time against Chiang. The plot to assassinate Chiang by Ch'en, a terrorist working for the local communists, results in Ch'en's arrest and execution, followed by Chiang's wholesale slaughter of every communist in Shanghai. Katov, the Russian, is executed with all the rest, and Kyo, who continued to organize resistance, commits suicide after he is arrested.

When *Man's Fate* appeared in 1933, it was hailed as a groundbreaking, new lesson in the struggle between communism and capitalism. The political Left, especially, recognized the novel as the greatest fictional history of social unrest in the twentieth century. On one level, readers found in the novel the anatomy of a revolution, many of which were going on around them in 1933, as the old order gave way to the new. On another level, readers saw the psychology of many individuals in a society where revolution was happening. It attempted to answer the question of how one behaves when the world is turning upside down. The worst only want to hang on to power at any price. Then there are those who change the way we see the world. Finally, there are those who act, not always wisely, for social change.

No less a figure than the Russian revolutionary Leon Trotsky, read Malraux's sequence of revolutionary novels, of which *Man's Fate* is the most widely known. In answer to Trotsky's criticism that Malraux's characters abandon communist ideology, Malraux claimed that he was primarily interested in individual psychological struggles rather than politics. On this level, readers saw the adequacy or inadequacy of various courses of action: Konig, the sadistic police chief who only gets satisfaction from humiliating and torturing his victims because he himself had been tortured by the Russians in

his youth; the communist terrorist Ch'en, who inherits the fervor of the Lutheran teachers of his childhood but none of their love or faith; the old intellectual Marxist Gisor, who escapes in opium; and the disreputable Westerner Clappique, who escapes into alcohol.

Most characters are figuring out not only how to act in a revolution but also how to act in the full knowledge that life is essentially meaningless and absurd.

The answer suggested by Malraux was a new set of outlooks, new values, a new set of myths for the revolutionary world in which the lowliest person is valued and where work is not a punishment but a dignified role in a common struggle. In stressing the value to society of individual action, Malraux brought a new perspective to existentialism.

Additional Readings: Charles D. Blend, *André Malraux: Tragic Humanist* (Columbus: Ohio State University Press, 1963); Harold Bloom, ed., *André Malraux* (New York: Chelsea House Publishers, 1988).

85. *Nausea* (*La Nausea*), by Jean-Paul Sartre (France, 1938). Jean-Paul Sartre, one of the most highly regarded social and metaphysical philosophers of the twentieth century, had an immense impact on the thinking of his readers throughout the world. His best-known work of fiction, in which he embodied existentialism, is *Nausea*, a work that was originally titled *Melancholia*. The novel was written and published against a background of post–World War I disillusionment and despair, rampant capitalism and worldwide economic depression, and the rise of aggressive, militaristic fascism.

Presented as a found diary, *Nausea* is the story of a spiritual/intellectual quest by a scholar named Roquentin, who has returned to France to study an eighteenth-century figure. He is a solitary person and has no social life but is, at first, completely engrossed in his books. Gradually, however, he abandons the plan of reviving the dead man who is the object of his quest and turns to examine meaning in the present. His life, he realizes, is entirely without center or foundation. He has no real home and feels that everything is in transition. In the course of his quest, he has repeated epiphanies, sudden moments of enlightenment, as, for example, when he chats with a casual acquaintance, a socialist and a pederast, who, having failed to find his own answers in real life, looks for answers in books. Roquentin's quest continues as he takes an aimless ride on a streetcar, as he looks around him in a public garden, finally leaving for Paris, where he is abandoned by a former mistress, listens to jazz, and finally plans to write a book about his quest that will make others ashamed of their delusions and, at the same time, explain himself. The truth to which his quest takes him is so grim and unsettling that it repeatedly brings on disgust or nausea, at times a paralysis of the intellect. The plot is not one of action and event but solely of mental twists and turns.

The importance of *Nausea* came from its presentation of existential philosophy in a form accessible to the reader of fiction. Readers in the backwash of a war so devastating for England and France were introduced by the novel to a hard, stark vision of the world as they asked, as Roquentin does, "What is the reason for all this suffering?" The answer they are given is not comforting nor pleasant, except in that the reader may see that it has the ring of truth: There is no meaning, no great pattern, no divine plan. There are no absolute values and no foundation. These things are human inventions. All is nothingness, absurd, and human beings have to face this awful truth and create their own meaning, as Roquentin does in planning his book. Basically, people are called upon to accept responsibility for their own actions and make their own free choices, outside of traditional values, social mores, and religious faith.

In expressing the importance of Sartre's thought, as it was expressed in *Nausea* and other works, Catharine Savage Brosman writes that he "gave a name to experiences of dread, shame, hostility, solitude, embodiment, emptiness, and others which readers recognized as their own" (*Dictionary of Literary Biography* 72, p. 353).

The necessity of creating one's own mean-

ing, as it is finally expressed in *Nausea*, forms the foundation of the radical political action to which Sartre and others, especially Marxists, devoted themselves. The power of his personal political commitment was expressed when in 1964 he was awarded the Nobel Prize for Literature and refused it, believing that accepting such an award by the establishment would weaken his image and effectiveness as a revolutionary.

Nausea was very favorably received by the public at the time of its publication, was translated into a number of languages, was regarded as a very successful work, and is still read and studied regularly over sixty years after its first appearance.

Additional Readings: Catharine Savage Brosman, *Jean-Paul Sartre* (Boston: Twayne, 1983); Edith Kern, ed., *Sartre: A Collection of Critical Essays* (Englewood Cliffs, NJ: Prentice-Hall, 1962).

86. *The Plague* (*La Peste*), by Albert Camus (France, Algeria, 1947). *The Plague*, published in 1947 and set in Oran, Algeria, has reference to the early 1940s in France during World War II, beginning with the German invasion of France in the spring of 1940. As the German army moved across France, the French government fell, and a puppet government, whose strings were pulled by the German occupiers, was established in Vichy, France, under an aged ex-soldier named Marshall Petain. Many Frenchmen cooperated with their German occupiers with varying degrees of enthusiasm. But when the Germans invaded, a strong underground resistance movement arose, nominally spearheaded by Charles de Gaulle, who had escaped to London from where he led a relatively small collection of French soldiers and sailors committed to continued resistance in France.

There were, as well, significant numbers of civilians who worked in hundreds of loosely organized, local resistance groups to undermine the German occupiers. They served as journalists, messengers, spies, and saboteurs and in lesser ways made the occupation less comfortable for the Germans.

With the successful invasion of Normandy and the liberation of France by the Allies in 1944, de Gaulle reentered France to set up a provisional government. After the war in Europe ended, in 1945, infighting began between factions in the resistance, who struggled with the problem of how to set up a new government and how to deal with Frenchmen who had collaborated with the Nazis.

Albert Camus, who had been a pacifist before Germany's invasion of France, decided when the Germans invaded that there were only two possible courses of action—either collaboration or resistance. A French Algerian, he moved to Paris and joined the underground in 1942, writing for *Combat*, the underground resistance newspaper. Typically, few particulars are known about his resistance work beyond his newspaper work. As a writer for *Combat*, he saw his purpose as countering German and Vichy propaganda, being a source of accurate information about the war, and assuring its readers that an Allied victory was inevitable. For several years after the war, until poor health forced him to leave, he continued to be a leading political voice within the resistance through his editing of *Combat* and other activities.

His influence also continued with the publication of his second novel, *The Plague*, written in the years immediately after the war and published in 1947. On the surface, it is the story of an Algerian town where the European inhabitants have been going about their lives in the usual way—working hard during the day and socializing at night. They are utterly oblivious to signs of an approaching plague: a proliferation of rats and increasing cases of sickness. As a consequence, they do nothing to avert disaster. Then, almost instantly, the entire town is consumed by a fatal plague that no one can stop and no one can survive, once infected. Its insidiousness is seen in its pattern of lying dormant for a time and then resurfacing. Three men work tirelessly and courageously to alleviate suffering, one of them, Dr. Rieux, approaching tragic heroism in the classical sense in that he continues to struggle even though he knows it will be futile in the end.

One hundred thousand copies of *The Plague* were sold within three weeks of its publication. By 1980, Camus's French publishers estimate that 3.7 million copies of the novel had been sold worldwide, making the novel one of the most financially successful novels ever published in France.

The plague in Camus's novel was immediately and universally understood to represent Nazism, in particular, and the human condition, in general. By inferring the German occupation, the reader could focus intensely upon certain human problems that occur in the face of adversity and isolation. As the plague suddenly broke out in the Algerian village, so Germans crept up on an insufficiently prepared France. France was isolated as if in quarantine, and everyone, having to look death in the face, suffered because of it. Comparatively few fought back with courage. But eventually, from despair came renewal and lucidity in both the fictional Algerian town and the real postoccupational France, where the opportunity arose for a more just and democratic form of government than had existed before the war.

For many Frenchmen, however, Camus's analogy was very unsettling, for he raised questions that had to be in the back of everyone's minds after the war. What responsibility do we bear in having participated in mass murder through our silence or inaction? Can a decent person struggle for his survival without hurting others? What good does it do to give up one's life in the struggle against evil?

By analogy, the book excoriated collaborators who had actually helped spread the plague/Nazism. At issue were the French, who by implication held a sense of political responsibility. It was also aimed at French leaders who had failed to avert the invasion in the first place. Rightist sympathizers with the Vichy government believed they were under attack in the novel, but so did many communists who saw Camus's intended analogy of the plague with Soviet imperialism. Moreover, many French intellectuals rightly concluded that Camus was attacking them as well.

Yet many of his readers found that Camus

alone had provided them with an unflinching articulation of France's predicament in the occupation and the effects of tyranny, both Left and Right. In the postwar confusion of setting up a just, free government, readers found hope in *The Plague*. Happiness came not just from surviving but from helping humankind, cursed with perpetual plagues. In the struggle we can be united and renewed.

Despite his critics, no writer enjoyed greater popularity throughout the Western world in the 1950s, 1960s, and 1970s, those years of emerging social action. In 1957 he was awarded the Nobel Prize for Literature. In the United States, Camus was more read and discussed than any French author had ever been. It was recognized that in *The Plague* Albert Camus had written no less than the myth of modern man.

Additional Readings: Bettina L. Knapp, *Critical Essays on Albert Camus* (Boston: G.K. Hall, 1988); Emmett Parker, *Albert Camus: The Artist in the Arena* (Madison: University of Wisconsin Press, 1965).

87. *Molloy*, by Samuel Beckett (Ireland, France, 1951). Samuel Beckett is one of the most original thinkers of the twentieth century, and *Molloy* is his most significant fiction, a work that dramatizes his philosophy regarding modern man's alienation in a universe ruled by a roll of the dice.

Molloy is told from the point of view of two men whose identities become one by the end of the novel. The first narrator, Molloy, explains that he must give what he has written of his story every week to a man who comes by to collect it, because his inability to walk has trapped him in his mother's room. He tells of being arrested on his way to his mother's house, then of being attacked by a mob after running over a dog on his bicycle. He is befriended by a poor workman in a forest whom he later proceeds to kick and hit with his crutch before emerging from the forest, falling in a ditch from which he is rescued, and being taken to his mother's house, bringing his part of the story full circle. The second narrator, Moran, is sent by his super-visor to find Molloy. His son goes with him, and on the way, he makes camp and receives two visitors, one of whom is suddenly dead. Moran hides the body, is intercepted and sent home by his supervisor, and finds, as he sits in his room writing his report, that his clothes and health have been steadily deteriorating. At the end, he is planning to leave on another mission.

Samuel Beckett's influence in this, his best-known novel, lies in its ability to illustrate philosophical musings about the human condition in the modern world. Although the characters of the novel are scarcely realistic, they reflect a kind of unhappy truth that Beckett introduced to his readers. The world of Molloy and Moran is like no other. These characters are the refuse of society, society's wounded, the down-and-outers: beggars, hoboes, cripples, the homeless, and the insane. Yet the reader, though he or she may be introduced to such characters for the first time through this novel, recognizes that they are emblematic of all human beings who are, in effect, all damaged.

Readers of the novel noticed that the other distinctive quality of the characters in *Molloy* is their absolute solitude of soul, their utter loneliness. Even though Moran has a son and Molloy speaks of a mother, the two men seem as alienated from their kin and everyone else as they would be from utter strangers. In this, too, readers saw something of their own loneliness.

Not only are the characters in *Molloy* unable to know other human beings; they are unable to know any absolute truths about the world or any universal meaning. The universe of Molloy's world seems run by chance. The good life of one person and the poor life of another comes to them randomly. Nothing *causes* good or bad fortune. It exists as no part of any divine plan. It has no reason.

In light of the pessimism reflected in the lives of its characters, the readers of *Molloy* are struck by the ludicrous pretensions of human beings to knowledge of God, of absolute meaning, and of their own importance. Understandably, enthusiastic readers of *Mal-*

loy have indicated that no one can come away from the novel unchanged.

For his plays, especially "waiting for Godot," as well as for *Molloy*, Beckett was awarded the Nobel Prize for Literature in 1969.

Additional Readings: Porter H. Abbott, *The Fiction of Samuel Beckett: Form and Effect* (Berkeley: University of California Press, 1973); John Fletcher, *The Novels of Samuel Beckett* (London: Chatto and Windus, 1964).

88. *The Mandarins* (*Les Mandarins*), by Simone de Beauvoir (France, 1954). *The Mandarins* is the best-known and most popular fiction of Simone de Beauvoir, the celebrated French feminist of existentialism and the French radical Left.

The background of the novel is formed by the post–World War II years between 1944 and 1947, in a time when leftist writers were fighting among themselves as they attempted to come to terms with the French resistance and France's collaboration with the Nazis during the war, the materialistic capitalism of the postwar Allies in the West, the plight of Third World peoples, and the growing aggression and rumors of purges in Stalinist Russia.

The plot involves characters at the center of the intellectual world of France after the liberation: a psychiatrist named Anne Dubreuilh, her husband Robert, a journalist named Henri Perron, and an American writer named Lewis Brogan. Many readers saw this as an autobiographical fiction about de Beauvoir herself, Jean-Paul Sartre, Albert Camus, and Nelson Algren, though the author denied any such intention. The theme is the philosophical, personal, and political problems that beset the group and place a strain on their friendships. The enduring theme of the novel is the multiplicity of political stances that divided the "mandarins" after their united stance in liberating France was behind them. The center of the action is Paris but, illustrating their increasing globalism, includes several trips to other countries.

The Mandarins was immediately both a popular and a critical success. In the first month after publication, the novel sold 40,000 copies. In 1954 the novel received the Prix Goncourt for the year's finest French novel, thus stimulating a renewed surge upward in sales. Translated into fifteen languages, the book's renown went well beyond the borders of France. Curiously, both the communist and capitalist press reviewed the novel positively, both convinced that the novel portrayed their political views in the best light and condemned their adversaries. Testimony to the novel's influence were the flood of letters to de Beauvoir that it generated.

The novel provided its readers with a lesson in current global political attitudes. It is the first novel to clarify the divisive issues among the political Left after World War II. Here was a group of compatriots and friends who had once been united in a very clear purpose during the war. Afterward, however, the world situation became hopelessly complex, primarily because they were interested in issues that went beyond France alone and because the wartime Allies were now divided into the opposing camps of the U.S.-dominated West and the Soviet-dominated East. Neither side had a monopoly on morality or humane actions.

Each character represents a different political stance. Though not a member of the Communist Party, Robert, Anne's husband, is a Marxist who cooperates with the communists but has an aversion to the party line. Henri has serious differences with Robert with regard to communism, especially as stories about the Soviet labor camps come to light. He comes to be more sympathetic with the Americans. Yet in their little group there are members of the Communist Party, those who are disgusted with all politics, and those who use politics for their own self-advancement.

Readers at the end of the novel have a sense of the divisive issues but no final answer, no preferred political solution.

Additional Readings: Carol Ascher, *Simone de*

Beauvoir: A Life of Freedom (Boston: Beacon, 1981); Konrad Bieber, *Simone de Beauvoir* (Boston: Twayne, 1979).

89. *Night* (*La Nuit*), by Elie Wiesel (Romania, France, 1958). Although Elie Wiesel's novel *Night* is classified as fiction, he insists that all the events are true and that the work is autobiographical in nature, deriving from his own experiences in the 1940s, as a victim of the Holocaust.

The Holocaust, which is the novel's subject, resulted from Nazi Germany's extermination of Europe's Jews. When Adolf Hitler came to power in 1933, the first step in Germany was to divest the country's Jews of all economic power and participation. In 1938, during "the Night of the Broken Glass," all German synagogues were burned, Jewish-owned shop windows were smashed, and thousands of Jews were arrested. In Poland, the Holocaust began in 1939, when Germans invaded Poland and forced all Jews into ghettos. Jews in German-occupied portions of the USSR were systematically killed in 1941. By 1941, with most of Europe under German control, official Nazi policy called for the extermination of Jews throughout Europe. In 1941 and 1942, death and work camps were set up in Poland with the intention of gassing Jews. Three hundred thousand Jews were taken to the camps from the Warsaw ghetto alone.

Countries throughout Europe, sympathetic to or invaded by the Nazis, began turning their Jewish citizens over to Germany for extermination. Hungary capitulated in 1944.

Auschwitz in Poland was the largest death camp, where, over 1 million Jews were gassed. A large population of Jews and a much smaller number of Gypsies were the only prisoners specifically targeted for the gas chambers in all the camps. Other prisoners—Slavs, homosexuals, communists, and Jehovah's Witnesses—were among the non-Jews who died in the camps of starvation, disease, and Nazi guns.

The novel begins in 1940, as the young Eliezer is receiving religious instruction from a popular and honored Jew named Moshe. Eliezer's seeming idyllic life is disrupted when Moshe is banished from the town by the authorities because he is of foreign birth. Moshe and other citizens, primarily Jews, were then forcibly displaced by the Nazis and shipped to Poland, where they were made to dig their own graves before being shot. Having miraculously escaped, Moshe returns to relate his story, attempting to raise an alarm among the Jewish community concerning things to come. But his warnings fall on deaf ears. His hearers refuse to take his story seriously.

Subsequently, in 1944, the Nazis arrive to occupy Eliezer's village. They arrest all Jews, including Eliezer, during Passover, force them to wear a yellow star, and confiscate all their property before relegating them to a ghetto. Nevertheless, the Jews continue to have hope that Russian soldiers will shortly arrive to liberate them. Before this can happen, however, they are transported like cattle to the concentration camp at Auschwitz. In Auschwitz they are separated into groups at the direction of the infamous Nazi sadist Dr. Joseph Mengele. One group will immediately be sent to be gassed. Eliezer and his father are placed in the group that has a momentary reprieve so that they can be worked. Within the camp, Eliezer sees perpetual death and inhumane cruelty. They experience starvation and killing labor.

With the Russian army coming closer, the prisoners are relentlessly marched in brutal ice and snow, without clothing or food, toward another infamous camp—Buchenwald. In Buchenwald, after experiencing unspeakable horrors, Eliezer sees his father die but cannot mourn him. Finally in April 1945, he is liberated. When he looks into a mirror, he sees an unrecognizable corpse.

While Anne Frank's diary was one of the first works to draw attention to the day-to-day fears and deprivations of Jews in hiding, Wiesel's novel was the first widely distributed concentration camp novel written about conditions in the camps by an actual survivor. The novel resulted in renewed widespread awareness of the Holocaust, which had, heretofore, only been available in fragmentary court testimony.

Readers of *Night* found many tragic complexities in the story, especially in the dehumanizing effect of extreme physical and psychological torture. All humane feeling seemed to be muted or destroyed.

Operating on the theory that those who ignore history are doomed to repeat it, Wiesel accomplished his purpose of bringing information about the Holocaust to the attention of a large audience, many of whom had not been born or were children when the Nuremberg Trials took place.

The influence of the publication of *Night* is seen in the establishment of many memorials to victims of the Holocaust and numerous museums about the horrors, designed to keep alive the memory of what happened. The development of the largest single museum began in Washington, D.C. in the 1980s with Wiesel serving as chairman of the President's Commission on the Holocaust.

Largely as a result of *Night*, but also other work for human rights, Wiesel received the Nobel Prize for Literature in 1985. In the same year he received the Congressional Gold Medal of Honor.

Additional Readings: Jack Kolbert, *The Worlds of Elie Wiesel* (Cranberry, NJ: Susquehanna University Press, 2001); Robert Krell and Marc I. Sherman, *Medical and Psychological Effects of Concentration Camps on Holocaust Survivors* (New Brunswick, NJ: Transaction Publishers, 1997).

90. *The Planet of the Apes* (*La Planete des singes*), by Pierre Boulle (France, 1963). *The Planet of the Apes* is a science-fiction masterpiece that portrays a future in which simians have replaced *Homo sapiens* as the intelligent, "sapient" creatures in life. However it is not ordinary science fiction, in the sense of using scientific possibilities to project the future, in the manner of Jules Verne. It is rather social commentary, a satire, more fantasy than science, used to excoriate the savage tendencies of modern life, in the manner of Jonathan Swift's *Gulliver's Travels* or Voltaire's *Micromegas*.

The story within a story begins as two hol-

iday adventurers find a manuscript in a bottle floating in space. The author of the manuscript, Merou, a twenty-fifth-century journalist, tells of his expedition with eminent scientists to a distant galaxy, hoping to find a world "different" from their own. They reach their destination in two years, landing in a field where they find a beautiful naked woman who is unable either to speak or to think. Merou calls her Nova. All her people prove to be like her. Soon Merou and his associates are hunted down by a race of creatures who have both superior intelligence and language: These higher beings are apes.

In the course of the story, the survivors are placed in cages, as in a zoo, and are then studied the way humans customarily observe nonhumans in a laboratory.

Ultimately, Merou gets to learn the language of the apes. He discovers that, as in human society, they are divided essentially into three groups: the gorillas, who represent authority and power; the pedantic, unoriginal orangutans, who represent official science and are in effect the enemies of progress, intent on preserving tradition; and the chimpanzees, who represent the genuine intellectuals in society and who befriend Merou.

Merou, while on an archeological expedition, learns that at one time the "humans" were intelligent, like his own people, and the apes were the lower animals, but that after centuries of apathy and of failure to use their brains the humans turned into the mindless creatures that he sees around him, while the apes, constantly striving and using all their faculties, rose to predominance.

Boulle's novel is recognized as one of the most trenchant satires of human society in the modern age. In particular, the novel attacks two targets: the modern world's arrogant science and technology, which had risen to eclipse all other disciplines, and the intellectual apathy and passivity of the human race. Boulle articulated the problem of nuclear weapons and proposed that science itself might destroy the world. Boulle says that the threat to civilization will come not from without but from within. In this novel, humankind has been made so unthinking and mute by its reliance on static instruments of help and by so-called entertainment that all mental activities, including speech, finally atrophy, like a leg left motionless for so long that it ceases to function. Man's enslavement or obliteration comes from his own empti-ness and failure to use his faculties, rather than from an atomic holocaust.

One indication of the enthusiasm with which Boulle's novel was greeted is in its choice for many screen incarnations, including films in 1968 and 2001.

Additional Reading: Lucille Frackman Becker, *Pierre Boulle* (New York: Twayne, 1996).

Germany

❧

Johann Wolfgang von Goethe, *The Sorrows of Young Werther*, 1774

Thomas Mann, *The Magic Mountain*, 1924

Hermann Hesse, *Steppenwolf*, 1927

Erich Maria Remarque, *All Quiet on the Western Front*, 1929

Lion Feuchtwanger, *Success*, 1930

Theodor Plevier, *Stalingrad*, 1948

Heinrich Boll, *Billiards at Half-Past Nine*, 1959

Günter Grass, *The Tin Drum*, 1959

Christa Wolf, *Divided Heaven*, 1963

❧

TIMELINE

1700s   In the eighteenth century, Germany was a loose connection of over 300 separate states held together by ties of language, culture, and the fading Holy Roman Empire and dominated militarily by Protestant Prussia in the north and Catholic Austria in the south. In literature it was dominated by the principality of Weimar, which attracted, among others, the poet Johann Wolfgang von Goethe, the philosopher Johann Gottfried von Herder, and the novelist Jean Paul Richter.

1740–86   Frederick the Great makes Prussia a great power in Europe.

1766–67   Johann Gottfried von Herder, leader of the *Sturm und Drang* movement, publishes *Fragments on Recent German Literature*.

1767   Moses Mendelssohn, a German Jewish philosopher who advocated tolerance, breadth of knowledge, and nobility of mind, produces *Phadon*, his most influential work.

1770   Goethe meets Herder, the man who has profoundly influenced him.

1770–80   *Sturm und Drang* [Storm and Stress], a youth-oriented form of German romanticism, geared to youthful suffering and social revolt and greatly influenced by ideas of

Herder and Jean-Jacques Rousseau, flourishes in Germany.

1773	Goethe's produces *Götz von Berlichingen*, a drama.
1774	Johann Wolfgang von Goethe's *The Sorrows of Young Werther* is published.
1775	Goethe settles in Weimar.
	Under the influence of Lillo's *The London Merchant* and Samuel Richardson's *Clarissa*, Gotthold Ephraim Lessing produced his play *Miss Sara Sampson*, a milestone in German theater.
1775–1800s	The Werther cult is in full flower.
1781	Immanuel Kant produces *Critique of Pure Reason*. Kant's subjectivist theory of knowledge gave a philosophical basis to German individualism that flourished in the Storm and Stress period. It also showed the difficulties of a rationalist theology.
	Friedrich Schiller has his play *Die Rauber* ("The Robbers") printed, using his own money. The play that damned virtually every aspect of civilization was a tremendous success.
1786–97	Frederick William II permits Prussia to become comparatively weak; ends religious toleration.
1787	*The Sorrows of Young Werther* is revised and republished.
1792	Francis II of Austria is elected to head the Holy Roman Empire.
1797–1807	In Frederick William III's reign, Prussia partially regains its strength.
1804	Schiller's *William Tell* becomes a rallying cry for German nationalism.
1806	Prussia is decisively defeated by French armies.
1807	The Edict of 1807 abolishes serfdom and permits individuals to rise

in society by merit. It also opens up trades and professions to all classes.

Jerome Bonaparte (twenty-three years old) becomes king of Westphalia.

1808	J.G. Fichte delivers a series of *Addresses to the German Nation*. Adopting Herder's idea of a *Volksgeist* ("folk spirit"), which negates the individual spirit in favor of a communal one embracing the spirit of a whole nation, Fichte declared the existence of a special German spirit, superior to all the others.
	Goethe writes *Faust*, Part I.
1809	Goethe writes *Elective Affinities*.
	Jacob Grimm becomes the king's librarian.
1810	University of Berlin is founded.
1812–15	The Brothers Grimm edit and publish *Grimms' Fairy Tales*, originally called "Children- and Household Tales," which becomes a part of German national heritage.
1812–16	George Wilhelm Hegel's *The Science of Logic* is published. Hegel wrote of the organic evolution of society: Institutions grow to maturity, achieve a purpose, then give way to others, in a pattern of "dialectic," and finally produce a "synthesis," a process that makes the state ("God walking upon earth") the source of all social and moral values, unhampered by international law or the interests of the individual.
1815	Napoleon is defeated at Waterloo.
1817	At Wartburg Castle, Student Societies (*Burschenschaften*,) march on behalf of "union" and "freedom." Though officially repressed, they reappear in the 1820s and the 1830s.
1848	Revolutions occur in Germany, as throughout most of Europe.
1850–70	Otto Edward Leopold von Bismarck rises to power.

1854–56	The Crimean War is fought.
1854–74	Richard Wagner produces *The Ring of the Nibelung*, operas based on the German epic *Song of the Nibelungs*, attempting to recreate the conditions of ancient Greek drama by fusing all the elements of art into one form while making theater a religious occasion (*Festspiel*) and using national legends for subject matter.
	In 1872, Ludwig II enabled him to establish the *Festspielhaus* at Bayreuth.
1862	Bismarck becomes minister-president.
1870–71	Germany defeats France in the Franco-Prussian War.
1871	In the great Hall of Mirrors at Versailles, Bismarck proclaims the formation of the German Empire, established with William I of Prussia as emperor. Otto Edward Leopold von Bismarck becomes chancellor. The government is marked by anti-Catholic and anti-socialist measures and strong nationalism.
1878	Germany acquires colonies in Africa and the Pacific.
1882	Germany enters into an alliance with Italy and Austria-Hungary.
1890	With the political rise of the socialists and Bismark's increased repression, he is dismissed by William II, the new emperor.
1899	Philosopher Houston Stewart Chamberlain's *The Foundations of the Nineteenth Century* is published. This work, by a man who was born in Germany of English parents and became a German citizen, becomes a major piece of propaganda, arguing for the superiority of the Aryan race and the need for cleansing Western culture of Jews and people of color—a stance that would be adopted by Germans after World War I and

would inspire Hitler in the creation of extermination camps during World War II.

1907	An alliance counter to Germany is formed by France, Britain, and Russia.
1914	World War I begins.
1918	Germany is defeated. William II abdicates.
1919	The Treaty of Versailles forces Germany to cede territory, pay reparations, and dismantle its military.
	The German Empire is dismantled and replaced with the Weimar Republic with Friedrich Ebert as president.
	Reforms include universal suffrage, freedom of speech, press and association, and the plan to nationalize vital industries.
	The Bavarian Revolution is a Socialist attempt to overthrow Weimar. Reprisals are brutal.
1922	The devalued Reichsmark produces damaging inflation.
1924	Thomas Mann's *The Magic Mountain*, set in pre–World War I Germany, is published.
1925–34	An aged war hero named Paul von Hindenburg is president of the Weimar Republic.
1926	Germany joins the League of Nations.
	Adolf Hitler becomes the leader of the Nazi Party, using a corps of brownshirts or storm troopers to attack what the Nazis decided were enemies of Germany. These included communists and Jews.
1927	Hermann Hesse's *Steppenwolf* is published.
1929	Erich Maria Remarque's *All Quiet on the Western Front*, with a setting in World War I, is published.
	The book is confiscated by U.S. Customs in Chicago.

Thomas Mann wins the Nobel Prize for Literature.

1930   The opening of a film of *All Quiet on the Western Front* enrages Nazis, who storm and disrupt the theater.

With a setting between 1919 and 1923, Lion Feuchtwanger's *Success* is published.

1930s   A devastating economic depression results in the rise of communist radicals on the Left and fascist radicals on the Right.

1933   Hitler is made chancellor of Germany. The Communist Party is banned. The Enabling Act is passed, giving government absolute, totalitarian powers.

Concentration camps are built to house Jews, Gypsies, communists, homosexuals, and criminals.

Mann's novel is burned; he is declared an enemy of the state; and he loses his citizenship.

Remarque's novel is burned.

Steppenwolf is burned.

Success is burned.

1934   All political parties excepting the Nazi Party are forbidden. A large army is developed, and propaganda and indoctrination are favored policies.

1935   Nazis pass the Nuremberg Laws to deprive Jews of citizenship and civil rights. The property of Jews is also confiscated.

Germany leaves the League of Nations and becomes militarized.

1938   Nazis, in a particularly horrendous rampage, known as "The Night of the Broken Glass," kill over ninety Jews, torch temples, and break the windows of Jewish businesses.

1939   The first shot of World War II is fired by the Germans at Danzig to annex it to the Third Reich.

With Germany's invasion of Poland, Britain and France enter the war.

Polish Jews are sent to ghettos.

1940   Other European countries are invaded and overcome by Germany, including Denmark, Norway, and France.

1941   Hitler invades Russia and sends death squads to kill 1 million Russian and Ukrainian Jews.

1942   The Nazis agree on a final solution to what they called "the Jewish problem" and begin extermination of Jews and other "undesirables." Some 6 million Jews are killed.

The United States enters the war against Germany.

Hitler renews his push into Russia.

1943   German forces surrender to Russians at Stalingrad.

1944   British and U.S. forces land in German-occupied France and liberate Paris.

1945   With Allied forces moving in to Berlin from the west and Soviet tanks moving in from the east, Hitler commits suicide and Germany surrenders.

As the Allies liberate concentration camps, the full horror of the Holocaust becomes known to the world.

Germany is divided into military zones. The Allies have control of the south and west, what will become the Federal Republic of Germany. The Soviet Union controls the east. Berlin is also divided into sectors.

Hermann Hesse is awarded the Nobel Prize for Literature.

1945–46   The Nuremberg Trials bring Nazi leaders before an international tribunal for war crimes against humanity.

1947	After two years of economic hardship in Europe, the U.S. Marshall Plan puts Europe, including West Germany, back on its feet. Within two years the West Germany economy is one of the most vigorous in Europe.
1948	The Soviets attempt a blockade of Berlin.
	Theodor Plevier's *Stalingrad* is published.
1949	The United States sends supplies by air over the blockade, and the Russians lift the ineffectual blockade after eleven months.
	West Germany becomes the Federal Republic of Germany.
1952	The West ends its military occupation of West Germany.
1959	Heinrich Boll's *Billiards at Half-Past Nine* is published.
	Günter Grass's *The Tin Drum* is published.
1961	Soviet East Germany constructs the Berlin Wall to prevent the heavy migration of poverty-level East Germans to the prosperous West Germany.
1963	Christa Wolf, from East Germany, publishes *The Divided Heaven*.
1972	Boll wins the Nobel Prize for Literature.
1989	The Berlin Wall comes down.
1990	East Germany collapses and both East and West Germany are unified as the Federal Republic of Germany.
1994	The Russian military leaves East Germany after fifty years of occupation.
1999	Günter Grass wins the Nobel Prize for Literature.

91. *The Sorrows of Young Werther* (*Die Leiden des jungen Werther*), by Johann Wolfgang von Goethe (Germany, 1774; rev. 1787)**. *The Sorrows of Young Werther*, a novel that had a profound effect on both England and France, first appeared in a Germanic culture markedly different from that of the rest of Europe. Unlike France or England at the time, Germany was not a unified nation. It was a federation of semiindependent states, places small enough to be successfully governed and controlled by local princes. Germany also had no viable middle class in the eighteenth century; and since the greatest threat to the aristocracy usually came from the middle class, as it did in France, the power structure in Germany remained undisturbed. The Church and the nobility cooperated to keep all other classes inferior and powerless. Like the aristocracy, the Church preached "divine right" and "obedience" in a country of devout believers. In Germany, princes and churches ruled, and peasants obeyed. While the French were moving toward revolution, Germany, with no intervening "Age of Reason," was moving directly to Romanticism with its emphasis on *Sturm und Drang* (Storm and Stress). Thus, when rebellion occurred, it took the form of speculative philosophy and wild romanticism, not political challenge to existing institutions. With all the restrictions imposed on rebellious action, the German intelligentsia turned to excessive idealism, to "inward" freedom and the triumph of spirit over external reality. The time and the place were ripe for Johann Wolfgang von Goethe's story of an inwardly tortured idealist.

Goethe was one of the early progenitors of *Sturm und Drang*, writing first a stormily heroic play, *Götz von Berlichingen*, in 1773 and then the novel, *The Sorrows of Young Werther*, in 1774, the former covering the heroism of storm and stress, the latter its romantic love.

The story of the hero, young Werther, is told through his letters, until a presumed editor injects a third-person narrative shortly before the end. The letters show him to be sensitive, intelligent, attractive, and perceptive, often given to "fantastic dreams" and "speculative thinking." The letters also reveal certain traits suggesting the emotional disintegration that brings about his end. Before its publication, Goethe noted that Werther becomes "unhinged" through "unhappy passions." His agony begins in a typically untamed, romantic rural setting, when he falls madly in love. Finding his unhappy passions vain, unrealizable, excruciatingly painful, he at last puts a bullet through his head.

Werther's disintegration is previewed through the use of parallel and contrasting episodes in the two parts of the novel. First, Werther carries the *Odyssey*, the classic story of a hero who learns to control himself and his desires as he wanders home from the Trojan War. Then he carries *Ossian*, a wild tale of untamed and violent passions (supposedly written by the legendary Irish hero but discovered later to have been written by James McPherson). His suicide is presaged by the suicide of a young girl who has been seduced and by a clerk driven mad by his hopeless love.

The novel may be considered in part semi-autobiographical, with the author as the young dreaming lover, in that Goethe himself was constantly falling madly in love at various times—first with Gretchen, then with Annette, Charlotte, Lili, Mina, Ulrike, Friederike, and Maximiliane. He was also inspired by an actual romantic death: In October 1772, Wilhelm Jerusalem borrowed a pistol and shot himself in despair from hopeless love for the wife of a friend. Goethe wove these two elements together to form a psychologically complex hero.

Werther immediately became a wild sensation like no other in literature. Its publication was compared to an explosive storm, not only in Germany but throughout Europe. Readers, especially the young, adopted it as the triumphant standard of the entire Romantic movement. It was as if no other book had ever been published, for every young reader was consumed by *Werther*.

It was also hated as passionately as it was praised. The German clergy viewed it as a distinct threat because of its questionable morality and sympathetically presented suicide. Classic scholars berated the author for his uncontrolled romantic excess. But no amount of institutional criticism could dampen the rapture with which the young responded to Werther.

The Werther cult was so excessive as to be almost laughable at times. Young men rebelled by adopting strange clothes and bizarre haircuts, like those they imagined the romantic hero sported. One young man, in imitation of Werther, went around with his shirt open to the navel and his wild hair uncombed. The standard Werther outfit was, however, a blue frock coat and a yellow vest. Others wandered around, consumed for the first time with the need to write passionate verses, as Werther did.

Unfortunately, some members of the Werther cult carried their rapturous imitation to an extreme: The novel gave rise to an alarming spate of suicides among the young.

On a fundamental level, Goethe's novel validated for his readers that cornerstone of romanticism: feeling above all—above reason, duty, authority, and material success. One example is the French writer Madame de Staël, who echoed *Werther* in *D'Linfluence des passions*, stressing the importance of "feelings" and even praising suicide. She declared *The Sorrows of Young Werther* to be "the greatest book of all time." Napoleon Bonaparte carried three books with him to Egypt: One of those was *The Sorrows of Young Werther*, a book he admitted having read seven times.

The Sorrows of Young Werther, along with Rousseau's *New Heloise*, were the first books to reach such cult status that they spawned major industries in the production of mementos and commemorative editions.

Additional Reading: Stuart Pratt Atkins, *The Testament of Werther in Poetry and Drama* (Cambridge, MA: Harvard University Press, 1949).

92. *The Magic Mountain* (*Der Zauberberg*), **by Thomas Mann** (**Germany, 1924**). *The Magic Mountain* is the best-known and most influential work of Thomas Mann, considered by many to be Germany's greatest writer. The novel appeared in 1924, as various political philosophies were vying for ascendancy in Germany, a battle that was won by Hitler's Nazi Party in the early 1930s. The story is set in a seven-year back-wash of romantic idealism before the outbreak of World War I, including Germany, on one side, and France, England, and eventually the United States on the other.

The title refers to a transcendent spiritual life lived outside of time and history, in this case, literally a sanitarium for tuberculosis patients. Hans Castorp, the main character, can find a degree of philosophical and spiritual truth in this isolated place, removed from real life, to which he commits himself. Here, for example, he is exposed to different perspectives on pre–World War I politics and society: humanism, Catholicism, hedonism, and socialism. He also explores the allure and terror of sickness and death and their relationships to love. After Hans has passed the mythical seven years on the magic mountain, he leaves to fight in World War I. The novel ends on the battlefield.

The Magic Mountain marked a turning point in German thought. Ever since the eighteenth century, romantic idealism had been the prevailing philosophy of Germany. As Hans leaves the sanitarium and the romanticism that it represents, so the German people would be led by the novel to move beyond romanticism. *The Magic Mountain* was a repudiation of three aspects of romanticism in particular: the fascination with and idealization of death and illness; the romanticizing of the pastoral and rural; and the recommendation of sustained transcendence and repudiation of the world. Each of these ideas can be found in Germany's preeminent novel of romanticism, Goethe's *The Sorrows of Young Werther*.

In Mann's novel, readers saw the preoccupation with sickness and death, on the part of the sanitarium workers and the protagonist, as the ultimate "sickness." Settembrini, one of the regular visitors to the sanitarium, presents the healthier attitude of approaching life through reason and humanism.

While the romantic would have recommended remaining in transcendence on the magic mountain forever, the novel projects the need to go through a time of intense and intellectual and spiritual self-scrutiny. Mann makes clear to the reader the inherent danger of a long-standing escape from time, history, reality, action, and responsibility. Hans's decision to become a soldier seems an affirmation of humanism and of full involvement with society and history. Clearly, Mann's readers saw that the choice of eternal transcendence and contemplation is a choice of death.

On another level, the sanitarium itself was seen as representative of Germany, the sickness of the sanitarium representative of Germany's aloofness from human concerns and the rest of the world. From this point of view, Germany's romantic ideals are a form of darkness that stresses the past and brings on social destruction.

Mann also provided a running and unresolved argument between two dominant social theorists: one a rational humanist and the other a radical reactionary. Though neither side "wins" the argument, the discussion clearly shows the dangers presented by radical groups that were already growing in Germany and Italy and would ultimately result in the rise of Hitler's Nazism.

Five years after publication of *The Magic Mountain* and chiefly on the strength of that novel, Mann became the first German writer in seventeen years to win the Nobel Prize for Literature. But the satisfaction of having received worldwide fame after publication of the novel was tempered by the German fascists' denunciation of the novel's portrayal of reactionaries. The attacks on his work and character, which had begun immediately after the appearance of *The Magic Mountain*, increased dramatically as the Nazis rose to power. Within a year of Hitler's rise to power, Mann was declared an enemy of the state, his citizenship was revoked, his works were banned, and his honorary doctorate from the University of Bonn was rescinded.

Ironically, after World War II, he would also be attacked in the United States, the country to which he had fled for asylum. During the Cold War years of communist hunting in the United States, Mann was spied upon by the Federal Bureau of Investigation, and Senator Joe McCarthy and his associates combed every spoken and written word of Mann's for reference to "social justice," which they interpreted as sympathy with communism.

Additional Readings: James Cleugh, *Thomas Mann: A Study* (New York: Russell and Russell, 1968); Henry Caraway Hatfield, ed., *Thomas Mann: A Collection of Critical Essays* (Englewood Cliffs, NJ: Prentice-Hall, 1964).

93. *Steppenwolf* (*Der Steppenwolf*), by Hermann Hesse (Germany, 1927). No author has ever equaled the sensation created by German writer Hermann Hesse among young people over thirty years after the first publication of his novel. And the social relevance of *Steppenwolf*, his novel that has received the most critical attention, is more the story of the United States in the 1960s than it is of Germany in the 1920s, when the action of the novel occurs.

Harry Haller, the main character of the novel and a thinly fictionalized portrait of Hesse himself, is a man in personal crisis who feels his own dislocation in German society between the wars—a country that is itself dislocated within the world. The spiritual quest he takes in response to crisis ironically leads him to the extremes of sensuality, notably alcohol, sex, and hallucinatory drugs, which all figure in his friend Pablo's "Magic Theater." In the climatic evening with Pablo and another friend Hermine, a prostitute, Haller hallucinates his own murder of Hermine, conversations with Mozart, and his own trial for murder. His experiences become a psychological quest to distinguish between the real and the ideal, between mere appearance and ultimate reality.

The issues that arise in the course of the novel are the character's spiritual dislocation, his repudiation of a middle-class, thoroughly materialistic society and its values, the discovery that he and his kind are outside society's mainstream, the importance of psychoanalysis, the escape through his discovery of sensuality and sex without boundaries, and the psychedelic experience.

Steppenwolf was eagerly embraced by a body of Hesse's admirers among the young in Germany in 1927, but he was immediately attacked by the older generation of Germans. By 1933, his character was being attacked in the Nazi press for poisoning the minds of youth with his Freudian psychoanalysis. A few years later, all his books, including *Steppenwolf*, were banned throughout Germany, and no new editions of the novel were issued. But at the end of the war *Steppenwolf* was revived, and Hesse was awarded the Nobel Prize for Literature in 1945. This was followed by numerous other awards in Germany during the 1950s.

In the 1960s, however, interest in *Steppenwolf* skyrocketed in the United States in one of history's most bizarre literary trends, for Hesse began to be regarded by many as one of the most relevant and important writers of the century. Fifteen million copies of Hesse's works were sold between 1961 and 1971, producing a literary phenomenon unheard of in America. *Steppenwolf* became the frequent subject of university courses and journalistic and academic articles alike. The fascination with Hesse became known as a cult and a virus, especially among the "hippies" of the 1960s. The popularity of the book was also reflected in the frequency with which *Steppenwolf* was invoked by businesses appealing to the young. There was a Steppenwolf bookstore in Aspen, a Steppenwolf bar and a Magic Theater in Berkeley, and a Steppenwolf Rock Quintet. Well after the initial 1960s Hesse craze, a movie called *Steppenwolf* was made in 1974.

The appeal of Hesse was in large measure a reaction among the young of the United States to societal pressures for middle-class conformity and material success that had made them cynical and disillusioned during the 1940s and 1950s. *Steppenwolf*, by contrast, presented the outsider as hero and focused on a positive individualism. The young saw articulated in the novel the emptiness produced by a superficial life lived in a society that spelled success in terms of material accumulation. Hesse directed attention to the inner life, which alone held the truth of the self.

Hesse also articulated the disillusion and criticism of the social establishment. *Steppenwolf* was easily relevant to a time when the establishment had begun and continued to perpetuate the Vietnam War.

On a more specific level, *Steppenwolf* gave comfort and hope in a society in which LSD and birth control had created youthful revolutions of a personal nature with regard to sexuality and drugs.

Additional Readings: G.W. Field, *Hermann Hesse* (New York: Twayne, 1970); Carlee Marrer-Tising, *The Reception of Hermann Hesse by the Youth in the United States* (Bern: Lang, 1982).

94. *All Quiet on the Western Front* (*Im Westen nichts Neues*), **by Erich Maria Remarque (Germany, 1929).** *All Quiet on the Western Front*, a portrayal of World War I from the point of view of a German soldier, by an author who had experienced its horrors, is one of the most influential war novels ever written. Written in 1927–28, ten years after the end of World War I, it was published in 1929, only a few years before the final collapse of Germany's Weimar Republic.

Stark statistics reveal much about the truth of World War I. In the first weeks of battle, the Russians lost 300,000 men at Tannenberg. The Austrians suffered 250,000 casualties in Galicia, and 100,000 others became prisoners of war. In the first six months, the French lost 800,000 men. The small state of Serbia, determined to "hold the pass" against the Central Powers in the Balkans, had at least one tenth of its entire population killed. At Gallipoli, an entire Australian army was destroyed and achieved nothing. On the Western Front, trenches stretched for 600 miles across France and Belgium, 30,000 miles of filthy trenches total in all the fields of war. There they sat for years, filled with new waves of soldiers, while attacks rocked back and forth, slaughtering each other. Rain collected in the trenches, eternally, and the endless mud was knee-deep. While rats swarmed through all the miles of trenches, and lice and fleas crawled over the men, disease spread pandemically.

The novel both captures the emptiness of war as experienced by common soldiers and by suggestion conveys something of the intense skepticism felt by most of Europe in the years that followed.

The plot is simple. Paul Baumer, age eighteen, volunteers for service and is sent to France. He and his friends spend the first half of the book largely behind the lines in reserve, with only sporadic action, and the second half engaged in almost constant action, building up to the death of Paul, just as the war ends. Remarque achieves a timeless quality by seldom giving the battles names and by steadily accelerating the intensity of action against German forces.

Paul, briefly home on leave, realizes that he is forever cut off from the traditional values of his past and that hope for the future is vain and delusional. The only value in the useless bloodbath he has experienced is comradeship, the common bond among soldiers, who alone know the real truth.

The reading public all over the world received the antiwar novel enthusiastically. Within three months of its publication in Germany, it sold half a million copies; by the end of a year, it had sold 1 million. This success was repeated worldwide. It sold 3.5 million copies in eighteen months, going into twenty-five translations and being repeatedly pirated as well. Remarque's novel eventually became one of the most popular novels in history. It has been maintained that it has sold more than any other book in history except for the Bible, becoming one of the most recognized titles in the world. Despite its popularity in the United States, it was from the first subject to censorship by its publishers, Little, Brown, who in order to secure Book-of-the-Month Club selection expunged references to a latrine and a scene of lovemaking between a long separated married couple. It was banned in Boston and confiscated by the U.S. Customs Office in Chicago in 1929 and is still often banned on the grounds that it contains obscenities.

In Remarque's own Germany, the reaction of political ideologues was less positive than the general response in the United States. German ultranationalists damned it because it implicitly condemned German capitalists, politicians, and the military. Left-wingers condemned it because it did not. Right-wingers claimed that Remarque was actually a Jew: Citing the name "Remark" (his birth name) in reverse as evidence, they maintained that his real name was thus "Kramer" (shopkeeper). Leftists condemned it because it did not take a sufficiently strong stand politically. Socialist critic Arnold Zweig attacked the novel because it had not shown the economic and social origins of the war. Others attacked his military service. He was also attacked by the Nazis for much the same reasons, and it was one of the first books to be burned after the Nazis came to power.

The long-term impact of the novel was enormous, especially in two respects: It articulated the reasons for the loss of faith and meaning in the years following the war; and for several generations of men, including those who fought in World War II, it provided a view of what modern warfare had become.

The book, dedicated to the "Lost Generation," articulated for its readers the disillusionment that followed the war. Remarque's readers saw the reason for their own loss of faith and meaning in the experience of the soldiers in the novel, in the evidence that this war was the greatest disaster, the greatest betrayal, and the greatest butchery in history.

This novel, more than any other single source, provided an iconoclastic view of war by undermining the romance and heroism of war. War was walking across open, denuded spaces into machine-gun fire, in obedience to orders. It was neither romantic nor glorious nor clean nor fair. There were no heroes, heroics, or winners in this action; there were only absurdity and chaos, with all the morality of a slaughterhouse where animals are butchered without thought and compunction. The influence of the novel was magnified with the production of the American film version in 1930. The star of the film, a young Lew Ayers, became a conscientious objector in World War II.

The premier of the film in Berlin once more caused trouble, just as had the novel.

Over the objections of the Defense Ministry, claiming that it cast aspersions on the German army, German censors permitted its showing. On the day after the premier, Joseph Goebbels, soon to become one of Adolf Hitler's chief advisers, showed up with some 200 followers to throw stink bombs and sneezing powder, release white mice, and storm through the theater to alarm the audience.

But having absorbed the stark realism of Remarque's *All Quiet on the Western Front*, American and English soldiers entered World War II with a greater gravity and realism than their fathers had taken to World War I.

Additional Readings: Christine R. Barker and R.W. Last, *Erich Maria Remarque* (London: Oswald Wolff, 1979); Richard Arthur Firda, *All Quiet on the Western Front: Literary Analysis and Cultural Context* (New York: Twayne, 1993).

95. *Success* (*Erfolg*), by Lion Feuchtwanger (Germany, 1930). *Success*, the first fictional condemnation of Adolf Hitler, was the beginning of Feuchtwanger's status as an antifascist idol. The novel is thoroughly grounded in Feuchtwanger's experiences in Germany, during the years when Hitler was amassing power.

Fighting between Germany and the Allies in World War I continued until November 1918, after Germany had formed a new government and surrendered. The terms under the Treaty of Versailles specified that Germany surrender land (Alsace-Lorraine, West Prussia, and all colonies), money ($30 million in gold), and its coal, trains, merchant ships, and navy. The crushing ignominy of the treaty caused immediate, long-lasting, and intense bitterness, paving the way for the fanatical nationalism of Adolf Hitler's Nazi Party, which was strong enough by 1920 to stage an unsuccessful revolt.

Immediately after the war, the German Empire was collapsed and a democratic republic—the Weimar Republic—was formed, first under the leadership of Frederick Ebert, a reformer, then in 1925 under Paul von Hindenburg, an aging general. This weak government, despised universally as a symbol of surrender and defeat, made Germany vulnerable to manipulation by the fanatical Right, both in and out of government, as well as the Left. In 1919, a group of socialists, which included many prominent German artists and intellectuals, staged a coup to unseat the Weimar Republic. Known as the Bavarian Revolution, it was quickly put down by the government, and with the instigation and cooperation of the fascists, leftists were pursued and persecuted. When Hitler came to power in 1933, his Nazi party, with less than 38 percent of the vote, outlawed the Communist Party and decreed that Hitler would have dictatorial power.

Success, published with the subtitle *The History of a Province*, is a portrait of Munich, including an immense cast of characters, in the turbulent years between 1919 and 1923, as Hitler was coming to power, as artists on the Left were being persecuted, and as many others without firm political commitments were attempting to establish their own political and artistic philosophies from the chaos and heated discussions surrounding them. The suspenseful narrative has as its frame the attempt by Johanna Krain to secure the release of art critic Dr. Kruger who has been arrested following the Bavarian Revolution. A subplot, predicting the full-scale persecution of the Jews by Adolf Hitler, involves Kruger's lawyer, Dr. Sigbert Geyer, whose illegitimate part-Jewish son Ernst follows Hitler until his ethnicity becomes an issue and he is murdered by Hitler's troops. The novel's protagonist is Tuverlin, a young artist and the author's mouthpiece, who attempts to listen to various ideologues and determine his own stance.

The immediate reception of the novel in Berlin was mildly favorable. But Munich reacted with character slurs, wholesale castigation, and howls of protest. Seen as a vicious attack on the city, the novel was subtitled "Book of Hatred" by one reviewer. Feuchtwanger had presented in *Success* the first, extremely laughable caricature of Adolf Hitler, and the Nazi press screamed, "Jew Feuchtwanger" and "Traitor Feuchtwanger."

Although Tuverlin, who represented the

author's point of view, decidedly rejected the role of politics in an artist's life, after the publication of this novel, he was no longer viewed as a moderate. While Feuchtwanger was castigated at home, he soon found that the novel had brought him celebrity status outside Germany, especially in Britain and the United States. Upon accepting the Nobel Prize, for example, Sinclair Lewis had mentioned Feuchtwanger by name as one equally deserving of the prize.

The great influence of *Success* lies in the fact that Feuchtwanger presented his readers with the first picture of the ineffectiveness and shocking injustices of the Weimar Republic, the first picture of the conditions that gave rise to Hitler, and the first characterization of Hitler's ideology and tactics.

Feuchtwanger's novel laid bare the destructiveness of the authoritarianism, militarism, hero worship, and nationalism so fundamental to German character. He showed that Hitler would exploit these very characteristics to bring Germany to his feet. The novel also provided his readers with insight into the back room political maneuvers, especially with regard to finance and the patterns of oppression on both Left and Right. Ever devoted to the balanced, objective picture, Feuchtwanger showed his readers both the rewards and the costs of revolutionary action.

Success was immediately rejected by German booksellers and in the 1930s was burned in Germany, along with most of Feuchtwanger's other books. As a Jew and hated author, he was forced to leave Germany, leaving behind his possessions and papers, which were all destroyed. After setting up residence in France, he was arrested and placed in a concentration camp from which he was able to make a daring escape and another daring escape across the Pyrenees and onto a boat for the United States.

After World War II, he was invited to report on the Nuremberg Trials of Nazis, on the strength of *Success* and his status as a symbol of anti-Nazism. But he declined. But his days of persecution were not over: In the Cold War that ensued after the war, he was attacked by communists and other leftists for failing to take a strong stand with the radical Left in *Success*. Worse, he was spied on in the United States and accused of having been "premature" in his attack on fascism in his novel *Success*, proving to the satisfaction of the Federal Bureau of Investigation that he was a communist sympathizer. His ten-year appeal for U.S. citizenship was never accorded.

Additional Readings: Alex de Jonge, *The Weimar Chronicle: Prelude to Hitler* (New York: New American Library, 1978); Lothar Kahn, *Insight and Action: The Life and Work of Lion Feuchtwanger* (Madison, NJ: Fairleigh Dickinson University Press, 1975); John M. Spalek, ed., *Leon Feuchtwanger: The Man, His Ideas, His Work. A Collection of Critical Essays* (Los Angeles: Hennessey and Ingals, 1972).

96. *Stalingrad*, by Theodor Plevier (Germany, 1948). In June 1941, when 3 million of Adolf Hitler's German troops first invaded the Soviet Union, Theodor Plevier had been living in Russia for seven years, ever since he had gone there to attend a literary conference in Moscow and had not been allowed by the Nazis to return to his native Germany. Throughout 1941, both Germany and Russia suffered great losses—dead, wounded, and prisoners of war. But in the spring of 1942, despite all advice to the contrary, Hitler, eager for rich Soviet natural resources, insisted on continuing his push into Russia. Half of the German forces in Russia headed for Stalingrad in late summer of that year. Upon reaching the city in November, Germany's Sixth Army and part of the Fourth Panzer Army found themselves surrounded by Soviet forces. In the bitter January of 1943, without fuel or food, the German forces at Stalingrad were forced to surrender, with a loss of 200,000 troops.

Plevier's novel is an immediate account of the 1943 German Sixth Army's defeat in the Battle of Stalingrad. Largely told from the German point of view, the protagonists are a common German soldier named August Gnotke and a German officer, Major Vilshoven. Gnotke, who embodies the nobility

of the common man, has become thoroughly disillusioned with both the war and his military superiors. He survives both morally and psychologically by throwing all his energy into taking care of a dying fellow soldier.

Major Vilshoven is also presented sympathetically, as an officer who has been made bitter and cynical by the German high command. He is finally driven to oppose his superiors who needlessly sacrifice the lives of the German soldiers in order to please Hitler and obey his order to make any sacrifice by fighting to the finish in a hopeless situation.

Hopeless carnage and losses, not only to military action but to cold, disease, and starvation, all are directly attributable in the novel to Hitler's bungling and the army's insistence on being loyal and obedient rather than using their own intelligence. First, it made military sense for the Germans to break through the Russian lines before they were hopelessly encircled, but Hitler had given orders to the contrary, so the Germans waited, with winter coming, until it was too late. Second, they should have admitted defeat when it became clear that they could not win, that they could in no way win the battle, and that the only sure result would be the suffering and loss of more soldiers.

It is not surprising to learn that Plevier's novel was banned in Germany, where his early works had been burned on May 10, 1933. But it became immensely popular throughout Europe and eventually sold close to 3 million copies in Germany, going through a number of editions. It has also enjoyed extremely good sales throughout other countries, especially in Russia, to which he was exiled during World War II and where the book was written.

Plevier's book was perceived as a serious threat in 1945 because, from a German point of view (formed by reading the letters of Germans written during the campaign), he presented facts and impressions about the Battle of Stalingrad that exposed the stupidity and culpability of the German government and military, a perception expressed by most German soldiers who had fought there. Even though he used the quite valid point of view of two German soldiers, the work was seen as very favorable to the Russian position.

Through the use of discussions between German soldiers, Plevier was able to reveal to his novel's audience the more fundamentally flawed and ruinous political premises and policies that lay behind Hitler's plan to conquer Europe. Sometimes readers formed their opinions of the Third Reich through German characters who damned themselves and their country through their own words, arguing that anyone who is too sick or weak to endure is of inferior racial stock.

Additional Reading: Dieter Sevin, "Theodor Plevier," in Wolfgang D. Elfe and James Hardin, eds., *Contemporary German Fiction Writers* (Detroit, MI: Gale Research Co., 1988), pp. 242–47.

97. *Billiards at Half-Past Nine* (*Billard um halb zehn*), by Heinrich Boll (Germany, 1959).

Billiards at Half-Past Nine is a chronicle of the Federal Republic of Germany by Heinrich Boll, unquestionably the most popular writer of contemporary Germany and a 1972 winner of the Nobel Prize for Literature.

Boll grew to manhood in the chaotic years after World War I while the Nazis were coming to power. He was drafted into the military during World War II, served on several fronts, was wounded numerous times, and finally deserted shortly before the war was over. After the war, as Boll was trying to make a career for himself as a writer and support his growing family by working as a carpenter, Germany was being divided into Eastern and Western zones. After an initial period of economic hardship, from 1945 until 1947, Western Germany profited from the decision by England and the United States to rebuild the economy and industry of the country, transforming it into what would become in the 1950s the most prosperous country in Europe. In September 1949, West Germany was officially formed into the Federal Republic of Germany, with self-government and a new capital in Bonn. Military occupation by the Allies came to an end in 1952, and the Republic was allowed to rearm.

During the years when Boll's novel was being written, after he had already established his reputation as a writer of consequence, business and private investment in Germany grew enormously, the growth of the country coming to be labeled "the economic miracle." By 1960 the country had an export surplus of $1 billion.

Billiards at Half-Past Nine, first published in 1959 at the height of Germany's economic resurgence, is the story of Germany's history and three generations of a single middle-class German family, the Fahmels, over a period of fifty years. The story is told, however, within an eight-hour frame on a September day in 1958. The day, a special one for the family in that it is the eightieth birthday of the patriarch, Heinrich Fahmel, turns ugly when Heinrich's wife attempts to shoot a high government official with a Nazi past.

The three generations of Germans are explained by their relationship to the local Roman Catholic church. The first generation of the Fahmel family, who rose to prominence after World War I, built the church. The male heir in the next generation, the generation of Nazi soldiers, bombed it. And the representative of the new generation of the Fahmel family, having no strong feelings about religion, ponders whether he should tear it down or reconstruct it.

Although Boll's chief competitor in Germany, Günter Grass, is considered to be the finer writer, Boll's popularity with the public is far greater than any other contemporary author. He has 31 million books in print, translated into forty-five languages. In the 1970s Boll, largely as a result of his novel and short fiction, was listed fourth by Germans as the man who most completely represented the highest order of the German conscience.

The novel had an enormous effect on the way that Germans and non-Germans regarded the history of Germany and the Federal Republic of Germany. Readers found in the novel an insistence that Germans continue to confront the Nazi past. Boll, as a member of a group of writers called the *Trummerliteratur*, translated as "rubble literature," believed that the only possible stance for a German artist was to create from the rubble of history, facing head-on the tradition of aggressive militarism, tyranny, and sadistic intolerance. In this novel, readers also saw the perniciousness of capitalism and the new German wealth and the inappropriate materialism of the Church, which Boll, at the time, was moving away from. The novel also proposed the alternative to capitalism of socialism, which Boll was also beginning to embrace at the time.

Finally, in the Fahmel matriarch's attack on a government official, readers saw a hopeful move against German bureaucratic corruption.

Additional Readings: Robert Conrad, *Heinrich Boll* (Boston: G.K. Hall, 1981); Enid MacPherson, *A Student's Guide to Boll* (London: Heinemann, 1972).

98. *The Tin Drum* (*Die Blechtrommel*), by Günter Grass (Germany, 1959). Günter Grass, winner of the 1999 Nobel Prize for Literature, is considered by many to be the most important novelist of post–World War II Germany. *The Tin Drum*, a story of the rise and defeat of Nazism, is his unquestionable masterpiece and the first of three novels about Germany that subsequently came to be known as the *Danzig Trilogy*.

The history of the city of Danzig, Grass's hometown, is essential to *The Tin Drum*. In 1899, when the mother of the novel's protagonist is conceived, Danzig was a Prussian city, but with the defeat of Germany in World War I, Danzig, still a city of German language and culture, became a free city, surrounded by Poland. By the time of the birth of the novel's protagonist in 1924, a bitter and defeated Germany is on the rise, and diverse political ideologies are vying for dominance, Adolf Hitler's Nazi Party prominent among them. In 1933, without a majority of support, Hitler assumed power under the Third Reich. The aim of the Nazis to bring the free city of Danzig "home to the Reich" was soon accomplished, and the first shot of

World War II was fired in Danzig in September of 1939 with the attack on the Polish Post Office there as Danzig was annexed to the Third Reich. After World War II, with Germany's surrender, Danzig, renamed Gdansk, became part of Poland.

The Tin Drum, Grass's novel covering these events, begins in a post–World War II mental institution in West Germany, where a dwarf named Oskar Matzerath, the chief narrator and protagonist, recalls his past in Danzig, with the help of a family photograph album and a drum, on which he beats to conjure up memory. His story begins with his parents and his childhood in Danzig where the Nazi Party is gaining a foothold. Oskar is in Danzig when the post office is attacked. Each of Oskar's characteristics and experiences is linked to Hitler's army: For instance, his impotent "wallowing" is compared to the German army's impotent "wallowing" in mud outside Moscow at the same moment; the suicide of a Danzig pederast is seen as Germany's suicidal attack on Russia; Oskar's blue eyes, beating on a drum, and belief that he is the messiah are like Hitler himself.

Through a series of complex events, Oskar finds himself on the beaches of Normandy in France during the Allied invasion of Germany-held France. He is also in Paris, amusing German troops and officers with his marvelous gift of breaking glass with his voice, graduating from beer bottles to cathedral windows. He returns to Danzig in time for the bombing and invasion of the Russians. In the meantime, he is implicated in several murders and continues to wreak havoc and destruction everywhere he goes. From Danzig he heads to West Germany and participates in the economic prosperity fostered by Western world capitalism, eventually becoming heir to a fortune. But he is accused of murder and is placed in a mental institution where he has been for two years. As the novel ends, he senses the arrival of the Black Cook, the greatest terror of his life, coming now from out of the future rather than the past.

The Tin Drum, greeted as a phenomenal success, made Günter Grass famous. Sales of the novel were extremely good in Europe and the United States. He immediately received the Berlin Critic's Prize and the prestigious Gruppe 47 award of 1958. In 1999, chiefly on the strength of his 1959 novel *The Tin Drum*, Grass was awarded the Nobel Prize for Literature.

Immediately after its appearance, however, the novel was excoriated as decidedly as it was later to be praised, largely for unearthing a Nazi past that Germany had successfully avoided talking about since the war. Both the novel and its author were forbidden in Gdansk, and the senate of the city of Bremen refused to allow the writers of the city to give Grass its literary prize. Throughout East and West Germany, *The Tin Drum* was publicly deplored by many people as obscene, blasphemous, and treasonous.

The enormous impact on many readers came from its being the first comprehensive and measured study of the rise of Hitler's dictatorship, the war, including the Holocaust, and the emergence of a postwar Germany, all from the point of view of a disillusioned German who had served as a Nazi soldier. Its readers saw a Germany presented as devoid of meaning and shaped by a capitalism that has its roots in Nazi horror. Oskar—dwarfed, infantile, impotent, destructive, pathological, and obscene—is at different times identified with Hitler, with Nazism, with Germany. His messianic delusions are parallel to Germany's own delusion of Nordic supremacy.

Additional Readings: W. Gordon Cunliffe, *Günter Grass* (New York: Twayne, 1969); Alan Frank Keele, *Understanding Günter Grass* (Columbia: University of South Carolina Press, 1988).

99. *Divided Heaven* (*Der geteilte Himmel*), by Christa Wolf (Germany, 1963).

Christa Wolf, once a citizen of what was East Germany, is one of the most prominent writers of post–World War II Germany. She was the first writer to address a matter of pressing concern in Europe: the anxiety created by Germany's division into two countries, a situation to which her title makes reference. Though a citizen of West Germany in the

1960s and early 1970s, Wolf's political commitments and much of her professional ties were to East Germany. In 1976, she moved to East Berlin. *Divided Heaven*, her second novel, published in 1963, plummeted her to a position as the best-known author in what was once called the German Democratic Republic or communist-controlled East Germany.

After Germany surrendered at the end of World War II, the USSR had occupied the Eastern part of the conquered Germany, and the Allies had occupied the Western part. Germany remained divided into two countries, even after formal occupation was officially over, the Communist bloc still controlling East Germany and making it difficult for East German citizens to travel outside the boundaries of the country. In the months when Wolf was writing her novel before its publication in 1963, East Germany was in economic and political decline and turmoil. West Germany had a booming economy, while East Germany's failing economy and political repression had resulted in the loss of thousands of skilled and professional labor. In August 1961, the inability of the country to stem the continual loss of manpower prompted East Germany's construction of the Berlin Wall, separating East and West Germany. The result of this despotic measure was even greater animosity within East Germany's borders among its citizenry and increased economic hardships from the untold damage to the image and reputation of East Germany. Another consequence of the building of the wall was an expansion of the Cold War between capitalistic and communistic countries and anxiety worldwide that another war was eminent.

Wolf's novel takes place against a cruelly divided Germany that tore apart relationships and heightened the tension and isolation in everyday life. The plot of the novel is primarily a flashback, a reverie of an East German teacher-in-training named Rita Seidel who is recuperating from what the reader only knows as an "accident." Although she thinks back on her childhood briefly, the main narrative is of the past two years of her life: a love affair with Manfred Herrfurth, a chemist, her leave-taking of the small village in which she grew up, her adjustment to city life, and her work in a factory as well as a teacher trainee. The reader gathers from the ambiguously told tale that Rita's accident has followed shortly after Manfred fled East Germany, just before the erection of the Berlin Wall in 1961.

Wolf's novel was enthusiastically received by both East and West German readers. Although the novel was clearly critical to much in the East German situation, the official position on the novel by the East German authorities and their sanctioned critics was unusual. They tended to stress the fact that the novel's heroine continues to live and work hard within the confines of East Germany, that her lover deserts both her and his country for the lure of gold in West Germany. Little mention was made of problems created by the building of the wall, and the whole matter of Rita's "accident" was ignored, Wolf having left the exact nature of the accident ambiguous. Wolf received East Germany's highest award for literature: the Heinrich Mann Prize. Subsequently, East German critics would castigate her for failing to integrate socialist ideals into her fiction.

In West Germany, the novel was more searchingly discussed and more enthusiastically received. These and other of Wolf's novels opened up discussion of the matter of self-censorship. In order to be published in East Germany, Wolf had obviously chosen to keep Rita's accident ambiguous. West German critics, however, read the novel as highly critical of political oppression in the East, of ruinous economic problems, and of the callous division of families and friends by the Berlin Wall, all of which led to what non–Eastern bloc audiences interpreted as Rita's suicide attempt. It was, however, the last time Christa Wolf received a strong endorsement from the West. She was shortly to be accused of literary cowardice in failing to criticize East Germany strongly enough before the government fell.

Wolf obeyed the directives of East Germany in gaining experience in factories and on farms in order to give a firsthand account of labor in her fiction, one of the first successful East German writers to do so. But despite a convenient ambiguity, the novel provided readers in the East and West with the first artistically rendered picture by a socialist writer of just why East Germany built the Berlin wall (for example, to halt the exodus of farmers from East Germany escaping collectivization) and the effect the wall had on a citizen like Rita who is suddenly trapped in East Germany after the escape of a loved one.

Additional Readings: George Buehler, *The Death of Socialist Realism in the Novels of Christa Wolf* (Frankfurt: Lang, 1984); Marilyn Sibley Fries, ed., *Responses to Christa Wolf: Critical Essays* (Detroit, MI: Wayne State University Press, 1989).

Ireland

༒

Jonathan Swift, *Gulliver's Travels*, 1726

Maria Edgeworth, *Castle Rackrent*, 1800

Charles Maturin, *Melmoth the Wanderer*, 1820

Bram Stoker, *Dracula*, 1897

Robert Tressell, *The Ragged Trousered Philanthropists*, 1914

James Joyce, *Ulysses*, 1918, 1919, 1922

༒

TIMELINE

1169   Norman-Welsh forces under Richard de Clare, known as "Strongbow," invade Ireland after an ousted king in eastern Ireland appealed for help in regaining his throne.

1171   Strongbow and Henry II accept feudal homage from Irish leaders. For several hundred years thereafter, three zones of influence dominated Ireland: The "Pale," extending for about thirty miles around Dublin, was ruled effectively by English; to the far east, locals were generally independent; in between, a tangled web produced both chaos and independence.

1649   When the duke of Ormond (the Lord Lieutenant) unites Irish Catholic and Protestant forces in opposition to Parliament, Cromwell sends some 15,000 men to wipe out all opposition. The result was a brutal slaughter at Drogheda (they massacred the garrison, killed people in the streets, and deliberately burned some seventy people to death in a church where they had gone for refuge) and the institution of a land settlement that produced eternal resentment: From two thirds to three quarters of the land outside Ulster was given to Protestant English landlords.

1726   Jonathan Swift's *Gulliver's Travels* is published.

1782   In the growing age of revolutions, limited home rule for Ireland, along with some prosperity, was accompanied by endemic horrors that resulted in violence and rebellion: In a Catholic country, Catholics were excluded from government and forced to pay rent to English landlords and to contribute tithes to an established Protestant church.

1797   When Irish rebels appealed to revolutionary France for help, the English sent a violent Protestant militia to stamp out rumored mutiny: People were hanged, beaten, and shot in the streets.

1798   Rebellion erupted in the south, with vengeful rebels exacting brutal revenge on conquered militia. Ruthless slaughter included the burning to death in a barn of some 200 men, women, and children.

1800   In a population of an estimated 4,550,000 in Ireland, some 3,150,000 are Roman Catholic. They are not allowed to hold office, and only a few (since 1793) were able to own land. Most paid rent to absentee landlords and paid taxes to the Anglican Church.

Maria Edgeworth's *Castle Rackrent* is published.

1801   The Act of Union joins Ireland to England.

1803   Ireland continues to have very real grievances. Robert Emmett, Irish revolutionary, leads an attack on Dublin Castle in an attempt to secure Irish independence.

1820   Charles Maturin's *Melmoth the Wanderer* is published.

1837   Poor harvests throughout the British Isles create great hardships for the poor.

1840s   The "Hungry Forties" result in starvation throughout the British Isles.

1845–47 A devastating famine ravages Ireland. One million people die, reducing its population by 25 percent. John Henry Cardinal Newman, once an Oxfordian and

Anglican convert to Roman Catholicism, publishes his *Essay on the Development of Christian Doctrine*.

1848   Revolutions occur throughout Europe.

1867   The Fenians, a secret Irish society, actively seek to overthrow British rule of Ireland. Charles Stewart Parnell becomes the charismatic Irish leader in Parliament.

1890   Irish leader Charles Stewart Parnell is deposed.

1897   Bram Stoker's *Dracula* is published.

1902   The Irish revolutionary party Sinn Fein is formed aggressively to fight for Irish independence from England.

1903   The Gaelic League is organized in Ireland with the aim of recapturing Irish language and culture.

1904   June 16, "Bloomsday," the setting of James Joyce's *Ulysses*, will in the last of the century become an annual literary celebration.

1912–22 Ireland escalates its struggle for independence in what becomes known as the Irish Revolution.

1914   Robert Tressell's *The Ragged Trousered Philanthropists* is published.

1916   On Good Friday, Sir Roger Casement, who had been knighted for outstanding work in Africa, was landed on the Irish coast by a German submarine; he was captured, tried for treason, and ultimately hanged.

In the Easter Rebellion in Ireland, a splinter group of the Sinn Fein who oppose World War I and support more aggressive measures in fighting for Irish independence seize Dublin. Their unsuccessful struggle ends with the execution of nationalist leaders by the British.

1918   Home Rule for Ireland passes Parliament but will not go into effect until after the world war is over. The revolutionary Sinn Fein wins 73 of the 106 Irish seats in the English Parliament.

Serial publication of episodes 1–14 of James Joyce's *Ulysses* begins.

1919   The Sinn Fein proclaims Irish independence with Eamon De Valera as president.

Britain sends special operatives called the Black and Tans in to police Ireland. The Irish Republican Army (IRA) begins wholesale attacks on them, and hundreds on both sides are killed.

1919–20   James Joyce's *Ulysses* is banned by U.S. postal authorities.

1920   Parliament passes a Government of Ireland bill providing for separate Irish Parliaments: one for Northern Ireland and one for the rest of Ireland.

1922   *Ulysses* is published on Joyce's fortieth birthday. Five hundred of 2,000 copies of *Ulysses*, intended for distribution in the United States, are burned.

All of Ireland except Northern Ireland is declared the Irish Free State but is still part of the English Commonwealth.

Civil war issues in Ireland between the English-supported provisional government and the Sinn Fein. Hundreds of Irish are killed, including the leader of the provisional government, Michael Collins.

The Supreme Court of the United States declares that *Ulysses* is not pornography and should no longer be banned by the federal government.

De Valera begins his sixteen-year leadership of the Irish Free State with its agenda of ending Britain's involvement in Irish affairs.

1937   The Irish Free State becomes Eire.

1949   Eire becomes the Republic of Ireland. England decrees that Northern Ireland is still part of the United Kingdom.

1965–1980s   As relations between the Republic of Ireland and England improve, the more radical IRA increases acts of terrorism, especially in Protestant-dominated Northern Ireland.

1973   The IRA begins a policy of bombing public sites in England.

100. *Gulliver's Travels*, by Jonathan Swift (Ireland, 1726). *Gulliver's Travels*, a book filled with scatological images and harsh, even brutal allusions, written by an aging misanthrope, has been recognized as the most savage satire ever written.

Appearing at a time of political turmoil and revolutionary change in an eighteenth-century society when an old way of life was crumbling, the book is cynical and disdainful of religion and philosophy and presents both the human race and civilization itself as hopelessly fouled. This novel is especially pertinent to the recent rise of political parties in England.

Something of the origin of the names of the political parties may indicate the temper of the times. The word *Tory* was an Irish word for "robber," applied to the Court Party by Titus Oates in 1680. *Whigs*, short for Whiggamore, originally referred to a band of Scots active against Charles I in 1648. As the historian G.M. Trevelyan noted: "And as soon as one side thus called its opponents after the Catholic bandits who waylaid the Saxon settlers among the Irish bogs, it was an obvious retort to hurl back the name of the Covenanted 'Whigs' who murdered bishops on the Scottish moors" (*England Under the Stuarts* [New York: Putnam, 1926], p. 411).

In 1725, after a series of personal disasters, Swift began writing *Gulliver's Travelers*. One year later it was published. Part I tells of Gulliver's visit to Lilliput, the most familiar part of the story. Here the Lilliputians are six inches tall, and Gulliver enjoys immense superiority. Political parties are distinguished by the wearing of high heels or low heels, religious factions by the breaking of an egg at the Big End or the Little End. In Part II, he visits Brobdignag, where the situation is reversed: The locals are sixty feet tall. The king mistakes Gulliver for an insect and thinks Europe is an anthill. In Part III, Gulliver is pulled up to a floating island, Laputa, in a bucket, where scientists and philosophers working at the Academy of Lagado produce fantastic and absurd inventions. Moving to the land, he finds a place where criminals are sentenced not to death but to immortality. In Part IV, Gulliver visits the land of the Houyhnhnms, where the intelligent, reasonable, and truly cultured creatures are horses. They have as their menials human beings called Yahoos who are stupid, brutal, and deformed in both mind and body and whose favorite amusement is climbing trees and defecating on each other.

The book was an immediate success. The straight, simple language, never heavily Latinized, the fantastic adventures, and the humor and wit enchanted its readers. Many even considered it to be factual. The aging widow of the duke of Marlborough, whom Swift had excoriated once, years earlier, praised it as an accurate view of kings, ministers, and other hangers-on at court. Some were critical of the topical allusions and others of what were called its filthy images.

By the nineteenth century, the first part had become a children's classic. The Victorians, while deploring the language and images of the whole, retained the visit to the Lilliputians as incisive and admirable.

It has been read, too, as provocation for the study of ideas, especially of Utopian and Dystopian fiction, and as stimulation for discussions of culture and civilization, progress and disintegration.

Part IV has become a springboard for evaluations of civilization and culture. The Lilliputians, because of their smallness in matters of politics and religion, as well as physical size, have raised discussions of morality.

By the twentieth century, the adventure in Part I was firmly established as a classic. It

continued to sell well, was standard reading fare in college and university histories of English literature, and was made into many successful films, the most recent a 1996 made for television movie. The most convincing evidence for its influence is the fact that words from the novel have entered the English language, especially "Lilliputian" as a concept for noting and for measuring the value of mere size alone.

Additional Readings: John Cannon, ed., *The Whig Ascendancy* (New York: St. Martin's Press, 1981); Richard Gravil, ed., *Swift: "Gulliver's Travels"* (London: Macmillan, 1974); Brean S. Hammond, *Gulliver's Travels* (Philadelphia: Open University Press, 1988).

101. *Castle Rackrent,* **by Maria Edgeworth (Ireland, England, 1800).** *Castle Rackrent,* ostensibly a comedy of manners, was a revelation to English readers of antiquated manorial life and flagrant injustice in Ireland, its troubled "colony." As such, it served as a warning of tribulation to come with the forthcoming so-called union of England and Ireland. Edgeworth's novel both entertained and educated English readers at an alarming time in their history.

In 1800, Ireland had a population of about 4,550,000 people. Some 3,150,000 of these were Roman Catholic; the rest were either Anglican or dissenting Protestant. In this overwhelmingly Catholic country, Catholics could not hold high office or become members of the Irish Parliament. They were forbidden from owning land until 1793 when a few stepped upward to ownership. The rest worked in factories at starvation wages (as did all workers) or toiled on farms that someone else owned. They paid rents to absentee owners and tithes to a state-supported Anglican church that they could not accept. In addition, they then paid tithes to their own Catholic church. When they voted, they were forced to choose their representatives from among Protestant electors. It was a situation guaranteed to produce humiliation and seething hatred and to mount violent rebellion, as the commoners did at the onset of the American Revolution and, later, the French Revolution.

In 1797–98, opportunity for an Irish rebellion presented itself. The British fleet mutinied, while the Bank of England suspended specie payment, and on the continent, France was universally victorious in its war against England. The heads of British government stationed at Dublin Castle in Ireland learned of the planned rebellion and, to quell it, sent an unruly Protestant militia against a traditional and bitter foe. The English militia was eager to settle old scores. Irish men and women were stripped and punished on the street merely for wearing a green ribbon, the mark of a revolutionary. They were beaten, shot, or hanged in massive numbers. But Irish rebels in the south got their revenge: They massacred militia companies in their barracks; in one case, they slaughtered nearly 200 men, women, and children trapped in a barn.

A French invasion fleet to assist the Irish, arranged by young Irish patriot Wolfe Tone, sailed for Ireland on a cold December morning, only to be destroyed by a gale. Remnants of the French force attempted battle on land, hoping to raise local forces to rebellion. Sufficient support did not come, however, and the French force was destroyed or dispersed. The rebels were finally defeated at Vinegar Hill in a battle characterized by barbarous butchery. The young patriot Wolfe Tone forestalled his destined hanging by cutting his own throat in prison in November 1798.

A song from the time in lilting melody contains still familiar lines:

It's the most distressful country that ever I
have seen,
They're hanging men and women for the
wearing of the green.

At this time, Maria Edgeworth produced an "Irish" novel for English readers. The story, narrated by Thady Quirk, an old retainer with a sharp eye for detail, and by a presumed editor who occasionally intrudes to explain allusions and language, tells of the slow but sure (and sometimes wildly humorous) decay of three generations of Rackrents, each of whom, in one way or another, is totally irresponsible. Sir Patrick is a drunken gambler; Sir Murtaugh, his son, is stingy and useless; his younger brother Kit, who inherits the estate, irresponsibly raises the rent, marries for money, locks his wife up, carouses, and finally dies in a duel; Sir Conolly, a distant relative, inherits and sells the estate to Thady's son Jason, a lawyer.

The decline of this family, as well as graphic details of the life as it is lived, is told with humor, irony, and sharp, realistic details, all of which introduced a new element to English readers, whose country was about to absorb, by force, another country that they had abused for centuries and about which they knew little or nothing. The book shows the terrible exploitation of the Irish by an inept, antique manorial system dating back to the Middle Ages that was badly in need of reform.

The novel was published in January 1800, just before the Act of Union, which was to "unite" Ireland and Britain constitutionally. In the contents of the short novel as well as in the preface, Edgeworth conveys the warning that such a union will not be easy, that it will be fraught with trouble. The subtitle and the fictional editor convey that the story is true to life, that the tale was not embellished for dramatic effect.

In a time of great trouble, while Wolfe Tone and Robert Emmett preached violent rebellion and martyrdom, Edgeworth's double perspective served to mute discontent. The old retainer is faithful to the last and shows no signs of attempting to rise above his station. Although he is not an entirely reliable narrator, his commentary on the decaying Rackrents is subtly ironic. The "editor's" comments are replete with double entendres that describe the Irish situation. For example, his comments on the troubles of marriage are intended to be a warning of the dangers in the forthcoming union of England and Ireland.

The novel earned the praise of both King George III and the prime minister. It also reached the English people, inspiring them to ameliorate the evils. The trouble did not vanish, but Edgeworth's was one of those enduring novels that changed the way many Englishmen viewed the Irish.

Additional Readings: Marilyn Butler, *Maria Edgeworth: A Literary Biography* (Oxford: Clarendon Press, 1972); Tom Dunne, *Maria Edgeworth and the Colonial Mind* (Dublin: National University of Ireland, 1984); Tadhg Foley and Sean Ryder, eds., *Ideology and Ireland in the Nineteenth Century* (Dublin: Four Courts Press, 1998).

102. *Melmoth the Wanderer,* by Charles Maturin (Ireland, 1820). *Melmoth the Wanderer,* by Irish clergyman and novelist Charles Maturin, stands as one of the greatest of the Gothic genre and established a tradition of its own. In Maturin's novel, he developed the type of the dark, brooding man, cursed by his own Satanic pact, doomed always to stand alone as an eternal observer of the mass of humankind.

By the time Maturin wrote his novel in 1820, the Tories, with the exception of one brief interlude, had been in power for more than thirty years. After Napoleon's defeat, the victors at the Congress of Vienna fought, conspired, wildly reveled in the celebration of triumph, and divided the spoils. The keynote of everything became the reinstitution of the status quo. In England, the keynote was repression, under the guise of law, order, peace abroad, and above all, discipline. The result was the rescinding of many hard-won liberties. The government passed post facto laws repealing the Habeas Corpus Act, heavily taxing newspapers, and in every way attempting to stamp out radical ideas. The horrors of industrialism flourished in England without any protective legislation to diminish profits. The Gothic tradition itself became politicized, while the British government, especially after the years of the Terror in France, became increasingly immovable. After about 1800, the optimism of reformers began to fade; at the same time, the age of Romanticism and of romantic rebels against the forces of power comes to the fore.

In this atmosphere, hope went underground. Social protest was revealed fictionally in undercurrents of flight and pursuit, of threats by some dark, overwhelming power equivalent to the repressive social system. In his novel, Maturin is said to have critiqued romantic individualism, referring indirectly to the French Revolution.

Melmoth is set in Ireland where tension grew, undispelled by the 1800 Act of Union, joining Ireland and England. In Ireland, Maturin said that he found the extremes of refinement and barbarism, congenial with the Gothic, which made his wild, romantic tale plausible.

Maturin opens the novel with a peaceable, if melancholy, scene of contemporary Ireland. To be at the side of his dying uncle, John Melmoth interrupts his study at Trinity College, Dublin, to return to the family estate, which was taken by force during the rule of Cromwell. John Melmoth then learns of his ancestor, the wandering Melmoth who lived in the time of Cromwell and had made a pact with the Devil: an agreement by which he would be granted an exceedingly long life along with certain powers in exchange for his soul. In his wandering Melmoth visits multiple scenes of great suffering and torture, a catalog of the human soul and human society in extremes of violence, injustice, and pain, including the Spanish Inquisition and London's Bedlam. Along the way he critiques many instances of oppressive ideologies and institutions. At last Melmoth comes back to Ireland to face his fate.

One important stipulation is attached to Melmoth's contract with the Devil: He can pass off his contract to someone else if anyone is willing to do so. But no one will accept his offer, and no one rescues him.

Both critics and the public admired the book, attesting to its power. *Melmoth* exerted a major influence not only on the development of classic horror stories but on the general concept of romantic individualism in opposition to society and on the early formation of psychology. The Faustian figure of Melmoth, the dark hero of Romanticism standing alone on a mountaintop, defiant and alienated from the world, became a recognizable and admired type in Western culture. The psychological influence of the novel is manifested in its delineation of the double personality and of the dark, concealed urges at the center of the human personality.

Additional Readings: Henry William Hinck, *Three Studies on Charles Robert Maturin* (New York: Arno Press, 1980); Glenn R. Hueckel, *The Napoleonic Wars* (New York: Garland, 1985); Dale Kramer, *Charles Robert Maturin* (New York: Twayne, 1973).

103. *Dracula*, by Bram Stoker (Ireland, England, 1897). Many critics have made the argument that Bram Stoker's Dracula is the most popular literary figure in history. Author Phyllis Rose contends that "the sheer number of works with 'Dracula' in their title tempts me to argue that no other single work, with the exception of the Bible, has so influenced Ango-American culture" (p. 30).

The plot of Stoker's enduring story begins with a young Englishman's trip to Transylvania to conduct business with an insidious Count Dracula, whose name in Slavic means "dragon," an agent of the devil. Through his Count Dracula, Stoker popularized the traditional vampire myth of the walking dead who is hurt by sunlight, sleeps in a coffin by day, and comes out at night to feed on the blood of the living, who, as a result, become vampires themselves. This is what Dracula's English guest, Jonathan Harker, discovers. The story continues later in England where the attractive but forbidding Count infects civilized society, including several angelic heroines who fall to his charms. Only when a stake is driven through this vampire's heart are the good people of London able to stem this powerful but charming evil.

The novel was not immediately the grand success that Stoker hoped for. As a theater man, he recognized its dramatic possibilities from the first and did stage readings of his novel in the year of its publication to protect the theatrical copyright to his material. Although the novel has never been out of print, only after Stoker's death in 1912 did the story he created become the phenomenally influential myth intrinsic to Western culture. For it was the stage and screen versions of Stoker's novel, rather than the novel itself,

that provided Stoker with immortality. The first was the 1922 German film *Nosferatu*; the second was the 1927 English play, starring Bela Lugosi; and the third was the 1931 film starring Lugosi.

Although stories of vampires existed before Stoker wrote his novel, and many have appeared since then, the popularity of Stoker's novel has meant that, in the mind of the public, "vampire" has been identified with Stoker's Count Dracula. Since 1897, Stoker's book has never been out of print. One reason why the novel has endured is that Stoker was the first to construct a vampire story in which past and present and myth and science come together.

In the twentieth century, over 1,000 novels, plays, and short stories have been written using Stoker's fictionalization of the Dracula myth. Numerous films have been produced using Stoker's idea, and the novel has spawned what has been described as a small industry of academic Dracula books. The persistency of Dracula as a symbol of evil, over eighty years after the publication of Stoker's novel, is manifested in the many works of literature featuring Stoker's Count which appeared in the closing decades of the twentieth century.

One reason for the consistent popularity of the novel has been its adaptability to different ages and contexts. In the beginning, its appeal came from its pitting of evil, in the form of Dracula, against innocence, in the form of Lucy, in its frequent specific references to "the New Woman" who was emerging at the time, and in its oblique references to English imperialism, in which Stoker, an Irishman, was intensely interested. As the psychological age evolved, the novel took on a more complex meaning as the embodiment of dark sexuality.

The book has never enjoyed greater popularity than it has at the beginning of the twenty-first century, feeding a new cult of the Gothic, a subculture estimated to number in the hundred thousands throughout the world whose members worship the concept of satanic darkness and death and wear black clothes and fake fangs. Many of its members claim to relish the drinking of human blood.

Additional Readings: Margaret L. Carter, ed., *"Dracula": The Vampire and the Critics* (Ann Arbor, MI: UMI Research Press, 1991); Frank Mort, *Dangerous Sexualities* (London: Routledge and Kegan Paul, 1987); Phyllis A. Rose, *Bram Stoker* (Boston: Twayne, 1982).

104. *The Ragged Trousered Philanthropists,* **by Robert Tressell (Ireland, England, 1914).** *The Ragged Trousered Philanthropists,* by Robert Tressell (pen name of Irishman Robert Noonan), though not well known in the United States, has been the most widely read, enthusiastically championed and influential proletarian novel in English history. Set in the fictional town of Mugsborough (a thinly veiled version of Hastings, where Noonan lived and worked as a painter), the novel shows the appalling conditions of life under which workers lived in Edwardian England, at a time when the privileged life of the few was about to fade under the onslaught of the world war and the slow but steady and violent rise of Labour in English politics.

While featuring as the main character a socialist propagandist, Frank Owen, the novel has no conventional plot, no love theme, and no aesthetic/dramatic development of characters. The story rather chronicles a year in the lives of a group of men who work for a decorating firm called Rushton & Co. Detailed pictures of the men and their families, especially the poverty and neglect under which they exist, provide the drive of the story. Driven by fierce competition and fear of dismissal, skilled craftsmen are forced to take shortcuts that leave them with no pride in their work. Workers are troubled constantly by fear of dismissal. Ignorance, poverty, and hunger, along with mutual suspicion and fear, lead to something like self-perpetuating desolation. The title comes from Owen's attempts to explain to his fellow workers that they are the "philanthropists" who work (for very little pay) to make their employers rich. When Owen attempts to explain socialism as a remedy for these abominations, he is rebuffed or sneered at. Owen himself is asked because of special skills to decorate a room with a Moorish motif, to design it and create it himself. And while he is paid only the standard rate for the job, he achieves some sense of satisfaction that makes him momentarily forget his disintegrating health and material hardships. While the novel centers on the workers, Tressell also covers the lives and the hypocrisies of politicians, religious leaders, and others in the town; all exhibit patterns of corruption and protection of vested interests. He particularly attacks the sanctified hypocrisy of the Church and entrenched establishment versions of Christianity, while at the same time honoring those who are genuinely religious.

The book illustrates a common theme among those who perceptively observe human life: If men are to wait in ignorance and poverty until they are wise and good, they will wait forever. And if workers and reformers sit and wait, immobile, for the rulers of the world voluntarily to relinquish their reigns of power, the workers will still be sitting there when the final horn blows. Tressell thus provides practical suggestions for socialism and for a workable and vastly improved system of education, both of which have proved effective and have, in one way or another, entered into the fabric of British life. He also maintains throughout the story a fine sense of humor, which is often the sharpest arrow.

The novel has appeared in three different versions. Studies of Tressell's papers have revealed that the 1914 version was considerably abridged. A 1918 edition was further abridged. Then in 1955, an edition edited by Fred Ball largely restored Tressell's original manuscript. With paperback editions emerging in the 1960s, sales of the book soared. From the very first the novel had an immense, and eager, following. Alan Sillitoe describes how, as a nineteen-year-old national serviceman, he had an enthusiastic friend, a Glasgow wireless operator, push the book at him, declaring, "You ought to read this. Among other things, it is a book that won the 1945 election for Labour" (quoted in

Martin's Seymour Smith's "Introduction" to the edition of the novel published by Citadel Press).

The book has been dramatized on stage in at least two versions. It has been adapted for films. And it has been the subject of a major documentary by the BBC. The author himself has become the subject of a center of study and of an annual festival at Hastings, his hometown. Today the citizens there commemorate with entertainments, tours, photographs, scholarly papers, political appreciations, and similar activities the landing of William the Conqueror almost a thousand years ago and the life there of Robert Tressell about a hundred years ago, along with the appearance of his novel. Since 1981 there has been a series of Robert Tressell Memorial Lectures in Hastings. In addition, Tressell has been mentioned in actions by the Trades Union Congress and the William Morris Internet Archive. The Tressell Centre has dedicated one of its annual meetings to the theme of educational reform, stressing the ideas brought out by Tressell in the book. The book has distinctly been one of the most influential of the modern age in the United Kingdom.

Additional Readings: F.C. Ball, *One of the Damned: The Life and Times of Robert Tressell, Author of The Ragged Trousered Philanthropists* (1973; London: Lawrence & Wishart, 1979); Jack Mitchell, *Robert Tressell and the Ragged Trousered Philanthropists* (London: Lawrence & Wishart, 1969); Sidney Pollard, *Labour History and the Labour Movement in Britain* (Brookfield, VT: Ashgate, 1999).

105. *Ulysses*, by James Joyce (Ireland, 1918, 1919, 1922).

James Joyce's *Ulysses*, widely regarded as the greatest novel of the twentieth century, is a psychological novel that is, nevertheless, thoroughly grounded in the turbulent history of Ireland. The oppressive anti-Catholic measures mandated by the English and the long-standing exploitation of Ireland's land and peasantry by the Irish aristocracy, working in league with absentee English landlords, had resulted in numerous uprisings throughout the nineteenth century.

Ireland's struggle for home rule, that is, independence, from England, escalated in the closing decades of the nineteenth century. The greatest Irish political leader, whose presence looms in the background of Joyce's novels, was Charles Stuart Parnell, a leader of the Irish Home Rule Party and a member of Parliament who was deposed in 1890, following pressure from the English government and Ireland's Roman Catholic Church, after he was named as correspondent in a divorce trial. The Sinn Fein, a revolutionary party working for Ireland independence, was formed in 1902, and the Gaelic League, an attempt to recapture the Irish past—its culture and language as distinct from England's—was formed in 1903.

The novel takes place in this turbulent social setting on June 16, 1904, just one year after the formation of the Gaelic League. The hero is Leopold Bloom, a Jewish advertising executive, a parodic parallel to Homer's Ulysses, who makes the rounds of Dublin, echoing Homer as he listens to the barmaids who sing a siren song, watches a young "Circe" play on the beach, and listens to the drunken ranting of a Cyclops in a bar. Two other characters lend their consciousness to the novel. One is Stephen Dedalus, central character of Joyce's earlier novel, *Portrait of the Artist as a Young Man*, who is looking for a father figure, which he finds in the end in the person of Bloom. The other is Molly Bloom, Leopold's lusty wife and an opera diva, whose affirmation of earth, life, and love closes the novel.

Ulysses has often been called one of the most admired and most despised books of all time. The book, which was first published in Paris in serial form, was roundly attacked, even before it appeared as a completed book, on the grounds that it parodied Ireland, attacked the Church, and used coarse language. The book was called indecent because it made reference to Bloom's masturbation and defecation and ended with the lyrical, erotic reverie of Molly Bloom. On grounds of indecency, in 1919 and 1920, sections of the serialized book were seized and burned by the U.S. postal authorities. A formal complaint, lodged by the New York Society for the Suppression of Vice, resulted in fines and official warnings to block further distribution. Some 500 of the 2,000 copies in English, intended for distribution in 1922, were burned by the postal authorities; 499 of 500 copies intended for shipment to the United States were destroyed by British customs. Not until 1932 did the U.S. Supreme Court defend legal distribution of Joyce's novel, on the grounds that a book could not be banned by the government as indecent because it contained "dirty words."

Since that time *Ulysses* has drawn a wide and admiring readership. It is the subject of more studies than any other modern novel, having been the sole subject of numerous books. It has stimulated the publication of annotated editions, encyclopedias, catalogs, maps, and pictorial guides. June 16, 1904, "Bloomsday," is now celebrated annually as a festival in Dublin. Some indication of the importance of the work is shown in the fact that in 2001, twenty-seven sheets of the handwritten manuscript of *Ulysses* brought $1,546,000 at auction.

Much of the novel's influence came from the attention it drew to Dublin and Ireland itself. The artifacts of everyday Dublin life brought the city and the culture alive for many readers (just as it enraged the Irish). Perhaps for the first time in modern literature, readers were led to see mythic meaning in mundane, even seedy, daily existence.

On the other hand, the novel articulated the distaste and frustration that many readers, who lived in small Dublins throughout the world, had felt concerning the stifling parochialism of their lives. Joyce's recommendation of linkage with a world outside the small community struck a chord in the hearts of many who read the novel.

Ulysses exposed its readers to the need to embrace a wider world than that in which the young Stephen Dedalus had grown up. The Dublin of the novel is hampered by the narrow theology and morality of the Catholic Church, by the blind allegiance and violence of Irish nationalism, and by the backward-looking attempt to legitimize a dead language and a dead culture. Through Stephen, who tries to free himself of the parochialism of the Church and nationalism, and through Leopold Bloom, whose Jewishness makes him an outsider, necessarily beyond the usual Irish categories, the novel affirmed for many readers openness, variety, inclusion, and toleration.

Additional Readings: Arnold Bruce, *The Scandal of "Ulysses": The Sensational Life of a Twentieth-Century Masterpiece* (New York: St. Martin's Press, 1992); Frank Budgen, *James Joyce and the Making of Ulysses and Other Writings* (London: Oxford University Press, 1972); James Connolly, *Labour and Easter Week*, ed. Desmond Ryan (Dublin: At the Sign of the Three Candles, 1966).

Italy

❧

Ignazio Silone, *Bread and Wine*, 1936

Elio Vittorini, *Men or Not*, 1945

Italo Calvino, *The Path to the Nest of Spiders*, 1947

Renata Vigano, *Agnese Goes to Her Death*, 1949

❧

TIMELINE

1919–22 Italy, still a monarchy nominally ruled by Victor Emmanuel, is plagued by social and political upheaval and economic disaster. Violent animosity breaks out between various groups: Socialists and Communists, Christian Democrats, the Catholic Popular Party, and the Fascists.

1922 Benito Mussolini, the Fascist leader, forces Victor Emmanuel to appoint him the country's political leader.

1924 Violent elections cause Mussolini to suspend constitutional government, the concrete beginning of his reign of fascist tyranny that takes all effective power from the legislature, makes Mussolini answerable to the king alone, and suspends the freedom of the press.

1926 Mussolini outlaws all political parties other than his own.

1928 All power is given to the Fascist Grand Council responsible to Mussolini.

1933 Fascists come to power in Germany under Adolf Hitler. Although Mussolini is initially suspicious of Hitler's breaking of the Treaty of Versailles and attempts to invade Austria in 1934, Hitler acknowledges Mussolini as a model.

1935 Italy invades Ethiopia, prompting the United Nations to impose economic sanctions on Italy.

1936 Mussolini annexes Ethiopia and names King Victor Emmanuel emperor of what he calls "the New Rome."

Mussolini enters into an alliance with Germany.

Ignazio Silone's *Bread and Wine* is published and is immediately banned in Italy and Germany. It continues to be banned until the end of the war.

1937	Italy withdraws from the League of Nations and signs a pact with Germany and Japan.
1937–39	Mussolini lends Italian forces to support General Francisco Franco during the Spanish Civil War.
1938	Italy now refuses to interfere with Germany's invasion of Austria.
	The Italian government begins policies of discrimination and harassment of Jews.
1939	Italy annexes Albania and signs a military assistance pact with Germany.
	World War II begins, but Italy does not immediately enter the war.
1940	Italy enters World War II. The Italian army attacks British Somaliland, Libya, and Greece.
	Italian military decisions begin to be made in Germany.
1941	Greece is occupied by the German military.
	Italy declares war on the United States after the Japanese attack Pearl Harbor.
1941–45	An underground brigade of guerrillas, largely communists, forms to undermine fascist control.
1942	Germany begins to control the Italian government as well as the military.
	Italian forces suffer heavy losses on all fronts, and citizens in Italy suffer from starvation and economic hardships.
	Allied forces invade Italy, and bombing raids on Italy begin.
1943	In the face of a groundswell of opposition to Mussolini, his Fascist Grand Council gives him a vote of no confidence, and he is placed in prison.
	Southern Italy is invaded by the Allies.
	Italy signs an armistice with the Allied nations.
	Italy is invaded by German forces, which occupy Rome, and rescue Mussolini from prison.

	The Italian government in exile declares war on Germany.
1944	The Allies liberate Rome, and a coalition government, of liberals, Roman Catholics, socialists, and communists, is formed to deal with an economic disaster in a ravaged country.
1945	The Allies defeat the last of the German armies in Italy.
	Elio Vittorini's *Men or Not* is published.
	Mussolini and his mistress and a few close supporters are captured by Italians and executed.
	Massive retaliation against Mussolini's supporters follows. Thousands are executed.
1946	The leadership of Italy is assumed by Alcide De Gasperi, a Christian Democrat.
	The first democratic election is held.
	The Italian king abdicates and leaves the country.
1947	Allied forces withdraw from Italy.
	Italo Calvino's *The Path to the Nest of Spiders* is published.
1948	The Cold War, which will rage throughout the 1950s, begins to intensify between leftists and conservatives.
	The head of the Italian Communist Party survives an assassination attempt; a national strike is called; and demonstrations erupt throughout Italy, necessitating the calling out of 300,000 troops to restore order.
1949	Renata Vigano's *Agnese Goes to Her Death* is published.
2000	Ignatio Silone becomes a subject of public controversy.

106. *Bread and Wine* (*Brot und Wein*), by Ignazio Silone (Italy, 1936). *Bread and Wine*, a twentieth-century novel of modern Italy, became one of the most influential novels of the era, making its author a cult figure. Silone, an icon of antifascist resistance and integrity, is one of those writers whose life and actions are so entwined with the vision of his novels as to be virtually inseparable.

Bread and Wine was written in 1935, the year that saw fascist Italy's bloody conquest of Ethiopia and the beginning of the New Rome, as Mussolini called it. A worldwide perception at the time held that democracies were weak and congenitally unable to solve the overwhelming problems that plagued Europe, notably the universal economic depression. Mussolini's solution was to conquer weaker nations abroad and install a monolithic system of government at home. In Italy his fascists arrested dissidents, tortured prisoners, destroyed presses, and in other ways stifled all opposition. The horrifying efficiency with which Mussolini ran the country is suggested in part by noting that Adolf Hitler, in forming the German Third Reich, patterned the machinery of his Nazi domestic policies after those of Benito Mussolini. Mussolini's military conquest began in Africa. His modern army slaughtered stone-age warriors who were still using bows and arrows. His aviator son described with pleasure, as he dropped bombs onto masses of Ethiopians, the sight of bloody body parts, he said, blossoming like a rose. While Italian crowds lined up to cheer departing soldiers, and bishops came out to bless them, the world and the League of Nations looked on in consternation and futility. These were some of the events that led to the union of the Axis Powers and brought on World War II. These years also marked a crisis in the life of Ignazio Silone.

Secondino Tranquilli, born in 1900 of a landowning family in central Italy and orphaned at fifteen, rebelled against perceived injustice and cruelty in the world around him at an early age. He moved to Rome, where he became actively involved in socialist circles and helped form the Italian Communist Party, over the years rising to positions of power, both locally and nationally. In 1928 his younger brother died after having been abused by fascist police on suspicion of a bombing.

In 1930, feeling that he was substituting one vicious tyranny for another, he dropped all affiliations with the Communist Party and retired to Switzerland. There, broke, friendless, beaten by life, and in poor health, he began to write novels, drawing from his experiences as a young man. He also at this time underwent therapy under Carl Jung and adopted a primitive type of Christianity outside organized religion. In effect, Secondino Tranquilli vanished, and Ignazio Silone was born.

As Secondino Tranquilli was reinventing himself and his values after a tortuous division of soul, so in *Bread and Wine* his protagonist, a communist organizer, in the end forsakes the party and turns to primitive Christianity. The hero, a thinly veiled idealization of the author himself, Pietro Spina ("Peter Thorne"), an antifascist and member of the party, returns to Italy and, to escape arrest, is forced to retreat to a remote village, where he pretends to be a convalescent priest, under the name of Paulo Spada ("Paul Sword").

Published first in Switzerland in German as *Brot und Wein*, the novel was, from the first, an enormous success, selling almost 2 million copies and making Silone a wealthy man and the hero of antifascists throughout the world, becoming an inspiration and rallying cry for antifascists in Spain. And during World War II, Allied armies circulated the novels free to Italian troops near the front, when they moved into Italy. Silone's prestige continued until his death in 1978.

Not surprising, the book was immediately banned in Germany and Italy. It was not available in Italy until after World War II. Even so, despite the phenomenal influence the novel enjoyed in other countries, it was still rarely read in Italy long after the war was over, reportedly because its antifascist stance created dis-ease among postwar intellectuals who had failed to oppose Mussolini.

His readers, many born and bred as Christians, found in the novel an argument for a new socially conscious Christianity with which they could sympathize. Furthermore, he articulated for those in sympathy with the underground a kind of sacred fraternity that he cast in Christian terms. For example, at the wake of a martyred man in the novel, his friends and family eat bread and drink wine in his honor as in the Eucharist. This bread and wine of Holy Communion become symbols of brotherhood.

While the novel reaffirmed basic religious beliefs, at the same time it articulated disappointment in the institution of the church. And despite its antifascist message, it has also been said that no book so graphically conveyed to its readers the sorrowful failure of socialism as well. As a result of his unflinching message delivered from exile, Silone was described in the press as a moral hero and a secular saint.

The saga of Ignazio Silone was not over yet, however. In the late 1990s the literary and political world was rocked by two Italian historians who claimed to have uncovered evidence in the secret files of Mussolini's government indicating that from 1919 until 1930, for all the years during his rise to power in the Communist Party, Secondino Tranquilli had been a secret informant for the fascist police. The conclusions of these historians were subsequently and convincingly rebutted in June 2000 by another student of Italian history in the 1920s and 1930s who demonstrated that the historical documents had been mishandled and that there was good reason to believe that Silone was acting under orders of antifascist forces.

Additional Readings: Peter Brand and Lino Pertile, eds., *The Cambridge History of Italian Literature* (New York: Cambridge University Press, 1996); Robert S. Dombroski, *Properties of Writing: Ideological Discourse in Modern Italian Fiction* (Baltimore: Johns Hopkins University Press, 1994).

107. *Men or Not* (*Uomini e no*), by Elio Vittorini (Italy, 1945). In Italy, a country where the novel as a moving social and philosophical force was slow to develop, the rise of fascists, before, during, and after World War II, was one of the richest periods of enduring novels. From the 1920s to the mid-1940s, Italy was an ideological battleground

where fascists, Christian Democrats, and Marxists warred for control. Fascism rapidly took the stage, promising to bring efficiency and prosperity to a backward economy. Soon, however, many people realized that the price to be paid for order was oppression, imprisonment, and war with the Allies. The armed resistance against fascism began in 1943 with isolated strikes across Italy and the Italian Fascistic Council's ouster of Benito Mussolini, a move of which most of Italy's population approved. But hope was short-lived because the German Nazis moved in, took over Italy, freed Mussolini from prison, and helped him reassume power. To combat both German and Italian fascism, working-class Italians formed an underground resistance movement to sabotage the work of occupying Germans.

This perilous and tumultuous period in Italy gave birth to the resistance novel. One of the most influential was Elio Vittorini's *Men or Not*, published in the year the Allies defeated the fascists.

The novel is set in 1944, just one year previous to its publication. Its subject is the resistance to German Nazis and Italian fascists by Milanese saboteurs. The title has reference to Vittorini's theory that such a struggle separates the men from the boys, or the human beings from the nonhumans, antifascism being in the author's opinion an assertion of humanity. His characters do not act from political conviction but from humanitarian impulses and moral necessity. Their enemies are automatons and sadists in whom the fire of human compassion has gone out. His main character, code-named N2, renews his strength to combat the enemy through occasional encounters with the woman he loves.

Vittorini's *Men or Not* articulated the painful questions that had begun to trouble readers in Italy, especially those who, like himself, had initially supported Mussolini. Through the novel, readers were forced to confront troubling questions: How had they allowed their country to surrender its humanity and its freedoms to a dictator? What had made it possible for Mussolini to rule Italy for twenty-one years?

Men or Not also voiced for its Italian readers, and explained to the rest of the world, both the pride and the shame that had dominated Italian life for two decades, for it discussed the conditions and attitudes that had moved Vittorini himself in the 1920s to support a dictator. It also portrayed the extraordinary courage on the part of the resistance leaders, especially those among the laboring people, who worked for Mussolini's defeat.

In a culture heretofore dominated by poetry and romance, Vittorini's novel was also a breakthrough in the realistic portrayal of the brutalities that tyrannical politics and modern warfare inflict on the civilian population.

Additional Readings: Sergio Pacifici, *The Modern Italian Novel from Manzoni to Svevo* (Carbondale: Southern Illinois University Press, 1967); Frank Rosengarten, "The Italian Resistance Novel, 1945–1962," in *From Verismo to Experimentalism*, ed. Sergio Pacifici (Bloomingdale: Indiana University Press, 1969).

108. *The Path to the Nest of Spiders* (Il sentiero dei nidi di ragno), by Italo Calvino (Italy, 1947). The setting for Italo Calvino's novel is war-torn Genoa, Italy, beginning in September 1943, the month when Germany invaded Italy and rescued Benito Mussolini from prison after his ouster by the Italian Fascist Grand Council, in response to widespread discontent and strikes. The Italian resistance was given great impetus during this year and stymied the German invaders with various acts of sabotage—blowing up their bridges, roads, trucks, and trains to impede Nazi operations and destroying German equipment and installations wherever they were found. Other resistance activity, scarcely less dangerous, included the printing and circulation of dozens of underground antifascist newspapers.

Calvino's protagonist is a Huckleberry Finn–type character, a fourteen-year-old boy named Pin. He was typical of the lower-class, apolitical urchins from the city slums, scorned by people of every class. Among the stereotypical communist organizers and working-class resistance soldiers, he is an anomaly: an outcast orphan who keeps himself alive with petty thievery and whose chief companions are the disreputable homeless men who haunt Genoa's streets and amuse themselves at his expense.

Pin is a convincing character to honor the resistance, which by 1947 was then being attacked by revisionist historians. Pin has no political ax to grind and, in the beginning, sees little difference between the invading German soldiers and the native Italians with whom he associates. They all abuse him. When almost by accident he falls in with resistance members, however, he discovers a type of character he can respect for the first time, although most are as outcast and disreputable as he is.

Unlike many Italian resistance novels, *The Path to the Nest of Spiders* ends on an affirmative note as Pin walks arm in arm with a comrade he considers to be his adopted "cousin," significant in that Pin in this bedraggled group of resistance fighters has finally found the family he never had before.

Calvino's novel found many readers and advocates in a time when the resistance was under a postwar attack. Although sales of this first novel were not impressive by today's standards, they were phenomenally good for the postwar years in Italy because readers of any class and political persuasion were able to find themselves included in the humane movement lauded there. It was not a novel that insisted on a class struggle. This can be seen in the words of one character who says the resistance is "an elementary, anonymous struggle for human redemption from all our humiliations: for the workers from exploitation, for the peasant from ignorance, for the petit-bourgeois from his inhibitions, for the pariah from his corruptions."

The Path to the Nest of Spiders was one of a group of highly influential resistance novels that redeemed the history of the left wing and its efforts in World War II. It helped break the power of the rich, politically reactionary European aristocrats and bourgeoisie, and it gave impetus to the rise of left-wing and working-class politics in the 1950s. Furthermore, the Allied presence in Italy in World War II had created a wider interest in Italian culture and history, which made possible considerable interest in Calvino's novel among non-Italians.

Additional Readings: Gunter Berghaus, *Futurism and Politics: Between Anarchist Rebellion and Fascist Reaction 1909–1944* (Providence, RI: Berghahn Books, 1996); JoAnn Cannon, *Italo Calvino: Writer and Critic* (Ravenna: Longo, 1981); Beno Weiss, *Understanding Italo Calvino* (Columbia: University of South Carolina Press, 1993).

109. *Agnese Goes to Her Death* (L'Agnese va a morire), by Renata Vigano (Italy, 1949). This resistance novel by Vigano is set in Italy in the years 1943 to 1945, during which time she was a member of a communist partisan brigade, following her ten years as an active antifascist in the underground. The 1930s in Italy, which serve as a background to the action, were marked by bitter ideological struggles between many political factions. One of these factions, the fascists, had in this early period gained the support of a populace convinced that Mussolini would revitalize a moribund Italian economy and bring much needed efficiency to government and the military. Christian Democrats and communists, who lost in their attempts to keep fascism at bay, were persecuted throughout the war and prewar years and relegated in their activities to the underground.

The title character of Vigano's novel, set in the Mussolini years, is an aging peasant woman, fearlessly and practically committed to the communist cause, though she knows nothing of its theoretical underpinnings. Her activism begins when the Germans, who have invaded Italy, after the surrender to the Allies, throw her husband into a labor camp where he dies. Her fierce and heroic actions in the resistance end with her murder by a German soldier.

In the middle of the Cold War between North Atlantic Treaty Organization (NATO) nations, led by the United States, and the Soviet bloc communism, Vigano's novel impressed on her readers the positive role that communists had played in the fight against Mussolini and Hitler in the 1930s and 1940s. While the procommunist message of the novel was received with antagonism in much of the Western world, it was greeted sympathetically by many intellectuals and working-class readers in postwar Italy and France where communists worked openly and were gaining some political power even in the legislature.

The novel was a clear boost to the communist cause in showing the unmistakable support and sense of purpose given to working-class Italians in the face of fascist terror. Her readers saw in the novel a repudiation of the NATO attitude that lumped fascism and communism together. Instead, they were exposed to the argument that communism was in practice the antithesis of fascism. Her characters were only passingly interested in ideology and conversion but had put their lives on the line, as no other group had done, to rid their country of a foreign invader. The novel reminded Italians that it was the communists who had worked more effectively than any other group and that, unlike fascism, which drew its support from the wealthy and powerful, communists had toiled in the trenches with the working people. Despite Vigano's care to stand clear of economic, ideological theory, her uneducated, humble main character, who has never even heard of Marx or Lenin, conveyed to the novel's readers the sense that in the philosophical struggle even then going on throughout the world it was the communists who had proven their willingness to embrace the common people.

Vigano's skill in presenting a simple tale, free of obvious proselytizing on the part of the narrator and characters, protected her from charges of propagandizing. Still the timing of her story was crucial, for by 1949, Italy had tended to fall into a languid conservatism, led by a powerful aristocracy and a wealthy upper middle class. Working-class organizers were again being labeled as troublesome and extreme. Vigano's book reminded her readers that it was not the

Germans only who had been the villains: Powerful Italian families had financed the fascist goon squads that had terrorized the common people.

Italy and the other European countries deeply affected by the novel were traditionally Roman Catholic. Despite this—in a real sense *because* of this—Vigano's novel had a marked impact, for the novel impressed on readers that good and evil were clear realities that could be redefined. Curiously, God was on the side of the atheists in this story, and

evil was in evidence in the mass murder and terror perpetrated by the fascists and Nazis with whom the Church in Rome had an unsettling accommodation.

Additional Readings: Ivanoe Bonomi, *From Socialism to Fascism: A Study of Contemporary Italy* (London: Hopkinson, 1924); Sergio Pacifici, *The Modern Italian Novel from Manzoni to Svevo* (Carbondale: Southern Illinois University Press, 1967); Frank Rosengarten, "The Italian Resistance Novel, 1945–1962," in *From Verisimo to Experimentalism*, ed. Sergio Pacifici (Bloomington: Indiana University Press, 1969), pp. 212–37.

Russia

◈

Nikolai Gogol, *Dead Souls*, 1842

Ivan Turgenev, *Fathers and Sons*, 1862

Leo Tolstoy, *War and Peace*, 1863–69

Fyodor Dostoevsky, *The Possessed*, 1872

Fyodor Dostoevsky, *The Brothers Karamazov*, 1880

Leo Tolstoy, *Resurrection*, 1899

Maxim Gorky, *Mother*, 1906

Mikhail Sholokhov, *Quiet Flows the Don*, 1928–40

Aleksandr Solzhenitsyn, *One Day in the Life of Ivan Denisovich*, 1962

Mikhail Bulgakov, *The Master and Margarita*, 1966–67

◈

TIMELINE

1801   Russian Czar Paul I, the despotic son of Catherine the Great, is murdered.

1801–25   Paul I's son Alexander I reigns in Russia, promising but not delivering reform. This is a period marking the rise of intellectuals and reformers seeking civil liberties, wider suffrage, and improvement in the condition of the serfs.

1812   During the Napoleonic Wars, Napoleon Bonaparte of France invades Russia and is driven back. The most famous battle between Napoleon's forces and Russia is the Battle of Borodino, which Leo Tolstoy depicts in *War and Peace.*

1825   With the death of Alexander I, the Decembrists, a group of military officers, attempt to control the czarist government and enact reforms but are overturned by the repressive new czar Nicholas I.

1825–55   Nicholas I subdues reformers with his police state and heavy censorship.

1842   Russian serfs who die after the census is taken are counted as officially alive until the next census appears.

Nikolai Gogol's *Dead Souls* is published. It refers to these literally but not officially dead serfs.

1854–55 Russia is ignominiously defeated by the Turks in the Crimean War.

1855–81 Alexander II, known as the czar liberator, rules Russia.

1861 Alexander II frees Russia's 40 million serfs but fails to enact needed land reforms, thus angering both landed aristocracy and radicals.

1862 Ivan Turgenev's *Fathers and Sons* is published.

1863 Leo Tolstoy's *War and Peace* is published. Its setting is Napoleon's invasion of Russia.

1872 Fyodor Dostoevsky's *The Possessed* is published.

1880 Fyodor Dostoevsky's *The Brothers Karamazov* is published.

1881 Alexander II is killed by a bomb.

Alexander III comes to the throne, brutally oppresses reformers, and suspends civil liberties.

1894 Nicholas II comes to the throne.

1898 Maxim Gorky is imprisoned for political activity.

1899 Leo Tolstoy's *Resurrection* is published.

This novel is expurgated and censored in Russia for thirty-eight years.

By this time the number of political prisoners sent to Siberia each year reaches 10,000.

1901 Tolstoy is excommunicated by the Russian Orthodox Church.

Maxim Gorky is again imprisoned.

1903 The Bolshevik movement is formed under the direction of Vladimir Ulyanov, known as Lenin.

1904–05 In the Russo-Japanese War, Russia is defeated.

1905 In a bloody massacre near the Winter Palace, the Cossacks join other government troops in slaughtering and injuring hundreds of striking demonstrators.

Gorky, who is among them, is imprisoned, joins the Bolsheviks, meets Lenin, and then flees the country until 1913.

After Bloody Sunday, Nicholas is forced to enact some reforms. Nevertheless, another insurrection occurs before the end of the year and is crushed by an army loyal to the czar.

1906 Gorky publishes *Mother* while in exile.

1914 Russia reluctantly enters World War I to stem Germany's aggression.

1917 The czarist regime is overturned in the Russian Revolution. Nicholas II and his family are imprisoned and eventually killed.

In June, Alexander Kerensky becomes provisional prime minister.

In October, the Bolsheviks, under Lenin seize power from Kerensky.

1918 Russia withdraws from World War I, taking huge losses.

1918–20 Russia is torn by Civil War between the Red Army of the Bolsheviks and the White Russians supported by the Cossacks. After winning the Civil War, the Bolsheviks establish the Union of Soviet Socialist Republics.

The Cossacks are dismantled and dispossessed.

1924 Lenin dies, and Leon Trotsky and Joseph Stalin compete for power. Stalin emerges victorious as the USSR's supreme leader and begins converting the economy to heavy industry.

1927 Leon Trotsky is expelled from the party and banished.

1928–40 Mikhail Sholokhov's *Quiet Flows the Don* is published. Its subject is the Cossacks, and its setting is between 1912 and 1922.

1934	Stalin begins purging opponents through execution and imprisonment in Siberian labor camps (the Gulag). Several million Russians are arrested; 1 million are shot; and 2 million die in the camps.
1936	Gorky is killed by government assassins on Stalin's orders.
1936–38	The purges, which are part of Stalin's rule from the beginning, reach their height, and prison sentences in Siberia increase.
1939	Stalin signs a Non-aggression Pact with Nazi Germany.
1940	The USSR continues its expansion through Poland, Finland, Latvia, Lithuania, Estonia, and the Balkans.
	Trotsky is assassinated in Mexico on Stalin's orders.
1940s–50s	The Cold War between the USSR and capitalist nations rages.
1941	Sholokhov's novel wins the Stalin Prize.
	Germany invades the USSR.
1941–45	Aleksandr Solzhenitsyn serves in the Russia army during World War II.
1943	Russia is able to turn Germany back.
1945	By the end of World War II, Russia has lost 28 million people.
1945–53	Solzhenitsyn is arrested on false charges and serves time in Siberia for eight years.
1946	Winston Churchill of England warns of the menace of the USSR in his "Iron Curtain" speech.
1948	Eastern bloc countries come under Russia control.
1953	Josef Stalin dies.
1958	Upon coming to power, Nikita Khrushchev reviews the outrages of Stalin's regime and "de-Stalinization" begins.
1960	Russia proclaims the "Year of Tolstoy."
1961	Stalin's body is removed from its place of honor.

1962	Solzhenitsyn's *One Day in the Life of Ivan Denisovich* is published and immediately banned in the USSR.
1965	Solzhenitsyn's papers are confiscated by the government.
	Sholokhov wins the Nobel Prize for Literature.
1966–67	Mikhail Bulgakov's novel *The Master and Margarita* is published posthumously.
1969	Solzhenitsyn is expelled from the USSR.
1970	Solzhenitsyn wins the Nobel Prize for Literature.
1982	Mikhail Gorbachev becomes head of state.
1986–89	Gorbachev revolutionizes the USSR with his policy of glasnost, or openness and candor, and perestroika, or reform of the system and support of elections, freedom of expression, and freedom of assembly.
	The Soviet Union's republics begin to declare their independence from Moscow.
1991	Boris Yeltsin elected the first president of Russia.
	The USSR is officially dismantled.
	Charges of treason against Solzhenitsyn are dropped.
1994	Solzhenitsyn returns to Russia to live.

110. *Dead Souls* (*Mertvye dushi*), by Nikolai Gogol (Russia, 1842). *Dead Souls* was written during the repressive reign of Czar Nicholas I. It plays on an actual, ridiculous government practice. In Russia in 1842, all serfs—literally slaves—at the time of one census were officially still alive until the next census, ten years later, even if their residences meanwhile had become the graveyard. In Gogol's novel, a traveling rogue, Pavel Ivanovich Chichikov, taking advantage of this fact, buys these "dead souls" from provincial landowners to promote a land scheme that he will use to acquire real estate and money.

The seemingly honest thief calls on a wide variety of provincial types to purchase dead men, while people in the capital, assuming he must be a millionaire, fawn over him. However, his scheme is discovered, causing riots of suspicion and speculation, and Chichikov decides to run for the exit, at which point his life is laid bare. He races off in a flying troika, which the author now identifies with the fate of Russia: "And you, Russia, do you not hurtle forward too, like some spirited troika that none can catch?"

Gogol's strategy of using comedy as social commentary proved that laughter is the sharper sword. He led his readers to ridicule and scorn every powerful entity in Russian society, viewing many that had been considered sacrosanct as just grotesque comic types, which became legendary in Russian culture. In his novel, landowners, for instance, lie, pretend, shout, bang chairs, claim to have access to government contracts, and, in general, act like madmen. Greed and self-importance bring out the worst in a great variety of human types in this world where seeming imbeciles walk about masquerading as minor savants.

When it first appeared, *Dead Souls* was regarded as a savage satire of nineteenth-century upper-class rural society. Critics at the time commented that, in this narrative play on the idea of reality versus illusion, the novel had removed the attractive masks that covered the privileged class. For instance, Chichikov himself seems to be well mannered, fastidious, polite, trustworthy, and competent; but that masks his crude, greedy corruption. And the people who fawn over him, while genteel on the outside, are moneygrubbing on the inside.

Everyone saw around them every day the stupidity of the ruling class, but only *Dead Souls* brought the blundering out into open discussion. Before the novel, Gogol wrote to a friend, it was as if all Russia were dead souls who refused to speak the truth. Ironically, though Gogol himself was a politically conservative supporter of the monarchy, his satire strongly reinforced the thinking of left-wing social activists and radical writers of

his day, who saw themselves as working "under Gogol's overcoat." Liberal critics saw it as the embodiment of a cruel and nonsensical world they wanted to sweep away. To some, it revealed a tumor at the heart of the society.

The aspects of the novel that inspired social reformers and revolutionaries were its social relevance, its great love of the common people, and its reformist intent, but during one period at the beginning of the twentieth century, literary critics attempted to leach the social realism from the novel and see it primarily as a fantasy. However, at least one man, the revolutionary Lenin, continued to regard it as a purposeful social satire and its author as a kindred soul and reformers as insightful for recognizing the value of Gogol's portraits that had stimulated reformist zeal.

During the 1930s and 1960s, readers of social conscience reclaimed Gogol as one of their own for his realistic satire of Russian landowners and serfs in the 1840s. The Soviet Union also recognized Gogol as inspiring and reinforcing the land reforms and economic changes that broke the power of the landlords and gave Russian serfs a fighting chance.

Despite Gogol's personal conservatism, the indisputable fact remains that *Dead Souls* exercised an enormous influence on the way in which ordinary Russians regarded the privileged class, on the actions of the most powerful revolutionaries of the twentieth century, and on the thinking of millions of others who, like Gogol's infamous dead souls, have remained voiceless.

Additional Readings: D.C.B. Lieven, *Empire: The Russian Empire and Its Rivals* (New Haven, CT: Yale University Press, 2001); Robert A. Maguire, *Exploring Gogol* (Stanford: Stanford University Press, 1994); William Mills Todd, *Fiction and Society in the Age of Pushkin; Ideology, Institutions, and Narrative* (Cambridge, MA: Harvard University Press, 1986).

111. *Fathers and Sons (Ottsy i deti)*, by Ivan Turgenev (Russia, 1862). *Fathers and Sons* is a chronicle of Russia at a time when it was a vast, backward country, more Asian than European, with an unbridgeable gulf between the rich aristocracy and the brutalized serfs, all governed by an autocratic Czar. The aristocrats learned French and adopted French manners, while the peasants or serfs were illiterate and lived in poverty, oppression, and ignorance, eternally tied to the soil. While serfs were officially freed by the czar in the 1860s, their conditions remained unchanged without genuine land reform. Indeed, their freedom only intensified agitation.

The artists' freedom from censorship, combined with the belief that art must adhere to truth and social purpose, led novelists, above others, to express the turmoil of Russian life. And Turgenev, a mild-mannered, nonviolent man, wrote the first Russian novel to ignite the century's social unrest. That novel was *Fathers and Sons*.

It begins as a young student, Arkady Kirsanov, brings a charismatic friend, Basarov, home to his family's country house. There Basarov, a "nihilist," encounters Arkady's father Nicolay, an aging man who loves the gentle life, and Nicolay's brother Pavel, a vain, pompous ex-army officer who had once been a dandy in his upper-class social circle and is now merely a stuffy and bored nonentity who essentially does nothing. The story concerns the clash between Basarov and the others, representing conflicting points of view on the urgent problems of the day. Basarov eagerly rushes into the breach when he recognizes a philosophical adversary in Pavel. He explains the ramifications of nihilism, the belief that scornfully regards scientific, measurable truth as the only objective in life. Basarov values above all else strength and willpower, not sentimentality for a dead past. It is essentially a cruel philosophy that condones ruthlessness in the accomplishment of its goals.

Turgenev's work had already had an astounding influence on Russian life. *A Sportsman's Sketches* (1852), for instance, had reportedly so stirred the czar concerning the brutalities of serfdom that he resolved to free the serfs. *Fathers and Sons* was seen by Russian readers as another assault on the consciousness of the privileged class. Reactions

were intense, both positive and negative. Many viewed the novel as representing the best interests of the working classes. It was hailed as an incisive look at the issues touching injustice and the various faces of revolution, which could be both courageously constructive and wildly destructive. Many recognized in the novel a calm warning that was needed at the time: the danger to the culture of obliterating everything from the past, whether immediately harmful or not. And looking back, later readers have seen that it was Turgenev, even more than Tolstoy and Dostoevsky, who accurately predicted the future.

The novel also succeeded in alienating many Russians: those on the Left, the Right, the Center, the young, the old, the traditionalists, and the reformers. They could not agree on what it stood for and were angered by what they saw as either Turgenev's attacks or ambiguities. Was Basarov a parody? An ideal to be emulated? Did the author approve of his arguments? Did he scorn them? All sides felt betrayed. Author Isaiah Berlin noted that the novel "caused the greatest storm among its Russian readers of any novel before or, indeed, since" (p. 280).

Turgenev was caricatured and ridiculed by all sides. In the left-wing press Basarov was presented as a vicious Mephistopheles. An old friend saw him as a kind of Genghis Khan, a "wild beast symptomatic of the savage condition of Russia" (quoted in Isaiah Berlin, p. 283). Others labeled Turgenev's efforts as "too fair." Berlin notes that Basarov, scarcely a wholly admirable character, "affected the young as did Werther, in the previous century, influenced them, like Schiller's *The Robbers*, like Byron's Laras and Giaours and Childe Harold in their day" (p. 285).

When Turgenev was buried in Russia, in October 1883, the crowds attending the ceremonies were on a massive scale, and representatives from all classes attended. The government was so fearful of outbreaks of terrorism that workers' organizations were not permitted to identify themselves on the wreaths they sent. While his novel had offended or disappointed so many, his death still brought readers forward to honor the man. And his reputation still had the power to strike fear into the heart of the government.

Additional Readings: Isaiah Berlin, *Fathers and Children: Turgenev and the Liberal Predicament* (Oxford: Clarendon Press, 1972); Jane T. Catlow, *Worlds within Worlds: The Novels of Ivan Turgenev* (Princeton, NJ: Princeton University Press, 1990).

112. *War and Peace* (*Voina i mir*), by Leo Tolstoy (Russia, 1863–69).

War and Peace, regarded universally as Russia's great epic and considered by many as the greatest novel of all time, is thoroughly grounded in Russian history. In the background of the story, focused on the Napoleonic Wars, is Russia's nineteenth-century history under the czars, beginning with the reign of Alexander I, which culminated in Napoleon's invasion of Russia in 1812 and forced his retreat.

Alexander's son, Nicholas I, came to the throne, planning from the first to use his secret police to suppress reform. His downfall came with Russia's defeat in the 1854 Crimean War against the Turks. After the failure of repeated attempts to limit the monarchy and eliminate serfdom and after two years of useless slaughter in the Crimea, the Russian people were openly rebellious.

Alexander II, the son of Nicholas I, who ascended the throne in 1855, was called the Czar Liberator because he freed some 40 million serfs in 1861, among other reforms. But the displeasure of both landed aristocracy and radical reformers created instability and anarchy, and in 1881 Alexander was killed by a bomb.

The plight of the working class and intelligentsia worsened with the succession of Alexander III, a Slavophile antagonistic to reformers. Unlike his father, a firm believer in autocracy, he used every brutal measure available to suppress reform. During his reign, in 1865, at the time of the appearance of the first chapters of *War and Peace*, Russia was in tremendous turmoil. The lives of serfs were little changed after their emancipation

because of the failure to enact land reforms. Kept ignorant and uneducated and in unspeakable poverty, regarded as little more than beasts, used as cannon fodder in senseless wars outside their borders, they seethed with generations of injustice. Large segments of the population, running across class lines, were infuriated with the czar's gross economic and social wrongs. Trouble came now not from a few aristocratic reformers and students but from a wide base. The bourgeoisie were increasing in strength and dissatisfaction, as were conservative reformers. The split between various political positions widened, and violent disagreement erupted over whether Russia should be defined primarily as Slav or European.

Set in the period just before, during, and after Napoleon's 1812 invasion of Russia, the grand sweep of Tolstoy's novel is shown in its huge cast of more than 500 characters. The primary focus is on four young aristocrats: Pierre, the large, congenial, bearlike man who contains the novel's hope for democracy and equality; the intellectual and disillusioned Prince Andre, who detests war but must defend his country when it is invaded; Natasha, the desirable young woman who betrays Andre, her true love, returns to care for him while he is dying, and after the war, marries Pierre; and Nikolai, Natasha's brother. The novel ends in 1815, after Napoleon has been forced to retreat. Interspersed throughout the novel are essays on the nature of history.

Completed in 1869, it became an instant success that stirred not only the nation but the world. The influence of Tolstoy's novel has been exceedingly far-reaching and can be discussed on several different levels: its reenforcement of Russian nationalism, including a reinterpretation of events in the Napoleonic War; its provocation of discussion about determinism and the "Great Man" view of history; and its validation of the group over the individual in Soviet life.

War and Peace was the first great expression of the new nationalism that had arisen in the 1860s, accomplished by having at its center a time when all Russians had united to devastate the French invader, which had subdued all of Europe. As such, the novel was an antidote to the defeat at the hands of the Turks in the Crimean War and the chaos of political turmoil.

Nationalism was also served by Tolstoy's reinterpretation of two events in Russian history. He turned a general, regarded at the time as a bungling failure, into a warrior genius. The Battle of Borodino, therefore, was turned by Tolstoy into a Russian success rather than a failure, as it had generally been presumed to be.

The theory of history, retold in *War and Peace*, had its greatest worldwide influence in debunking the Great Man theory, whereby history is seen as the shadow cast by one great man of any given period. In the case of the novel, the man is Napoleon. Tolstoy shows, for example, that at Austerlitz, Napoleon's victory had nothing to do with Napoleon's grand plan but with the actions of thousands of men at individual crossroads and bridges. In Tolstoy's view, great men are merely thrown up on the wave of events; they do not guide history.

The result of this theory was to place greater importance on the group. In the novel, this means the large group of citizens from all classes, working together in ordinary life. Such a view reinforced the socialism that followed the publication of the novel. Tolstoy's determinism in the novel, which he personally denied but which readers continually see there, was also in accord with the economic determinism of Marx and Lenin.

Although Tolstoy's novels were sometimes banned before the Russian Revolution, afterward *War and Peace* came to be revered as a sacred national text. To illustrate: 1960 was designated by the Soviet Union as the "Year of Tolstoy." Between 1917 and 1958, some 5,000 books and articles were written on Tolstoy—500 on *War and Peace* alone.

Tolstoy's pacifism, which began to be expressed in *War and Peace*, altered world history by influencing Mahatma Gandhi's nonviolent leadership, resulting in independence for India and, through Gandhi, the

nonviolence of Martin Luther King and the civil rights movement in the United States.

Additional Readings: Isaiah Berlin, *The Hedgehog and the Fox: An Essay on Tolstoy's View of History* (New York: Weidenfeld and Nicholson, 1954); R.F. Christian, *Tolstoy's War and Peace* (London: Oxford University Press, 1962).

113. *The Possessed*, or *The Devils* (*Besy*), by Fyodor Dostoevsky (Russia, 1872). *The Possessed* is a novelistic commentary on the turbulent political agitation in Russia in the 1860s in the reign of Czar Alexander II. Alexander had inherited numerous problems from his father, Nicholas I—problems of corruption and poverty that had outraged the working people and separated the nation's leaders even more from the rest of Russia. But during Nicholas I's reign, a group of younger intellectuals and reformers had arisen to address the problems of the serfs. During the reign of Alexander II, one of the more enlightened czars, some of their radical reforms were made, the chief of which was the legal emancipation of the serfs from their landholding owners. The czar also improved the legal system, created representative government at the local level, modernized the army and the bureaucracy, and eliminated much of the old censorship. But the seeds of discontent had already been planted, and the anger among Russians was growing because the reforms did not go far enough. The emancipation of the serfs, for example, meant little without land reforms. There were still no meaningful limits to the czar's power and, despite the easing of censorship, no civil liberties to speak and write one's mind. Finding it impossible to work peaceably within the system, reformists adopted the tactics of disobedience and terror. Throughout the 1860s, those devoted to socialism, anarchy, and nihilism conspired against the government and each other, creating havoc in Russian society. At the time of the publication of *The Possessed*, the organization of Russians devoted to terrorists' tactics had become formidable and effective and culminated in the bombing of Alexander II's carriage in 1881.

The plot of *The Possessed*, based in part on

actual events, is the story of two men: a ruthless revolutionary named Verhovensky, who is the son of an intellectual, and Stavrogin, his guilt-ridden, aristocratic associate who is without religious faith and incapable of love. Verhovensky, who declares that he will use any tactics to bring about the revolution, wants to use the reluctant Stavrogin, a man from a noble family, to front for the group Verhovensky leads.

The chief force in the life of Stavrogin, the classic Dostoevsky sinner, is guilt over his abuse of a twelve-year-old girl who subsequently committed suicide. This does not keep him, however, from destroying other women in the course of the novel. It does lead him to punish himself by marrying Marya, a simple-minded girl, whom his friend Verhovensky has killed because she would be a political liability for Stavrogin. Stavrogin is responsible for other murders in the cause of revolution. Despite his machinations to retain control and eradicate his enemies, Stavrogin's organization falls apart, and he, himself, disappears. At the same time, the guilt-ridden Stavrogin kills himself, leaving his father to contemplate a society without religious faith or love.

Dostoevsky's novel appearing against the background of nihilist chaos, made apparent in the real-life murder of a young student by a group of revolutionaries to which he had belonged, heightened the novelist's avowed purpose to present an antinihilistic argument. The first reaction to the novel was loud outrage from the political Left, which denounced Dostoevsky and the novel for demeaning the courageous efforts of young intellectuals who were working for a better life for those less fortunate than themselves and for freedom of expression for all Russians. They criticized the novel for painting a whole generation of young people as heartless fanatics. Many readers made clear in their reviews of the novel that they were disappointed in Dostoevsky's betrayal of the cause of reform. In response, he wrote a column, protesting that he had been inspired by and had worked for one of the leading older liberals venerated by the Left. S.G. Nechaev,

whose group had murdered one of their own members, had been his mentor at one time.

Nor were the author's clearly recognizable models for his characters appreciated. In some cases, he caricatured Russian intellectuals of considerable stature: Not only Nechaev but also the highly regarded writer Ivan Turgenev.

Many readers saw this novel, written by one of Russia's preeminent literary figures who, in his youth, had had firsthand experience with revolutionary groups, as indiscriminately undermining all political reform in Russia, which Dostoevsky showed as having been infected by Western Europe.

Others believed that the once radical author was merely criticizing a kind of spiritual nihilism that had infected the reform movement. What often got lost in this cast of caricatures was his real point—that reformists, by losing sight of moral and religious values, had corrupted human progress. Without God and without order, Dostoevsky believed, any human effort will be base and destructive.

The novel was received far more favorably by the right wing than the left wing and was taken up as an inspiration especially by those who wanted a return to national, that is, Russian, values, situated in Christian faith and national order. As audiences have become distanced from the actual political circumstances surrounding the novel, they have found more value in Dostoevsky's religious theme.

Additional Readings: Joseph Frank, *Dostoevsky: The Miraculous Years, 1865–1871* (Princeton, NJ: Princeton University Press, 1995); Irving Howe, "Dostoevsky and the Politics of Salvation," in *A Collection of Critical Essays*, ed. Rene Wellek (Englewood Cliffs, NJ: Prentice-Hall, 1962); Walter Moss, *A History of Russia* (New York: McGraw-Hill, 1997).

114. *The Brothers Karamazov* (*Brat'ia Karamazovy*), by Fyodor Dostoevsky (Russia, 1880). *The Brothers Karamazov* was one of the last of the great nineteenth-century novels and one of the most highly regarded. It is a huge, comprehensive work that attempts to probe the depths of human psychology in Imperialist Russia, a reality that for Dostoevsky was revealed in examining passionate, intense people undergoing the most intense pressures. Thus he wrote about souls in extremis: criminals, saints, prostitutes, psychologically fierce or unhampered people who attempt to achieve goodness but through accidents or human passions find themselves in the darkest pits of human endeavor.

In *The Brothers Karamazov*, four passionate sons of a drunken, dissolute, violent, and evil father, Fydor Karamazov, each in turn, in his own way, passionate and extreme, plunges into his own dark night of the soul. There is Alyosha, the "saintly" brother, who wants only to be like the saintly priest Father Zossima; Ivan, the intellectual skeptic, who seeks to penetrate the meaning of life through reason, even while he struggles with his own soul; Dymitri, the lover of the good life through all things physical and hearty, food, drink, women, good times, and unhampered intensity; and finally Smerdyakov, the illegitimate son of a servant woman and probably of old Karamazov, a vile, negative man. The predicament unfolds with the crime of patricide, when one of the sons violently murders the old man. It is a moral tale, classified as a realistic fantasy, that explores such things as the meaning of good and evil, the nature of God, and the meaning of Satan and Hell. With graphic and excruciating description, Ivan describes a tiny child who calls out for his father after having been brutally beaten by him for no reason, prompting the skeptic to ask what kind of God could willfully bring about or even permit such torture of small children in this world?

All of the novel's characters question the meaning of life; and they do so having experienced the lowest depths of life and the saddest horrors that men can inflict upon each other. Dostoevsky explores the motives not just of evil men who are travesties of humanity but of good men, men caught in the extremities of life.

Dostoevsky's own experience had provided him with the outward boundaries of human existence. When he was a child, his father, a surgeon, was murdered, probably by his serfs. As a young man, he was arrested and condemned for anti-government activity, and was facing a firing squad when, at the last minute, a messenger galloped up with a reprieve. The whole thing turned out to have been a staged performance ordered by the czar. He spent four years at hard labor in Siberia, followed by four more years of military service at the lowest rank. He was an epileptic and a compulsive gambler (suffering huge losses that forced him to beg for loans from friends) and was tortured by his own repeated adultery. Finally, even after he became famous, he had to work constantly to avoid overwhelming debts.

The Brothers Karamazov was very enthusiastically received. Dostoevsky was already a celebrated, though poor, Russian novelist, and the advent of his new novel was regarded as the chief literary event of the year.

To read Tolstoy's *War and Peace* or his later works is to live in a world of light or to see characters struggling for light. To read Dostoevsky is to descend into some cosmic darkness that contains most of the troubles that have haunted the human mind. One evidence of his lasting influence can be shown by an anecdote. After a speech honoring Russian poet Aleksandr Pushkin in 1880, he wrote his wife telling how, as he left the platform, "a host of people, youths, graybeards and ladies" had surrounded him, saying, "You're our prophet. We've become better people since we read *The Karamazovs*" (Robin F. Miller, *"The Brothers Karamotzov": Worlds of the Novel* [New York: Twayne, 1992], p. 7). These nameless people may be said to represent hosts of others, of every nation and political persuasion, who found that the descent into the depths influenced or changed their lives as it presented them with a parable of modern life.

Sigmund Freud, the father of psychoanalysis, after reading *The Brothers Karamazov*, declared that Dostoevsky had instinctively probed the darker corners of human psychology. In the era of disillusionment following World War I, the novel enjoyed a surge of popularity as an expression of a desperate, and seemingly futile, search for meaning and for God in a cruel world.

Russian scholar Nicholas Berdyaev, in a fit of mad exaltation, wrote: "So great is the worth of Dostoyevsky that to have produced him is by itself sufficient justification for the existence of the Russian people" (Miller, p. 8).

Additional Readings: Robin Feuer Miller, *"The Brothers Karamatzov": Worlds of the Novel* (New York: Twayne, 1992); Rene Wellek, ed., *Dostoevsky: A Collection of Critical Essays* (Englewood Cliffs, NJ: Prentice-Hall, 1962).

115. *Resurrection (Voskreseniye)*, by Leo Tolstoy (Russia, 1899). Tolstoy's novel *Resurrection*, in protesting the abuses of capital punishment and the prison system, actually challenges the social and religious foundations of Russian life. Supported by the powerful Russian Orthodox Church, the czarist regime had for centuries maintained a class system of landed aristocrats and serfs, the last of which lived in wretched hopelessness, even after they were belatedly freed in 1861. Failure to enact land reforms kept them exploited and in penury and did little to change the government's view of them as little more than beasts of burden, unfit for education, and inherently immoral and criminal. The growing class of industrial workers did not fare much better. As in all societies, these lower-class citizens in Russia felt most keenly the harsh and unjust policies of the police and the legal and prison system. In Russia, members of the working classes, along with insurgents of every class, were sent to prisons in Siberia, where the work they were forced to perform was made health- and life-threatening by the harsh, barren landscape and the bitterly cold climate. By the time of Tolstoy's novel, more than 10,000 Russians were exiled to Siberia each year, many, like Joseph Stalin, Vladimir Lenin, and Leon Trotsky, for political activities.

The plot of *Resurrection* begins with the trial of a domestic servant named Katusha Maslova whose life has been ruined many years earlier because of her seduction by an aristocrat, Prince Dmitri Ivanovitch Nekhludof, and her subsequent pregnancy. Now a prostitute, she is on trial for a robbery and murder she declares she did not commit. By coincidence, Prince Nekhludof, who recognizes her, is on the jury that acquits her of the crime. However, through a bureaucratic error, she is sentenced to hard labor in Siberia. As atonement for his responsibility in causing her fall, Nehludof joins her in Siberia and decides that the criminality among the peasants is caused largely by the actions of the upper classes, government, and Church. He renounces his own land, turning his estate over to his peasant workers to operate as a commune. He also renounces the Church when he becomes a true follower of Jesus. Maslova is released from prison, but despite their newfound love for each other, she must marry someone of her own class rather than Nekhludof

Because of Tolstoy's reputation, the novel had instant and wide-ranging success. The reception by ordinary readers in Russia was wildly enthusiastic. Moreover, translations appeared in England, France, Germany, and the United States at the same time it was appearing in Russia. In addition to the official versions of the novel, many illegal versions appeared throughout the world. In Germany twelve different translations circulated in 1900, fifteen editions in France.

By the time of the publication of this incendiary novel, Tolstoy was such an internationally celebrated figure that the government regarded his person as untouchable. However, the perceived threat posed by the novel is seen in its being heavily censored in Russia. Not until 1936 did a complete and unexpurgated edition appear there. And in 1901, the Russian Orthodox Church excommunicated him because of the novel's heresy.

It was said of Tolstoy after the publication of *Resurrection* that he was the only man in Russia sufficiently courageous and respected to criticize the government as he had done. In short, no one else had so openly brought to public attention the injustices suffered by prostitutes, by lower-class women in general, by workers accused of crimes, by imprisoned criminals, and by serfs in their everyday lives.

Although the revolutionary government would continue their own policies of oppression and Siberian labor camps, many of the injustices that led to the Revolution of 1917 were publicly expressed in *Resurrection* and helped give shape to the class and land reforms that followed.

Additional Readings: Nicholas Valentine Riasanovsky, *A History of Russia*, 6th ed. (New York: Oxford University Press, 2000); Ernest J. Simmons, *Introduction to Tolstoy's Writings* (Chicago: University of Chicago Press, 1968); Edward Wasiolek, *Tolstoy's Major Fiction* (Chicago: University of Chicago Press, 1978).

116. *Mother* (*Mat'*), **by Maxim Gorky (Russia, 1906).** Maxim Gorky is one of Russia's most widely known political writers, and *Mother* is considered to be his masterpiece and his most polemical novel. Gorky, who had a very hard childhood and young manhood, having to perform difficult physical labor, became a Marxist and began working in the cause of revolution in his late teens, during the repressive reign of Alexander III. Revolutionary activity was provoked by the czar's absolute refusal to tolerate public participation in government or civil liberties of speech, press, assembly, or legal recourse. When the czar ascended the throne in 1894, he also withheld civil liberties and did nothing to alleviate the suffering of peasants and factory workers, earning the animosity of most segments of the Russian population and increasing radical protests, of which Gorky was a part. By 1898, despite his beginning fame as a writer, Gorky was imprisoned for his political activity. He was also arrested and imprisoned in 1901 and in 1905, after his involvement in what was known as "Bloody Sunday," on January 9, when the government killed and wounded hundreds of striking workers demonstrating for reforms near the czar's Winter Palace. In that year, Gorky joined the Bolshevik Party and met Lenin. He helped build the barricades in Moscow for the December uprising in 1905, and

knowing that arrest was eminent, he fled the country and was in exile for eight years, during which time he wrote and published *Mother*.

Gorky's novel is the story of an old woman who is converted to the socialist cause by her son, Pavel Vlasov, a young political activist. In the background of her perilous activities are a cast of characters from many different walks of life who are dedicated to the cause of reform. They include middle-class factory owners, factory workers, aristocrats, and artists. After her conversion, the mother assumes bold risks to spy for the revolutionaries and distribute their literature. Finally, her son, whom she loves more than any being on earth, is tried in a kangaroo court, after articulating in a speech the message of the novel, and then is shipped to a living death in Siberia. The mother brazenly distributes hundreds of copies of the speech to the gathering crowds while she shouts out incendiary truths: "We perish all our lives, day after day in toil, always in filth, in deceit. And others enjoy themselves and gormandize themselves on our labor; and they hold us like dogs on chains, in ignorance." She is not just a character; she becomes symbolic of Mother Russia. And in the middle of her speech, the police arrive to beat her into silence, and she dies.

At the time of the novel's first appearance, readers on the Left reviewed the novel favorably. Many, out of sympathy with his cause, accused him of having created Marxist propaganda rather than art. But the eyes of many readers were opened to the desperation, courage, and determination of revolutionaries in Russia in the decade preceding the Russian Revolution. The political Left was given hope, and the Right was alarmed at discovering just how extensive underground support for the cause was across class lines. It was largely this novel that made Gorky beloved in his native Russia and caused him to be seen as a formidable enemy by both czarist and revolutionary tyrants. Lenin extended the novel his approval, but Gorky's subsequent criticism of some of Lenin's policies led him to censure Gorky's work. Gorky's sudden death in 1936 is believed by many to have been murder, carried out by Joseph Stalin's secret police on Stalin's orders.

Although he continued to be viewed critically by many literary reviewers, by the late 1950s Gorky had come to be regarded in what was then the Soviet Union as one of the greatest writers the country had produced.

Additional Readings: F.M. Borras, *Maxim Gorky the Writer: An Interpretation* (Oxford: Clarendon Press, 1967); Paul Dukes, *A History of Russia* (Durham, NC: Duke University Press, 1998); Barry Scherr, *Maxim Gorky* (Boston: Twayne, 1988).

117. *Quiet Flows the Don* (*Tichy Don*), **by Mikhail Sholokhov (Russia, 1928–40).** *Quiet Flows the Don* chronicles the lives of the Don Cossacks, one of the most colorful and distinctive peoples in pre-Revolutionary Russian.

The Cossacks, historically known as fierce warriors, superb horsemen, and free spirits, had settled along the Don, Dneper, and Ural Rivers centuries before after having escaped serfdom, and, being too troublesome to be conquered, had won from the czars land and other benefits in exchange for military service. In 1905, they had charged into the throngs of striking peasants demonstrating at the czar's Winter Palace.

They also played a role in the civil war that followed the Russian Revolution. Following the Revolution of February 1917, a provisional government was established under Alexander Kerensky. He, in turn, was replaced in October by Bolsheviks led by Lenin. Then civil war broke out as the Red Army of the Bosheviks fought against the counterrevolutionary White Russians, supported by the Cossacks. By 1920 the White Russians had been soundly defeated by the Bolsheviks, and the Cossacks' old way of life began to vanish rapidly. Their estates were broken up, their military power was dismantled, and they were dispersed throughout Russia and the rest of the world: some in Europe serving in private cavalries, a few in Hollywood, working as stunt riders.

It is this Cossack culture that Sholokhov describes, covering 1912 to 1922, from pre–World War I days on through the revolution to the end of the civil war that followed. The huge novel, patterned structurally after Tolstoy's *War and Peace*, gives an epic sweep to the Cossack's story of heroism, devastation, nobility of purpose, and divided loyalties. Like Tolstoy, Sholokhov used documentary materials and historic interpolations to support the actions of an enormous cast. Unlike Tolstoy's novel, however, it ends in defeat for the Cossacks. A melancholy tone permeates the broad sweep of action, which concentrates on great movements rather than on individuals.

Sholokhov himself was born in the Cossack region of the Don to a Ukranian mother and a Russian father. Sholokhov joined the Red Army when war reached the upper Don; there he witnessed the anti-Bolshevik uprising and participated in the campaign against guerrilla remnants of the White Army. He later used these experiences to portray the civil war with realism and integrity and to show sympathy with the Cossack cause.

The protagonist of the novel is Grigor Melekhov, a Cossack, with a divided conscience and a sense of duty. Grigor wavers, first supporting the White Russians, then joining the Red Army, and finally returning to fight with partisan guerrillas of the White Army. Finally, in his native region, the White Army is defeated by the Bolsheviks. His doom is sealed when, once more at home, he is destroyed by a former friend, now an ardent communist.

The novel was originally published in serialized form between the years 1928 and 1940, despite continual trouble with Soviet functionaries over his sympathy for the White Russians, especially in Book Three, which included graphic accounts of Red Army brutality. After a personal audience with Stalin, however, publication was resumed. The book won the Stalin Prize in 1941.

The novel met with immediate success in Russia and throughout the world, where it retained its popularity for decades. It has long been required reading in the curriculum of every schoolchild in Russia. As of 1984, when Sholokhov died, the novel had been translated into seventy-three languages. In 1996, a definitive edition was published in Great Britain and the United States, with all abridgments and all material cut by Soviet censors reinserted.

Sholokhov, who insisted that he was a communist first and a writer second, pioneered socialist realism, which is characterized by the use of art to glorify socialism. Few writers have been so enthusiastically lauded in Russia. On the strength of his political standing in the Communist Party, coupled with his authorship of this novel, Sholokhov received the Order of Lenin eight times and was named a "Hero of Socialist Labor" in 1967. In 1965, he received the Nobel Prize for Literature, the only officially sanctioned Soviet writer ever to be so honored. While controversy existed at first as to whether Sholokhov actually wrote the novel because of his nonliterary background, it is generally believed now that he did.

Recognized as a landmark in Russian fiction, Sholokhov's novel is, for readers throughout the world, the primary picture of the Don Cossacks and the Russian civil war. The book was crucial in showing that many Cossacks—indeed, many White Russians— were not counterrevolutionaries but were very torn during the civil war and found much to admire about the Bolsheviks. The novel also shows to the world that no one side had a monopoly on atrocities. It has been said that Sholokhov gave expression to the history of the USSR, unifying the new regime with an epic myth by presenting his countrymen with a balanced picture of the forces at war and giving an objective account of the choices before them. And while it is his only great novel, it is also the foremost artistic example of Russia's socialist realism.

In 1930, when Sholokhov finished reading to a meeting of communist workers from Part Six, concerning the funeral of Peter Melexov, a White Russian officer killed by the Bolsheviks, many in the audience were openly weeping.

Additional Readings: C.G. Bearne, *Sholokhov*

(Edinburgh: Oliver and Boyd, 1969); Paul Dukes, *A History of Russia* (Durham, NC: Duke University Press, 1998); David Hugh Steward, *Mikhail Sholokhov* (Ann Arbor: University of Michigan Press, 1967).

118. *One Day in the Life of Ivan Denisovich* (*Odin den iz zhizni Ivana Denisovicha*), **by Aleksandr Solzhenitsyn (Russia, 1962).** Solzhenitsyn's novel, one of the most highly controversial novels of the twentieth century, is based on his own experience in the forced labor camps of Russia's Siberia. Siberia, the frozen wasteland of Russia, had served as a prison and haven for runaway serfs throughout the nineteenth century. With the rise to power of Joseph Stalin in the 1920s, Siberia began to be a major, notorious area of activity. To exploit the metals, diamonds, and forests of the area, Stalin sent millions of people from Russia and Soviet Eastern bloc countries to prisons and work camps in Siberia. By any standard, life in Siberia was cruel and unusual punishment. The weather was brutal; the work was backbreaking; the food and supplies totally inadequate. Anyone remotely suspected of posing a threat to Stalin was condemned to Siberia or executed, often on spurious charges. Between 1936 and 1938, when purges were at their height, it has been estimated that as many as 7 million people were either executed or sent to Siberian prisons and camps. Even though the numbers of those arrested declined in 1938, war prisoners and suspected Russian dissidents continued to be exiled to Siberia. Even after Stalin died and was denounced, repressive measures continued. Aleksandr Solzhenitsyn, a former soldier during World War II, was sentenced to eight years in prison on the evidence that he had criticized Stalin in a letter to a friend.

The plot of the novel based on his experiences involves a typical day in the life of a former carpenter and Russian soldier in World War II who, after having escaped from capture by the Germans, is then imprisoned by the USSR on the grounds that he associated with the enemy. Although he believes that he will never come out of prison alive, he has not succumbed to despair and prides himself on being able to survive the brutal cold, starvation, and labor.

The book appeared in 1962, during a "thaw" in the Cold War before the fall of Nikita Khrushchev, the Soviet leader who denounced Stalinism. The book was actually printed with Khrushchev's permission, and he reportedly had wept upon reading it. Khrushchev was not alone. Few novels were greeted with such acclaim in the Soviet Union and the rest of the world. However, what has been called a re-Stalinization occurred in the late 1960s, and Solzhenitsyn ran afoul of the government. His novel had always been banned in the prison camps, though available to the population at large, but in the mid-1960s it became forbidden reading in the Soviet Union and was quietly withdrawn from libraries. In 1965 Solzhenitsyn's papers were confiscated, and in 1967 he publicly denounced censorship in the Soviet Union. In 1969, he was expelled from the Soviet Writers' Union and subsequently from the country itself. Not until glasnost in 1989 were his works again available in his country. This was not the fate of the novel in the rest of the world, however; by 1976, the novel had sold 30 million copies.

The book's controversy came from its obvious commentary on Soviet life even after the death of Stalin. Readers' eyes were opened to the parallels between Ivan's life in the prison and everyday Russian life in the collective farms and factories throughout the country: The prison has its wardens who are equivalent to the work bosses outside the prison; the work in and out of prison is backbreaking and falls without equality on certain shoulders; the young people are as eager to escape what they perceive to be the prison of the farm collectives as the Siberia prisoners are to escape their prison walls; corruption and bribery exist in both places, as do hunger and malnutrition.

In the light of Solzhenitsyn's denunciation of the whole system through his portrait of life in Siberia, readers split into two main groups, his book becoming the center of a worldwide debate. On one hand were main-line Soviets and philosophical Marxists and socialists throughout the world. On the other hand, one found political conservatives of every stripe. Conservatives praised the book, calling it a scourge of communism and Solzhenitsyn the conscience of Russia. The book influenced them not only as one of the first eyewitness pictures of what occurred in the camps under Stalin but as an accurate analogy of Soviet life. British aristocrat Lord Home saw the book as entirely consistent with British conservatism.

Many liberals, on the other hand, were angered by the book, arguing that it presented the world with a false picture of socialism and ignored the reforms that had been put into effect after Stalin's death. Soviets charged that the author, in demonizing the Soviet Union, had played into the hands of the United States and other Western world imperialists who were exploiting the book politically. Though many books have been written on Solzhenitsyn, it is almost impossible to find one that does not take a rigid position on one of these two extremes.

Additional Readings: Stephen Carter, *The Politics of Solzhenitsyn* (New York: Holmes and Meier, 1977); Christopher Moody, *Solzhenitsyn* (New York: Barnes and Noble, 1973); D.M. Thomas, *Alexander Solzhenitsyn: A Century in His Life* (New York: St. Martin's Press, 1999).

119. *The Master and Margarita* (*Master i Margarita*), by Mikhail Bulgakov (Russia, 1966–67).

The Master and Margarita, regarded by many as the greatest Russian novel of the twentieth century, was far too dangerous in its implications to be published in the author's lifetime. Early in his career Bulgakov had been expelled from the only statesanctioned writers' group in the country, the Soviet Writers' Union, so he no longer had either status or income as a writer toward the end of his life when he began work on his novel. Only in late middle age did Bulgakov have the confidence to give fictional form to the idea he had been mulling over for most of life and that he considered to be his masterpiece. Even so, the work could not be published in his lifetime and did not appear until 1966, some twenty-six years after his death in 1940. Too controversial to be published before Stalin had been denounced, it remained a closely guarded secret until Khrushchev came to power. Even then it appeared in censored form.

The context of the novel is Stalinist Russia, a time of heavy censorship of literature and newspapers, government spying on its own citizens, purges of Stalin's opposition, imprisonment in Siberia, suppression of religion, layer upon layer of corrupt party bureaucracy, and an impossible list of ideological demands exacted of every artist.

Knowing how explosive his work would be, Bulgakov disguised its real meaning through analogy in a three-part, overlapping story. The first is the story of a devil named Woland and his associate fiends who create havoc in the lives of stupid party-liners in a Moscow underworld as punishment for their greed and arrogance. The second is the story of a persecuted novelist (the master) who tries to burn his manuscript to save his life, even though that life is lived out in a state mental institution. His mistress, Margarita, bargains with the devil in a Faustian pact on behalf of her lover. The third plot, perhaps written by the master, perhaps by his friend "Homeless," perhaps told by Satan or Margarita, is the story of Christ and Pontius Pilate, who is tortured by his own cowardice.

The publication of the novel was an immediate sensation throughout Russia and around the world, reviving the West's interest in the Soviet Union. Western and dissident Russians lauded the book, but the party establishment in Russia reacted with dismay, especially members of the Writers' Union, which had been so decidedly parodied.

The disguised narrative parallels left the story open to a number of interpretations. Some readers have even argued that the story is actually friendly to Stalin, that Woland is a wise, heroic Stalin who has appeared to punish the middle-class materialists who have betrayed the party's cause. Still other readers

saw Woland as representative of Western capitalism, come to destroy Soviet society. But most readers were stunned to see that the sensational novel excoriated and ridiculed the greed, arrogance, and senselessness that they had been dealing with daily in Moscow for decades. To the outside world, the novel corroborated tales of discontent with Stalinism that began emerging during the Khrushchev years.

The novel's use of the figure of Jesus brought to the fore the efficacy of Christianity in an atheistic country that outlawed religion. Roman persecution seems to parallel Moscow persecution; Pilate parallels a cowardly people, including the master, who submit too easily to oppression. There is a hope of regeneration in the Christian story, but oppression of the human spirit and of truth in the Soviet Union, where humans become robots, makes regeneration impossible.

Finally, readers' eyes were opened to the problems facing artists in the Soviet Union. Every artistic work was required to fit into a narrow definition of art that reflected well on the Soviet Union. The operation of the Soviet Writers' Union was exposed, revealing their power to make or ruin the life of an artist, not on the basis of any work's independent artistic merit but on how well it reflected the Soviet line. Woland provided his Russian audience with the heretical view that true art cannot be destroyed. Manuscripts, he tells the reader, do not burn. But the temple of Soviet literature in the novel *does* burn down.

The work consistently receives critical attention throughout the world, and its power to influence readers is regarded as a threat in Russia, where parts of the novel are still censored.

Additional Readings: Andrew Barratt, *Between Two Worlds: A Critical Introduction to* The Master and Margarita (Oxford: Clarendon Press, 1987); Laura D. Weeks, ed., The Master and Margarita: A Critical Companion (Evanston, IL: Northwestern University Press, 1996).

Spain

୧୭

Miguel de Cervantes, *Don Quixote*, 1605, 1615

Benito Pérez Galdós, *Doña Perfecta*, 1876

Vicente Blasco Ibáñez, *The Cabin*, 1898

Ramón J. Sender, *Pro Patria*, 1930

José María Gironella, *The Cypresses Believe in God*, 1953

୧୭

TIMELINE

280(?)–337 A Latin document gives the Roman Catholic Church jurisdiction over all the Western Empire.

1056 The three centuries of Moorish rule of Spain ends with Ferdinand's conquest of Spain.

1478 The Inquisition, with an intricate force of its own spies, police, and justice system, begins a brutal campaign to purify religion of heretics, enforce Roman Catholicism as the state religion, and strengthen the monarchy, using execution, torture, and confiscation of property.

1492 In unifying Spain, Spanish monarchs Ferdinand and Isabella decree that only Roman Catholicism will be tolerated in Spain, forcing Spain's many Jewish and Muslim citizens to either convert or leave their homeland. Those who convert are distinguished from other Christians with the title "New Christians," as opposed to "Old Christians."

1516 Charles of Hapsburg comes to the Spanish throne.

1519 Charles is designated Charles V, Holy Roman Emperor. He leads the fight in suppressing the Protestant Reformation and cleansing the country of heretics.

1545–64 The Council of Trent affirms Roman Catholicism as the only true religion.

1547 Archbishop Juan Martínez Siliceo decrees the Statute of Purity of Blood, leading to the exclusion of New Christians from any positions of authority.

1556 Philip II comes to the Spanish throne.

1571	Spain, leading the Holy League, defeats the Turks in the Battle of Lepanto.
	Miguel de Cervantes is a soldier in this battle.
1575–80	Cervantes is held in captivity by the Moors.
1580	Spain has become the largest empire in the world.
1588	The Spanish Armada is defeated by the British in the English Channel.
1605	Miguel de Cervantes's *Don Quixote* is published. Passages objectionable to the Church are expunged at the time, and it will continue to be subjected to censorship up to the twenty-first century.
1609	King Philip III expels 250,000 Christianized Moors from Spain.
1621	Philip IV becomes king. In his reign, the arts and learning flourish, making this the Golden Age of Spain.
1810–13	A national assembly in Cádiz replaces the absolute power of the monarchy in Spain with a Parliament. It ends the Inquisition and limits the power of the clergy.
1814	King Ferdinand VII, who had fled Spain during the Napoleonic Wars, returns to Spain and negates the Cádiz constitution, restoring the absolute power of the king.
	The struggle between liberal reformers and Church-supported conservatives continues well into the twentieth century.
1868	In what came to be known as the Glorious Revolution, Queen Isabella, Ferdinand's daughter and a harsh absolute monarch, is deposed by liberal factions.
1869	A democratic constitution is put in place that guarantees freedom of conscience.
1873–74	After the brief reign of King Amadeo, the Spanish Parliament establishes Spain's first republic. The republic is plagued by dissension.
1874	The military ends the republic and places Isabella's son, Alfonso XII, on the throne.
1876	A Church-supported constitution rescinds freedom of conscience and declares Catholicism to be the only state religion.
	Benito Pérez Galdós's *Doña Perfecta* is published.
1890s	Republican reformist activities increase.
	Vicente Blasco Ibáñez becomes a leading activist for reforms of government and Church and is forced into exile.
1898	Vicente Blasco Ibáñez's *The Cabin* is published. The book angers both clerical and governmental authorities, and the author spends most of his time in exile in France.
1904	Spain occupies Morocco.
1906	France awards Blasco Ibáñez the Legion of Honor.
1909	Political leader Antonio Maura starts a violent rebellion when he tries to draft young men to march against Morocco.
1914–18	Spain remains neutral during World War I.
	Although Spain flourishes economically, there are strikes, agitation from several quarters for home rule, and agitation for greater republican rule by Spain's Parliament.
1919	Morocco revolts against Spanish occupation.
1921	The Moroccans defeat the Spanish army at Anual.
1923	Parliamentary government is overthrown in a military coup led by General Miguel Primo de Rivera, who is named by the king to head the government.

Writer Ramón J. Sender is drafted to serve in Morocco.

1926   Sender, after being decorated for bravery in Morocco, is jailed for political activity.

1930   Sender's novel about Morocco, *Pro Patria*, is published.

1931   As a result of elections that show strong support for a republican form of government, King Alfonso XIII leaves the country.

The Second Republic of Spain is formed and puts in place many reforms. All official government ties to the Church are severed.

1932   The republic begins important land reforms to break up large estates and place land in the hands of peasants.

1933   Elections result in a rightist government that enrages leftists by weakening land reform and modifying the separation of Church and state.

1936   After continual struggles between rightists and leftists, a left-wing coalition, including socialists and communists, form a Popular Front, win the election, and reinstate reforms. Internal upheaval continues, and the military seeks to overthrow the government.

The Spanish Civil War begins between the military, right-wing Nationalists in rural areas, and the left-wing Republican Loyalists in industrial areas. The Nationalists, under the leadership of General Francisco Franco, receive military aid from fascist Germany and Italy. The Republicans are aided by volunteers from throughout the world who form the International Brigades.

1938   Ramón Sender goes into exile from Spain.

1939   Spain's Civil War ends with defeat of the Republicans, Franco as absolute dictator, and reprisals against all Loyalists. Some 37,000 Loyalists are executed. The power of the Roman Catholic Church is restored as the official state religion, and Franco's Spanish Fascist Party becomes the official state party.

The novels of Galdós, Blasco Ibáñez, and Sender are banned.

1950   Although Franco's regime had been condemned and ostracized by Allied countries immediately after the war, when the Cold War gets under way, Franco's Spain is embraced by many of its former antagonists as a useful ally against communism.

1953   José María Gironella's novel about the Spanish Civil War, *The Cypresses Believe in God*, is published.

1975   Franco's death ends his forty-year dictatorship.

120. *Don Quixote* (*El ingenioso hidalgo Don Quijote de la Mancha*), by Miguel de Cervantes (Spain, 1605, 1615). Cervantes wrote his masterpiece *Don Quixote*, called the beginning of the modern novel, near the end of his life, during what is known as the Golden Age of Spain, the "Century of Gold" (1560–1660), characterized by Spain's great armies, its "invincible" fleet, the Armada, its powerful court, and intolerant religious establishment. The nonsensical and discriminatory division between ruling "Old Christians" and lowly "New Christians," the last composed of forced converts among Jews and Muslims, formed the basis of an unjust society.

Cervantes, who was poor most of his life, was perhaps the greatest of its geniuses. Out of necessity, he became a soldier and actively participated, and was wounded, in the Battle of Lepanto, between Western world forces and the Ottoman Empire, in one of the crucial battles of history. Later, having been captured by Moors on his return to Spain, he was a slave for five years, during which he vainly attempted to escape on four occasions, before being ransomed. When he wrote *Don Quixote*, he brought with him a lifetime of wisdom, acquired the hard way, and an infectious sense of humor.

Cervantes began *Don Quixote* as a satire on still-popular novels of chivalry, positing a lugubrious figure whose mind had been addled by too much ingestion of such wild impossible tales. His inclusion of Sancho Panza, however, and the vision of a matter-of-fact practical peasant as a companion for the Don, thus necessitating always a contrapuntal view of reality and of dreams, made it much more than a satire of popular novels. The episodic, rambling novel is filled with misadventures and numerous digressions, and neither the Don nor Sancho in the end can escape the buffets of a hard world. The story became, in effect, a vehicle not only for the wisdom and the varied experiences accumulated by the author in a long and varied life but a trenchant satire of Spanish society.

It seems clear that, in the book, Cervantes came at last to think of his addled Knight ("The Knight of the Woeful Aspect") as a saint as well as a madman. Don Quixote is courteous and kind throughout, and he attempts always to make right a world of wrongs. His last words for the world (his epitaph) are indeed memorable: "If I did not accomplish great things, I died in their pursuit."

From the first, Cervantes met with the usual stern ecclesiastical censorship that expunged scenes from the novel that appeared to ridicule the established Church and state. Despite the fact that the book has been plagued by censors ever since, it is easily the second bestselling book in the world.

The novel has been seen and interpreted differently in each age, depending on the varied values of the time. In the seventeenth century, the novel was seen as a wild burlesque. In the eighteenth century, it was read as a satire on those who defied common sense or reason. In the nineteenth century, it was seen as a portrait of a misunderstood idealist in a hostile world. The twentieth century incorporated all of the above, generally with a sense of admiration rather than ridicule—a trend that culminated in the Broadway musical *Man of La Mancha*, with the outstanding song "The Impossible Dream" representing the heart and the soul of the

Don. Don Quixote has been interpreted as Catholic, as Protestant, as neither, and as a Freethinker. The complexity of the novel has made divergent, somewhere contradictory, interpretations possible, even inevitable.

Don Quixote is a work that all peoples have responded to because it encompasses basic elements of human nature as well as a varied picture of Spanish life at the time and because Cervantes did it first and did it best. Arguably, no novel in Western literature has ever exerted a greater influence.

Readers at the time and in subsequent generations have never afterward been able to take seriously the romantic excesses of medieval sagas and tales of war. At the same time, the awkward, mentally addled gentleman of old Spain, who dons his absurd armor and mounts his ridiculous nag, seeing only the best of whatever triviality he looks upon, has struck readers as himself a noble figure of dreams, who lifts his readers up along with him, into something finer than the mundane, everyday world. The novel in fact becomes a paradigm of the human situation, the lowest animalism and the highest aspiration.

The novel inevitably raised certain questions for its readers as to the relationship of illusion to reality, the ability to turn illusion into reality or to transcend reality.

The novel's influence is also seen in its contribution to the culture of a myth or type in Don Quixote and its addition to the language of the figure of "tilting at windmills."

Additional Readings: Richard L. Predmore, *The World of Don Quixote* (Cambridge, MA: Harvard University Press, 1967); P.E. Russell, *Cervantes* (Oxford: Oxford University Press, 1985).

121. *Doña Perfecta*, by Benito Pérez Galdós (Spain, 1876).

Pérez Galdós is regarded as the most important of Spain's novelists after Cervantes, and *Doña Perfecta*, his polemical work criticizing sanctimonious and narrow-minded religious attitudes, elicited both positive and negative responses from his nineteenth-century audience.

As Galdós reached maturity the political landscape of his native Spain was changing rapidly. The Spain of powerful grandees and absolute monarchs had begun to decline as liberal forces came to the fore. A revolution of 1868 provided for freedom of conscience; and from 1873 to 1875, Spain was a republic. When a constitutional monarchy was established, the monarch, Amadeo de Saboya, abdicated, saying that "Spaniards are ungovernable." Finally, the Bourbons were restored under the leadership of Alfonso XII. Liberals shared power with Conservatives temporarily, but Conservatives inserted a clause in the new constitution rescinding the freedom of conscience that had been guaranteed in 1868. In 1876, the year the new constitution was promulgated, Galdós produced *Doña Perfecta*, the first of three novels attacking the intolerance now embodied in the constitution.

The hero is Pepe Rey, an idealistic young man with modern, progressive ideas who, with his father's encouragement, goes to Orbajosa, a remote and backward cathedral town, to meet and possibly to marry his cousin Rosario. Pepe learns to love Rosario, at the same time discovering that her narrowly pious mother, his aunt Doña Perfecta, secretly opposes the union, all the while concealing her real feelings behind a hypocritical facade. The mother's ally in this deception is Don Inocencio, the local priest, who shares her inclination to value form and power over substance. Pepe, who is very outspoken and lacking in tact, argues with the priest and criticizes church art and music. Ultimately he finds himself faced with overwhelming problems: lawsuits, loss of government commissions to survey the area for mining and irrigation projects, and most important, Doña Perfecta's determination to prevent his marriage to Rosario. When Pepe tries to elope with Rosario, Doña Perfecta has him killed by one of her men. As a result, Rosario, having become insane, is confined to an asylum, and Doña Perfecta is free to devote her life to religion without further interference.

The novel had an immediate, momentous effect on its Spanish readers. They saw the novel's timely purpose for what it was: a plea for tolerance and a bitingly satiric criticism of the new Church-sponsored constitution, which was put into effect while the novel was appearing in installments. In *Doña Perfecta*, the government's declaration that Catholicism was to be the state religion and the basis of the educational system had been made to appear ridiculous.

His readers were reminded of the iron link between the Church and the conservatives in government that seemed intent on resisting any reforms that would benefit the middle and lower classes. Typical of Pérez Galdós's works, this novel suggested to them that the bourgeoisie, a class that did not exist before 1850, was the hope for the future and that the aristocracy was backward and malicious.

As a result of this novel, Pérez Galdós was regarded as something of a devil by conservative readers, including the Church hierarchy. They saw Galdós as attacking the very foundation of religion and the centuries-old hold that the Church had exercised over European countries. He had scathingly satirized them by naming a maliciously flawed religious woman Doña "Perfecta" and an evil and manipulative parish priest Don "Inocencia." Because of Galdós's general high standing in Spain, it also put them on the defensive.

Yet the book rang true for many other Spanish readers. It openly revealed that narrow religious attitudes were contributing to the backwardness of the government and to official repression. The novel verified what many had begun to suspect, that orthodox religion as it was then practiced was destructive, that it was a narrow form of religion above all else that formed or "deformed" Spanish society, that the Church limited the perception and the life of the great mass of Spaniards, and that the doctrines and practices of institutional religion betrayed Christianity's original message of love and hope. Religious people, the novel showed, could often silence the voices of their consciences with religious ceremony. *Doña Perfecta*, through its condemnation of religious intolerance and fanaticism, contributed to a revolutionary movement in Spain that shaped history.

When Galdós died on January 4, 1920, some 30,000 people paid homage to him at

City Hall, and many thousands of ordinary, common people lined up along the route to the cemetery, openly paying their tribute to the man who had championed their rights. Perhaps it was a tribute, too, that Carlist-oriented newspapers abused him while Liberal papers heaped praise upon him. As one of Spain's greatest and most popular novelists, his influence on the attitudes of Spanish people was significant.

It was also enduring, for the Constitution of 1978, established after the Franco regime ended, is also a tribute to Pérez Galdós in that it brought about, at last, a realization of many of the causes for which he and others had worked. It established a democratic, constitutional monarchy, eliminated official state endorsement of the Church, and instituted a more tolerant attitude.

Additional Readings: Peter Bly, *Galdós's Novel of the Historical Imagination: A Study of the Contemporary Novels* (Liverpool: Cairns, 1983); Stephen Gilman, *Galdós and the Art of the European Novel* (Princeton, NJ: Princeton University Press, 1981); Geoffrey Ribbans, *History and Fiction in Galdós's Narratives* (Oxford: Oxford University Press, 1993).

122. *The Cabin* (*La barraca*), by Vincente Blasco Ibáñez (Spain, 1898). The socioeconomic system of the closing years of the nineteenth century in Spain included the worst characteristics of a lingering medievalism and of the burgeoning Industrial Revolution. The vast majority of Spain's working poor were virtual slaves, laboring in the fields like serfs or else in the growing, unregulated industries dominated by mining, smelting, and shipbuilding. The wealthy Church, hostile to both modern science and social reform, found it easier to exploit the large labor force it required by keeping it in total ignorance. Several changing conditions only worsened the lives of rural peasants: a growing population of both native and emigrant laborers, who swamped the labor market and brought down the price of wages; the greed of a small but powerful monied middle class, which achieved status by buying Church land; and the political corruption of the

monarchy, which had been restored in 1874 and kept its power through the manipulation of elections.

By the 1870s, however, reform thinkers and political activists were attempting to break the hold of the Church and to inspire workers and peasants who rented land to organize against the aristocracy and wealthy bourgeoisie. Throughout the 1890s and early 1900s, Ibáñez was at the forefront as an elected representative, a publisher of reform journals, an orator, and a novelist. In reprisal, the government arrested him, jailed him, harassed him constantly, and forced him into exile.

The Cabin, generally considered his best-known and finest work, is set in the agriculturally rich area of Blasco's homeland in Valencia during the closing decade of the nineteenth century. Its subject is the effect of agrarian policies and worker resistance on the lives of individuals in the community. The workers lose, and the owners win with the help of a corrupt court.

The impact of *The Cabin*, reinforced by the personality of its author, was both immediate and long-standing, not only in Spain but throughout the world. In Blasco's own country of Spain, where feelings ran high both for and against him, the book had sales of 112,000 copies by 1928 and over 1 million copies to date. The book's immense popularity gave birth to a new word—*blasquismo*—meaning an impassioned dedication to the land reforms it urged. Although the Church and ruling class hated the book and literary critics railed against it as propagandistic and defeatist, so wild was the enthusiasm of the common people for the novel that *blasquismo* was said to be at the center of public life in Valencia for over fifty years, culminating in an eight-day festival in the author's honor in 1921. The book's influence was even more profound outside of Spain, in the United States, in South America, and in Europe, especially France where Blasco was awarded the Legion of Honor in 1906.

In general, *The Cabin* gave clarity to the complex problem of farmworkers, land reform, and social activism throughout the world, a situation that was just as acute in the so-called progressive United States as it was in Latin countries, even though it was not until the 1930s that an American author, John Steinbeck, drew similar attention to the problems in his two novels *In Dubious Battle* and *The Grapes of Wrath*. Many readers for the first time discovered the humanity of the Spanish peasant in the human interaction within a caste system. Readers also discovered the dangerous consequences for all classes in the unjust and inequitable land system. The politically naive, in countries where open discussion of progressive ideas was not tolerated, were introduced by *The Cabin* to several competing social theories, primarily Marxism and anarchism, which had arisen to correct the problems the novel raises.

Blasco's *The Cabin* is credited with having led to specific reforms during the Second Spanish Republic, which came to power in 1931, three years after his death. The new constitution borrowed from the novel's progressive ideas in addressing problems the novel had identified, in effect eliminating the feudal system and putting in its place an equitable system of landownership, largely based on socialist philosophy. For example, it broke up large estates and distributed parcels to peasant farmers. It articulated needs and encouraged modern reform consciousness among the masses. Article One of the new constitution sounded as if it could have come from the mouth of one of the reformers in *The Cabin*: "Spain is a democratic Republic of Workers of all classes, organized under the rule of Liberty and Justice." Under Section Three the Second Republic attempted to lessen the power and budget of the Church and clergy.

Blasco's novel is also credited with preparing for the Spanish Civil War that was waged to depose the fascist Francisco Franco—a war that was fought to preserve the ideals and reforms inspired by *The Cabin*. With the loss of the Loyalist cause and Franco's long reign, it is scarcely surprising that Blasco's novel was no longer available in Spain, although it continued to be read to inspire needed reforms in Latin America and Europe. Because

of his anticlerical, antimonarchical stance, the Spanish government and pro-establishment intellectuals did all that they could to silence Blasco. It is a negative testimony to his power that even today in Spain his work is regarded as so threatening that standard histories of Spanish literature rarely mention him or his novel and that it is hard to find versions of *The Cabin* that have not been expurgated or censored. No respectable study of his work has yet appeared in Spain. Nevertheless, sales of the novel are testimonies to the vast, continuing popularity of the novel throughout the world and among the general populace in Spain.

Additional Readings: Christopher L. Anderson, *Primitives, Patriarchy and the Picaresque in Blasco Ibáñez* (Potomac, MD: Scripta Humanistica, 1995); Jeremy Medina, *From Sermon to Art: The Thesis Novels of Vincente Blasco Ibáñez* (Valencia: Albatross Ediciones, 1998).

123. *Pro Patria* (*Iman* **in Spain;** *Earmarked for Hell* **in England), by Ramón J. Sender (Spain, 1930).** Ramón J. Sender, one of the most widely read and prolific writers produced by Spain, lived as an independent thinker and rebel through the most turbulent times in Spanish history. The events of 1921 through 1923 are the setting for his first and most influential novel *Pro Patria*. Spain had remained neutral during World War I (1914–18), but bloody battles between Spain's working classes and its government were being waged on its own streets at home. Nor did Spain's neutrality during the war preclude the existence of an enormous Spanish military force. Much of the trouble in Spain stemmed from conflicting interests over Spain's presence in Morocco, where it had maintained a substantial military presence since 1904. Spain's leaders, hungry for power and economic gain, were eager to increase the military there, even in the face of formidable opposition on the part of native Morocco's striving for independence and Spain's own working people who were being conscripted to serve in the military there in a cause in which they had no interest. In 1921 one of many tribal rebellions was waged against Spanish colonial policies and occupying forces in Morocco during which a Spanish fort was decimated and 12,000 Spanish troops died. In Spain, two years later, a military coup wrenched power from the parliamentary government, and General Miguel Primo de Rivera placed Spain under a military directorate. In that same year, Ramón Sender was conscripted as a private to serve in the military in Morocco. He fought in some of the most brutal battles imaginable as Spain sought to regain reputation and territory lost two years earlier and was decorated for bravery in action upon his return to Spain fourteen months later. Four years later he was imprisoned for three months by the Spanish government; thirteen years later he was fighting in the Spanish Civil War against General Francisco Franco who had accumulated power as the commander of Spain's forces in Morocco; and sixteen years later he had to flee the country as an exile.

Pro Patria, a naturalistic treatment of Spain's wars in Morocco in the early 1920s, was based on Sender's experiences as a soldier in Africa. It is the story of Viance, a private in the occupying Spanish army in Morocco who, even in peaceful times, endures horrible privations, then sees the tribal Moors kill every Spanish soldier in the town of Anual and every Spanish fort in the desert and track down and kill every soldier who escapes. Viance, who is captured and escapes from the Moors, is the sole survivor. Terrorized and half dead and insane from hunger, thirst, and injuries, he stumbles into a Spanish fort that has been spared, where he is treated worse by his own leaders than he was by the Moorish captors. The final scenes show Viance, back in Spain at last, on the point of suicide with his home gone, unable to get a job, and cursed and mistreated by townspeople.

The novel was considered an immediate and brilliant success after its publication in 1930. An inexpensive edition published in Spain in 1933 sold 30,000 copies. Despite this record of success in Spain, the novel was even more popular in other countries. It was translated into eleven languages in just a few

years, in Germany selling 30,000 copies in less than a year. The power of the novel and the perceived threat it posed to Franco's government is attested to by the fact that *Pro Patria*, along with Sender's other works, was banned in Spain for over twenty-five years. In 1968, almost thirty years after Sender's banishment, he was invited back to his native land for the first time. However, it was a moment of Basque unrest, and when the government learned that a delegation of workers intended to greet him at the airport, it canceled his return.

Pro Patria had a profound influence—both negative and positive—on its readers worldwide on several fronts. At the basic level, it was one of the first European novels to have a lower-class, peasant hero. For much of the novel, the action and the musing and sensitive philosophizing over that action are seen through his eyes. Viance does not just follow orders without thinking; he considers the metaphysical meaning of the horrors he has observed and the losses he incurs. For its readers, most of whom were products of devout Catholicism in Europe and Protestantism in the United States, Sender had a shocking revelation: In the horror that Viance experiences, it is difficult for even this simple peasant to avoid the observation that the forces that rule the universe are either cruel or uninterested in humankind's suffering.

On a social level, the novel introduced its readers to the reality that common people are used as cannon fodder in wars and that wars are often waged for no other reason but to make their leaders rich. Sender went one step further than most antiwar novelists in showing that behind wars lie the greed and sadism of a government and a ruling class who feel no responsibility for the soldiers they use so carelessly and basely. For his readers in the 1930s, Sender's book was a realistic eye-opener to the horrors of military service. Even before the attack by the Moors, the Spanish soldiers get so thirsty they are reduced to drinking their own urine. They are half killed with work, live in utter filth, and are subjected to gross injustice on the part of their officers. The treatment of Viance by his superiors after his horrendous ordeal following the destruction of Anual is symbolic of the treatment of all peasants by the ruling class. He is not allowed medical treatment, he is not given food or drink, and he is forced to sleep in the street.

Additional Readings: Ronald Schwartz, *Spain's New Novelists, 1950–1974* (Metuchen, NJ: Scarecrow Press, 1976); Anthony M. Trippett, *Adusting to Reality* (London: Tamesis Books, 1986).

124. *The Cypresses Believe in God* (*Los Cipreses creen en Dios*), **by José María Gironella (Spain, 1953).** In 1953, Gironella produced an epic-sized novel about the Spanish Civil War titled *The Cypresses Believe in God*. The enormous success of the novel is attributed to the fact that it provided Spanish people with their first comprehensive, historically detailed picture of the chaos that led up to the war.

The background of the war begins in the late nineteenth century. In ultraconservative, traditionalist Spain, dominated still by aristocratic grandees and the Roman Catholic Church, the loss of the Spanish-American War in 1898, while damaging prestige abroad and morale at home, intensified a murderous factionalism that produced a century of chaos.

Neutral Spain had profited from expanded sales to the Allies in World War I but then, unable to compete in the postwar world, had faced serious depression and, in addition, had bungled and lost a senseless war in Morocco. Following this, General Primo de Rivera, with the tacit approval of King Alphonso XIII, formed a dictatorship in 1923, making some gains but generating intense hostility. Then in 1929 an even more severe international economic depression came, again creating massive unemployment, low wages, and grinding poverty. De Rivera resigned in 1930, and republican parties won the subsequent election in 1931. With the resignation of Alphonso, a new government was formed—the Second Republic. Momentary successes only exacerbated mutual fears, and

finally, in July 1936, after a series of political murders, civil war broke out. This war killed at least 600,000 people, totally devastated a country just on the eve of World War II, and produced a harsh dictatorship that endured for almost forty years, keeping Spain backward and retarded until Franco's death in 1975. Both censorship and life in Franco's Spain were harsh. Art and ideas that even seemed to criticize the government or the government's past were thoroughly suppressed.

On both the political Right and Left in the conflict—ultimately designated Nationalist and Loyalists—numerous mutually hostile parties who constantly squabbled among themselves, temporarily cooperated from necessity to form opposing armies that fought each other for three years.

It was this situation that Gironella attempted to portray as a novelist, in a story mixing fiction, history, and echoes of his own personal experience. That experience included his growing up in Gerona, an area sympathetic to Franco's Nationalists, and his service in the Ski Patrol in the Nationalists army. After the war, he produced two undistinguished novels and suffered a nervous breakdown. In 1953, he wrote his masterpiece.

The Cypresses Believe in God took place between April 1931 and July 30, 1936, the period that saw the growth and death of the Second Republic and the beginning of actual fighting in the civil war. The focus is on the Alvear family, who live in an apartment overlooking the Ter River in Gerona: Matias, the father, a local clerk; Carmen, the mother, a devout Catholic; Cesar, a physically weak intellectual who becomes a priest; Pilar, a quiet, protected girl; and Ignacio, the main character, seventeen years old at the beginning and intending to become a priest.

Ignacio is not a politically aligned ideologue. He is introduced instead as an idealistic, well-meaning boy who wants to do good and to help the poor and who, like the country as a whole, was ignorant of the horrors to come. He is a young student on the verge of awareness and of life, and he learns the complexities of the time gradually.

Gironella's novel is important in two respects: It broke the barrier of censorship in Spain, and it explained to the Spanish people a very complex and chaotic period in their recent experience. The novel, about the civil war, was published at a time when the civil war was one of many forbidden subjects in Spain. However, several things worked to Gironella's advantage in avoiding being censored. Franco was trying to please the Americans and the rest of Europe in order to enter the European Union and to apply to the United States for aid, in exchange for allowing Americans to locate bases in Spain. And Franco had every reason to suspect that Americans were unhappy with his oppressive censorship. It certainly did not damage Gironella's case that he had fought on the side of Franco in the civil war. For all these reasons, Gironella managed to break the barrier of censorship, writing of the causes and effects of the war on ordinary people. He thus came to the fore in the battle for freedom of expression, inspiring other novelists to take up the theme of the war, as well as other previously forbidden subjects. The great popularity of his novel paved the way.

The chaos and pain of the period seemed to many who lived through it impossible to make sense of. Many readers found that Gironella made some sense of the many conflicting historical details and the conflicting ideological tensions of the time in showing the war as it hits Ignacio's native Gerona—the strikes, the failure of the Second Republic, and the general sense of anarchy.

In its use of a devout family, the selfless service to humanity of the hero who wanted to be a priest, and the martyrdom of his brother who is studying to be a priest, the novel resulted in a return of many Spanish people to the Roman Catholic Church and a reaffirmation of Catholic values.

The novel, while one of the bestselling books in Spanish history, was not without enormous controversy. Many in 1953 believed the novel proved Gironella a traitor to Franco's cause. Others criticized his interpretation of events, especially in the scene in which Cesar, Ignacio's brother, is slaughtered by a Revolutionary firing squad.

Additional Readings: Ronald Schwartz, *José María Gironella* (New York: Twayne, 1972); Ronald Schwartz, *Spain's New Wave Novelists, 1950–1974* (Metuchen, NJ: Scarecrow Press, 1976).

NORTH AMERICA

Canada

Sinclair Ross, *As for Me and My House*, 1941
Gabrielle Roy, *The Tin Flute*, 1945
Margaret Atwood, *The Handmaid's Tale*, 1985

TIMELINE

1914–18   During World War I, 60,000 Canadians lose their lives.

1919   General strikes sweep Canada.

1920s   Canada experiences economic difficulties in absorbing returning soldiers and converting war industries to peacetime industry.

1929   The Great Depression hits Canada.

1930   A killing drought worsens as the 1930s continue.

   Debts and displacement plague farmers.

1931   The Statute of Westminster makes Canada a sovereign state.

1933   One third of Canada's workers are unemployed; factories close or drastically cut production; wages are cut; and the cost of living falls.

   A 65 percent fall in wheat prices is a killing blow to Canadian agriculture.

The socialist Co-operative Commonwealth Federation, led by J.S. Woodsworth, a Methodist minister, gains influence with its proposal for nationalizing industry and health care.

1935   As "Bennett buggies" crowd the roads—cars pulled by horses named for the conservative prime minister—and the displaced crowd into work camps, citizens make an "On to Ottawa Trek" to confront the government. This results in arrests and riots.

   Conservatives are soundly defeated in the elections.

1941   Ross Sinclair's *As for Me and My House* is published.

1945   Gabriella Roy's *The Tin Flute* is published.

1953   Equal Pay measure passes in the United Nations.

1960   Gender discrimination on the job is addressed by the United Nations.

Women flood the workforce in Canada.

1961 Televangelist Pat Robertson founds the Christian Broadcasting Network, which airs his *The 700 Club* and will grow into one of the largest national networks in the United States.

1966 The National Organization for Women is established in the United States.

1971 The National Action Committee on the Status of Women is formed in Canada to address feminist issues including equal pay for equal work and abortion.

Jerry Falwell, a fundamentalist television evangelist, expands his television empire and establishes a college.

1973 Jimmy Lee Swaggart, a Louisiana evangelist, expands his media empire to television, which will shortly include a recording studio and a production organization. He also founds a Bible college and a printing and mailing industry.

1977 Robertson founds Regent University and a cable television station.

1979 Falwell founds a political organization called the Moral Majority. His first activity on the national scene is to ensure the election of Ronald Reagan in 1981 and 1989.

Falwell lends his political clout to the support of Ferdinand Marcos of the Philippines.

1980s Television evangelists Jim and Tammy Faye Bakker rise to prominence with their own television network and an extravagant amusement park.

1985 Margaret Atwood's *The Handmaid's Tale* is published.

1987 The Bakkers are found to be involved in financial and sexual scandals, and Jim Bakker is sent to prison.

1989 Robertson founds a conservative political action group known as the Christian Coalition. Its purpose is to influence policy and elections.

1990 A film of *The Handmaid's Tale* is the occasion for demonstrations by conservative religious groups.

1991 Swaggart's ministry experiences a setback when his regular solicitation of prostitutes is revealed.

125. *As for Me and My House*, by Sinclair Ross (Canada, 1941). *As for Me and My House* is the story of an unhappy marriage, set in the Canadian prairie town of Horizon in the period between the wars, a time of economic hardship and gloom in isolated, struggling communities.

The novel was originally published in 1941, following the Great Depression, when a German victory seemed imminent in World War II. Britain, at the time, stood tenuously alone following the fall of France and the German blitz of London.

The story is narrated in the form of a diary, by a person we know only as Mrs. Bentley. The diarist is the wife of the Rev. Philip Bentley, minister of a Protestant church in a small western town. The time is unspecified, but the circumstances suggest the depression years of the 1930s. The reader learns that Philip Bentley, illegitimate and poor, had, as a youth, been unable on his own to afford the expense of a college education, but when a visiting friend of his father's told him that the church would pay for his education if he agreed to become a minister, he accepted. There, in a theology college at the university, located "in the Middle West" of Canada, he meets and marries his wife. When they met, she was a music student who was desperately hoping to save enough to spend a year in "the East," possibly even in Europe. Instead, she relinquishes her ambitions to marry Bentley.

She is never given a name other than "Mrs. Bentley," even though we see the story entirely through her eyes. This contributes to her anonymity, which helps provide the underlying tension and the accumulating unhappiness and frustration that pervade the novel. Once a budding musician, and obviously a skilled writer, nurtured on dreams of European culture, she now exists only as the nameless minister's wife, in the small prairie town where life is a matter of horses and crops and ministerial drudgery.

Her husband Philip is himself an artist—a painter—yet Mrs. Bentley feels that his art and his personal inclinations are really worldly and mundane, that he lacks a deeply religious or spiritual dimension. In one of his sessions, according to Mrs. Bentley's account, he has an affair with a young woman, Judith West. Judith gives birth to a baby and dies in childbirth. The anger and hurt Mrs. Bentley feels because of this intensifies her sense of inadequacy.

There is a pervasive sense of anonymity about her entire existence: Philip preaches in an unnamed church ("Protestant," or "the Church"); they attend an unnamed university, located in an unnamed city; and during the sermons people listen mostly to the message of the wind, constantly blowing outside and covering pews and hymnals with dust.

And at the end the couple hope to escape the poverty and isolation of the village and return to the unnamed city where they were once students.

The book was completed well after the years of the Great Depression, when neither publishers nor critics nor the reading public seemed particularly interested in a gloomy novel of the Canadian west. While original reviewers in Canada felt that the novel was well written, and some hailed the author as a young writer of great promise, Americans dealt mostly with plot summaries and characters, and nobody urged readers to buy it. As a consequence, the book was largely ignored at the time of publication. Only much later, after a silence of some thirty years, did the novel come back to life, to become recognized as a major contribution to Canadian literature. In one of the most remarkable twists of fortune in modern literature, the novel went on to become one of the genuine classics of modern Canadian literature. As David Stouck has pointed out, circumstances changed, dramatically, and the novel came to represent something essential not only about Canadian literature but also about Canadian

culture. By the end of the twentieth century, it had become a cornerstone of Canadian studies in colleges and universities, was the subject of symposiums and conferences, and, in general, had pervaded Canadian culture, a chronicle of a key time and place in Canadian history.

It has been hailed for its portrayals of the fate of artists in the modern world, its dichotomy of East versus West in North America, the problems of isolation, the monotony of prairie life, and the constant factors of wind and snow.

Additional Readings: John Moss, ed., *From the Heart of the Heartland: The Fiction of Sinclair Ross* (Ottawa: University of Ottawa Press, 1992); David Stouck, *Sinclair Ross's* As for Me and My House: *Five Decades of Criticism* (Toronto: University of Toronto Press, 1991).

126. *The Tin Flute* (*Bonheur d'occasion*), **by Gabrielle Roy (Canada, 1945).** The setting of Gabrielle Roy's novel of Quebec, Canada, takes place in a poor, working-class urban neighborhood at the end of the economic depression of the 1930s, as World War II is beginning. It is a time when both rural and urban populations in Canada, as elsewhere, had been ravaged by unemployment and its consequences—hunger and displacement. The institution of the family was placed under a particular strain as husbands deserted their families to escape the burdensome responsibilities they were unable to carry, and teenage children were forced out of the home to alleviate pressure on their families. During this time, opportunities for women declined. Money was so limited that when it was available for a child's education or advancement, it went to the males in the family rather than the females. Other laws and practices limited jobs, when they were available, to a sole male breadwinner. However, as World War II loomed, the economy improved. War was, ironically, the salvation of many workers. Men without jobs flocked into the army; the war machine, demanding new and constant goods, produced jobs and improved the economy; and the decline in male workers, now in the armed forces, gave women opportunities in jobs that had been closed to them before. One need only note the phenomenon of "Rosie the Riveter." But these changes meant that the family only disintegrated further.

The Tin Flute is about the Lacasse family—a mother, father, and their large family. Like their neighbors, they have been ravaged by the depression, but now war brings them a small ray of hope. The father finds his opportunity for a job in the army that will eventually provide him with a pension in his advancing age. His son and his daughter's husband-to-be also consider enlistment in the army to be their sole opportunity for economic survival. Another son and the daughter's lover are also rescued by the war: They find jobs in the munitions industry.

The novel, which is classified as social realism, is critical of two aspects of French Canadian society: the military-industrial capitalists whose misuse of powerless workers makes their service to the God of War preferable to their peacetime humiliations, and the religious and social traditions of Quebec that teach women that their fulfillment must only be found in marriage. The novel undermines traditional marriage by showing that the mother of the family has long ago lost sight of her aspirations in order to be the mainstay of her large family. One of her daughters chooses the religious life over marriage, and the other tries unsuccessfully to go her independent way, eventually finding that this society will not allow her to survive unless she accepts the constraints and self-sacrifice demanded by marriage.

The Tin Flute became an instant, international success, has been translated into nine languages, and brought Roy numerous honors. As a result of the publication of this book alone, she was awarded the Richelieu Medal, the Prix Femina, the Governor General's Award, and the Royal Academy's Lorne Pierce Medal. The Literary Guild of America chose it as a Book of the Month, and Universal Pictures bought the film rights.

The novel's impact came from its revolutionary turn away from the idyllic rural scene in Canada. It drew attention for the first time to the harsh realities of urban life. Its social realism and social protest, new to French Canadian literature, was a type that did not come into its own in Quebec until some twenty years after *The Tin Flute* was published. The theme of war as salvation was one that many ordinary people experienced at the time, but few writers had explored.

The novel also pioneered looking at traditional Canadian society through a feminist perspective, drawing attention to gender inequities, the dynamics between mother and daughter, and the limitations under which women struggle.

Additional Readings: Paul Gilbert Lewis, *Traditionalism, Nationalism and Feminism: Women Writers of Quebec* (Westport, CT: Greenwood Press, 1985); Patricia Smart, *Writing in the Father's House: The Emergence of the Feminine in the Quebec Literary Tradition* (Toronto: University of Toronto Press, 1991).

127. *The Handmaid's Tale*, by Margaret Atwood (Canada, 1985). *The Handmaid's Tale*, a bestseller that received the Arthur C. Clarke Award for Science Fiction and that was short-listed for a Booker Prize and adapted for film in 1990 by playwright Harold Pinter, was written in the 1980s during a time of rampant televangelism. Fundamentalist ministers flocked to the airways to stage extravagant religious services, sometimes involving so-called faith healing, and to openly and passionately solicit their far-flung audiences for money. The large majority of these performers were successful enough to build enormous financial organizations that included media, entertainment, and educational enterprises, designed to cultivate followers and collect even more funds. Even the more subtle televangelists had family mansions, churches the size of European cathedrals attached to spacious campuses or on expensive properties in the middle of cities, and private airplanes. Some, like the Reverend Jerry Falwell and the Reverend Oral Roberts, were able to establish thriving institutions of higher learning in comprehensive communities, largely under their control.

Such was the draw of Oral Roberts that he could amass millions of dollars by threatening to "go to heaven" if his listeners didn't send him sufficient money by a designated date.

The reign of televangelism diminished with a plethora of scandals, most of which started as sex scandals and later revealed financial malfeasance and ties to organized crime. The most notorious was that of Jim Bakker, whose arrest for fraud brought down a multimillion-dollar complex that included a theme park to rival Disney World.

Especially pertinent to *The Handmaid's Tale* is the persistent mixing of religious sectarianism in politics and public policy in, for example, the presidential aspirations of the Reverend Pat Robertson, chief executive officer of an international corporate empire, and the persistent incursion of "the moral majority" or Religious Right in legal and political affairs.

Atwood's novel, appearing in the brief heyday of televangelism, supposes a society taken over by militaristic televangelists who have determined that they alone know how to save the world. They now run the United States, renaming it Gilead, according to their religious dictates. Women in this society have been placed in a variety of categories to serve different functions needed by the men. Wives, who are in charge of the house and the family's social life, are distinct from the handmaidens whose function is to bear children. The narrator and main character, named Offred, is an official "handmaiden" whose function in this futuristic society is to bear children to revitalize the new nation once poisoned by pollution. She looks back to a past in which she was an independent woman with a job and a family. But in the new, highly stratified theocracy, she has been forced to service some of the ruling "Commanders." As she makes her way around a city, she notes the wall where dissidents are continually being executed and thinks of the secret service that knows and reports all to the bullying police force. As a handmaiden, she is denied all contact with friends and fam-ily and forbidden all entertainment, including reading.

Her life changes when she is transferred to a different commander. He does not require sex of her, treats her as a companion instead, and allows her to read in his study. The problem is his infertility and, thus, her inability to produce his child, a situation that, if discovered, will consign her as a cleaning woman in old radiation dumps. To avert disaster for both of them, her commander arranges for her to sleep with his chauffeur in order to become pregnant. But in the end officials come for her, and she has no way of knowing whether she is being arrested by police or rescued by the resistance.

The Handmaid's Tale was instantly successful and instantly controversial when it first hit bookshelves. It incurred the disapproval of many organizations, including the Roman Catholic Church. So threatening was the novel that demonstrations were launched against the book and the film adapted from it in major cities throughout the world.

Many critics, as well as readers, felt that the novel carried the same cautionary message of the dangers of totalitarianism that George Orwell's *1984* had warned of. Especially alarming was the possible intrusion of sectarianism into the life of a complex and varied society, in a way that was happening among Muslim fundamentalists in Iran at the time of the novel's publication.

Also noted by readers and critics was the "Historical Notes" that closed the novel in which the author compares the situation of blacks and women in Gilead by reporting on a female equivalent of the Underground Railroad, by which women, like pre–Civil War slaves, escaped to Canada.

Readers noted Atwood's warning that both men and women are damaged when women are reduced to sexual slaves or household drudges. Unfortunately, though the "Historical Notes" at the end makes clear that Gilead is dead, its psychological aftereffects linger in the all-male conference where presenters' remarks, demeaning to women, are met with easy and insensitive laughter by the audience.

Additional Readings: Don Gillmor, *Canada: A People's History* (Toronto: McClelland and Stewart, 2000); Coral Ann Howells, *Margaret Atwood* (London: Macmillan, 1996); Judith McCombs, ed., *Critical Essays on Margaret Atwood* (Boston: G.K. Hall, 1988).

Mexico

⁓

Carlos Fuentes, *The Death of Artemio Cruz*, 1962

⁓

TIMELINE

1800s–1900s The Europeans who had conquered Mexico in the sixteenth
century continue to enslave the
poor natives. The natives are decimated by disease, used as enforced labor, and sometimes
intermarry with Europeans. Roman Catholic missionaries, who
have come with the Spanish, continue to accumulate great wealth
and property and enforce religious
compliance.

1804 Spain's actions against the Roman
Catholic Church anger Mexican
residents.

1810–13 Revolutions against social and racial inequality are led by Catholic
priests. They are unsuccessful.

1820 A successful revolution brings
Mexican independence and a limited monarchy.

1823 A military revolt results in the formation of a Mexican republic
under Mexico's first president,
Guadalupe Victoria.

1833 Antonio Lopez de Santa Anna
elected president.

1836 The war between Mexico and
Texas comes to an end with Santa
Anna's defeat by the forces of Sam
Houston at the Battle of San Ja-
cinto. The Mexicans retreat south
of the Rio Grande.

1847 The Mexican War with the United
States over California and New
Mexico ends with Mexico's defeat.

A Caste War of the Yucatan is
waged by Mayan natives against
whites.

1855 Reformers assume control under
the leadership of Native American
Benito Pablo Juarez. They topple
the dictatorship of Santa Anna.
The new constitution creates a republic with representative government.

1861 France invades Mexico and makes
Maximilian king.

1867 The French withdraw, and Maximilian is executed.

1872	Reformer Juarez dies in office after a stormy term following the withdrawal of the French.
1877	After repeated revolutionary attempts at toppling the government, Porfirio Díaz assumes presidency.
1888	Díaz's courtship of foreign investors reaches an extreme when he engineers large amounts of foreign capital.
1888–1911	During these years of Díaz's government, landholders are favored, peasants fall into peonage to landholders, and the concentration of wealth into the hands of the very few increases. The result is unending rebellion against the government.
1910	By 1910, 90 percent of the rural population is without land. The large majority of Mexicans live in extreme poverty, and the richest 20 percent receive 57 percent of the income and control the nation's politics. Few countries in the world have such an unbalanced economy. This situation continues throughout the twentieth century.
1911	Díaz is thrown out and forced into exile.
1910–20	Revolution in Mexico rages with three factions, often antagonistic to each other: those led by Madero, those led by Emiliano Zapata, and those led by Pancho Villa.
1920–40	The revolution forces extensive reforms in reducing the wealth and power of the Church, redistributing land, and instituting social reforms to rescue those in poverty.
1923	Plutarco Elías Calles becomes president.
1926–28	Calles withstands a revolt on the part of the clergy and establishes an official political party, which will be known as the Partido Revolucionario Institutional (PRI).

This party retains power for seventy years.

1934	Lázaro Cárdenas, as a revolutionary reformer president, returns more land to the peasantry.
1936	In a blow to foreign investors, the government takes over foreign oil companies.
1946	When Miguel Alemán becomes president, he opens the door for more foreign investment in Mexico, and a dual economy develops with a great chasm between capitalized industry and agricultural wealth, on one hand, and armies of poorly paid labor, on the other.
1953	Women are first allowed the vote in Mexico, but repression and corruption continue.
1962	Carlos Fuentes's *The Death of Artemio Cruz* is published. Its setting ranges from 1889 to 1960.
2000	Vicente Fox becomes the first president of Mexico to defeat the old PRI party.

128. *The Death of Artemio Cruz* (*La muerte de Artemio Cruz*) by Carlos Fuentes (Mexico, 1962). The most famous of Carlos Fuentes's novels is also the most political. Through the memories of Artemio Cruz, the dying family patriarch, the novel raises a number of key social and political issues in Mexico's history, beginning with the birth of the main character in 1889, a feudal era when a few large landholders of Spanish descent enslaved armies of the poor who were descended from Indians and black slaves. The story moves to a time of peasant revolutions against long-standing tyranny, culminating in the Mexican Revolution of 1914. The story proceeds to cover the years from the revolution until the death of the protagonist in 1960, showing the loveless union of Old World aristocracy to the new ruthless and greedy revolutionary, the last of whom burdened Mexico with a different sort of financial corruption. The country was plundered in the industrial growth that followed, a result of the collusion between foreign imperialists, like the United States and Japan, with ruthless Mexican businessmen. International tycoons continue to exploit the working poor, who constitute over half of Mexico's population.

Artemio Cruz, symbolic of the "new order" in Mexico following the revolution, narrates his life story as he lies on his deathbed, recalling his mother, a lower-class mulatto who was raped by his father, a wealthy landowner. As a teenager, he fights on the side of the Rebels against the Federals in the Mexican Revolution, becoming enraged and grief-stricken when the Federals kill his lover Regina.

After the revolution, he uses information he receives from a fellow prisoner, an aristocratic scion of the wealthy Bernal family, to maneuver his way into the good graces of his young friend's rich and powerful father, taking over the management of the Bernal family's business enterprises and, through underhanded means, securing the old man's daughter, Catalina, for his wife, even though there is no love between them. Through the years, as he becomes more powerful and corrupt in his business dealings, he and Catalina make life miserable for each other. The only person he loves and respects is his son, Lorenzo, who dies in the Spanish Civil War. Artemio dies, cursed by his wife and daughter, who are only interested in their inheritance.

Artemio Cruz was seen as a symbol of the greed and corruption that replaced revolutionary fervor and reform in Mexico. The novel was a shocking criticism of the PNR, the National Revolutionary Party, which controlled Mexico from the late 1920s until the year 2000, its name changing to the PRI (the Partido Revolucíonario Institucíonal) in 1946. Fuentes boldly drew attention to the government's corruption, its favoring of big business and rich foreign investors, and its complete abdication of its responsibility toward the nation's poor. It is credited with encouraging significant social and political change in Mexico, changes that the government brutally resisted. Government retaliation culminated eight years later in a massacre of hundreds of demonstrators, ten days before the 1968 Olympics in Mexico. Opponents of the PRI were systematically murdered in the next two decades. Not until the year 2000, forty years after the publication of Fuentes's novel, was the PRI voted out of office, after a seventy-one-year reign.

Fuentes's novel was one of the first novels critical of the government, written by a respected author of distinction in Mexico. As such, it encouraged a school of writers who, taking Fuentes as a model, saw a revolutionary role for the Latin American writer.

Additional Readings: Robert Brody and Charles Rossman, eds., *Carlos Fuentes: A Critical View* (Austin: University of Texas Press, 1982); Brian R. Hamnett, *A Concise History of Mexico* (Cambridge: Cambridge University Press, 1999); Raymond Leslie Williams, *The Writings of Carlos Fuentes* (Austin: University of Texas Press, 1996).

United States

1700–1899

∾

James Fenimore Cooper, *The Last of the Mohicans*, 1826

Herman Melville, *Typee*, 1846

Nathaniel Hawthorne, *The Scarlet Letter*, 1850

Herman Melville, *White Jacket*, 1850

Herman Melville, *Moby-Dick*, 1851

Harriet Beecher Stowe, *Uncle Tom's Cabin*, 1852

William Wells Brown, *Clotel: or The President's Daughter*, 1853, 1854

Timothy Shay Arthur, *Ten Nights in a Bar-room and What I Saw There*, 1854

Rebecca Harding Davis, *Life in the Iron Mills*, 1861

Horatio Alger, *Ragged Dick*, 1867

Louisa May Alcott, *Little Women*, 1869

Anna Sewell, *Black Beauty*, 1877

Henry James, *Portrait of a Lady*, 1881, 1908

Mark Twain, *Adventures of Huckleberry Finn*, 1884–85

Helen Hunt Jackson, *Ramona*, 1885

Edward Bellamy, *Looking Backward*, 1888

William Dean Howells, *A Hazard of New Fortunes*, 1890

Stephen Crane, *The Red Badge of Courage*, 1895

Kate Chopin, *The Awakening*, 1899

∾

1700–1899: TIMELINE

1607	Englishmen settle Jamestown, Virginia.
1620	Puritans settle at Plymouth Plantation in Massachusetts.
1626	Englishmen settle Salem, Massachusetts.
1628	English Massachusetts Bay Company, led by Puritans, settles New England with a center in Boston.
1636–38	Controversy rages over the preaching of Anne Hutchinson, resulting in her banishment to Rhode Island.
1675–76	War wages as French and Indians, the latter led by a chief named King Philip, fight English settlers.
1690	Indian attacks at Schenectady, New York, and other outposts result in the death of hundreds of settlers.
1692	Trials for witchcraft begin in Salem, Massachusetts.
1754	The French and Indian War begins.
1757	Fort William Henry falls to the French, and English troops and settlers are slaughtered on their way to Fort Edward, despite promises of protection.
1773	In one of the most dramatic acts of rebellion against the British, Bostonians throw imported tea from British ships into the harbor to protest taxes on tea.
1775	The American Revolution against the British begins as William Dawes and Paul Revere ride to Lexington to warn colonists of the arrival of Redcoats.
1776	The Declaration of Independence is signed in Philadelphia.
1794	Sections of Benjamin Franklin's *Autobiography* are published.
1803	The United States makes the Louisiana Purchase.
1804	Meriwether Lewis and William Clark set out to map the western part of North America, opening up the west to settlement.

1808	Congress puts an end to the importation of slaves.
1812	The British attack Washington, D.C. but are repelled.
1820	Washington Irving publishes *Rip Van Winkle.*
	The Missouri Compromise allows the admission of Missouri as a slave state and denotes where slavery can and cannot exist.
1822	A slave rebellion fails in South Carolina.
	Liberia is established as a refuge for freed slaves.
1823	The Monroe Doctrine is enacted to protect the Americas from European powers.
1826	James Fenimore Cooper's *The Last of the Mohicans* is published. The setting is the 1750s.
1829–43	The Indian Removal Act forces Native Americans living east of the Mississippi to move to Oklahoma. Their land is confiscated.
1830	The Book of Mormon is published by Joseph Smith.
1830s	Many states begin passing laws giving married women the right to retain their own property.
1831	Nat Turner's slave rebellion fails in Virginia.
	William Lloyd Garrison's publication of *The Liberator* starts the abolitionist movement.
1832	Andrew Jackson is elected the seventh president of the United States.
1836	Ralph Waldo Emerson publishes *Nature*, a book that becomes the "Bible" of Transcendental philosophy.
1837	A long economic depression begins in the United States, resulting in the closing of businesses and banks.
	The first college for women, Mount Holyoke Female Seminary, opens in Massachusetts.

1839   Herman Melville goes to sea as a cabin boy on the *St. Lawrence*, a merchant ship sailing from New York City to Liverpool. He will write of this adventure in *Redburn*.

1841   Herman Melville sets sail for the South Seas on the whaler *Achushnet*.

The first large expedition sets out for California.

1842   Melville lives among cannibals in the Marquesas Islands, an experience he will fictionalize in his first novel, *Typee* (1846). His visit to Tahiti, later in the same year, will be the basis for *Omoo* (1847).

1843–44   Melville sails from Hawaii to Boston on a military vessel, the *United States*, an experience from which he draws material for *White Jacket* (1850).

1845   Women working in the Lowell, Massachusetts, textile mills form the Female Labor Reform Association, a precursor of much union activity.

Frederick Douglass's *Narrative of the Life of Frederick Douglass* is published.

John Charles Fremont leads an expedition to California.

1845–46   Henry David Thoreau lives in a cabin he builds on Walden Pond.

1846   The United States' war with Mexico begins.

Melville publishes *Typee*.

Dred Scott, a slave taken out of the slave states, sues for his freedom.

Mormons move west to Salt Lake City after their leader Joseph Smith is lynched in Illinois.

1848   Thoreau delivers his lecture on "Civil Disobedience" in Concord, Massachusetts.

A Women's Rights Convention is held in Seneca Falls, New York, and includes a demand for suffrage.

Mexico cedes California to the United States.

James Marshall discovers gold on Sutter's California spread.

1849   The discovery of gold on Sutter's spread begins a massive rush to California.

Riots occur in and around the Astor Place Opera House in New York City between rabid American nationalists and upper-class American Anglophiles. The immediate issue is a feud between an English and an American actor.

1850   Melville publishes *White Jacket*.

Flogging is outlawed by Congress.

Property rights for women are passed in six states.

The Fugitive Slave Act, forcing the return to slavery of slaves who have escaped to freedom, is passed.

Nathaniel Hawthorne publishes *The Scarlet Letter*.

California is admitted to statehood.

1851   Melville's *Moby-Dick* is published.

Harriet Tubman begins her many trips on the Underground Railroad, secretly helping slaves escape.

Mormon leader Brigham Young proclaims himself governor of Utah.

1852   Harriet Beecher Stowe's *Uncle Tom's Cabin* is published.

Polygamy is officially sanctioned by the Mormons.

1853   William Wells Brown's *Clotel* is published in England.

1854   Thoreau's *Walden* is published.

Timothy Shay Arthur's *Ten Nights in a Bar-room* is published.

The Kansas-Nebraska Bill rescinds the Missouri Compromise and leaves the decision to allow slavery in any territory up to its voters, opening Nebraska to white settlers.

Fugitive slave George Burns is arrested in Boston.

1857   Slavery is protected by the *Dred Scott* decision of the U.S. Supreme Court. The ruling decrees that no slave has legal rights.

In Mountain Meadow, Utah, a Mormon fanatic and his followers massacre 120 settlers traveling to California. They attempt to shift the entire blame for this on Indians.

1859   John Brown leads an abolitionist raid on the arsenal at Harper's Ferry.

1860   Abraham Lincoln is elected the sixteenth president of the United States.

South Carolina secedes from the Union.

1861   Rebecca Harding Davis's *Life in the Iron Mills* is published.

J.P. Morgan is sufficiently wealthy to donate $62 million to help restore U.S. gold reserves. His United States Steel is one of the first billion-dollar companies in America.

1861–65   The Civil War begins and rages for four years.

1862   The Homestead Act encourages settlement on the frontier.

1863   The Emancipation Proclamation frees slaves in rebel states.

1864   On William Tecumseh Sherman's march to the sea in November and December, he orders that the city of Atlanta be burned. His soldiers go amok, not only burning commercial enterprises but also plundering and burning private homes and food. This is the setting for Margaret Mitchell's *Gone With the Wind*.

1865   Robert E. Lee surrenders to Ulysses S. Grant at Appomattox, Virginia. The war has cost 600,000 lives.

1865–77   The South is totally subjugated during Reconstruction.

1866   Henry Bergh establishes the New York Society for the Prevention of Cruelty to Animals.

The Fourteenth Amendment to the Constitution gurantees equal protection under the law.

The National Labor Union is organized—the first attempt to unite all trade unions into one organization.

1867   Horatio Alger's *Ragged Dick* is published.

Nebraska achieves statehood.

1868   George Thorndike Angell establishes a Society for the Prevention of Cruelty to Animals in Massachusetts.

The Fourteenth Amendment makes ex-slaves citizens.

1869   Louisa May Alcott's *Little Women* is published.

The Knights of Labor is organized.

1870s   The Women's Crusade against Rum gains in numbers and influence.

The Fifteenth Amendment gives male former slaves the vote.

1874   A secret union called the Molly Maguires clashes with mine owners, buttressed by Pinkerton police. Ten Molly Maguires are hanged.

1875   The Society for the Prevention of Cruelty to Children is established in New York City by Elbridge T. Gerry.

1876   The Sioux defeat U.S. forces under George Armstrong Custer at the Little Big Horn in Montana.

1877   Anna Sewell's *Black Beauty* is published.

Chief Joseph and his people are captured as he attempts to flee into Canada and is sent to an Oklahoma compound where most die.

The Great Rail Strike occurs.

The Socialist Labor Party is founded in the United States.

After Reconstruction, the South enforces segregation, sets up contract and convict systems that continue black servitude and dependence on whites, and enforces discrimination.

1878   Two hundred blacks migrate to Liberia in Africa.

Hundreds of Ute Native Americans die in an Oklahoma compound where they have been imprisoned.

John D. Rockefeller controls 90 percent of U.S. oil refineries.

1879   The Wyoming Stock Growers Association protects a group of ranchers with large spreads against small, struggling ranchers, sheep growers, and the government.

Twenty thousand blacks leave the South for the western frontier.

1880   A violent fight between wheat farmers and the Southern-Pacific Railroad occurs at Mussel Slough.

1880s   These are the days of the great cattle trail drives out West.

The Women's Christian Temperance Union becomes extremely active in closing saloons.

Andrew Carnegie's monopoly was at this time valued at $400 million.

1881   Henry James publishes *The Portrait of a Lady.*

The American Federation of Labor is organized. Its first leader is Samuel Gompers.

1884–85   Mark Twain publishes *Adventures of Huckleberry Finn.*

1885   Mark Twain's book is banned from public libraries throughout the United States, including those in Concord, Brooklyn, Denver, and Omaha.

Helen Hunt Jackson's *Ramona* is published.

1886   The Dawes Severalty Act ceded 160 acres to each Native American family.

In this year there are 10,000 labor strikes in the country. The New York traction strike of transportation workers provides William Dean Howells with material for a novel. The McCormick Harvester strike leads to the Haymarket Riot.

1888   Edward Bellamy's *Looking Backward* is published.

1889   White settlers rush into Oklahoma in a frenzied grab for land that had earlier been ceded to Native Americans.

1890   William Dean Howells's *A Hazard of New Fortunes* is published. The subject is the 1886 traction strike in New York City.

Steelworkers and other factory workers labor under hazardous conditions, without breaks, for twelve-hour shifts, seven days a week, for $10 a week.

The struggle for women's suffrage becomes especially active at the state level with the organization of the National American Woman Suffrage Association.

The census shows that 65,000 vagrant children, most of them girls under sixteen, live on the streets of New York City.

Mississippi is the first southern state to require literacy tests and poll taxes to deny blacks the vote.

The Sherman Anti-Trust Act is passed to limit activity of monopolies.

1890s   There are 1,200 documented lynchings of blacks in the United States, the great majority in the South.

1892   Steelworkers strike at Homestead, Pennsylvania. In the conflict that follows, union members are locked out; ten are killed and hundreds injured.

The Johnson County War wages in Wyoming where wealthy cattlemen hire Texas gunmen to protect their interests against smaller farmers. In the vigilante justice that prevails, several men are lynched by the gunmen. Although the government intervenes, no one is brought to justice.

1894   The American Railway Union strike erupts in violence.

Labor leader Eugene Debs is arrested and sent to prison.

1895	Stephen Crane's *The Red Badge of Courage* is published. The setting is the Civil War.
1896	The U.S. Supreme Court, in *Plessy v. Ferguson*, makes segregation legal.
1898	The Spanish-American War is waged and won by Americans over Cuban independence from Spain.
1899	Kate Chopin's *The Awakening* is published.
	Andrew Carnegie controls 25 percent of all the country's iron and steel production.

129. *The Last of the Mohicans*, by James Fenimore Cooper (United States, 1826). *The Last of the Mohicans* was the most popular, highly regarded novel of the author, who, in the 1820s, was regarded as the first and most representative of American novelists. The narrative is set in the 1750s, during the war between the British and French over the Canadian border. The novel is also pertinent to the period in which it was written, the 1820s, when America was struggling for a cultural identity apart from England.

In 1754, the French and Indian War began, with different Indian tribes aligning themselves with one or the other side. On August 9, 1757, the French laid siege to and ultimately achieved surrender of Fort William Henry. After much killing (as revealed in Cooper's novel) English General George Munro, in accordance with terms of a truce, was permitted to take some troops to Fort Edward, some fifteen miles down river. However, the Indians allied with the French attacked the troops, slaughtering most of them in the forest.

Fenimore Cooper's novel, based on the 1757 massacre during the French and Indian War, was a successful attempt through fiction to create a defining legend peculiar to America. The story opens in 1757 with two sisters who, with their soldier escort, have attempted to seek a place of safety during the impending attack on Fort William Henry, over which their father has command. They are, instead, betrayed into ambush by their Indian scout Magua. Hawkeye, the frontiersman and protagonist of this and other Leatherstocking novels, along with his Indian friend, the Mohican Chingachgook, and Chingachgook's son Uncas, rescue the women. The action of the novel turns on the fate of the party as they are moved around, attacked, and escape. Uncas, the last of the Mohicans, is finally killed by Magua.

Cooper, who was already a successful novelist by this time, enjoyed even greater success with this novel, which sold enough copies to rescue him from debt and allow him to move to Europe for a time to continue writing full-time. The novel continued in popularity through the twentieth century when it was published in numerous editions and made into several movies and television scripts, the last a major motion picture of the 1990s.

The novel that Cooper wrote about Fort William Henry was conceived in the 1820s, a time when the new nation was struggling to assert its own cultural identity, separate from the British from whom they had won their political independence in 1783. Many Americans still looked to English tradition for respectable works of art to define the culture, disparaging fiction, poetry, and art produced on American soil.

The novel gave American culture its distinctive hero and a defining legend, as nothing else had done, in capturing dramatic events in the founding of the country. Cooper patterned Natty Bumppo, or Hawkeye, in part on the legend of Daniel Boone, particularly an episode in which Boone rescued his daughter from the Indians. The type he created in Natty Bumppo was seen as the archetypical American democrat. Thus the novel promoted nationalism by making viable an identity separate from England.

Moreover, Cooper's novel elevated those values that would help the country identify itself as nature's nation: Natty's friendship with a Native American; the reinforcement of the idea of the Noble Savage; the attempt to validate the ordinary American through the recreation of his speech; and the reinforcement of the values of individualism, natural physical ability, ruggedness, and freedom from Europeanized civilization.

Additional Readings: Charles M. Andrews, *The Colonial Background of the American Revolution* (New Haven, CT: Yale University Press, 1934); William P. Kelley, *Plotting America's Past: Fenimore Cooper and the Leatherstocking Tales* (Carbondale: Southern Illinois University Press, 1983); Daniel H. Peck, ed., *New Essays on "The Last of the Mohicans"* (Cambridge: Cambridge University Press, 1992).

130. *Typee*, **by Herman Melville (United States, 1846).** In 1846, Herman Melville published his first novel, based on his experiences as a sailor on a whaling ship and in the Marquesa Islands. Few people in the West had any knowledge of this part of the world, though their appetites had been whetted for information by the voyages of such explorers as James Cook and Louis Antoine de Bouganville and reports brought back by whaling ships such as the *Essex*. South Seas culture was as compelling and mysterious as it was forbidding. Stories of cannibalism and disfiguring embellishments were mixed with Rousseauistic beliefs in the Noble Savage, holding a grim fascination for the reader.

At the same time, the so-called civilized world regarded all people in non-European cultures as little more than lower animals, without human intelligence or anything recognizable as religion.

Christian fervor, and the influence of the clergy in the century, was especially great. As a consequence, some of the most active cultural forces in America and England were missionary societies, supported largely by upper- and middle-class women in association with the clergy, whose aim it was to convert natives in non-European areas such as Hawaii.

Another characteristic of nineteenth-century culture relevant to Melville's novel was the general prudishness with regard to the body and sex. It was a time when young ladies in polite society never rode in a carriage or visited in a parlor alone with a young man. Women and girls were covered from head to toe with clothes, even on the warmest days. Physicians were even hindered in making accurate diagnoses because modesty dictated that they examine their female patients fully clothed.

Melville, who was thoroughly familiar with these conventions, wrote *Typee* after he had lived on some of the roughest ships on the seas, with their international crews from every corner of the civilized and uncivilized earth. He had also actually lived briefly in the Marquesas, spent time in Tahiti, and run a business in Hawaii. So his perspective, as he wrote *Typee*, was at variance with that of most of his prospective readers.

Typee is a story, based on his own experience, of a young man who signs aboard a whaler and becomes so distressed at the food, living quarters, medical care, labor, and method of justice aboard the ship that he jumps ship with a friend near the Marquesa Islands. As they wander around one of the islands, the main character falls and breaks his leg; his friend Toby goes for help; the hero is found by a tribe native to the islands and taken back to their village of Typee. Here he is treated like visiting royalty as they take great pains to bring him back to full health. Most memorable are his outings on the lake with the beautiful native woman Fay-a-way. The narrator declares that he could have remained there forever but for several discoveries. First, he enters the temple after one of their brief skirmishes with another tribe and finds the half-eaten remains of a slaughtered enemy. Second, as his leg heals and he becomes mobile, he suspects that the tribe will attempt to keep him with them as a favored pet. Finally, he hears their plans to tattoo him as they themselves are richly decorated, a prospect that fills him with horror. And so he escapes to another commercial whaling ship.

Typee was an enormously popular novel in both England and America because it gave its audiences a picture of an unknown culture, rendered very sympathetically, something no writer had done in just this way. The success almost did Melville in, however, in that readers and publishers began to doubt that such a tale of kindly, attractive, and clever cannibals could possibly be true. They claimed it was a story totally imaginative, with no basis in fact, which Melville had passed off as an accurate picture of life in the Marquesas.

Publishers in England threatened to pull it off the market. Fortuitously, however, the shipmate whom Melville had called Toby, and whom he had never heard from again, was living in New York state and wrote a letter to a newspaper corroborating Melville's story. Thereafter, *Typee* was accepted as having a basis in fact and transformed the views that many readers had of South Sea natives.

Other readers reacted in diverse ways to Melville's comparisons of his cannibals to the owners and operators of the whaling ships, a comparison that was more to the credit of the cannibals. For those open to the Rousseauistic idea of the Noble Savage, this novel was convincing proof that civilization dehumanized man and that it was the Europeanized man who was the real barbarian. For other, more orthodox churchgoers, Melville's comparison was an irreligious outrage. It struck at the very reason for the missionary effort to say that the cannibals had a perfectly humane moral code and that their own religion was just as valid as Protestantism—that they, therefore, had no need for conversion.

Similarly, readers reacted variously to the candid bawdiness of Melville's book, parts of which had to be expunged before publication. Some readers came to see that different cultures had valid ways of dealing naturally and openly with the body that was far from sordid, even though their attitudes were unlike those of Puritan-engendered New England. But many were shocked that a New England young man would have experienced and then written about such things as a native queen throwing her muumuu over her head to display proudly her bare tattooed bottom to a tattooed sailor onboard ship. For Melville to have rowed in a boat alone with the beautiful, topless Fay-a-way was bad enough, but to write of it was unconscionable.

Additional Readings: Merlin Bowen, *The Long Encounter: Self and Experience in the Writings of*

Herman Melville (Chicago: University of Chicago Press, 1960); Wai-chee Dimock, *Empire for Liberty: Melville and the Poetics of Individualism* (Princeton, NJ: Princeton University Press, 1991).

131. *The Scarlet Letter,* by Nathaniel Hawthorne (United States, 1850). Puritan New Englanders settled the northern United States in the seventeenth century and for almost 100 years thereafter officially reached into every aspect of colonial life. Two hundred years later, the Puritans no longer had political control, but little in American life was free of their influence. Several aspects of life in the 1850s are pertinent to Nathaniel Hawthorne's novel set in Puritan times, especially (1) the continuing power of the Protestant Church and the clergy; (2) society's view of sex, and (3) society's view of women.

To the first point, we find that the Protestant Church still dominated American life. Women, especially, were active in churches and missionary societies and regarded New England clergymen as saintly, spiritual figures to whom they could turn for guidance and comfort. To the second point, society's view of sex, one finds that the old Puritans' intellectual emphasis on things of the spirit, their suspicion of this world, and their fierce punishments of extramarital sex had turned in the nineteenth century to extreme prudery in sexual matters. Sex was a matter of shame and a subject not to be spoken of. For example, when Nathaniel Hawthorne's wife Sophia edited his journals after he died, she expunged from them any comment he had made that had a sexual suggestion, including his description of a woman alone on the street at night. This was the age of euphemism when new words were coined to replace old words that had the slightest sexual connotation. The word *leg* was replaced with "limb," for example. The third point has to do with the place of women in Hawthorne's society. The good woman was a dependent, largely sexless being for whom men did the thinking and decision making. Each of these entities are addressed in *The Scarlet Letter.*

Nathaniel Hawthorne's novel, set in

seventeenth-century Boston during the time of Puritan rule, is about a young matron named Hester Prynne who conceives and bears a daughter, Pearl, before her husband joins her in the New World. She refuses to tell the community the name of the child's father. After she is released from jail, she is given a cottage to live in on the outskirts of town and forced to pin the letter "A," for adultery, on her dress. Two other characters are involved in her life: her husband, Roger Chillingsworth, who arrives in Boston on the day she is publicly upbraided for her behavior, and Arthur Dimmesdale, the father of her illegitimate child. Chillingsworth exacts a promise from her that she won't reveal his true identity. From these entangled lives, the themes of revenge, guilt, and pride are developed through the characters' relationship to their Puritan society.

Hawthorne takes the Puritan clergy off its pedestal. The older clergymen are presented as narrow-minded, cruel buffoons. The young clergyman is an ambitious and cowardly, self-deceived person who has gotten one of his young parishioners with child and refuses to own up to it until he is on his deathbed. By contrast, Hester, an adulteress, is sympathetic. So the novel's heroine is everything a model Victorian woman is not: She is sexual (even an adulteress); she lives alone and supports herself and her daughter; she is much more decisive and stronger than her former lover, the Reverend Dimmesdale; and she is intellectual, becoming a religious skeptic. The subject of sex is central to the plot and the theme, and unlike the usual cautionary, moral novel of his day, the work makes no attempt to urge youth to be chaste. The minister, while pretending to sainthood, had not only gotten a young married woman pregnant; he seemed continually plagued with sexual feelings, leading him to whip himself in private. Hester, on the other hand, has not only had an adulterous affair; she tells Dimmesdale many years later that there was nothing wrong in what they did.

Local readers were outraged by Hawthorne's introduction of his story of Hester

with a blistering portrait of the Salem of his own day, in which he portrayed the "venerable" pillars of Salem with whom he worked as idiotic and corrupt old men. Even for outsiders, his antipatriarchal sentiments were shocking.

The immediate reaction to Hawthorne's novel was mixed. He was one of the first writers to show the Puritan fathers in an unsympathetic light. Many churchgoers were especially outraged that he would present a minister as a partner in adultery. Much of the public objected to the portrait of Hester and the frank use of the topic of adultery. Hawthorne, they charged, took no moral stand in his novel. Hester, the scarlet woman, was presented sympathetically, and the wronged husband was presented as a cruel demon. The loudest immediate objections to the book, however, came from Salem, Massachusetts, Hawthorne's own hometown, and were leveled at the withering satire of his novel's introduction, titled "The Custom-House." Despite the public outrage and threats, Hawthorne defiantly asserted in print that as long as he lived, he would always see that every word of "The Custom-House" was included with *The Scarlet Letter*.

Today, the novel is regarded as an American classic. Despite critics who have taken pains to discredit Hawthorne's whole history by claiming that he erred on some minor historical point in his story, his portrait has become the official version of the Puritans to the present day. Hester Prynne, her scarlet letter, and the Puritans as they were portrayed in his novel have become part of our national mythology, have made their way into our symbolic language, and are points of reference that contemporary culture immediately recognizes as the prototypical suffering adulteress, a society-imposed badge of shame, and self-righteous intolerance. It has been rewritten, frequently staged and filmed, and often parodied.

Additional Readings: Richard H. Brodhead, *The School of Hawthorne* (New York: Oxford University Press, 1986); Samuel Chase Coale, *In Hawthorne's Shadow* (Lexington: University of

Kentucky Press, 1985); Claudia Durst Johnson, *Understanding "The Scarlet Letter"* (Westport, CT: Greenwood Press, 1995).

132. *White Jacket,* by Herman Melville (United States, 1850).

On August 17, 1843, in Hawaii, Melville signed aboard a U.S. Navy frigate, the *United States,* which brought him home to New York on October 14, 1844. *White Jacket,* which Richard Henry Dana had encouraged him to write, is explicitly about abuses in the U.S. Navy, derived from his experience aboard this military vessel.

What Melville learned firsthand was that there was no social caste more despised and exploited than that of a sailor in the military. The work was grueling and dangerous for men who were considered cannon fodder in wartime. They were often young boys who had been unwillingly impressed, or kidnapped, from port cities or other ships to serve as virtual slaves, especially in the British navy. Common sailors were not provided with the basic necessities of life, often subsisting on insect-infested "hardtack," biscuits so hard that they had to be soaked in liquid before they could be consumed. Living under these circumstances, they were subject to disease and wounds for which they received inadequate treatment. The code, especially the Articles of War, under which they lived was brutal and capricious and was a matter of law even in peacetime. And punishments, as cruel and unusual as those found in any medieval dungeon, were administered for the most trivial infractions. Men who sailed with Melville could remember "keel-hauling," a practice of pulling a sailor by a rope under the entire length of the ship. During this ordeal barnacles tore him to shreds, and he drowned. When Melville served aboard the *United States,* flogging was still a common, universally approved punishment. A sailor could be sentenced to flogging through the ship, in which every man aboard was expected to beat him severely with a cat-o'-nine-tails (a rope with nine thongs at the end, sometimes containing lead). There were even occasions when a miscreant would be whipped not only through the ship but "through the fleet."

When reformer and nurse Florence Nightingale objected to these practices in the British navy in the late 1850s and 1860s and suggested that sailors be taught to read and write and manage their wages, she was ridiculed by upper-class officers who told her in no uncertain terms that sailors were subhuman and could only be managed with brutality. These were the conditions in the British navy twenty years after *White Jacket,* and Melville declares in his novel (and most reviews corroborated his judgment) that conditions in the U.S. Navy were much worse than the British navy.

Melville's *White Jacket* appeared in 1850, ten years after the famous book by Richard Henry Dana titled *Two Years before the Mast.* His intention was to lay bare the abuses in the navy and to argue that the system flagrantly violated every precept of a democracy. The abuses run from the serious physical and psychological effects of floggings and sadistic medical treatments to the hundreds of petty nonsensical rules designed to suit the whims of the captains and commodores but that make life difficult for the sailor. Among the less severe complaints were being forced to eat all meals in the course of eight hours and being forbidden to "sing out" while doing heavy labor.

The greatest emphasis was on flogging. Many men died from this brutal punishment. Others were unable to perform their duties for months afterward. In his short time aboard the *United States,* Melville saw 163 men flogged.

Melville's chief target was the system itself, which reduces men to automatons, children, dogs, or slaves. This is the kind of individual, Melville says, that the navy wants working for it—creatures who will subject themselves without question to the lord of the manor, which is to say, the captain. The old royal European system remained alive and well on a man-of-war. The Articles of War, which removed all rights from common sailors, was designed to produce such an individual. Rarely, however, were these rules applied to officers. How, in a democratic country, he asks, are "thousands of Americans . . . subjected to the most despotic usages?"

Very good sales and reviews indicate that Melville's novel had an immediate and largely positive impact on its readers. A minority of reviewers declared that just because Melville had been to sea, he was not necessarily fit to recommend the abolition of flogging or to question the Articles of War, both of which served good purposes. But the majority agreed with two reviewers, one in April and one in June, who recommended that a copy of the book should be put into the hands of every member of Congress. Another said that what Melville observed firsthand and wrote about was enough to sink the whole naval military system—"ships, officers, and all, to perdition" (see Tony Tanner's "Introduction" and John Rugdale's "Explanatory Notes" to the edition of *White-Jacket* published by Oxford University Press in 1990). The most concrete evidence that Melville's book changed the course of naval history is that on September 28, 1850, six months after the novel appeared, the U.S. Congress outlawed flogging in the navy.

As readers noted at the time, Melville changed the way that life at sea was regarded. He, himself, like many another boy, had run away from the constrictions of civilization and anticipated adventure by going to sea. Melville dispelled the romance of sailoring, treating the subject of sailing ships and sailors realistically, without melodrama and without romance, leading one reviewer to declare that there should be "a copy of *White-Jacket* in every village library wherever the English language is spoken," because, as another writer noted, Melville lifted "the veil which covers the . . . real 'life below stairs' " (see Tanner's "Introduction").

But the book was not just an exposé of the navy—it was one of the first books by an established American writer to show realistically the inhuman conditions under which the lower classes lived in a country that proclaimed democratic ideals.

Additional Readings: Richard H. Brodhead, *Hawthorne, Melville, and the Novel* (Chicago: University of Chicago Press, 1976); Brian Higgins and Hershel Parker, eds., *Herman Melville: The Contemporary Reviews* (New York: Cambridge University Press, 1995).

133. *Moby-Dick*, by Herman Melville (United States, 1851). Herman Melville's *Moby-Dick* is considered by many readers to be the greatest novel that America ever produced. In scope it mirrored the vast country in which it was written, the sea being the ultimate frontier, removed from civilization and where mankind is at the mercy of nature's most horrific forces. It was also a commentary on the social, economic, and philosophical character of America at mid-nineteenth century.

The mercantile nature of the country, which rested on the backbreaking and often dangerous labor of the working class, is pertinent to the novel, as is the exploitation of the seemingly boundless natural resources available at that time. Also pertinent to the novel are the two most prominent religious and philosophical positions taken in the country at the time: (1) the nineteenth-century Protestant view of a benevolent creator and the Protestant Ethic and (2) the Transcendentalist nature philosophy articulated by Ralph Waldo Emerson.

The hunt for the lucrative whale oil was a fitting emblem for American enterprise, for, as Melville points out, their products brought light to the entire world. Few capitalists made greater profits than the owners of whaling ships. Often, America's pursuit of profit was encouraged by the religious establishment, which, in Melville's novel, is represented by the Quaker owners of the whaler who calculate ways to exploit their laborers at the same time that they read their Bibles. A man who enjoys riches was, it was thought, a hard worker beloved and approved of by God. Their immense profits, pursued at any cost, were garnered on the backs of the working poor.

The sailors who hunted whales were fitting representatives of nineteenth-century slaves and working-class Americans in that, on a whaling ship, every country and race in the world was represented. Their work was the most perilous undertaken in the world. Casualties aboard whalers were notoriously high. At the same time, such men were regarded as little more than animals.

Moby-Dick is the story, told by a former schoolteacher named Ishmael, of a whaling voyage he goes on, underwritten by the ship's avaricious owners and led by a maniacal captain named Ahab. The tale has numerous interwoven strands. One is the story of the love between Ishmael, an American, and Queequeg, a native South Sea islander who seems always destined to be a stoical rescuer and savior of his fellow man. The contrasting story is Ahab's, the captain who will sacrifice and destroy anyone and anything in seeking his revenge on the white whale, Moby-Dick, who has taken off Ahab's leg on an earlier voyage. This voyage, sent out by so-called peaceloving Quakers, is dedicated to the violent plundering of nature.

Melville's novel was not a clear success. It gained neither the reading public nor the critical acclaim that his earlier novels on the South Seas had received. Nor did he receive any sizable profit from his big novel. When Melville died, though his modest obituary in a New York newspaper mentions only this one work, *Moby-Dick*, the book had long been out of print. It was not reprinted until over twenty years after Melville's death. Soon after that, however, it came to be commonly recognized as America's greatest novel and has never since been out of print. It is a standard classic included in university courses on American literature, and it has been repeatedly adapted for stage, film, and television. A highly touted television version was broadcast in 1998.

Moby-Dick's social relevance has impressed itself on readers. It was the first important novel in America to chronicle in considerable detail the actual work and life of the common laborer in the nineteenth century. Every phase of whaling, with all its dangers and the intricate skills required in the performance of the work, is described in careful and colorful detail.

Furthermore, the work was regarded as a commentary on work in America's factories. As the sailor in *Moby-Dick* falls into the carcass of the whale, so many an urban landlubber lost life or limb by falling into machinery.

Readers also found in the novel discussions and images of American commerce, fueled by money from the greedy and pious owners who try to attract sailors at the lowest possible price. A similar metaphoric reference to commerce is the doubloon, staked on the mast of the ship, to lure men to risk their lives for money.

More recent readers have seen in the novel a foreshadowing of trouble that humans have created in plundering nature, on the theory that human beings are greater in importance than any other of God's creatures.

The novel has had the greatest influence, however, in shaping philosophical and psychological rather than social ideas. Melville, who jokingly referred to it as a wicked book, presents an existential or nihilistic suggestion that there is nothing beyond the wall of nature—no divine being and no reason, only mindlessness. Only the saving humanism of Queequeg prevails.

The greatest influence of the novel is seen in its psychological study of obsession. Not even the Shakespearean models that inspired Melville's creation have been so firmly impressed on the human consciousness as the apotheosis of maniacal obsession as has Ahab. He is America's most important tragic hero. And *Moby-Dick*—which captures the spirit of the country, the fear and attraction of nature, the necessity of action, the love of adventure, the virtue of brotherhood—is rightly considered to be the epic of America.

Additional Readings: Richard H. Brodhead, ed., *New Essays on "Moby Dick"* (Cambridge: Cambridge University Press, 1986); Michael Paul Rogin, *Subversive Genealogy: The Politics and Art of Herman Melville* (New York: Knopf, 1983).

134. *Uncle Tom's Cabin*, **by Harriet Beecher Stowe (United States, 1852).** Slavery in the American colonies began in the seventeenth century with the importation of slaves into Virginia and New England. By the middle of the eighteenth century, most slaves were located in the Southern states because black slave labor was not economically feasible in the commerce and small acreage farms of the North. Furthermore, many of the prominent Northern leaders had always believed that slavery was immoral and had taken steps to abolish it in their jurisdictions. Moreover, the struggle for power between the rural South and the industrial North, that is, their votes in Congress, soon rested on the extent to which new states would be admitted as "slave" or "free." In the six-year period before Harriet Beecher Stowe's novel appeared serially (before its book publication in 1852), controversies over a number of admissions to the Union were being argued, and other turning points in the history of slavery had occurred. In 1845 an escaped slave named Frederick Douglass, whom Stowe consulted extensively, published a narrative of his life as a slave. In 1846, a slave, Dred Scott, who had been taken from slave to free territory, sued for his freedom. A new, notorious Fugitive Slave Law passed in 1850. This controversial act allowed slaveholders to pursue their slaves even in free territory and declared that those helping slaves escape were liable for prosecution as criminals. This law led to continual controversy and violence.

The main characters of *Uncle Tom's Cabin* are an elderly slave named Tom, a young slave named Eliza, and her son Harry. The secondary plot follows Eliza's escape to Canada with her son, who has been sold and is about to be taken from her. In the main plot Uncle Tom is sold by Mr. Shelby, a well-meaning master who has fallen on bad economic times, and is bought by and lives with a kind family, the St. Clares, where he cares for his owner's child, Little Eva, and her African American playmate Topsy. At the death of Mr. St. Clare, he is sold to the epitome of evil, Simon Legree, and eventually dies from a beating. The novel ends as Shelby's son, George, frees all of the Shelby slaves. To the novel is appended Stowe's plea for an end to

slavery in accordance with Christian ideals and a commitment to educate and improve the lives of freed slaves.

Stowe's work was immediately and enthusiastically received and became one of the bestselling novels in America. Despite the earlier appearance of *Narrative of the Life of Frederick Douglass*, Stowe's book was the first account of the plight of slaves to reach a wide audience. Her millions of readers throughout the world were deeply moved by a story that gave slavery a human dimension and revealed the conditions under which slaves lived. When Southern apologists for slavery challenged her facts, she wrote another account, documenting every situation she had described in the novel.

Stowe illustrated that even slaves belonging to a benevolent master were in constant jeopardy: The master's suddenly reduced economic situation (like Shelby's) or death (like St. Clare's) left his slaves exposed to the danger of being sold to a cruel monster. For the first time, Stowe's readers became aware of the hideous system of slave traders, overseers, and the slave market where human beings were treated as animals. Nor had many people at the time had any inkling of the sexual abuse of slave women at the hands of slave owners, a matter the Victorian Stowe treats with great delicacy.

Much of what humanized and created sympathy for the slaves in the eyes of Stowe's audience was the separation of slave families. And this was a new dimension that Frederick Douglass had not explored, because, in actuality, slave owners usually separated children and parents in early childhood to keep emotional ties from developing. This was a careful calculation on the part of owners to avoid trouble when they separated families.

Stowe also articulated the argument that slavery was anti-Christian, a stance that is primarily presented through the words of Little Eva and in the author's addendum. However, the link between Christianity and abolitionism was not a simple one to maintain. Ministers, especially in the South, were some of the most vocal apologists for slavery, maintaining that slavery was sanctioned in the Bible and that black people were not fully human. Furthermore, the forerunner of *Uncle Tom's Cabin*, *Narrative of the Life of Frederick Douglass*, had graphically shown that the most religious people were the cruelest slaveholders and that Christians had made Bible Schools for slaves illegal. Even Stowe had shown that, of all Christian groups, it was only the Quaker minority that actively assisted in the Underground Railroad. She also demonstrated through her characters that it was often difficult for slaves to cling to any religious faith under such a brutal system. To make her argument, she had to append it in her own words.

Stowe's novel had the immediate effect of educating and motivating many people who had not taken a stand against slavery, especially in the North. Readers credited the novel with prompting them to take an active role in the abolition of slavery.

Stowe is also credited with hastening the outbreak of the Civil War. Tradition has it that President Abraham Lincoln, upon meeting Stowe in the early 1860s, supposedly told her, "So you're the little lady who caused the great war!"

The story of Uncle Tom was perpetuated in the phenomenally popular dramas of the story that many resident and traveling companies played throughout the country. As a result, the names of some of Stowe's characters have entered the language: a "Tom," meaning a black man intent on appeasing his oppressors, and "Simon Legree," meaning any cruel sadist.

Additional Readings: Elizabeth Ammons, ed., *Critical Essays on Harriet Beecher Stowe* (Boston: G.K. Hall, 1980); Thomas F. Gossett, *Uncle Tom's Cabin and American Culture* (Dallas, TX: Southern Methodist University Press, 1985).

135. *Clotel: or The President's Daughter*, by William Wells Brown (United States, 1853, 1864). *Clotel*, which first appeared in England in 1853, well before the American Civil War, was the first African American novel, a fictional argument against slavery, written by a black man who had escaped from his former owner. Set in colonial Virginia, the novel was published in England the year after Harriet Beecher Stowe's *Uncle Tom's Cabin* appeared in the United States and a year after a group called the Pro-Slavery Group published a volume of their arguments in support of slavery.

Pro-slavery arguments presented to justify the buying and selling of human beings were profuse at this time, coming from the North as well as the South. A disproportionate number of pro-slavery arguments came from the pens of ministers who based their arguments on the Bible. The extreme arguments claimed that blacks were not true human beings, that they were the sons of Ham who were damned by God, that slavery was necessary to allow more cultivated Christians to rise in the world, and that Bible figures themselves owned slaves.

Economic and "legal" arguments also prevailed, proponents of slavery arguing that the economic growth of the country depended on slavery, that wholesale emancipation would bankrupt the country, that owners treated their slaves well for the most part, and that slaves led better lives as slaves than they would lead as free men. It was also argued that working against slavery or failing to return escaped slaves to their owners was a breach of the law.

Clotel countered these arguments with fictional portraits of what life was like for humans in bondage. In the original version, Clotel is a mulatto slave, the daughter of Thomas Jefferson and his housekeeper, a slave named Currer. When Jefferson assumes his position as president in Washington, D.C., he sells at auction the mother of his child and his child, both of whom look white. Clotel is sold to a man named Horatio Green, who makes her his mistress. The daughter she has by Green is also white. Both women are assumed to be white until Green decides to marry someone else, who finds out that Clotel has black blood in her veins. Clotel is then sold, and Mary, her daughter, becomes a servant in her father's house. Clotel's new owner intends her to be his mistress also, but she escapes with a man named William and goes back to Virginia to rescue

Mary. Along the way, however, she drowns herself. Suicide is also the way out of slavery for Clotel's sister and her daughters.

While Thomas Jefferson is in Washington expounding on the need to abolish slavery, his mulatto daughter and lover meet their deaths.

Mary, his granddaughter, helps a rebel slave named George go free by exchanging clothes with him. He escapes to Europe, but she is "sold South," the worse fate a slave could have. On the way, however, she is rescued by a Frenchman, who takes her to Paris where they marry. After her husband dies, Mary coincidentally runs into George in Paris. The novel ends with their marriage.

Clotel first appeared in England the year after *Uncle Tom's Cabin*. It was not published in the United States until 1864. In the American edition, the patrimony of the leading character is changed. She is no longer the daughter of a president but the daughter of a senator. Even this modification was not sufficient to secure for *Clotel* the hearing in the United States that it deserved. Even former abolitionists, while they appreciated the antislavery arguments, were made uncomfortable by the sexual misconduct of white owners against slave women and especially by Brown's implication of a senator, let alone a revered president, in such misconduct.

Brown was not only the first African American novelist to give slavery a human face in fiction; he was the first writer on slavery to present openly the sexual misuse of women by their white owners as a frequent fact of slave life. Such misconduct had been implied in a couple of instances in accounts by Frederick Douglass and Harriet Beecher Stowe, but Brown based his entire story on the irony that the daughter of the president of the United States was a slave by his enslaved housemaid. Thus, there were no American reviews of the novel, not even in the abolitionist journal *The Liberator*. Black readers in the early decades of the twentieth century also ignored the book, largely because the subject of slavery had become an embarrassment to them. The novel continued to be ignored until the 1960s when the study of

African American life and the capturing of the African American past came to the fore in Black Studies in colleges and universities.

The novel then, along with other writing, instigated a revision in American history, illustrating the horrible irony of people in a country who recommended freedom and liberty for all but who held slaves. Like Douglass, Johnson was most outraged by ministers who called themselves Christian yet held slaves. His final chapter documents the number of ministers in various religious denominations who bought and sold slaves.

Although slaves had been freed at the time Brown's book appeared in the United States, the pro-slavery, pro-South argument persisted, and his book, written by one who had actually been a slave, illustrated that slaves had not been generally treated decently, had not been better off as slaves, and were fully human, intelligent beings, often with more white blood in their veins than black.

Brown also, curiously, proposed that Jefferson had had children by a slave, a question that arose in controversy for years until the matter was finally resolved when a DNA test confirmed it.

Additional Readings: William Edward Farrison, *William Wells Brown: Author and Reformer* (Chicago: University of Chicago Press, 1969); Lucile Schulberg Warner, *From Slave to Abolitionist: The Life of William Wells Brown* (New York: Dial Press, 1976).

136. *Ten Nights in a Bar-room and What I Saw There*, by Timothy Shay Arthur (United States, 1854). The famous temperance novel by Timothy Shay Arthur is one of the landmarks in America's nineteenth-century reform movement and second only to Harriet Beecher Stowe's *Uncle Tom's Cabin* in its popularity and impact on that world.

One can only grasp the enormity of the impact of Arthur's novel and the impetus for his writing it by examining the world in which it appeared: first, the toll that industrialism had taken on the vast urban armies of factory and home workers and, second, the response of reformers to the evils of the system.

With the advent of industrialization, abuses inevitably followed the factories and mills. Great masses of ordinary laborers in an increasingly class-ridden society sank into a dehumanized horror that almost defies comprehension: They made starvation wages; worked at backbreaking labor from predawn to after darkness, often over dangerous machinery or with poisonous chemicals; lived in festering slums, with little or no hope of escape; and died from inadequate diet and poor health care.

Many tried to cope with the hopelessness and pain of their lives by staying in an alcohol-induced stupor that destroyed their families and led them to an early death.

Reformers, made up primarily of evangelical Christians and secular idealists, responded to the abuses of the factory system as well as a variety of issues in the nineteenth century. Many of these reforms were interrelated. The three most prominent social movements to emerge in the nineteenth century were abolition of slavery, women's rights (especially suffrage), and temperance. But other reforms, associated with these issues, were also part of attempts to save the bodies and souls of the poor—for example, attempts to protect children and animals from cruelty and exploitation, to rescue many who had been forced into prostitution, and to rehabilitate criminals. The women's movement and temperance were especially close because alcohol was seen primarily as a man's problem, causing domestic violence and economic disaster.

Arthur's novel is about a traveler who in periodic visits to the town of Cedarville notices the deterioration caused by the Sickle and Sheaf saloon owned by Simon Slade. At the same time that Slade becomes rich, the families of those who frequent his saloon become poor. However, Slade, himself, eventually sinks into poverty and decay.

Many disasters either occur in the saloon or happen as a result of drunkenness. The most notorious is the murder of little Mary Morgan, daughter of a drunkard named Joe Morgan; when she goes to the saloon to bring her father home, she is hit by a glass thrown by Slade in a fight. Willy Hammond, a gambler, is also killed in the saloon by a drunk Harvey Green, when Hammond discovers him cheating. Mrs. Slade goes insane as a result of her son's disreputable life; and Slade's son also finally murders his father.

After this the citizens are finally aroused. At a mass meeting, they decide to forbid the sale of liquor and destroy the liquor in stock at the saloon, feeling hopeful that they can change the town for the better.

The book sold over 1 million copies in the course of a few years and was immediately adapted to the stage in one of the most popular plays of the century. Its chief influence is seen in the boost it gave to the already thriving prewar temperance movement. In the year following publication of the novel, several states, following the famous Maine law that placed limitations on the making and selling of liquor, passed laws forbidding the sale of alcoholic beverages.

Along with the play *The Drunkard* and the various plays of *Uncle Tom's Cabin*, the adaptation of Arthur's novel for the stage was instrumental in giving the theater respectability and in drawing into the theater many religious people who had avoided it as a den of iniquity. The success of Arthur's novel, and the play based on it, had an immense cultural impact in that it spawned a spate of temperance entertainments, especially songs and plays.

Additional Readings: Anonymous, *T.S. Arthur, His Life and Work by One Who Knows Him* (Philadelphia: J.M. Stoddart, 1873); J.C. Furnas, *The Life and Times of the Late Demon Rum* (New York: Putnam, 1965); Mark E. Lender, *Dictionary of American Temperance Biography* (Westport, CT: Greenwood Press, 1984).

137. *Life in the Iron Mills*, by Rebecca Harding Davis (United States, 1861). The Industrial Revolution was fully under way in the United States in 1861. Workers had been lured in great numbers from farms and from Europe to work in factories where jobs were becoming more plentiful. The most prominent industries were several varieties of textile, paper, and iron mills. At the same time there was little regulation of industry, in the interest of workers or the environment. Most of the concern for workers came from private charitable organizations. Hours were killingly long, and machinery and vats of chemicals posed constant dangers. Weary workers who became careless often lost lives or limbs during work hours and received nothing from owners in recompense. On top of long hours there were "speed-ups" during which managers and owners demanded that work be performed at a killing pace. There were no breaks, no vacations, and no sick days. To miss work for any reason was to put one's livelihood in jeopardy.

A combination of these conditions meant that all a worker had strength to do was survive physically. There was not the time or strength to maintain a spiritual or social life, to exercise one's creativity, or to aspire to a better life. Workers were regarded as little more than beasts, writers at the time unabashedly categorizing them as members of "the dangerous classes."

Rebecca Harding Davis's novella, set in Virginia, first appeared in serial form in 1861. The main characters are two iron mill workers, Deborah and Hugh. Careful attention is given to Deborah's squalid home life, her frailty and exhaustion, as well as her affection and self-sacrifice for her cousin, Hugh, a Welch furnace tender. The scene turns from the house and streets where Deborah lives to the factory itself. Hugh, who carves powerful artistic works from smelting refuse, is observed like a laboratory animal by several men who are taking a tour of the factory. They are especially drawn to his unfinished, impressionistic statue of a woman. Each of the upper-class men represents a different social viewpoint: a mill administrator who claims that such people as Hugh must be—are meant to be—sacrificed for the country's economic progress; a young cynic who recognizes Hugh's plight but asserts philosophically that nothing can be done about it; and a physician who demands that something be done to help this artist but backs away when he is challenged to assume this burden himself. Through no intention to rob anyone, Hugh finds himself in possession of the doctor's wallet, which Deborah gives him and urges him to keep. Before Hugh can return it, he is arrested and sentenced to nineteen years of hard labor. In desperation, he slits his wrists with some tin he hones in his prison cell. Deborah, who has also been imprisoned as his accomplice, is rescued by a Quaker woman who moves her away from the factory to a tranquil rural setting. Their story ends on a bleak note, as the outlook for other, similar workers continues to be hopeless—as anguished and incomplete as Hugh's beautiful sculpture.

Davis's work was a pioneer effort to present the lives of working people realistically. The large readership of the *Atlantic* was exposed for the first time in literature to the grinding poverty and dehumanizing labor of the factory worker. It also drew attention to the industrial worker as a human being capable of creativity and affection and to the futility of their aspirations to gain a better life or to see their creativity flower.

Moreover, Davis pinpointed for the reader the heartlessness of the factory system, the justifications that allowed the perpetuation of the system, and the hypocrisy of the parlor liberal who is generous with words and sentiment but refuses to act.

Life in the Iron Mills has been seen as the first of a long line of "proletarian" novels in America, like *The Jungle* and *The Grapes of Wrath*, which took up the cause of the working man and woman.

Additional Readings: Sharon M. Harris, *Rebecca Harding Davis and American Realism* (Philadelphia: University of Pennsylvania Press, 1991); Jane Atteridge Rose, *Rebecca Harding Davis* (New York: Twayne, 1993); Linda Wagner-Martin and Cathy N. Davidson, eds., *The Oxford Book of Women's Writing in the United States* (Oxford: Oxford University Press, 1995).

138. *Ragged Dick*, by Horatio Alger (United States, 1867). In 1867, at the time

Horatio Alger serially published *Ragged Dick*, the most famous of scores of his tales for boys, cities in the East were nightmares for poor children. With the end of the Civil War two years before, the United States was rapidly becoming an industrial nation, and cities were inundated with youths from farms and immigrant families seeking a means of survival. The crushing poverty of such families forced their children to begin hard physical labor almost as soon as they could walk. There was no federal and only scant state regulation of child labor. Malnourished and working long hours in dangerous conditions, these children rarely rose above poverty as they grew to adulthood. There were, however, a few isolated cases in which poor street children became successes as adults. Orphans and children abandoned by their poor families became a major urban problem, which private charitable institutions struggled to ease, at different times separating orphan siblings and sending them out west to dubious fates with farmers and ranchers who needed extra work hands. One identifiable urban group that emerged after the Civil War was composed of young boys between the ages of five and fifteen, whose families had died or deserted them and who found themselves alone on the city streets. In bitterly cold winters, these homeless boys slept under newspapers, over steaming grates near city buildings. They picked up money by collecting rags, blacking shoes, running errands for businesses, selling matches, and selling newspapers. Uneducated and unprotected, they were frequent victims of disease, cold, starvation, and abuse. These were the boys about whom and for whom Horatio Alger's narratives were written.

Ragged Dick, his first novel of a type he made famous, was the initial novel in one of several series. The pattern he established here was one he would repeatedly follow: In this case, a city street urchin survives as a boot black, through "luck and pluck" (the name of another Alger series). His handsomeness, though he is dirty and ragged, and his hard work and basic honesty attract the attention of a benefactor who keeps an eye on him and eventually finds him a clerical position in a counting house. Dick is determined and ambitious, so it is no surprise to his pals when he achieves fame and wealth as an adult.

The first installment in a boy's magazine was a tremendous success, attracting more fan mail than any story ever had. Even before the second installment appeared, publishers, who had once dismissed Alger, were clamoring for his next fictions. The sale of the book and those it spawned was phenomenal, totaling some 20 million copies. Boys who could read, read the book to those who could not. Those who couldn't afford to buy the book, which first sold for $1.25 and was reduced to 10¢ after 1900, haunted libraries for an available copy. When it first appeared, Sunday Schools ordered thousands of copies to distribute as moral instruction for their young parishioners. Alger was often hyperbolically described as the best-loved author in the world. For thirty years, no other books matched the sales of his.

The popularity of *Ragged Dick* derived in part from the hunger for entertaining, uplifting literature after the Civil War scarcity of reading material. But Alger was an innovator in several ways. First, he provided boys with stories about people and settings that they knew, with heroes with whom they could identify, and he gave dignity to the lowly boy's work of polishing shoes and selling matches.

Furthermore, *Ragged Dick* was a story that gave his young readers hope that they, too, could persevere through hard work and honesty, qualities that the book encouraged them to value (along with the ultimate goal— money).

Finally, the novel called attention to the plight of destitute boys. For this reason, Charles Loring Brace, a wealthy benefactor of children and founder of the Children's Aid Society, visited Alger shortly after the novel appeared and enlisted his help as a chaplain and tutor in the Newsboys Lodging House, with which Alger remained associated for the rest of his life.

Additional Readings: Carol Nackenhoff, *The Fictional Republic: Horatio Alger and American Political Discourse* (New York: Oxford University Press, 1994); Gary Scharnhorst, *Horatio Alger, Jr.* (Boston: Twayne, 1980).

139. *Little Women,* **by Louisa May Alcott (United States, 1869).** In 1869 the society inhabited by women was a circumscribed one with very few choices. After the elementary years, schooling was segregated by sex, and relatively few girls received formal educations beyond the eighth grade. Upper- and middle-class girls typically had a specialized education that included painting, music, sometimes French, and fancy handwork like lace-making and embroidery. Schools of higher education were not available to women until 1837, and even then only a very few were open to them. Eventually some women were able to receive advanced training in mathematics, languages, history, and the classics, but even after public colleges were established for women in the late nineteenth century, the only profession for which they were trained was teaching. There was simply no choice, even for the educated middle-class woman. Schools of medicine, engineering, law, and science did not accept women.

The upper-class woman was expected to marry and only with her family's approval of a husband of her class. Typically, she bore children who were reared by a servant. She oversaw the housework and spent her time in social calls, doing fine needlework, and either planning or going to extravagant parties or attending church and missionary society meetings. The renegade upper-class wife sometimes involved herself in charity work. Typically, middle-class women had slightly more actual work to do, but only within the confines of the house or church.

Circumstances often dictated that even many upper- or middle-class women had to become breadwinners for themselves and their families: Sometimes women never married, their families fell on hard economic times (when, for example, their husbands fell ill), or they were widowed or abandoned by

their husbands. For such women work opportunities were extremely limited. To remain respectable, they had to produce incomes from their homes by teaching or sewing or cooking marketable products.

As her novel demonstrates, Louisa May Alcott and her sisters led lives in many ways unexceptional for their time in that they and their mother labored under the limitations placed on their sex. In other ways, not apparent in the novel, the Alcott women had a father who took the education of his four daughters very seriously. They were formally taught, not only by their father, one of the leading philosopher/teachers of his time, but also by Henry David Thoreau, the most prominent naturalist in nineteenth-century America. Furthermore, they grew up hearing the greatest thinkers in America converse in their living room.

But the world beyond the Alcott household was not always prepared to offer them the opportunities commensurate with their abilities. Their mother, an educated woman, supported the family at times working as a laundress, seamstress, and housekeeper, as did Louisa May herself.

Little Women, Alcott's novel for girls, which drew on her own childhood, is one of the most popular, enduring novels of all time. Her heroine is young Jo March, a high-spirited young woman who grows up in a household of her mother and sisters, her father having been absent much of the time fighting in the Civil War. Jo turns down the offer of marriage to a wealthy young man who has been a family friend since young boyhood—a character in part based on Nathaniel Hawthorne's son Julian, who lived next door to the Alcotts. Jo chooses instead to seek a new independent life on her own in the city, where she begins to write. There she meets an older man who becomes her mentor and friend and who gives her advice about her manuscript. Jo must suddenly move back home when one of her sisters falls sick, but her older friend eventually seeks her out, reveals that he has gotten a publisher for her book, and declares his love for her. They marry and together start a school for boys.

Why did this story become so extremely popular among young girls at the time? And why has it remained so popular, many women today declaring that this character in an 1869 novel is their model? Why has it inspired so many dramatizations, including one, as a popular film, in the 1990s that put this 1869 novel briefly on the *New York Times* bestseller list over 120 years later?

The answer probably lies in the character of Jo March herself. Young women continue to find inspiration in her strength, her determination, and her independence, yet strong sense of family responsibility. Her readers see Jo as a rebel who chose a path unthinkable in her day and that perhaps few women would have the fortitude to follow even today. She was offered everything that society dictated that a young woman could desire: that is, marriage to a handsome, personable young man with a comfortable living who could take care of her forever and allow her to follow her vocation as a writer without ever having to worry about where money came from. Instead, she turned him down and pursued her own course independently. Readers could understand how she might want to try her own wings, to find out just what she could do and who she was.

Readers for generations have seen that, to the extent that Jo refuses to let her life as a woman be predictable, she takes on the heroic qualities admired by classical thinkers.

Additional Readings: Ruth K. MacDonald, *Louisa May Alcott* (Boston: Twayne, 1983); Martha Saxon, *Louisa May: A Modern Biography of Louisa May Alcott* (Boston: Houghton Mifflin, 1977); Madeleine Stern, ed., *Critical Essays on Louisa May Alcott* (Boston: G.K. Hall, 1984).

140. *Black Beauty*, by Anna Sewell (United States, 1877). In the *Encyclopedia of Animal Rights and Animal Welfare* published by Greenwood Press in 1998, *Black Beauty*, by Anna Sewell, is referred to as the most influential anticruelty novel of all time. Cruelty to animals persists even in the twenty-first century, as anyone who reads the newspaper knows. But the difference between such acts today and in 1877, when the novel *Black Beauty* appeared, is that such acts are much rarer now, and when they do occur, they make headlines in newspapers. Then and now, human attitudes toward animals promote or allow cruel behavior. It derives from the notion that Man is the supreme creature, favored by God, and is free to use animals as he wants. Cruelty has also been justified by the argument that animals have no real feelings and no intelligence, that animals are property that a person has a sacred right to deal with as he pleases.

Writers in the nineteenth century record cruelty to animals that is sadistic and without reason. In the *Adventures of Huckleberry Finn*, for instance, men set fire to a dog on whom they have poured turpentine and "sic" dogs on a nursing sow. And then, as today, people cause unusual pain to animals in providing themselves with food: raising chickens or calves for veal in pens that restrict movement, castrating or branding cattle without anesthesia. Fashion and fad, like docking a dog's tail or cropping its ears, also continue today.

The American father of anticruelty law in America was Henry Bergh, who in 1866 founded the American Society for the Prevention of Cruelty to Animals (ASPCA) and saw the first anticruelty legislation enacted (in New York State) in the same year. The second most active ASPCA was established in Massachusetts in 1868 by George Thorndike Angell.

Many works of literature have been written to promote a change of heart in the cruel treatment of animals, but the first one of significance and the one with the widest impact was without a doubt Anna Sewell's *Black Beauty*, a work dictated by the author to her mother and published posthumously. In the novel's subtitle, a comparison is made between Sewell and Harriet Beecher Stowe, between *Black Beauty* and the most important social protest, antislavery novel in America: The subtitle, "*The Uncle Tom's Cabin* of the Horse," suggests that Sewell's novel will help liberate animals from cruelty, just as Stowe's novel helped liberate the slaves.

To accomplish her purpose, Sewell told

her story from the point of view of the animal, Black Beauty, with the effect of giving the animal human feelings and thoughts. This episodic narrative with scant plot moves from one scene of cruelty to animals to the next, from one testimony of cruelty to the next. The emphasis is on accepted human practices in the treatment of horses and dogs—practices that were not deemed cruel: tail bobbing, risky jumping during fox hunts; and the use of blinkers, double-bits, and check reins. But reference is also made to cruel treatment of animals other than horses, for example, the hunting of rabbits and foxes for sport. Sewell, through the voice of Black Beauty and other horses in the novel, generates the greatest outrage over mutilations in the name of fashion. Many readers realized for the first time that the docking of horses' tails left them no way to flick away flies and that the clipping of dogs' ears left their inner ears unprotected.

The publication of *Black Beauty* was sponsored by the Massachusetts ASPCA and was introduced by Angell Thorndike. Its phenomenal success was credited with boosting the activity and interest in anticruelty societies and anticruelty legislation across the nation. For decades 250,000 copies were sold annually. Throughout the twentieth century, it continued in print, going through numerous editions. It has also been made into films.

The novel also heightened public awareness of what constituted cruelty, especially toward animals who were beaten or overburdened with heavy loads. The public also became aware that it was usually human abuse that made many animals bad-tempered.

Many procedures to which Sewell objected are retained even today, especially on specialized animals such as walking horses, hackney ponies, quarter horses, and race horses. She was not able to save dogs from tail and ear mutilation. But her novel, told from the point of view of the horse, led to a more compassionate attitude toward animals in general and to legislation that outlawed the more egregious cruelty to animals like rubbing kerosene on the feet of horses to cause

them to pick up their feet and draining the blood of quarter horses to make them trot slower.

Moreover, Sewell's novel has been responsible for generations of young people falling in love with horses and maintaining a lifelong affection for animals.

Additional Readings: George T. Angell, *Autobiographical Sketches and Personal Recollections* (Boston: Franklin Press, 1884); Susan Chitty, *The Woman Who Wrote Black Beauty* (London: Hodder and Stoughton, 1971); Ellen B. and Anne Grimshaw, *The Annotated Black Beauty* (London: J.A. Allen, 1989).

141. *The Portrait of a Lady,* **by Henry James (United States, England, 1881, 1908).** *The Portrait of a Lady* is the story of an American woman's interaction with Europe in the second half of the nineteenth century. The entire culture at the time had felt the impact of the new science and skepticism in general. In an intellectual climate that encouraged the questioning of tradition, post–Civil War America was struggling to define its own culture as distinct from that of England and Europe. At the same time there was still the perception that European art and education were superior to that of America. Whereas America seemed to be a place of action and nature, Europe was a place of civilization and the mind. America came to represent a kind of innocence, while Europe came to represent experience. James, who excelled in the novel of the American abroad, was especially sensitive to the complexities of national identities.

Sigmund Freud's modern psychoanalysis was yet to make itself known in the nineteenth century, but interest in the intricacies of the human mind and character was very much in the atmosphere as James was writing his most famous novel. At the time, his brother William, with whom he was closely associated, had already established his reputation as a lecturer on psychology, a blending of theology and medicine.

The Portrait of a Lady reveals James's interest in the newly developing psychology and national identities. The protagonist of the novel is Isabel Archer, a young, inexperienced American woman who, through the endeavors of her friend Ralph Touchett, suddenly finds herself in possession of a tidy fortune. Although Touchett likes and admires Isabel, his motives in arranging for her to receive the money are not wholly benevolent: He says that he is curious to see what she will do, what will happen to her, should she become an heiress. Unfortunately, the money does not work to her advantage. She becomes the target of a skilled, charming fortune hunter whom she is duped into marrying. Not until she has developed a great affection for Pansy, his young relative, does she learn his true nature, that he is a faithless philanderer and that Pansy is his daughter by his mistress. Furthermore, there seems to be no satisfactory physical union between Isabel and her husband. Long after she has been married, it is a steadfast young American admirer who seems to sexually awaken Isabel with a kiss. When the moment presents itself for Isabel to make the decision to leave her husband for the man who really loves her, she decides to stay with her husband for the sake of his daughter Pansy.

James's novel was immensely popular, but from the start, it quickly became an American classic. The influence of the novel does not lie in the fact that it addresses a particular social issue (as his more feminist *The Bostonians* did); instead, it introduces his readers to a story that is entirely psychological in its action, leading to a redefinition of "adventure." In short, the novel insists that internal action is of greater significance than physical action and that psychological courage is more important than physical courage.

Despite James's own choice to be a resident of England, spending much of his time in the rest of Europe, as a writer, he provided America with an admirable national identity by contrasting the American with the European. In *The Portrait of a Lady*, it is the Americans who, while naive and unpolished, still display the greater qualities of honesty, openness, ability, and energy.

Additional Readings: Millicent Bell, *Meaning in Henry James* (Cambridge, MA: Harvard University Press, 1991); Daniel Mark Fogel, ed., *A Companion to Henry James Studies* (Westport, CT: Greenwood Press, 1993).

142. *Adventures of Huckleberry Finn*, by Mark Twain (United States, 1884–85). The most famous work by Mark Twain, America's realist/humorist, is one of the darkest, most complex books in the American canon. It is also, without question, one of the most influential books ever written, in that it defined and differentiated American culture as distinct from England and Europe and challenged every conceivable nineteenth-century value and tradition. The United States into which the novel appeared was a divided country, having just barely survived a barbarous civil war between North and South over the question of slavery. Although the war had officially ended slavery, freed blacks in the South were free in name only. They still labored under the conditions of a system of convict labor and contract arrangements that were often worse than slavery. Southern gentry, while much reduced in circumstances, still clung to the romantic ideals of Sir Walter Scott, calling themselves "colonels," clinging steadfastly to an appearance of aristocratic grace, and violently challenging as a matter of "honor" anyone who "insulted" them.

These were some of the values and situations that Twain brought into question. His radical masterpiece has a deceptively simple picaresque plot that has led many people to miscategorize it as a carefree boy's book. During Huck's and Jim's adventures they encounter ruthless criminals aboard a sinking ship called the *Walter Scott*, two scoundrels who call themselves "the king" and "the duke," two families who are determined to exterminate each other in a feud, and a "colonel" who shoots down an unarmed drunk in the street. In the final chapters, Jim is captured and held as a runaway slave on the Phelps farm. Tom Sawyer arrives to join Huck and to insist on a painfully protracted game of freeing Jim according to the rules of romance novels, even though he has known all along that Jim has been freed by his owner. At the last, Huck turns his back on civilization and heads out west.

The immediate reaction to the book was mixed. Most of the public and reviewers, both North and South, were outraged. Libraries refused to have it on their shelves. As late as 1907, teachers and libraries were being instructed to steer clear of the book. The board of the Concord, Massachusetts, library in 1885 was typical. They described it as immoral, exhibiting coarse humor, rough, and inelegant. During Twain's lifetime it was banned from the public libraries of Brooklyn, Denver, and Omaha, to name a few. Every Boston newspaper, plus the *Century*, the *Republican*, the *Critic*, the *Chicago Tribune*, and many others, condemned the book unfit for young people because its hero was dirty, uncouth, and uneducated, scratched himself, and used the word "sweat" instead of "perspiration." He smoked, skipped school, spoke ungrammatically, lied, and stole. In an age of religious fervor, not only did the book's hero not go to church, but he inadvertently mocks prayer, heaven and hell, churchgoers, temperance, revivals, and Bible stories. Its unsavory scenes included one of a naked dead man in an abandoned whore house, the dragging of a river for Huck's body, vicious child beatings, thieves planning to kill one of their own gang, animal torture, the shooting down of an unarmed man, the digging up of a corpse at midnight, and the tarring and feathering of two con men.

Twain's book ranks ninth in the thirty most frequently banned books in America. Although the most admirable person in the book is a black man, and the author's chief message is a condemnation of his slavery, at mid-twentieth century, the book began to be challenged once more on the grounds that the characters it contained spoke the racial epithets common to its day and included unflattering stereotypes of black people.

On the positive side, the work, which has endured as few others have, had a profound influence on most of its readers. Readers found in it a condemnation of the labor systems of the defeated South that, like Tom Sawyer, had perpetuated the enslavement of an emancipated people. It also emphasized the hypocrisy and bloody violence of the prevailing Walter Scott code of honor in the episode in which Colonel Sherburn shoots down an unarmed man in the street and a white-suited patriarch encourages a bloody feud.

The greatest impact the book had was as a cultural declaration of independence for Americans. His readers realized for the first time that the American experience could be the stuff of great art. Although well-known American writers before Twain placed their action and characters in the United States, earlier novels were, for the most part, anglicized. But in Twain readers found American landscapes, characters, and regional dialects. They were also exposed to a book that deflated the pomposity of English and European models (in its characters called the king and the duke, for example, and in Tom's destructive games inspired by French and English literature). Twain's American revolution was based on turning attributes associated with Europe and England upside down. So civilization, associated with the Old World, is cruel and senseless when compared with Nature, associated with the New World. And pernicious European civilization encompasses traditions of honor and chivalry, organized religion, manners, rigid class distinctions, and a perverse code of morality that tells Huck it is wrong to help a runaway slave. In short, Twain's book reached a wide audience and completely changed the way Americans regarded themselves, inspiring the confidence in national character that Ralph Waldo Emerson had hoped to do in "The American Scholar."

Additional Readings: Shelley Fisher Fishkin, ed., *Lighting Out for the Territory: Reflections on Mark Twain and American Culture* (New York: Oxford University Press, 1996); Maxwell Geismar, *Mark Twain: An American Prophet* (New York: McGraw-Hill, 1970); Claudia Durst Johnson, *Understanding the Adventures of Huckleberry Finn* (Westport, CT: Greenwood Press, 1996).

143. *Ramona*, by Helen Hunt Jackson (United States, 1885). One of the most influential books of late-nineteenth-century America was written by a woman committed to helping the Native American at a time of high drama in relations between Indians and whites. Nine years before the appearance of the novel, Custer's defeat at the Little Big Horn had inflamed anti-Indian feeling, permitting the roundup of the Sioux Indians into prison compounds and reservations. In 1877, Chief Joseph had led the surviving Nez Perce tribe just short of safety in Canada when they were overtaken by the U.S. cavalry and sent to an Oklahoma compound, where they died. The next year, the same fate awaited the Utes. By then most Indians had been forced onto reservations; if they left, they were caught and dragged back. In 1885, the year in which the novel appeared, great pressure was being placed on the federal government to open Oklahoma lands to whites; Oklahoma was at the time the last Indian stronghold, a place to which Indians from all over the East Coast had been forced before the Civil War by Andrew Jackson.

The history most directly relevant to the novel's plot, however, occurred shortly after thousands of people from the East arrived in California just after 1849, looking for gold. Many who abandoned all hope of finding a fortune in gold to take back with them to families in the East squatted on land in California owned by Native Americans and Mexicans. Some of these ranches included vast acreage; some did not. No matter the size, the white settlers' claims on land in California, which achieved U.S. statehood soon after the gold rush started, meant that land titles remained matters of controversy well into the twentieth century.

Ramona is the story of a young woman, daughter of an Irish father and a Native American mother, who is raised by a wealthy Mexican landowner. At the death of her foster parents, she is moved to the house of her foster mother's sister, Señora Morena, a woman who dislikes her because she is part Indian.

Ramona falls in love with an Indian named Alessandro. When Señora Morena threatens to send Ramona to a convent to stop the marriage, she and her lover elope. But his people have been driven from their village by whites who want their land. The couple must go to San Diego to look for work. When they accumulate enough money, they buy a farm. All goes well with them until white settlers want their farm, too. As a result, they are forced to move to the mountains, where a confused and depressed Alessandro is mistakenly shot dead.

Ramona, near death, is rescued by her childhood friend, a wealthy Mexican, who nurses her back to health. Upon taking Ramona back to his house and ranch, however, he discovers that white settlers are also moving in there. The couple, now married, decide to move to Mexico, convinced that their land will be taken, no matter where they decide to live in the United States.

Ramona, which had a phenomenally large readership, was one of the most popular novels of the 1880s. Its influence was immediate, practical, and political, as well as artistic and cultural. When it appeared, it was immediately compared in its impact to Harriet Beecher Stowe's *Uncle Tom's Cabin* and described as one of the most ethical works of the nineteenth century. It is credited with essentially changing the way that a public (long used to Indian hating) viewed Native Americans, creating great sympathy for their plight through the suffering of Ramona.

The novel was directly responsible for the passage of the 1886 Dawes Severalty Act. By means of this legislation, 160 acres of land were given to each Indian family but held in trust by the government for twenty-five years to keep Indians from being tricked or cheated out of what was rightfully theirs, as they had been so many times before. Unfortunately, despite decent motives in the passage of this act, it somehow made it easier for whites to assume Indian land.

Ramona also had a tremendous influence on tourism and settlement of California as many settlers and visitors from the East indicated that they had been attracted to the West by their reading of the book and its lush descriptions of the southern part of the state.

Many readers of the book found the "mission style" described there romantic and attractive, and creations of mission-style buildings, which they had learned about in *Ramona*, sprang up all over the United States.

Ramona's influence was spread through stage and screen productions, including a song with enduring popularity, titled "Ramona."

Additional Readings: Evelyn I. Banning, *Helen Hunt Jackson* (New York: Vanguard Press, 1973); Valerie Sherer Mathes, *Helen Hunt Jackson and Her Indian Reform Legacy* (Austin: University of Texas Press, 1990).

144. *Looking Backward*, by Edward Bellamy (United States, 1888). *Looking Backward* is a utopian novel in which the author, by projecting his hero into the future (the year 2000), criticized the capitalist system of his own day (in the year 1887). *Looking Backward* dramatically influenced American thought and particularly American socialist reformers for the next half century. Its impact has been compared to that of *Uncle Tom's Cabin*.

It appeared in 1888, in a time of great industrial poverty, labor unrest, violence, terrible slums, and the wretched hovels and dead-end alleys without hope in which the unfortunates lived as the nineteenth century neared its end—the kind of places that Jacob Riis exposed in searing photographs and other reformers (called "Muckrakers" by Theodore Roosevelt) wrote about in blistering articles. In New York City a girl of six worked from predawn darkness till after nightfall to earn six cents a day, went home where her large family lived in one small basement room. The normal work schedule was a sixty-hour, six-day week. At the same time the richest church in New York earned a great part of its fortune as the largest owner of the most terrible slums, collecting rent from the same wretches that its religion enjoined it to love. Employers used every means possible to prevent labor from organizing and to keep wages at starvation level. The greatest troop mobilization since the

Civil War was required to prevent working people from organizing.

At the same time, capitalists generally admired the success of men like J.P. Morgan, Jay Gould, Andrew Carnegie, Rockefeller, the collective Robber Barons, and those others who gathered in Newport for weekend parties and spread hidden diamonds as party favors for elegant guests to find in their sandpiles.

The novel is the story of Julian West who finds himself in the year 2000, when all the old world's problems have been solved: All competition has vanished, and the government now runs everything as "one great business corporation." Money no longer exists. Neither does poverty. One makes purchases in accordance with his own share of the national system. Education, now efficient and excellent, is provided for all. In contrast to the limited possibilities for young women in 1887, society in 2000 provides opportunities for female workers as well, giving them time off from careers to have children if they choose. Furthermore, all jobs are considered equal, so there are no fractious class distinctions and no quarrels. Those who do not work are jailed. All this is run by an industrial army, a universal organization that sees to the running of the system. In the new order, private enterprise has vanished. Each citizen is now an employee of the state. The collective organization has eliminated crime, poverty, warfare, and many diseases. And they have raised the cultural level of the country. The real impact comes from Bellamy's trenchant criticism of the capitalistic, and egregiously barbaric, life in his own world of 1887 and in his complementary suggestions that problems can actually be solved.

For the new utopia, there must be a massive conversion—not just material manipulation but a true conversion to a new ethical awareness.

The book sold 60,000 copies the first year; the second year it sold over 100,000. By 1897, the number reached 400,000. It was wildly received in Europe, especially in Russia. It has never been out of print.

The book's influence on a variety of reformers was phenomenal. Educator John Dewey and historian Charles Beard declared that, as a social philosophy, Bellamy's book was second in importance only to Karl Marx's *Das Kapital.* Among others who felt the impact of the book were Norman Thomas, head of the American Socialist Party, and Upton Sinclair, author of *The Jungle.* Labor pioneer Eugene Debs said that the book made him a socialist, and Clement Atlee, former British prime minister, claimed that the British Labour Party was founded on Bellamy's principles. Not only did the book profoundly influence the labor movement in the United States, but writer Maxim Gorky even considered Bellamy an influence on Russian radicals. Ironically, the principles of the book were eventually reflected in U.S. economic theory.

"Bellamy" or "Nationalist" clubs were formed by people, impatient with talk alone, to promote the kind of reforms that he had written about. In Boston, the first club was sponsored by the *Globe* and the labor editor of the *Herald.* Membership included a varied group: theosophists, Christian socialists, and militarists. By 1890, some 500 Nationalist clubs had been formed throughout the country.

In addition to success on the East Coast, floods of orders came from the West and from the Farm Belt. Clergymen used it as topics for sermons. While not everyone agreed with its implied recommendations for the future, all wrestled with the ideas.

The novel is consistently included on lists of the ten most important and influential books written.

Additional Readings: Sylvia Bowman, *Edward Bellamy* (Boston: G.K. Hall, 1986); *Looking Backward, 1988–1888,* ed. Daphne Patai (Amherst: University of Massachusetts Press, 1988).

145. *A Hazard of New Fortunes,* **by William Dean Howells (United States, 1890).** *A Hazard of New Fortunes,* which Howells considered his most important work, was the first great novel about the new urban-industrial turmoil in the United States, a narrative that gave direction to America's progressive thinking at the turn of the century. Events in the 1880s forced this nonviolent man to confront the prospect that violence was the inevitable result of the class struggle. *A Hazard of New Fortunes* was the culmination of his alarm over the potential for violence.

In the last years of the 1880s, social unrest erupted everywhere. In 1886 alone, 10,000 strikes seriously disrupted the American economy. Howells had the dubious opportunity of observing a particularly rancorous strike, the New York traction strike, at close hand. He noted the reasonable demands on the part of the workers and the intransigence of large corporations who controlled the city's transportations system. One day during this strike, Howells saw a penniless immigrant grab a dirty piece of bread from the gutter and devour it hungrily. He was appalled at the existence of such hunger, such massive poverty in a rich and productive country like the United States.

A Hazard of New Fortunes was strongly influenced by the Haymarket Riot of 1886 and Howells's own futile attempt in the wake of that event to marshal the country's reformers in the cause of justice. In 1886, when workers at the McCormick Reaper Works in Chicago, subjected to a general lockout, picketed the plant, a clash between workers and scab replacements led to police interference. Several workers were brutally beaten and two died. The next evening protesters, including workers, political radicals, and the mayor of Chicago, gathered at Haymarket Square. After an uneventful evening and following the mayor's departure, the police moved with force to hasten an already dispersing crowd. A bomb went off, killing one policeman, fatally wounding six others, and injuring dozens more. The police then began firing into the crowd, wounding many.

The result was national hysteria, fomented largely by a sensational press; eight anarchists were tried and convicted, not because they were guilty but because they were anarchists. Seven of them were sentenced to hang. In the wild mood that followed, socialists, anarchists, radicals, "foreign" agitators of all sorts, and even mild reformers became incarnate devils in the public mind, threatening and undermining everything America held dear. Howells, unable to marshal his former abolitionist publishers and friends to the cause of the anarchists, went out on a limb alone to denounce the courts publicly, but only a few days afterward, the anarchists were executed.

A Hazard of New Fortunes, set in New York City where Howells had moved from New England to work for *Harper's*, reflects the new urban face of America, to which myriad immigrants, exploited by industrialism, had brought the more revolutionary European approach to social problems. This novel was a graphic portrayal of a great city pulled apart by social strife and the dilemma of an artist torn between the demands of art and his social conscience. Basil March, the novel's main character, is like Howells, himself, in many ways—a journalist committed to observing with fascination and apprehension the effect of immigrants on the political scene and to the necessity of drawing the attention of his readers to the plight of the urban poor. The novel introduces a theme of fatalism and determinism in both personal relationships and in the larger economic structure of the society, as financial pressures place impossible strains on the city's families.

A Hazard of New Fortunes sold twice as many copies, Howells noted, as had any of his previous novels. Sales reached 19,000 in the first six months and exceeded 23,000 in the first year: a significant and impressive figure when popular romances were increasingly dominating the market.

The reputation that Howells already enjoyed at the time of the novel's appearance guaranteed that his new novel would be taken seriously. In many ways it registered a turning point in his thinking that profoundly influenced his readers, themselves struggling with the outrage at social injustice as well as fear of working-class violence.

Howells had, through his fiction and criticism, drawn attention to the problems of rampant capitalism, materialism, and class

conflict, but he had always recommended optimism and faith in the human spirit. To these ends, he had refused to exploit sordidness (as France's Emile Zola had) or to condone violent revolution (as radical Russian writers had done). But the events leading up to *A Hazard of New Fortunes* had tempered his views in many ways. Through this new novel, by a man with a reputation for being reasonable and responsible, the country saw more vividly the character and result of industrial capitalism after the Civil War, the formation of large monopolies, the grinding poverty, the decline in morality, and the stress on profit alone. In *A Hazard of New Fortunes* Howells emphasized the strain the system had placed on all traditional forms and values and the human tragedy that resulted when economic, political, social, and philosophical changes created havoc for the poor and the powerless.

Through the novel, readers were also shown that socialism was a reasonable approach to current problems, a suggestion that was considered heretical at the time.

Howells's old optimism was muted by the incipient determinism of the novel, the suggestion that characters are at the mercy of forces beyond their control.

Finally, readers saw the novel as a warning that while violence was deplorable and futile, it was inevitable as long as reasonable social reforms were rejected.

Howells's immense influence was acknowledged repeatedly, especially on the occasion of his seventy-fifth birthday celebration, when he was praised by no less a dignitary than the president of the United States, William Howard Taft.

Additional Readings: John W. Crowley, *The Late Career of William Dean Howells, the Dean of American Letters* (Amherst: University of Massachusetts Press, 1999); Kermit Vanderbilt, *The Achievement of William Dean Howells* (Princeton, NJ: Princeton University Press, 1968).

146. *The Red Badge of Courage*, by Stephen Crane (United States, 1895). Stephen Crane's famous novel about the American Civil War, one of the first complex works about the horrors of war, has served as an antiwar testament for over 100 years. The world into which the novel made its first appearance was deeply colored by the Civil War. Every community, North and South, contained many men who had seen battle. By the time of the novel's publication, stories of the utter devastation and suffering during the war had begun to fade and were being transformed by Union soldiers into exciting tales of danger and bravery. In literature as well as retold personal memories, what was called the genteel tradition prevailed. The usual characters in the tradition were either romantic farmers or members of polite, upper-class society. The hero of war stories in this tradition was usually the upper-class, romantic young officer who never wavered in his devotion and courage. Any unpleasantness in general was brushed over and sufficiently covered up to keep the hearer or reader from discomfort.

Every boy, like Crane himself in this postwar period, grew up listening to stories told by the veterans in their villages. To the surprise of many readers at the time, who were convinced by the novel's authenticity that Crane had fought in the Union Army, he was not even born until 1871, some six years after the war ended; at the time, he wrote that his novel had never even "smelled the powder of a sham battle." For generations of soldiers the novel articulated the multiple sensations that surface in time of battle: the impulse to protect one's reputation, the nature of courage, the fear of extinction, the nature of heroism, the pressures exerted on the individual by the group, the impersonal character of nature and "the gods," and the role of warfare or any momentous tragedy in coming to manhood. These themes are present in the story of young Henry Fleming, opening near a battlefield as he wonders how he will meet the challenge of face-to-face combat. The first time he meets the chaos of battle, he is proud of himself for standing firm and continuing to fire his rifle. But after a brief respite he and his comrades are again sent into battle. This time he throws down his gun and flees. Before he can return to his

regiment, he is himself hit over the head with a rifle by a fellow soldier, sees one of his friends die, deserts a man who is near death, and attempts to rationalize his own cowardice. The next morning when he again goes into battle, he is fiercer than all the rest. After numerous battles and lulls in the fighting throughout the day, he contemplates his own behavior, both his cowardice and bravery.

The novel has had an enduring influence on its readers as a deflation of bravery. Readers had been used to the novels of Thomas Nelson Page and Charles King who romanticized the Civil War as a noble adventure of brave and handsome officers made even more attractive by their wounds. But Crane diminished the concept of bravery and the glory of war itself. Henry Fleming suspects that his bravery has a common source with his cowardice, that it is all pure instinct over which he has had little control. Both his heroism and his cowardice seem to come from his lowest, animal side. He also fears that he and the other soldiers have little choice in what they do. Their paths seem determined by nature, by blind gods, by the government, by the officers. Not until the writing of Ernest Hemingway would bravery be so effectively brought into question.

The novel also showed its readers through stark naturalism—the first time in English—that war is not genteel and glorious. The usual comment on the part of astute reviewers and readers was that Crane gave them a new view of war. For example, he describes a soldier's corpse in unblinking detail—his eyes staring and dull, his lips yellowed, and ants running over his lips.

On a more mundane level of iconoclasm, the novel undermined for its readers what were once inevitably regarded as the soldier's noble leaders—the officers. These men curse the young soldiers, derisively call them "mule-drivers," and gallop around pretentiously on horseback, sometimes running down the wounded men, who fear them as much as the enemy.

The immediate response to the novel was not entirely commendatory. The *New York Tribune* and *The Philadelphia Press* are illustrative of the outrage generated by the novel. The novel struck them as tedious and grotesque. The chief complaint was about the naturalism of the novel: its "brutal coarseness," "decadent morbidity," and profanities. Others complained that the book would worsen relations between North and South.

Despite these reactions, the initial response to the novel was largely very positive from both soldiers and literary reviewers, on the grounds that it was the first starkly true study of the psychology of war. A number of Union veterans even mistakenly bragged that Stephen Crane had served in their outfits.

The popularity of the novel has never diminished in its hundred-year history. Each generation, which finds itself fighting wars, has turned to Crane's work, increasingly finding antiwar arguments in it that were rarely mentioned by earlier readers. After both world wars, Crane's novel had an increase in readership. During the Vietnam War *The Red Badge of Courage* was read more avidly than ever before by those who found it to be America's first antiwar novel. Soldiers were amazed to find that this sixty-year-old novel gave expression to their own feelings about the conditions of battle and its psychological pressures.

Additional Readings: Sculley Bradley, Richmond Croom Beatty, and E. Hudson Long, eds., *Norton Critical Edition of* The Red Badge of Courage (New York: W.W. Norton, 1976); Claudia Durst Johnson, *Understanding* The Red Badge of Courage (Westport, CT: Greenwood Press, 1998).

147. *The Awakening*, by Kate Chopin (United States, 1899). Kate Chopin's novel appeared in 1899, at the end of the Victorian era, a century marked by excessive prudishness, repressed sexuality, and restrictions of many kinds on female behavior. Polite society and Victorian medicine taught that decent ladies were not sexual, intelligent, or independent of men in any way. Only prostitutes enjoyed sex; decent women submitted to sex in marriage only to please their husbands. It was believed that considerable mental activity was not natural to a woman and

that too much thinking would make her physically and mentally ill. Reading and engagement with the world outside the house were regarded as morally risky and physically and mentally disabling. When physicians were puzzled by a woman's disorders, they often ordered that she have no intellectual stimulation and take to her bed and stay there. Every aspect of a woman's character and life was supposed to be subordinated to, engulfed by, her husband's. The upper- and middle-class wife was typically regarded as a commodity and a convenience, required by men to bear their children, keep their houses in order, and when appropriate, arrange a social life that would advance their husbands in their businesses.

Kate Chopin's novel, strongly influenced by the French writer Gustave Flaubert, boldly challenged these views of women and marriage. Her main character, Edna Pontellier, is the "trophy wife" of a well-to-do New Orleans businessman. He is not a bad man or a bad husband. But he has his own life apart from her, believes that her whole purpose in marriage is to serve him, and is not unusual for his time in treating her as if she were a child.

A combination of events begin to "awaken" Edna. For the first time, she begins to learn to swim and is attracted to a young artist who converses with her as if she is an intelligent human being. Gradually she experiences the awakening of her independent self, first refusing to entertain her husband's business associates, then moving out of the house to her own modest quarters. She takes up serious painting, offers comfort to a friend who is, unlike herself, a natural mother-woman, and entertains her younger male friend. Whether they consummate their love is left ambivalent, but she feels a sexual awakening for the first time when he kisses her. By the novel's end, society is threatening to place her in a bind. Edna cannot fulfill her duty to herself at the same time she fulfills her duty to the sons she loves. So she swims out into the sea, which has come to symbolize freedom, and drowns.

When Kate Chopin's novel first appeared,

it was considered a scandalous flaunting of conventional morality and social convention. Here was a sympathetic portrayal of a woman who had turned her back on her marriage and children. Moreover, Chopin's novel depicted female passion as neither immoral nor sick. The book was thoroughly condemned by major newspapers, especially those in her home area of the Midwest. It was described as a morbid, unhealthy book. The book seemed to have few admirers. The publication of *The Awakening* literally killed Kate Chopin's career as a writer. At the time of the book's appearance, she had signed a contract with a publisher to issue her book of short stories, *A Vocation and a Voice*. But after *The Awakening*, the contract was summarily canceled. Within six years, the novel was out of print. Not until 1961 was *The Awakening* reissued.

Only at this point did Kate Chopin's novel begin to have an impact, and its influence was and continues to be exceptional. Ironically, it was her novel, written in the nineteenth century, that awakened the twentieth-century woman to her own possibilities. Even though it was written so many years before, it was the first work of fiction to reach women with a message of independence and fulfillment beyond motherhood and the confines of the home.

The message of woman's double-bind, no less true in the last half of the twentieth century than it was at the end of the nineteenth, is articulated by the physician in *The Awakening* who says to Edna that woman's biology entraps her in a family with children before she has an opportunity to grow up. It was a message that reached scores of women with the growth of women's studies beginning in the 1960s, for *The Awakening* was included not only in women's studies courses throughout the country but in all standard college anthologies of American literature. The book, which had disappeared from print in 1906, reappeared half a century later to become the foundation of modern feminism.

Additional Readings: Lynda S. Boren and Sara deSaussure Davis, eds., *Kate Chopin Reconsidered: Beyond the Bayou* (Baton Rouge: Louisiana State University Press, 1992); Emily Toth, *Kate Chopin: A Life of the Author of "The Awakening"* (New York: Morrow, 1990).

1900–1939

෧෨

Theodore Dreiser, *Sister Carrie*, 1900

Frank Norris, *The Octapus. The Story of California*, 1901

Owen Wister, *The Virginian: A Horseman of the Plains*, 1902

Andy Adams, *The Log of a Cowboy*, 1903

Jack London, *The Call of the Wild*, 1903

Upton Sinclair, *The Jungle*, 1906

James Weldon Johnson, *The Autobiography of an Ex-Colored Man*, 1912

Zane Grey, *Riders of the Purple Sage*, 1912

Willa Cather, *My Antonia*, 1918

Edith Wharton, *The Age of Innocence*, 1920

Sinclair Lewis, *Babbitt*, 1922

Theodore Dreiser, *An American Tragedy*, 1925

F. Scott Fitzgerald, *The Great Gatsby*, 1925

Ernest Hemingway, *A Farewell to Arms*, 1929

William Faulkner, *The Sound and the Fury*, 1929

John Dos Passos, *U.S.A.*, 1930–38

Erskine Caldwell, *Tobacco Road*, 1932

Henry Roth, *Call It Sleep*, 1934

James T. Farrell, *Studs Lonigan*, 1932, 1935

Margaret Mitchell, *Gone With the Wind*, 1936

Zora Neale Hurston, *Their Eyes Were Watching God*, 1937

John Steinbeck, *The Grapes of Wrath*, 1939

1900–1939: TIMELINE

1900	Thirty-eight U.S. cities have a population of over 100,000 people, illustrating the shift from rural to urban living.
	Theodore Dreiser's *Sister Carrie* is published.
Early 1900s	Social and political life in the United States was dictated by the laissez-faire economics that had prevailed since the rise of the Industrial Revolution in the nineteenth century. Free enterprise, the sacredness of the profit motive, and the belief that government should not interfere with commerce had led to appalling abuses of workers, including children, and massive poverty. It had also led to monopolies that destroyed competition and placed the wealth of the nation in the hands of a few.
1901	A new Socialist Party is formed, led by Eugene V. Debs.
	Frank Norris's *The Octopus* is published. It is about events that occurred in 1880.
	Industrialist Andrew Carnegie sells the U.S. Steel Corporation for $250 million.
1902	Theodore Roosevelt breaks up railroad monopolies, beginning to bring them under federal control.
	Owen Wister's *The Virginian* is published. It is set in the 1880s and 1890s in Wyoming.

Statistics are published showing that for the past three years, two black people on average are lynched every week in the United States.

At this time, black workers make one third the money that whites take home for the same work.

1903	The Federal Court gives the government increasing power to regulate the country's railroads.
	Andy Adams's *The Log of a Cowboy* is published. It is set in the 1880s and 1890s.
	Jack London's *The Call of the Wild* is published.
	Henry Ford founds Ford Motor Company. The assembly line he inaugurates starts the Second Industrial Revolution.
1904	By this time 2 million U.S. workers are union members.
1904–08	During Theodore Roosevelt's administration, forty-three suits are filed against trusts; one of the results is an order to dissolve Standard Oil of New Jersey.
1905	The Industrial Workers of the World (the IWW, or Wobblies) organize. They are much more aggressive than most other unions, and many of their members belong to the Communist Party.
1906	Theodore Roosevelt uses the term "muckrake" in association with journalists and reformers who focus on the corrupt and unpleasant side

of American life. Reformers eagerly take on the name "Muckrakers."

The courts give the federal government the power to regulate interstate commerce.

Upton Sinclair's *The Jungle* is published.

As a result of investigations into the meatpacking industry, inspired by Sinclair's novel, the first Pure Food and Drug Law is enacted.

1907   A run on banks is caused by a money panic.

1909   W.E.B. Du Bois founds the National Association for the Advancement of Colored People.

1911   John D. Rockefeller's Standard Oil is ordered broken up into separate corporations by the U.S. Supreme Court.

Job efficiency, not always to the benefit of the worker, is promoted by Frederick W. Taylor's *The Principles of Scientific Management.*

1912   Zane Grey's *Riders of the Purple Sage* is published. The setting is the 1870s.

James Weldon Johnson's *The Autobiography of an Ex-Colored Man* is published.

J.P. Morgan, who owns a monopoly of steel production and other industries and businesses, is investigated by the House of Representatives.

Theodore Roosevelt bolts the Republican Party and forms the Progressive Party, popularly known as the Bull Moose Party.

1913   James Clark McReynolds, appointed as attorney general by Woodrow Wilson, oversees the prosecution of the United and Pacific Railroads and antitrust suits against International Harvester, American Telephone and Telegraph, and the New York, New Hampshire, and Hartford Railroads.

1914   The Federal Trade Commission is created to curb the unfair impediments to free trade by trust formation, and the Clayton Act legalizes some union activity.

1917   The United States enters World War I.

1918   Willa Cather's *My Antonia* is published.

Fighting in World War I ends with the defeat of Germany. U.S. casualties include 130,174 dead and 203,460 wounded. The United States has spent almost $42 billion dollars fighting World War I.

1919   World War I ends formally with the Treaty of Versailles.

An iron and steel strike involving 370,000 workers fails and damages union growth.

The American Communist Party is organized in Chicago, Illinois.

1920   Union membership reaches 5.1 million.

Suffrage for women is finally ratified by the Nineteenth Amendment to the Constitution.

Prohibition officially begins, eventually bringing with it a rise in criminal activity; notable are speakeasies (where illegal alcohol is sold), bootlegging, and rampant gangsterism.

1920s   Per capita income rose by 9 percent except for the richest 1 percent of the population, whose income rose by 75 percent. Corporate profits rose by 62 percent; dividends, by 65 percent; and wages, by only 9 percent.

Management meets falling profits by cutting wages and increasing workers' hours. Every two weeks many workers are called upon to work twenty-four-hour shifts.

Small independent farmers are neglected and do not share in the economic boom.

Edith Wharton's *The Age of Innocence* is published. It is set in the 1870s.

1921   Total farm income falls from a high of $17.7 million in 1919 to $10.5 million.

1922   Sinclair Lewis's *Babbitt* is published.

1924   Norman Thomas begins his leadership of the Socialist Party, which will contribute to policies embodied in Franklin Roosevelt's New Deal in the 1930s.

A constitutional amendment is offered to the states to regulate child labor, but an insufficient number of states adopt the measure, and it dies.

1925   Theodore Dreiser's *An American Tragedy* is published.

F. Scott Fitzgerald's *The Great Gatsby* is published.

In one of the most notorious trials of the century, which is in essence a trial about ideas, schoolteacher John T. Scopes is found guilty of a crime in teaching the theory of evolution.

1927   Radicals Nicola Sacco and Bartolomeo Vanzetti are executed after having been found guilty of a bombing, on questionable evidence.

1929   In Chicago, Illinois, a hotbed of Prohibition-type gangsterism, henchmen of leading gangster Al Capone seize control of underworld business by murdering seven people in Bugsy Moran's rival gang.

The stock market crashes, financially ruining many people who have taken out loans to buy stocks.

The average income for farm and factory workers in the United States is $750 a year. Henry Ford's income is $14 million a year.

Dreiser's *An American Tragedy* is banned in Boston.

Ernest Hemingway's *A Farewell to Arms* is published.

William Faulkner's *The Sound and the Fury* is published.

Thomas Wolfe's *Look Homeward, Angel* is published.

Huey Long, a flamboyant but highly effective Louisiana populist, begins his rise to power.

1930   A second banning in Boston of Dreiser's novel leads to attempts to reform Massachusetts obscenity laws, all of which fail to pass.

Sinclair Lewis becomes the first American to win the Nobel Prize for Literature.

Wages for backbreaking "stoop" labor in the fields of California are as low as ten cents an hour. The average pay for pea pickers is fifty-six cents a day.

Some 1,352 banks fail, causing financial disaster for the millions of people with money saved or invested in them.

Altogether 26,355 large corporations fail.

1930s   Throughout the Great Depression, 90,000 large businesses fail, putting millions of people out of work.

Production drops by 50 percent.

Thirty-seven percent of nonagricultural workers are unemployed.

It is common to find wages of five cents an hour or seventy-five cents a week.

Dust storms rage in the Bread Basket of the country, blowing away tons of topsoil and making farming impossible.

1930–36   John Dos Passos's *U.S.A.* is published.

1931   Some 2,294 banks fail.

Bank customers lose $531,774,004 in this year alone. In this year 28,285 corporations fail.

Panic causes U.S. citizens to take more than $250 million in gold out of the country in Herbert Hoover's last week in office.

One of the most notorious trials of the century begins when nine young black men are charged with raping two white women who are later found to have lied. The case doesn't have its final chapter until 1976 when, after repeated guilty findings and court reversals, the last of the Scottsboro "Boys" is pardoned.

1932 Sharecroppers have an average income of $100 a year.

An estimated 250,000 people lose their homes this year.

The public's anger is leveled particularly at law enforcement officers, who are often used by business owners against workers during strikes and at banks that have lost the life savings of customers and regularly foreclose on mortgages. Such is this anger that outlaws who rob banks become public heroes. In this year, for instance, Pretty Boy Floyd robs the bank in his hometown of Sallisaw, Oklahoma, in broad daylight, after casually announcing his plan to random friends he meets on the street.

Erskine Caldwell's *Tobacco Road* is published.

1933 Prohibition ends.

New York City welfare officials report that 139 children had died of starvation in the city this year.

The Tennessee Valley Authority is established to provide affordable power to the rural poor.

Before the year is out, President Roosevelt has enacted numerous radical reforms to improve the economy and alleviate the suffering of workers.

The stage version of Caldwell's *Tobacco Road* opens on Broadway and has a phenomenal run of 3,182 per-

formances, at the time the longest-running show in Broadway history.

1933–34 Ninety-nine strikes by farmworkers are recorded in a two-year period, involving 87,364 workers.

In California especially, owners and law enforcement officers react with violence, killing, wounding, and kidnapping union members and imprisoning hundreds of workers.

The National Industrial Recovery Act, one of many measures proposed by Franklin Roosevelt and passed by Congress to alleviate the suffering of workers, is declared unconstitutional by the Supreme Court.

1934 A General Strike of union members occurs throughout the United States. In San Francisco, California, demonstrators are shot by police in the streets. And in other places, strikers are intimidated, beaten, and sometimes killed.

Henry Roth's *Some Call It Sleep* is published.

1935 The CIO (Congress of Industrial Organizations) is formed. This will become the most effective association of labor unions.

James T. Farrell's *Studs Lonigan* is published.

1936 John Steinbeck's *In Dubious Battle* is published. It is an account of an agricultural strike and farmworkers organizing in California.

The Spanish Civil War, which pits antifascists against Francisco Franco, begins. It is a precursor of World War II and draws many volunteers from throughout the world, including the Abraham Lincoln Brigade of American men and women.

Margaret Mitchell's *Gone With the Wind* is published. The setting is the American Civil War and Reconstruction.

1937 Zora Neale Hurston's *Their Eyes Were Watching God* is published.

The novel is attacked by many African Americans and ignored by white readers until the 1970s.

1938   In the beginning of official harassment of social radicals that will continue for over two decades, the House of Representatives sets up a committee to investigate "un-American" activities.

The Fair Labor Standards Act is passed to protect workers by providing for the eight-hour day and forty-hour week.

1939   John Steinbeck's *The Grapes of Wrath* is published.

Carey McWilliams's exposé of the agricultural industry, *Factories in the Fields*, is published.

With Adolf Hitler's help, Franco wins in Spain. The deaths of Abraham Lincoln Brigade members have been heavy, and the returning veterans are routinely harassed by the U.S. government.

148. *Sister Carrie*, by Theodore Dreiser (United States, 1900).

Sister Carrie chronicles the rise from obscurity to fame of a young girl in a hard, cold, materialistic society at the turn of the twentieth century.

The story takes place in the nineteenth century, which saw the rise of an industrialism that was, for the worker, bitter, brutal, hard, and often hopeless. By the time Dreiser wrote, the system was at its worst, especially for female laborers like the young Carrie of his novel. The sweatshop system required women and girls to sew in factories all day, carry heavy loads home in the evening, and sew at home all night for a few cents a day. In factories, as late as 1893, women worked in damp basements and were exposed constantly to dangerous machinery and chemicals that ate through the skin on their fingers. Poor women who eked out meager livings were regarded as fair game for sexual exploitation, largely because the public believed that women who worked outside the home were morally suspect. Ironically, the most

disreputable work of all, performing in the theater, as Carrie comes to do, paid women better wages than anything else. The average pay for a clerking job such as Carrie's was $5 a week. At the same time Andrew Carnegie took in $25 million in profits from his steel mills. J.P. Morgan bought out Carnegie for $440 billion and was so powerful that he was able to challenge the president of the United States. Money ruled with an iron fist.

The plot centers primarily on three figures: Carrie Meeker, an eighteen-year-old girl seeking her fortune in Chicago and later New York; Charles Drouet, an affluent salesman with whom she lives in an effort to escape grinding poverty; and George Hurstwood, manager of an elegant saloon, whom Carrie accepts as a lover as a means of advancing herself. Hurstwood's downward spiral begins when he steals money for the saloon, money he is forced to return after he is discovered. In New York, where Hurstwood and Carrie have fled, he gradually sinks into poverty while Carrie, rising on the force of her youth and beauty, becomes first a chorus girl and finally an actress. The novel ends with Hurstwood's suicide and Carrie's triumphant success.

Dreiser's landmark novel had an inauspicious and unpromising beginning. The publisher, upon reading the whole manuscript, did everything he could to back out of the contract. Initially only 558 copies were bound for distribution. Some 500 unbound copies were burned and remaindered. Major journals ignored it. Critics of the day who did review it generally condemned the novel. Most critics found no beauty and no moral value in the novel, viewing it as an inducement to vice. A few, favoring revolt against the genteel tradition, increasingly praised it. Only when British publications gave enthusiastic reviews to a highly cut version did American critics become interested in the novel. By the end of the century, however, it had become one of the great, influential novels of the age. Since then, it has been widely taught and written about widely in academe. Its influence, as one of those novels that helps explain the complexities of modern man in the modern world, has spread dramatically.

One of Dreiser's innovations, which so profoundly shocked contemporary reviewers, was his refusal to express disapproval for the self-seeking life that Carrie led. Carrie is not at all concerned with morality or immorality. She is like a force of nature, moving to winds of change in a world where implacable currents leave individual beings little or no choice as to the pattern of their lives. The only thing that sets Carrie apart is her youth and beauty. Her chemical attractiveness carries her ever upward in this society. Readers were introduced to the view that in their world morality had nothing to do with the life force, or with success or failure or survival. In the early 1900s Dreiser's view of an amoral universe, driven by chance, was unacceptable, but in the late twentieth century, when views of a hostile or disinterested fate had long since been introduced, the novel began to rise in prestige and influence.

Although readers tended to have great sympathy for Carrie and for all Dreiser's lower-class laboring people, they found in his novel scant impetus to reform. Instead they found an amoral world in which one is driven like a leaf in a wind. Carrie and Hurstwood do not really struggle; they drift.

Dreiser was the first American novelist to expose his readers to the kind of naturalism made famous in France by Emile Zola; but while shaped by European models, the novel's naturalism derived primarily from Dreiser's own experiences growing up in poverty, as the eleventh of twelve children in a German immigrant family, and working in his formative years as a newspaper reporter in various places throughout the Midwest and in New York, while reading voraciously.

It was also Dreiser's *Sister Carrie* that introduced to America a novelistic application of Spencerian evolution to social situations. Dreiser, influenced by Charles Darwin's theory of evolution, was especially drawn by Herbert Spencer's philosophy based on it— the Social Darwinism of the "survival of the fittest," as Spencer called it, by means of which all of creation was seen as a congeries of implacable forces that gradually eliminated the weak and elevated the strong, without consideration of human morality. This was the pattern that Dreiser consistently portrayed and that earned him fame.

Additional Readings: Michael Davitt Bell, *The Problem of American Realism: Studies in the Cultural History of a Literary Idea* (Chicago: University of Chicago Press, 1993); Donald Pizer, ed., *New Essays on "Sister Carrie"* (New York: Cambridge University Press, 1991).

149. *The Octopus. The Story of California,* by Frank Norris (United States, 1901). Frank Norris, the father of American "muckraking," wrote *The Octopus*, the first of a planned trilogy, to expose corruption and exploitation in the wheat and railroad industries. The specific incident that inspired Norris and that he incorporated into the novel was the Mussel Slough massacre of 1880 in the San Joaquin Valley of California, which resulted when officials of the railroad tried to evict wheat farmers from land that the farmers had been promised. The wheat farmers had long suffered under the dishonest policies of railroad owners, who were allowed to buy up thousands of prime acreage on either side of the railroad itself with the promise that farmers could eventually buy the land at reasonable prices. When, added to the ever-higher charges for shipping grain by railroad, the Southern Pacific Railroad asked small fortunes for the land they owned, the farmers rebelled, and considerable bloodshed resulted.

At the same time, California wheat farmers were also becoming gigantic businesses, largely by paying their workers rock-bottom wages, providing them with slum housing, and requiring long hours.

Against this backdrop, Norris's book takes place. His title refers to the many arms of the railroad, like the tentacles of an octopus, which reach into every area of American life and, as Norris writes, go into the very soil. The book's three major characters are Vanamee, an immigrant shepherd; Annixter, a wealthy rancher; Behrman, a villainous railroad representative; and Presley, a poet turned reformer. At first, Presley refuses to come to the aid of farmhands who approach him with their grievances because he feels that he is sensitive and superior and they disgust him.

With ill-feeling rising among the farmworkers, against the wheat farmers, a different dispute arises between the railroad officials and the wheat farmers. The railroad continues to raise shipping prices, believing that if the farmers are making profits, they can pay more for shipping. Largely because of the railroad's machinations, one farmer, Dyke, goes bankrupt, becomes a criminal, and goes to prison.

Incensed at what he discovers about railroad practices, the poet Presley abandons the writing of an epic and writes a social protest poem called "The Toilers," which he publishes in the daily newspaper.

The situation worsens when the railroad refuses to sell land to the farmers at reasonable prices, as it had promised. Wheat growers even then lived on railroad land and had improved it. In a protracted war, the wheat farmers become as corrupt and ruthless as the railroad.

When the railroad officials try to evict the farmers, a gun battle ensues, in which the rancher Annixter is killed. His widow and daughter are left bankrupt and are forced to look for work in the city. They eventually die there of starvation outside a railroad banquet hall in San Francisco.

Presley throws a bomb into a railroad representative's house but then decides to reject violence. He slips out on a wheat ship to India, which is suffering a horrible famine. Behrman, the villainous railroad representative, slips into the wheat-filled ship's hold and suffocates.

The Octopus brought to the public's attention the underhanded dealings of the Southern Pacific Railroad in California at a time when unhappiness with railroads throughout the United States was widespread. He illustrated the human cost of industrial greed and was able to influence public opinion with his information about the railroad's monopoly, its political power, and its ability to set whatever prices it liked. That mood forced Congress to allow Theodore Roosevelt in the spring of 1902 to break up railroad monopolies and bring them under federal control. By 1903, the federal court gave government the power to prohibit certain practices as well as to regulate business, and in 1906 legislation was allowed that regulated interstate commerce.

Norris's book introduced what would become the commonplace idea that agriculture and industry were at odds with one another, that neither was interested in the public good, and that the public interest should take precedence over private profit. With *The Octopus*, the public mistrust of corporate America became more widespread. Norris's book can be credited with showing the need for government regulation of industry in general to protect the public, an idea that exploded on the scene with Franklin Roosevelt's New Deal.

Although many interpreted the book as a simple fight between decent farmers and big business, *The Octopus* was ahead of its time in showing the perfidy of California agribusiness and its exploitation of farmworkers. In the next few years, the beginning of a fight against farmers would ensue and would be marked by violence throughout the twentieth century.

Moreover, Norris led the way for American authors who wanted to address specific issues, especially the so-called Muckrakers like Upton Sinclair and writers of the 1930s such as John Steinbeck.

Additional Readings: William B. Dillingham, *Frank Norris: Instinct and Art* (Lincoln: University of Nebraska Press, 1969); Joseph R. McElrath, Jr., *Frank Norris Revisited* (New York: Twayne, 1992).

150. *The Virginian: A Horseman of the Plains,* **by Owen Wister (United States, 1902).** Owen Wister's *Virginian* was largely responsible for establishing the myth of the western frontier in the United States and throughout the world. For his story, Wister turned to the territory of Wyoming near the close of the nineteenth century. From its inception in 1869, the Wyoming territory had encouraged the development of large cattle ranches; the first laws passed included protection of cattle ranchers. By 1879, wealthy ranchers, many of them absentee, were a well-organized and protected group known as the Wyoming Stock Growers Association; they resisted federal regulation and mounted well-funded campaigns to keep out sheep farmers and small cattle ranchers by denying them association membership and accusing them of stealing. By the late 1880s, a series of natural and economic events had weakened the cattle business; large ranchers became convinced that their troubles arose from small ranchers who were stealing their cattle. Conflict erupted in 1892 in what came to be known as the Johnson County war, when wealthy ranchers in Wyoming hired gunmen from Texas to enter Wyoming, run down suspected thieves, and take justice into their own hands. In the course of this vigilante justice, two men were killed, while other county residents turned on the Texas vigilantes and the Wyoming ranchers who had hired them. Further violence was avoided when the government intervened and arrested the gunmen and wealthy ranchers responsible. However, they were freed, and no one was ever brought to trial. (A few years later, the controversial scout and lawman turned gunman Tom Horn was tried and executed for murder, in the same area.)

The title of the novel refers to the protagonist's place of origin and has nothing to do with the story's actual setting, which takes place in 1884, in this period of intense hatred between ranchers in Wyoming. A visitor from the East, who comes to Medicine Bow, Wyoming, where "the Virginian" works on Judge Henry's ranch, narrates the story. During a trip to the ranch, the narrator is able to observe the many attributes of the ranch hand: his social skills, his cunning, his mastery of his cowboy's skills, his card playing, and his success with the ladies. In this trip, the major plot is initiated. This is the romance between the eastern aristocratic Molly Wood and the Virginian. The subplot is also introduced on the trip to Judge Henry's

ranch: the Virginian's confrontation with the villainous rustler Trampas, who, when he insults the Virginian, is warned, "When you call me that, *smile*."

The chief escapades include the following: the Virginian is made foreman on the judge's ranch; he beats up a man who abuses animals; he is attacked by Indians and rescued by Molly; he wins Molly's affections; he discovers that his friend Steve is a rustler and is forced to hang him; Trampas challenges the Virginian on his and Molly's wedding day; to defend his honor, the Virginian kills Trampas; he marries Molly, visits her family in the East, and charms them.

When this novel was published, the subject of the western was regarded as low-brow and unfashionable. No one, including the publisher, foresaw the success of the novel. But two months after it was published, it had become a raging success, selling 50,000 copies and leading all the bestseller lists. In three months, it had sold 100,000 copies. By the end of 1902, it was declared the most popular book in America. Wister, who had dedicated the book to Theodore Roosevelt, was lionized in every quarter, invited to the White House repeatedly, and feted at Harvard University, his alma mater, as well as in houses of the rich in New York City and Newport. Wister's opinions on a wide range of topics were sought and treated with respect. At the same time, some of the novel's ideas were soundly criticized, especially the Virginian's lynching of his friend Steve. It was charged that Wister had condoned, perhaps even glorified violence—that he had condoned a lynching in Wyoming that would have been denounced, had it taken place in the South.

The novel has continued in popularity. For sixty years it was the most widely read western ever written. Wister was chosen to write a stage version shortly after the novel appeared. Although it had only modest success on Broadway, it was one of the most successful traveling stage shows in the first half of the twentieth century. In 1914, the first of four highly acclaimed movies based on the novel appeared. In the era of television, producers capitalized on the title and characters' names for a television series that aired from 1962 to 1970 on NBC.

Wister, more than any other person, including Roosevelt, made the western frontier a respectable subject for literature and study. Moreover, it was this novel that popularized the figure of the western hero, a national myth that appeared in and often dominated every form of media, every art form.

Not only did *The Virginian* create a ceaseless demand for cowboy heroes; it articulated the values that caused the Virginian to become a role model for many men. Those values, often contrasted with the culture of the eastern United States, included personal confidence, charisma, a high level of professionalism, physical attractiveness, and strength.

Additional Readings: John L. Cobb, *Owen Wister* (Boston: Twayne, 1984); Loren D. Estleman, *The Wister Trace* (Ottawa, IL: Jameson Books, 1987).

151. *The Log of a Cowboy,* **by Andy Adams (United States, 1903).** One of the most exciting and authentic accounts of a cattle drive, from Texas to Montana at the height of trail driving days, is *The Log of a Cowboy* by Andy Adams.

Though born in Indiana in 1859, to cultured Scotch Irish pioneer parents, Adams made his mark as a working cowman in Texas, at a time when great ranches had formed and frontier conditions still existed on the plains. As a young man in the early 1880s, he signed on as a cowhand with a herd driving north from the Rio Grande. Adams spent eight of the next ten years in Texas as a trail driver. By the time he quit in 1890, he was a foreman. After two more years in Texas, he tried gold mining in Colorado and Nevada, ultimately settling down in Colorado Springs.

He began writing his *The Log of a Cowboy* at age forty-three. By this time, the days of the old trail drives were only a memory, and romance was already replacing the dust-and-heat reality of the cattle drive. Adams wrote to set the record straight, to describe those days as they really were. The title derives

from the fact that cowboys often kept a log or journal—an account of daily events on the trail, similar to the log kept by sailors on ships.

The initial chapter describes the end of the Civil War, the fictional family's disasters in Georgia in the wake of Union General Sherman's destruction of everything in his path, and Robert E. Lee's surrender. Like so many other Southern families, they headed west. Tommy, the cowboy, after hearing his brother Robert's exciting tales of leading a herd to the far north, signs on with a trail boss named Flood. In 1882, they picked the herd up at the mouth of the Rio Grande, near Brownwood or Matamoras, their destination being Fort Benton and the Blackfoot Agency in Montana. The novel describes daily events of life along the trail and the nature and the character of the men who drive the herd. The action includes all the details of an arduous life: slow, plodding days, moonlit nights, days when cattle all but perish from thirst in a dry and dusty land without water, stampedes, river crossings, and other daily hardships. The action includes a passage through Dodge City when it was still wild, a meeting with Indians, and trips through a section called No Man's Land. Adams includes many details, such as the information that Americans count the herd by putting knots in a string, whereas Mexicans count them by dropping pebbles in a pan. Over 3,000 head of cattle are counted in this manner.

After the Civil War, as once-huge herds of buffalo began to vanish from the plains, great herds of cattle took their place; and the Great Plains (once known as the Great American Desert) became a chain of ranches and cattle drives heading north. As this facet of westward expansion became internationally publicized—in tales of the "Wild West," photographs, novels, histories, and finally, films—the myth of the American cowboy became, for a time at least, the myth of America, worldwide. Among all these almost infinite accounts, this one book stands alone, combining the excitement of trail drives through dangerous country with the reality of factual details upon which the myth was created. Generations of readers have looked to this novel for both elements.

Adams's novel has assumed the status of history and is cited by virtually every historian of western cattle trails. While sales have not been exceptional by bestseller standards, they have been steady, and it has never been out of print, having become the standard by which other accounts are judged and often upon which they are based. Indirectly at least, the influence of this novel has been incalculable, as it has impacted upon those who read of the Old West or watch western films.

Historian J. Frank Dobie borrowed from Adams, and Walter Prescott Webb, in his history *The Great Plains* (Lincoln: University of Nebraska Press, 1981), devotes several pages to Andy Adams because Adams was the most reliable source. Adams, he noted, put "the spirit and the facts of the trail into his book" (p. 462). There was "but one novel of the cattle country that is destined to become a classic," Webb wrote (p. 462). And if anthropologists and critics had ignored it, he concluded, that was "perhaps because they lack the basis of judgment."

Additional Readings: J. Frank Dobie, *Andy Adams, Cowboy Chronicler* (Dallas, TX: Southern Methodist University Press, 1926); Wilson Mathis Hudson, *Andy Adams: Storyteller and Novelist of the Great Plains* (Austin, TX: Steck-Vaughn, 1967).

152. *The Call of the Wild*, by Jack London (United States, 1903). Jack London's most famous book appeared in a time when attitudes toward nature were in transition. There were still advocates of the early-nineteenth-century approach to nature as the embodiment of beatific spirit, a view preached by both the English Romantics and American Transcendentalists. Philosophers of this stripe would agree with Ralph Waldo Emerson that nature never did betray the heart that loved her, that the natural man was inevitably the good man, and that the way to God was through nature. A more sentimentalized view of nature had developed in the highly popular animal stories of the period,

going back to Anna Sewell's *Black Beauty*, a story seen through the eyes of a kind hearted horse who makes note of the cruelties of civilization.

Another, more unpleasant view of nature, largely counter to Transcendentalism, had intruded itself in the nineteenth century. This was Charles Darwin's theory of evolution with its idea of nature not as spiritual idyll but as a tooth-and-claw fight for survival and included the notion that all advanced creatures, including man, had evolved from lower forms.

It is against this background that Jack London wrote his famous nature (or animal) book, *The Call of the Wild*. Like the animal books so popular in his day, London's main character is an animal, a dog, who is highly anthropomorphized and sympathetic. He has a brain that works very much like a human's, and he exhibits affections very much as a human does. For example, he remembers year after year the death of his friend John Thornton at the hands of a Native American tribe.

But London's is no animal story in the usual, romantic nineteenth-century fashion, for his tale is thoroughly grounded in the scientific determinism of Charles Darwin. First, it is apparent that Buck's Yukon world is a brutal world: A pack of starving wild dogs there tear apart their tamer counterparts. It is a world where only the strongest survive, where injured or maimed dogs are slaughtered by the pack. And in this god-forsaken landscape, he wrote, a dog or a man might remember the early strains from which he has evolved.

This novel, brutal and grim in many ways, became an immediate bestseller and was largely responsible for making its creator the best-known and highest-paid writer of his day.

There were a few reviews in which the book was disparaged, primarily because of its stark realism or the anthropomorphism of its canine main character. Still, the immediate response to the novel was overwhelmingly positive. Although the book's importance in the literary canon has declined in America, it continues to be a work of scholarly significance in Europe and Asia and remains as one of the popular works among the general public in America, especially among young adult readers.

The book has had enormous influence on several fronts. It appeared on the scene when the general public's typical view of Darwin was expressed by a cartoon featuring a man with a baboon for a grandfather. London's novel was one of the first works read by the general public that gave validity to Darwin's theory of evolution. Through Buck's experience and his sense of kinship with a wilder ancestor, the new science was made more understandable and palatable to this novel's readers.

His readers lived at the end of a culture brought up on Sir Walter Scott and his disciples. London turned his readers to the living natural world for romance and adventure rather than to a fanciful past. As such, *The Call of the Wild* made popular what were called red-blooded American adventure stories in place of the gentlemanly frolics of European knights. In short, it gave adventure fiction a new orientation.

The animal book as a genre began to take a more complex and realistic turn with *The Call of the Wild*. It became a prototype of further stories based on science rather than sentiment.

The book inadvertently introduced and reinforced for its readers two political movements: the societies opposed to the cruelty toward animals and the environmental movement. In the 1980s and 1990s, the book provided fuel to enactments to restore the wolf to its natural habitat and to save wild animals from extinction.

Additional Readings: Claudia Durst Johnson, *Understanding* The Call of the Wild (Westport, CT: Greenwood Press, 2000); Earle Labor and Jeanne Campbell Reesman, *Jack London*, rev. ed. (New York: Twayne, 1994); Jacqueline Tavernier-Courbin, The Call of the Wild: *A Naturalistic Romance* (New York: Twayne, 1994); Earl J. Wilcox, ed., The Call of the Wild *by Jack London: A Casebook with Text, Background Sources, Reviews, Critical Essays, and Bibliography* (Chicago: Nelson-Hall, 1980).

153. *The Jungle*, by Upton Sinclair (United States, 1906). *The Jungle*, the single most recognizable and influential work of the New Journalism School, or what Theodore Roosevelt called the Muckraker School, was written by Upton Sinclair, a socialist who wrote with the purpose of indicting American capitalism and presenting a brief for socialism at a time when an unbridled quest for profit had led to unspeakable exploitation of both the American worker and the American public. In preparation for his novel, Sinclair lived for seven weeks in Chicago's stockyards district, where many of the workers were immigrants from Eastern Europe. The story he wrote, dedicated to "The Workingmen of America," accurately depicted the living and working conditions of the workers and the way in which food was prepared for the American people.

The plot involves Jurgis Rudkus, his fiancée, and their families who emigrate from Lithuania to the United States where, they have heard, good-paying jobs are available for workers. Working at his first job of sweeping away cow entrails, he is able to afford a modest house for the families, only to find that they have been cheated. The financial emergency that this brings forces the whole family to go to work, including Rudkus's elderly father, the women, and the children. Exploitation and grinding poverty result in the loss of their house, Jurgis's arrest, debilitating illnesses and accidents, and the deaths of Jurgis's father, wife, and two children. For a time he is reduced to begging and stealing, just as a cousin is reduced to prostitution. At the end of one day, he attends a political rally and is persuaded by a rousing speech by a socialist. Jurgis's story comes to a close as he gets a more respectable job from a humane boss and is given hope that socialism will bring the worker a better life than the one he initially found in the stockyards.

Sinclair exposes many unjustices suffered by the Chicago workers: unregulated wages and hours, unsafe and unsanitary conditions, lack of any safety net for the injured or sick or laid-off worker, and sexual abuse of workers by managers. Sinclair also, in the course of the story, uncovered unsanitary practices that reached into any home in the United States that bought meat that they did not prepare for themselves: the processing of diseased animals, the unsanitary preparation of meat, the use of unsafe chemicals to disguise rotten meat, the grinding up of poisoned rats and sweepings into sausages, and the failure to interrupt the processing when a worker, himself, fell into the grease where his body was rendered into lard with the rest of the organic matter and distributed across the country.

The book first appeared serially in the Socialist press, but the five publishers to whom it was initially submitted rejected it on the grounds that it was too controversial and inflammatory. Only after a thorough check of Sinclair's allegations did Doubleday agree to publish it. Sinclair's fear that the book would be met with a conspiracy of silence turned out to be totally unfounded, for it was an immediate bestseller, its subject monopolizing the conversation of an appalled public for months.

The Jungle was one of the most influential books by any reformer in that the reaction to it was swift and practical. Meat products distributed by the Big Five Chicago meatpackers fell 50 percent. President Theodore Roosevelt, despite his demeaning name for reformers like Sinclair, ordered an immediate investigation of the meatpacking industry. Reforms of the industry, especially regarding the inspection, handling, and labeling of meat, were shortly forthcoming, and the Pure Food and Drug Act was quickly passed. As J.C. Furnas writes in his social history of the United States titled *The Americans* (Putnam, 1969), "that little blue-ink U.S. inspection stamp on a cut of meat at the supermarket represents an inadvertent great service done you by Upton Sinclair" (p. 872).

But the real issue Sinclair had written the novel to address, justice for the American worker, was long in coming. Jack London, in his introduction to the work, had predicted that the novel would bring great masses to the cause of socialism, but such was not the case. In a frequently quoted assessment, Sinclair often said that he had wanted to touch the hearts of his readers but instead had turned their stomachs. Although the novel did not immediately make great converts to socialism as an organized political party, its lingering influence was felt in the 1930s when, after the Great Depression, the government under Franklin Roosevelt began to regulate industry and public services controlled by private enterprise.

Additional Readings: William A. Bloodworth, *Upton Sinclair* (Boston: Twayne, 1977); John Bartlet Brebner, *Canada, a Modern History* (Ann Arbor: University of Michigan Press, 1970); Raindra Nath Mookerjee, *Art for Social Justice: The Major Novels of Upton Sinclair* (Metuchen, NJ: Scarecrow Press, 1988).

154. *The Autobiography of an Ex-Colored Man,* **by James Weldon Johnson (United States, 1912).** James Weldon Johnson presented his purely fictional novel as an autobiography in order to make his story more credible to the world of violent race relations in which it appeared. The United States in the late nineteenth and early years of the twentieth century might well be labeled the era of lynching. It has been estimated that, on average, two black people were lynched every week in America between 1889 and 1902. Lynching continued well into the 1930s. Other matters involving race at the time are also pertinent to his story. In the year in which Johnson's novel appeared, black workers made one third the money that whites made and were barred from most labor unions, which might have provided avenues for redressing their grievances. Segregation existed to some degree in every aspect and in every area of the United States, from sports and the arts to housing and transportation.

The story that takes place in a racial climate characterized by violence and discrimination is about an unnamed narrator, the son of an African American mother and a white father whom he has never seen. He is a man of light complexion who has been reared in a black culture by his mother. A musician, the protagonist first plans to become a famous composer to prove to the world that black people are not inferior. However, on a trip to the South, the direction of his life changes. On his mission to collect the music of southern black musicians, he runs upon and observes a lynching. So terrified is he by what he observes that he decides to renounce his past and his race and live the rest of his life as a white man. In his new identity he also leaves behind his career as a musician in order to make money, rise to social prominence, and produce a family with a white wife.

Although he enjoys success and happiness and says that he has never doubted the wisdom of his actions, especially as it affects his children, he begins to suspect that he has "chosen the lesser part, that I have sold my birthright for a mess of pottage."

Johnson's anonymously published novel, perhaps because it was assumed to be a true account, received considerable attention at the time and opened the way for other black writers of the Harlem Renaissance. However, it fell into obscurity as did many other seminal works by black writers at the time.

In many quarters, its subject of a black man passing for white, a story that necessarily touched on miscegenation, not to mention integration, was regarded as scandalous, crude, immoral, and illegal. In the late 1960s, however, the novel was rediscovered and reissued, with the emergence of African American studies. It subsequently became a standard work for the study of African American studies and literature.

Its influence on American life can be seen in several ways. For example, Johnson was one of the first writers, along with Zora Neale Hurston, to convince his audience of the value of African American culture. The first chapters of his novel comprise an advertisement for the black folk art that Johnson spent his life promoting.

The novel also provided the shocking picture of a man so traumatized by racial violence and worn down by discrimination that he would rather relinquish his identity, culture, and art than to live as a black man in America. Although the narrator is presented as sympathetic, he and the reader are led to see his actions as a moral failing. The novel continues to be important as a study of the damage that results from a black man's denial of his race and history.

Finally, the novel raised several questions for its readers, both black and white, about the effect of racism on white people, a racism that led them to devote massive amounts of energy on a sorry cause.

Additional Readings: Eugene D. Levy, *James Weldon Johnson: Black Leader, Black Voice* (Chicago: University of Chicago Press, 1973); Kenneth M. Price and Lawrence J. Oliver, eds., *Critical Essays on James Weldon Johnson* (New York: Hall, 1997).

155. *Riders of the Purple Sage*, by Zane Grey (United States, 1912). For more than fifty years *Riders of the Purple Sage* was the bestselling novel by the man whose western fiction shaped the popular image of the West and the ideals of early-twentieth-century America.

When this novel appeared, America was facing the problem of unfettered industrialization, which had lured many young people from rural America to impersonal urban areas. The growth of factories had brought sweatshop labor and exploitation, produced slums, attracted floods of immigrants who, like the displaced rural natives, worked in horrifying conditions for starvation wages and lived on the edge of existence in festering slums. Not surprisingly, it was an age of social unrest and disdain for authority—even to the point of widespread admiration for those who flaunted the rich man's law.

Like Theodore Roosevelt, who became a rancher to improve his health, Grey believed that the novelist should be a crusader, like Victor Hugo. He turned to the subject of the West to convey the frontier values so in contrast to the industrialism of his own era. His story took place on the frontier in 1871, a time when the United States was still nature's nation, when the Native American, whom Grey presented sympathetically, still lived close to nature in the West, when wild life was abundant, and when a person could still shed European social restrictions and transform himself on the frontier without the constraints of traditions, laws, and wealth, or lack of it. The West of the novel, in contrast to the overcivilized world of the city and factory, is an Eden and is fast being threatened by civilization. In *Riders of the Purple Sage*, this threat comes in the form of the Mormons, portrayed as an intolerant and narrow religious sect with unacceptable practices that they attempt to inflict on anyone who comes within their sphere of influence. They had brought their own parochial brand of civilization to Utah under the leadership of Brigham Young, who installed himself as governor in 1851 and in 1852 officially sanctioned polygamy, a practice that Grey was not alone in considering coercively abusive. In addition, at the time of the novel, the notorious Mountain Meadow massacre, in which Mormons dressed as Indians had slaughtered members of a wagon train heading west, still endured as a living memory.

The story takes place in the relatively new Mormon settlement in what is now Utah, during a period of intense hostility between the Mormons and the rest of the people of the West, whom the Mormons called "gentiles." Jane Witherspoon, a young Mormon heiress who has inherited a fortune from her father, has earned the disfavor of Mormon elders first by befriending a non-Mormon, Berne Venters, and second, by refusing the advances of Elder Tull, who wants her to become one of his wives. A group of church officials are preparing to whip Venters when Lassiter, a loner and accomplished gunman from Texas, arrives and prevents it. Thus Lassiter also earns the Mormons' intense hatred.

Lassiter has come north to seek his sister, Millie Erne, and to exact revenge on the men who, eighteen years before, had lured her away from her husband and then seduced and betrayed her. A love affair develops between two philosophical opposites: Jane, a strong-willed woman who wants to live in peace according to her own conscience, and Lassiter, who above all wants revenge and be-

lieves that guns and skill at using them are necessary on this or any frontier.

Another love affair develops between Venters and Bess, the mysterious daughter of an outlaw, who nurses Venters back to health after he is wounded. Venters also discovers a secret valley so arranged by ancients that the disturbance of a balancing stone would seal the entrance, preventing any presumed enemies from entering. This is the place into which Lassiter and Jane escape at last from pursuing Mormons.

Riders of the Purple Sage was an instant bestseller. Domestic sales of the book totaled well over a million copies in the forty years after publication. Considering the copies borrowed from lending libraries, this most popular of Zane Grey's books reached several million readers. The novel helped to secure his reputation as the most widely read living author in the 1920s. From 1915 to 1924, he was on the bestseller list nine times; for three years he headed the list. His books have sold 40 million copies and been translated into twenty-seven languages. Grey's readership totals well over 250 million people. As late as 1960, his novels still sold more than a million copies a year.

In 1950, one year after the triumph of Mao in China, the U.S. State Department planned to translate *Riders of the Purple Sage* into Annamese, the language of Indo-China, and distribute it for propaganda purposes, to represent the American way of life.

Riders of the Purple Sage influenced American culture by articulating a myth of America's frontier with characters who became consistent archetypes: the outsider, sometimes outlaw, who takes on the established community authorities alone; the strong, independent outdoorswoman, capable on the frontier of doing a man's work but clinging to an ideal of peace; and villains who use their own perverse form of law to exploit nature and their fellow human beings for their own selfish ends. Embedded in his characters and stories was nostalgia for a time when Americans lived and were taught by nature. It articulates and encourages frontier virtues:

personal freedom, rugged individualism, simplicity, honesty, and humane action.

Throughout the world Zane Grey largely determined the image of the American West. And in this capacity, he helped shape the face of his century.

Additional Readings: Carlton Jackson, *Zane Grey* (Boston: Twayne, 1989); Stephen J. May, *Zane Grey. Romancing the West* (Athens: Ohio University Press, 1997).

156. *My Antonia*, by Willa Cather (United States, 1918). Willa Cather's frequent depiction of life on the Nebraska frontier of her youth has sometimes earned her the label of a regional novelist. The setting for *My Antonia* is a rural community, farmed by Native Americans and a variety of immigrants from the eastern United States and Europe. White travelers first saw Nebraska territory, chiefly the domain of Native Americans, on their way farther west, but in 1854 the Kansas-Nebraska Act opened Nebraska to white settlement, and the Homestead Act of 1862 was a further encouragement to settlement. Statehood was finally approved for Nebraska in 1867, and within fifteen years, almost all Native Americans had been removed to other areas outside of Nebraska. The population of Nebraska in the closing decades of the nineteenth century and well into the twentieth century consisted primarily of Union veterans of the Civil War and immigrants from Germany and Sweden. But settlers from other northern and central European countries arrived as well. Most of the settlers were farmers who raised livestock and grains.

Life was hard for the early settlers who first lived in sod houses and always struggled with brutal winters and droughts, low farm prices, and high operating expenses.

Despite the mutually hard frontier conditions suffered by all segments of Nebraska life so far away from established society, village and rural life was often highly divided by class consciousness in which poor European immigrants were discriminated against by more prosperous settlers from the eastern United States.

Cather's novel, set in Nebraska in the early twentieth century, is told from the point of view of Jim Burden, a middle-aged lawyer whose childless marriage has failed and who looks back on life in the pioneer settlement days of the northern prairie, at the turn of the twentieth century when, at the age of ten, he arrived in the town of Black Hawk to be cared for by his grandparents. His rosy memory of those days centers on the character of Antonia Shimerda, a vibrant young girl, several years his senior, who has arrived in Black Hawk with her immigrant family at about the same time. In their youth, Jim and Antonia represent contrasting cultures, both struggling in a wild landscape that is foreign to them both. Jim's family is straitlaced, Protestant, comfortably situated economically, educated, and willing to share what they have to help the Shimerdas. Antonia's family is poor, Catholic, struggling, distinctly Old World, and somewhat wild and free compared with the Burdens. Jim and Antonia develop a bond in what he remembers as their idyllic youth. But while Jim is nurtured and educated by his family, Antonia must be the support of her family after her distraught father kills himself. She is able to escape some of the extreme poverty of her bleak farm life when the Burdens secure her a domestic position in the village. While Jim goes off to law school, Antonia loses ground. She has a love affair, is deserted, bears a child, and returns to her rural home, but with her dignity intact.

Twenty years later, Antonia and Jim, now a successful attorney, meet again. She is still the spirited, magical woman he remembers, even though she has married a humble laborer and has a large family.

The novel was popular with the reading public from the first. With the rise in interest in American Studies and Women's Studies in the 1960s, the novel became an even more frequent subject of study in the classroom and in scholarly journals.

Its influence derives chiefly from its creation of a realistic history of the northern prairie at the turn of the century. When it first appeared, in the wake of World War I, many writers, both American and European, were incorporating into their fiction the disillusionment brought on by the meaningless slaughter that had just occurred. But *My Antonia* offered its readers an alternative stance, no less valid, no less true to reality. While Jim Burden enters the story as a lonely and unhappy man, he finds meaning and hope in his personal childhood history, united in innocence to Antonia and nature. The values he remembers from that time endure: that is, all that is natural, various, nurturing, eager, and loving.

Readers continue to find in the novel an antidote to the essentially rosy picture of the frontier in Laura Ingalls Wilder's *Little House on the Prairie*. The dark side of frontier life was intense isolation and hopelessness that often created distorted self-images, suspicion, small-mindedness and bitterness. It is a world barren of most high art but retaining much of the community snobbery of the civilized East.

Readers also found the novel to be an exception to the usual male-centered stories of the West popularized by Zane Grey, Owen Wister, Emerson Hough, and others, which presented the extraordinary feats of cowboys and gunfighters. Cather's is the everyday domestic world of children and wives and unheroic farmers. It was, she once said, a story of the "other side of the rug"—the hidden, unremarkable side of frontier life.

Additional Readings: Philip Gerber, *Willa Cather* (New York: Twayne, 1995); Sharon O'Brien, *Willa Cather: The Emerging Voice* (New York: Oxford University Press, 1987).

157. *The Age of Innocence*, by Edith Wharton (United States, 1920). *The Age of Innocence*, generally regarded as Edith Wharton's greatest novel, is both a satire and a chronicle of an age. Wharton wrote the novel in the wake of the literal, psychological, and philosophical devastation of World War I, setting her novel in New York City in the 1870s, the time and place of her own youth. Both settings are pertinent to the impact of the novel. At the time Wharton began writing the novel, the world had been turned upside down by a world war that had undone traditional values and meaning and rendered individuals without roots and without certitude. The old limitations and rules that had circumscribed the world before the war were now gone. Every religious and moral idea that had once been a conviction was now an uncertainty.

From this position of postwar unease, Wharton looked back to her childhood, placing her novel in the 1870s, a time for her of the comfort and certitude that came of clearly understood traditional social boundaries and moral rules. The world of the novel is limited to the lives of the super rich in the city where 400 of the world's oldest elite families ruled supreme. The unquestionable bases from which they governed were ancient social position and immense wealth. Materially they vied with one another for the most lavish furnishings, fashions, and houses, keeping one mansion in the wealthiest section of the city, one vacation house in Newport, and a sumptuous flat or house in Europe. It was the era in which "keeping up with the Joneses" became an obsession. Much thought and energy went into enforcing self-made rules designed to protect their class from outsiders, and they admitted into it neither nouveau riche pretenders to high society nor bohemian artists and intellectuals.

Their philosophy of class identity and family wealth was conveniently joined to their religious beliefs, in that they were sincerely convinced that inherent moral superiority had caused them to be blessed with material goods and social power.

Into this setting, Wharton placed a love triangle composed of Newland Archer, a successful lawyer from an eminent old upper-class New York family; his fiancée May Welland, a virtuous young woman dedicated to upholding the morals of her class at any cost; and May's cousin, the unorthodox Countess Ellen Olenska, who has recently returned to New York from Europe. Ellen alarms May, other relatives, and their friends with her shocking lifestyle. She dresses unconventionally, chooses to live in an unfashionable neighborhood, and cultivates friends whom her relatives find unacceptable. Her chief outrage, however, is deciding to divorce her brutal husband.

May and the rest of Ellen's family determine to stop her, chiefly because they believe that a divorce will embarrass them socially. Newland, in his capacity as a lawyer, is pressed into talking Ellen out of the divorce. He argues convincingly that the desires of the individual must be subordinated to the group, especially in the interests of the family and its children.

When Newland falls in love with Ellen, he changes his mind, wanting her to divorce and marry him. But giving in to social and family pressure, he follows his own earlier advice and, sacrificing his own happiness to the group, marries May instead. After their marriage, he reconsiders and asks Ellen to be his mistress, but May secures her husband by lying to Ellen, telling her that she is pregnant. Ellen refuses Newland's offer and leaves New York for Paris. Even years later, after May dies, Newland cannot bring himself to contact Ellen, despite his son's encouragement to do so.

Wharton's novel was an immediate success, selling 100,000 copies right away and bringing her, in addition, $18,000 in serialization rights. In 1921, it garnered her the Pulitzer Prize for Literature. Within two years, she had made $50,000 from sales and $9,000 from film permissions. The novel has been steadily popular but enjoyed a surge of attention beginning in the 1980s with the establishment of Women's Studies programs. In 1993, it was again the subject of a major motion picture.

The novel continues to contribute to its readers the picture of a formative era in museum-like particularity. Thanks to Wharton's eye for detail, the novel includes graphic pictures of the architecture of the day, the interior design of houses, the mode of entertainment, the fashion in clothes. It is also a chronicle of the values of one aspect of our national character.

But what began as a chronicle of an orderly age of rules and strict morals, written as the Roaring Twenties approached, turned into a satiric exposé of the shallowness and greed of that age. Wharton had turned after World War I to write about what she regarded as the innocence of her youth, in a time of comforting traditions and verities. Many people, including the Pulitzer committee, even saw the novel as morally uplifting. But what Wharton came to see and what she has conveyed to most readers is the irony of a society behind whose innocence lay cruelty and self-interest and whose rules comprised the letter of morality without its charitable spirit.

It is also powerful as a novel of a life that because of social conventions goes unlived.

Additional Readings: Irving Howe, ed., *Edith Wharton: A Collection of Critical Essays* (Englewood Cliffs, NJ: Prentice-Hall, 1962); Linda Wagner-Martin, *Age of Innocence: A Novel of Ironic Nostalgia* (New York: Twayne, 1996).

158. *Babbitt*, by Sinclair Lewis (United States, 1922). *Babbitt*, a book of satiric social history, made its appearance in 1922, marking an era between World War I and the great economic depression of the 1930s. The 1920s were, stereotypically, a time of great material prosperity, rapid social change, superficiality, and spiritual poverty. Politically, the era was often marked by a mindless patriotism joined with fear and hatred of "outsiders," whether they were foreign immigrants or "un-American" radicals. Culturally, it was a time of antiintellectualism, social conformity, and challenges to traditional sexual mores and the role of women. The 1920s are also identified with the 1919 Prohibition Amendment, outlawing the sale of liquor, a law that did little to temper the drinking habits of Americans but did much to foster hypocrisy and gangsterism.

George F. Babbitt, the title character of Lewis's novel, is a middle-aged real estate salesman who is caught up in a shallow, unstable social milieu of the 1920s. While he is materially successful and socially acceptable in his Midwest hometown of Zenith, something fundamental is missing in his life, leading him eventually to clash with the society that has shaped him. The novel opens on a town and characters who uphold conformity, the status quo, and social acceptability above other virtues, including honesty and integrity. Babbitt, for instance, thinks nothing of using shady business practices to sell real estate, if selling more property brings him into better standing within the community. He deplores trade unions and, speaking against the "closed shop," believes that no one should be forced to belong to a union, but everyone should be forced to join the Chamber of Commerce in order to fight unions. However, beneath the bravado and slogans is emptiness.

The initiating circumstance, which begins to dispel Babbitt's jolly self-deception, is the crisis of his friend Paul, who, desperately unhappy at having relinquished a career as a violinist to marry and become a roofing salesman, flaunts social mores, takes a mistress, shoots his wife in the shoulder, and goes to jail. Babbitt, subsequently, also goes through a time of rebellion, taking up with liberal thinkers and sympathizing with striking workers. But when the new Babbitt finds himself ostracized and desperately alone, he decides, at least outwardly, to conform again and join the conservative Good Citizen's League in order to gain community support once again. Inwardly, however, he keeps something of his newfound independence and advises his son to follow his heart.

Babbitt was an immediate popular success throughout the world. The Nobel Committee in Sweden made clear that their choice of Sinclair Lewis for the Nobel Prize was made chiefly on the strength of this novel.

George Babbitt has become a national archetype of the materialistic, superficial, and conforming middle class. The impact made by Lewis's satire is attested to by the fact that "Babbitt" and "babbittry" have taken their place as nouns in English-language dictionaries worldwide, appearing in lectures, articles, books, and even book titles, as an instantly recognizable type—one who is wary of foreigners, radicals, the young, and bohemians and who loses his identity in groups of his own kind, turning churches into businesses and valuing mediocrity.

Additional Readings: Sheldon Norman Greb-stein, *Sinclair Lewis* (New York: Twayne, 1962); Mark Schorer, ed., *Sinclair Lewis. A Collection of Critical Essays* (Englewood Cliffs, NJ: Prentice-Hall, 1962).

159. *An American Tragedy,* by Theodore Dreiser (United States, 1925). Theodore Dreiser's classic indictment of the American Dream can be seen in the context of American intellectual history. Benjamin Franklin wrote of the American Dream as the opportunity for even a poor boy like himself to rise to a position of influence in the United States. But by the twentieth century, runaway industrialism had created a different vision of success, materialistic values, and a highly stratified social structure. A class of wealthy owners were at the top of the range and, at the bottom, a class of hopeless working-class poor, sometimes referred to as "the dangerous classes." Opportunities to rise above one's class were very few indeed, for poor wages made it difficult to even survive, much less accumulate the capital to secure an education or to set oneself up in business. In the 1920s, when Dreiser's novel appeared, World War I had weakened the country's traditional humane values, replacing them with materialism. Economic laissez-faire and technology had opened the way for the rich to become richer on the stock market. Poor factory workers and farmers were already experiencing the economic depression that would hit most of the populace in the 1930s.

Within this context, Clyde Griffiths, Dreiser's protagonist, struggles for the American Dream. In Book One of the novel, Clyde, as a young boy from a poor family in Kansas City, begins to have his differences with his fanatically religious parents who expect him to help them in their street corner ministries. Like the ambitious Ben Franklin, Clyde works hard, getting better and better jobs. Unlike Franklin, however, Clyde adopts a wild, lawless lifestyle and is in a stolen car when it hits and kills a child. Clyde eludes the police and escapes to Chicago. Book Two takes place in Chicago where he works hard at multiple jobs, rising to a position at an exclusive club. Through a family connection he goes on to secure a good job in a factory in New York City but finds himself initially socially ostracized by his rich uncle's family. Clyde begins an affair with a factory worker named Roberta and shortly after falls in love with a wealthy woman named Sondra who introduces him to the high society that scorns him.

Possibilities for his great success collapse when Roberta becomes pregnant and asks him to marry her. When he refuses, she threatens to expose him. He finds he can't go through with his plan to kill her but accidentally kills her with a camera while they are in a boat, and she falls overboard and drowns. He swims to shore and fails to report what has happened. Clyde is found out, arrested, and eventually executed.

An American Tragedy has long been regarded as a classic of American leftist literature. When it appeared, in what seemed to be flush times, it drew attention, as few works ever had, to the rigid divisions in U.S. society. The novel impressed on its readers that the American Dream of equality and opportunity can easily turn into a nightmare.

The reading public was shocked to see the implicit charge that the misplaced materialism in society led to greed and crime.

The novel was also prophetic in the sense that four years later the imbalance and lack of control in the economy led to economic collapse, which destroyed families, careers, and livelihood and even caused widespread malnutrition.

Four years after the novel first appeared, *An American Tragedy* was banned in Boston on grounds of obscenity. Evidence at trial was restricted to passages taken out of context. The decision was appealed and upheld again in 1930. As a result of the trial, legislation was introduced in Massachusetts to revise the state's censorship laws, requiring consideration of objectionable passages in context. The proposal was twice advanced and twice defeated.

Additional Readings: Alfred Kazin and Charles Shapiro, eds., *The Stature of Theodore Dreiser: A Critical Survey of the Man and His Work* (Bloo-

mington: Indiana University Press, 1955); Ellen Moers, *Two Dreisers* (New York: Viking Press, 1969).

160. *The Great Gatsby*, by F. Scott Fitzgerald (United States, 1925). *The Great Gatsby* is the most enduring of a series of works by Fitzgerald that made him an international figure and shaped the age, following World War I, known as the Roaring Twenties.

World War I, which ended in 1918, dramatically altered the Western world countries that participated in it. The jingoism and false national honor among world leaders that gave rise to the war and the senseless slaughter of common soldiers on the battlefields shattered all Old World ideals, all meaning, all verities. As some historians have noted, God himself died on the battlefields of Germany and France. The mass disillusionment in attitudes that led to such tremendous suffering for seemingly no reason at all ineffably led to a breakdown in older values and morality. Some people reacted to the disillusionment and erosion of meaning by discarding the capitalistic ideals on which the country was built and committing themselves to political radicalism. Others—usually the more socially or financially privileged—indulged themselves irresponsibly in reaction to the momentary and superficial boom in the economy and the pervasive moral decay caused by the war. For these privileged few, the postwar 1920s held few checks on personal behavior, sexual gratification at any cost, material opulence, thoughtless spending, drunkenness, in short, a self-indulgent life lived at high speed.

The novel presents the story of such a social group. The protagonist is Jay Gatsby, a self-created man of mysterious means now living on a palatial estate on Long Island who idealizes Daisy Buchanan, a married woman living across the lake from Gatsby's house. He had known and loved her for many years, when she was Daisy Fay, a girl whose family money and status put her far above him. Gatsby's story is told by a narrator named Nick Carroway, also his neighbor, a man who can objectively view both Gatsby and the entangled world that he longs to enter—and from which he is forever barred. While the Buchanans and their friends are Old Money, Gatsby's fortune is newly acquired, and old prejudices will never bend. It is a carefully woven tale of love, infatuation, status, corruption, materialism, and defeat. The cast of characters includes a coterie of drunken friends, bootleggers, gangsters, mistresses, and blackmailers. The plot thickens with the revelation that the husband of Daisy, the ideal woman in Gatsby's eyes, has a mistress and, finally, that Daisy herself allows another person to take the blame when she kills a character with her car.

Although Fitzgerald had leaped into national prominence with his first novel, and he and his new bride, Zelda Sayre, had become high priest and priestess of the age of rebellious youth, *The Great Gatsby*, now often called the great American novel because it so accurately delineates the American Dream, was not an instant success. It sold only about 25,000 copies in 1925 and was out of print when Fitzgerald died in 1940. It was republished after his death, and with a Gatsby revival by scholars in the 1950s, the novel became a popular classic, having sold some 300,000 copies by 1980. Three film versions of the novel have been issued.

The immense influence of the novel came from its delineation of the American Dream of material excess as it was defined in the postwar 1920s among those who could afford to pursue it. Fitzgerald not only lived this dream; he defined the age it engendered, when people literally had money to burn on cars, clothes, houses, and entertainment. Largely as a result of *The Great Gatsby*, Fitzgerald was and remains an icon inseparable from the Roaring Twenties or the Jazz Age, as he named it. It was this book that portrayed that peculiar society of excess in a shifting world where old values seemed no longer relevant. While this novel focuses on the aspirations of young men, it was the unhampered conduct of young women that gathered most of the attention, because life

for them, only a few years before, had been tightly controlled.

Paradoxically, the novel also changed the public's idealized way of regarding the age that both made and destroyed Jay Gatsby and F. Scott Fitzgerald. Daisy Buchanan became a symbol for all that was superficially alluring in the 1920s culture. Gatsby's moment of truth with regard to Daisy parallels the reader's disillusionment with the whole age and its values. It was Fitzgerald who painted the emptiness and lovelessness at the heart of the era, who saw the essential self-centeredness and greed to which he and his characters had succumbed.

Additional Readings: Ronald Berman, *"The Great Gatsby" and Modern Times* (Urbana: University of Illinois Press, 1994); Dalton Gross and MaryJean Gross, *Understanding "The Great Gatsby"* (Westport, CT: Greenwood Press, 1998).

161. *A Farewell to Arms*, by Ernest Hemingway (United States, 1929).

Hemingway's war story *A Farewell to Arms* has been one of the most influential and enduring novels of our age. The author had already come to prominence with *In Our Time* (1925), a book of short stories, and *The Sun Also Rises* (1920), a novel dealing with restless and disillusioned émigrés living in Paris in the backwash of World War I who tried to fill the emptiness of their lives with rounds of drinking and temporary pleasures. *A Farewell to Arms* catapulted him into international fame and made him one of the major figures of his age.

The post–World War I age was a special one. For many thinking people, it was a time of sudden moral and spiritual bankruptcy, a time when, as one of the characters of Hemingway's contemporary F. Scott Fitzgerald, says "Very few things matter, and nothing matters very much" (*This Side of Paradise* [New York: Scribner's, 1920]).

The staple values of the Western world had been under assault for centuries. New science and logic, and the Age of Reason, had shattered the sure beliefs of the Middle Ages while introducing revolutions and new ideals. The nineteenth century had produced a bitter clash of science and religion. Theories of Darwin, Marx, and Freud—making the individual the product of eons of evolution or of historical necessity or of illusive psychological traumas—had tended to deprive humankind of individual responsibility and to take from humans the surety that God was in His heaven and all was right with the world. The twentieth century had begun in a long twilight. Hope was still strong and progress was steady. Men still believed before World War I that they could go away in a romantic haze of patriotism to a war that would last only a few months, and they would come home then to honor and adulation, having served God and country.

However, they did not come home from that war with honor or great expectations. They came home with nightmares, from a devastating, destructive, and useless slaughter. There was no starry sky above and no moral law within—only emptiness and betrayal.

A Farewell to Arms tells the story of Frederick Henry who, like Hemingway, has volunteered to serve in World War I with Italians in Italy. When he becomes injured, he is taken to a hospital, where he meets and has an affair with Catherine, a nurse. They soon marry and he rejoins the action. Then, in the disastrous retreat from Caporetto, seeing the useless killing of men ahead, Frederick plunges into the river to escape, joining Catherine, who is now in Switzerland and pregnant with their child. The end comes with Catherine's death in the hospital, after which Henry leaves, devastated, an event described with simplicity and feeling in one of the most famous lines in modern literature: "After a while I went out and left the hospital and went back to the hotel in the rain."

The great influence of Hemingway comes from his decision in this novel to face the war head-on and his ability to give his readers a sense of why the postwar generation lost its faith. Writers of the postwar world tried to find meaning in many different ways. F. Scott Fitzgerald leaped into the frenzy of the Age of Jazz (a term he created), a time of wild flappers, free sex, and endless drinking

binges. John Dos Passos plunged into a socialistic world that would totally condemn the war and accuse capitalists of a vicious conspiracy. William Faulkner retreated into the past, creating his imaginary clans of Southern Gothic decay. Only Ernest Hemingway, in *A Farewell to Arms*, actually faced and analyzed the war and portrayed the world the victims came back to.

He was able to convey to his readers an iconoclastic view of war. His hero, for example, is a deserter. And the war spells the "farewell" to many things, not just to munitions and fighting but to love (the arms of Catherine), to peace of mind, to meaning itself in the absence in this hostile universe of all the old props.

The novel gave to the world a totally new approach to courage. No longer was it defined as the bravado of running into battle; its new definition was a stoical endurance in the face of a loss of love and meaning that cannot be hidden behind a barrage of rhetoric.

Hemingway's influence was enormous, in part stemming from his spare innovative style, in part from his public persona as reporter, adventurer, big game hunter, and war correspondent. The influence of his most powerful novel, *A Farewell to Arms*, was ubiquitous as a representative of an age and as a conveyer of values in times of chaos.

Additional Readings: Carlos Baker, *Hemingway: The Writer as Artist* (Princeton, NJ: Princeton University Press, 1952); Scott Donaldson, ed., *New Essays on Hemingway's "A Farewell to Arms"* (Cambridge: Cambridge University Press, 1990); Linda Wagner-Martin, ed., *Ernest Hemingway: Seven Decades of Criticism* (East Lansing: Michigan State University Press, 1998).

162. *The Sound and the Fury,* **by William Faulkner (United States, 1929).** In the background of William Faulkner's most famous novel is the Southern region of the United States, looking nostalgically back on a largely fraudulent picture of plantation glory and medieval honor before the Civil War, while at the same time it struggled after the war to enter the mundane world of commerce by any means, largely on the backs of poor whites and blacks. As the first narrative of the novel opens, Southern poor whites are beginning to find their own voices and trades, independent of the old aristocrats, and African American organizations are beginning to seek votes and legal equity for themselves.

Philosophically, throughout the Western world, it was a time of change as the old eternal verities seemed doomed to perish under the weight of war and science.

The Sound and the Fury, a single story told repeatedly using four different sources, is the history of an old and wealthy Mississippi family, the Compsons. Each retelling of the story increases the reader's perspective on the related events. The first account is told in stream-of-consciousness fashion by a thirty-three-year-old Benjy, a man with the mind of an infant, whose most pleasant thought is of his sister, Candace or Caddy, and who wanders near a stretch of land once intended as his inheritance but then sold to make a golf course. Part two is told by the protagonist of the novel, Benjy's brother, Quentin Compson, a sensitive, cerebral Harvard student. Quentin is obsessed with the past and with his sister Candace. Unable to convince himself of ontological certainty, even at the risk of taking on guilt for his incestuous urges, he moves steadily toward suicide. The third section is told by the third brother, Jason, a crass materialist who represents and foreshadows the worst of the New South. The family servant, Dilsey, a religious woman of great heart and loving insight, relates the fourth section.

Although *The Sound and the Fury* is often called Faulkner's best work and is the work that Faulkner himself regarded with greatest affection, the novel did not receive immediate widespread recognition. Not until the Faulkner revival, occasioned by Malcolm Cowley's 1946 issuing of *The Portable Faulkner* and the subsequent growth of the field of Southern literature, did the book become a classic. When national attention did arrive, it was countered by Southern outrage at what was perceived as the smearing of the

region by one of its own. Only shortly before Faulkner's death, with the award of the Nobel Prize for Literature in 1950, did Faulkner's own region begin to embrace him and, later, turn him into an icon and a cottage industry in his hometown of Oxford.

The great influence of *The Sound and the Fury* derives not only from its innovative style but from its innovative approach to the history of the South. Until this novel's appearance, the American South had been represented chiefly by romantic narratives like those written by Faulkner's great-grandfather, William Clark Faulkner, which portrayed the romance of plantation life before the war. Faulkner's novel is a corrective, a portrayal of myriad aspects of the South, represented by the main characters that include the beguiling but destructive Southern belle and the hard man of commerce who seize the opportunity to rebuild a devastated region in the image of a mall. Quentin is the intellectual and artist who is torn between the horrors and beauties of the past and present South, protesting to his Harvard roommate, "I don't hate it!"

The Sound and the Fury is also influential in being one of the first novels ever to present with a good deal of accuracy and sympathy the relationship of white Southerners and newly freed black slaves in the New South. Dilsey, the family servant, is the only "whole" human being in the novel, as well as being the only nurturer the family has known.

The relevance and influence of the novel extend far beyond the regional commentary, however. It addresses the universal ontological malaise of the era as is suggested by the title, taken from Shakespeare's *Macbeth*. Life, for modern humankind, had become a "tale told by an idiot, full of sound and fury, signifying nothing." Quentin learns that the worst thing in life is not the burden of sin but the suspicion that his sin does not matter, that, in effect, *nothing* matters.

Additional Readings: Richard P. Adams, *Faulkner: Myth and Motion* (Princeton, NJ: Princeton University Press, 1968); Michael Millgate, *Faulkner's Place* (Anthens: University of

Georgia Press, 1997); Noel Polk, ed., *New Essays on "The Sound and the Fury"* (Cambridge: Cambridge University Press, 1993).

163. U.S.A., by John Dos Passos (United States, 1930–38). In *U.S.A.*, a trilogy consisting of *42nd Parallel* (1930), *1919* (1932), and *The Big Money* (1936), Dos Passos presents a multifaceted history of the first third of twentieth-century America from the perspective of an idealistic individualist, focusing on the struggles of socialist labor against an all-powerful and brutal capitalist world. By including different forms of popular culture (songs, newsreels, biographies, movies, the "Camera Eye," daily headlines, prose-poems, as well as autobiography) in a narrative that stresses mass movements, he was able to show common people being swept along by great tides over which they have little, if any, control. In this way, Dos Passos achieved great power in a unique form and, in effect, stood as an important socialist voice of his generation. His influence, as such, was enormous.

In the late 1920s, Dos Passos began writing a novel (which ultimately became the trilogy) to explain, in fictional form, precisely what had happened in twentieth-century American history to bring about the controversial and, to most liberal thinkers, tragic executions of the anarchists Nicola Sacco and Bartolomeo Vanzetti. Like the victims of the Haymarket Square riot in the late nineteenth century, Sacco and Vanzetti were convicted on weak, and many thought, trumped-up evidence, not because murder had been proved but because they were anarchists, sops to the popular mood of hatred and fear generated at the end of the Roaring Twenties. Business was booming for businessmen, if not for laborers and farmers. Americans were experiencing a postwar malaise, along with fear of all conspiratorial foreigners and "entangling alliances."

Dos Passos ultimately began to see three distinct eras in his chosen period. The center was World War I, the great watershed that shattered old assumptions. The time before World War I, called the Progressive era, was a time of great hope, which was ironically doomed to fail. The final phase covers the period of cynical disillusionment following the war and the frenetic pace of the 1920s, the so-called Jazz Age. Dos Passos deals with the conflict between labor and capital at a time when the workers were generally defeated and those who rose to power in the capitalist world were generally corrupt, when only material success and Big Money mattered. He portrays a world of waste, cynicism, greed, and amorality, a time of enormous change and massive turmoil, ending in the economic collapse of October 1929 and the Great Depression.

Dos Passos's novel about the prewar years was called *42nd Parallel*, a title that refers to the jet stream winds that sweep across the North American continent and suggests tumultuous, traumatic changes to come. Leftist political movements—socialism, syndicalism, the Industrial Workers of the World, or Wobblies, and other reformist movements—were gaining strength. Among a variety of characters and vignettes, this novel shows the failure of a Wobbly named Mac and the success of a public relations man named J. Ward Moorehouse.

The title of the novel about the second period, *1919*, referred to the year after World War I ended. Its subject is the war itself and the unstable peace that followed. Dos Passos, who served in the war first as a volunteer at Verdun and then with the Red Cross in Italy, hated the war passionately and considered it a betrayal of the American people. The war is presented as a capitalist plot to defeat socialism, and its brutality achieves nothing. The author's chief villain, among a host of characters, is President Woodrow Wilson. Joe Williams, a major character, dies at sea after various misadventures, both here and in South America; Richard Ellsworth Savage, a Harvard man, goes to France to join an ambulance corps and, in a complete moral collapse, eventually joins J. Ward Moorhouse. Other characters suffer similar defeats.

The Big Money, based on the third period, portrays rampant greed, exploitation, and violence, a time in which money controls everything and displaces all other values. In this final novel, Mary French, an idealistic woman engaged in leftist causes, becomes involved in the defense of Sacco and Vanzetti.

For the publication of the trilogy in 1938, Dos Passos added a character called "Vag," who serves to frame the story, appearing at the beginning and the end: a ragged, beaten vagabond, a symbol of terrible economic times, wandering alone down a dusty road leading to nowhere, a symbol, too, of the results of a vicious system that destroys men as well as hope and leaves only the corrupt and the empty to prosper.

The critical reception and the effect of the novels, published both separately and as a trilogy, were electrifying. Dos Passos became the voice of the times, and for the future, a model as well as a standard for socialist workers and other reformers. The work, often called an epic drama of American life, influenced several generations of European and American thinkers.

Additional Readings: Townsend Luddington, *John Dos Passos: A Twentieth Century Odyssey* (New York: Dutton, 1980); Thomas Strychacz, *Modernism, Mass Culture, and Professionalism* (Cambridge: Cambridge University Press, 1993).

164. *Tobacco Road*, by Erskine Caldwell (United States, 1932). *Tobacco Road*, as novel, play, and film, made Erskine Caldwell rich and famous and made the title and the concept household words throughout the United States and the world.

Caldwell's achievement as a novelist is intimately tied to his early background. The only child of a Reformed Presbyterian minister who served as an official mediator for troubled churches in rural Georgia, Caldwell, born in 1903, spent his own childhood traveling from one community to another, always temporary, always an outsider, and being thrown generally upon his own resources and the care of his mother. This itinerant life, while putting a great strain on his mother, enabled Caldwell to observe, firsthand, the daily life of poor, bottom-level, starving farmers in rural Georgia: the kind of people he wrote about in *Tobacco Road*.

Historically, the postwar world of the 1920s, which was the setting of the novel, saw a great boom in American economic life—a boom for almost everybody except the small farmer, who saw the land decay while the cost of production grew often to exceed the price of what was sold; and there was no government help, not even money to upgrade the land. For small southern farmers, the Booming Twenties was a disaster; and the result was a wholesale migration of people, black and white alike, from the farms to the great cities. In *Tobacco Road*, Caldwell writes about a family that tried to remain on the farm.

The novel is the story of a farm family headed by Jeeter Lester, a poor, limited, and worn-out Georgia farmer, living on land that they will soon lose and existing in the last stages of disintegration, facing literal starvation after having suffered malnutrition, lack of education, and even lack of hope in many years of deprivation. Jeeter has fifteen children in all, most of them gone and working in town. The family members are equally hampered or limited in their outlook and equally doomed. Sixteen-year-old Dude has a passionate ambition to own a car. Ellie May, the plain, handicapped daughter, falls in love with Lov Benson, who is married to Jeeter's twelve-year-old daughter Pearl. Ada, Jeeter's wife, worries about her daughter who has gone. Jeeter tries desperately to save the farm, but clearly he is doomed from the start. He has not been able to plant cotton in six years.

In the action, Lov (carrying a load of turnips) comes to get Jeeter's aid in getting Pearl to sleep with him but is distracted by Ellie May. While this is happening, Jeeter steals Lov's turnips. The Jeeter family then eat the turnips, joined by Sister Bessie Rice, a widowed preacher, who afterwards leads them all in a prayer of penitence.

This squalid story, told with humor, brought Caldwell literary distinction and respect. Some readers and critics have noted that although Caldwell portrayed his downtrodden sharecroppers with great sympathy, he wrote nevertheless with a tone of condescension. However, this subtle, if real, weakness did not vitiate the popularity or the influence of the novel.

In addition, the story was dramatized by Jack Kirkland one year after the novel appeared. The play, opening in New York in 1933, was a sensational success. It ran for seven and a half years—3,182 performances; and when the curtain fell on its closing night, it was the longest-running play in the history of Broadway. In 1941, it was also turned into a very successful film, directed by John Ford, one of the great directors of the age.

Caldwell's characters and his title, his setting for fictional representations, passed into folklore. The very name "Tobacco Road" became a metaphor for characters or situations representing degradation.

Perhaps the ambivalence of this influence—by a man who wrote with sympathy but who achieved, in the popular mind, at least a large element of farce and even of grotesquerie—can be illustrated by an event on that first opening night on Broadway. Caldwell paced outside the front of the theater with a companion, apprehensive about what the audience would think of the play. When the curtain descended, he realized that his story had been greeted enthusiastically, but at the same time, he was appalled by another factor: the overwhelming laughter. He is reported to have wept that while he had intended to evoke sympathy for his characters, the audience had greeted them as farces.

This, in fact, is the element about Caldwell's novel that passed into the history of American life: the ludicrousness of its situations and characters. Only the rare perception would see the interior anguish beneath the facade.

Caldwell's later work did not live up to expectations, but the impact of *Tobacco Road* was unparalleled.

Additional Readings: Edwin T. Arnold, ed., *Erskine Caldwell Reconsidered* (Jackson: University Press of Mississippi, 1990); Dan B. Miller, *Erskine Caldwell* (New York: A.A. Knopf, 1995).

165. *Call It Sleep*, by Henry Roth (United States, 1934). *Call It Sleep,* by Henry Roth, has been widely acclaimed as the American classic of immigrant literature. Set in the Lower East Side of New York City in the first decade of the twentieth century, the novel covers roughly two years in the life of a sensitive young boy, the son of Austrian Jewish immigrants. The child, David Schearl, learns that his father, Albert, had first come to the United States and secured a job as a printer before his mother, Genya, had joined him with their twenty-one-month-old son. Upon seeing the infant, Albert, possessed of a dangerous jealous streak and a violent temper, grabs the child's hat and throws it into the sea.

David is tortured by his father's constant mean-spirited cruelties toward him and toward his loving mother. In response, the family becomes increasingly isolated. David is also spitefully bullied at school, especially by the Gentile boys. The boy begins increasingly to turn for support and companionship to his mother.

Despite his suffering, David's view of his parents as idealized superhumans keeps him on something of an even keel. One day, however, overhearing a conversation between his mother and her newly arrived sister, he learns that even his parents are flawed. His aunt speaks of a romance his mother had had when she was a girl and also of a shameful moment in the life of his father when he had been too paralyzed with fear to intervene when a bull attacked his own father, who had died as a consequence.

Devastated by what he learns, David begins to lose his grip on his own life as he realizes his parents' frailties. He returns to a transportation rail where he had often played alone and ends up electrocuting himself, being taken to a hospital where he almost dies. The book ends as his parents, horrified at the thought of losing him, gather round him to show their love.

When Roth's book first appeared, it received many laudatory reviews and had a respectable reading public. Over the years, a small coterie of admirers continued to hold the book in high regard, their fervor rising to what some have described as cult status.

But the economic situation at the time of its appearance did not encourage a huge readership. Nor did the depression sustain Roth's publisher, who went bankrupt during the depression. Despite a small group of devoted fans, the novel virtually disappeared.

A number of general readers and literary critics, especially those who had themselves been raised in immigrant families in the first several decades of the twentieth century, continued to draw attention to the novel as a masterpiece. Finally, in 1960 the book was reissued in hardcover and in 1964 was issued in paperback. At the time of its reintroduction in print, it was featured on the first page of the *New York Times Book Review*. It was immediately hailed as a masterpiece, sold over 1 million copies, and was translated into dozens of languages.

The novel has had an immense influence on several fronts. Although Roth had been a communist for a brief period in the 1930s, he was unable to write social protest literature in the same way that other radicals had done. Still, his novel stands as the first chronicle of the slums of the Jewish Lower East Side in New York. It is one of the most authentic pictures of the lives of immigrants and the heavy price they paid for their dislocation and pursuit of the American Dream. It is also, wrote critic Leslie Fiedler, probably the best single book about the Jewish experience ever written.

Roth is also credited with chronicling the multiple dialects of the Jewish immigrants, most of which were influenced by Yiddish and have long since disappeared.

Roth's novel is generally classified by the public not as a social novel but as a psychological one. *Call It Sleep* is credited with both introducing to American readers the internal monologue earlier used by James Joyce and applying Freudian psychology, including the Oedipus complex, to Jewish life.

With the urge of ethnic groups to seek out their roots in the 1960s and 1970s, and with the rise of interest in multiculturalism and Jewish studies, Roth's book has become a mainstay in college and university curricula.

Additional Readings: Bonnie Lyons, *Henry*

Roth: The Man and His Work (New York: Cooper Square, 1976); Hana Wirth-Nesher, *New Essays on "Call It Sleep"* (Cambridge: Cambridge University Press, 1996).

166. *Studs Lonigan*, by James T. Farrell (United States, 1932, 1935). James T. Farrell's status as a major novelist rests on the great success of *Studs Lonigan*, a grim story of Irish Catholics in Chicago slums, told naturalistically, with vivid scenes of slum life, a multiplicity of characters, and realistic dialogue, and centered on the growing up and final decline of young William "Studs" Lonigan. Though told with great power and force and realistic humor, it is a bleak, harsh, and desolate picture of life for its Irish characters. Its protagonist is not a hero at all; he is a struggling, physically strong, and potentially talented boy whose life becomes a pattern of unrelieved decay and waste. Written in the heart of the Great Depression (*Young Lonigan* appeared in 1932, *The Young Manhood of Studs Lonigan* in 1934, *Judgment Day* and the trilogy in 1935), Farrell aimed in this trilogy to give a total experience of life.

Naturalism, stemming from theories of Emile Zola in France and utilized in America by Theodore Dreiser, Jack London, and others in the twentieth century, was strongly influenced by Social Darwinism. It attempted to fuse science with art, to combine all relevant scientific knowledge with sociological observation in a total presentation of life: life according to "nature," to that which is natural. Man is a product of his world, his environment, and his training as well as inherent genetic factors. Thus, if man is deprived, he should look to himself for help, not to his stars. The purpose of a novelist, then, becomes to throw light into the dark corners.

While naturalism died in Europe in the early twentieth century, various factors in America prolonged its useful life. The Great Depression, the rise of unions, brutal confrontations between owners and workers, the growing awareness of an underprivileged class in a harsh industrial environment (much later developing in America than in England), the increased tension between religion and science—all this prolonged the elements and conditions under which naturalism flourished.

Not unexpectedly, *Studs Lonigan*, in the mid-1930s, hit the literary world and American society with enormous force.

The trilogy covers the period from 1916 to 1931. In the beginning, it is summer. Studs is fifteen. Just graduated from St. Patrick's Grammar School, he is eager to become a "big guy," uncertain about his future, concerned with fighting, dreaming of sex, urged by his mother to become a priest and by his father to continue his education. In one memorable scene, Studs sits with lovely and respectable Lucy Scanlan in a tree, in all innocence, dreaming and drifting away the afternoon, a moment that he always remembers.

In Volume two—April 1917—Studs attempts to enlist in the war but is too young. He skips school most of the time, hangs out at pool halls, gets involved in a robbery, and is employed by his father as a painter. He spends his time fighting, drinking, and whoring. Reprimanded by both family and church, he sees his companions fall prey to venereal disease and decay. He also goes steadily downward, winding up on New Year's Eve of 1919 collapsing in a street, drunk and badly beaten.

The third volume, which begins twelve years later, chronicles the final decay of Studs as the stock market collapses; his father goes bankrupt; his younger brother takes the same path to decay that Studs has taken; and Studs has a heart attack, plans to get married, and then, broke and out of a job as well as in poor health, dies of pneumonia.

Farrell used his trilogy not just to show a particular man and a family but also to represent an entire class of people, the Irish Catholics of Chicago. It is a grim, harsh portrayal. They are not heroic, not romantic, not quaint, not charming. They are violent and often stupid, "bone-heads." They hate and envy Poles, Jews, blacks, and others who are different. Technically, the pure naturalism is relieved by use of devices such as newspaper stories, movie plots, surrealistic conversations, letters, and sermons.

More than the physical squalor of Irish neighborhoods in Chicago, more than the economic disasters, Farrell impressed upon his readers the spiritual poverty of Lonigan's existence.

The novel was a sensational, scandalous success. It was met with expressions of shock and outrage throughout the United States for decades, shunned or deplored as a filthy book. Teachers and parents made no secret of trying to keep the novel from the eyes of children. In many small public libraries, it was placed out of sight, fit for only a select few patrons to see.

Despite the controversy, the novel achieved the status of a modern classic. It came to stand alone as the representation of certain aspects of its time and place. And the name Studs Lonigan came to be a universally recognized metaphor for a life of total waste. Until the day he died in 1979, Farrell was still a widely recognized celebrity and in great demand as a lecturer.

Additional Readings: Kathleen Farrell, *Literary Integrity and Political Action* (Boulder, CO: Westview Press, 2000); Michael Sadleir, *Studs Lonigan* (London: Constable, 1936).

167. *Gone With the Wind*, by Margaret Mitchell (United States, 1936). The story that unfolds in Margaret Mitchell's novel *Gone With the Wind* (retold in the classic movie made from it in 1938) is a historical epic of the nineteenth century and one of the most readily recognizable narratives in the world. The setting is the South during and after the American Civil War, beginning with a conflict—fired by romance—over the region's need to maintain the slavery on which depended a lucrative plantation economy, the fruits of which were enjoyed by a powerful few.

The opening chapters of the novel include an array of rationales among upper-class Southerners for joining the fray: the romantic appetite for any contest on the part of two young brothers; the reluctant sense of noblesse oblige, family duty, regional loyalty, and sense of honor on the part of the idealist who despises war; and the opportunity to profit from the war on the part of the realist, who eventually joins the conflict as a soldier just when it becomes apparent that the South's cause is a lost one.

The novel concentrates on the lives of plantation women during the war. Having subsisted on the labor of others and occupied themselves with dances and parties before the war, they are obliged afterward to dodge enemy shells; to serve in what was regarded as the disreputable activity of nursing the sick and wounded; to protect themselves with cunning and firearms, if necessary; and to forage for their own sustenance, largely independent of the help of their husbands, fathers, and slaves.

The novel also embraces the years immediately following the South's defeat, during and after Reconstruction, when the characters returned to poverty and burned and gutted rural plantations to which few former black slaves or former poor white workers now felt allegiance. In the social upheaval, poor whites are often portrayed as the new adversaries of the former lords and ladies of the plantation, and blacks are seen as the war's chief victims. The final setting shows the socioeconomic rise of the "New South," based on unscrupulous urban-industrial capitalism.

Against a historical background, from a Southern perspective, Mitchell placed characters that have become national icons, in scenes that are universally recognized. Even lines from the novel are instantly recognizable by most literate Americans, making Rhett's last lines to Scarlett an opportunity for parody.

Chief among its characters are Ashley and Melanie Wilkes, the embodiments of genteel idealism, the fading delicate flowers of a bygone era, who are too weak to help themselves, let alone anyone else; Rhett Butler, the dashing opportunist who is not quite corrupt enough to triumph over every adversity; and most of all, Scarlett O'Hara, who learns quickly, if painfully, how to be the archetypal survivor.

Gone With the Wind was said to have been the fastest-selling book in publishing history, selling 30,000 copies in one day. Within six months of its publication, 1 million copies had been sold. Fifty years later, it had sold more than 25 million copies and gone through 185 editions in twenty-seven languages. Through its classic translation on film, often called the greatest movie ever made, the story of *Gone With the Wind* reached billions of people.

The novel's immediate influence was part and parcel of the Great Depression in the United States, which by 1938 had left 13 million workers unemployed and had torn apart countless families whose breadwinners had deserted to hit the road as hobos and whose children felt obliged to leave to support themselves when they entered their teens. Mitchell's novel was not only a much needed entertaining diversion; it was a story of assurance—the possibility of survival after a horrendous disaster. Many who suffered through the depression could empathize with a heroine—however manipulative and selfish—who declared, "I'll never be hungry again." Others looked with nostalgia on a way of life that the depression seemed to have inevitably destroyed.

Although Mitchell's novel was not the first or the last to take its subject from the Civil War, *Gone With the Wind* did more to create the world's view of the South and the conflict that transformed it than any single work of literature. For the first time, readers saw in a work of literature an unromanticized view of the devastating effect of war on this society. This wildly popular story, with its sympathetic interpretation of a controversial era of Southern history, was as restorative of a bludgeoned Southern psyche as Scarlett was of her home plantation, Tara. Its vision of attractive, gracious antebellum plantation owners, of scalawagish poor whites, and of "quality" blacks who lived only to serve their former enslavers has yet to find an equally convincing popular corrective. But the enduring reputation of the novel was underscored in 2001 when publication of Alice Randall's *The Wind Done Gone*, a retelling of the story from a black slave's perspective, was delayed by the courts.

Additional Readings: Gone With the Wind *as Book and Film*, ed. Richard Harwell (Columbia: University of South Carolina Press, 1983); Elizabeth I. Hanson, *Margaret Mitchell* (Boston: Twayne, 1991).

168. *Their Eyes Were Watching God,* by Zora Neale Hurston (United States, 1937). Hurston's novel of life in a small African American town is reflective of a patriarchal African American society within a larger white-dominated society in the 1920s and 1930s. One of the novel's characters explained the dynamics of power at the time in this way: The white man throws down his burden for the black man to pick up, and the black man throws it down for the black woman to pick up. The black woman, she says, is the mule of the universe. Here, in a nutshell, is the problem of the novel.

The most obvious theme of the novel is the relationship between black men and women from the woman's point of view. Pertinent to the novel is the historical use of black women for the convenience and pleasure of men. They had no life apart from waiting on their fathers, husbands, lovers, and sons. The black woman's aspiration was never allowed to go beyond her husband's domestic sphere or a white family's field or kitchen. Her role was obedience and self-sacrifice. She was not expected to use her brain or her imagination except in serving her men.

Although the main conflict at issue is relations between men and women, this theme is played out in the context of race relations in a Jim Crow world of discrimination and segregation in the South.

The main character of the novel is Janie Crawford, who tells her friend about her three marriages. Her first husband, Logan Killicks, is a man chosen for her by her grandmother, though Janie has no love or admiration for him. Logan sees her as a young woman whom he has every right to

control completely; so it is no surprise when Janie runs away with Joe Stark to another town in Florida where Joe becomes mayor and owner of a general store. With his new power in the community, Stark also tries to manipulate Janie by refusing to allow her to have any friends in the community, where he feels that he is superior to everyone else. Moreover, as Joe's wife, she completely loses her identity: Joe insists that she be called "Mrs. Mayor." After Joe dies of an illness, Janie meets a younger man named Tea Cake who is her soul mate. This marriage seems made in heaven. Tea Cake encourages Janie to be her own person and to relax and enjoy life. This idyllic union is not to last, for Janie is forced to shoot Tea Cake when he contracts rabies and attacks her. At first she is charged with murder but is eventually acquitted.

Hurston's novel had little positive impact when it was first published in 1937, during the Great Depression. Its negative impact, however, was immediate and devastating. Most important black writers, notably Richard Wright, vehemently denounced the novel as a work that pandered to white stereotypes of black people. The dialects and folklore, which anthropologist Hurston had attempted to capture with accuracy, were damned as demeaning to African Americans. Wright was joined by many other black intellectuals in declaring that all Hurston's novel did was to make white folks laugh. The novel was also strongly criticized on other grounds, namely, that it did not, like other black novels of the day, mount any kind of social protest.

Largely as a consequence of these damaging reviews, the novel immediately went out of print. It was not reprinted for thirty years. It was then reintroduced to readers by novelist Alice Walker in the 1970s, but again it languished until a few years later it was brought into print chiefly because of the growth of the new Women's Studies movement. The book has been called the first feminist novel by an African American. Since its reintroduction, it has become a regular offering in courses in the comparatively new fields of Women's Studies and African American Studies. Moreover, the novel itself was a powerful impetus to the development of both these specialties in which long-ignored materials are being introduced and studied.

The novel is greatly responsible for reinventing African American culture. Before Hurston was taken seriously, distinctive African American culture was regarded by whites as comical, by blacks as an embarrassment. In this novel, Hurston, who had returned to her home to look again at her culture with an anthropologist's trained eye, presented the reader with a compendium of black culture. After the novel came to be taken seriously, there was a greater tendency for readers to value the wisdom, variety, and beauty in African and African American art and folklore.

Additional Readings: Robert S. Hemenway, *Zora Neale Hurston: A Literary Biography* (Urbana: University of Illinois Press, 1977); Neal A. Lester, *Understanding Zora Neale Hurston's* Their Eyes Were Watching God (Westport, CT: Greenwood Press, 1999).

169. *The Grapes of Wrath*, by John Steinbeck (United States, 1939). Few novels have been so decidedly products of their age and, at the same time, have had a greater immediate impact on the society in which they appeared. In 1939, the United States had suffered through a decade of nightmarish economic depression, made all the worse by a natural disaster across the middle of the continent where topsoil had blown away in blinding dust storms. People across all walks of life were thrown out of work. Families lost their mortgaged homes and their farms to the banks. Death from starvation and malnutrition were commonplace. Families split apart as older children had to leave to support themselves and heads of households abandoned their families in desperation. Whole households, deprived of work and homes, lived out of their automobiles or in makeshift shelters. Moreover, divisions between the wealthy, governing class and the lower and middle classes widened. In such a situation, the law came to be regarded as

heartless, policemen seen as no better than outlaws, and outlaws seen as heroes. No group of people suffered more than the nation's small family farmers, especially those who had been trying to eke out a living in the Dust Bowl areas of the nation's heartland, which included the states of Arkansas, Oklahoma, Kansas, and Texas. These people, deprived of their farms, were lured west, to what they understood was nothing less than a Garden of Eden, in the state of sunny California, a place of many opportunities for work and advancement. For the overwhelming majority, however, this place of large corporate farms became a greater hell than they had ever imagined.

Steinbeck addresses the multiple problems of the system in the course of his narrative, into which he weaves journalistic-style chapters of actual occurrences as they were reported in the small radical presses during the 1930s. These problems include: unsanitary living conditions in the camps provided for workers; the practice of luring more workers to their farms to keep salaries low; inadequate pay; lack of health care; lack of any reliable system of communication regarding jobs and employers; child labor and lack of provisions for educating children; the practice of cheating their workers; brutal law enforcement tactics; the destruction of food surpluses in the face of starvation. The cruel suppression of any farmworkers' efforts to organize is shown through the characters of the former preacher Jim Casy and the former convict Tom Joad.

The impact of this timely novel was immediate and explosive. Ordinary people who had no knowledge of migrants and the situation in the California fields were alarmed at what they read. The book gave legislators, under the direction of Senator Robert LaFollette of Wisconsin and John Tolan of California, the incentive and the public support to begin conducting hearings at once in California. After reading the novel, Eleanor Roosevelt, the president's wife, came to California in April 1940 to observe conditions for herself. More than once in the three years of public hearings, passages from *The Grapes of Wrath* were read into the record. The chief measure that the novel prompted the Senate committee to work toward was the inclusion of farmworkers in protections of the Wagner Act and the National Industrial Relations Act (NIRA). In 1938 the NIRA guaranteed improved working conditions for labor, a maximum number of hours in the workweek, and a minimum wage. But farmworkers and all child labor had been specifically excluded from its protections. The Wagner Act, which protected the rights of labor to organize, had also excluded farmworkers. Law enforcement officers firebombed or shot into union meetings. The conditions laid out for the public in Steinbeck's novel resulted in a recommendation to the U.S. Senate by the LaFollette, committee, in 1941, that farmworkers receive the same right to organize as industrial workers. Unfortunately, by that time, World War II was under way, and legislators were too preoccupied with world affairs to fight the California farm owners on behalf of farmworkers. So the measure failed to pass the Senate.

Not all the public reaction to Steinbeck's *The Grapes of Wrath* resulted in praise for the author and sympathy for the cause of the farmworker. The reaction from California growers was furiously negative. In farm-rich areas of the Southwest every effort was made to ban the book from libraries. The Associated Farmers and the California Citizens Association and their powerful backers funded several books intended to discredit Steinbeck's novel. One of the more infamous attempts was *Grapes of Gladness*, written by M.V. Hartranft. *The Grapes of Wrath* was banned in Oklahoma, where Steinbeck's reasons for the economic disaster infuriated those in power. There were other reasons for the negative public reception of the book in Oklahoma. Many of the state's citizens believed that what Steinbeck thought was a sympathetic portrait of "Okies" was, in fact, a humiliating caricature. Many Oklahomans and Californians from Oklahoma continued to believe that they were maligned by Steinbeck as immoral and stupid.

In other parts of the country, the book was condemned as pornography. Cardinal Spellman of the Roman Catholic Church, for example, ordered all members of the Catholic faith to avoid it as a filthy abomination. If you take the coarse parts out, said some reviewers, you would have a book of blank pages. Although original objections to the book were made on political and economic grounds, its language has made it a continual subject of debate and attempted censorship, the latest recorded in 1993.

Although the book's impact was greatest immediately after its publication, it influenced television journalist Edward R. Murrow's documentary *Harvest of Shame* and the work of Cesar Chavez in organizing farmworkers in the 1950s and 1960s. It has never been out of print and has never ceased to exert an influence. Never would Americans view in the same way the system by which food was placed on their tables.

Additional Readings: John Ditsky, *Critical Essays on Steinbeck's* The Grapes of Wrath (Boston: G.K. Hall, 1989); Claudia Durst Johnson, *Understanding* The Grapes of Wrath (Westport, CT: Greenwood Press, 1999); David Wyatt, ed., *New Essays on* The Grapes of Wrath (Cambridge: Cambridge University Press, 1990).

1940–1990

∾

Richard Wright, *Native Son*, 1940

Walter Van Tilburg Clark, *The Ox-Bow Incident*, 1940

Robert Penn Warren, *All the King's Men*, 1946

J.D. Salinger, *Catcher in the Rye*, 1951

Ralph Ellison, *Invisible Man*, 1952

James Baldwin, *Go Tell It on the Mountain*, 1953

Ray Bradbury, *Fahrenheit 451*, 1953

Jack Kerouac, *On the Road*, 1957

Ayn Rand, *Atlas Shrugged*, 1957

William J. Lederer and Eugene Burdick, *The Ugly American*, 1958

Harper Lee, *To Kill a Mockingbird*, 1960

Joseph Heller, *Catch-22*, 1961

Ken Kesey, *One Flew Over the Cuckoo's Nest*, 1962

Sylvia Plath, *The Bell Jar*, 1963

Chaim Potok, *The Chosen*, 1967

N. Scott Momaday, *House Made of Dawn*, 1968

Kurt Vonnegut, *Slaughterhouse-Five*, 1969

Ernest J. Gaines, *The Autobiography of Miss Jane Pittman*, 1971

Edward Abbey, *The Monkey Wrench Gang*, 1975

Leslie Marmon Silko, *Ceremony*, 1977

Alice Walker, *The Color Purple*, 1982

Sandra Cisneros, *The House on Mango Street*, 1983

Toni Morrison, *Beloved*, 1987

Amy Tan, *The Joy Luck Club*, 1989

1940–95: TIMELINE

1940 Richard Wright's *Native Son* is published.

Walter Van Tilburg Clark's *The Ox-Bow Incident* is published.

Germany continues to build concentration camps.

1941 On December 7 Pearl Harbor is attacked without warning by the Japanese. Subsequently Congress declares war on Japan. Four days later, Italy and Germany declare war on the United States.

Jews, who are being forced to wear Stars of David badges as stigmas in Germany and whose livelihoods and property have already been confiscated, begin to be imprisoned throughout Nazi-conquered countries, including Vichy France.

1945 Germany is defeated, and the war in Europe is over.

Allied soldiers, including many Americans, liberate concentration and death camps, finding living corpses, thousands of unburied dead, and gas chambers. It will later be determined that millions of people deemed undesirable by the Nazis were killed, including 6 million Jews.

The United States drops the first atomic bombs on Hiroshima and Nagasaki, Japan, prompting the surrender of Japan.

1945–46 After World War II is over, union activity accelerates as 5 million workers strike for wage increases.

1946 Robert Penn Warren's *All the King's Men* is published.

1947 Congress passes, over President Harry Truman's veto, the Taft-Hartley Act, which limits workers' freedom to strike.

Under the "Marshall Plan" instituted by President Truman and named for

Secretary of State George C. Marshall, the United States provides funds to rehabilitate the economies of European countries.

In a Cold War with communist countries, President Truman sets up loyalty boards to investigate government employees.

The House Un-American Activities Committee begins investigations of communism in the movie industry.

Jackie Robinson is the first black ballplayer to integrate professional baseball.

1948   President Truman seeks to end segregation in schools and discrimination in employment.

Israel becomes an independent state.

President Truman forces an end to segregation in the armed forces and discrimination in federal jobs.

Anticommunist hysteria mounts with the case of Alger Hiss.

Communist North Korea declares that the whole of Korea should be united under communist rule.

1949   William Faulkner wins the Nobel Prize for Literature.

1950   When South Korea is invaded by communist-led North Korea, the United Nations intervenes and the United States takes a strong, active military role in the Korean conflict.

Senator Joe McCarthy of Wisconsin escalates the Red hysteria by falsely claiming that he has the names of many communists in high government places.

The Bureau of Indian Affairs begins a policy of withdrawing federal assistance to tribes. Its intent is to sell reservation land and relocate Indians in a few large cities, a policy that is universally opposed by the tribes themselves.

1951   J.D. Salinger's *Catcher in the Rye* is published.

1952   Ralph Ellison's *Invisible Man* is published.

The United States explodes the first hydrogen bomb.

The Supreme Court rules that subversives can be fired from jobs as teachers in public schools; in New York City, eight teachers are fired on those grounds.

Anne Frank's *Diary of a Young Girl* is published.

1953   James Baldwin's *Go Tell It on the Mountain* is published.

Ray Bradbury's *Fahrenheit 451* is published.

An armistice is reached in the Korea War.

Joseph Stalin, seen as the archenemy of capitalism as well as a brutal tyrant, dies.

Convicted spies Julius and Ethel Rosenberg are electrocuted for treason, a charge they deny to the end.

Senator McCarthy keeps up a continual tirade against those he believes to be communists, including, he says, many in Truman's administration.

1954   In *Brown v. Board of Education* the Supreme Court rules that racially segregated public schools are unconstitutional and orders that segregation in public schools be dismantled.

The United States begins sending military assistance to South Vietnam to keep it out of the hands of communists.

As a result of anticommunist decrees, 2,600 civil servants are dismissed on specious evidence.

Senator McCarthy is condemned by his congressional colleagues.

Ernest Hemingway wins the Nobel Prize for Literature.

1954–68   There are forty recorded lynchings of black people in the United States.

1955   After a black woman named Rosa Parks refuses to give up her seat on a bus to a white man, she is arrested, and a boycott of buses in Montgomery Alabama, proceeds, eventually to be led by Martin Luther King.

1956   The University of Alabama enrolls a black student, Autherine Lucy, and after three days of violence expels her.

1957   Jack Kerouac's *On the Road* is published.

Ayn Rand's *Atlas Shrugged* is published.

Soviet Union launches *Sputnik* spacecraft on October 4, effectively beginning the "space race" with the United States.

Congress passes the Civil Rights Act to investigate refusal to register and allow African Americans to vote.

1958   William J. Lederer and Eugene Burdick's *The Ugly American* is published.

A bomb thrown into a church in Birmingham, Alabama, kills four African American children.

1960   Harper Lee's *To Kill a Mockingbird* is published.

Black students stage a sit-in in Greensboro, North Carolina, to desegregate eating establishments.

By this time, only 765 of the 6,676 southern school districts had been racially integrated.

The federal government initiates a plan to encourage economic development in areas where Native Americans live.

A survey reveals that farmworkers throughout the country are still paid poverty-level wages and have no indoor plumbing and scant educational opportunities and medical care.

1961   Joseph Heller's *Catch-22* is published.

President John F. Kennedy expands military involvement in South Vietnam.

Freedom Rides to assist blacks in registering and voting begin.

1962   Ken Kesey's *One Flew Over the Cuckoo's Nest* is published.

Rachel Carson's *Silent Spring* is published, warning of the danger of pesticides. This is the real beginning of public awareness of dangers to the environment.

John Steinbeck receives the Nobel Prize for Literature.

1963   The average women's salaries in the United States are about 58.9 percent of those of men's.

The Equal Pay Act passes, making it illegal to pay different wages to men and women who are doing the same work.

Sylvia Plath's *The Bell Jar* is published.

In Washington, D.C., 250,000 people demonstrate against violence and discrimination.

President John F. Kennedy is shot and killed in Dallas, Texas. His vice president Lyndon Baines Johnson assumes the presidency.

After a staged standoff, two African American students are allowed to enroll at the University of Alabama.

Betty Friedan's *The Feminine Mystique* is published and becomes a defining text of new feminism.

1964   The Civil Rights Act of 1964 bars discrimination on the basis of sex, race, color, or national origin and establishes the Equal Employment Opportunity Commission to enforce its provisions.

Three civil rights workers are kidnapped and murdered in Mississippi.

The war in Vietnam escalates.

The Free Speech movement, protesting administrative control of press and speech, is born on the campus of the University of California in Berkeley.

Congress passes the Wilderness Act to preserve wilderness areas.

1965	Some 3,200 black and white protesters march in Selma, Alabama. Two hundred state troopers attack a group of 525. Four days later a black minister in Selma is beaten to death.

U.S. forces in Vietnam grow to 125,000 troops.

Race riots break out in Watts, a suburb of Los Angeles, resulting in the death of 34 and the arrest of thousands.

1967   Malcolm X is assassinated in New York City. Chaim Potok's *The Chosen* is published.

Frustration with the lack of real progress in stopping racial discrimination results in riots in thirty U.S. cities.

By this time military involvement in the Vietnam War has escalated. Five hundred thousand troops have been committed to the war.

A march on the Pentagon to protest the war in Vietnam involves some 35,000 protesters, 647 of whom will be arrested.

Congress passes the Air Quality Act.

The Environmental Defense Fund is established.

1968   N. Scott Momaday's *House Made of Dawn* is published.

Congress creates the National Council of Indian Opportunity to improve education and medical care for Native Americans.

The acknowledged leader of the civil rights movement, Dr. Martin Luther King, is shot and killed in Memphis, Tennessee. Riots erupt in black neighborhoods throughout the country, leaving fifty people dead.

Friends of the Earth is established to work for the environment.

Congress adopts the Wild and Scenic Rivers Act.

1969   A U.S. spaceship—dubbed "The Eagle" by its Apollo 11 crew—lands on the moon. Astronaut Neil Armstrong becomes the first man to walk on the moon.

Kurt Vonnegut's *Slaughterhouse-Five* is published.

A group of Native Americans seize the abandoned prison island Alcatraz as rightfully belonging to them.

Two hundred and fifty thousand people come to D.C. to protest the Vietnam War.

1970   With news of the U.S. invasion of Cambodia, students demonstrate on many campuses, including Kent State University, where the National Guard opens fire, killing four students.

The first Earth Day is launched to protest business and government abuse of the environment.

Greenpeace is established and takes an aggressive stand in protecting the environment.

The Natural Resources Defense Council is established.

The Environmental Protection Agency is established.

The Clean Air Act is passed.

1971   The Sierra Club Legal Defense Fund is established.

Ernest J. Gaines's *The Autobiography of Miss Jane Pittman* is published.

1972   What comes to be known as the Watergate scandal begins with a break-in at Democratic headquarters. Hearings will unfold, and gradually a complex web of unethical and illegal actions sanctioned by President Richard Nixon will come to light.

Title IX of the Higher Education Act forbids sexual discrimination in federally funded education programs.

Six hundred members of the American Indian Movement converge on the Bureau of Indian Affairs in D.C. to demand help for Indians, particularly those relocated to cities.

The Environmental Protection Agency bans DDT, a toxic chemical pesticide.

The Clean Water Act is passed.

1973   The Supreme Court decrees in *Roe v. Wade* that states cannot forbid abortions in the first six months of pregnancy.

Members of the American Indian Movement occupy the town of Wounded Knee, South Dakota, which they hold for two months.

The complete withdrawal of American troops from Vietnam begins.

1974   With impeachment facing him, President Nixon resigns.

1975   Edward Abbey's *The Monkey Wrench Gang* is published.

The Resource Conservation and Recovery Act is passed.

1977   Leslie Marmon Silko's *Ceremony* is published.

1980   The "Superfund" is established to clean up hazardous waste sites.

1981   An Earth First! demonstration at Glen Canyon Dam alarms industry and government with its threat of violence.

1982   Alice Walker's *The Color Purple* is published.

The Equal Rights Amendment, proposed to end discrimination against women, fails when it does not receive the ratification of thirty-eight states.

1983   Sandra Cisneros's *The House on Mango Street* is published.

1987   Toni Morrison's *Beloved* is published.

1989   Amy Tan's *The Joy Luck Club* is published.

1993   Toni Morrison wins the Nobel Prize for Literature.

1995   Women's salaries are now 71.4 percent of men's.

170. *Native Son*, by Richard Wright (United States, 1940). Richard Wright's landmark novel about the African American experience in Chicago in the 1930s appeared in the context of several events: the migration of African Americans from rural southern areas to urban centers in the North and the nationwide economic collapse of the 1930s. In the 1920s, even before the Great Depression hit the nation, small farmers in the South were already experiencing serious economic woes. Black farmers and farmworkers in the South were not only suffering from immediate hunger; they were also laboring under job discrimination and segregation. Their hopelessness was intensified by their inability to vote or to secure education for their children. As a consequence, they began trying their luck in many northern cities—Detroit, Chicago, Washington, Philadelphia, New York—where, they were told, labor was in demand and discrimination was not as overt. Some experienced a brief reprieve from poverty, but by the early 1930s, the Great Depression had devastated northern cities as well as southern farms. In the intense competition for jobs, African Americans lost ground. Opportunities dried up quickly. Northern laws were not as discriminatory as southern ones, but discrimination existed nonetheless. They lived in segregated slums, which bred anger, despair, and crime. Many found themselves without the financial and moral support of their extended families, who had been split up in the migration.

For his novel, Wright created a character shaped by this situation. Bigger Thomas is angry and hopeless, in the beginning taking out his frustration on his fellow African Americans by accosting them and robbing them. His life changes when he is hired by a wealthy man as a chauffeur. His encounter with the man's daughter brings on disaster. He inadvertently kills the drunken girl in trying to keep her quiet. In attempting to conceal his crime, he also kills his girlfriend Bessie. Finally, he is arrested, defended by the Communist Party, and eventually sentenced to die in the electric chair.

It was a Book-of-the-Month Club selection, the initial run of copies being sold out within hours of its appearance. In three weeks it sold 215,000 copies, in six weeks, 250,000 copies, and the novel was lauded as one of the great works of twentieth-century literature. It was and is, however, one of America's most controversial novels. At the time of its appearance, it was attacked by many black readers for making a violent bully and murderer the novel's protagonist, in effect reinforcing one of the oldest and most unpleasant stereotypes of black people and making white people even more frightened of blacks. The portrait of the Communist Party was also denounced by many readers sympathetic to the cause of black people.

Nevertheless, the novel was also highly praised, and credited with changing the way America viewed race. In the 1960s, interest in the novel was revived by the civil rights movement and the growth of African American Studies programs.

It has been said to have changed forever the way the nation viewed race relations. It was the first detailed and realistic portrayal of race relations in the North. It was the first view of an urban ghetto from the point of view of one of its inhabitants. And it was the first serious, realistic account of the life of African Americans in urban slums, bringing attention for the first time to the reality of discrimination and poverty among African Americans in the North and suggesting that white society would pay dearly for perpetuating slums and injustice.

Additional Readings: Henry Louis Gates and Anthony Appiah, eds., *Richard Wright: Critical Perspectives Past and Present* (New York: Amistad, 1993); Keneth Kinnamon, ed., *Critical Essays on Richard Wright's "Native Son"* (New York: Twayne, 1997).

171. *The Ox-Bow Incident,* **by Walter Van Tilburg Clark (United States, 1940).** Walter Van Tilburg Clark's novel about a lynching, while it has an Old West setting, resonated with meaning for 1938 and 1939 and later assumed other references in the civil rights struggles of the 1950s and 1960s. At the time the novel was written in 1938, the world was beginning to be aware of the rise of Adolf Hitler and fascism in Germany, which would soon result in the invasion of Austria, Czechoslovakia, and Poland and the setting up of extermination camps.

Van Tilburg Clark's novel, with its fascistic bullies, had relevance to developments in Germany, but, as he has said, it also spoke to repressive authoritarianism in recent U.S. history. Of particular importance to the novel were the many actual lynchings that occurred after the Civil War, most of them of black people in the South. Years after the novel's publication, as the civil rights movement grew in the 1950s and 1960s, lynchings increased as well, reviving interest in Clark's novel about a lynching. Between 1954 and 1968, forty people were lynched in the South, including two white men and one black man working to register black voters in 1962.

The Ox-Bow Incident, set 100 years earlier in the Old West of the nineteenth century, is the story of a group of men who, in the absence of the sheriff, embark on a mission to find rustlers who have, reportedly, killed a cowboy named Kincaid. The group includes men with a variety of different views regarding their mission. Some, out of macho egotism, are hotheadedly intent on vengeance and on taking the law into their own hands. Others are unenthusiastic about the project but join the group to protect themselves. Others are pressured into participating or accompany the posse with the hope of turning them back. Eventually, three men are found and lynched, one suffering hideously from the botched job. On the way home, the lynching party encounters the sheriff and the cowboy whose murder they thought they were avenging. In the denouement, one of the reluctant lynching party participants and his father, the ringleader, kill themselves.

The novel, often considered an "anti-Western," marked a turn in America's value system. It seemed to many readers to contradict the spirit of violence, decisive action, and manliness found in the older westerns, causing a reexamination of what had once been called frontier values. Unlike the typical western, Van Tilburg Clark's novel has no real hero. Its sympathetic characters who argue against the lynching—Osgood, the minister, Davies, the merchant, and Gerald Tetley, the young man forced by his father to participate—are ineffectual weaklings, easily intimidated or overcome by the cruel egotists who believe that their honor rests on the successful pursuit and lynching of supposed culprits.

Interest in the novel, and the highly successful 1943 film adapted from it, was revived in the 1960s when a new edition was published. The novel became an argument against the violence growing throughout the South as whites joined blacks to encourage voter registration and integration.

Additional Readings: Martin Kich, *Western American Novelists*, vol. 1 (New York: Garland, 1995); Max Westbrook, *Walter Van Tilburg Clark* (New York: Twayne, 1969).

172. *All the King's Men*, by Robert Penn Warren (United States, 1946). *All the King's Men* enjoys a unique status in American history: It is a political novel with a timely subject (the rise of a popular and feared dictator), but it has endured as a universal consideration of power and justice and the relationship, in human terms, of good and evil.

The fictional Willie Stark, a brilliant, charismatic, and manipulative man of the people who rises from obscurity to become governor of the state, was inspired by and based on the career of governor of Louisiana Huey Long. Long rose to power in 1928, in a spectacular campaign in which, like Willie Stark, he represented the voiceless common people fighting against the entrenched power of a wealthy class that had dominated politics in Louisiana for more than a hundred years and had showed no sign of ever relinquishing one iota of privilege.

The federal government, under the presidency of Calvin Coolidge, who believed that "the business of America is *business*," promoted corporate welfare and did nothing for the small farmer, who saw both his profits and his land slipping away. Nor did the state

of Louisiana help until Long was elected. Long went on, as governor, to make himself an absolute dictator, controlling virtually every aspect of life, even shaping the judiciary through his personally appointed attorney general. When the legislature, in anger, attempted to impeach him in 1929, he circumvented it with trickery and force and went on to solidify his power. While being accused by history of both demagoguery and corruption, Long nevertheless did much for the common man in Louisiana. Among his improvements were building hospitals and bridges, paving roads, dramatically improving education, and issuing free textbooks.

The novel, narrated by Jack Burden, describes the rise and the final fall of Willie Stark, ending with his assassination. It details both his potential for good, shown in his consistent motivation to benefit the common people, and the incipient evil in his inevitable abuse of power. The book concentrates, in the final analysis, not so much on Willie Stark as on the intelligent, perceptive, and passionate observer who, inevitably, as part of the human race, becomes involved in the web of power and deceit.

Published first in August 1946, the novel became an immediate bestseller. An initial run of 7,500 copies was sold immediately; then followed four more printings, each selling as rapidly as the first. An Armed Services paperback edition was distributed to servicemen. A *Time* Magazine Reading Program edition was published in 1963; a Franklin Library edition came out in 1976; and an abridged edition with a limited vocabulary was issued. By 1949, 40,000 copies had been sold. By 1955, it has been estimated, some 2 million copies were in circulation. The novel went through more than fifty printings and was translated into twenty-four languages.

In 1949, it was made into a movie, which received international acclaim and won the New York Film Critics Award, a Golden Globe Award, and an Academy Award as the Best Picture of the Year. A 1958 television version appeared starring Neville Brand.

The novel was a departure in fictional portrayals of the South. The post–Civil War history of the South, and Louisiana in particular, had dealt with the settlement of great plantations, the coming of the Civil War, Reconstruction, discriminatory freight rates, the resurgence of the Bourbons and the nouveau riche intruders, the White League, political machinations, and the rise of industry. It was a history fraught with suffering and emptiness, a history in which the common people have rarely been represented, in a culture fixated on the romantic or the sensationalistic, in such literature as *Gone With the Wind* or *So Red the Rose* or *Tobacco Road*. Robert Penn Warren, while not dealing with the common people per se (the way Harriet Beecher Stowe represented slaves in *Uncle Tom's Cabin*), at least recognized their plight in his portrayal of the rise of Willie Stark and in the sources of Willie's appeal.

The novel exerted considerable influence by raising for the first time in a modern setting Shakespearean questions of political accomplishment. How does one go about achieving good? How can a people suffer 100 years or more of brutal and consistent abuse without eventually turning to violence and dishonesty themselves? Are men like Willie Stark courageous men of the people, fighting valiantly for human rights? Or are they manipulative human beings, lusting after power? Is the power one needs to change the world always necessarily corrupting?

From the first the novel was controversial and generated discussion of the character of power. In the beginning, at a time when Adolf Hitler, Benito Mussolini, and the Japanese emperor were fresh in the public mind, critics focused on the figure of Willie Stark as a similar dictator, encompassing all the horrors that dictatorship represented. Was it not reprehensible of Warren to present such a man in sympathetic terms? Should he not have distinctly expressed his disapproval?

As time passed, readers began to see the universality and complexity of Warren's portrayal, seeing it in terms of moral relativism and noting its philosophical and theological implications. They began, in short, to broaden the scope of a work that demon-

strated both a wider and deeper influence on the American mind. Instead of narrowing or being increasingly forgotten, the work became more and more to be a cogent representation of an American dilemma, with ramifications not limited to time and place.

Additional Readings: Harold Bloom, ed., *Robert Penn Warren* (New York: Chelsea House, 1986); Harold Woodell, All the King's Men: *The Search for a Useable Past* (New York: Twayne, 1993).

173. *Catcher in the Rye*, by J.D. Salinger (United States, 1951). *Catcher in the Rye* is a product and an omen of an internally troubled people living in an externally carefree country following World War II. Soldiers were home from a terrible war that the Allies had won. The economic prospect for the country was optimistic. Capitalism was booming. Individuals and the country were at work. More people than ever were enjoying material plenty. The family was idealized. Women were on their pedestals and in their places within the home. Racial minorities were in their places and relatively quiet. Young people were presumably untroubled and untroublesome, idealized in many family television shows like *Ozzie and Harriet*. Churches were enjoyable social clubs. Conformity was valued and demanded.

Holden Caulfield was one of America's first glimpses of the turbulence that seethed beneath the bland, happy surface of the culture after World War II. In a picaresque plot, Holden, an antihero in the tradition of Huckleberry Finn, leaves yet another hated prep school where his wealthy parents have deposited him to take a troubling journey through New York City. As the story is told by Holden, as if to a psychiatrist, the journey is internalized and interpreted.

Holden's story reminded his adult audience that even in this affluent society adolescence was not, and never had been, a carefree time. In many ways his is a universal story of adolescent angst as he tries to come to grips with the unavoidable realities of adult life—sex, the loss of innocence, solemn and heavy responsibilities, and death. These are the leitmotifs that run through his journey. He worries about his little sister, all children, in fact, and the girls his age, whom he cherishes. He dreads their exposure to the confidence men and obscenities of the modern world. He feels the heavy responsibility to protect them, to be a "catcher in the rye." And he is troubled by intruding mortality, mourning still the untimely death of his older brother and betraying his obsession with a favorite expression of being amused, "It killed me."

Because of the novel, readers began to view their own world in a different light because it was also a commentary on a particular time in history. Although Holden is an unreliable narrator, limited in self-awareness and judgment, he is able to pinpoint troubling aspects of his society. He sees that far too much importance is placed on external show, extravagant displays of material wealth, physical prowess, physical appearance, and social clout. The readers found in the book a warning, that to live so completely on the surface in a superficial culture, as does Holden's Hollywood brother D.B., is to lose all individualism, all sense of true self. Salinger's book showed them that such people, who seem in this age to live only on the surface more than ever, are the most contemptible of humans; they are life's "phonies" whose characters are untrustworthy and unknown even to themselves.

Catcher in the Rye articulates for a large audience a largely Emersonian message, which proclaimed an inner, spiritual reality, which society—especially postwar society—was always attempting to undermine. Holden has not yet been co-opted; he, like many others with vague feelings of dissatisfaction, still has religious and spiritual needs that the world happily ignores and refuses to fulfill. The book was part of an underground revival of Transcendentalism that produced a renewed interest in Eastern mysticism, a determination on the part of some people to "drop out" of commercialized society, to commit themselves to "beatific" transcendence. In short, there is a direct line from Salinger's book to the 1950s Beat Generation.

Catcher in the Rye inspired and marked a radical change in the attitude of young people in America in a number of ways: (1) It fostered a suspicion of the "establishment," especially one in which individualism was lost to commercial society's demands for conformity; and (2) it encouraged the role of youthful rebellion and, in a sense, created the generation gap in the 1950s, making it the norm rather than the exception in society.

The book defined and articulated adolescence as it would be perceived for decades. Adolescence was no longer just an extension of childhood. It was a separate category. It was no longer seen as a time when young people were mentored and shaped by wise and loving parents, as in the popular television series *Father Knows Best*. Instead, adolescence was equated with rebellion against all authority. The difference can be seen in changes in the image of the adolescent. In the 1950s, one had the picture, albeit an ideal, of the young man, very like the Nelson brothers, who wore neatly pressed shirts and pants and sported a crewcut. He ate regular meals with the family and spent most of his free time and his vacations with his family. Adolescence was, in a real sense, an extension of childhood. When Holden Caulfield turned his "hunting cap" around, he also reversed the image of the young man. In its place came the picture of a surly, weirdly dressed, resentful rebel who, at his best, is rarely found at family gatherings and, at worst, is involved with drugs and sex.

Fifty years after its publication, the novel continues to sell over 250,000 copies a year. But *Catcher in the Rye* has also increased in controversy over the years and has been more often the subject of censorship than any book young people read. It has been the subject of challenges and banning in every year since 1955, when it became apparent that this was an enormously popular book with an unmistakable impact. Although much of the censorship of the book was prompted by its language, the more significant, underlying objection is to a sympathetic presentation of an adolescent who questions authority and who objects to the hypocrisy of his elders.

Additional Readings: Warren French, *J.D. Salinger, Revisited* (Boston: Twayne, 1988); Sanford Pinsker, *"The Catcher in the Rye": Innocence under Pressure* (New York: Twayne, 1993); Joel Salzberg, ed., *Critical Essays on Salinger's "The Catcher in the Rye"* (Boston: G.K. Hall, 1990).

174. *Invisible Man*, by Ralph Ellison (United States, 1952). Ralph Ellison's *Invisible Man* has often been praised as the finest novel of post–World War II America. Although mythic and universal in scope, its impact derives from its unfolding of the African American experience in the Deep South and New York City's Harlem in the 1940s. It was a time when racial segregation prevailed throughout the United States. In its most unrelieved form in the southern states, laws kept the races separate in every aspect of life, and the vote was denied black citizens. The educational and job discrimination African Americans faced in the South sent many families to northern cities for opportunities. Harlem, a black neighborhood in New York, was frequently their destination.

Harlem also engendered many social and political movements intended to redress the inequalities and injustices of African Americans throughout the country. Among these was Marxism, which had racial justice as an expressed aim but which was often criticized as being racist and sexist in its operation. In the South, the struggle for improvement in the lives of African Americans in the 1940s and 1950s was concentrated on the right to vote and to serve on juries. In the North, reformers were addressing segregation.

This is the setting in which *Invisible Man* unfolds. It is about the African American who is in, but not of, the larger white culture and thus has difficulty defining himself. The protagonist narrates his history from his self-imposed prison in an underground room lit by 1,369 lightbulbs. His story begins with his high school graduation. As a reward for his valedictorian speech recommending racial humility and accommodation, he is given a college scholarship. After he is expelled by the treacherous president of the all-black college, he goes to Harlem, where he becomes disillusioned by both black radicals and white Marxists, the last of whom he had earlier joined. After a bloody riot in which the two forces collide, he finds that his skin is turning white. Whites trying to escape blacks are turning black, he finds, and blacks trying to escape whites are turning white. The truth is he and most of his kind are invisible. After a prolonged time underground, he anticipates rebirth into the world.

Ellison's novel was an instant success, winning the National Book Award in 1953. Moreover, the novel has grown in importance throughout the twentieth century and brought Ellison the Medal of Freedom in 1969. Nevertheless, it was highly controversial and received many negative reviews at its first appearance. Not surprisingly, the targets of his scathing satire, the Communist Party and black nationalists, published their outrage when the book first appeared. But he was also criticized by both white and black moderate reformers for failing to advance the social and political issues then so crucial to black advancement. The novel was also denounced by many activists in the late 1950s and 1960s as the work of an "Uncle Tom."

But the enduring influence of *Invisible Man* derives from its presentation of a black protagonist as a complex human being with a full range of human refinements and foibles, ambiguities, and paradoxes, rather than as a narrow stereotype or a narrowly drawn victim or an abstraction.

The novel is also influential in, for the first time in literature, using the black experience to create a universal hero undergoing classical tribulations and grappling with the universal problem of human identity.

Additional Readings: John Hersey, ed., *Ralph Ellison: A Collection of Critical Essays* (Englewood Cliffs, NJ: Prentice-Hall, 1974); Eric Sundquist, ed., *Cultural Contexts for Ralph Ellison's "Invisible Man"* (Boston: Bedford, 1995).

175. *Go Tell It on the Mountain*, by James Baldwin (United States, 1953). James Baldwin, an electrifying new talent, burst on the scene in 1953, encompassing in his first fiction a segment of life in America entirely foreign to most readers. The novel speaks to issues pertinent to its setting in the late 1920s and early 1930s as well as to the time of its appearance in the 1950s. Looming in the consciousness of the African American characters are the years of black slavery in the South as well as the great displacement of blacks forced by economics to follow the more promising vocational opportunities held out by northern cities, leaving the support of their extended families far behind them. The action of the narrative takes place in Harlem, in New York City, where so many black southerners settled. Some of these displaced settlers did find better lives, but for most, the cities—Chicago, Philadelphia, Detroit, Washington, D.C.—like New York, were not the utopias African Americans were seeking. Harlem, for example, was a mecca for writers and musicians; its churches gave its residents meaning and solace. But Harlem was, nevertheless, a ghetto, filled with the poor, who felt exploited by absentee landlords, businessmen, and employers. Many felt betrayed when the dream of beneficence and equality that had lured them north was exposed as fraudulent. The frustrations were often played out through physical and psychological violence within the family unit.

In *Go Tell It on the Mountain*, the destructiveness wrought by history and played out within the family is directed against a young boy, despised by his stepfather for his physical smallness, lack of beauty, and the uncertainty of his sexual identity. Despite having what are regarded as handicaps, the boy has indisputable gifts that his stepfather lacks—a quick intelligence, skill as a writer and student, and heightened spirituality—and that make the stepfather's hatred even keener. Parts One and Three of the novel are presented from the boy's point of view, while Part Two is from the point of view of other key characters, including his stepfather.

The highly emotional Pentecostal church is the center of this family's life, and John's apparent visitation by the Holy Spirit on the occasion of his baptism lifts him up above his stepfather, a lay minister, to a position of power and respect in the congregation,

which recognizes the magnitude of his spiritual gifts.

Baldwin's novel was well received by the white and the black critical establishments and by many readers as well. Its influence lay in its being one of the first brutally realistic looks inside the urban African American family where the violence that the black race had suffered at the hands of white society reverberates at the hands of the black patriarch.

The novel also brought to its audience the first portrait from an African American of the powerful black urban church and the ambivalence with which many regarded that institution that seems both comforting and emotionally exploitative and that encouraged in its disciples the humility of Jesus in their relations with whites.

Finally, the novel connected for its readers the history of slavery and the Great Migration to mid-twentieth-century life lived by urban African Americans, in effect, warning of the racial violence to come.

Additional Readings: Fern Marja Eckman, *The Furious Passage of James Baldwin* (New York: Evans, 1966); Trudier Harris, ed., *New Essays on "Go Tell It on the Mountain"* (Cambridge: Cambridge University Press, 1996); Stanley Macebuh, *James Baldwin: A Critical Study* (New York: Third Press, 1973).

176. *Fahrenheit 451*, by Ray Bradbury (United States, 1953). When Ray Bradbury's popular futuristic novel appeared, the United States was involved in the Cold War with the Soviet Union. In its frenzied fear that communism would invade the country, the government had throughout much of the 1940s and 1950s been vigilant to a fault in ferreting out citizens whom it believed to be in sympathy with leftist causes—causes that were automatically labeled as dangerous to democracy and the country. Much of this policing centered on printed information. Citizens lost their jobs and reputations for having subscribed to book clubs or real journals that were frowned upon by the government as friendly to communism. And many writers, like the "Hollywood Ten" screenwriters and playwright Arthur Miller, were persecuted for writing materials of which the government disapproved.

Although Bradbury's novel takes place at some future time in the United States, it also focuses on the government's intolerance of books, a practice that at one time had included only selected volumes but had come to include all books of any kind. The novel, coming at the height of the Cold War, projects a dystopia where the intellect and emotion are disparaged and citizens no longer have the normal connections with nature or one another. The chief characteristic of the country is the ban the government places on all books. Indeed, the main work of the country's firemen, the chief law enforcement officers, is not to extinguish fires but to start them, as a means of destroying books. The title of the novel derives from the temperature at which paper burns.

With no emotion and no thought, their lives are spent, appropriately, sitting in front of giant televisions. Their only interaction is with the screen, not with each other.

The chief character of the novel is Guy Montag, a fireman who has begun to steal books from some of the collections the firemen are supposed to burn.

Guy is married to a woman who, normal for this society, regards television characters as her true family and isolates herself from Guy by keeping her headphones turned on. In contrast to Guy's wife is another young woman named Clarisse who is treated as an outcast because of her unconventional behavior and attitude—that is, she loves nature and openly expresses her feelings.

When Guy begins to question the ban on books, he is told that books cause trouble and unhappiness, especially among minorities, and that it is best for all citizens to just ban books. But true complications begin when Guy's wife turns him in to the authorities because he has books in their house. In Guy's confrontation with his chief who insists that his house and books must be burned, the chief is killed. A fugitive at the end, Guy joins an underground group of older men who have each memorized a great work of literature in the assurance that one

day they will be allowed to publish and make them available for everyone to read.

Fahrenheit 451 was an enormously popular work that ran to multiple printings and was adapted into a highly successful film in 1966. One of the strongest indictments of censorship and a highly popular work of literature, it has relevance even today as books are still taken off library shelves and textbooks are still expurgated. Ironically, Bradbury's frank treatment of issues controversial in the 1950s and 1960s caused his own publisher to cut or modify parts of the book without his knowledge. No one realized for many years that two versions of the book were being marketed—one for schools and one for adult readers.

Fahrenheit 451, and the censorship of the book, was the single biggest influence in the setting up of the American Library Association's Intellectual Freedom Committee, which brought pressure to bear on publishers who tried to expurgate books to promote sales.

Bradbury's book made the connection between censorship and the dehumanization and degeneration of society. The book also warned that minorities initiated far too much censorship, whether they be African Americans asking for the removal of Mark Twain's *Adventures of Huckleberry Finn* from the classroom or evangelical Christians urging that Charles Darwin's *The Origin of Species* be removed from science curricula.

Moreover, Bradbury prophesied, at a time when television was in its infant stage and the Internet a complete unknown, that an entire society would one day devote itself to staring at various screens, living their lives vicariously and interacting more intensely with personages on and through the screen than with flesh and blood people.

Additional Readings: Harold Bloom, ed., *Ray Bradbury* (Philadelphia: Chelsea House, 2001); Wayne L. Johnson, *Ray Bradbury* (New York: Frederick Ungar, 1980); William F. Nolan, *The Ray Bradbury Companion* (Detroit: Gale Research, 1975).

177. *On the Road*, by Jack Kerouac (United States, 1957). *On the Road*, a picaresque chronicle of America's Beat Generation, takes place in the late 1940s and early 1950s, a post–World War II era that ushered in great prosperity, new technology, quick fixes, and wider-based education. These advances, however, also brought with them conformity, standardization, an emphasis on materialism, and intolerance of the foreign, the eccentric, and the "abnormal." Religious institutions in these years often tended to place more emphasis on the happiness that derives from social and material success than on spiritual fulfillment. The Cold War that developed between Western capitalist nations, the United States in particular, and the Soviet Union and its satellite countries further homogenized American social thought by treating with suspicion those whose political leanings were too liberal. The clothes, the houses, and the leisure time of Americans did not admit of much variety. Movies and the new medium of television seemed to accentuate homogeneity. The old rugged individualism of the American frontiersman had given way to conformity.

On the Road is the story of a journey by automobile. It is as much spiritual and emotional as physical, pushing ever westward toward a frontier that, ironically, lies in Eastern philosophy and drugs and inside the human psyche. The journey is undertaken by the novel's chief protagonists, Sal Paradise, the narrator, and Dean Moriarty—wild, young bohemian men identified as members of the Beat Generation, the term "beat" deriving from the word *beatific*.

Despite the novel's hostile reception by literary critics, Kerouac's novel took America by storm, not only in its huge sales but in its frenzied generation of fads and cults. Kerouac was immediately besieged with offers to appear on television, to be interviewed by popular and fashionable magazines. He was offered $100,000 for the screen rights to his story, which he accepted. In imitation of its characters, Americans are said to have bought thousands of pairs of Levis and hit the road. The merchandising of *On the Road* continued into the twenty-first century, as Kerouac's picture and name are used in ads for

clothes and demand remains high for Kerouac memorabilia. Some indication of its continuing popularity is shown in the fact that in 2001 a scroll on which Kerouac wrote the novel was auctioned off at $2.43 million.

The novel, with its alternative lifestyle and attitudes, answered a great need in many Americans for the freedom and largeness of an unconventional life out of the mainstream. It held up the values of adventure and risk for the ordinary person as well as for the artist. It ridiculed the newer conformity of the postwar years and affirmed the country's older virtues of individualism and adventure. It also affirmed the importance of a life of the spirit, in contrast to consumerism and materialism.

Though often criticized for failing to take a political stance, especially in its focus on spiritual transcendence, some social thinkers believed that the book, in celebrating difference, made way for the involvement of young white Americans in the civil rights movement. Many young political radicals who surfaced in the 1960s confessed that Kerouac's *On the Road* was their original inspiration to challenge a discriminatory system.

Additional Readings: Ann Charters, ed., *The Beats: Literary Bohemians in Postwar America*, 2 vols. (Detroit: Gale Research, 1983); Tim Hunt, *Kerouac's Crooked Road: Development of a Fiction* (Hamden, CT: Archon, 1981); Barry Miles, *Jack Kerouac, King of the Beats: A Portrait* (New York: Holt, 1998).

178. *Atlas Shrugged*, **by Ayn Rand (United States, 1957).** The formative background of the novel, which created a cult of followers of "Objectivism" and of its author Ayn Rand, begins in pre-Revolutionary Russia and ends in the Cold War of the United States in the 1950s. Rand was born in Russia in 1905, during a turbulent time when, after centuries of slavery and the subjugation of working people in fields and factories, the common people were expressing a growing dissatisfaction with the ruling class. In 1917, when Rand was twelve years old, the revolution against the czar and the Russian aristocrats began. The new communist government under Lenin confiscated private land and broke the power of upper-class families so that wealth could be redistributed for the common good. Rand's family was among those dispossessed by communism, and by the time she left for the United States in 1926, Josef Stalin was already gaining control of Soviet Russia and beginning his notorious purges.

The United States to which Rand came in 1926 was also undergoing radical change. The devastating economic depression, brought about largely by unbridled capitalism and characterized by intense labor unrest, was soon to hit the country. To alleviate problems the administration of Franklin Roosevelt instigated greater government control in the 1930s. By the end of his administration, the Social Security Administration, for example, had set up an effective system for helping injured, jobless, and retired workers, and laws had been enacted to protect factory workers from unsafe, unhealthy working practices, starvation wages, killing hours, and management attempts to thwart union organizing. Businesses were also beginning to be regulated by antitrust measures.

Rand viewed such measures as dangerously creeping communism, much like she had witnessed in the Soviet Union and that had led to the downfall of her family. In the Cold War years of the 1950s when the U.S. government carried out an intense campaign against political leftists of all sorts, she wrote her novel to attack the power of the state, labor unions, and restrictive measures to control capitalism. In *Atlas Shrugged*, her futuristic novel, the good guys are businessmen and women—capitalistic "prime movers," angered by government regulation. They secretly congregate in a hidden refuge to bide their time and make plans to take over the country themselves. The chief value, the novel insists, is the individual, who is more important than the rest of society, the state, or God.

The publication of *Atlas Shrugged* brought Rand instant, worldwide attention. The fol-

lowers of Objectivism, a philosophy first outlined in the novel, constituted a fervent and sizable cult. As a result of the novel, the Nathaniel Branden Institute was set up by, and named for, one of her admirers to perpetuate her ideas, offering courses and lectures on her philosophy. It was later renamed the Ayn Rand Institute. Part of the work of the institute was the publication of a newsletter and a magazine containing political and social essays and book and film reviews. The institute also offered a mail order book service.

However, the book also had the effect of alienating many conservatives and splitting the conservative movement into what were called true conservatives and libertarians, the party that Rand's book is given credit for helping establish. This split was caused largely by the novel's firm recommendation of rationalism, atheism, sexual freedom, separation of church and state, and the nontraditional family.

At the beginning of the twenty-first century, the American Philosophical Association still includes an active Ayn Rand society, and a television movie of *Atlas Shrugged* is in development.

Additional Readings: James Thomas Baker, *Ayn Rand* (Boston: Twayne, 1987); Allan Gotthelf, *On Ayn Rand* (Belmont, CA: Wadsworth, 2000).

179. *The Ugly American*, by William J. Lederer and Eugene Burdick (United States, 1958). The episodic novel, which Lederer and Burdick expressly wrote as a criticism of how Americans in official positions overseas dealt with Asians, in particular, was set in Southeast Asia in the 1950s at a time when communism was being introduced to Third World countries and was spreading with a speed that the United States and Great Britain found alarming.

The modern association of the United States with Vietnam, a key country in Southeast Asia, began during World War II, when troops under the leadership of Ho Chi Minh entered into an alliance with the United States to drive the Japanese out of their territory. When the Japanese surrendered in

1945, Ho Chi Minh declared his country's independence from France, which had claimed Vietnam as a colonial possession. But Ho Chi Minh's communist sympathies caused the United States, then obsessed with the dangers of communism, to denounce Ho and align itself with France. Despite the active help of the United States, France, whose citizenry were out of sympathy with their government's continuing presence in Vietnam, lost and made plans to leave Vietnam, a country that was now divided into the northern half led by Ho Chi Minh and the southern half led by a European-supported emperor. The United States continued to influence affairs in Southeast Asia, refusing to allow South Vietnam to participate in elections in 1955 and vowing to keep South Vietnam, Laos, and Cambodia free of communism, at all costs.

Set in an area near Vietnam, when the United States, European countries, and Russia all maintained a strong presence there, the novel shows the superior attitude of Americans who refuse to learn the languages of the countries they occupy, refuse to socialize with the Asians native to the host countries, and remain doggedly ignorant of the problems of their poor. The Western military officers and diplomatic corps look with horror on communism as an evil ideology and are incapable of understanding why the Asian masses find communism so compelling.

By contrast, the Russians of the novel make valiant attempts to learn Asian languages, to post signs and distribute literature in both Russian and Asian languages, and to treat the natives as their equals.

There are four major American characters in the novel. Homer Atkins is an engineer who has been hired to oversee officially approved jobs of building dams and roads to accommodate military vehicles, projects that will obviously help the Americans but not the people who live there. He is ridiculed and humiliated for offering instead his own plan of local low-cost projects to help the ordinary people achieve a measure of self-sufficiency. Finally, Atkins pulls out and works directly with the local farmers on small projects to pump water to fields. Another character Jonathan Brown, a U.S. senator on a fact-finding visit, is deluded by the military and diplomatic personnel who misrepresent facts to him, are careful to mistranslate conversations, shield him from any opinion that would give him the impression that they are not being successful in suppressing communism, and divert his attention with numerous lavish parties. Two ambassadors in the novel are Gilbert MacWhite, who is fired from his job, and Louis Sears, who demonstrates the worst qualities of the system of appointing ambassadors. He is wealthy, makes big political contributions, and doesn't raise controversies.

The Ugly American brought to public attention the incompetence and misguided motives of the U.S. presence in Asia and actually led to official congressional hearings on U.S. policies. Specifically, it resulted in members of Congress taking a closer look at the way in which foreign aid to Asia was being used. Some changes in approach were recommended. Although the book changed the minds of many citizens interested in Asian affairs, especially impressing on them the danger of these countries being converted to communism by Russians who dealt with them in a more humane and effective way, few fundamental changes were made in the behavior or policies touching Asia. One year after the novel was published, U.S. involvement in the Vietnam War began.

The book, however, made many Americans aware of how they presented themselves in *any* foreign country. As a result of the book, the term "ugly American" entered the language as a term for describing the clumsy, ignorant, and rude tourist on foreign soil. The novel inspired a movie in 1963, starring Marlon Brando.

Additional Readings: George C. Herring, *America's Longest War . . . 1950–1975* (New York: Wiley, 1979); Stanley Karnow, *Vietnam* (New York: Foreign Policy Association, 1983).

180. *To Kill a Mockingbird*, by Harper Lee (United States, 1960). African American struggles for justice and equality, and the resultant conflict, had reached a critical phase in the United States, and especially in the American South, at the time of the publication of Harper Lee's *To Kill a Mockingbird*. In 1954, decades of segregation in education were legally ended with the Supreme Court's ruling in *Brown v. Board of Education*. Then in 1955, after Mrs. Rosa Parks was arrested for refusing to sit in the back of a Montgomery, Alabama, bus, a citywide boycott began, eventually ending segregation of public transportation. Other civil rights demonstrations throughout the South were usually accompanied by violence against blacks. The homes and churches of black ministers were bombed; peaceful demonstrators were attacked by police with dogs and fire hoses; civil rights workers were killed; and black children and adults seeking to integrate schools and universities were threatened and pelted with rocks and eggs. Much of the violence in the 1950s was occurring in Alabama, the state that is the setting for Lee's novel.

Into this climate, *To Kill a Mockingbird* appeared in 1960. Set in a small village south of Montgomery, Alabama, in the 1930s, it is the story of three children who observe and are fundamentally changed by the trial of a black man on a charge of rape, a story that echoes a notorious trial, also in the 1930s and also in Alabama, in which nine black men were falsely accused and found guilty of rape by two white prostitutes. The leading character of *To Kill a Mockingbird* is Atticus Finch, a small-town southern lawyer who defends Tom Robinson, the accused man. As the plot proceeds, attitudes toward race and class and long-standing traditions of inequality and injustice are exposed. Lynchings, for example, are a way of life in this community, some of whose citizens attempt to take justice into their own hands before Tom Robinson's trial. Racial hatred is too ingrained in the largely dirt-poor jurors for them to resist the arguments offered by the district attorney or the testimony of Tom's poor white accuser, even though clear evidence is presented to the contrary. The reader learns that only two of the many black citizens in the

area know how to read, that blacks never serve on juries, that they are segregated in the balcony of the courtroom and in a damp jail where white criminals are never incarcerated. Venomous measures are also taken against Atticus Finch for his defense of a black man. Just as the novel offered the reader a sympathetic perspective on the lives of southern African Americans, it also provided its readers with a fresh view of southern whites who were becoming increasingly distressed at the injustices of the place they called home. Atticus Finch was a hero, however flawed, unlike the stereotypical southerner usually perpetuated by both northern and southern writers.

The immediate responses to the book swung from one extreme to the other. On the negative side, the book was denounced and banned from some libraries and public school curricula because it questioned adult, white, and governmental authority and used ungrammatical and profane language. On the positive side was a popular outpouring of praise that resulted in Lee's being awarded a Pulitzer Prize. An Academy Award–winning movie was also made from the novel, released in 1962 and starring Gregory Peck as Atticus Finch.

Few works have had a greater immediate or long-term impact on readers than has *To Kill a Mockingbird*. In its forty-year history, it has never been out of print. Within a year of its publication, 600,000 copies had been sold, and it had been translated into ten languages. A study of bestselling books, from 1895 to 1975, found that it was the seventh bestselling book in America. By 1982 over 15 million copies of the book had been sold. By 1982, over 18 million in paperback books alone had sold. It has consistently been one of the most frequently taught texts in high schools since its appearance in 1960.

In 1991, the Library of Congress found that among American readers surveyed the novel was listed second only to the Bible as a book that had most decidedly changed the lives of its readers. And in England, in 1997, newspapers found that their readership listed

To Kill a Mockingbird as one of the best ten novels ever written.

For decades the book has changed the way many southerners view their society, opening their eyes to a history and to attitudes that they had never seen in their own backyards. Arguments continue to the present over whether or not black characters in the novel are stereotyped, and for that reason primarily, the novel is still consistently challenged and banned. But many white and black readers alike contend that their first encounter in literature with multidimensional black characters came with their reading of Harper Lee's novel. The stereotypical black character in literature had been either a shuffling "Tom" or a diabolical fiend. This novel was one of the first by a white author to present a fully realized black character with whom one could identity and sympathize.

The novel dispelled another stereotype of the time—that of the white southern male, portrayed either as a tobacco-chewing redneck or as a Kentucky colonel. Atticus Finch was neither. He eschewed the gun culture of his region, devotedly fostered tolerance, benevolence, and reason in his children, and read omnivorously.

The novel has had a special impact on lawyers and journalists who list Atticus Finch as a role model. In a literary age of the antihero, this novel recasts our definition of the hero as one who struggles against the society to which he belongs. Ironically, the novel, which challenged consistent stereotypes, also created a persistent, frequently imitated stereotype—that of the southern crusader.

Additional Readings: Claudia Durst Johnson, To Kill a Mockingbird: *Threatening Boundaries* (New York: Twayne, 1994); Claudia Durst Johnson, *Understanding* To Kill a Mockingbird (Westport, CT: Greenwood Press, 1994).

181. *Catch-22*, by Joseph Heller (United States, 1961). *Catch-22* appeared in 1961 at a time when America was convinced that it had just fought for and won a victory for democracy against fascism in the 1940s, and had for some time turned to fight communism to save its economic system, seen as the foundation of democracy, which was being assailed at every turn.

Americans looked back with considerable pride on a war against Japan and fascist Germany and Italy, a war in which Joseph Heller had been an active participant as a U.S. Air Force bombardier. The war was not just a defense of democracy; it was a preservation of free enterprise upon which it was assumed that democracy depended.

When the war was over, the Cold War began against Russian and Chinese communism, seen as the new enemy threatening the nation's capitalism, that is, "the American way of life." The trouble was that the enemy was seen as within: people who had expressed sympathy for communists, people with socialist leanings, workers who organized in labor unions. Congress sought to ferret out these undesirables through its own House Committee on Un-American Activities. In the course of Senator Joseph McCarthy's investigations, he declared that General George Marshall and even President Harry Truman were traitors.

Heller's book challenged these assumptions about the military during World War II and about the merits of capitalism during the Cold War. In the narrative about Air Force Captain John Yossarian, Heller claims classic and biblical myth for comment on the contemporary world. Yossarian has flown the maximum number of bombing missions and yet must continue flying because of "Catch-22": You can only get out of flying more missions if you are insane, but if you plead insanity, you are obviously quite sane. There is, in short, no way out. He continues to be tortured by the deaths of his fellow flyers and the general insanity of the system, especially by the actions of one Milo Minderbinder who lives to make money on the black market in any way possible and at the cost of many lives if necessary. There is one thing Yossarian will not do to get out of flying more missions: He will not agree to return home as a spokesman for the war effort. Finally, the book's hero deserts during time of war, planning to reach the neutral sanctuary of Sweden.

Although the novel appeared to considerable praise in 1961, it was the escalation of the war in Vietnam, beginning in 1964, that gave *Catch-22* cult status, for it was finally recognized and appreciated widely as an antiwar novel, written well before the antiwar stance had become popular. Those who read it saw that even the good guys in a war destroyed not only innocent children but their own men, fighting on the same side. Parallels were drawn between Vietnam and the novel, the final escape of Yossarian compared to draft resisters fleeing to Canada.

Readers during the Vietnam War also correctly saw that *Catch-22* was not only an antiwar novel but also an anti*military* novel. The novel's military is madness personified. Its blundering is laughable on the surface but at the core sinister and destructive. Many veterans of World War II claimed that Heller had scarcely exaggerated, that they could match each of the novel's absurdities from their own experience. The conclusion the novel reaches is that the United States used its own brand of fascism to conquer Hitler's fascism.

Only after the Vietnam War was over did it register with readers that Heller's real target was rampant capitalism, represented in the novel by Milo Minderbinder. Furthermore, there can be little doubt that the novel contained devastating criticism of the Red-baiters who had taken over the country in the 1950s. At one point, Milo, like the U.S. government on occasion, had entered into a pact with fascists to run his syndicate called M and M Enterprises. When the guards try to confiscate the German planes he's using, he justifies his fascist connections and shrieks, "Is this Russia?"—implying that he is much more comfortable dealing with the fascists than with the communists. He makes deals with the Americans to bomb German installations and deals with the Germans to bomb his own people, doing it all in the name of "private enterprise." In the novel, it is Milo's greed that creates much of the nonsensical devastation as, for example, his bombing of the airfield of his own base and killing his comrades in the process.

In a mythological episode, after the death of young Snowden in Yossarian's plane, the flyer sheds his uniform and sits naked in a tree, looking down on the activities of the base, in what is not just a repudiation of the war and the military but an attempt to return to an Edenic innocence outside the bombing raids and the killing, outside the commercial greed that perpetuates the war. However, Milo, the epitome of capitalism, finds Yossarian and, like Lucifer tempting Adam with an apple, tries to tempt him to eat and enjoy some chocolate-covered cotton he has invested in, a scene that sets up Milo as Lucifer or Satan, tempting mankind toward the Fall. Throughout the novel, one finds scenes equating Milo's blatant black marketeering to Wall Street profiteering—and at a time when the people who voiced much milder criticisms of capitalism were being blacklisted or jailed for their pains. One assumes that readers were too busy laughing to catch the dangerous reproach.

In any case, the supreme measure of the influence exerted by any work is its effect on the language, and the phrase "Catch-22" has entered the dictionary as a description of all ridiculous double-binds. A highly praised film was made, based on the novel, in 1970.

Additional Readings: Robert Merrill, *Joseph Heller* (Boston: Twayne, 1987); David Seed, *The Fiction of Joseph Heller* (New York: St. Martin's Press, 1989).

182. *One Flew Over the Cuckoo's Nest,* by Ken Kesey (United States, 1962). Ken Kesey's novel, from the first recognized as a classic of the 1960s counterculture, is rooted in the complacency of the 1950s and the rebellion of the 1960s. The 1950s in America, despite the Cold War, the Korean conflict, and the Red Scare, were, at least superficially, tranquil, happy years. College students and other young people were as acquiescent, on the whole, as were most of the rest of the population. Jobs were plentiful, capitalism and business were booming, and material comfort seemed to be at the fingertips of anyone who desired it. Sociologists, surveying the scene, pronounced "conformity," "materialism," "patriotism," "capitalism," and "advertising" to be the key words to describe the society.

The 1960s produced a sharp reaction to the conformity and acquiescence of the 1950s, becoming a decade of turbulent, sometimes violent civil disobedience on the part of significant numbers of Americans. There were social protests across the nation's college and university campuses as students reacted against the old en loco parentis administration policies that censored their expression and treated them as children. Many young people, both white and black, became involved in the civil rights protests. Members of a counterculture, the old beatniks and younger hippies gathered in the nation's cities to adopt lifestyles in marked contrast to middle-class materialism. Finally, the catalyst for much unhappiness was the Vietnam War. Organizations that worked in the antiwar cause included Students for a Democratic Society, the Congress of Racial Equality, the Student Non-Violent Coordinating Committee, and the National Organization of Women.

Ken Kesey's novel was a scathing satire of the society of the 1950s, presented, in part, as an institution for the insane where all outsiders, rebels, and society's cast-offs were incarcerated. The main characters are an Indian named Chief Bromden, who finally escapes from the institution to rejoin his people, and McMurphy, whose rebelliousness and cunning bring liberation to the other inmates but is finally destroyed by the system, which administers a lobotomy, forcing Chief Bromden to liberate his friend by killing him.

Kesey's novel became enormously successful, established him as a cult figure in the 1960s, and secured its place as a modern classic. In the twenty years after it first appeared, it went through sixty-eight printings, selling 7 million copies, and the 1975 movie based on the novel, starring Jack Nicholson as McMurphy, won five Academy Awards.

The influence of Kesey's novel was enormous in its expression of the individual's struggle against a society that tries to turn all people into machines. In this sense it reaffirmed as saving values virtues that many had once seen as fundamental to America: independence and heroism, in a clear parallel with James Fenimore Cooper's Leatherstocking Tales.

The book was also influential in its optimism: McMurphy, in Christ-like fashion, is able to overcome the fascistic society to help his friends, and most of the inmates, including Bromden, are finally liberated.

Additional Readings: Barry H. Leeds, *Ken Kesey* (New York: F. Ungar Publishers, 1981); George J. Searles, ed., *A Casebook on Ken Kesey's "One Flew Over the Cuckoo's Nest"* (Albuquerque: University of New Mexico Press, 1992); Stephen Tanner, *Ken Kesey* (Boston: Twayne, 1983).

183. *The Bell Jar*, by Sylvia Plath (United States, 1963). A central text in the modern tradition of autobiographical fiction, Sylvia Plath's widely read novel was first published in England under the pseudonym Victoria Lucas, only later appearing under her true name in an American edition.

The novel takes place in 1953 and speaks to woman's restricted place in a 1950s culture, a time when she was often viewed as an ornament, with great stress placed on her appearance, as if "prettiness" was somehow a virtue. This too-frequent attitude led quite naturally to the expectation that women use every means to get themselves married, as they were believed to be truly fulfilled only in the role of wife and mother. As a homemaker, her life was consumed ideally by activities such as cooking, laundering, housecleaning, and baby-sitting. Even as late as the 1950s, unmarried, educated women were restricted largely to schoolteaching and clerical work. Many women suffered psychologically from these attitudes and limitations.

This is the background of attitudes and practices behind Plath's novel *The Bell Jar*. The central characters of the novel are a young college student named Esther Greenwood, her longtime boyfriend, and her mother. Esther, an aspiring writer, wins a spot, with several other students, as guest editor at a New York City fashion magazine. Her time is spent acquiring an acceptable wardrobe for one being groomed as an ornament and being set up with dates with men who humiliate and mortify her. The experience is so surreal that Esther finds herself increasingly removed from reality, the bell jar begins to descend over her, and her own behavior becomes increasingly bizarre. Back home in a suburb of Boston, her confidence is finally shattered by her failure to be accepted into a college writing workshop. Her low point is reached when she swallows a bottle of sleeping pills and hides beneath the house. She is found only after several days, is finally treated by an intelligent and sympathetic psychiatrist in a decent hospital, and is able to return to her old college life—but still wondering when the bell jar might again descend.

The novel, which first appeared only a month before Plath committed suicide at the age of thirty, shortly achieved a place as a classic portrayal of the descent into despair, more brutally graphic than similar novels like J.D. Salinger's *Catcher in the Rye* and Ken Kesey's *One Flew Over the Cuckoo's Nest*, with which it has been compared. The novel was largely responsible for elevating Plath to a cult figure.

Feminists, who have added the novel to the standard college and university reading lists of Women's Studies courses, have compared the influence of Plath's *The Bell Jar* to Betty Friedan's *The Feminine Mystique* as an articulation of the devastating consequence of the demeaning attitude toward women. Of the classic literature about the insanity arising from the adolescent's lack of power or adaptability to the modern world, only *The Bell Jar*'s main character is a woman.

Many, who see the novel primarily as inseparable from Plath's own suicide, have harshly denounced the seeming martyrdom of an artist who, as they see it, irresponsibly gives in to suicide, presenting suicide in the book as deceptively and somewhat romantically alluring, almost a necessity for a tortured artist. Other readers, for somewhat the same reason, have sharply criticized the placing of the book on high school reading lists because it tends to romanticize suicide.

Finally, however, the novel has been seen by many as going past the situation in the 1950s, going beyond the woman question to present the universal despair of the sensitive, creative individual in a cruel and impersonal commercial society.

Additional Readings: Pat Macpherson, *Reflecting on "The Bell Jar"* (London: Routledge, 1991); Linda Wagner-Martin, *"The Bell Jar," a Novel of the Fifties* (New York: Twayne, 1992).

184. *The Chosen*, by Chaim Potok (United States, 1967). The historical setting of Chaim Potok's *The Chosen* is a Jewish community in Brooklyn between 1944 and 1948. The characters in the novel belong chiefly to one of two groups of Jews antagonistic to one another: the Hasidic and Orthodox branches of Judaism. Hasidic Jews are originally from Poland and the Ukraine, are considered far more right wing than other Jews, dress in distinctive clothes and wear long side locks of hair, and worship by feverish dancing and singing in the synagogue rather than by careful study of Scripture. Hasidic Jews may try to convert other Jews to their way of thinking, believing that other arms of Judaism have gone astray. Orthodox Jews, on the other hand, are considered to be in the mainstream of Judaism and American life, though they keep the Sabbath and eat only kosher food, unlike more liberal wings of Judaism.

During the time of Potok's story, a number of issues regarding the fate of Jews were very much in the public eye: First, of course, was World War II and the battle against the anti-Semitism of Adolf Hitler. Second was the Holocaust, the full implications of which were not known to the world until after the war was over. Third was the rise of Zionism, or the creation of a Jewish state.

The title of the novel comes from the idea that the Jews were God's chosen people. In the Jewish community in Brooklyn the ill feeling between Hasidic and Orthodox Jews reaches a crucial point during a "war" between their baseball teams. Reuven Malter, a young man from an Orthodox Jewish family, is deliberately beaned in the head by Danny

Saunders, the son of the leader of the local Hasidic Jews. As a result of the attack, Reuven is hospitalized and in danger of losing his eye. Danny, appalled at what he has done, visits the hospital to ask Reuven's forgiveness, which, after long contemplation, Reuven is able to extend, and the boys become lifelong friends.

Tensions come between the boys, however, when Danny's rigid Hasidic father refuses to allow Danny to associate with an Orthodox Jew. However, Mr. Malter, Reuven's father, is able to soften Reuven's dislike of Danny's father by explaining how Mr. Saunders had saved the lives of his followers by getting them out of Europe before Hitler consolidated his power there. Although Mr. Saunders finally relents and welcomes Reuven into his house, he again refuses to allow the boys to be friends when he discovers that Mr. Malter, Reuven's father, is a passionate Zionist.

An even greater conflict between father and son occurs over the issue of Danny's future. He balks at assuming religious leadership of the Hasidic sect, as he had always been expected to do. Much to his father's horror, Danny is interested in Darwin and Freud and wants to become a psychologist. Ironically, however, Reuven plans to become a rabbi.

The book ends as both young men prepare, with their fathers' blessings, to enter the fields they have chosen for themselves.

The Chosen immediately became a bestseller, spending thirty-nine weeks on the *New York Times* bestseller list. It was also on the short list for the National Book Award. In the next ten years, four hundred thousand copies were sold in cloth cover and 3 million in paperback. In 1982, a successful movie version created even more sales of the book, and in 1988, a musical version of the novel was adapted for the New York stage.

Potok's book was considered to be a blockbuster, introducing the American public to the special world of Jewish fundamentalism from a Jewish American perspective. Most works about Jewish life up to this time had had little to do with religious life. For the first time, as well, readers of the novel saw the impact of the American dream of professional progress on the religious Jew.

Additional Readings: Edward Abramson, *Chaim Potok* (Boston: Twayne, 1986); Sanford Sternlicht, *Chaim Potok: A Critical Companion* (Westport, CT: Greenwood Press, 2000).

185. *House Made of Dawn*, **by N. Scott Momaday (United States, 1968).** One of the first novels by a Native American writer about modern Native American life to receive worldwide attention, *House Made of Dawn* confronts the problems of identity facing men and women on the reservations of the Southwest. These problems had their beginnings in the appearance of Europeans in the Western Hemisphere. Clashes of culture occurred from the beginning as the Europeans brought with them the concept of private ownership of land and resources to a continent of people who believed that land and resources should be held in common by various tribes. As the Europeans, armed with superior technology, settled farther and farther west, Indians were pushed ahead of them. Not only did the number of Indians decrease dramatically, but attempts to "civilize" them put a great strain on their own traditions and religion. In 1830, the Indian Removal Act marked a downward turn for Native Americans. By means of this act, Native Americans were rounded up and, in forced marches during which many died, were relocated west of the Mississippi to what is now Oklahoma. By the middle of the century, Native Americans throughout the United States were largely herded onto reservations that have often been described as little more than concentration camps. The Dawes Act of 1887, intended to put more land in the hands of individual Native Americans, actually made more Indian land available for white settlement. Not until 1924 were Native Americans allowed U.S. citizenship. Less than twenty years later, however, they were being drafted to serve in World War II.

The story that Momaday situates on the Jicarilla Reservation in New Mexico is essentially the identity crisis of a Kiowa Indian who is surrounded by a white culture of which he is also a part. The main character is Abel, steeped in the culture of a tribe that is rapidly losing its meaning. Even as a young man he experiences conflict, as when he objects to the tribal treatment of a captured eagle and animals that are hunted down. Moreover, he is removed from the tribal community because his father, of whom he has little knowledge, was an outsider. With the death of his brother and mother, his angst increases. He feels that he must leave the tribe to get some sense of his own identity within it. Eventually he enters the white world where he is just as emotionally troubled, violent, and isolated as he had been among his own people. In the army, engaged in war, he knows little of the camaraderie felt by his fellow soldiers. Instead, they regard him as a type. When he returns home, he has degenerated into a violent, ill-tempered, deeply troubled drunk. He is unable to find meaning in the potentially healing ceremonies of the tribe and ends up killing a man whom he perceives to be an evil witch. For this crime, he goes to prison. Six and a half years later, out of prison, he is "relocated" from the reservation to the city of Los Angeles. His redemption and embrace of his own identity within the tribe begin when a social worker involves him in a tribal ceremony called the Night Chant. Abel's journey ends as he listens to his grandfather's healing stories. At this moment Abel enters the House Made of Dawn, the Navajo image of the cosmos.

The House Made of Dawn won the Pulitzer Prize for fiction in 1969, in part because, as the committee explained, the novel marked "the arrival on the American literary scene of a matured, sophisticated literary artist from the original Americans." The novel's chief influence has been to introduce audiences to the rites and rituals, social traditions, and supernatural beliefs of the Jemez and Navajo cultures. It also gave its readers, long used to the rationalism of the naturalistic novel, a sense of the tangible power of myth.

It was also an introduction to the problems of the Native American in the last half of the twentieth century and especially among veterans of World War II. These were men who were taken from the relative simplicity of the tribe where life was nature centered and forced into a world of war and chaos, in a strange culture with strange values shaped by technology and business. They and life on the reservations suffered when, in huge numbers, these men failed to return to work among their people. The novel also introduced readers to the problems of alcoholism, violence, and general disintegration among members of the tribe.

Additional Readings: Susan Scarberry-Garcia, *Landmarks of Healing. A Study of "House Made of Dawn"* (Albuquerque: University of New Mexico Press, 1990); Matthias Schubnell, *N. Scott Momaday. The Cultural and Literary Background* (Norman: University of Oklahoma Press, 1985).

186. *Slaughterhouse-Five*, by Kurt Vonnegut (United States, 1969). Kurt Vonnegut's novel, based in part on his own experience as an American soldier in World War II, is a story of the bombing of Dresden, used as a commentary on all war, especially the United States' war in Vietnam, which was still under way at the time of the novel's publication, having begun in 1964. In the course of World War II, on February 13, 1945, Allied planes began the first of three bombing raids of Dresden, a German city chiefly used to hold prisoners of war and so militarily inconsequential that it was not defended by either guns or fighters. As a consequence of the bombing, the inner city was obliterated by fire bombs, and an estimated 70,000 people, almost all civilians, were killed. The Allies may have had three objectives, though none was ever officially announced: It was a "morale bombing" as part of the psychological war; the target was the 400,000 German civilian refugees fleeing east Germany; it had a political motive to show the Russians how powerful the Allies were just before the Yalta Conference. For twenty years after World War II ended, published military history in the United States ignored the bombing of Dresden altogether, and documents about the raid continued to be classified.

Four years before the publication of Vonnegut's novel, the United States became engaged in the war in Vietnam, so divisive of the United States and so destructive of the Vietnamese people and their land as well as of young American soldiers that, in retrospect, it appears to be the single overriding issue in the country from 1964 to 1973. The story of the war can be traced to the end of Vietnam's colonial control by the French, when it was divided into two countries, with the communists controlling North Vietnam. When North Vietnam attacked noncommunist South Vietnam, the United States became involved in what critics called an internal matter, a civil war, in order to stem the tide of communism in Asia. U.S. forces began bombing North Vietnam. In 1965, draft quotas doubled, President Lyndon Johnson asked Congress for an additional $1.7 billion to carry on the Vietnam War, and American forces in Vietnam were planned to reach 125,000. By the time of the publication of *Slaughterhouse-Five*, 541,000 soldiers were fighting in Vietnam. Public displeasure with the war was escalating rapidly, and frustration was expressed with increasing frequency and often through outbreaks of violence. Finally 57,000 Americans had died, and thousands more were physically and psychologically maimed in a war that was lost to the North Vietnamese and that had had little political support in America.

The narrative by Vonnegut, questioning all wars but specifically World War II and the war in Vietnam, is told by a former American prisoner of war (POW) who witnessed the firebombing of Dresden and who returns to Germany with a friend many years later. His chief character is another Dresden POW named Billy Pilgrim who innocently (all wars are fought by children, the narrator reminds us) stumbles through mindless battles, is entertained with a theatrical by jolly British POWs, is threatened by hoodlums in his own outfit, and finally ends up in Dresden where the Allies' bombs boil alive schoolgirls who are bathing in a water tower and turn every human being in their paths into "little logs." Billy comes home, psychologically crippled, to escape history with time travel, onto a planet called Tralfalmadore, an Edenic place where the only book is Jacqueline Suzanne's soap opera about drugs, *The Valley of the Dolls*. Meanwhile, Billy's son, who had been something of a juvenile gangster, is a highly successful Green Beret, serving in Vietnam.

Twenty years later Billy shares a hospital room with an Air Force Reserve brigadier general who, in reading an English book on the Dresden bombing, ridicules those who criticize the bombing and endorses other military arguments that the United States should not work for nuclear disarmament.

Vonnegut's book, and its exposé of military nonsense during wartime, was a powerful enabler of the antiwar movement in the United States, and it was given credence by the fact that its author had served in the front line in World War II battles and had actually been in Dresden when it was bombed. The book, along with Stephen Crane's *The Red Badge of Courage* and Joseph Heller's *Catch-22*, became the antiwar canon of the 1960s and early 1970s, being invoked in the increasing number of antiwar demonstrations that occurred in the last two years of the 1960s and the first four years of the 1970s. The book carried a message of historical involvement. Poor, psychologically wounded souls like Billy Pilgrim escaped into an ahistorical world of science fiction or Eastern mysticism or drugs. But the narrator is the model of behavior, heroically confronting history and reality, as painful as it is, by facing head-on the horror of war in what he calls his "Duty-Dance with Death."

This was the philosophy that galvanized social involvement of all kinds, notably demonstrations against the Vietnam War, which was at its height in 1968. These include massive demonstrations during the Democratic Convention in Chicago in 1968 when protesters were beaten by police and antiwar activists were silenced or barred from the convention floor. It also included protests on many college campuses, resulting in repressive action against demonstrators. Massive arrests were made at Harvard University, San Francisco State University, New York City

College, the University of California at Berkeley, and many other campuses. On November 15, 1969, 250,000 people gathered in Washington, D.C., to protest the Vietnam War. And on May 4, 1970, in a war protest demonstration at Kent State University, four college students were killed and nine seriously wounded by National Guardsmen.

The novel, one of the most frequently censored books of the last twenty-five years, has been damned for being unpatriotic, antiwar, anti-American, and defiant of the government. Some citizens have unwittingly revealed the power of the book in objecting that young men who read the book may resist fighting for their country.

Additional Readings: Peter G. Jones, *War and the Novelist: Appraising the American War Novel* (Columbia: University of Missouri Press, 1976); Marc Leeds and Peter J. Reed, eds. *Kurt Vonnegut* (Westport, CT: Greenwood Press, 2000); Stanley Schatt, *Kurt Vonnegut Jr.* (Boston: Twayne, 1976).

187. *The Autobiography of Miss Jane Pittman,* **by Ernest J. Gaines (United States, 1971).** Ernest Gaines's 1971 novel, presented as an autobiography based on fictional interviews, appeared at the end of a turbulent era in race relations in the United States. In 1960, demonstrations that began in Greensboro, North Carolina, desegregated public eating places across the country. The next year, the Congress for Racial Equality began sponsoring Freedom Riders, black and white citizens who went south to integrate interstate transportation. They were met with continual violence and arrests. In 1963, nonviolent demonstrators protesting the prohibition of voting rights for African Americans and racial discrimination were attacked with pressure hoses, billy clubs, and attack dogs. Three civil rights workers were beaten and shot in Mississippi in 1964. Riots broke out in black neighborhoods in Los Angeles' Watts in 1965, followed in 1968 with the largest number of urban riots on record, following the assassination of Dr. Martin Luther King, Jr. In 1970, shortly before the appearance of Gaines's novel, police in Jackson, Mississippi, machine-gunned a black college campus, killing two students.

Gaines's novel first appeared against this background of struggle and violence. The novel is structured as a historian's interview with 110-year-old Jane Pittman, covering her life from the Civil War to 1962 when the Civil rights movement in the United States was getting under way.

Miss Pittman's story begins during the Civil War on a plantation in Louisiana where she is a slave. Even as a ten-year-old, Jane exhibits a strength and rebelliousness that results in continual corporal punishment. When the war ends, she is determined to join others who want to press on to the North, but her companions are killed on the way and Jane can't find her way. Instead of going north, she goes farther south, having to work on another plantation where the conditions are even worse than they were before Emancipation. Ned, the young boy she has raised and who eventually goes north to be educated, returns to Louisiana with a missionary's zeal about the liberating and uplifting effects of black education. Not surprisingly, he is killed for his actions. The novel closes when another young black man of Jane's acquaintance becomes an activist and is killed when he comes to the defense of a young black woman who is arrested for daring to drink at a whites-only water fountain.

Gaines provided his readers with the first comprehensive overview of history in which the African American is given a human face and in a form designed to appeal to the general public. The influence of the novel can be found in the rational it gave for both nonviolent protest and violent riots that occurred shortly before the novel's publication.

The novel, appearing at the height of efforts to establish Black Studies programs in universities, gave his audience a perspective that defined many of the issue that arose in shaping programs: the necessity of having black historians present history from an African American perspective; the necessity of confronting racial stereotypes openly; and the necessity of confronting the reality of slavery, something African Americans had been reluctant to do.

Gaines's novel also raised an issue that would continue to be controversial for decades—the cultural necessity to acknowledge the guiding strength of African American women in the black family and community.

Additional Readings: Valerie Melissa Babb, *Ernest Gaines* (Boston: Twayne, 1991); David C. Estes, ed., *Critical Reflections on the Fiction of Ernest Gaines* (Athens: University of Georgia Press, 1994).

188. *The Monkey Wrench Gang*, by Edward Abbey (United States, 1975). Edward Abbey, author of many books on the environment, is recognized as the pioneer of modern environmental activism with his foremost novel *The Monkey Wrench Gang.* Although the Beat writers of the 1950s had drawn attention to environmentalism, in the 1950s and 1960s, the environment had taken a backseat to the more politically critical problem of the Vietnam War. Before the publication of Abbey's book, environmentalism's chief spokesman was the peaceable Sierra Club. Individual warnings about the decimation of forests and animal species were generally passed off as the ravings of crackpots. Little consideration was given to the disastrous ecological effects of pesticides.

Abbey's book is about a group of environmentalists called the monkey wrench gang who use violent means ("monkey-wrenching") to save the ecology of the deserts in the American West. Their dangerous tactics include the blowing up of a train and a bridge across a canyon, setting billboards on fire, and disabling power lines, geological sensors, and the engines of bulldozers. They try to shift the blame for their deeds to Native American activists and are pursued by a Mormon bishop. Though they are arrested, they never admit their involvement and never serve time.

Few books have had such an immediate and unmistakable impact. *The Monkey Wrench Gang* was directly responsible for the wholesale use of violence on the part of environmental activists. Abbey came to be called the cult hero to environmentalists. By romanticizing violence in the cause of protecting the environment from developers, Abbey provided the environmental movement with clear justification for violent action. The book also popularized a new term, *ecotage*, a wedding of "ecology" and "sabotage." It inspired the formation of a group called Earth First! who were committed to violent solutions when no other remedies had brought results. Admittedly galvanized by Abbey's novel, Earth First! declared the necessity of blowing up dams and bridges. Like its counterpart organization Green Peace, the actions of Earth First! were regarded as an interference in normal governmental and business activities, and its troublemaking trespassing was seen as a nuisance and an embarrassment. As a direct response to the publication of the novel, Earth First! staged a media event that was neither violent nor destructive but still disturbing in its symbolism. Taking their cues from Abbey and his novel, in 1981 the founders of Earth First! surreptitiously climbed onto the Glen Canyon Dam, the dam that the monkey wrenchers of the novel had dynamited to save the desert. But instead of blowing up the dam, they unfurled a huge black plastic "crack" over the side of the dam in what was regarded as a threatening gesture. Members of the group apprised Abbey of their intentions and invited him to accompany them and watch from a ringside seat on a nearby bridge. As the crack appeared against the bridge, Abbey shouted, "Earth First!" and "Free the Colorado."

Environmental activism at the beginning of the twenty-first century owes a direct debt to *The Monkey Wrench Gang*, having been motivated by the novel to use such effective maneuvers as lying in the path of logging trucks, pulling up survey stakes, chaining themselves to trees, and driving iron spikes into trees to make it dangerous to saw them down.

In the year 2000, the most prominent participants in three large demonstrations in American cities were members of the nonviolent Ruckus Society, a spinoff of Earth

First!—the society inspired by *The Monkey Wrench Gang.*

Additional Readings: Garth McCann, *Edward Abbey* (Boise, ID: Boise State University Press, 1977); Philip Shakecoff, *A Fierce-Green Fire* (New York: Hill and Wang, 1993); Susan Zakin, *Coyotes and Town Dogs: Earth First! and the Environmental Movement* (New York: Penguin Books, 1993).

189. *Ceremony,* by Leslie Marmon Silko (United States, 1977). Silko's novel *Ceremony* is a presentation of the Native American mind and life from a Native American point of view, intertwining songs, stories, poems, and incantations of the culture to produce a distinctive prose form that she uses to explore psychological as well as social and political issues pertinent to life on the reservation.

The novel, consistent with the old culture she writes about, has as its main focus the group and the landscape rather than a single hero. The novel begins with Tayo, a veteran of World War II whose physical and emotional problems have not been improved by the postwar hospitals and psychiatrists. He remains confused and unable to synthesize the things that he experiences and observes. Yet his problems are not his alone but symptomatic of troubles that surround him, specifically a killing drought that has been visited on the group. The drought is the result of earth's displeasure not only with modern man in general, who has engaged in a world war, but with Tayo specifically because he once cursed the rain after his friend died while they were prisoners of the Japanese in the Philippines. Unlike his contemporary Emo who has adopted a cynical European outlook, Tayo, a half-breed, is hampered by his inability to reconcile the European world with his tribal view of the universe. The one promising remedy for his pain that goes through his head is to go through "a good ceremony."

Back home after the war, after the hospitals, Tayo searches without success for the right tribal story that will show him how others before him survived such tribulations. He wants to return to the army hospital and disappear. But his grandmother is convinced that while white medicine has failed, tribal medicine will cure Tayo. Her suggestion causes discord in a family where some members are now Christians who don't want some of the family's dirty linen aired in public. But the grandmother prevails, and the medicine man is invited in to produce a ceremony and a healing story but fails. In the course of searching for a cure for Tayo, he must explore his childhood, his war experiences, and his family history and encounter directly his own community, as well as tribal magic. Finally, he knows the tribal story of boundlessness, unity, pattern, and returns to his native home to convey what he has learned to his family.

Silko's novel was enthusiastically received by the public and the literary critics alike, leading in 1981 to a MacArthur Prize Fellowship award.

Ceremony was one of the first novels to reach a general readership that combined Native American literary forms with a modern setting and modern events, specifically the events of World War II and after. The novel also introduced many readers to the social problems of the contemporary Native American in the form of Tayo and his friends who were treated with some respect during the war but then came home to discrimination and squalor.

Many readers also saw the intricacies of Native American healing practices for the first time. Such was Silko's use of these traditions that some Native American writers took her to task for revealing to the general public sacred secrets that were not meant to be revealed outside the tribe.

The novel has often been classified as an environmental novel that affirms the sacredness of the land, which has a voice and must not be subdued. This view was presented in the novel against the background of the white man's heedless endangerment of the earth: the mining and the nuclear bomb development in New Mexico.

Silko's worldview in the novel was a radical

departure from the European preoccupation with and deification of the lonely self. In this novel, from the Native American point of view, the emphasis is not on the lonely, free ego but on the necessity for submerging the ego into the group and becoming one with the earth.

Additional Readings: Gregory Salyer, *Leslie Marmon Silko* (New York: Twayne, 1997); Per Seyersted, *Leslie Marmon Silko* (Boise, ID: Boise State University Press, 1980).

190. *The Color Purple*, by Alice Walker (United States, 1982). *The Color Purple*, one of the most controversial novels about the African American experience, is set in rural Georgia in the early decades of the twentieth century.

The plot unfolds through the letters of Celie, the main character, to her sister Nellie and to God. It begins when Celie, a plain-looking girl, is fourteen years old and lives with her mother and Alphonso, her stepfather. Alphonso has repeatedly raped Celie, and she gives birth to two children by him. His atrocities against her continue when he wrenches the babies from her and gives them away. At the death of Celie's mother, Alphonso forces Celie to marry an older man named Albert, who prefers Celie's prettier younger sister Nettie. Albert is as much of a sadist as Alphonso. He physically and psychologically abuses Celie and drives Nettie away by attempting to seduce her. Celie is devastated by the loss of the only people she cares for in the world: her children and her sister. As a further abomination, Albert moves his beautiful and worldly wise mistress Shug Avery into his house with Celie. However, this change actually becomes Celie's salvation because she and Shug learn to love each other, and Shug begins tenderly to give Celie self-esteem. Celie considers Albert's worst crime against her to be his concealment from her of her sister Nettie's precious letters. For this she cannot forgive him. She eventually finds the letters, discovering that Nettie has found Celie's two children and has married a missionary.

Celie's miserable life takes a turn for the better when she and Shug eventually leave Albert and move in together. Shug continues to guide and support Celie, helping her establish financial independence as a dressmaker. Her new trade soon brings Celie success and friends. At Alphonso's death, Celie also inherits his farm by default. At the end of her story, she is reunited with Nettie and her two children and their families.

Walker's novel was highly successful and continues to enjoy impressive sales. It is also a standard work required of college students studying American literature, African American Studies, and Women's Studies. In 1983 the novel won a Pulitzer Prize, and in 1985 it was adapted as a successful motion picture.

The Color Purple is one of the most controversial works written by an African American author. It brought into the foreground from the shadows issues of child rape, spousal abuse, and lesbianism. It provided sympathetic characters with whom many black and white readers could share their anguish and who helped them recognize the loss of self-esteem produced by abuse. The novel also provided a healthy and happy picture of strong women in affirming relationships and assured women that the damage done by abuse could be overcome.

However, the novel was received with harsh and sometimes violent negative reactions for several reasons. Counter to the usual African American protest novel, in this work the role of whites was comparatively obscure. The real target of the novel's social criticism was the African American male, represented by Alphonso and Albert. Both are sadistic, brutish, and lazy. Some very vocal readers accused Walker of dividing the African American community that badly needed to unite in a common goal of fighting inequality.

After the novel's publication, both academics specializing in African American literature and public figures interested in race bitterly debated issues raised by the work. Throughout the country, the opening of the movie, based on the novel, was picketed.

Additional Readings: Henry Louis Gates Jr. and K.A. Appiah, eds., *Alice Walker: Critical Perspectives Past and Present* (New York: Amistad, 1993); Donna Haisty Winchell, *Alice Walker* (New York: Twayne, 1992).

191. *The House on Mango Street,* **by Sandra Cisneros (United States, 1983).** With *The House on Mango Street* Sandra Cisneros became one of the first Chicana novelists to attract worldwide attention. This, her autobiographical novel, takes place in a poor Puerto Rican urban neighborhood in the city of Chicago. In forty-four episodes, held together by the common setting and the consciousness of an adolescent narrator, a young girl named Esperanza, life in the barrio and the painful growth toward self-confidence unfold. Unlike many of her friends, Esperanza is more prone to become disillusioned with what life in the ghetto holds for her and tends to question her community's expectations of her and the other girls. Her sensitivity, creativity, and aspirations also set her apart. Fittingly, Esperanza tells the reader that her name in English means "hope," something that few young people in the barrio dare indulge in.

Much of the action of the novel involves the constant themes of love and death in the ghetto: the untimely death of young men and women, the death of the older neighbors and family who seem to take something of a lost culture away with them, the adolescent chatter of young girls learning about sex and love, examples of the transition into adulthood, and the disillusionment that comes from seeing the role that Hispanic life expects its women to play. Episodes that show the steps that Esperanza takes in growing up include a description of her first job, the first wedding of one of her friends (in the eighth grade), and her first community dance as a young woman. In this last crucial test, she feels initially embarrassed by the clothes she wears, so at variance with the other girls' dress. Her discomfort soon vanishes, however, when she realizes that she is being admired for her grace as a dancer.

The characters she introduces are extraordinarily colorful yet, the reader understands, typical of the barrio. There are eccentric old Mexican men and women, living in a Spanish island in the middle of the Midwest, who have never known a word of English. There are young men who, even as children, seem doomed to tragic ends. Most of all, there are girls, eager for life, who gradually see their torpid, small futures foretold in the drudgery of their mothers and aunts.

Esperanza comes to an awareness of her need for her own house, not the ugly house on Mango Street, meaning her own identity, not the role that Hispanic society expects of its women. As she leaves Mango Street, taking with her precious memories of her past, she declares, "I have begun my own kind of war. Simple. Sure. I am one who leaves the table like a man, without putting back the chair or picking up the plate."

The House on Mango Street was immediately recognized as bringing a new perspective to a largely unknown aspect of American life and has been generally recognized as the first Hispanic novel to become successful in the United States. The novel easily made its way into high school, college, and university curricula and often became the cornerstone of the emerging Chicana Studies programs throughout the country.

Until the appearance of *The House on Mango Street*, the situation of the Hispanic woman in the United States had largely been ignored by feminists and Women's Studies programs. It was Cisneros's novel that brought the social and cultural lives of a large segment of the United States into full consideration. Consistent with this, the novel also brought attention and respectability to Chicana life as a subject of study, a subject for art.

Additional Readings: Julian Olivares, "Sandra Cisneros' *The House on Mango Street,* and the Poetics of Space," in Maria Herrera-Sobek and Helena Maria Viramontes, eds., *Chicana Creativity and Criticism: Charting New Frontiers in American Literature* (Houston, TX: Arte Público Press, 1988), pp. 160–70; Yvonne Yarbro-Bejarano, "Chicana Literature from a Chicana Feminist Perspective," in Maria Herrera-Sobek and Helena

Maria Viramontes, eds., *Chicana Creativity and Criticism: Charting New Frontiers in American Literature* (Houston, TX: Arte Público Press, 1988), pp. 139–45.

192. *Beloved*, by Toni Morrison (United States, 1987).

Based on a true occurrence in 1856 in the antebellum South, Toni Morrison's novel has in its background the devastating effect of slavery on family life. In an effort to produce more workers, slaves were bred like cattle, without regard to ties of affection. To make the buying and selling of slaves less troublesome for slaveholders, every effort was taken to keep family feeling from taking hold. For example, laws throughout the slave states forbade slaves to marry, and infants were often taken from their mothers as soon as possible to prevent the normal ties between mother and child from developing, thus, it was believed, forestalling objections and trauma if one member of a family was to be sold away from the other. Yet family feeling could not always be suppressed entirely. Young lovers would risk their lives to meet against their masters' orders. Again and again, families, upon learning that they were to be separated by sales, would risk their lives to escape. On more than one occasion, mothers, to protect their children from the ravages of slavery, attempted to kill them and commit suicide. One such case, documented later by Harriet Beecher Stowe, appears in *Uncle Tom's Cabin*.

Beloved, which takes place after Emancipation and the Civil War, involves a mother named Sethe and her daughter Denver, both former slaves. The two women are now haunted by a two-year-old child, Denver's sister, who had died before Emancipation when Denver was an infant. The infant ghost becomes quiet, however, when a visiting friend named Paul D. orders her to leave. Almost immediately after the ghost's disappearance, a sickly twenty-year-old woman named Beloved appears at the house and asks Sethe to help her. Sethe, who seems to be under the woman's spell, takes her in and nurses her. Bizarre occurrences happen when Beloved moves into the house. Paul, who is

suspicious of the newcomer, begins to act in strange ways against his will, finding himself seduced by Beloved. The two women of the house become convinced that Beloved is the manifestation of the ghost, Sethe's long-dead child who once haunted the house. The newcomer has obviously assumed her name from her tombstone: "Beloved daughter of ———."

Sethe reveals the mystery of her child to Paul: When she was a slave she had attempted to protect her children from a sadistic slave owner by killing them. However, she was able to dispatch only the two-year-old before she was stopped. The revelation of this gruesome tale drives Paul from the house, leaving it to the machinations of Beloved, who becomes Sethe's tyrant, almost as if she has been reborn as the sadistic slave owner. Sethe willingly and lovingly performs all the tasks that Beloved puts to her, happy to have her child back.

But Denver's concern for her mother's well-being brings the women of the community to the house to drive the ghost away through prayer. As they converge on the house, so does a white man, apparently intent on removing Beloved. Sethe, remembering the horror of another white man who had, in effect, taken away her child, attacks the man with a knife but is stopped by the women. Beloved, as woman and ghost child, vanishes, and Paul returns to comfort a devastated Sethe.

The novel, often compared with *Uncle Tom's Cabin*, won the Pulitzer Prize in 1988 and was the basis for Morrison's being awarded the Nobel Prize is 1993. Readers have seen in the novel the complex issues of slavery and ownership and of confronting the past in order to move on with one's life. Some readers regarded it as an example of "Holocaust literature."

The novel has been a controversial one because it fails to exonerate its black characters for the pain they cause each other. Readers were both drawn to and repelled by Morrison's painful portrait of infanticide and by the cruelty in Beloved's haunting of and tyranny over her mother. The dean of Nigerian letters, Chinua Achebe, who ranks *Beloved* as one of the greatest novels of the African and African American experience, believes that its impact has come from its metaphoric probing of the African diaspora, that scattering of Africans as slaves throughout the world, and from the challenge the novel poses about the responsibility that Africans themselves must assume for what occurred in the nineteenth century (Somini Sengupta, "A Literary Diaspora Toasts One of Its Own," *New York Times*, November 6, 2000, p. B1).

Additional Readings: Henry Louis Gates Jr., and K.A. Appiah, eds., *Toni Morrison: Critical Perspectives Past and Present* (New York: Amistad, 1993); Nellie McKay, ed., *Critical Essays on Toni Morrison* (Boston: Hall, 1988); Wilfred Samuels, *Toni Morrison* (Boston: Twayne, 1990).

193. *The Joy Luck Club*, by Amy Tan (United States, 1989). Asians have immigrated to Western world cities in great numbers since the middle of the nineteenth century. Nowhere has the effect of that immigration made itself felt so profoundly as in the area around San Francisco, California, where the many immigrants from China just before and after the Cultural Revolution found in the United States a long-established, ready-made Chinese American subculture. If they wished, Chinese-born adults could submerge themselves in a society surprisingly free of Western language and tradition. At the same time, their American-born children felt the strain of existing in two competing cultures.

Amy Tan, herself born in Oakland, California, of Chinese parents, writes in *The Joy Luck Club* of the psychological and social pressures and reconciliation in the daughter-mother relationships of Chinese families in California.

The Joy Luck Club of the title is a social club, formed in 1949 by four Chinese women immigrants as an excuse to get together to play mahjongg, eat, and talk, chiefly about their daughters. The Joy Luck Club is, of course, much more than a social gathering; it is a vital support group for the four women. At the opening of the story,

one of the daughters, June Woo, has been conscripted to take her deceased mother's place at the table. The story is told from the point of view of the older women and each of their daughters.

Implicated in the difficulty that the older women and their daughters have in their relationships with one another is the older women's reconciliation with their Chinese pasts and the younger daughters' acceptance of their Chinese identities, culminating for one daughter, June, in a trip to China.

Each of the chapters in the book begins with a parable that throws light on the story of the modern-day characters that follows. The chapters explore the mothers' lives in China, marked by family humiliation, repression, wartime atrocities, and triumph over gender discrimination. Contrasted with the daughters' childhoods in the United States and their identities as Americans are the mothers' fears of oblivion, expressed as the loss of family and Chinese tradition.

Amy Tan's novel was an instant and phenomenal success with both literary critics and the general reading public, appearing on the *New York Times* bestseller list within a month of its publication. It remained on the bestseller list for nine months, rising within the year to the fourth-highest position, selling over 4 million copies. The novel was shortlisted for several awards, including the National Book Award for Fiction, was translated into over twenty languages, and in paperback rights alone, has brought Tan $1.2 million since its publication.

A 1993 stage adaptation played in academic and regional theaters and in various cities in China. Tan also wrote the screenplay for a major motion picture in 1994.

The novel was not only widely read but widely influential in dealing with the frequent theme of mother-daughter relationships, first from the mother's point of view. More than anything else, however, was her readers' exposure for the first time to a modern history of women in China and to Chinese American culture.

More than any other work of literature, Tan's novel has been credited with creating the phenomenal interest in Chinese American writing that followed, including a spate of novels and short stories by Chinese American writers.

Additional Readings: E.D. Huntley, *Amy Tan: A Critical Companion* (Westport, CT: Greenwood Press, 1998); Elaine Kim, *Asian American Literature: An Introduction to the Writings and Their Social Context* (Philadelphia: Temple University Press, 1982).

SOUTH AMERICA

Brazil

ᗖᗙ

Aluisio Azevedo, *Mulatto*, 1881

Jorge Amado, *Gabriela, Clove and Cinnamon*, 1959

ᗖᗙ

TIMELINE

1600–1700S	Brazil's commerce, directed by Portuguese invaders, consists chiefly of trade in slaves, captured from among native Indians.
1756–78	During these years some 28,000 African slaves are imported to Brazil.
1770s	The suitability of Brazil for cotton growing is discovered. Large plantations are established for the growing of cotton. Portuguese companies begin to finance even larger schemes for the wholesale importation of African slaves to work on the cotton plantations.
1812–20	Thirty-six thousand African slaves imported to Brazil.
1819	The number of slaves in Brazil is double the number of free whites.
1820s–30s	The major crop changes from cotton to sugar.
1822	Brazil gains its independence from Portugal.
1830	The slave trade is declared illegal but continues largely unabated until 1850.
1850	The international slave trade is effectively abolished, but trading slaves remains legal within the country's boundaries.
1871	The Rio Branco Law frees all children born to slaves after 1871.
1875	Bernardo Guimarãe's abolitionist novel *The Slave Isaura* is published.
1881	Aluisio Azevedo's *Mulatto* is published.
	Azevedo is forced to flee his home in Maranhao, Brazil.
1888	Slaves in Brazil are emancipated.
1889	Brazil's first republic is established, guaranteeing separation of church and state.
1891	A new constitution eliminates the monarchy, provides for an elected

legislature, and gives the vote only to literate, adult males.

1894   The first elections are held, but a small class of elite composed of coffee planters and landed aristocracy controls all politics.

The majority of the population, made up of former slaves and their descendants, are still impoverished and have no voice.

1911–15   A flood of 600,000 European immigrants arrives in Brazil.

1915   Brazil's first important feminist novel, *The Year* by Rachel de Queiroz, appears.

1920s   Urban and industrialized areas spring up, populated by working- and middle-class Brazilians who still have no political voice.

1922–24   Revolts by reformers among the military officers are successfully put down.

1929   The worldwide economic depression hits Brazil and is marked by a steep decline in coffee exports.

1930   A successful revolution is launched by military officers who have been joined by urban workers.

1930–34   A coalition transitional government under Getulio Vargas controls Brazil.

1934   Vargas becomes president.

1937–45   Vargas, who has now become dictator, institutes limited reforms, encourages commerce.

1945   A military coup forces Vargas to resign.

1946   A new constitution gives power to Brazil's individual states, shifting power from the elite to the masses.

1950   Former President Vargas returns to power in a general election. Vargas again centralizes power.

1954   Confronted with the prospect of being thrown from office after a scandal, Vargas commits suicide.

1958   Jorge Amado's *Gabriela, Clove and Cinnamon*, with a setting in 1925, is published.

194. *Mulatto* (*O Mulato*), by Aluisio Azevedo (Brazil, 1881). Azevedo, recognized as Brazil's first naturalist, drew attention to several social problems in *Mulatto*, an unflattering picture of provincial society in the northern province of Maranhao.

The history of this region of Brazil, which sets it apart from the rest of the country, is constantly in the background of Azevedo's fiction. Like all of Brazil, Maranhao had been a Portuguese colony. Its poor soil, lack of economic development, and general isolation made the area more backward than the rest of Brazil. So by the seventeenth century its chief business was hunting down Indians to be sold as slaves. Slavery continued to be a prominent feature of the area throughout the eighteenth century, growing by leaps and bounds in the 1770s when it was discovered that cotton growing was suitable to the climate. At that time, a Portuguese company began to finance the importation of African slaves and the establishment of plantations to assist in the growing of cotton. Between 1756 and 1778, 28,000 African slaves were imported to the Maranhao province alone; and between 1812 and 1820, 36,000 slaves were imported. By 1819, the population of the region consisted of 133,000 slaves and 60,000 free whites.

In 1822, Brazil gained independence from Portugal, but in Maranhao province, many of the upper-class citizens deplored the separation from Portugal, and maintained Portuguese traditions and cultural and business ties with Europe. By contrast, the middle and lower classes identified themselves as Brazilians.

In the 1820s and 1830s, cotton growing moved to the southern United States, and the region changed their main cash crop to sugar. In 1830, the slave trade was declared illegal but nonetheless continued until 1850, when the importation of slaves was effectually abolished. Trade in slaves, however, continued internally. In 1871, a small step toward manumission was taken with the Rio Branco Law, which freed all children born to slaves after 1871. It was well known, however, that the clergy helped owners get around the law by backdating birth certificates.

By 1881, when *Mulatto* was published, considerable racial mixing had occurred, and Brazilians prided themselves on having established a racial paradise.

Also pertinent to the novel's background is the class struggle that continued in the province and the gross corruption on the part of individual Roman Catholic clergy to gain more personal power for themselves by interfering in personal, family, and community activities underhandedly, by currying favor with the wealthy, and by manipulating the emotions of their parishioners.

Mulatto has several interwoven plots: clergyman Canon Diogo's manipulation of the community to secure more power for himself; the belabored rise to power, self-awareness, and social consciousness of mulatto hero Raimundo; and Raimundo's star-crossed love affair with the wealthy merchant's daughter, Ana Rosa. Diogo is evil personified, a man of God who is a liar, seducer, and thief, who tries to talk Ana Rosa into an abortion and arranges for the murder of Raimundo. The highly educated, upperclass Raimundo only learns in adulthood that his mother was a black slave. It is then that he becomes an articulate spokesman for abolition. As an unreligious, antimonarchical, sophisticated man of science, he is in direct contrast to Diogo and the rest of the town's privileged citizens. The town's bigots, learning of his parentage, call him by the name usually given to mulattos—*cabra*, or goat. Ana Rosa, mistakenly convinced that her family will relent to marriage with Raimundo if she becomes pregnant, seduces him. At the moment when she realizes that he has been shot by a jealous clerk in her father's business, she miscarries.

The book was published to critical acclaim in literary circles, but most Brazilians, especially those in Maranhao, were enraged and scandalized at the young Azevedo's satire of the middle and upper class and at his devastating portrait of a clergyman. The outcry against him was so strong that he was forced to leave Maranhao within the year.

The book exercised tremendous influence in dispelling the myth that Maranhao, the community of Portuguese-philes, was the "Athens of Brazil," by portraying its citizens as backward, ignorant, mean-spirited individuals whose chief occupations were participating in small-minded local intrigues. In his pictures of the humiliations, poverty, and punishments suffered by blacks and mulattos, Azevedo also dispelled once and for all the myth of Maranhao as a racial paradise.

The book is also credited with having an influence on the outlawing of slavery and the freeing of the slaves in 1888, seven years after the publication of *Mulatto*.

Additional Readings: Dorothy Scott Loos, *The Naturalistic Novel of Brazil* (New York: Hispanic Institute, 1963); Daphne Patai and Murray Graeme MacNicoll, "Introduction," to Aluisio Azevedo's *Mulatto* (Rutherford, NJ: Fairleigh Dickinson University Press, 1990); Thomas E. Skidmore, *Brazil: Five Centuries of Change* (New York: Oxford University Press, 1999).

195. *Gabriela, Clove and Cinnamon (Gabriela, cravo e canela)*, by Jorge Amado (Brazil, 1958). *Gabriela, Clove and Cinnamon* is one of the most popular and controversial novels of Jorge Amado, Brazil's most widely read novelist. Amado, a political radical who was imprisoned in Brazil and then exiled, incorporated his political causes into his fiction, which was banned and burned in Brazil.

Amado uses his usual satire and humor in *Gabriela* for serious purposes. The social commentary of the novel touches on the trauma of adjusting to the more decadent and impersonal world of the cocoa port city of Ilheus, as opposed to the inland villages from which most of the characters have traveled. But Amado also uses his 1925 setting to comment on the hardships that Brazil's feudal view of women placed on both men and women. The absence of a mother figure in the novel underscores the controlling power of the patriarchy in which women are regarded as uneducable, base, needing constant supervision, and unfit for work or any other life outside the home. A Brazilian woman's husband, Amado writes, "was her owner, her lord and master; he dictated the laws and was to be obeyed and respected. He had all the rights, she the duties."

The central plot is the murder of a seemingly pious, meek, churchgoing housewife whom her brute-of-a-husband finds in the arms of another man. The unwritten law of Brazil required such a husband to kill his wife, even if she were suspected of adultery, in order to preserve his masculine image and the honor of his name. Rarely did the courts find such a man guilty. In Amado's novel, however, the community is stunned when the upper-class husband is found guilty of murder and sentenced to prison.

The novel is also a commentary on the system of prostitution and concubinage demanded by the males, who rationalized their illicit sex by claiming that it protected their wives from the men's too-active libidos.

A series of female portraits in the novel illustrate rebellions against tradition. The nineteenth-century aristocrat Ofensia d'Avila lives in memory in the town as a woman who refused the suitors pushed on her by her brother and rebelled by remaining a virgin all her life. One of the many concubines of the husband found guilty of murder also feels entrapped and contrives ways to escape her prostitution. The most successful rebellion is waged by Malvina, an upper-class student, who finally makes her escape from her boarding school to the city, where she lives on her own, works in an office by day, and goes to school by night.

The title character Gabriela, who subtly influences lives behind the scenes, runs away from her hard-earned prison of respectability, returning only when her lover agrees to accept her as an equal.

The novel was one of Amado's greatest successes and was translated into twenty-four different languages. Amado, a political radical, had drawn attention to several social problems in his earlier novels. *Gabriela* was the first novel by a highly popular writer to speak openly about the continuing problems Brazilian women faced with the tradition of sexism and seclusion. In particular, Amado was praised for exposing the unwritten law, which continued to be followed to the end of the twentieth century. Many hailed the book as an important precursor of later feminist fiction.

But the novel has also been excoriated for doing more harm than good to the cause of women. Many readers argue that the humor, with which Amado draws his portraits, tends to trivialize the very problems he cites and that he perpetuates male stereotypes of women, continuing to regard woman's liberation and fulfillment solely in terms of sexual pleasure.

The novel's popularity in Brazil was so great that hotels, bars, restaurants, and products were named for Amado's characters.

Additional Readings: Bobby J. Chamberlain, *Jorge Amado* (Boston: Twayne, 1990); Ann Pescatello, "The Brazileira: Images and Realities in Writings of Machado de Assis and Jorge Amado," in *Female and Male in Latin America: Essays*, ed. Ann Pescatello (Pittsburg: University of Pittsburg Press, 1973), pp. 29–58; Thomas E. Skidmore, *Brazil: Five Centuries of Change* (New York: Oxford University Press, 1999).

Chile

෴

Isabel Allende, *The House of the Spirits*, 1982

෴

TIMELINE

1933   Salvador Allende founds the Socialist Party in Chile.

1937   Allende is elected to the lower house of the legislature where he becomes a spokesman for the poor.

1939–42   Allende serves as minister of health.

1942   Allende is chosen as the leader of the Socialist Party.

1945   Allende is elected to the Senate from where he continues his mission to address the problems of lower-class Chileans.

1970   Allende is elected the first socialist president of Chile.

His agenda calls for peaceful reform and less power for foreign companies and large landholders. He begins a policy of land reform by reallocating land and begins a program of national health care.

1970–73   The United States actively blocks economic assistance.

The Central Intelligence Agency (CIA) sends $10 million to support Allende's opponents.

1973   A military coup violently overthrows the Allende government, and Allende himself is found shot.

1974   General Augusto Pinochet takes power.

Isabel Allende, niece and goddaughter of Salvador Allende, works tirelessly in a dangerous underground operation to assist in the escape of threatened citizens.

1974–88   Pinochet declares himself absolute dictator and turns Chile into a police state. He bans political opposition, cancels constitution and Congress, and enforces censorship. Thousands are arrested; prisoners are routinely tortured; some 3,200 are reported dead or missing; and thousands are forced to flee the country.

1975   Isabel Allende is forced to flee the country.

1982   Allende sees her novel *The House of the Spirits* into print. The book is banned in Chile.

1990   Pinochet is deposed from his Senate position, flees the country, and is brought to trial for crimes against humanity.

2000   Pinochet is returned to Chile where his fate continues to be a matter of judicial and political controversy.

196. *The House of the Spirits* (*La casa de los espiritus*), by Isabel Allende (Chile, 1982). *The House of the Spirits*, by Chilean writer Isabel Allende, is a partially autobiographical account of several generations in an unnamed South American country. Structurally the novel follows the lead of Gabriel Márquez's *One Hundred Years of Solitude* and shows echoes of Márquez's "magic realism" in its mixture of fantasy and brutal reality; but whereas Márquez portrays a male society, Allende concentrates on feminist themes.

Clara, the daughter of politician Severo del Valle and his suffragette wife Nivea, is a clairvoyant who ultimately marries Esteban Trueba, a small ranch owner and sometimes brutal man who rose from poverty to right-wing senator for the Conservative Party. They produce three children, all alienated from their father and all embracing some form of socialism: Jaime becomes a doctor for the poor (and is thus labeled a "hopeless loser"); Nicolas becomes the leader of a religious group that fights for civil rights and is forced to leave the country; and Blanca, becoming pregnant by Pedro Tecero Garcia, the socialist son of Esteban's foreman, sees her lover attacked by her father and is forced to marry a French count, Jean de Satigny. The marriage dissolves and Blanca gives birth to Alba. Alba also grows up to become involved in socialist causes.

It is at this point that echoes of recent history become predominant. When the Liberal Party defeats the Conservatives in a presidential election, military men rebel and establish a brutal dictatorship. While Esteban Trueba initially supported this coup d'état, he recants after seeing the true horror of an absolute rule that is not temporary but permanent and is marked by unparalleled cruelty and depri-

vation of civil rights. His granddaughter Alba (whom he loves) is imprisoned, tortured, and repeatedly raped before finally gaining release, while pregnant. Symbolically, Alba looks forward to a future with some hope and without being consumed by a desire for vengeance.

The story is told from three points of view: Esteban's granddaughter, in the present, opens the novel and closes it; in addition, having found a journal of her now-deceased grandmother Clara, she narrates large portions of the story from the third-person point of view. And in between these narrations, Esteban, the conservative grandfather, tells his own story from a first-person point of view. The same line thus opens and closes the novel.

In addition to reflecting the early life of the author, the novel is a stern indictment of recent Chilean history. In 1970, Salvador Allende Gossens, the cousin and godfather of the author, won the presidential election on a socialist ticket that included communists in its coalition of reformist elements. While the communists quickly dropped out of the resulting government, Allende's genuine reforms continued. He redistributed income, raised wages, controlled prices, and undertook other programs designed to improve the condition of the poor and simultaneously diminish the iron control of big corporations and large private landowners. The U.S. government and the CIA, under the presidency of Richard Nixon, took drastic steps, both open and secret, to undermine the government as well as the reforms of Allende's administration. They hampered the economy and sent millions of dollars into the coffers of Allende's enemies. At last, they succeeded. A military junta led by General Augusto Pinochet Ugarte led a violent revolt and established a dictatorship. They destroyed Chilean democracy, destroyed the government, and destroyed Allende—with the help of the U.S. government and the CIA. It was officially reported that Allende committed suicide when he saw the troops of the junta pounding into his room, but it is generally believed that he was murdered. In Pinochet's seventeen-year regime that followed Allende's death, 3,200 people were reported dead or missing, and thousands more escaped from Chile.

The novel, with its realistic details of Chilean life, was an international success, written by one whose life and family were close to the seats of power and who could report on what life was like in those years leading up to and including the actions of a truly brutal and horrendous dictatorship. With the help of the United States, Pinochet's government had influenced the international press to discredit Allende's government with continual stories of a negative and libelous nature. Isabel Allende's novel had an enormous influence throughout the world in countering what had become the standard picture of a corrupt and oppressive Allende government. As such, *The House of the Spirits* mustered international condemnation of Pinochet and his crimes—a series of crimes in which the U.S. government had a strong and dirty participation.

Isabel Allende risked her life repeatedly in helping dissidents escape Pinochet's regime until she herself had to flee the country in 1975 after being marked by Pinochet's military. She continues to write novels, including others that patently and emotionally condemned the Pinochet government of torture and violence; but it is *The House of the Spirits* that first captured international attention and was cited as an influence in bringing down Pinochet in 1990 and finally bringing him to justice in the year 2000.

Additional Readings: Patricia Hart, *Narrative Magic in the Fiction of Isabel Allende* (Rutherford, NJ: Fairleigh Dickinson University Press, 1989); Patricia Politzer, *Fear in Chile* (New York: Pantheon Books, 1989); Sonia Riquelme Rojas and Edna Aguirre Rehbein, eds., *Critical Approaches to Isabel Allende's Novels* (New York: Lang, 1991).

Colombia

Gabriel Garcia Márquez, *One Hundred Years of Solitude*, 1967

⨍⨎

TIMELINE

1863   The United States of Colombia is established. It reinforces an 1853 constitution guaranteeing certain civil rights and separation of church and state.

1880–1930   Conservative policies prevail.

1886   The country's name is changed to Colombia, and the Roman Catholic Church becomes the country's official religion.

1890s   The United Fruit Company arrives in Colombia to exploit the country's natural resources and cheap labor. Known as the Octopus, the company invades every avenue of Colombian life.

1899–1902   Civil wars ravage the country.

1903   Panama, once part of Colombia, is declared an independent state.

1928   After striking for more humane working conditions and living wages, banana workers are slaughtered by a government directed by the United Fruit Company.

1936   The government finally assumes power to regulate foreign businesses for the good of Colombia. Workers are given the right to strike, and the Catholic Church is declared to be no longer the official state religion.

1944   Further benefits are guaranteed: a minimum wage, health care benefits for workers, and the right to organize.

1948–2000   Marauding bands composed of rebels, soldiers, and gangsters terrorize the countryside, killing hundreds of thousands of people.

Government is continually in chaos or paralyzed by feuding liberals and conservatives.

1959   The Cuban Revolution occurs, giving Colombians hope for a similar reorganization and reform, which, unfortunately, never happens.

1959–61   Gabriel Garcia Márquez, a newspaperman, works for a Cuban news agency.

1960–80   Márquez is forced into exile from Colombia.

1967	Márquez's *One Hundred Years of Solitude* is published. The novel explores nineteenth- and twentieth-century Colombia. The banana workers massacre of 1928 is a particular focus of the action.
1970–2000	Drug cartels gain a foothold in government and seriously disrupt the country even further with their violence.
1980	Márquez returns to Colombia from exile.
1982	Márquez receives the Nobel Prize for Literature

197. *One Hundred Years of Solitude* (*Cien años de soledad*), by Gabriel Garcia Márquez (Colombia, 1967). *One Hundred Years of Solitude* is recognized as the most important work of "La Boom," translated as "the explosion," in Latin American literature in the 1960s. La Boom was marked by a turning away from realism and by political subject matter, often connected ideologically with the 1959 Cuban Revolution, a defining moment for all Latin America.

The novel explores much of Colombian nineteenth- and twentieth-century social and political history, including civil wars between conservatives and reformers, the laying of the first railroad, the establishment of North American influence with the arrival of the United Fruit Company at the end of the nineteenth century, the arrival and influence of the first cinema and the first automobiles, and the slaughter of thousands of banana workers as retaliation for a strike in 1928. Although not mentioned specifically, in the background of the novel is what was known as "The Violence" in Colombia, from 1948 forward, in which an estimated 200,000 people died at the hands of different marauding groups, from gangsters to soldiers.

The novel is the story of six generations of a South American family, the Buendias. The story begins with the Buendias family patriarch, José Arcadia Buendia, who in fantasy-like fashion is troubled by the ghost of a man he has killed, loses all sense of time, begins speaking in Latin, a language he has never been taught, and through his own calculations, discovers that the earth is round. Despite the so-called progress brought to the solitude of this once idyllic settlement by different characters, including a band of gypsies, the eccentricities of various family members endure throughout the ages. The fall of the family paradise is complete with the main historical event, which follows the economic development of their village: that is, the wholesale massacre of striking banana plantation workers. The government's way of dealing with the slaughter is to deny officially that the dead workers ever existed, a ruse that had proved successful, even when the workers were alive, to avoid paying them adequate wages and following modest regulations. Now officials tell the relatives of the dead strikers that they must be dreaming that the strikers ever worked in Macondo or were killed. Eventually, all official records are expunged of any reference to a banana company's operation.

The book was an immediate and overwhelming success, was translated into twenty-seven languages, went through hundreds of editions, and won four international prizes. At one point in 1967, demand for the book was so great that new editions were appearing at the rate of one a week. Chiefly on the strength of this novel, Márquez received the Nobel Prize in 1982. Between 1967 and 1984, the novel was the subject of some 285 scholarly articles. It is said that it is the second most popular book ever written in Spanish, after Miguel de Cervantes's *Don Quixote*.

However, neither *One Hundred Years of Solitude* nor Márquez's other journalistic writings were popular with Colombian dictators, and Márquez had even more reason after the publication of his novel to remain in exile with his family throughout the 1970s when the international fame he had garnered from the novel had made him a wealthy man. Though he was offered diplomatic posts by Colombia, only in 1980 did he feel it was sufficiently safe to return there.

Márquez's novel was immensely influential

in raising the political consciousness of readers with regard to Latin America, for his nameless fictional country is understood to be not just Colombia but all of Latin America. The historical slaying of native Indians and pillage by the Spanish in the novel led to the establishment of countries that are, in turn, easily pillaged by North Americans. The United Fruit Company is a case in point. The slaughter in the book, though based on a true event, represents the continual imperialist intervention and government retribution in such countries as Argentina and Nicaragua.

The Cuban Revolution made possible a new perspective on the Latin American history that Márquez introduces in the novel. Before the revolution, there had been the tendency to say that exploitation, inequality, and corruption were inevitable in every Latin American society. It was a kind of institutionalized despair. The novel revealed a different attitude, reinforced by the Cuban Revolution—that poverty and class discrimination were not inevitable. Nor were they ordained by God. Those in power in South America had manipulated history and memory to maintain a fatalistic myth. And other nations with influence in South America had bought into the official view.

Additional Readings: David Bushnell, *The Making of Modern Colombia* (Berkeley: University of California Press, 1993); Bernard McGuirk and Richard Cardwell, eds., *Gabriel Garcia Márquez* (Cambridge: Cambridge University Press, 1987); George McMurray, *Gabriel Garcia Márquez* (New York: Ungar, 1977).

Cuba

〰️

Reinaldo Arenas, *The Palace of the White Skunks*, 1975

〰️

TIMELINE

1898	The United States declares war on Spain over Spanish atrocities in Cuba and with the expressed purpose of liberating Cuba from Spain.
	After fourteen months, the war ends, Spain is ousted from Cuba, and the United States occupies the island.
	The Cuban rebels who had begun the rebellion against Spain are not welcome in the new government.
1902	U.S. military occupation of Cuba comes to an end but only after Cuba agrees to the Platt Amendment. This prohibits Cuba from making alliances with other countries, guarantees the United States military bases in Cuba, and forces Cubans to allow the United States to intervene there whenever the United States determines that such action is necessary.

Despite a new constitutional government, economic hardship continues as wealthy foreigners buy Cuban land and business, and laborers from nearby countries flood in to work for substandard wages.

1906, 1912, 1917	U.S. Marines land in Cuba to protect U.S. interests and to dispel rebellious factions seeking to unseat corrupt governments.
1925	Individuals living in the United States own half of Cuba's sugar plantations and land.
1930	The once-reformist government of Gerardo Machado is criticized for Cuba's economic disasters during the depression. Machado responds with police tactics.
1933	Machado is forced to resign, and his successor, Carlos Manuel de Cespedes, is overthrown by the radical Student Directorate and the

military, under the leadership of Sergeant Fulgencio Batista y Zaldívar. Ramón Grau San Martín becomes president and institutes needed economic reforms, including redistribution of land.

1934   Assisted by the United States, Batista leads a coup to overthrow Grau.

1944   Batista and his handpicked successor lose the election.

1944–52   Cubans suffer under two governments, unparalleled in corruption and incompetence. Public funds land in the hands of the wealthy and many foreigners.

1952   Batista returns from retirement in the United States to take over Cuba by force, invalidate the constitution, and make himself dictator.

1953   Fidel Castro rises to power on a platform of land and economic reforms, including health care and social security. He leads an unsuccessful rebellion against Batista. Sixty-eight of his followers are tortured and killed, and he is sentenced to a fifteen-year prison term.

1954   Batista, elected unopposed to a new term, frees political prisoners, including Castro.

1954–58   Batista refuses to hold free elections. Castro's rebel forces operate first out of Mexico, then out of the mountains in Cuba.

1958   Batista, failing to retain even a modicum of support, leaves Cuba secretly. A rebel government supported by Castro comes to power.

1959   Castro becomes prime minister. His reforms include reducing large real estate

and corporate profits, redistributing wealth, setting up farm cooperatives, providing health care, and seeing that all citizens became literate.

1959–61   A million Cubans—most of them professionals and large landowners—leave Cuba in exile.

Reinaldo Arenas, who has essentially been sympathetic with the revolution, refuses to politicize his fiction and is thus censored and labeled a counterrevolutionary.

1975   Reinaldo Arenas has his novel, *The Palace of the White Skunks*, secretly published abroad. It first appears in French.

198. *The Palace of the White Skunks* (*Le palais des tres blanches mouffettes*), by Reinaldo Arenas (Cuba, 1975). The setting of Reinaldo Arenas's *The Palace of the White Skunks* is the turbulent period in the late 1950s when Fulgencio Batista found that his dictatorship in Cuba was in jeopardy, despite the support he enjoyed from the United States, his powerful neighbor to the north. Although the United States urged him to make needed reforms to protect himself, Batista refused to allow free elections in a country that for decades had seen a steady rise in abject poverty, an erosion of all social relief, and a concentration of wealth and property in the hands of fewer and fewer people. In 1953 a young lawyer named Fidel Castro began his rise to power as the leader of one of the larger rebel groups in opposition to Batista. Castro and his band made as the chief planks in their platform a plan to alleviate the suffering of the poor by redistributing wealth and providing social services for the poor. In July 1953, however, Castro's band of followers staged an unsuccessful attack on Batista's government. Many of the rebels, including Castro, were captured, and sixty-eight of them were tortured and executed. Castro, himself, was sentenced to fifteen years in prison. In the next year, he was released, along with many other political prisoners, and resumed his armed opposition to Batista, first from a base in Mexico and later from the mountains of southeast Cuba, from where his band of rebels made attacks on Batista's military bases. A reporter for the *New York Times*, who visited Castro's headquarters, drew attention to rebel grievances, and as a result, other rebels and reformers joined him. By March 1958, forty-five different organizations had publicly come to the support of Castro. Batista was losing on both political and military fronts. His attack on Castro's stronghold in May was unsuccessful, allowing Castro's supporters to emerge from their mountain base and begin to win control of cities on the Cuban plains. Finally, in January 1959, Batista fled the country, and Castro assumed control.

The family, upon which Arenas's experimental novel focuses, is a reflection of Cuba itself in the days before the revolution. Poverty, political oppression, hunger, and hopelessness have left all of its members confused, despondent, and though they all suffer the same indignities, fighting among themselves. The grandfather, Polo, who had come to Cuba from Spain to find a better life, is, like the rest of Cuba, mired in poverty and tries to make ends meet by running a produce stand. Disappointed in having sired only daughters, he abdicates any responsibility toward his family, leaving his wife to toil alone in bitterness. Only one of their daughters is able to struggle on behalf of the family. The others have either gone mad or abandoned them. The novel ends as Fortunato, Polo's young grandson, attempts to join Castro's

army in order to escape his poverty and his family.

Arenas was the first novelist to provide the world with a balanced, subjective view of the revolution that had rocked the Western world, especially Latin America. While the novel attests to the brutal conditions created by Batista's dictatorship, it also attempts through surrealism to illustrate the murky complexities of family and national politics. This has been his chief contribution to post-Revolutionary literature. Readers who hoped to see a clear condemnation of Castro by a Cuban writer were disappointed by his very real picture of the hardships and injustices perpetrated by Batista. Those who hoped that Arenas would join the ranks of social realists in Communist Cuba were disappointed to find that he does not present the revolution as an ideal answer to the family's and the country's problems. He refuses, at least in this novel, to demonize or glorify Castro.

Arenas received an award from Castro's government for his first novel, but he quickly fell into disfavor. Although Arenas's hero plans to join Castro's forces and dies at the hands of Batista's forces, his novel, like his other works, remain banned in Cuba because of his express refusal to allow his writing to serve the cause of the revolutionary government. The manuscript for *The Palace of the White Skunks* was smuggled out of the country and published first in French. Five years later, he escaped to the United States from Cuba.

Additional Readings: Roberto Gonzalez Echevarria and Enrique Pupo-Walker, eds., *The Cambridge History of Latin American Literature*, vol. 3 (Cambridge: Cambridge University Press, 1996).

Peru

༺ༀ༻

Ciro Alegría, *Broad and Alien Is the World*, 1941

༺ༀ༻

TIMELINE

1845–51, 1855–62 During the presidential terms of Ramón Castillo, slavery is abolished, a liberal constitution is enacted, and commercial advances take place.

1879 Peru gains its independence.

1883–1908 Peru is ruled by a series of absolute dictators.

1900–2000 By 1900, Native Indian Peruvians had been relegated to the unarable Andean Highlands, to the eastern jungle, or to other areas of poor land. Even into the twenty-first century, 45 percent of Peru's population is made up of Indians, 37 percent of mixed blood, and 18 percent of European descent. Political power, resources, and arable land remain largely in the hands of the latter.

1908–12 Augusto Leguía becomes a reform president of Peru.

1919 After seven years out of office, Leguía seizes power and declares himself dictator.

1924 To counter the tyranny of Leguía, the American Popular Revolutionary Alliance (APRA) is founded, with the express purpose of improving the lives of the Native American majority in Peru. Leguía promptly bans the party.

1930 Leguía is overthrown.

Ciro Alegría joins the APRA and in the 1930s is twice imprisoned.

1933 A new, more liberal constitution is instituted. The new president, Luis Sánchez Cerro, is assassinated.

1934 Ciro Alegría is banished from Peru.

1939–40	President Manuel Prado y Ugarteche is forced to institute further reforms regarding Native Americans.
1941	Alegría's *Broad and Alien Is the World* is published. It has a setting in the years between 1912 and 1926.
1948	Alegría is allowed to return to Peru, where he again becomes politically active.

199. *Broad and Alien Is the World* (*El mundo es ancho y ajeno*), **by Ciro Alegría (Peru, 1941).** Regarded as the first classic work of Peruvian fiction, *Broad and Alien Is the World* was written about the hardships and struggles of Native American Peruvians during a time of political turmoil between 1912 and 1926.

By the nineteenth century, Peru's 45 percent Native American population, many descended from the Inca, were largely relegated to the Andean Highlands, to the jungles of eastern Peru, and to poor rural land, the well-to-do Spanish landholders having confiscated all fertile arable and mineral-rich land in the country.

Although slavery was abolished in mid-nineteenth century, the plight of the country's large population of Indians continued to worsen. Augusto Leguía y Salcedo, president of Peru during the time of Alegría's novel, was a dictator committed to wholesale economic and business advances for the ruling classes, which he protected by means of brutal oppression of all opposition. Leguía was interested in bringing Peru into the international business community by marketing its natural resources, but he had no patience with the plight of Peru's poor.

Leguía's chief opposition within the country was the American Popular Revolutionary Alliance, the APRA, which was formed in 1924 by exiled Peruvian activists. Their main objective was to see radical improvements made in the lives of Peru's Native Americans. Leguía's method of dealing with the orga-nization was to ban it and imprison its leaders. Although even Peru's dictators, who followed Leguía, continued to ban the APRA, it managed to flourish as one of Peru's most influential political parties. Ciro Alegría, author of *Broad and Alien Is the World*, joined the APRA in the 1930s and was twice imprisoned for his political activity before being banished from Peru in 1934.

His novel, written in 1941, addressed the problems of the Native Americans in Peru by focusing on the hardships suffered by the people of Rumi, a small native village, between 1912 and 1926. His cast of characters include Rosendo, the highly regarded mayor of the village, Rosendo's adopted son Castro, the bandit Vasquez, and a Spanish don named Amenabar, who owns a plantation adjoining the valley where the village is located.

The initiating circumstance is Don Amenabar's greed for the native land and for their labor on his plantation and in his mine, leading him to claim their land in court. By paying informants and bribing the judge, local governor, and witnesses, he wins his case, and the natives are forced to relocate on the cold, arid, unarable mountainside. Many of them are forced to leave for work in urban areas where they are cheated and, enslaved for debt, made to labor in rubber and coca plantations. There many of them die of malaria and snakebite.

Not satisfied with taking the Indians' land in the valley, Don Amenabar steals their cattle as well. This prompts their mayor, Rosendo, to retrieve their bull, but he is arrested and imprisoned indefinitely for stealing and for collaborating with a local bandit named Vasquez, whose wife lives in his village. In jail he meets many other Indians, one of whom, Prieto, sends a letter to Peru's president to inform him of the injustices they are suffering. But contrary to his expectations, the president sends him a perfunctory reply and nothing changes.

The bandit Vasquez then decides to take vengeance against every person who has collaborated with Don Amenabar, but Amenabar escapes and Vasquez is arrested and placed in a cell with Mayor Rosendo. After Vasquez escapes, Rosendo is beaten to death by the police. Rosendo's adopted son Castro, now home from the army, helps the community create some arable land on the mountainside, helps them relocate, and persuades them to relinquish some of their superstitions in order to survive, but the court answers the Indians' appeal for return of their valley by giving Amenabar their mountainside as well. When the villagers led by Castro protest, most are slaughtered. As Castro dies, his wife wonders where she will go and what she will do.

This was the first fiction in a major subgenre in Peru called "indigenism." Its purpose was to call attention to the economic exploitation and entrenched injustice suffered by Native Americans in Peru. The instant, worldwide sympathy evoked by the novel was instrumental in buttressing the APRA and forcing some economic reforms for Peruvian Indians during the office of President Manuel Prado y Ugarteche in the 1940s.

The novel was also one of the earliest fictions to present the clash of cultures in Peru and to show that, despite the attempts of a powerful Spanish culture to obliterate Indian culture, Native American ways were sufficiently ingrained to survive for centuries after the Spanish conquest. Alegría also presented in the novel the astonishing argument that native culture was equal in importance to European culture.

Alegría's novel, like all literature of indigenism, was criticized by many, more radical proponents of the cause of native Peruvians, who argued that it was a book written by a Spanish Peruvian for a Europeanized audience. The book's ending even suggests, it was argued, that native Peruvians did not have the capacity to help themselves. The liberation of native Peruvians would come only when they themselves created their own stories from their own culture.

The novel, while it was received enthusiastically throughout the world and especially in the United States, which offered and provided Alegría asylum, was denounced in Peru. Not until 1948 was he allowed to return to his own country and participate in its politics.

Additional Readings: Eileen Early, *Joy in Exile: Ciro Alegría's Narrative Art* (Washington, DC: University Press of America, 1980); Luis Martin, *The Kingdom of the Sun: A Short History of Peru* (New York: Charles Scribner's Sons, 1974).

Trinidad

❦

V.S. Naipaul, *A House for Mr. Biswas*, 1961

❦

TIMELINE

200. *A House for Mr. Biswas,* **by V.S. Naipaul (Trinidad, India, United Kingdom, 1961).** V.S. Naipaul inhabits and writes of a world ravaged by British colonialism, a world that leaves societies fragmented and its characters rootless and isolated long after the battles for political independence have been won.

The setting for this, his first novel, is the West Indies, where a history fueled by greed has mangled the area and its inhabitants, most of whom are blacks whose ancestors were brought from Africa and Indians whose ancestors were brought from India to work on sugar plantations. Europeans had occupied the area from the seventeenth century, searching first for gold in the New World and then making their fortunes from sugar growing and slave trading. They made no attempt to create a society or to foster a culture. From the point of view of the East Indians, these islands were nobody's home but just a place populated by exiles, a place to work and make enough money to survive.

Mr. Biswas, the lower-class Indian hero of Naipaul's novel, attempts to do what appears from the first to be impossible in this place inhabited by those uprooted from their homelands: He attempts to create a home in a place where no one is really at home, to learn to belong where no one really belongs, to have wholeness of being in a place that has been fragmented by history.

Biswas rejects the fatalism of his Hindu grandfather who has told him that they are doomed to and must accept that they must always work hard and never aspire to ownership. Biswas must quietly struggle against the Tulsi family that rules the community with the same tyranny that nineteenth-century plantation owners ruled their slaves. At one time, his impediments become so overwhelming that he has a mental breakdown. Yet despite all the discouragements of the protagonist's religion, class, and economic situation, he determines to improve his lot in life, trying to create in other ways by writing and painting, though each is a failure. His creation of self-meaning in this place is primarily represented by the dream of building a house. He does build two humble houses, but both must be vacated when they are threatened by flood and then fire. It is only shortly before his death that he actually completes his beautiful house and garden.

The influence of this Naipaul novel, one of the most widely read books in the Western world by a writer in exile, has been formidable—both positive and negative at the same time. The book angered many political writers who believed that Naipaul, one of the first colonized writers to speak out about colonized people, adopted a British viewpoint, making disparaging remarks about his own people. In their view, he tended to blame the victims of colonization rather than the colonizers for the inadequacies of the conquered societies like Trinadad and India. On the other hand, Naipaul's novel generated great interest in the West Indies, this novel being seen as a metaphoric history of the area and a fictional story of what the Indian has been able to accomplish in the face of overwhelming odds in the West Indies. In 2001, Naipaul received the Noble Prize for Literature.

Additional Readings: *V.S. Naipaul* (London: Longmans, 1975); Robert K. Morris, *Paradoxes of Order: Some Perspectives on the Fiction of V.S. Naipaul* (Columbus: University of Missouri Press, 1975); Fawzia Mustafa, *V.S. Naipaul* (Cambridge: Cambridge University Press, 1995); Timothy Weiss, *On the Margins: The Art of Exile in V.S. Naipaul* (Amherst, MA: University of Massachusetts Press, 1992); Landeg White, *V.S. Naipaul* (New York: Macmillan, 1975).

Appendix: Additional Protest Novels

ALBANIA

Kadare, Ismail, *The Pyramid*, 1992 (hierarchy and absolute dictatorship)

ALGERIA

Camus, Albert, *The Stranger*, 1942 (superficial and hypocritical morality)

Mammeri, Mouloud, *The Sleep of the Just*, 1955 (cultural conflict and nationalism)

Wattar, Tahir Al-, *The Ace*, 1974 (the promise of socialism in an area of Western capitalism)

AUSTRALIA

Grenville, Kate, *Lilian's Story*, 1985 (oppression of women)

Keneally, Thomas Michael, *Bring Larks and Heroes*, 1967 (the convict system and the Vietnam War)

Keneally, Thomas Michael, *The Chant of Jimmy Blacksmith*, 1972 (the plight of Aborigines)

Tennant, Kylie, *The Joyful Condemned*, 1953 (working women in Sydney slums)

Tennant, Kylie, *Tiburon*, 1935 (the outsider, unemployment, and the police)

AUSTRIA

Ebner-Eshenbach, Marie von, *Their Pavel*, 1887 (lives of the rural poor)

Jelinek, Elfriede, *Women as Lovers*, 1975 (the stratified social structure and restricted lives of women)

Musil, Robert, *The Man without Qualities*, 1930–43 (the dangers of encroaching fascism)

BELGIUM

Mallet-Joris, Françoise, *Beguine Rampart*, 1951 (a sympathetic treatment of lesbian passion)

BOTSWANA

Head, Bessie, *A Question of Power*, 1973 (patriarchal and white oppression)

BRAZIL

Fagun Telles, Lygia, *The Girl in the Photograph*, 1973 (military rule in Brazil)

Guimaraes, Bernardo, *The Slave Isaura*, 1875 (abolition of slavery)

Queiroz, Rachel de, *The Three Marias*, 1939 (the restricted spheres of women in Brazil)

CANADA

Atwood, Margaret, *The Edible Woman*, 1969 (issues affecting women)

Godbout, Jacques, *Knife on the Table*, 1965 (Quebec nationalism)

Jasmin, Claude, *Ethel and the Terrorist*, 1964 (multiethnic tensions in Quebec)

Leacock, Stephen, *Sunshine Sketches of a Little Town*, 1912 (criticism of provincial life)

Marchessault, Jovette, *Mother of the Grass*, 1980 (male domination and the salvation of the matriarchy)

CHINA

Ba Jin, *Family*, 1931 (authoritarianism in government and family)

Dai Houying, *Ah Humanity*, 1981 (humanism over class struggle)

Gao Xingjian, *Soul Mountain*, 2000 (the cultural revolution)

Liu E, *Travels of Lao Can*, 1904–07 (dangers in the socialist revolution)

Luo Guangbin, *Red Crag*, 1962 (reasons behind the revolution in China)

Wang Lin, *The Blue and the Black*, 1958 (Taiwanese anticommunist argument)

Ye Shengtao, *Ni Huanzhi* 1928–29 (the need for revolution and educational reform)

CUBA

Calvo, Lino Novas, *The Slave Trader*, 1933 (the nineteenth-century slave trade in Cuba)

Sarduy, Severo, *Gestures*, 1963 (the dictatorship of Batista)

CZECHOSLOVAKIA

Capek, Karel, *The Absolute at Large*, 1922 (religious intolerance and political oppression)

Capek, Karel, *Krakatit*, 1924 (the threat of nuclear disaster)

Sramek, Frana, *Telo*, 1919 (the ravages of war)

Vaculik, Ludvik, *The Czech Dreambook*, 1980 (police harassment and brutality during Soviet occupation after World War II)

DENMARK

Andersen-Nexo, Martin, *Pelle the Conqueror*, 1906–10 (the plight of agricultural workers and rise of unions)

Branner, Hans Christian, *Toys*, 1936 (dangers of rising Nazism)

Ditlevsen, Tove, *Someone Harmed a Child*, 1941 (the abuse of children)

Rifbjerg, Klaus, *Witness to the Future*, 1981 (the horrors of war and threat of nuclear holocaust)

Thorup, Kirsten, *Baby*, 1976 (sexual degradation)

ENGLAND

Ainsworth, W.H., *Jack Sheppard*, 1839 (the criminal justice system)

Allen, Grant, *The Woman Who Did*, 1895 (morality and marriage)

Amis, Martin, *Money*, 1984 (Thatcherism and its antisocialist agenda)

Bage, Robert, *Hermsprong*, 1796 (need for political reform inspired by French Revolution)

Bulwer-Lytton, Edward, *Paul Clifford*, 1890 ("Newgate" prison and its criminals)

Butler, Samuel, *Erewhom*, 1872 (the threat of mechanization)

Carter, Angela, *The Passions of the New Eve*, 1977 (sexual identity and perversity in a dystopian society)

Cobden, John, *The White Slaves of England*, 1853 (living and working conditions of factory workers)

Dacre, Charlotte, *Zofloya*, 1806 (corruption of the aristocracy)

Dickens, Charles, *Little Dorret*, 1857 (debtor's prison)

Dickens, Charles, *Oliver Twist*, 1838 (the poor law, houses for the poor and orphanages)

Disraeli, Benjamin, *Sybil or the Two Nations*, 1845 (the chasm between rich and poor in England)

Eliot, George, *Felix Holt the Radical*, 1865 (the moral dilemma of political activism)

Elizabeth, Charlotte, *Helen Fleetwood*, 1841 (slums, factories, and the ten-hour bill)

Gaskell, Elizabeth, *North and South*, 1855 (details of industrial life)

Gissing, George, *Demos*, 1886 (socialism, the factory system, and poverty)

Gissing, George, *The Nether World*, 1889 (living conditions of the poor)

Greene, Graham, *The Power and the Glory*, 1940 (conflict between social revolution and the established church)

Greenwood, Walter, *Love on the Dole*, 1933 (lives of the laboring poor)

Haslam, James, *The Handloom Weaver's Daughter*, 1904 (a working-class view of English industry)

Jones, Lewis, *We Live*, 1939 (a miner's view of working conditions, unemployment, and unionism)

Kingsley, Charles, *The Water-Babies*, 1863 (child labor)

Lennox, Charlotte, *The Female Quixote*, 1752 (criticism of lowly place of women in patriarchy)

Moore, George, *Esther Waters*, 1894 (a society abusive and exploitative of women)

Morris, William, *News from Nowhere*, 1890 (a radical answer to Bellamy's *Looking Backward*)

Morrison, Arthur, *Child of the Jago*, 1896 (London's poor and the need for reform)

Reade, Charles, *Cast Yourself in His Place*, 1870 (trade unions)

Reade, Charles, *It's Never Too Late to Mend*, 1853 (social problems of the very poor)

Rymet, James Malcolm, *The White Slave*, 1844 (living and working conditions of industrial workers)

Sillitoe, Alan, *Saturday Night and Sunday Morning*, 1958 (spiritual and economic poverty in post–World War II England)

Stone, Elizabeth, *William Longshawe: The Cotton Lord*, 1842 (problems in the textile industry)

Trollope, Frances, *Jessie Phillips. A Tale of the Present Day*, 1843 (the New Poor Law)

Trollope, Frances, *Jonathan Jefferson Whitlaw*, 1836 (slavery and abolition)

Upward, Edward, *Journey to the Border*, 1938 (the need for radical political change)

White, William Hale, *The Revolution in Tanner's Lane*, 1887 (a working-class view of English industry)

FINLAND

Haanpaa, Pentti, *Exercise Field and Barracks*, 1928 (brutality of military training)

Hemmer, Jarl, *A Fool of Faith*, 1931 (atrocities committed during the civil war)

Linna, Vaino, *Unknown Soldier*, 1954 (Lapland War and resultant war crimes trials)

Sillanpaa, Frans Eemil, *Meek Heritage*, 1919 (poverty and hardship brought on by the civil war)

FRANCE

"Colette," Sidonie-Gabrielle, *The Vagabond*, 1911 (female sexuality and lesbianism)

Simon, Claude, *The Flanders Road*, 1960 (the economic causes of war and its atrocities)

Zola, Emile, *Nana*, 1880 (corruption in France's Second Empire as told through the story of a diseased and dying prostitute)

GERMANY

Brentano, Bernard von, *Theodor Chindler*, 1936 (rise of fascism and corruption between the wars)

Graf, Oskar Maria, *Prisoners All*, 1927 (the leftist Munich Revolution of 1918–19)

Mann, Heinrich, *The Patrioteer*, 1921 (leftist opposition to the Reich and incipient Nazism)

Travern, B. *March to Caobaland*, 1933 (the enslavement of Indians in the Mexicans timber industry)

Viebig, Clara, *The Village of Women*, 1900 (female victims of industrialism and poverty)

GREECE

Tsirkas, Stratis, *The Club*, 1960 (Greeks exiled in Italy during World War II)

Vassilis, Vassilikos, *Z*, 1966 (corruption and oppression of military government Greek monarchy)

GUATEMALA

Albizures, Miguel Angel, *Time of Sweat and Struggle*, 1987 (violence and oppression during a Coca-Cola strike)

Montejo, Victor, *Testimony: Death of a Guatemalan Village*, 1987 (military massacre of a rural village)

Morales, Mario Roberto, *Men under the Trees*, 1994 (military massacres of Indians)

GUYANA

Weber, A.R.F., *Those That Be in Bondage*, 1917 (enslavement of plantation workers)

HUNGARY

Jokai, Mor, *The Dark Diamonds*, 1870 (environmental and worker problems caused by industrialization and the mining of coal)

Kaffka, Margit, *Colors and Years*, 1912 (woman's uneasy place in society)

Konrad, Gyorgy, *The Case Worker*, 1969 (social injustice and poverty after World War II)

INDIA

Ghosh, Amitav, *The Shadow Lines*, 1988 (destructiveness of colonialism)

Satthianadhan, Krupa, *Kamala: A Story of Hindu Life*, 1894 (child marriage and widows, including the practice of suttee in which a widow is burned on her dead husband's pyre)

INDONESIA

Lubis, Mochtar, *A Road with No End*, 1952 (complicated moral questions arising in the fight for independence)

Toer, Pramoedya Ananta, *Corruption*, 1954 (corruption and disintegration among the ruling classes)

IRAN

Ahmad, Jalal Al-e, *By the Pen*, 1961 (an attack on the shah of Iran)

Daneshvar, Simin, *Savushun*, 1969 (woman's limitation and social activism in Arab society)

IRELAND

Johnston, Jennifer, *Shadows on Our Skin*, 1977 (the troubles in Ireland between Protestants and Catholics)

McCourt, Frank, *Angela's Ashes*, 1996 (poverty in Ireland)

ISRAEL

Grossman, David, *The Smile of the Lamb*, 1983 (the Intifada and Israeli-occupied West Bank)

ITALY

Bassani, Giorgio, *The Garden of the Finzi-Continis*, 1962 (oppression of Jews in Italy under fascism)

Levi, Carlo, *The Skin*, 1949 (the moral decline during American occupation of Italy after World War I)

Manzoni, Allesandro, *The Betrothed*, 1825 (Austrian oppression in Italy)

Moravia, Alberto, *Two Women*, 1959 (the effect of war on civilians in Italy)

Sciascia, Leonardo, *The Day of the Owl*, 1961 (the power of the Mafia)

JAMAICA

Brodber, Erna, *Jane and Louisa Will Soon Come Home*, 1980 (psychological conditioning of women by colonizers)

McKay, Claude, *Banana Bottoms*, 1933 (racism and social conflict in the Caribbean)

JAPAN

Masuji, Ibuse, *Black Rain*, 1965 (nuclear warfare)

KENYA

Thiong'o, Ngugi wa, *A Grain of Wheat*, 1967 (postcolonial corruption and complexity, misplaced heroism, and Marxism)

MEXICO

Azuela, Mariano, *The Underdogs*, 1916 (prorevolutionary account of Mexico)

Campobello, Nellie, *Someday the Dream*, 1994 (life in the garbage dumps of Mexico City)

Garro, Elena, *Recollections of Things to Come*, 1963 (oppression of women and minority groups)

Guzman, Martin Luis, *The Eagle and the Serpent*, 1928 (the many complex faces of revolution)

Lizardi, José Joaquin Fernandez de, *The Itching Parrot*, 1816 (denunciation of colonialism)

Lopez y Fuentes, Gregorio, *The Indian*, 1935 (the struggle of Mexico's indigenous peoples)

Rulfo, Juan, *Pedro Paramo*, 1955 (dictatorship)

Yanez, Agustin, *The Edge of the Storm*, 1947 (church and state intolerance and oppression of the common people)

MOROCCO

Chraibi, Driss, *The Simple Past*, 1954 (clash of cultures, assimilation into Western culture)

Ghallab, 'Abd al-Karim, *Master Ali*, 1981 (political oppression in French-occupied Morocco)

NETHERLANDS

Bordewijk, Ferdinand, *Blocks*, 1930 (dictatorship)

Bordewijk, Ferdinand, *Character*, 1938 (tyranny within family and state)

Dekker, Eduard Douwes, *Max Havelaar*, 1860 (Dutch colonialism in Indonesia, poor and powerless natives)

Hermans, Willems Frederik, *The Dark Room*, 1958 (reactions of Dutch to Nazis)

NIGERIA

Achebe, Chinua, *Arrow of God*, 1960 (colonialism and African stereotyping)

Tutuola, Amos, *The Palm Wine Drinkard*, 1952 (national cultural identity and cultural conflict)

NORWAY

Nedreaas, Torborg, *The War Hands*, 1952 (the North Atlantic Treaty Organization [NATO] and its implications for Norway)

Sigurd Evensmo, *Boat for England*, 1945 (harshness and injustice of postwar trials of collaborators)

PERU

Llosa, Mario Vargas, *The Notebooks of Don Rigoberto*, 1997 (militarism, machismo, and religious intolerance)

PHILIPPINES

Rizal, José, *Subversion*, 1891 (corruption and power of the Church in suppressing the poor)

POLAND

Glowacki, Janusz, *Give Us This Day*, 1981 (politics involved in the workers' uprising in Gdansk)

Gombrowicz, Witgold, *Ferdydurke*, 1938 (class hostility)

Gombrowicz, Witgold, *Insatiability*, 1930 (totalitarianism on the Left, notably in Russia and China)

Rudnicki, Adolf, *The Golden Windows*, 1943 (the Warsaw ghetto)

Siejak, Tadeusz, *The Deserter*, 1992 (Communist-inspired martial law to put down dissidents)

Tyrmand, Leopold, *The Man with White Eyes*, 1955 (the power of the Mafia)

RUSSIA

Chernyshevskii, Nickolai, *What Is to Be Done?*, 1863 (radical examination of marriage, socialism, and role of women)

Dudintsev, Vladimir, *Not by Bread Alone*, 1956 (post-Stalinist Russia)

Radischev, Alexander, *A Journey from St. Petersburg to Moscow*, 1790 (life in czarist Russia)

SOMALIA

Farah, Nuruddin, *Maps*, 1986 (occupation and brutal patriarchies of Africa's civil wars)

SOUTH AFRICA

Gordiner, Nadine, *July's People*, 1981 (racial injustice and inequality under minority rule)

SPAIN

Aub, Max, *The True History of the Death of Francisco Franco*, 1960 (the Spanish Civil War)

Delibes, Miguel, *Five Hours with Mario*, 1966 (social strife during the Spanish Civil War)

Sender, Ramon, *Mr. Witt among the Rebels*, 1935 (political dissension over the Spanish Civil War)

SWEDEN

Lo-Johansson, Ivar, *Breaking Free*, 1933 (living and working conditions of laborers and need for reform)

Martinson, Moa, *Women and Appletrees*, 1933 (living and working conditions of day laborers)

Moberg, Vilhelm, *When I Was a Child*, 1944 (socialist view of war)

SWITZERLAND

Keller, Gottfried, *Martin Salander*, 1886 (social satire in service of conservative republicanism)

TRINIDAD

James, C.L.R., *The Black Jacobins*, 1938 (anticolonialism)

James, C.L.R., *Misty Alley*, 1936 (friction between middle and peasant classes)

Naipaul, V.S., *The Mimic Men*, 1967 (racism in the Caribbean and Europe)

UNITED STATES

Algren, Nelson, *The Man with the Golden Arm*, 1949 (drug addiction and the culture of drugs)

Anderson, Sherwood, *Beyond Desire*, 1932 (an abortive and violent textile strike in North Carolina)

Baldwin, James, *Another Country*, 1962 (gay culture and sexual identity)

Bird, Robert Montgomery, *Nick of the Woods*, 1837 (Indian fighter as brutal rather than romantic)

Cable, George Washington, *The Grandissimes*, 1880 (race and class conflict in the Deep South)

Cahan, Abraham, *Yekl, a Tale of the New York Ghetto*, 1896 (New York City's Jewish slums)

Capote, Truman, *In Cold Blood*, 1966 (crime and the criminal and the world that produced them)

Chestnutt, Charles Waddell, *The House behind the Cedars*, 1900 (a black man's attempt to "pass" as white)

Churchill, Winston, *The Dwelling Place of Light*, 1917 (plight of immigrant mill workers)

Cobb, Humphrey, *Paths of Glory*, 1935 (antiwar novel about World War I)

Cozzens, James Gould, *Guard of Honor*, 1948 (racism in the military)

Crane, Stephen, *Maggie, a Girl of the Streets*, 1893 (the prostitute as victim rather than siren)

Dreiser, Theodore, *Jennie Gerhardt*, 1911 (a good woman destroyed by society's injustice)

Fast, Howard, *Freedom Road*, 1944 (political intolerance)

Friedman, Isaac K., *By Bread Alone*, 1901 (oppression of immigrant mill workers)

Galarza, Ernesto, *Barrio Boy*, 1971 (Mexican American life in the slums)

Gold, Mike, *Jews without Money*, 1930 (working-class troubles in a sordid life on New York City's East Side)

Hemingway, Ernest, *For Whom the Bell Tolls*, 1940 (the Spanish Civil War)

Holmes, Oliver Wendell, *Elsie Venner*, 1861 (biological determinism)

Howells, William Dean, *The Rise of Silas Lapham*, 1885 (perils of capitalism without conscience, money without morality)

Jones, James, *From Here to Eternity*, 1951 (the U.S. regular army and the military system)

Koestler, Arthur, *Darkness at Noon*, 1941 (anticommunist critique during the War)

Lewis, Sinclair, *Elmer Gantry*, 1927 (religious opportunism and hypocrisy)

London, Jack, *The Iron Heel*, 1908 (socialist view of working-class life)

McKay, Claude, *Banjo*, 1929 (racial injustice and inequality)

Morrison, Toni, *The Bluest Eye*, 1970 (destructive forces within and without an African American family)

Naylor, Gloria, *The Women of Brewster Place*, 1982 (lives of African American women)

Norris, Frank, *McTeague*, 1899 (inhumanity that results from rampant capitalism)

Olsen, Tillie, *Yonnondio*, 1974 (radicalism during the Great Depression)

Rand, Ayn, *The Fountainhead*, 1943 (follies of socialists and religious people)

Roth, Philip, *Portnoy's Complaint*, 1969 (Jewish identity crisis and cultural assimilation)

Trumbo, Dalton, *Johnny Got His Gun*, 1939 (personal damage caused by war)

Twain, Mark, *Pudd'nhead Wilson*, 1894 (sociology and psychology of race)

Twain, Mark, and Charles Dudley Warner, *The Gilded Age*, 1873 (vulgar materialism of postwar United States)

Wouk, Herman, *The Caine Mutiny*, 1951 (military despotism)

Wright, Richard, *Black Boy*, 1945 (childhood and race)

YUGOSLAVIA

Cosic, Dobrica, *A Time of Evil*, 1985–90 (suffering of Yugoslav communists after World War II)

Vasic, Dragisa, *Red Fogs*, 1922 (physical and psychological suffering in World War I)

Author Index

Title Index

Geographical Index

Numerals correspond to entry numbers

AUSTRALIA

Boldrewood, Rolf, *Robbery under Arms*, 23
Clarke, Marcus, *For the Term of His Natural Life*, 22
Franklin, Miles, *My Brilliant Career*, 24
Prichard, Katharine Susannah, *Coonardoo*, 25
Shute, Nevil, *On the Beach*, 26

BRAZIL

Amado, Jorge, *Gabriela, Clove and Cinnamon*, 195
Azevedo, Aluisio, *Mulatto*, 194

CANADA

Atwood, Margaret, *The Handmaid's Tale*, 127
Ross, Sinclair, *As for Me and My House*, 125
Roy, Gabrielle, *The Tin Flute*, 126

CHILE

Allende, Isabel, *The House of the Spirits*, 196

CHINA

Bei Dao, *Waves*, 16
Lu Xun, *The True Story of Ah-Q*, 15

Ts'ao Hsueh-ch'in, *Dream of the Red Chamber*, 13
Tseng P'u, *Flower in an Ocean of Sin*, 14

COLOMBIA

Márquez, Gabriel Garcia, *One Hundred Years of Solitude*, 197

CUBA

Arenas, Reinaldo, *The Palace of the White Skunks*, 198

CZECHOSLOVAKIA

Hasek, Jaroslav, *The Good Soldier Svejk and His Fortunes in the World War*, 27
Kafka, Franz, *The Trial*, 28
Kundera, Milan, *The Unbearable Lightness of Being*, 29

EGYPT

Mahfouz, Naguib, *The Cairo Trilogy*, 1
Saadawi, Nawāl El, *God Dies by the Nile*, 2

ENGLAND

Austen, Jane, *Pride and Prejudice*, 32
Bunyan, John, *The Pilgrim's Progress*, 30

ZIMBABWE

Issues Index

Numerals correspond to entry numbers

Child Labor and Abuse

Delinquency and Gangs

Orphans

CLASS AND CASTE INEQUITIES AND CONFLICTS

Class Privilege

Class Subjugation

COLONIALISM, IMPERIALISM, AND FOREIGN INTERVENTION

CONFORMITY

CRIME, LAW ENFORCEMENT, AND THE JUSTICE SYSTEM

CULTURE CLASHES AND CULTURAL ERADICATION

DISLOCATION AND DIASPORA

GOVERNMENT ISSUES

Censorship

Corruption

Government Reprisal

IMMIGRANTS

POLICE STATE TACTICS

POLITICS

POVERTY AND SLUMS

Hunger

Native American Religion

Religious Hypocrisy

Religious Persecution and Intolerance

State-Mandated Religion

Televangelism

RESERVES, RESERVATIONS, AND GHETTOES

SPIRITUAL ISSUES

Alienation

Disillusionment

Existentialism

Meaninglessness

Skepticism and Atheism

STRUGGLE FOR INDEPENDENCE

SUFFRAGE AND REPRESENTATION

TRIBALISM

TYRANNY, OPPRESSION, AND DENIAL OF CIVIL LIBERTIES

Circumcision

Discrimination, Subjugation, and Denial of Rights

Feminism

Isolation

Property and Inheritance

Prostitution

About the Authors

CLAUDIA DURST JOHNSON, former chairperson of English at the University of Alabama, is currently a freelance scholar and writer in Berkeley, California. She is the author of books on American history and literature, as well as theater history. She is also series editor for Greenwood Press's Exploring Social Issues through Literature Series and the Literature in Context Series, for which she has authored several volumes including *Understanding To Kill a Mockingbird* and *Understanding The Grapes of Wrath*.

VERNON JOHNSON, a graduate of Vanderbilt University, has wide experience as an author, theater director, and professor of world literature. He is co-author of *Understanding The Crucible*. He now resides in Berkeley, California where he continues to write and teach.